KIA

OPTIMA
2001-10 REPAIR MANUAL

CHILTON'S

I0805252

Covers All U.S. and Canadian models of Kia Optima 2001 through 2010

by Mike Stubblefield

CHILTON Automotive Books

PUBLISHED BY HAYNES NORTH AMERICA, Inc.

Haynes ®

APA AUTOMOTIVE PARTS & ACCESSORIES ASSOCIATION MEMBER

Manufactured in USA

ISBN-13: 978-1-56392-946-5
ISBN-10: 1-56392-946-5
Library of Congress Control Number: 2012936315

Haynes Publishing Group
Sparkford Nr Yeovil
Somerset BA22 7JJ England

Haynes North America, Inc
861 Lawrence Drive
Newbury Park
California 91320 USA

ABCDE
FGHIJ
KLMNO
PQRST

Contents

INTRODUCTORY PAGES

Photographer and mechanic with a Kia Optima

ACKNOWLEDGEMENTS

Wiring diagrams originated exclusively for Haynes North America, Inc. by Valley Forge Technical Information Services.

12-400

About this manual

ITS PURPOSE

The purpose of this manual is to help you get the best value from your vehicle. It can do so in several ways. It can help you decide what work must be done, even if you choose to have it done by a dealer service department or a repair shop; it provides information and procedures for routine maintenance and servicing; and it offers diagnostic and repair procedures to follow when trouble occurs.

We hope you use the manual to tackle the work yourself. For many simpler jobs, doing it yourself may be quicker than arranging an appointment to get the vehicle into a shop and making the trips to leave it and pick it up. More importantly, a lot of money can be saved by avoiding the expense the shop must pass on to you to cover its labor and overhead costs. An added benefit is the sense of satisfaction and accomplishment that you feel after doing the job yourself.

USING THE MANUAL

The manual is divided into Chapters. Each Chapter is divided into numbered Sections. Each Section consists of consecutively numbered paragraphs.

At the beginning of each numbered Section you will be referred to any illustrations which apply to the procedures in that Section. The reference numbers used in illustration captions pinpoint the pertinent Section and the Step within that Section. That is, illustration 3.2 means the illustration refers to Section 3 and Step (or paragraph) 2 within that Section.

Procedures, once described in the text, are not normally repeated. When it's necessary to refer to another Chapter, the reference will be given as Chapter and Section number. Cross references given without use of the word "Chapter" apply to Sections and/or paragraphs in the same Chapter. For example, "see Section 8" means in the same Chapter.

References to the left or right side of the vehicle assume you are sitting in the driver's seat, facing forward.

Even though we have prepared this manual with extreme care, neither the publisher nor the author can accept responsibility for any errors in, or omissions from, the information given.

➡ **NOTE**

A *Note* provides information necessary to properly complete a procedure or information which will make the procedure easier to understand.

⁂ CAUTION

A *Caution* provides a special procedure or special steps which must be taken while completing the procedure where the Caution is found. Not heeding a Caution can result in damage to the assembly being worked on.

⁂ WARNING

A *Warning* provides a special procedure or special steps which must be taken while completing the procedure where the Warning is found. Not heeding a Warning can result in personal injury.

Introduction to the Kia Optima

This manual covers 2001 through 2010 Kia Optima models. These vehicles are equipped with either a 2.4L four-cylinder engine or a 2.5L or 2.7L V6 engine.

The engine drives the front wheels through either a four or five speed automatic transaxle or a five speed manual transaxle via driveaxles.

Front suspension is independent, with coil-over shock absorbers used on 2006 and earlier models, and strut/coil spring assemblies on 2006.5 and later models. Rear suspension is independent as well, with coil-over shock absorbers used on 2006 and earlier models and conventional shock absorbers and coil springs on 2006.5 models. The rack-and-pinion steering unit is mounted on the suspension sub-frame.

The brakes are disc at the front and either disc or drum at the rear. Power assist is standard on all models. An Anti-lock Brake System (ABS) is standard equipment on some models and is available as an option on others.

➡ **Note: 2006 and 2006.5 models will both have a "6" in the tenth position of the VIN. To distinguish a 2006 model from a 2006.5 model, refer to the 8th position of the VIN (the engine code): A 2006 model will have a "6" (four-cylinder) or "8" (V6), while a 2006.5 will have a "3" (four-cylinder) or "4" (V6).**

Vehicle identification numbers

Modifications are a continuing and unpublicized process in vehicle manufacturing. Since spare parts manuals and lists are compiled on a numerical basis, the individual vehicle numbers are essential to correctly identify the component required.

VEHICLE IDENTIFICATION NUMBER (VIN)

This very important identification number is stamped on a plate attached to the dashboard inside the windshield on the driver's side of the vehicle (see illustration). It can also be found on the certification label located on the driver's side door post and on the right (passenger) side of the firewall. The VIN also appears on the Vehicle Certificate of Title and Registration. It contains information such as where and when the vehicle was manufactured, the model year and the body style.

VIN ENGINE AND MODEL YEAR CODES

Two particularly important pieces of information found in the VIN are the engine code and the model year code. Counting from the left, the engine code letter designation is the 8th digit and the model year code letter designation is the 10th digit.

On the models covered by this manual the engine codes are:

4 2.4L four-cylinder (2001)
6 2.7L V6 (2001)
6 2.4L four-cylinder (2002 through 2006)
8 2.7L V6 (2002 through 2006)
3 2.4L four-cylinder (2006.5 through 2009)
4 2.7L V6 (2006.5 and later)
8 2.4L four-cylinder (2010 and later)

On the models covered by this manual the model year codes are:

1 2001
2 2002
3 2003
4 2004
5 2005
6 2006
7 2007
8 2008
9 2009
A 2010

➡ Note: 2006 and 2006.5 models will both have a "6" in the tenth position of the VIN. To distinguish a 2006 model from a 2006.5 model, refer to the 8th position of the VIN (the engine code): A 2006 model will have a "6" (four-cylinder) or "8" (V6), while a 2006.5 will have a "3" (four-cylinder) or "4" (V6).

CERTIFICATION LABEL

The certification label is attached to the end of the driver's door post (see illustration). The plate contains the name of the manufacturer, the month and year of production, the Gross Vehicle Weight Rating (GVWR), the Gross Axle Weight Rating (GAWR) and the certification statement.

ENGINE NUMBER

On four-cylinder models, the engine identification number is stamped into a machined pad on the front passenger side of the engine block, under the exhaust manifold.

On V6 models, the engine identification number is stamped into a machined pad on the front left end (driver's side) of the engine block.

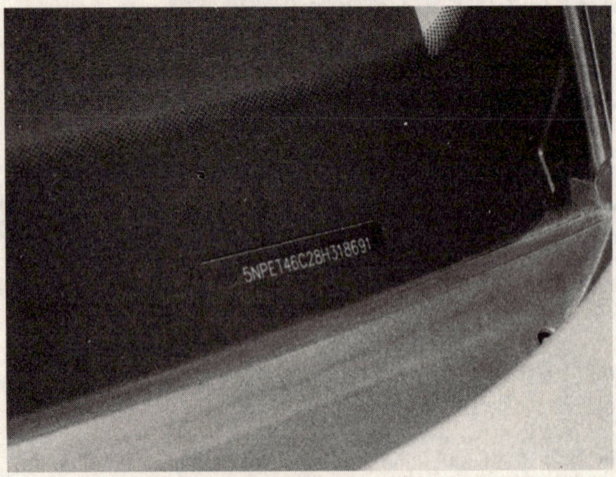

The Vehicle Identification Number (VIN) is located on a plate on top of the dash (visible through the windshield)

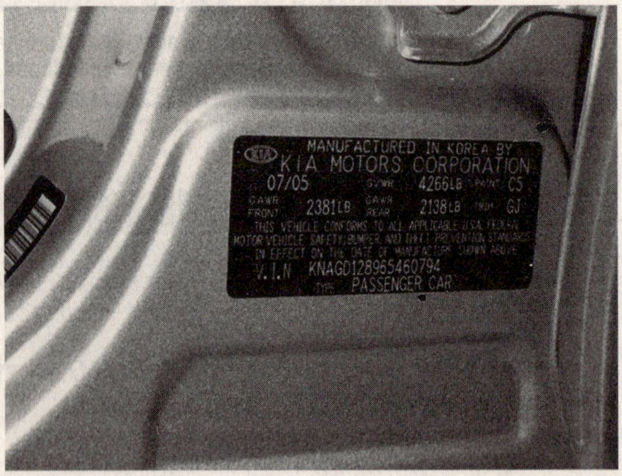

The vehicle certification label is located at the bottom of the driver's door post

Recall information

Vehicle recalls are carried out by the manufacturer in the rare event of a possible safety-related defect. The vehicle's registered owner is contacted at the address on file at the Department of Motor Vehicles and given the details of the recall. Remedial work is carried out free of charge at a dealer service department.

If you are the new owner of a used vehicle which was subject to a recall and you want to be sure that the work has been carried out, it's best to contact a dealer service department and ask about your individual vehicle - you'll need to furnish them your Vehicle Identification Number (VIN).

The table below is based on information provided by the National Highway Traffic Safety Administration (NHTSA), the body which oversees vehicle recalls in the United States. The recall database is updated constantly. For the latest information on vehicle recalls, check the NHTSA website at www.nhtsa.gov, www.safecar.gov, or call the NHTSA hotline at 1-888-327-4236.

Recall date	Recall campaign number	Model(s) affected	Concern
MAY 01, 2001	01V156000	2001 Optima	On some models, the side airbag harness for the driver position could be misrouted, which could result in it being pinched or cut by the seat cushion tilt mechanism. Damage to the wire harness could result in the side airbag not deploying in an accident.
JAN 19, 2003	03V067000	2002 Optima	On some models equipped with 2.7 liter V6 engines, the Crankshaft Position (CKP) sensor cases did not meet dimensional specifications. Internal gaps within the cases allowed epoxy to contact the printed circuit board, which resulted in cracking of the circuit board capacitor. A damaged CKP capacitor could result in engine stalling.
APR 08, 2004	04V180000	2002 Optima	Some models may contain a fuel tank assembly valve that may not close properly. If a vehicle with a fuel tank assembly valve that is not properly closed were to roll over, fuel spillage may occur. Fuel spillage in the presence of an ignition source could result in a fire.
MAY 26, 2009	09V183000	2002 Optima	Road salt applied in some states during the winter months may result in progressive, internal corrosion of the front subframe over time. Such subframe corrosion near the connection to the lower control arm can lead to wheel misalignment and/or other noticeable stress in steering, or accelerated abnormal tire wear. Corrosion of the front subframe could lead to separation, possibly resulting in a crash.

Buying parts

Replacement parts are available from many sources, which generally fall into one of two categories - authorized dealer parts departments and independent retail auto parts stores. Our advice concerning these parts is as follows:

Retail auto parts stores: Good auto parts stores will stock frequently needed components which wear out relatively fast, such as clutch components, exhaust systems, brake parts, tune-up parts, etc. These stores often supply new or reconditioned parts on an exchange basis, which can save a considerable amount of money. Discount auto parts stores are often very good places to buy materials and parts needed for general vehicle maintenance such as oil, grease, filters, spark plugs, belts, touch-up paint, bulbs, etc. They also usually sell tools and general accessories, have convenient hours, charge lower prices and can often be found not far from home.

Authorized dealer parts department: This is the best source for parts which are unique to the vehicle and not generally available elsewhere (such as major engine parts, transmission parts, trim pieces, etc.).

Warranty information: If the vehicle is still covered under warranty, be sure that any replacement parts purchased - regardless of the source - do not invalidate the warranty!

To be sure of obtaining the correct parts, have engine and chassis numbers available and, if possible, take the old parts along for positive identification.

Maintenance techniques, tools and working facilities

MAINTENANCE TECHNIQUES

There are a number of techniques involved in maintenance and repair that will be referred to throughout this manual. Application of these techniques will enable the home mechanic to be more efficient, better organized and capable of performing the various tasks properly, which will ensure that the repair job is thorough and complete.

Fasteners

Fasteners are nuts, bolts, studs and screws used to hold two or more parts together. There are a few things to keep in mind when working with fasteners. Almost all of them use a locking device of some type, either a lockwasher, locknut, locking tab or thread adhesive. All threaded fasteners should be clean and straight, with undamaged threads and undamaged corners on the hex head where the wrench fits. Develop the habit of replacing all damaged nuts and bolts with new ones. Special locknuts with nylon or fiber inserts can only be used once. If they are removed, they lose their locking ability and must be replaced with new ones.

Rusted nuts and bolts should be treated with a penetrating fluid to ease removal and prevent breakage. Some mechanics use turpentine in a spout-type oil can, which works quite well. After applying the rust penetrant, let it work for a few minutes before trying to loosen the nut or bolt. Badly rusted fasteners may have to be chiseled or sawed off or removed with a special nut breaker, available at tool stores.

If a bolt or stud breaks off in an assembly, it can be drilled and removed with a special tool commonly available for this purpose. Most automotive machine shops can perform this task, as well as other repair procedures, such as the repair of threaded holes that have been stripped out.

Flat washers and lockwashers, when removed from an assembly, should always be replaced exactly as removed. Replace any damaged washers with new ones. Never use a lockwasher on any soft metal surface (such as aluminum), thin sheet metal or plastic.

Fastener sizes

For a number of reasons, automobile manufacturers are making wider and wider use of metric fasteners. Therefore, it is important to be able to tell the difference between standard (sometimes called U.S. or SAE) and metric hardware, since they cannot be interchanged.

All bolts, whether standard or metric, are sized according to diameter, thread pitch and length. For example, a standard 1/2 - 13 x 1 bolt is 1/2 inch in diameter, has 13 threads per inch and is 1 inch long. An M12 - 1.75 x 25 metric bolt is 12 mm in diameter, has a thread pitch of 1.75 mm (the distance between threads) and is 25 mm long. The two bolts are nearly identical, and easily confused, but they are not interchangeable.

In addition to the differences in diameter, thread pitch and length, metric and standard bolts can also be distinguished by examining the bolt heads. To begin with, the distance across the flats on a standard bolt head is measured in inches, while the same dimension on a metric bolt is sized in millimeters (the same is true for nuts). As a result, a standard wrench should not be used on a metric bolt and a metric wrench should not be used on a standard bolt. Also, most standard bolts have slashes radiating out from the center of the head to denote the grade or strength of the bolt, which is an indication of the amount of torque that can be applied to it. The greater the number of slashes, the greater the strength of the bolt. Grades 0 through 5 are commonly used on automobiles. Metric bolts have a property class (grade) number, rather than a slash, molded into their heads to indicate bolt strength. In this case, the higher the number, the stronger the bolt. Property class numbers 8.8, 9.8 and 10.9 are commonly used on automobiles.

Strength markings can also be used to distinguish standard hex nuts from metric hex nuts. Many standard nuts have dots stamped into one side, while metric nuts are marked with a number. The greater the number of dots, or the higher the number, the greater the strength of the nut.

Metric studs are also marked on their ends according to property class (grade). Larger studs are numbered (the same as metric bolts), while smaller studs carry a geometric code to denote grade.

It should be noted that many fasteners, especially Grades 0 through 2, have no distinguishing marks on them. When such is the case, the only way to determine whether it is standard or metric is to measure the thread pitch or compare it to a known fastener of the same size.

Standard fasteners are often referred to as SAE, as opposed to metric. However, it should be noted that SAE technically refers to a non-metric fine thread fastener only. Coarse thread non-metric fasteners are referred to as USS sizes.

Since fasteners of the same size (both standard and metric) may have different strength ratings, be sure to reinstall any bolts, studs or nuts removed from your vehicle in their original locations. Also, when replacing a fastener with a new one, make sure that the new one has a strength rating equal to or greater than the original.

Tightening sequences and procedures

Most threaded fasteners should be tightened to a specific torque value (torque is the twisting force applied to a threaded component such as a nut or bolt). Overtightening the fastener can weaken it and cause it to break, while undertightening can cause it to eventually come loose. Bolts, screws and studs, depending on the material they are made of and their thread diameters, have specific torque values, many of which are noted in the Specifications at the end of each Chapter. Be sure to follow the torque recommendations closely. For fasteners not assigned a specific torque, a general torque value chart is presented here as a guide. These torque values are for dry (unlubricated) fasteners threaded into steel or cast iron (not aluminum). As was previously mentioned, the size and grade of a fastener determine the amount of torque that can safely be applied to it. The figures listed here are approximate for Grade 2 and Grade 3 fasteners. Higher grades can tolerate higher torque values.

Fasteners laid out in a pattern, such as cylinder head bolts, oil pan bolts, differential cover bolts, etc., must be loosened or tightened in sequence to avoid warping the component. This sequence will normally be shown in the appropriate Chapter. If a specific pattern is not given, the following procedures can be used to prevent warping.

Initially, the bolts or nuts should be assembled finger-tight only. Next, they should be tightened one full turn each, in a criss-cross or diagonal pattern. After each one has been tightened one full turn, return to the first one and tighten them all one-half turn, following the same

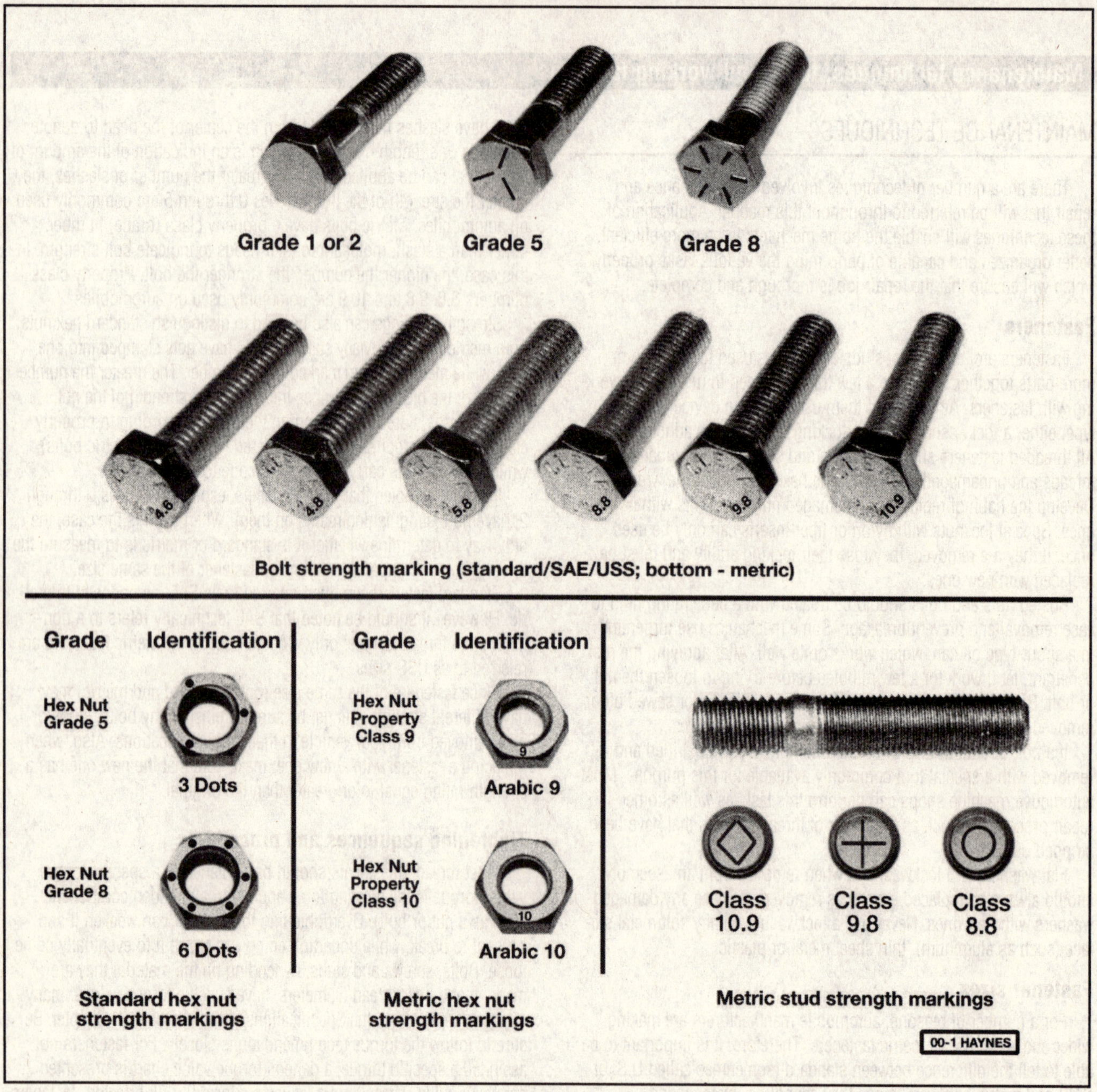

pattern. Finally, tighten each of them one-quarter turn at a time until each fastener has been tightened to the proper torque. To loosen and remove the fasteners, the procedure would be reversed.

Component disassembly

Component disassembly should be done with care and purpose to help ensure that the parts go back together properly. Always keep track of the sequence in which parts are removed. Make note of special characteristics or marks on parts that can be installed more than one way, such as a grooved thrust washer on a shaft. It is a good idea to lay the disassembled parts out on a clean surface in the order that they were removed. It may also be helpful to make sketches or take instant photos of components before removal.

When removing fasteners from a component, keep track of their locations. Sometimes threading a bolt back in a part, or putting the washers and nut back on a stud, can prevent mix-ups later. If nuts and bolts cannot be returned to their original locations, they should be kept in a compartmented box or a series of small boxes. A cupcake or muffin tin is ideal for this purpose, since each cavity can hold the bolts and nuts from a particular area (i.e. oil pan bolts, valve cover bolts, engine

Metric thread sizes	Ft-lbs	Nm
M-6	6 to 9	9 to 12
M-8	14 to 21	19 to 28
M-10	28 to 40	38 to 54
M-12	50 to 71	68 to 96
M-14	80 to 140	109 to 154
Pipe thread sizes		
1/8	5 to 8	7 to 10
1/4	12 to 18	17 to 24
3/8	22 to 33	30 to 44
1/2	25 to 35	34 to 47
U.S. thread sizes		
1/4 - 20	6 to 9	9 to 12
5/16 - 18	12 to 18	17 to 24
5/16 - 24	14 to 20	19 to 27
3/8 - 16	22 to 32	30 to 43
3/8 - 24	27 to 38	37 to 51
7/16 - 14	40 to 55	55 to 74
7/16 - 20	40 to 60	55 to 81
1/2 - 13	55 to 80	75 to 108

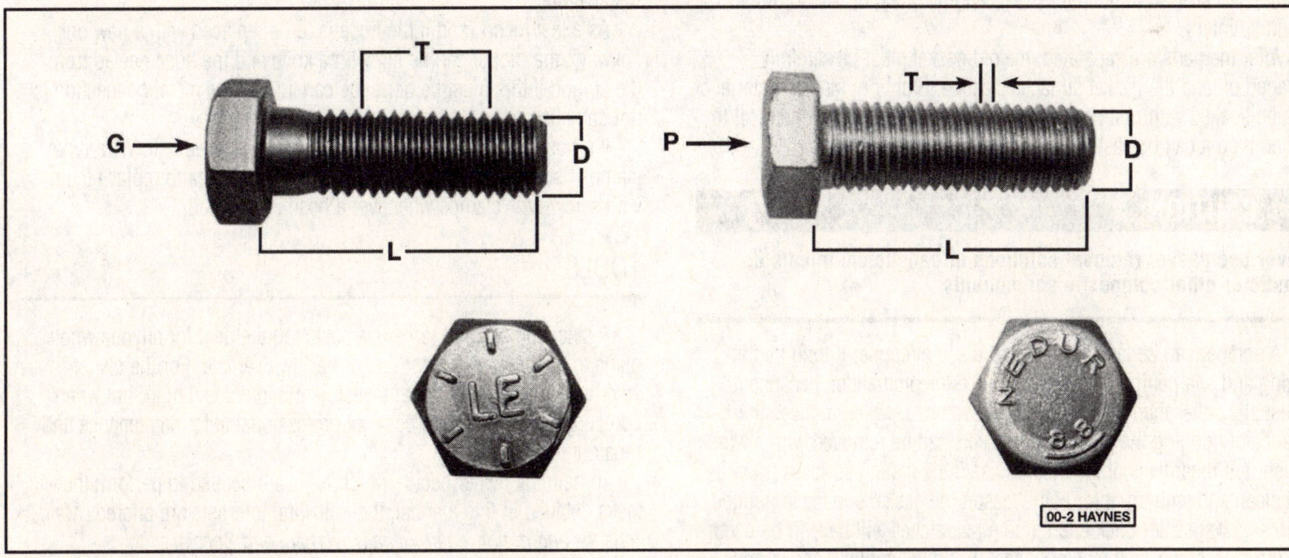

Standard (SAE and USS) bolt dimensions/grade marks

G *Grade marks (bolt strength)*
L *Length (in inches)*
T *Thread pitch (number of threads per inch)*
D *Nominal diameter (in inches)*

Metric bolt dimensions/grade marks

P *Property class (bolt strength)*
L *Length (in millimeters)*
T *Thread pitch (distance between threads in millimeters)*
D *Diameter*

mount bolts, etc.). A pan of this type is especially helpful when working on assemblies with very small parts, such as the carburetor, alternator, valve train or interior dash and trim pieces. The cavities can be marked with paint or tape to identify the contents.

Whenever wiring looms, harnesses or connectors are separated, it is a good idea to identify the two halves with numbered pieces of masking tape so they can be easily reconnected.

Gasket sealing surfaces

Throughout any vehicle, gaskets are used to seal the mating surfaces between two parts and keep lubricants, fluids, vacuum or pressure contained in an assembly.

Many times these gaskets are coated with a liquid or paste-type gasket sealing compound before assembly. Age, heat and pressure can sometimes cause the two parts to stick together so tightly that they are very difficult to separate. Often, the assembly can be loosened by striking it with a soft-face hammer near the mating surfaces. A regular hammer can be used if a block of wood is placed between the hammer and the part. Do not hammer on cast parts or parts that could be easily damaged. With any particularly stubborn part, always recheck to make sure that every fastener has been removed.

Avoid using a screwdriver or bar to pry apart an assembly, as they

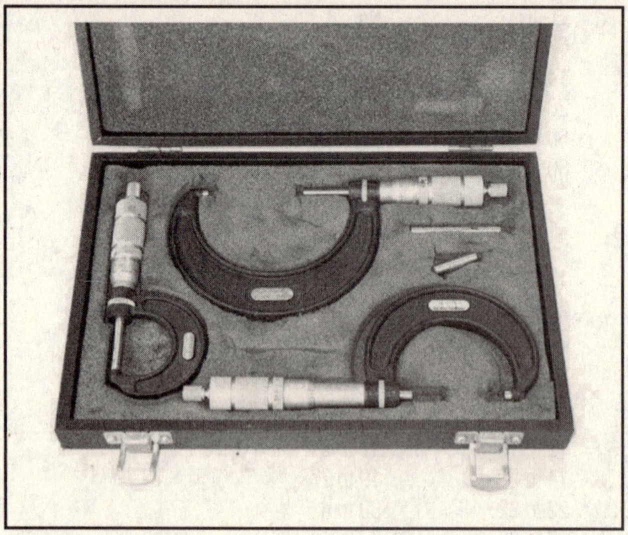

Micrometer set

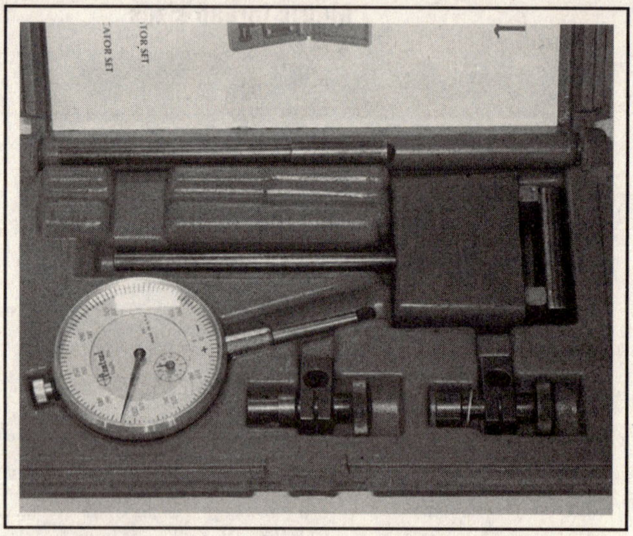

Dial indicator set

can easily mar the gasket sealing surfaces of the parts, which must remain smooth. If prying is absolutely necessary, use an old broom handle, but keep in mind that extra clean up will be necessary if the wood splinters.

After the parts are separated, the old gasket must be carefully scraped off and the gasket surfaces cleaned. Stubborn gasket material can be soaked with rust penetrant or treated with a special chemical to soften it so it can be easily scraped off.

⁂ CAUTION:

Never use gasket removal solutions or caustic chemicals on plastic or other composite components.

A scraper can be fashioned from a piece of copper tubing by flattening and sharpening one end. Copper is recommended because it is usually softer than the surfaces to be scraped, which reduces the chance of gouging the part. Some gaskets can be removed with a wire brush, but regardless of the method used, the mating surfaces must be left clean and smooth. If for some reason the gasket surface is gouged, then a gasket sealer thick enough to fill scratches will have to be used during reassembly of the components. For most applications, a non-drying (or semi-drying) gasket sealer should be used.

Hose removal tips

⁂ WARNING:

If the vehicle is equipped with air conditioning, do not disconnect any of the A/C hoses without first having the system depressurized by a dealer service department or a service station.

Hose removal precautions closely parallel gasket removal precautions. Avoid scratching or gouging the surface that the hose mates against or the connection may leak. This is especially true for radiator hoses. Because of various chemical reactions, the rubber in hoses can bond itself to the metal spigot that the hose fits over. To remove a hose, first loosen the hose clamps that secure it to the spigot. Then, with slip-joint pliers, grab the hose at the clamp and rotate it around the spigot. Work it back and forth until it is completely free, then pull it off. Silicone or other lubricants will ease removal if they can be applied between the hose and the outside of the spigot. Apply the same lubricant to the inside of the hose and the outside of the spigot to simplify installation.

As a last resort (and if the hose is to be replaced with a new one anyway), the rubber can be slit with a knife and the hose peeled from the spigot. If this must be done, be careful that the metal connection is not damaged.

If a hose clamp is broken or damaged, do not reuse it. Wire-type clamps usually weaken with age, so it is a good idea to replace them with screw-type clamps whenever a hose is removed.

TOOLS

A selection of good tools is a basic requirement for anyone who plans to maintain and repair his or her own vehicle. For the owner who has few tools, the initial investment might seem high, but when compared to the spiraling costs of professional auto maintenance and repair, it is a wise one.

To help the owner decide which tools are needed to perform the tasks detailed in this manual, the following tool lists are offered: *Maintenance and minor repair, Repair/overhaul and Special.*

The newcomer to practical mechanics should start off with the *maintenance and minor repair* tool kit, which is adequate for the simpler jobs performed on a vehicle. Then, as confidence and experience grow, the owner can tackle more difficult tasks, buying additional tools as they are needed. Eventually the basic kit will be expanded into the *repair and overhaul* tool set. Over a period of time, the experienced do-it-yourselfer will assemble a tool set complete enough for most repair and overhaul procedures and will add tools from the special category when it is felt that the expense is justified by the frequency of use.

Maintenance and minor repair tool kit

The tools in this list should be considered the minimum required for performance of routine maintenance, servicing and minor repair work. We recommend the purchase of combination wrenches (box-end and open-end combined in one wrench). While more expensive than open end wrenches, they offer the advantages of both types of wrench.

Combination wrench set (1/4-inch to 1 inch or 6 mm to 19 mm)
Adjustable wrench, 8 inch
Spark plug wrench with rubber insert

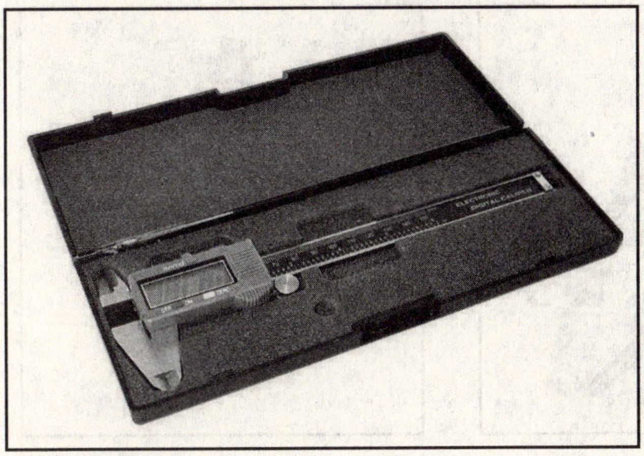

Dial caliper

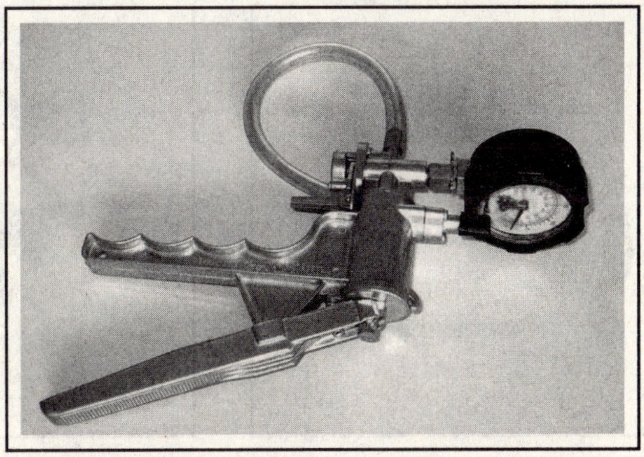

Hand-operated vacuum pump

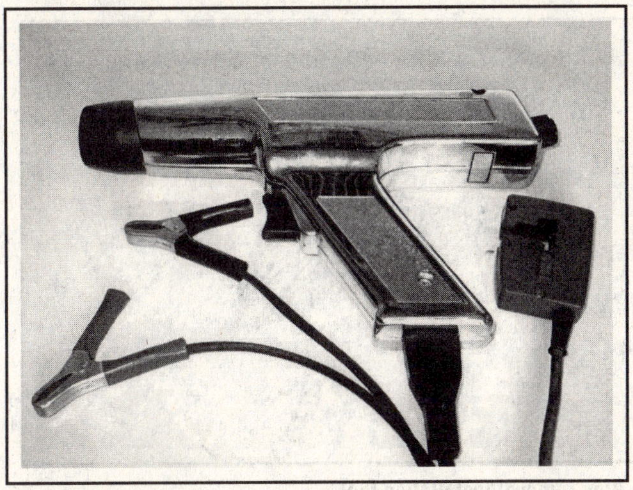

Timing light

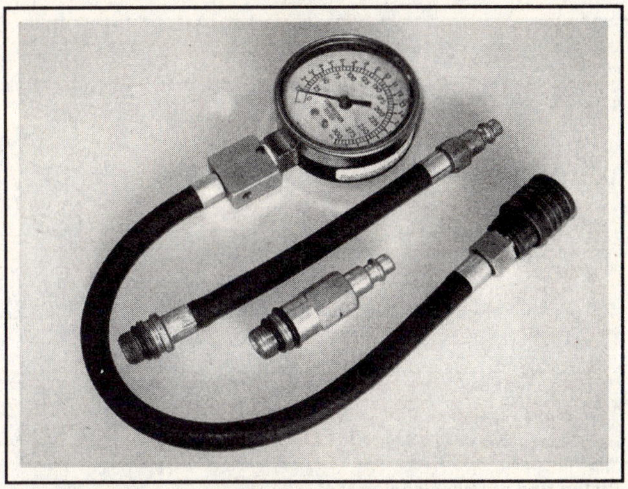

Compression gauge with spark plug hole adapter

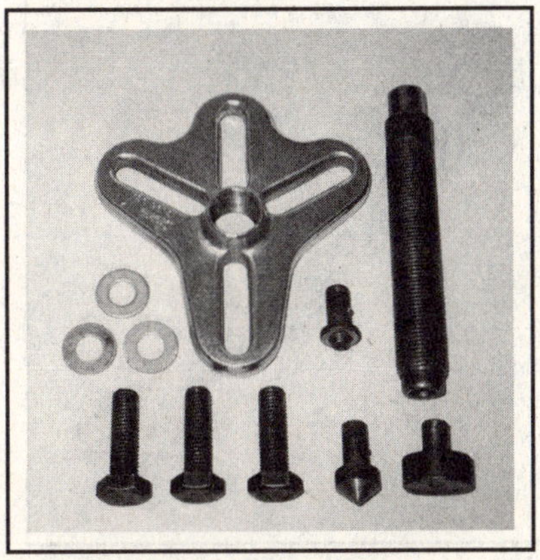

Damper/steering wheel puller

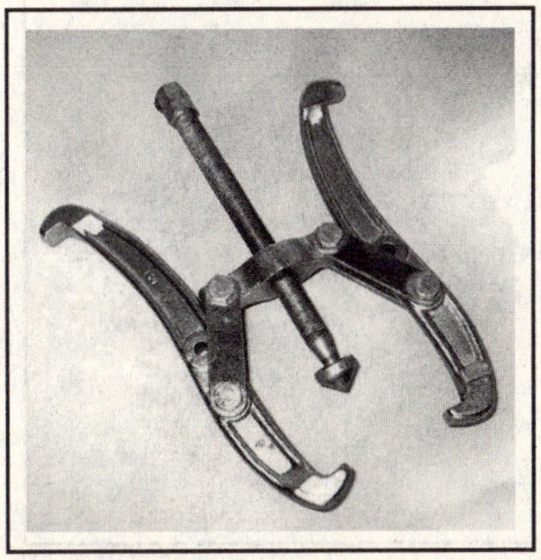

General purpose puller

Hydraulic lifter removal tool

Spark plug gap adjusting tool
Feeler gauge set
Brake bleeder wrench
Standard screwdriver (5/16-inch x 6 inch)
Phillips screwdriver (No. 2 x 6 inch)
Combination pliers - 6 inch
Hacksaw and assortment of blades
Tire pressure gauge
Grease gun
Oil can
Fine emery cloth
Wire brush
Battery post and cable cleaning tool
Oil filter wrench
Funnel (medium size)
Safety goggles
Jackstands (2)
Drain pan

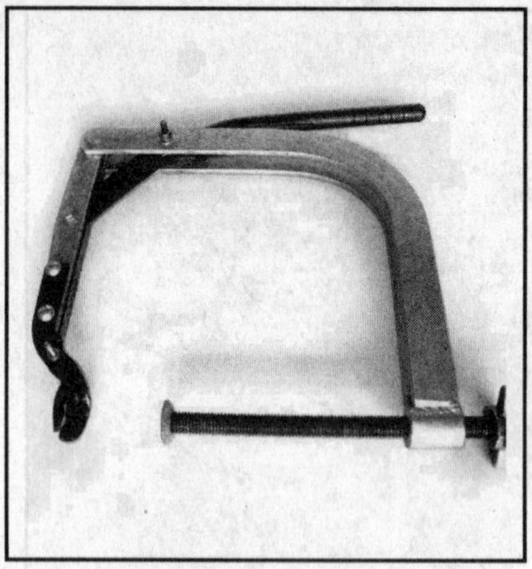

Valve spring compressor

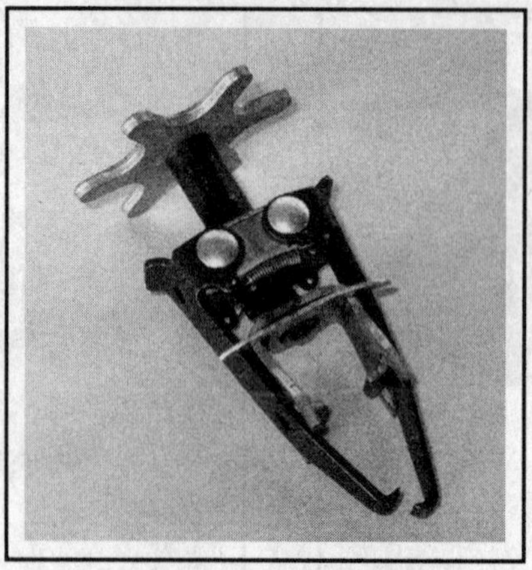

Valve spring compressor

Ridge reamer

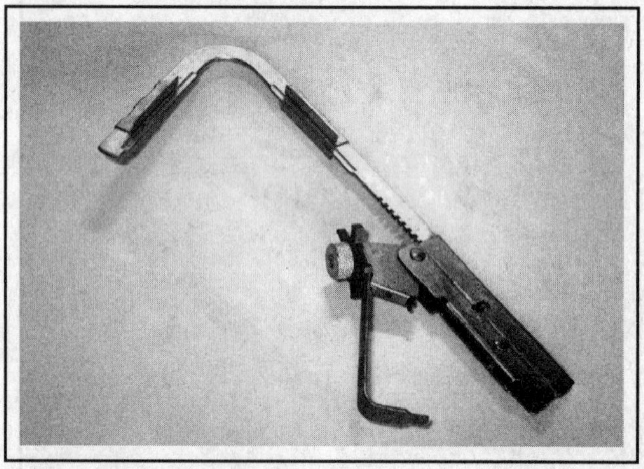

Piston ring groove cleaning tool

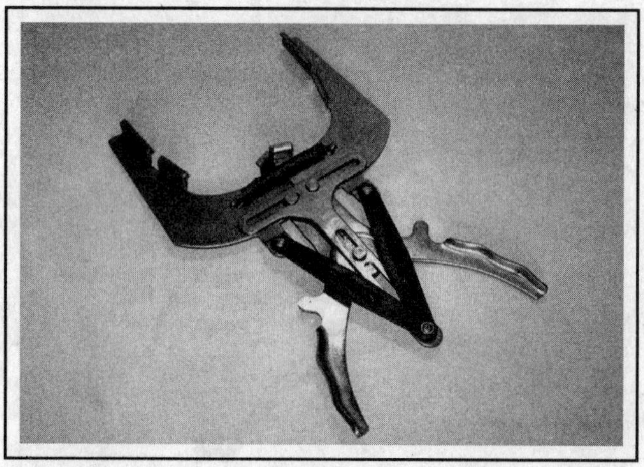

Ring removal/installation tool

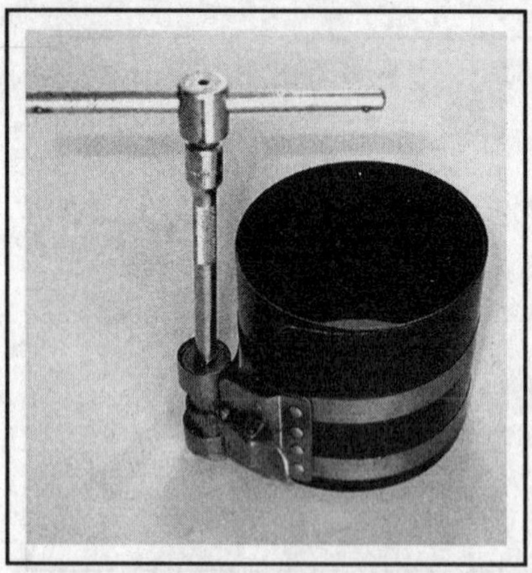

Ring compressor

Cylinder hone

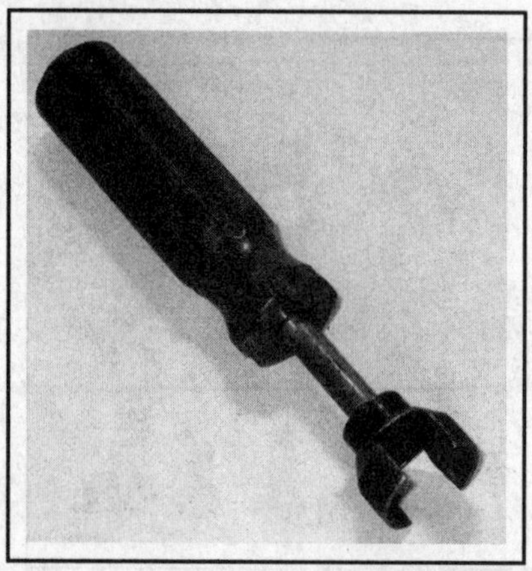

Brake hold-down spring tool

➡ **Note: If basic tune-ups are going to be part of routine maintenance, it will be necessary to purchase a good quality stroboscopic timing light and combination tachometer/dwell meter. Although they are included in the list of special tools, it is mentioned here because they are absolutely necessary for tuning most vehicles properly.**

Repair and overhaul tool set

These tools are essential for anyone who plans to perform major repairs and are in addition to those in the maintenance and minor repair tool kit. Included is a comprehensive set of sockets which, though expensive, are invaluable because of their versatility, especially when various extensions and drives are available. We recommend the 1/2-inch drive over the 3/8-inch drive. Although the larger drive is bulky and more expensive, it has the capacity of accepting a very wide range of large sockets. Ideally, however, the mechanic should have a 3/8-inch drive set and a 1/2-inch drive set.

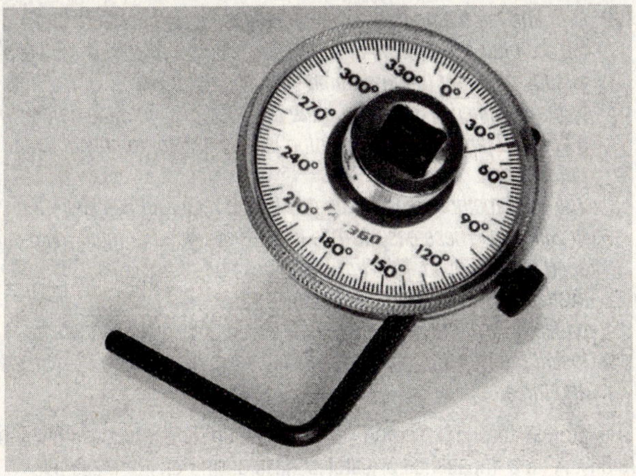

Torque angle gauge

Clutch plate alignment tool

Socket set(s)
Reversible ratchet
Extension - 10 inch
Universal joint
Torque wrench (same size drive as sockets)
Ball peen hammer - 8 ounce
Soft-face hammer (plastic/rubber)
Standard screwdriver (1/4-inch x 6 inch)
Standard screwdriver (stubby - 5/16-inch)
Phillips screwdriver (No. 3 x 8 inch)
Phillips screwdriver (stubby - No. 2)
Pliers - vise grip
Pliers - lineman's
Pliers - needle nose
Pliers - snap-ring (internal and external)
Cold chisel - 1/2-inch
Scribe
Scraper (made from flattened copper tubing)
Centerpunch
Pin punches (1/16, 1/8, 3/16-inch)
Steel rule/straightedge - 12 inch
Allen wrench set (1/8 to 3/8-inch or 4 mm to 10 mm)
A selection of files
Wire brush (large)
Jackstands (second set)
Jack (scissor or hydraulic type)

➡ **Note: Another tool which is often useful is an electric drill with a chuck capacity of 3/8-inch and a set of good quality drill bits.**

Special tools

The tools in this list include those which are not used regularly, are expensive to buy, or which need to be used in accordance with their manufacturer's instructions. Unless these tools will be used frequently, it is not very economical to purchase many of them. A consideration would be to split the cost and use between yourself and a friend or friends. In addition, most of these tools can be obtained from a tool rental shop on a temporary basis.

This list primarily contains only those tools and instruments widely available to the public, and not those special tools produced by the vehicle manufacturer for distribution to dealer service departments. Occasionally, references to the manufacturer's special tools are included in the text of this manual. Generally, an alternative method of doing the job without the special tool is offered. However, sometimes there is no alternative to their use. Where this is the case, and the tool cannot be purchased or borrowed, the work should be turned over to the dealer service department or an automotive repair shop.

Valve spring compressor
Piston ring groove cleaning tool
Piston ring compressor
Piston ring installation tool
Cylinder compression gauge
Cylinder ridge reamer
Cylinder surfacing hone
Cylinder bore gauge
Micrometers and/or dial calipers
Hydraulic lifter removal tool
Balljoint separator
Universal-type puller
Impact screwdriver
Dial indicator set
Stroboscopic timing light (inductive pick-up)
Hand operated vacuum/pressure pump
Tachometer/dwell meter
Universal electrical multimeter
Cable hoist
Brake spring removal and installation tools
Floor jack

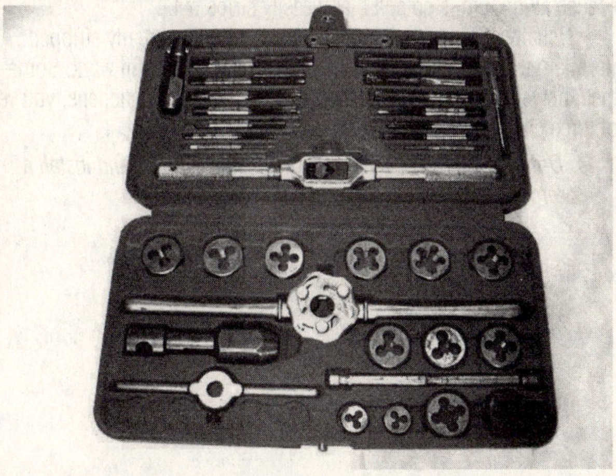

Tap and die set

Buying tools

For the do-it-yourselfer who is just starting to get involved in vehicle maintenance and repair, there are a number of options available when purchasing tools. If maintenance and minor repair is the extent of the work to be done, the purchase of individual tools is satisfactory. If, on the other hand, extensive work is planned, it would be a good idea to purchase a modest tool set from one of the large retail chain stores. A set can usually be bought at a substantial savings over the individual tool prices, and they often come with a tool box. As additional tools are needed, add-on sets, individual tools and a larger tool box can be purchased to expand the tool selection. Building a tool set gradually allows the cost of the tools to be spread over a longer period of time and gives the mechanic the freedom to choose only those tools that will actually be used.

Tool stores will often be the only source of some of the special tools that are needed, but regardless of where tools are bought, try to avoid cheap ones, especially when buying screwdrivers and sockets, because they won't last very long. The expense involved in replacing cheap tools will eventually be greater than the initial cost of quality tools.

Care and maintenance of tools

Good tools are expensive, so it makes sense to treat them with respect. Keep them clean and in usable condition and store them properly when not in use. Always wipe off any dirt, grease or metal chips before putting them away. Never leave tools lying around in the work area. Upon completion of a job, always check closely under the hood for tools that may have been left there so they won't get lost during a test drive.

Some tools, such as screwdrivers, pliers, wrenches and sockets, can be hung on a panel mounted on the garage or workshop wall, while others should be kept in a tool box or tray. Measuring instruments, gauges, meters, etc. must be carefully stored where they cannot be damaged by weather or impact from other tools.

When tools are used with care and stored properly, they will last a very long time. Even with the best of care, though, tools will wear out if used frequently. When a tool is damaged or worn out, replace it. Subsequent jobs will be safer and more enjoyable if you do.

HOW TO REPAIR DAMAGED THREADS

Sometimes, the internal threads of a nut or bolt hole can become stripped, usually from overtightening. Stripping threads is an all-too-common occurrence, especially when working with aluminum parts, because aluminum is so soft that it easily strips out.

Usually, external or internal threads are only partially stripped. After they've been cleaned up with a tap or die, they'll still work. Sometimes, however, threads are badly damaged. When this happens, you've got three choices:

1) *Drill and tap the hole to the next suitable oversize and install a larger diameter bolt, screw or stud.*
2) *Drill and tap the hole to accept a threaded plug, then drill and tap the plug to the original screw size. You can also buy a plug already threaded to the original size. Then you simply drill a hole to the specified size, then run the threaded plug into the hole with a bolt and jam nut. Once the plug is fully seated, remove the jam nut and bolt.*
3) *The third method uses a patented thread repair kit like Heli-Coil or Slimsert. These easy-to-use kits are designed to repair damaged threads in straight-through holes and blind holes. Both are available as kits which can handle a variety of sizes and thread patterns. Drill the hole, then tap it with the special included tap. Install the Heli-Coil and the hole is back to its original diameter and thread pitch.*

Regardless of which method you use, be sure to proceed calmly and carefully. A little impatience or carelessness during one of these relatively simple procedures can ruin your whole day's work and cost you a bundle if you wreck an expensive part.

WORKING FACILITIES

Not to be overlooked when discussing tools is the workshop. If anything more than routine maintenance is to be carried out, some sort of suitable work area is essential.

It is understood, and appreciated, that many home mechanics do not have a good workshop or garage available, and end up removing an engine or doing major repairs outside. It is recommended, however, that the overhaul or repair be completed under the cover of a roof.

A clean, flat workbench or table of comfortable working height is an absolute necessity. The workbench should be equipped with a vise that has a jaw opening of at least four inches.

As mentioned previously, some clean, dry storage space is also required for tools, as well as the lubricants, fluids, cleaning solvents, etc. which soon become necessary.

Sometimes waste oil and fluids, drained from the engine or cooling system during normal maintenance or repairs, present a disposal problem. To avoid pouring them on the ground or into a sewage system, pour the used fluids into large containers, seal them with caps and take them to an authorized disposal site or recycling center. Plastic jugs, such as old antifreeze containers, are ideal for this purpose.

Always keep a supply of old newspapers and clean rags available. Old towels are excellent for mopping up spills. Many mechanics use rolls of paper towels for most work because they are readily available and disposable. To help keep the area under the vehicle clean, a large cardboard box can be cut open and flattened to protect the garage or shop floor.

Whenever working over a painted surface, such as when leaning over a fender to service something under the hood, always cover it with an old blanket or bedspread to protect the finish. Vinyl covered pads, made especially for this purpose, are available at auto parts stores.

Jacking and towing

JACKING

The jack supplied with the vehicle should only be used for raising the vehicle for changing a tire or placing jackstands under the frame.

⁂ WARNING:

Never crawl under the vehicle or start the engine when the jack is being used as the only means of support.

When jacking the vehicle, the jack should be engaged with the rocker panel seam, between the two notches (see illustration).

The vehicle should be on level ground with the wheels blocked and the transmission in Park (automatic). Pry off the hub cap (if equipped) using the tapered end of the lug wrench. Loosen the lug nuts one-half turn and leave them in place until the wheel is raised off the ground.

Place the jack under the side of the vehicle in the indicated position. Use the supplied wrench to turn the jackscrew clockwise until the wheel is raised off the ground. Remove the lug nuts, pull off the wheel and replace it with the spare.

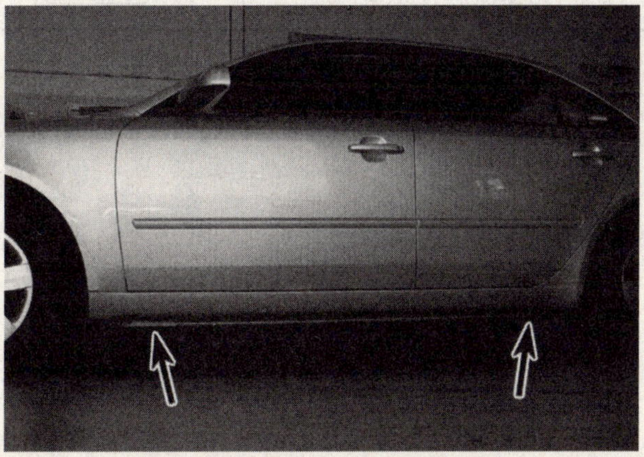

The jack fits between the notches in the rocker panel pinch-weld (there are two jacking points on each side of the vehicle)

With the beveled side in, reinstall the lug nuts and tighten them until snug. Lower the vehicle by turning the jackscrew counterclockwise. Remove the jack and tighten the nuts in a diagonal pattern to the torque listed in the Chapter 1 Specifications. If a torque wrench is not available, have the torque checked by a service station as soon as possible. Install the hubcap by placing it in position and using the heel of your hand or a rubber mallet to seat it.

TOWING

These models can be towed from the front with the front wheels off the ground, using a wheel lift type tow truck. If towed from the rear, the front wheels must be placed on a dolly. A sling-type tow truck cannot be used, as body damage will result. The best way to tow the vehicle is with a flat-bed car carrier.

The vehicle can be towed with all four wheels on the ground, provided that speeds don't exceed 30 mph and the distance is not over 15 miles. Before towing, check the transaxle fluid level (vehicles equipped with an automatic transaxle) (see Chapter 1). If the level is below the HOT mark on the dipstick, add fluid. Additionally, perform the following:

a) Release the parking brake
b) Place the shifter in the Neutral position
c) Place the ignition key in the OFF position (not the LOCK position)
d) Release the parking brake

⁂ CAUTION:

Never tow a vehicle with an automatic transaxle from the rear with the front wheels on the ground.

In an emergency the vehicle can be towed a very short distance with a cable or chain attached to one of the towing eyelets located under the front or rear bumpers. The driver must remain in the vehicle to operate the steering and brakes (remember that power steering and power brakes will not work with the engine off). Make certain that the vehicle is in neutral with the parking brake off.

Booster battery (jump) starting

Observe these precautions when using a booster battery to start a vehicle:

a) *Before connecting the booster battery, make sure the ignition switch is in the Off position.*
b) *Turn off the lights, heater and other electrical loads.*
c) *Your eyes should be shielded. Safety goggles are a good idea.*
d) *Make sure the booster battery is the same voltage as the dead one in the vehicle.*
e) *The two vehicles MUST NOT TOUCH each other!*
f) *Make sure the transaxle is in Neutral (manual) or Park (automatic).*
g) *If the booster battery is not a maintenance-free type, remove the vent caps and lay a cloth over the vent holes.*

Connect the red-colored jumper cable to the positive (+) terminal of the booster battery and the other end to the positive (+) terminal of the dead battery. Then connect one end of the black jumper cable to the negative (-) terminal of the booster battery, and the other end of the cable to a good ground, such as a bolt or bracket.

Start the engine using the booster battery, then run the booster vehicle at a fast idle for a few minutes to instill some charge in the dead battery. Let the engine idle, then disconnect the jumper cables in the reverse order of connection. The vehicle with the dead battery may have to be driven for 20 minutes or more to sufficiently recharge the battery for independent starting.

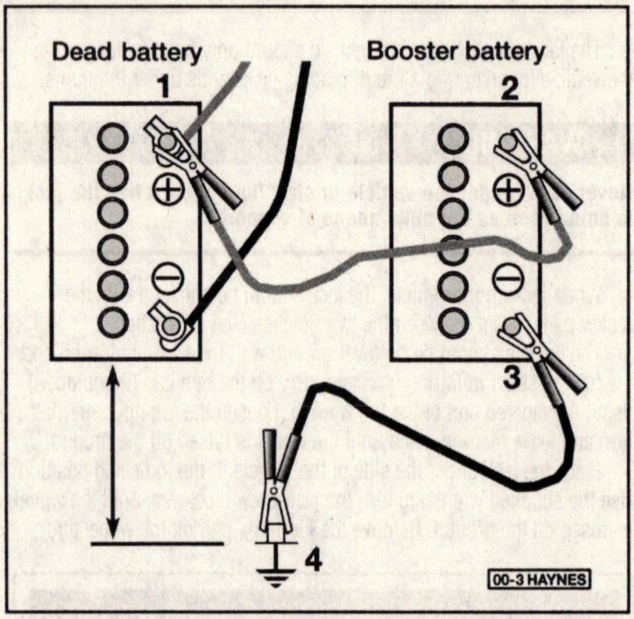

Make the booster battery cable connections in the numerical order shown (note that the negative cable of the booster battery is NOT attached to the negative terminal of the dead battery)

Automotive chemicals and lubricants

A number of automotive chemicals and lubricants are available for use during vehicle maintenance and repair. They include a wide variety of products ranging from cleaning solvents and degreasers to lubricants and protective sprays for rubber, plastic and vinyl.

CLEANERS

Carburetor cleaner and choke cleaner is a strong solvent for gum, varnish and carbon. Most carburetor cleaners leave a dry-type lubricant film which will not harden or gum up. Because of this film it is not recommended for use on electrical components.

Brake system cleaner is used to remove brake dust, grease and brake fluid from the brake system, where clean surfaces are absolutely necessary. It leaves no residue and often eliminates brake squeal caused by contaminants.

Electrical cleaner removes oxidation, corrosion and carbon deposits from electrical contacts, restoring full current flow. It can also be used to clean spark plugs, carburetor jets, voltage regulators and other parts where an oil-free surface is desired.

Demoisturants remove water and moisture from electrical components such as alternators, voltage regulators, electrical connectors and fuse blocks. They are non-conductive and non-corrosive.

Degreasers are heavy-duty solvents used to remove grease from the outside of the engine and from chassis components. They can be sprayed or brushed on and, depending on the type, are rinsed off either with water or solvent.

LUBRICANTS

Motor oil is the lubricant formulated for use in engines. It normally contains a wide variety of additives to prevent corrosion and reduce foaming and wear. Motor oil comes in various weights (viscosity ratings) from 0 to 50. The recommended weight of the oil depends on the season, temperature and the demands on the engine. Light oil is used in cold climates and under light load conditions. Heavy oil is used in hot climates and where high loads are encountered. Multi-viscosity oils are designed to have characteristics of both light and heavy oils and are available in a number of weights from 0W-20 to 20W-50.

Gear oil is designed to be used in differentials, manual transmissions and other areas where high-temperature lubrication is required.

Chassis and wheel bearing grease is a heavy grease used where increased loads and friction are encountered, such as for wheel bearings, balljoints, tie-rod ends and universal joints.

High-temperature wheel bearing grease is designed to withstand the extreme temperatures encountered by wheel bearings in disc brake equipped vehicles. It usually contains molybdenum disulfide (moly), which is a dry-type lubricant.

White grease is a heavy grease for metal-to-metal applications where water is a problem. White grease stays soft under both low and high temperatures (usually from -100 to +190-degrees F), and will not wash off or dilute in the presence of water.

Assembly lube is a special extreme pressure lubricant, usually containing moly, used to lubricate high-load parts (such as main and rod bearings and cam lobes) for initial start-up of a new engine. The assembly lube lubricates the parts without being squeezed out or washed away until the engine oiling system begins to function.

Silicone lubricants are used to protect rubber, plastic, vinyl and nylon parts.

Graphite lubricants are used where oils cannot be used due to contamination problems, such as in locks. The dry graphite will lubricate metal parts while remaining uncontaminated by dirt, water, oil or acids. It is electrically conductive and will not foul electrical contacts in locks such as the ignition switch.

Moly penetrants loosen and lubricate frozen, rusted and corroded fasteners and prevent future rusting or freezing.

Heat-sink grease is a special electrically non-conductive grease that is used for mounting electronic ignition modules where it is essential that heat is transferred away from the module.

SEALANTS

RTV sealant is one of the most widely used gasket compounds. Made from silicone, RTV is air curing, it seals, bonds, waterproofs, fills surface irregularities, remains flexible, doesn't shrink, is relatively easy to remove, and is used as a supplementary sealer with almost all low and medium temperature gaskets.

Anaerobic sealant is much like RTV in that it can be used either to seal gaskets or to form gaskets by itself. It remains flexible, is solvent resistant and fills surface imperfections. The difference between an anaerobic sealant and an RTV-type sealant is in the curing. RTV cures when exposed to air, while an anaerobic sealant cures only in the absence of air. This means that an anaerobic sealant cures only after the assembly of parts, sealing them together.

Thread and pipe sealant is used for sealing hydraulic and pneumatic fittings and vacuum lines. It is usually made from a Teflon compound, and comes in a spray, a paint-on liquid and as a wrap-around tape.

CHEMICALS

Anti-seize compound prevents seizing, galling, cold welding, rust and corrosion in fasteners. High-temperature anti-seize, usually made with copper and graphite lubricants, is used for exhaust system and exhaust manifold bolts.

Anaerobic locking compounds are used to keep fasteners from vibrating or working loose and cure only after installation, in the absence of air. Medium strength locking compound is used for small nuts, bolts and screws that may be removed later. High-strength locking compound is for large nuts, bolts and studs which aren't removed on a regular basis.

Oil additives range from viscosity index improvers to chemical treatments that claim to reduce internal engine friction. It should be noted that most oil manufacturers caution against using additives with their oils.

Gas additives perform several functions, depending on their chemical makeup. They usually contain solvents that help dissolve gum and varnish that build up on carburetor, fuel injection and intake parts. They also serve to break down carbon deposits that form on the inside surfaces of the combustion chambers. Some additives contain upper cylinder lubricants for valves and piston rings, and others contain chemicals to remove condensation from the gas tank.

MISCELLANEOUS

Brake fluid is specially formulated hydraulic fluid that can withstand the heat and pressure encountered in brake systems. Care must be taken so this fluid does not come in contact with painted surfaces or plastics. An opened container should always be resealed to prevent contamination by water or dirt.

Weatherstrip adhesive is used to bond weatherstripping around doors, windows and trunk lids. It is sometimes used to attach trim pieces.

Undercoating is a petroleum-based, tar-like substance that is designed to protect metal surfaces on the underside of the vehicle from corrosion. It also acts as a sound-deadening agent by insulating the bottom of the vehicle.

Waxes and polishes are used to help protect painted and plated surfaces from the weather. Different types of paint may require the use of different types of wax and polish. Some polishes utilize a chemical or abrasive cleaner to help remove the top layer of oxidized (dull) paint on older vehicles. In recent years many non-wax polishes that contain a wide variety of chemicals such as polymers and silicones have been introduced. These non-wax polishes are usually easier to apply and last longer than conventional waxes and polishes.

CONVERSION FACTORS

LENGTH (distance)						
Inches (in)	X	25.4	= Millimeters (mm)	X	0.0394	= Inches (in)
Feet (ft)	X	0.305	= Meters (m)	X	3.281	= Feet (ft)
Miles	X	1.609	= Kilometers (km)	X	0.621	= Miles
VOLUME (capacity)						
Cubic inches (cu in; in^3)	X	16.387	= Cubic centimeters (cc; cm^3)	X	0.061	= Cubic inches (cu in; in^3)
Imperial pints (Imp pt)	X	0.568	= Liters (l)	X	1.76	= Imperial pints (Imp pt)
Imperial quarts (Imp qt)	X	1.137	= Liters (l)	X	0.88	= Imperial quarts (Imp qt)
Imperial quarts (Imp qt)	X	1.201	= US quarts (US qt)	X	0.833	= Imperial quarts (Imp qt)
US quarts (US qt)	X	0.946	= Liters (l)	X	1.057	= US quarts (US qt)
Imperial gallons (Imp gal)	X	4.546	= Liters (l)	X	0.22	= Imperial gallons (Imp gal)
Imperial gallons (Imp gal)	X	1.201	= US gallons (US gal)	X	0.833	= Imperial gallons (Imp gal)
US gallons (US gal)	X	3.785	= Liters (l)	X	0.264	= US gallons (US gal)
MASS (weight)						
Ounces (oz)	X	28.35	= Grams (g)	X	0.035	= Ounces (oz)
Pounds (lb)	X	0.454	= Kilograms (kg)	X	2.205	= Pounds (lb)
FORCE						
Ounces-force (ozf; oz)	X	0.278	= Newtons (N)	X	3.6	= Ounces-force (ozf; oz)
Pounds-force (lbf; lb)	X	4.448	= Newtons (N)	X	0.225	= Pounds-force (lbf; lb)
Newtons (N)	X	0.1	= Kilograms-force (kgf; kg)	X	9.81	= Newtons (N)
PRESSURE						
Pounds-force per square inch (psi; lbf/in^2; lb/in^2)	X	0.070	= Kilograms-force per square centimeter (kgf/cm^2; kg/cm^2)	X	14.223	= Pounds-force per square inch (psi; lbf/in^2; lb/in^2)
Pounds-force per square inch (psi; lbf/in^2; lb/in^2)	X	0.068	= Atmospheres (atm)	X	14.696	= Pounds-force per square inch (psi; lbf/in^2; lb/in^2)
Pounds-force per square inch (psi; lbf/in^2; lb/in^2)	X	0.069	= Bars	X	14.5	= Pounds-force per square inch (psi; lbf/in^2; lb/in^2)
Pounds-force per square inch (psi; lbf/in^2; lb/in^2)	X	6.895	= Kilopascals (kPa)	X	0.145	= Pounds-force per square inch (psi; lbf/in^2; lb/in^2)
Kilopascals (kPa)	X	0.01	= Kilograms-force per square centimeter (kgf/cm^2; kg/cm^2)	X	98.1	= Kilopascals (kPa)
TORQUE (moment of force)						
Pounds-force inches (lbf in; lb in)	X	1.152	= Kilograms-force centimeter (kgf cm; kg cm)	X	0.868	= Pounds-force inches (lbf in; lb in)
Pounds-force inches (lbf in; lb in)	X	0.113	= Newton meters (Nm)	X	8.85	= Pounds-force inches (lbf in; lb in)
Pounds-force inches (lbf in; lb in)	X	0.083	= Pounds-force feet (lbf ft; lb ft)	X	12	= Pounds-force inches (lbf in; lb in)
Pounds-force feet (lbf ft; lb ft)	X	0.138	= Kilograms-force meters (kgf m; kg m)	X	7.233	= Pounds-force feet (lbf ft; lb ft)
Pounds-force feet (lbf ft; lb ft)	X	1.356	= Newton meters (Nm)	X	0.738	= Pounds-force feet (lbf ft; lb ft)
Newton meters (Nm)	X	0.102	= Kilograms-force meters (kgf m; kg m)	X	9.804	= Newton meters (Nm)
VACUUM						
Inches mercury (in. Hg)	X	3.377	= Kilopascals (kPa)	X	0.2961	= Inches mercury
Inches mercury (in. Hg)	X	25.4	= Millimeters mercury (mm Hg)	X	0.0394	= Inches mercury
POWER						
Horsepower (hp)	X	745.7	= Watts (W)	X	0.0013	= Horsepower (hp)
VELOCITY (speed)						
Miles per hour (miles/hr; mph)	X	1.609	= Kilometers per hour (km/hr; kph)	X	0.621	= Miles per hour (miles/hr; mph)
FUEL CONSUMPTION*						
Miles per gallon, Imperial (mpg)	X	0.354	= Kilometers per liter (km/l)	X	2.825	= Miles per gallon, Imperial (mpg)
Miles per gallon, US (mpg)	X	0.425	= Kilometers per liter (km/l)	X	2.352	= Miles per gallon, US (mpg)

TEMPERATURE

Degrees Fahrenheit = (°C x 1.8) + 32

Degrees Celsius (Degrees Centigrade; °C) = (°F - 32) x 0.56

****It is common practice to convert from miles per gallon (mpg) to liters/100 kilometers (l/100km), where mpg (Imperial) x l/100 km = 282 and mpg (US) x l/100 km = 235***

FRACTION/DECIMAL/MILLIMETER EQUIVALENTS

DECIMALS TO MILLIMETERS

Decimal	mm	Decimal	mm
0.001	0.0254	0.500	12.7000
0.002	0.0508	0.510	12.9540
0.003	0.0762	0.520	13.2080
0.004	0.1016	0.530	13.4620
0.005	0.1270	0.540	13.7160
0.006	0.1524	0.550	13.9700
0.007	0.1778	0.560	14.2240
0.008	0.2032	0.570	14.4780
0.009	0.2286	0.580	14.7320
0.010	0.2540	0.590	14.9860
0.020	0.5080	0.600	15.2400
0.030	0.7620	0.610	15.4940
0.040	1.0160	0.620	15.7480
0.050	1.2700	0.630	16.0020
0.060	1.5240	0.640	16.2560
0.070	1.7780	0.650	16.5100
0.080	2.0320	0.660	16.7640
0.090	2.2860	0.670	17.0180
0.100	2.5400	0.680	17.2720
0.110	2.7940	0.690	17.5260
0.120	3.0480	0.700	17.7800
0.130	3.3020	0.710	18.0340
0.140	3.5560	0.720	18.2880
0.150	3.8100	0.730	18.5420
0.160	4.0640	0.740	18.7960
0.170	4.3180	0.750	19.0500
0.180	4.5720	0.760	19.3040
0.190	4.8260	0.770	19.5580
0.200	5.0800	0.780	19.8120
0.210	5.3340	0.790	20.0660
0.220	5.5880	0.800	20.3200
0.230	5.8420	0.810	20.5740
0.240	6.0960	0.820	21.8280
0.250	6.3500	0.830	21.0820
0.260	6.6040	0.840	21.3360
0.270	6.8580	0.850	21.5900
0.280	7.1120	0.860	21.8440
0.290	7.3660	0.870	22.0980
0.300	7.6200	0.880	22.3520
0.310	7.8740	0.890	22.6060
0.320	8.1280	0.900	22.8600
0.330	8.3820	0.910	23.1140
0.340	8.6360	0.920	23.3680
0.350	8.8900	0.930	23.6220
0.360	9.1440	0.940	23.8760
0.370	9.3980	0.950	24.1300
0.380	9.6520	0.960	24.3840
0.390	9.9060	0.970	24.6380
0.400	10.1600	0.980	24.8920
0.410	10.4140	0.990	25.1460
0.420	10.6680	1.000	25.4000
0.430	10.9220		
0.440	11.1760		
0.450	11.4300		
0.460	11.6840		
0.470	11.9380		
0.480	12.1920		
0.490	12.4460		

FRACTIONS TO DECIMALS TO MILLIMETERS

Fraction	Decimal	mm	Fraction	Decimal	mm
1/64	0.0156	0.3969	33/64	0.5156	13.0969
1/32	0.0312	0.7938	17/32	0.5312	13.4938
3/64	0.0469	1.1906	35/64	0.5469	13.8906
1/16	0.0625	1.5875	9/16	0.5625	14.2875
5/64	0.0781	1.9844	37/64	0.5781	14.6844
3/32	0.0938	2.3812	19/32	0.5938	15.0812
7/64	0.1094	2.7781	39/64	0.6094	15.4781
1/8	0.1250	3.1750	5/8	0.6250	15.8750
9/64	0.1406	3.5719	41/64	0.6406	16.2719
5/32	0.1562	3.9688	21/32	0.6562	16.6688
11/64	0.1719	4.3656	43/64	0.6719	17.0656
3/16	0.1875	4.7625	11/16	0.6875	17.4625
13/64	0.2031	5.1594	45/64	0.7031	17.8594
7/32	0.2188	5.5562	23/32	0.7188	18.2562
15/64	0.2344	5.9531	47/64	0.7344	18.6531
1/4	0.2500	6.3500	3/4	0.7500	19.0500
17/64	0.2656	6.7469	49/64	0.7656	19.4469
9/32	0.2812	7.1438	25/32	0.7812	19.8438
19/64	0.2969	7.5406	51/64	0.7969	20.2406
5/16	0.3125	7.9375	13/16	0.8125	20.6375
21/64	0.3281	8.3344	53/64	0.8281	21.0344
11/32	0.3438	8.7312	27/32	0.8438	21.4312
23/64	0.3594	9.1281	55/64	0.8594	21.8281
3/8	0.3750	9.5250	7/8	0.8750	22.2250
25/64	0.3906	9.9219	57/64	0.8906	22.6219
13/32	0.4062	10.3188	29/32	0.9062	23.0188
27/64	0.4219	10.7156	59/64	0.9219	23.4156
7/16	0.4375	11.1125	15/16	0.9375	23.8125
29/64	0.4531	11.5094	61/64	0.9531	24.2094
15/32	0.4688	11.9062	31/32	0.9688	24.6062
31/64	0.4844	12.3031	63/64	0.9844	25.0031
1/2	0.5000	12.7000	1	1.0000	25.4000

Safety first!

Regardless of how enthusiastic you may be about getting on with the job at hand, take the time to ensure that your safety is not jeopardized. A moment's lack of attention can result in an accident, as can failure to observe certain simple safety precautions. The possibility of an accident will always exist, and the following points should not be considered a comprehensive list of all dangers. Rather, they are intended to make you aware of the risks and to encourage a safety conscious approach to all work you carry out on your vehicle.

ESSENTIAL DOS AND DON'TS

DON'T rely on a jack when working under the vehicle. Always use approved jackstands to support the weight of the vehicle and place them under the recommended lift or support points.

DON'T attempt to loosen extremely tight fasteners (i.e. wheel lug nuts) while the vehicle is on a jack - it may fall.

DON'T start the engine without first making sure that the transmission is in Neutral (or Park where applicable) and the parking brake is set.

DON'T remove the radiator cap from a hot cooling system - let it cool or cover it with a cloth and release the pressure gradually.

DON'T attempt to drain the engine oil until you are sure it has cooled to the point that it will not burn you.

DON'T touch any part of the engine or exhaust system until it has cooled sufficiently to avoid burns.

DON'T siphon toxic liquids such as gasoline, antifreeze and brake fluid by mouth, or allow them to remain on your skin.

DON'T inhale brake lining dust - it is potentially hazardous (see Asbestos below).

DON'T allow spilled oil or grease to remain on the floor - wipe it up before someone slips on it.

DON'T use loose fitting wrenches or other tools which may slip and cause injury.

DON'T push on wrenches when loosening or tightening nuts or bolts. Always try to pull the wrench toward you. If the situation calls for pushing the wrench away, push with an open hand to avoid scraped knuckles if the wrench should slip.

DON'T attempt to lift a heavy component alone - get someone to help you.

DON'T rush or take unsafe shortcuts to finish a job.

DON'T allow children or animals in or around the vehicle while you are working on it.

DO wear eye protection when using power tools such as a drill, sander, bench grinder, etc. and when working under a vehicle.

DO keep loose clothing and long hair well out of the way of moving parts.

DO make sure that any hoist used has a safe working load rating adequate for the job.

DO get someone to check on you periodically when working alone on a vehicle.

DO carry out work in a logical sequence and make sure that everything is correctly assembled and tightened.

DO keep chemicals and fluids tightly capped and out of the reach of children and pets.

DO remember that your vehicle's safety affects that of yourself and others. If in doubt on any point, get professional advice.

STEERING, SUSPENSION AND BRAKES

These systems are essential to driving safety, so make sure you have a qualified shop or individual check your work. Also, compressed suspension springs can cause injury if released suddenly - be sure to use a spring compressor.

AIRBAGS

Airbags are explosive devices that can CAUSE injury if they deploy while you're working on the vehicle. Follow the manufacturer's instructions to disable the airbag whenever you're working in the vicinity of airbag components.

ASBESTOS

Certain friction, insulating, sealing, and other products - such as brake linings, brake bands, clutch linings, torque converters, gaskets, etc. - may contain asbestos or other hazardous friction material. Extreme care must be taken to avoid inhalation of dust from such products, since it is hazardous to health. If in doubt, assume that they do contain asbestos.

FIRE

Remember at all times that gasoline is highly flammable. Never smoke or have any kind of open flame around when working on a vehicle. But the risk does not end there. A spark caused by an electrical short circuit, by two metal surfaces contacting each other, or even by static electricity built up in your body under certain conditions, can ignite gasoline vapors, which in a confined space are highly explosive. Do not, under any circumstances, use gasoline for cleaning parts. Use an approved safety solvent.

Always disconnect the battery ground (-) cable at the battery before working on any part of the fuel system or electrical system. Never risk spilling fuel on a hot engine or exhaust component. It is strongly recommended that a fire extinguisher suitable for use on fuel and electrical fires be kept handy in the garage or workshop at all times. Never try to extinguish a fuel or electrical fire with water.

FUMES

Certain fumes are highly toxic and can quickly cause unconsciousness and even death if inhaled to any extent. Gasoline vapor falls into this category, as do the vapors from some cleaning solvents. Any draining or pouring of such volatile fluids should be done in a well ventilated area.

When using cleaning fluids and solvents, read the instructions on the container carefully. Never use materials from unmarked containers.

Never run the engine in an enclosed space, such as a garage. Exhaust fumes contain carbon monoxide, which is extremely poisonous. If you need to run the engine, always do so in the open air, or at least have the rear of the vehicle outside the work area.

THE BATTERY

Never create a spark or allow a bare light bulb near a battery. They normally give off a certain amount of hydrogen gas, which is highly explosive.

Always disconnect the battery ground (-) cable at the battery before working on the fuel or electrical systems.

If possible, loosen the filler caps or cover when charging the battery from an external source (this does not apply to sealed or maintenance-free batteries). Do not charge at an excessive rate or the battery may burst.

Take care when adding water to a non maintenance-free battery and when carrying a battery. The electrolyte, even when diluted, is very corrosive and should not be allowed to contact clothing or skin.

Always wear eye protection when cleaning the battery to prevent the caustic deposits from entering your eyes.

HOUSEHOLD CURRENT

When using an electric power tool, inspection light, etc., which operates on household current, always make sure that the tool is correctly connected to its plug and that, where necessary, it is properly grounded. Do not use such items in damp conditions and, again, do not create a spark or apply excessive heat in the vicinity of fuel or fuel vapor.

SECONDARY IGNITION SYSTEM VOLTAGE

A severe electric shock can result from touching certain parts of the ignition system (such as the spark plug wires) when the engine is running or being cranked, particularly if components are damp or the insulation is defective. In the case of an electronic ignition system, the secondary system voltage is much higher and could prove fatal.

HYDROFLUORIC ACID

This extremely corrosive acid is formed when certain types of synthetic rubber, found in some O-rings, oil seals, fuel hoses, etc. are exposed to temperatures above 750-degrees F (400-degrees C). The rubber changes into a charred or sticky substance containing the acid. *Once formed, the acid remains dangerous for years. If it gets onto the skin, it may be necessary to amputate the limb concerned.*

When dealing with a vehicle which has suffered a fire, or with components salvaged from such a vehicle, wear protective gloves and discard them after use.

Troubleshooting

CONTENTS

This section provides an easy reference guide to the more common problems which may occur during the operation of your vehicle. These problems and their possible causes are grouped under headings denoting various components or systems, such as Engine, Cooling system, etc. They also refer you to the chapter and/or section which deals with the problem.

Remember that successful troubleshooting is not a mysterious black art practiced only by professional mechanics. It is simply the result of the right knowledge combined with an intelligent, systematic approach to the problem. Always work by a process of elimination, starting with the simplest solution and working through to the most complex - and never overlook the obvious. Anyone can run the gas tank dry or leave the lights on overnight, so don't assume that you are exempt from such oversights.

Finally, always establish a clear idea of why a problem has occurred and take steps to ensure that it doesn't happen again. If the electrical system fails because of a poor connection, check the other connections in the system to make sure that they don't fail as well. If a particular fuse continues to blow, find out why - don't just replace one fuse after another. Remember, failure of a small component can often be indicative of potential failure or incorrect functioning of a more important component or system.

ENGINE

1 Engine will not rotate when attempting to start

1 Battery terminal connections loose or corroded (Chapter 1).
2 Battery discharged or faulty (Chapters 1 and 5).
3 Automatic transaxle not completely engaged in Park (Chapter 7) or clutch pedal not completely depressed (Chapter 6).
4 Broken, loose or disconnected wiring in the starting circuit (Chapters 5 and 12).
5 Starter motor pinion jammed in flywheel ring gear (Chapter 5).
6 Starter solenoid faulty (Chapter 5).
7 Starter motor faulty (Chapter 5).
8 Ignition switch faulty (Chapter 12).
9 Starter pinion or flywheel teeth worn or broken (Chapter 5).

2 Engine rotates but will not start

1 Fuel tank empty.
2 Battery discharged (engine rotates slowly) (Chapter 5).
3 Battery terminal connections loose or corroded (Chapter 1).
4 Leaking fuel injector(s), faulty fuel pump, pressure regulator, etc. (Chapter 4).
5 Broken or stripped timing belt (Chapter 2A) or broken timing chain (Chapter 2B).
6 Ignition components damp or damaged (Chapter 5).
7 Worn, faulty or incorrectly gapped spark plugs (Chapter 1).
8 Broken, loose or disconnected wiring in the starting circuit (Chapter 5).
9 Broken, loose or disconnected wires at the ignition coil or faulty coil (Chapter 5).
10 Defective crankshaft or camshaft sensor (Chapter 6).

3 Engine hard to start when cold

1 Battery discharged or low (Chapter 1).
2 Malfunctioning fuel system (Chapter 4).
3 Faulty coolant temperature sensor or intake air temperature sensor (Chapter 6).
4 Faulty ignition system (Chapter 5).

4 Engine hard to start when hot

1 Air filter clogged (Chapter 1).
2 Fuel not reaching the fuel injection system (Chapter 4).
3 Corroded battery connections, especially ground (Chapter 1).
4 Faulty coolant temperature sensor or intake air temperature sensor (Chapter 6).

5 Starter motor noisy or excessively rough in engagement

1 Pinion or flywheel gear teeth worn or broken (Chapter 5).
2 Starter motor mounting bolts loose or missing (Chapter 5).

6 Engine starts but stops immediately

1 Loose or faulty electrical connections at ignition coil or alternator (Chapter 5).
2 Insufficient fuel reaching the fuel injector(s) (Chapters 1 and 4).
3 Vacuum leak at the gasket between the intake manifold/plenum and throttle body (Chapter 4).

7 Oil puddle under engine

1 Oil pan gasket and/or oil pan drain bolt washer leaking (Chapter 2).
2 Oil pressure sending unit leaking (Chapter 2).
3 Valve cover leaking (Chapter 2).
4 Engine oil seals leaking (Chapter 2).
5 Oil pump housing leaking (Chapter 2).

8 Engine lopes while idling or idles erratically

1 Vacuum leakage (Chapters 2 and 4).
2 Leaking EGR valve (Chapter 6).
3 Air filter clogged (Chapter 1).
4 Malfunction in the fuel injection or engine control system (Chapters 4 and 6).
5 Leaking head gasket (Chapter 2).
6 Timing belt or chain and/or sprockets worn (Chapter 2).
7 Camshaft lobes worn (Chapter 2).

9 Engine misses at idle speed

1 Spark plugs worn or not gapped properly (Chapter 1).
2 Faulty spark plug wires (Chapter 1).
3 Vacuum leaks (Chapter 1).
4 Incorrect ignition timing (Chapter 1).
5 Uneven or low compression (Chapter 2).
6 Problem with the fuel injection system (Chapter 4).

10 Engine misses throughout driving speed range

1 Fuel filter clogged and/or impurities in the fuel system (Chapters 1 and 4).
2 Low fuel pressure (Chapter 4).
3 Faulty or incorrectly gapped spark plugs (Chapter 1).
4 Leaking spark plug wires (Chapters 1 or 5).
5 Faulty emission system components (Chapter 6).
6 Low or uneven cylinder compression pressures (Chapter 2).
7 Weak or faulty ignition system (Chapter 5).
8 Vacuum leak in fuel injection system, intake manifold, air control valve or vacuum hoses (Chapters 4 and 6).

11 Engine stumbles on acceleration

1 Spark plugs fouled (Chapter 1).
2 Problem with fuel injection or engine control system (Chapters 4 and 6).
3 Fuel filter clogged (Chapters 1 and 4).
4 Intake manifold air leak (Chapters 2 and 4).
5 Problem with the emissions control system (Chapter 6).

12 Engine surges while holding accelerator steady

1 Intake air leak (Chapter 4).
2 Fuel pump or fuel pressure regulator faulty (Chapter 4).
3 Problem with the fuel injection system (Chapter 4).
4 Problem with the emissions control system (Chapter 6).

13 Engine stalls

1 Idle speed incorrect (Chapter 1).
2 Fuel filter clogged and/or water and impurities in the fuel system (Chapters 1 and 4).
3 Distributor components damp or damaged (Chapter 5).
4 Faulty emissions system components (Chapter 6).
5 Faulty or incorrectly gapped spark plugs (Chapter 1).
6 Faulty spark plug wires (Chapter 1).
7 Vacuum leak in the fuel injection system, intake manifold or vacuum hoses (Chapters 2 and 4).

14 Engine lacks power

1 Obstructed exhaust system (Chapter 4).
2 Defective spark plug wires or faulty coil (Chapters 1 and 5).
3 Faulty or incorrectly gapped spark plugs (Chapter 1).
4 Problem with the fuel injection system (Chapter 4).
5 Plugged air filter (Chapter 1).
6 Brakes binding (Chapter 9).
7 Automatic transaxle fluid level incorrect (Chapter 1).
8 Clutch slipping (Chapter 8).
9 Fuel filter clogged and/or impurities in the fuel system (Chapters 1 and 4).
10 Emission control system not functioning properly (Chapter 6).
11 Low or uneven cylinder compression pressures (Chapter 2).

15 Engine backfires

1 Emission control system not functioning properly (Chapter 6).
2 Problem with the fuel injection system (Chapter 4).
3 Vacuum leak at fuel injector(s), intake manifold, air control valve or vacuum hoses (Chapters 2 and 4).
4 Valve clearances incorrectly set and/or valves sticking (Chapter 2).

16 Pinging/knocking engine sounds during acceleration or uphill

1 Incorrect grade of fuel.
2 Fuel injection system faulty (Chapter 4).
3 Improper or damaged spark plugs or wires (Chapter 1).
4 Knock sensor defective (Chapter 6).
5 EGR valve not functioning (Chapter 6).
6 Vacuum leak (Chapters 2 and 4).

17 Engine runs with oil pressure light on

1 Low oil level (Chapter 1).
2 Idle rpm below specification (Chapter 1).
3 Short in wiring circuit (Chapter 12).
4 Faulty oil pressure sender (Chapter 2).
5 Worn engine bearings and/or oil pump (Chapter 2).

18 Engine continues to run after switching off

1 Idle speed too high (Chapter 1).
2 Excessive engine operating temperature (Chapter 3).

ENGINE ELECTRICAL SYSTEMS

19 Battery will not hold a charge

1 Alternator drivebelt defective or not adjusted properly (Chapter 1).
2 Battery electrolyte level low (Chapter 1).
3 Battery terminals loose or corroded (Chapter 1).
4 Alternator not charging properly (Chapter 5).
5 Loose, broken or faulty wiring in the charging circuit (Chapter 5).
6 Short in vehicle wiring (Chapter 12).
7 Internally defective battery (Chapters 1 and 5).

20 Alternator light fails to go out

1 Faulty alternator or charging circuit (Chapter 5).
2 Alternator drivebelt defective or out of adjustment (Chapter 1).
3 Alternator voltage regulator inoperative (Chapter 5).

21 Alternator light fails to come on when key is turned on

1 Warning light bulb defective (Chapter 12).
2 Fault in the printed circuit, dash wiring or bulb holder (Chapter 12).

FUEL SYSTEM

22 Excessive fuel consumption

1 Dirty or clogged air filter element (Chapter 1).
2 Emissions system not functioning properly (Chapter 6).

3 Fuel injection system not functioning properly (Chapter 4).
4 Low tire pressure or incorrect tire size (Chapter 1).

23 Fuel leakage and/or fuel odor

1 Leaking fuel feed or return line (Chapters 1 and 4).
2 Tank overfilled.
3 Evaporative canister filter clogged (Chapters 1 and 6).
4 Problem with the fuel injection system (Chapter 4).

COOLING SYSTEM

24 Overheating

1 Insufficient coolant in system (Chapter 1).
2 Water pump drivebelt defective or out of adjustment (Chapter 1).
3 Radiator core blocked or grille restricted (Chapter 3).
4 Thermostat faulty (Chapter 3).
5 Electric coolant fan inoperative or blades broken (Chapter 3).
6 Radiator cap not maintaining proper pressure (Chapter 3).

25 Overcooling

1 Faulty thermostat (Chapter 3).
2 Inaccurate temperature gauge sending unit (Chapter 3).

26 External coolant leakage

1 Deteriorated/damaged hoses; loose clamps (Chapters 1 and 3).
2 Water pump defective (Chapter 3).
3 Leakage from radiator core or coolant reservoir (Chapter 3).
4 Engine drain or water jacket core plugs leaking (Chapter 2).

27 Internal coolant leakage

1 Leaking cylinder head gasket (Chapter 2).
2 Cracked cylinder bore or cylinder head (Chapter 2).

28 Coolant loss

1 Too much coolant in reservoir (Chapter 1).
2 Coolant boiling away because of overheating (Chapter 3).
3 Internal or external leakage (Chapter 3).
4 Faulty radiator cap (Chapter 3).

29 Poor coolant circulation

1 Inoperative water pump (Chapter 3).
2 Restriction in cooling system (Chapters 1 and 3).
3 Water pump drivebelt defective/out of adjustment (Chapter 1).
4 Thermostat sticking (Chapter 3).

CLUTCH

30 Pedal travels to floor - no pressure or very little resistance

1 Master or release cylinder faulty (Chapter 8).
2 Hose/pipe burst or leaking (Chapter 8).
3 Connections leaking (Chapter 8).
4 No fluid in reservoir (Chapter 8).
5 If fluid level in reservoir rises as pedal is depressed, master cylinder center valve seal is faulty (Chapter 8).
6 If there is fluid on dust seal at master cylinder, piston primary seal is leaking (Chapter 8).
7 Broken release bearing or fork (Chapter 8).
8 Faulty pressure plate diaphragm spring (Chapter 8).

31 Fluid in area of master cylinder dust cover and on pedal

Rear seal failure in master cylinder (Chapter 8).

32 Fluid on release cylinder

Release cylinder plunger seal faulty (Chapter 8).

33 Pedal feels spongy when depressed

Air in system (Chapter 8).

34 Unable to select gears

1 Faulty transaxle (Chapter 7).
2 Faulty clutch disc or pressure plate (Chapter 8).
3 Faulty release lever or release bearing (Chapter 8).
4 Faulty shift lever assembly or control cables (Chapter 8).

35 Clutch slips (engine speed increases with no increase in vehicle speed)

1 Clutch plate worn (Chapter 8).
2 Clutch plate is oil soaked by leaking rear main seal (Chapters 2 and 8).
3 Clutch plate not seated (Chapter 8).
4 Warped pressure plate or flywheel (Chapter 8).
5 Weak pressure plate diaphragm spring (Chapter 8).
6 Clutch plate overheated. Allow to cool.

36 Grabbing (chattering) as clutch is engaged

1 Oil on clutch plate lining, burned or glazed facings (Chapter 8).
2 Worn or loose engine or transaxle mounts (Chapter 2).
3 Worn splines on clutch plate hub (Chapter 8).
4 Warped pressure plate or flywheel (Chapter 8).
5 Burned or smeared resin on flywheel or pressure plate (Chapter 8).

37 Transaxle rattling (clicking)

1 Release lever loose (Chapter 8).
2 Clutch plate damper spring failure (Chapter 8).

38 Noise in clutch area

1 Fork shaft improperly installed (Chapter 8).
2 Faulty bearing (Chapter 8).

39 Clutch pedal stays on floor

1 Clutch master cylinder piston binding in bore (Chapter 8).
2 Broken release bearing or fork (Chapter 8).

40 High pedal effort

1 Piston binding in bore (Chapter 8).
2 Pressure plate faulty (Chapter 8).
3 Incorrect size master or release cylinder (Chapter 8).

MANUAL TRANSAXLE

41 Knocking noise at low speeds

1 Worn driveaxle constant velocity (CV) joints (Chapter 8).
2 Worn side gear shaft counterbore in differential case (Chapter 7A).*

42 Noise most pronounced when turning

Differential gear noise (Chapter 7A).*

43 Clunk on acceleration or deceleration

1 Loose engine or transaxle mounts (Chapter 2).
2 Worn differential pinion shaft in case.*
3 Worn side gear shaft counterbore in differential case (Chapter 7A).*
4 Worn or damaged driveaxle inboard CV joints (Chapter 8).

44 Clicking noise in turns

Worn or damaged outboard CV joint (Chapter 8).

45 Vibration

1 Rough wheel bearing (Chapter 10).
2 Damaged driveaxle (Chapter 8).
3 Out-of-round tires (Chapter 1).
4 Tire out of balance (Chapters 1 and 10).
5 Worn CV joint (Chapter 8).

46 Noisy in neutral with engine running

1 Damaged input gear bearing (Chapter 7A).*
2 Damaged clutch release bearing (Chapter 8).

47 Noisy in one particular gear

1 Damaged or worn constant mesh gears (Chapter 7A).*
2 Damaged or worn synchronizers (Chapter 7A).*
3 Bent reverse fork (Chapter 7A).*
4 Damaged fourth speed gear or output gear (Chapter 7A).*
5 Worn or damaged reverse idler gear or idler bushing (Chapter 7A).*

48 Noisy in all gears

1 Insufficient lubricant (Chapter 7A).
2 Damaged or worn bearings (Chapter 7A).*
3 Worn or damaged input gear shaft and/or output gear shaft (Chapter 7A).*

49 Slips out of gear

1 Worn or improperly adjusted linkage (Chapter 7A).
2 Shift linkage does not work freely, binds (Chapter 7A).
3 Input gear bearing retainer broken or loose (Chapter 7A).*
4 Worn shift fork (Chapter 7A).*

50 Leaks lubricant

1 Side gear shaft seals worn (Chapter 7).
2 Excessive amount of lubricant in transaxle (Chapters 1 and 7A).
3 Loose or broken input gear shaft bearing retainer (Chapter 7A).*
4 Input gear bearing retainer O-ring and/or lip seal damaged (Chapter 7A).*

51 Locked in gear

Lock pin or interlock pin missing (Chapter 7A).*

** Although the corrective action necessary to remedy the symptoms described is beyond the scope of this manual, the above information should be helpful in isolating the cause of the condition so that the owner can communicate clearly with a professional mechanic.*

AUTOMATIC TRANSAXLE

➡ **Note: Due to the complexity of the automatic transaxle, it is difficult for the home mechanic to properly diagnose and service this component. For problems other than the following, the vehicle should be taken to a dealer or transmission shop.**

52 Fluid leakage

1 Automatic transaxle fluid is a deep red color. Fluid leaks should not be confused with engine oil, which can easily be blown onto the transaxle by air flow.

2 To pinpoint a leak, first remove all built-up dirt and grime from the transaxle housing with degreasing agents and/or steam cleaning. Then drive the vehicle at low speeds so air flow will not blow the leak far from its source. Raise the vehicle and determine where the leak is coming from. Common areas of leakage are:

a) Dipstick tube (Chapters 1 and 7)
b) Transaxle oil lines (Chapter 7)
c) Speed sensor (Chapter 6)
d) Driveaxle oil seals (Chapter 7).

53 Transaxle fluid brown or has a burned smell

Transaxle fluid overheated (Chapter 1).

54 General shift mechanism problems

1 Chapter 7, Part B, deals with checking and adjusting the shift

linkage on automatic transaxles. Common problems which may be attributed to poorly adjusted linkage are:

a) Engine starting in gears other than Park or Neutral.
b) Indicator on shifter pointing to a gear other than the one actually being used.
c) Vehicle moves when in Park.

2 Refer to Chapter 7B for the shift linkage adjustment procedure.

55 Transaxle slips, shifts roughly, is noisy or has no drive in forward or reverse gears

There are many probable causes for the above problems, but the home mechanic should be concerned with only one possibility - fluid level. Before taking the vehicle to a repair shop, check the level and condition of the fluid (Chapter 1). Correct the fluid level as necessary or change the fluid and filter if needed. If the problem persists, have a professional diagnose the cause.

DRIVEAXLES

56 Clicking noise in turns

Worn or damaged outboard CV joint (Chapter 8).

57 Shudder or vibration during acceleration

1 Excessive toe-in (Chapter 10).
2 Worn or damaged inboard or outboard CV joints (Chapter 8).
3 Sticking inboard CV joint assembly (Chapter 8).

58 Vibration at highway speeds

1 Out-of-balance front wheels and/or tires (Chapters 1 and 10).
2 Out-of-round front tires (Chapters 1 and 10).
3 Worn CV joint(s) (Chapter 8).

BRAKES

➡ **Note: Before assuming that a brake problem exists, make sure that:**

a) The tires are in good condition and properly inflated (Chapter 1).
b) The front end alignment is correct.
c) The vehicle is not loaded with weight in an unequal manner.

59 Vehicle pulls to one side during braking

1 Incorrect tire pressures (Chapter 1).
2 Front end out of alignment (have the front end aligned).
3 Front, or rear, tire sizes not matched to one another.
4 Restricted brake lines or hoses (Chapter 9).
5 Malfunctioning drum brake or caliper assembly (Chapter 9).
6 Loose suspension parts (Chapter 10).
7 Excessive wear of brake shoe or pad material or disc/drum on one side (Chapter 9).
8 Contamination (grease or brake fluid) of brake shoe or pad material or disc/drum on one side (Chapter 9).

60 Noise (high-pitched squeal when the brakes are applied)

Front brake pads worn out. Replace pads with new ones immediately (Chapter 9).

61 Brake roughness or chatter (pedal pulsates)

1 Excessive lateral runout (Chapter 9).
2 Uneven pad wear (Chapter 9).
3 Defective disc (Chapter 9).

62 Excessive brake pedal effort required to stop vehicle

1 Malfunctioning power brake booster (Chapter 9).
2 Partial system failure (Chapter 9).
3 Excessively worn pads or shoes (Chapter 9).
4 Piston in caliper or wheel cylinder stuck or sluggish (Chapter 9).
5 Brake pads or shoes contaminated with oil or grease (Chapter 9).
6 Brake disc grooved and/or glazed (Chapter 9).
7 New pads or shoes installed and not yet seated. It will take a while for the new material to seat against the disc or drum.

63 Excessive brake pedal travel

1 Partial brake system failure (Chapter 9).
2 Insufficient fluid in master cylinder (Chapters 1 and 9).
3 Air trapped in system (Chapter 9).

64 Dragging brakes

1 Incorrect adjustment of brake light switch (Chapter 9).
2 Master cylinder pistons not returning correctly (Chapter 9).
3 Restricted brakes lines or hoses (Chapter 9).
4 Incorrect parking brake adjustment (Chapter 9).

65 Grabbing or uneven braking action

1 Binding brake pedal mechanism (Chapter 9).
2 Contaminated brake linings (Chapter 9).

66 Brake pedal feels spongy when depressed

1 Air in hydraulic lines (Chapter 9).
2 Master cylinder mounting bolts loose (Chapter 9).
3 Master cylinder defective (Chapter 9).

67 Brake pedal travels to the floor with little resistance

1 Little or no fluid in the master cylinder reservoir caused by leaking caliper or wheel cylinder piston(s) (Chapter 9).
2 Loose, damaged or disconnected brake lines (Chapter 9).

68 Parking brake does not hold

Parking brake linkage improperly adjusted (Chapter 9).

SUSPENSION AND STEERING SYSTEMS

➡ Note: Before attempting to diagnose the suspension and steering systems, perform the following preliminary checks:

a) Tires for wrong pressure and uneven wear.
b) Steering universal joints from the column to the rack and pinion for loose connectors or wear.
c) Front and rear suspension and the rack and pinion assembly for loose or damaged parts.
d) Out-of-round or out-of-balance tires, bent rims and loose and/or rough wheel bearings.

69 Vehicle pulls to one side

1 Mismatched or uneven tires (Chapter 10).
2 Broken or sagging springs (Chapter 10).
3 Wheel alignment incorrect. Have the wheels professionally aligned.
4 Front brake dragging (Chapter 9).

70 Abnormal or excessive tire wear

1 Wheel alignment out-of-specification. Have the wheels aligned.
2 Sagging or broken springs (Chapter 10).
3 Tire out-of-balance (Chapter 10).
4 Worn strut damper (Chapter 10).
5 Overloaded vehicle.
6 Tires not rotated regularly.

71 Wheel makes a thumping noise

1 Blister or bump on tire (Chapter 10).
2 Improper strut damper action (Chapter 10).

72 Shimmy, shake or vibration

1 Tire or wheel out-of-balance or out-of-round (Chapter 10).
2 Worn wheel bearings (Chapter 10).
3 Worn tie-rod ends (Chapter 10).
4 Worn balljoints (Chapters 1 and 10).
5 Excessive wheel runout (Chapter 10).
6 Blister or bump on tire (Chapter 10).

73 Hard steering

1 Lack of lubrication at balljoints and/or tie-rod ends (Chapter 10).
2 Wheel alignment out-of-specifications. Have the wheels professionally aligned.
3 Low tire pressure(s) (Chapter 1).
4 Worn steering gear (Chapter 10).

74 Poor returnability of steering to center

1 Lack of lubrication at balljoints and tie-rod ends (Chapter 10).
2 Binding in balljoints (Chapter 10).
3 Binding in steering column (Chapter 10).
4 Lack of lubricant in steering gear assembly (Chapter 10).
5 Wheel alignment out-of-specifications. Have the wheels professionally aligned.

75 Abnormal noise at the front end

1 Lack of lubrication at balljoints and tie-rod ends (Chapters 1 and 10).
2 Damaged strut mounting (Chapter 10).
3 Worn control arm bushings or tie-rod ends (Chapter 10).
4 Loose stabilizer bar (Chapter 10).
5 Loose wheel nuts (Chapter 1).
6 Loose suspension bolts (Chapter 10).

76 Wander or poor steering stability

1 Mismatched or uneven tires (Chapter 10).
2 Lack of lubrication at balljoints and tie-rod ends (Chapters 1 and 10).
3 Worn strut assemblies (Chapter 10).
4 Loose stabilizer bar (Chapter 10).
5 Broken or sagging springs (Chapter 10).
6 Wheels out of alignment. Have the wheels professionally aligned.

77 Erratic steering when braking

1 Wheel bearings worn (Chapter 10).
2 Broken or sagging springs (Chapter 10).
3 Leaking wheel cylinder or caliper (Chapter 10).
4 Warped rotors or drums (Chapter 10).

78 Excessive pitching and/or rolling around corners or during braking

1 Loose stabilizer bar (Chapter 10).
2 Worn strut dampers or mountings (Chapter 10).
3 Broken or sagging springs (Chapter 10).
4 Overloaded vehicle.

79 Suspension bottoms

1 Overloaded vehicle.
2 Sagging springs (Chapter 10).

80 Cupped tires

1 Front wheel or rear wheel alignment out-of-specifications. Have the wheels professionally aligned.
2 Worn strut dampers or shock absorbers (Chapter 10).
3 Wheel bearings worn (Chapter 10).
4 Excessive tire or wheel runout (Chapter 10).
5 Worn balljoints (Chapter 10).

81 Excessive tire wear on outside edge

1 Inflation pressures incorrect (Chapter 1).
2 Excessive speed in turns.
3 Wheel alignment incorrect (excessive toe-in). Have professionally aligned.
4 Suspension arm bent or twisted (Chapter 10).

82 Excessive tire wear on inside edge

1 Inflation pressures incorrect (Chapter 1).
2 Wheel alignment incorrect (toe-out). Have professionally aligned.
3 Loose or damaged steering components (Chapter 10).

83 Tire tread worn in one place

1 Tires out-of-balance.
2 Damaged or buckled wheel. Inspect and replace if necessary.
3 Defective tire (Chapter 1).

84 Excessive play or looseness in steering system

1 Wheel bearing(s) worn (Chapter 10).
2 Tie-rod end loose (Chapter 10).
3 Steering gear loose (Chapter 10).
4 Worn or loose steering intermediate shaft U-joint (Chapter 10).

85 Rattling or clicking noise in steering gear

1 Steering gear loose (Chapter 10).
2 Steering gear defective.

Notes

Notes

1

TUNE-UP AND ROUTINE MAINTENANCE

Section

1 Kia Optima Maintenance Schedule

The maintenance intervals in this manual are provided with the assumption that you, not the dealer, will be doing the work. These are the minimum maintenance intervals recommended by the factory for vehicles that are driven daily. If you wish to keep your vehicle in peak condition at all times, you may wish to perform some of these procedures even more often. Because frequent maintenance enhances the efficiency, performance and resale value of your car, we encourage you to do so. If you drive in dusty areas, tow a trailer, idle or drive at low speeds for extended periods or drive for short distances (less than four miles) in below freezing temperatures, shorter intervals are also recommended.

When your vehicle is new, it should be serviced by a factory authorized dealer service department to protect the factory warranty. In many cases, the initial maintenance check is done at no cost to the owner.

EVERY 250 MILES (400 KM) OR WEEKLY, WHICHEVER COMES FIRST

Check the engine oil level (Section 4)
Check the engine coolant level (Section 4)
Check the windshield washer fluid level (Section 4)
Check the brake fluid level (Section 4)
Check the clutch fluid level (Section 4)
Check the power steering fluid level (Section 4)
Check the automatic transaxle fluid level (Section 4)
Check the tires and tire pressures (Section 5)

EVERY 3000 MILES (4,800 KM) OR 3 MONTHS, WHICHEVER COMES FIRST

All items listed above plus:
Change the engine oil and oil filter (Section 6)

EVERY 5000 MILES (8000 KM) OR 6 MONTHS, WHICHEVER COMES FIRST

All items listed above plus:
Check and service the battery (Section 7)
Rotate the tires (Section 8)
Inspect and replace if necessary the windshield wiper blades (Section 9)
Inspect and replace if necessary all underhood hoses (Section 10)
Check the cooling system (Section 11)
Inspect the brake system (Section 12)

EVERY 15,000 MILES (24,000 KM) OR 18 MONTHS, WHICHEVER COMES FIRST

All items listed above plus:
Inspect the suspension, steering components and driveaxle boots (Section 13)*
Inspect the exhaust system (Section 14)

EVERY 30,000 MILES (48,000 KM) OR 36 MONTHS, WHICHEVER COMES FIRST

All items listed above plus:
Replace the air filter (Section 15)*
Inspect the fuel system (Section 16)
Replace the interior ventilation filter (Section 17)*
Check and replace (if necessary) the PCV valve (Section 18)
Change the brake fluid (Section 19)

EVERY 50,000 MILES (80,500 KM) OR 60 MONTHS, WHICHEVER COMES FIRST

Service the cooling system (drain, flush and refill) (Section 26) (after the initial 100,000-mile [160,000 km] or 120-month service)
Replace the fuel filter (Section 21)

EVERY 60,000 MILES (96,000 KM) OR 72 MONTHS, WHICHEVER COMES FIRST

All items listed above plus:
Check and adjust if necessary the engine drivebelts (Section 20)
Change the automatic transaxle fluid (Section 22)**
Replace the manual transaxle lubricant (Section 23)**
Replace the timing belt (2006 and earlier four-cylinder and all V6 models) (Section 24)
Check and, if necessary, adjust the valve clearances (2006.5 and later models) (Section 25)

100,000 MILES (160,000 KM) OR 120 MONTHS, WHICHEVER COMES FIRST - THEREAFTER EVERY 50,000 MILES (80,500 KM) OR 60 MONTHS, WHICHEVER COMES FIRST

Service the cooling system (drain, flush and refill) (Section 26)

EVERY 120,000 MILES (193,000 KM) OR 144 MONTHS, WHICHEVER COMES FIRST

Replace the spark plugs (Section 27)
Check the ignition system components (Section 28)

* *This item is affected by "severe" operating conditions as described below. If your vehicle is operated under "severe" conditions, inspect all maintenance indicated with an asterisk (*) at 3000 mile/3 month intervals and perform maintenance or replace parts as necessary. Severe conditions are indicated if you mainly operate your vehicle under one or more of the following conditions:*
Operating in dusty areas
Idling for extended periods and/or low speed operation
Operating when outside temperatures remain below freezing and when most trips are less than 4 miles

** *If used for trailer towing, change the transaxle fluid every 30,000 miles (Section 22 or 23)*

Typical engine compartment layout, engine cover removed (2006 V6 model shown)

1 *Brake fluid reservoir*
2 *Air filter housing*
3 *Fuse/relay box*
4 *Battery*
5 *Radiator cap*
6 *Automatic transaxle fluid dipstick*
7 *Spark plugs (front cylinder head)*
8 *Engine oil dipstick*
9 *Engine oil filler cap*
10 *Windshield washer fluid reservoir*
11 *Power steering fluid reservoir*
12 *Engine coolant reservoir*
13 *Drivebelt*

Typical front underside components (2001 through 2006 models)

1 *Brake caliper*
2 *Brake hose*
3 *Inner driveaxle boot*
4 *Outer driveaxle boot*
5 *Balljoint*
6 *Lower control arm*
7 *Engine oil drain plug*
8 *Engine/transaxle subframe*

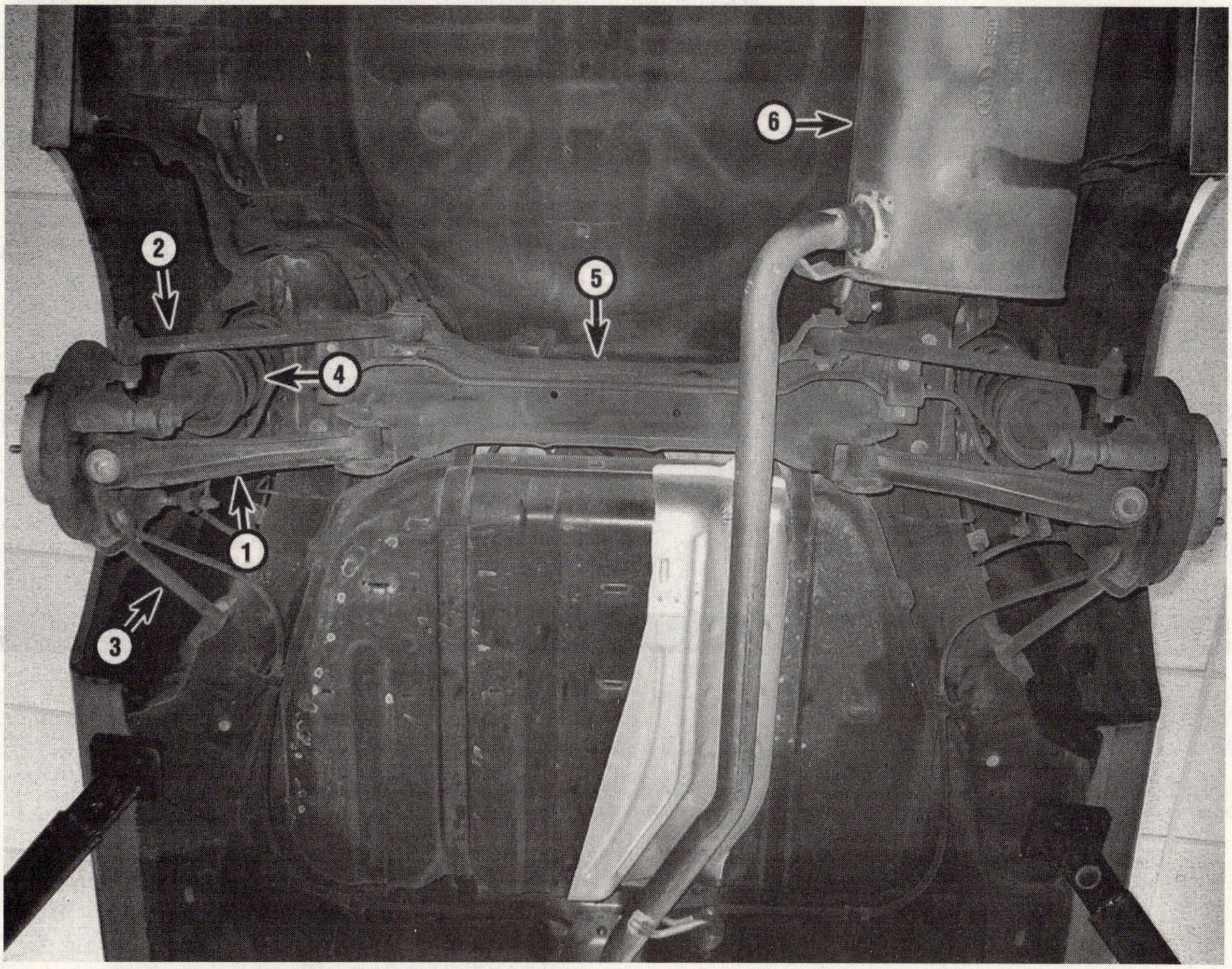

Typical rear underside components (2001 through 2006 models)

1 Front control arm
2 Rear control arm
3 Trailing arm
4 Coil spring
5 Rear suspension crossmember
6 Muffler

2 Introduction

This Chapter is designed to help the home mechanic maintain his vehicle for peak performance, economy, safety and long life.

Included is a master maintenance schedule, followed by sections dealing specifically with each item on the schedule. Visual checks, adjustments, component replacement and other helpful items are included. Refer to the accompanying illustrations of the engine compartment and the underside of the vehicle for the location of various components.

Servicing your vehicle in accordance with the mileage/time maintenance schedule and the following Sections will provide it with a planned maintenance program that should result in a long and reliable service life. This is a comprehensive plan, so maintaining some items but not others at the specified service intervals won't produce the same results.

As you service your vehicle, you will discover that many of the procedures can - and should - be grouped together because of the nature of the particular procedure you're performing or because of the close proximity of two otherwise unrelated components to one another.

For example, if the vehicle is raised for any reason, you should inspect the exhaust, suspension, steering and fuel systems while you're under the vehicle. When you're rotating the tires, it makes good sense to check the brakes and wheel bearings since the wheels are already removed.

Finally, let's suppose you have to borrow or rent a torque wrench. Even if you only need to tighten the spark plugs, you might as well check the torque of as many critical fasteners as time allows.

The first step of this maintenance program is to prepare yourself before the actual work begins. Read through all Sections pertinent to the procedures you're planning to do, then make a list of and gather together all the parts and tools you will need to do the job. If it looks as if you might run into problems during a particular segment of some procedure, seek advice from your local parts man or dealer service department.

OWNER'S MANUAL AND VECI LABEL INFORMATION

Your vehicle owner's manual was written for your year and model and contains very specific information on component locations, specifications, fuse ratings, part numbers, etc. The Owner's Manual is an important resource for the do-it-yourselfer to have; if one was not supplied with your vehicle, it can generally be ordered from a dealer parts department.

Among other important information, the Vehicle Emissions Control Information (VECI) label contains specifications and procedures for applicable tune-up adjustments and, in some instances, spark plugs. The information on this label is the exact maintenance data recommended by the manufacturer. This data often varies by intended operating altitude, local emissions regulations, month of manufacture, etc.

This Chapter contains procedural details, safety information and more ambitious maintenance intervals than you might find in manufacturer's literature. However, you may also find procedures or specifications in your Owner's Manual or VECI label that differ with what's printed here. In these cases, the Owner's Manual or VECI label can be considered correct, since it is specific to your particular vehicle.

3 Tune-up general information

The term tune-up is used in this manual to represent a combination of individual operations rather than one specific procedure.

If, from the time the vehicle is new, the routine maintenance schedule is followed closely and frequent checks are made of fluid levels and high wear items, as suggested throughout this manual, the engine will be kept in relatively good running condition and the need for additional work will be minimized.

More likely than not, however, there will be times when the engine is running poorly due to lack of regular maintenance. This is even more likely if a used vehicle, which has not received regular and frequent maintenance checks, is purchased. In such cases, an engine tune-up will be needed outside of the regular routine maintenance intervals.

The first step in any tune-up or engine diagnosis to help correct a poor running engine would be a cylinder compression check. A check of the engine compression (see Chapter 2 Part C) will give valuable information regarding the overall performance of many internal components and should be used as a basis for tune-up and repair procedures. If, for instance, a compression check indicates serious internal engine wear, a conventional tune-up will not help the running condition of the engine and would be a waste of time and money. Also in Chapter 2, Part C is information on checking engine vacuum, which also gives information on the engine's state-of-tune and condition.

The following series of operations are those most often needed to bring a generally poor-running engine back into a proper state of tune.

MINOR TUNE-UP

Check all engine related fluids (Section 4)
Clean, inspect and test the battery (Section 7)
Check all underhood hoses (Section 10)
Check the cooling system (Section 11)
Check the air filter (Section 15)
Check and adjust the drivebelts (Section 20)

MAJOR TUNE-UP

All items listed under Minor tune-up, plus . . .
Replace the air filter (Section 15)
Check the fuel system (Section 16)
Replace the spark plugs (Section 27)
Replace the fuel filter (Section 21)
Check the charging system (Chapter 5)
Check for the presence of stored diagnostic trouble codes (Chapter 6)

4 Fluid level checks (every 250 miles [400 km] or weekly)

1 Fluids are an essential part of the lubrication, cooling, brake, clutch and other systems. Because these fluids gradually become depleted and/or contaminated during normal operation of the vehicle, they must be periodically replenished. See *Recommended lubricants and fluids* and *Capacities* in this Chapter before adding fluid to any of the following components.

➡ **Note: The vehicle must be on level ground before fluid levels can be checked.**

ENGINE OIL

➧ **Refer to illustrations 4.2, 4.4 and 4.6**

2 The engine oil level is checked with a dipstick located at the front of the engine (see illustration). The dipstick extends through a metal tube from which it protrudes down into the engine oil pan.

3 The oil level should be checked before the vehicle has been driven, or about 5 minutes after the engine has been shut off. If the oil is checked immediately after driving the vehicle, some of the oil will remain in the upper engine components, producing a low reading on the dipstick.

4 Pull the dipstick from the tube and wipe all the oil from the end with a clean rag or paper towel. Insert the clean dipstick all the way back into its metal tube and pull it out again. Observe the oil at the end of the dipstick. At its highest point, the level should be between the lower and upper marks (see illustration).

5 It takes about one quart of oil to raise the level from the lower mark to the upper mark on the dipstick. Do not allow the level to drop below the lower mark or oil starvation may cause engine damage. Conversely, overfilling the engine (adding oil above the upper mark) may cause oil-fouled spark plugs, oil leaks or oil seal failures.

6 Remove the threaded cap from the valve cover to add oil (see illustration). Use a funnel to prevent spills. After adding the oil, install the filler cap hand tight. Start the engine and look carefully for any small leaks around the oil filter or drain plug. Stop the engine and check the oil level again after it has had sufficient time to drain from the upper block and cylinder head galleys.

7 Checking the oil level is an important preventive maintenance step. A continually dropping oil level indicates oil leakage through damaged seals, from loose connections, or past worn rings or valve guides. If the oil looks milky in color or has water droplets in it, a cylinder head gasket may be blown. The engine should be checked immediately. The condition of the oil should also be checked. Each time you check the oil level, slide your thumb and index finger up the dipstick before wiping off the oil. If you see small dirt or metal particles clinging to the dipstick, the oil should be changed (see Section 6).

4.2 The engine oil dipstick is mounted at the front right corner of the engine (V6 engine shown)

4.4 The oil level should be at or near the upper mark on the dipstick - if it isn't, add enough oil to bring the level to or near the upper mark (it takes about one quart to raise the level from the lower mark to the upper mark)

ENGINE COOLANT

➧ **Refer to illustrations 4.8a, 4.8b and 4.9**

⁂ WARNING:

Do not allow antifreeze to come in contact with your skin or painted surfaces of the vehicle. Flush contaminated areas immediately with plenty of water. Don't store new coolant or leave old coolant lying around where it's accessible to children or pets - they're attracted by its sweet smell. Ingestion of even a small amount of coolant can be fatal! Wipe up garage floor and drip pan spills immediately. Keep antifreeze containers covered and repair cooling system leaks as soon as they're noticed.

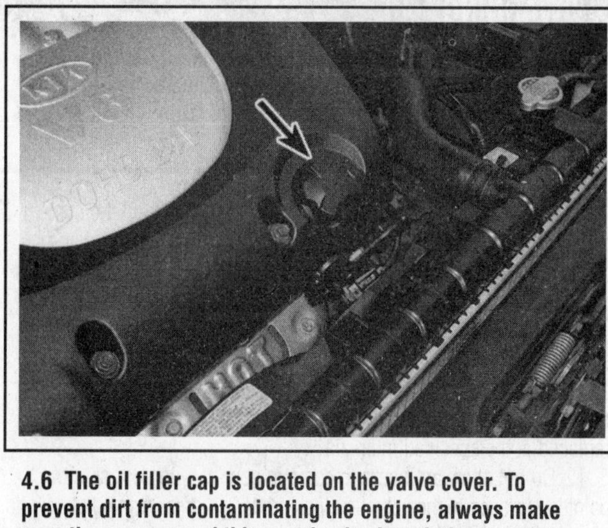

4.6 The oil filler cap is located on the valve cover. To prevent dirt from contaminating the engine, always make sure the area around this opening is clean before removing the cap (V6 engine shown)

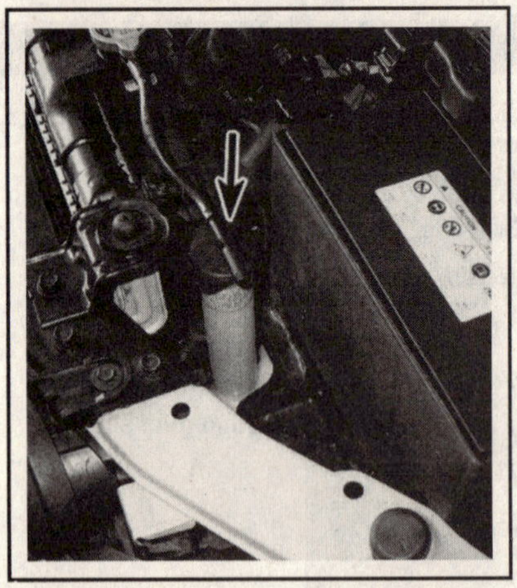

4.8a On 2001 through 2006 models, the coolant reservoir is located to the left of the radiator

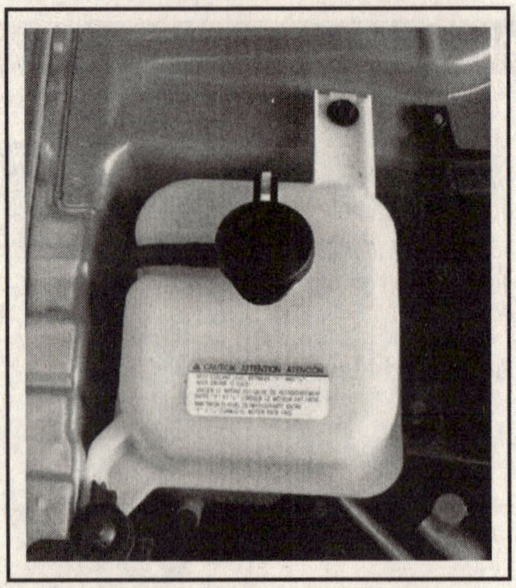

4.8b On 2006.5 and later models, the coolant reservoir is located on the right side of the engine compartment

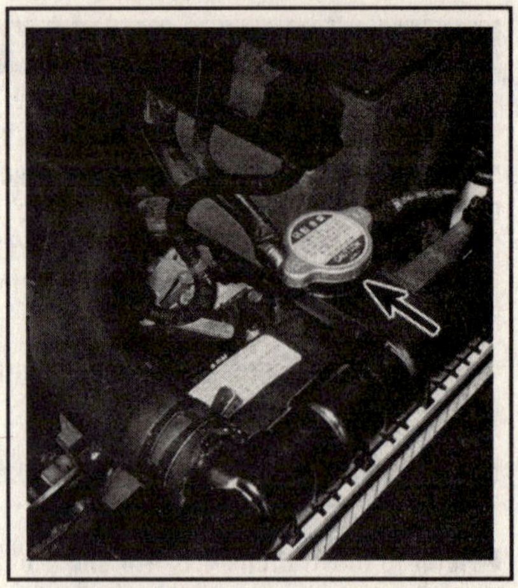

4.9 The radiator cap is located on the left side of the radiator

8 All models use a coolant reservoir tank connected by a hose to the top of the radiator (see illustrations).

9 The coolant level should be checked regularly. It must be between the Full and Low lines on the tank. The level will vary with the temperature of the engine. When the engine is cold, the coolant level should be at or slightly above the Low mark on the tank. Once the engine has warmed up, the level should be at or near the Full mark. If it isn't, allow the fluid in the tank to cool, then remove the cap from the reservoir and add coolant to bring the level up to the Full line. Use only the type of coolant listed in this Chapter's Specifications or in your owner's manual. Do not use supplemental inhibitors or additives. If only a small amount of coolant is required to bring the system up to the proper level, water can be used. However, repeated additions of water will dilute the recommended antifreeze and water solution. In order to maintain the proper ratio of antifreeze and water, it is advisable to top up the coolant level with the correct mixture. If the coolant level drops within a short time after replenishment, there may be a leak in the system. Inspect the radiator, hoses, engine coolant filler cap, drain plugs, air bleeder plugs and water pump. If no leak is evident, have the radiator cap pressure tested (see illustration).

⁂ WARNING:

Never remove the radiator pressure cap when the engine is running or has just been shut down, because the cooling system is hot. Escaping steam and scalding liquid could cause serious injury.

10 If it is necessary to open the radiator cap, wait until the system has cooled completely, then wrap a thick cloth around the cap and turn it to the first stop. If any steam escapes, wait until the system has cooled further, then remove the cap.

11 When checking the coolant level, always note its condition. It should be relatively clear. If it is brown or rust colored, the system should be drained, flushed and refilled. Even if the coolant appears to be normal, the corrosion inhibitors wear out with use, so it must be replaced at the specified intervals.

12 Do not allow antifreeze to come in contact with your skin or painted surfaces of the vehicle. Flush contacted areas immediately with plenty of water.

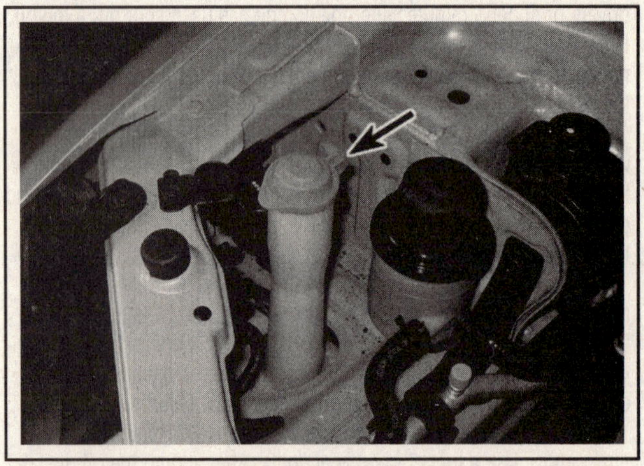

4.13 The windshield washer fluid reservoir is located at the right front corner of the engine compartment

WINDSHIELD WASHER FLUID

➧ Refer to illustration 4.13

13 Fluid for the windshield washer system is stored in a plastic reservoir that is located at the right front corner of the engine compartment (see illustration). In milder climates, plain water can be used to top up the reservoir, but the reservoir should be kept no more than two-thirds full to allow for expansion should the water freeze. In colder climates, the use of a specially designed windshield washer fluid, available at your dealer and any auto parts store, will help lower the freezing point of the fluid. Mix the solution with water in accordance with the manufacturer's directions on the container. Do not use regular antifreeze. It will damage the vehicle's paint.

BRAKE AND CLUTCH FLUID

➧ Refer to illustration 4.15

14 The brake master cylinder is mounted on the front of the power booster unit in the engine compartment. The clutch fluid reservoir is

4.15 The brake fluid should be kept between the MIN and MAX marks on the reservoir

mounted next to the brake booster.

15 To check the fluid level of either reservoir, simply look at the MAX and MIN marks on the reservoir (see illustration).

16 If the level is low, wipe the top of the reservoir cover with a clean rag to prevent contamination of the system before lifting the cover.

17 Add only the specified brake fluid to the reservoir (refer to *Recommended lubricants* and fluids in this Chapter's Specifications or your owner's manual). Mixing different types of brake fluid can damage the system. Fill the reservoir only to the dotted line - this brings the fluid to the correct level when you put the cover back on.

⁂ WARNING:

Use caution when filling the reservoir - brake fluid can harm your eyes and damage painted surfaces. Do not use brake fluid that has been opened for more than one year or has been left open. Brake fluid absorbs moisture from the air. Excess moisture can cause a dangerous loss of braking.

18 While the reservoir cap is removed, inspect the master cylinder reservoir for contamination. If deposits, dirt particles or water droplets are present, the system should be drained and refilled (see Chapter 8 or 9).

19 After filling the reservoir to the proper level, make sure the lid is properly seated to prevent fluid leakage and/or system pressure loss.

20 The brake fluid in the master cylinder will drop slightly as the brake pads at each wheel wear down during normal operation. If the master cylinder requires repeated replenishing to keep it at the proper level, this is an indication of leakage in the brake system, which should be corrected immediately. Check all brake lines and connections, along with the wheel cylinders and booster (see Section 12 for more information).

21 If, upon checking the master cylinder fluid level, you discover the reservoir empty or nearly empty, the brake system should be thoroughly inspected for leaks (see Chapter 9 for more information on the brake system).

POWER STEERING FLUID

➧ **Refer to illustration 4.25**

22 Unlike manual steering, the power steering system relies on fluid

4.25 The power steering fluid reservoir is located on the right side of the engine compartment. The reservoir is translucent, so the fluid level can be checked either hot or cold without removing the cap

that may, over a period of time, require replenishing.

23 The fluid reservoir for the power steering pump is located near the front of the engine.

24 For the check, the front wheels should be pointed straight ahead and the engine should be off.

25 The reservoir is translucent plastic and the fluid level can be checked visually (see illustration).

26 If additional fluid is required, pour the specified type directly into the reservoir, using a funnel to prevent spills.

27 If the reservoir requires frequent fluid additions, all power steering hoses, hose connections, the power steering pump and the steering gear assembly should be carefully checked for leaks.

AUTOMATIC TRANSAXLE FLUID

➧ **Refer to illustrations 4.32 and 4.34**

28 The level of the automatic transaxle fluid should be carefully maintained. Low fluid level can lead to slipping or loss of drive, while overfilling can cause foaming, loss of fluid and transaxle damage.

29 The transaxle fluid level should only be checked when the transaxle is hot (at its normal operating temperature). If the vehicle has just been driven over 10 miles (15 miles in a frigid climate), and the fluid temperature is 160 to 175-degrees F, the transaxle is hot.

⁂ CAUTION:

If the vehicle has just been driven for a long time at high speed or in city traffic in hot weather, or if it has been pulling a trailer, an accurate fluid level reading cannot be obtained. Allow the fluid to cool down for about 30 minutes.

30 If the vehicle has not just been driven, park the vehicle on level ground, set the parking brake and start the engine.

31 While the engine is idling, depress the brake pedal and move the selector lever through all the gear ranges, ending in Neutral.

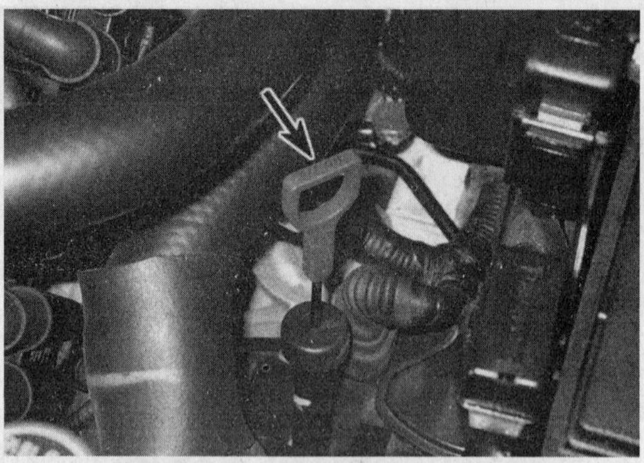

4.32 The automatic transaxle fluid dipstick is located to the left of the engine

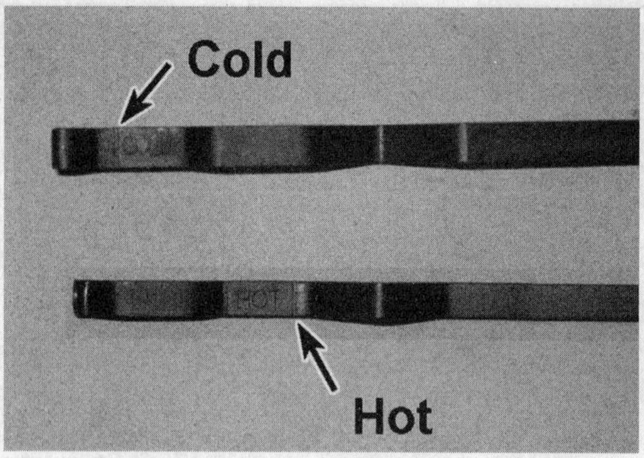

4.34 The automatic transaxle fluid should be in the Cold or Hot range, depending on its temperature

32 With the engine still idling, remove the dipstick from its tube (see illustration). Check the level of the fluid on the dipstick and note its condition.

33 Wipe the fluid from the dipstick with a clean rag and reinsert it back into the filler tube until the cap seats.

34 Pull the dipstick out again and note the fluid level (see illustration). If the transaxle is cold, the level should be in the COLD or COOL range on the dipstick. If it is hot, the fluid level should be in the HOT range. If the level is at the low side of either range, add the specified automatic transaxle fluid through the dipstick tube with a funnel.

35 Add just enough of the recommended fluid to fill the transaxle to the proper level. It takes about one pint to raise the level from the low mark to the high mark when the fluid is hot, so add the fluid a little at a time and keep checking the level until it is correct.

36 The condition of the fluid should also be checked along with the level. If the fluid at the end of the dipstick is black or a dark reddish brown color, or if it emits a burned smell, the fluid should be changed (see Section 22). If you are in doubt about the condition of the fluid, purchase some new fluid and compare the two for color and smell.

MANUAL TRANSAXLE LUBRICANT

➡ **Note: It isn't necessary to check this lubricant weekly; every 15,000 miles or 12 months will be adequate, or if leaks are noticed.**

37 Check the manual transaxle lubricant whenever there are signs of leakage.

38 Raise the vehicle and support it securely on jackstands.

39 Remove the transaxle fill plug and verify that the lubricant is near the bottom of the hole. If it isn't, add lubricant until it begins to flow out of the hole.

40 Reinstall the plug and lower the vehicle.

5 Tire and tire pressure checks (every 250 miles [400 km] or weekly)

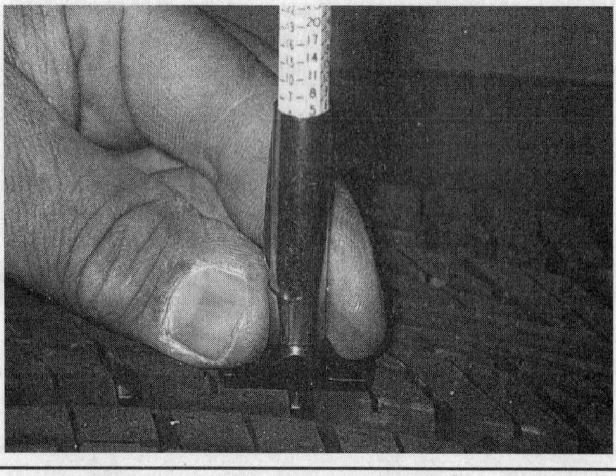

5.2 Use a tire tread depth gauge to monitor tire wear - they are available at auto parts stores and service stations and cost very little

➧ **Refer to illustrations 5.2, 5.3, 5.4a, 5.4b and 5.8**

1 Periodic inspection of the tires may spare you from the inconvenience of being stranded with a flat tire. It can also provide you with vital information regarding possible problems in the steering and suspension systems before major damage occurs.

2 Normal tread wear can be monitored with a simple, inexpensive device known as a tread depth indicator (see illustration). When the tread depth reaches approximately 1/16-inch, replace the tire(s) (preferably long before that).

3 Note any abnormal tread wear (see illustration). Tread pattern irregularities such as cupping, flat spots and more wear on one side than the other are indications of front end alignment and/or balance problems. If any of these conditions are noted, take the vehicle to a tire shop or service station to correct the problem.

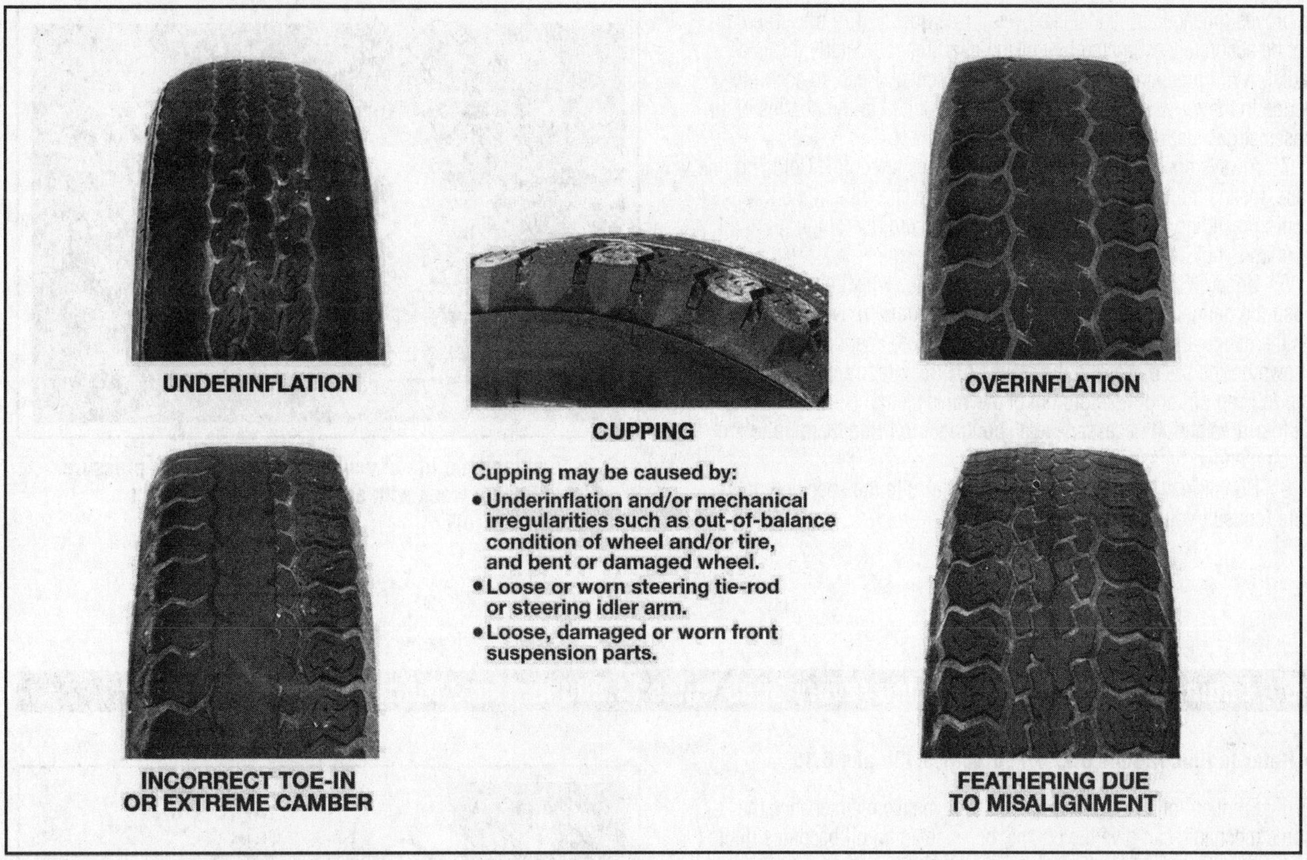

5.3 This chart will help you determine the condition of your tires, the probable cause(s) of abnormal wear and the corrective action necessary

4 Look closely for cuts, punctures and embedded nails or tacks. Sometimes a tire will hold its air pressure for a short time or leak down very slowly even after a nail has embedded itself into the tread. If a slow leak persists, check the valve stem core to make sure it is tight (see illustration). Examine the tread for an object that may have embedded itself into the tire or for a plug that may have begun to leak (radial tire punctures are repaired with a plug that is inserted into the hole). If a puncture is suspected, it can be easily verified by spraying a solution of soapy water onto the puncture area (see illustration). The soapy solution will bubble if there is a leak. Unless the puncture is inordinately large, a tire shop or gas station can usually repair the punctured tire.

5 Carefully inspect the inner sidewall of each tire for evidence of brake fluid leakage. If you see any, inspect the brakes immediately.

6 Correct tire air pressure adds miles to the lifespan of the tires,

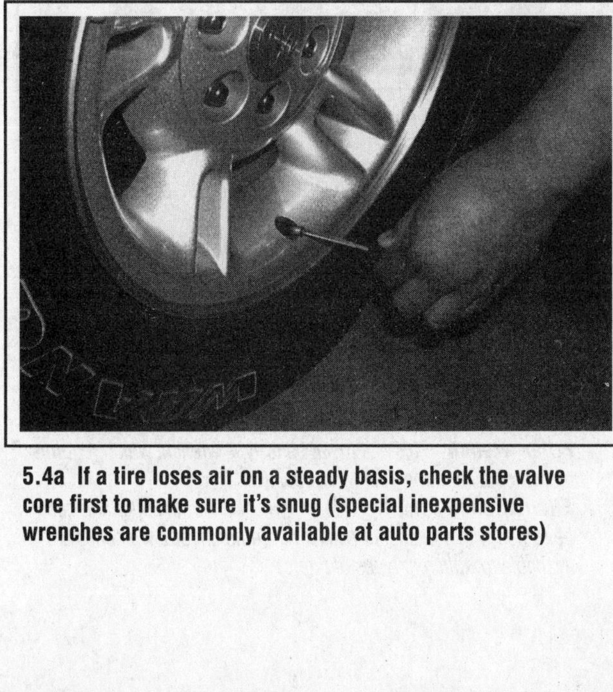

5.4a If a tire loses air on a steady basis, check the valve core first to make sure it's snug (special inexpensive wrenches are commonly available at auto parts stores)

5.4b If the valve core is tight, raise the corner of the vehicle with the low tire and spray a soapy water solution onto the tread as the tire is turned slowly - slow leaks will cause small bubbles to appear

improves mileage and enhances overall ride quality. Tire pressure cannot be accurately estimated by looking at a tire, particularly if it is a radial. A tire pressure gauge is therefore essential. Keep an accurate gauge in the glove box. The pressure gauges fitted to the nozzles of air hoses at gas stations are often inaccurate.

7 Always check tire pressure when the tires are cold. "Cold," in this case, means the vehicle has not been driven over a mile in the three hours preceding a tire pressure check. A pressure rise of four to eight pounds is not uncommon once the tires are warm.

8 Unscrew the valve cap protruding from the wheel or hubcap and push the gauge firmly onto the valve (see illustration). Note the reading on the gauge and compare this figure to the recommended tire pressure shown on the tire placard in the glove box. Be sure to reinstall the valve cap to keep dirt and moisture out of the valve stem mechanism. Check all four tires and, if necessary, add enough air to bring them up to the recommended pressure levels.

9 Don't forget to keep the spare tire inflated to the specified pressure (consult your owner's manual).

5.8 To extend the life of your tires, check the air pressure at least once a week with an accurate gauge (don't forget the spare!)

6 Engine oil and oil filter change (every 3000 miles [4,800 km] or 3 months)

➧ Refer to illustrations 6.2, 6.7, 6.13a, 6.13b and 6.15

1 Frequent oil changes are the best preventive maintenance the home mechanic can give the engine, because aging oil becomes diluted and contaminated, which leads to premature engine wear.

2 Make sure that you have all the necessary tools before you begin this procedure (see illustration). You should also have plenty of rags or newspapers handy for mopping up any spills.

3 Access to the underside of the vehicle is greatly improved if the vehicle can be lifted on a hoist, driven onto ramps or supported by jackstands.

⁂ WARNING:

Do not work under a vehicle which is supported only by a bumper, hydraulic or scissors-type jack.

4 If this is your first oil change, get under the vehicle and familiarize yourself with the location of the oil drain plug. The engine and exhaust components will be warm during the actual work, so try to anticipate any potential problems before the engine and accessories are hot.

5 Park the vehicle on a level spot. Start the engine and allow it to reach its normal operating temperature (the needle on the temperature gauge should be at least above the bottom mark). Warm oil and sludge will flow out more easily. Turn off the engine when it's warmed up. Remove the filler cap.

6 Raise the vehicle and support it securely on jackstands.

⁂ WARNING:

To avoid personal injury, never get beneath a vehicle when it is supported by only by a jack. The jack provided with your vehicle is designed solely for raising the vehicle to remove and replace the wheels. Always use jackstands to support the vehicle when it becomes necessary to place your body underneath the vehicle.

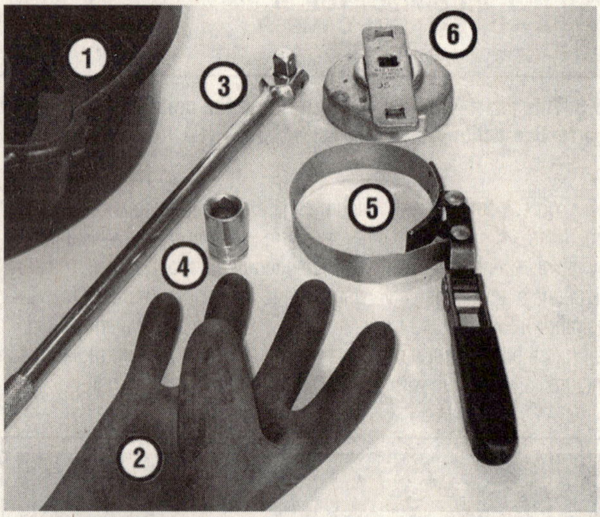

6.2 These tools are required when changing the engine oil and filter

1 ***Drain pan*** - *It should be fairly shallow in depth, but wide in order to prevent spills*
2 ***Rubber gloves*** - *When removing the drain plug and filter, it is inevitable that you will get oil on your hands (the gloves will prevent burns)*
3 ***Breaker bar*** - *Sometimes the oil drain plug is pretty tight and a long breaker bar is needed to loosen it*
4 ***Socket*** - *To be used with the breaker bar or a ratchet (must be the correct size to fit the drain plug)*
5 ***Filter wrench*** - *This is a metal band-type wrench, which requires clearance around the filter to be effective*
6 ***Filter wrench*** - *This type fits on the bottom of the filter and can be turned with a ratchet or beaker bar (different size wrenches are available for different types of filters)*

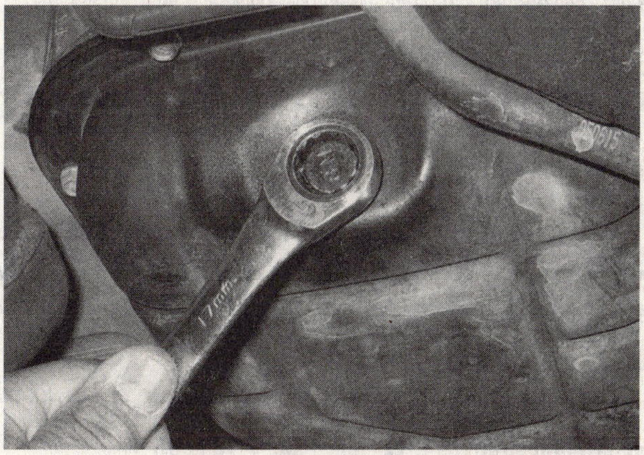

6.7 Use the proper size box-end wrench or socket to remove the oil drain plug without rounding off the corners

7 Being careful not to touch the hot exhaust components, place the drain pan under the drain plug in the bottom of the pan and remove the plug (see illustration). You may want to wear gloves while unscrewing the plug the final few turns if the engine is really hot.

8 Allow the old oil to drain into the pan. It may be necessary to move the pan farther under the engine as the oil flow slows to a trickle. Inspect the old oil for the presence of metal shavings and chips.

9 After all the oil has drained, wipe off the drain plug with a clean rag. Even minute metal particles clinging to the plug would immediately contaminate the new oil.

10 Clean the area around the drain plug opening, reinstall the plug and tighten it securely, but do not strip the threads.

11 Move the drain pan into position under the oil filter.

12 The oil filter is accessed from underneath the engine (see illustrations). Loosen the oil filter by turning it counterclockwise with an oil filter wrench. On most engines you will have to use the type of wrench that slips over the bottom of the filter and is turned with a ratchet. Just as the filter is detached from the block, immediately tilt the open end up to prevent the oil inside the filter from spilling out.

⁂ WARNING:

The engine exhaust manifold may still be hot, so be careful.

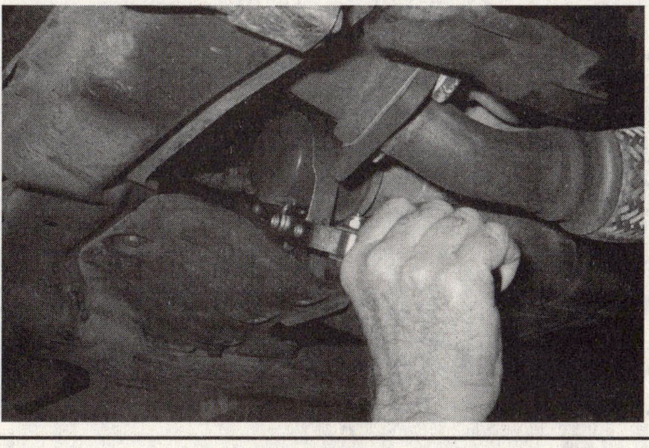

6.13b Use a special filter wrench that slips over the end of the filter (don't use the wrench when installing the new filter)

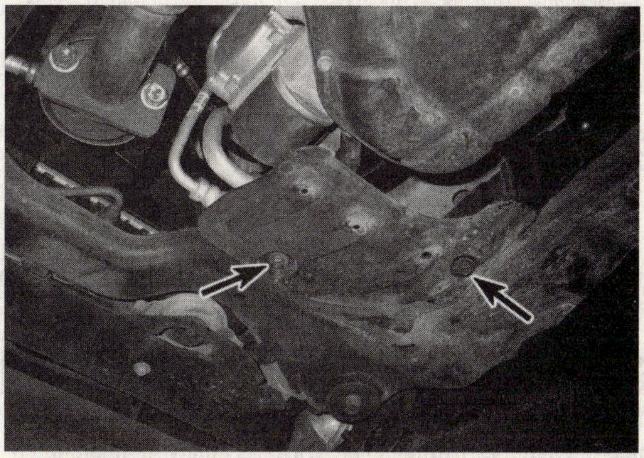

6.13a To access the oil filter on some models, remove these two bolts and this shield

Make sure that the old filter gasket does not remain stuck to the block.

13 With a clean rag, wipe off the mounting surface on the block. If a residue of old oil is allowed to remain, it will smoke when the block is heated up. It will also prevent the new filter from seating properly. Also make sure that none of the old gasket remains stuck to the mounting surface. It can be removed with a scraper if necessary.

14 Compare the old filter with the new one to make sure they are the same type. Smear some engine oil on the rubber gasket of the new filter and screw it into place (see illustration). Overtightening the filter will damage the gasket, so don't use a filter wrench. Most filter manufacturers recommend tightening the filter by hand only. Normally they should be tightened 3/4-turn after the gasket contacts the block, but be sure to follow the directions on the filter or container.

15 Remove all tools, rags, etc. from under the vehicle, being careful not to spill the oil in the drain pan, then lower the vehicle.

16 Add new oil to the engine through the oil filler cap in the valve cover. Use a funnel to prevent oil from spilling onto the top of the engine. Pour three quarts of fresh oil into the engine. Wait a few minutes to allow the oil to drain into the pan, then check the level on the oil dipstick (see Section 4 if necessary). If the oil level is at or near the F mark, install the filler cap hand tight, start the engine and allow the new oil to circulate.

17 Allow the engine to run for about a minute. While the engine is running, look under the vehicle and check for leaks at the oil pan drain plug and around the oil filter. If either is leaking, stop the engine and tighten the plug or filter slightly.

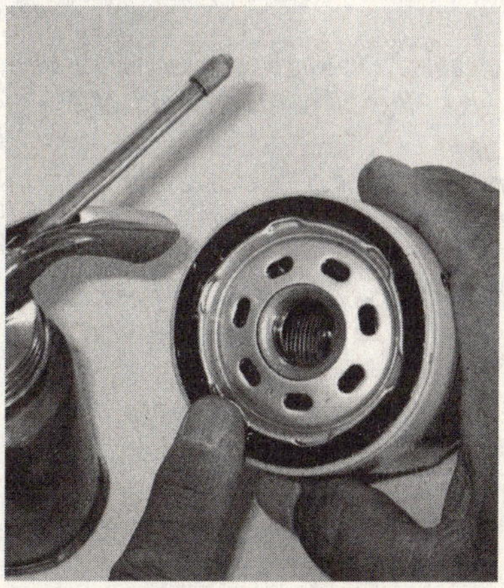

6.15 Lubricate the oil filter gasket with clean engine oil before installing the filter on the engine

18 Wait a few minutes to allow the oil to trickle down into the pan, then recheck the level on the dipstick and, if necessary, add enough oil to bring the level to the F mark.

19 During the first few trips after an oil change, make it a point to check frequently for leaks and proper oil level.

20 The old oil drained from the engine cannot be reused in its present state and should be disposed of. Check with your local auto parts store, disposal facility or environmental agency to see if they will accept the oil for recycling. After the oil has cooled it can be drained into a container (capped plastic jugs, topped bottles, milk cartons, etc.) for transport to one of these disposal sites. Don't dispose of the oil by pouring it on the ground or down a drain!

7 Battery check, maintenance and charging (every 5000 miles [8000 km] or 6 months)

WARNING:

Certain precautions must be followed when checking and servicing the battery. Hydrogen gas, which is highly flammable, is always present in the battery cells, so keep lighted tobacco and all other open flames and sparks away from the battery. The electrolyte inside the battery is actually dilute sulfuric acid, which will cause injury if splashed on your skin or in your eyes. It will also ruin clothes and painted surfaces. When removing the battery cables, always detach the negative cable first and hook it up last!

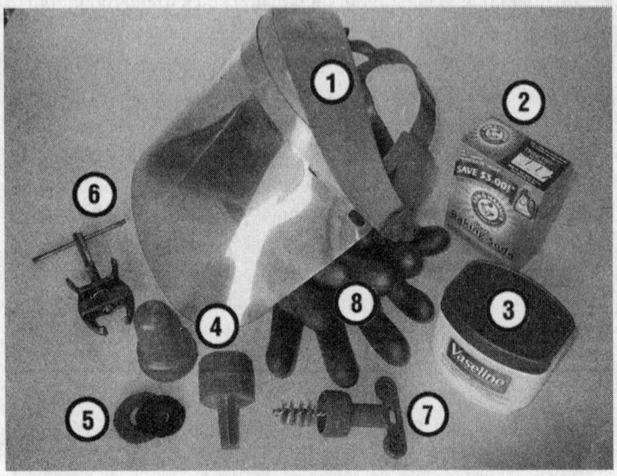

7.1 Tools and materials required for battery maintenance

1 ***Face shield/safety goggles*** - *When removing corrosion with a brush, the acidic particles can easily fly up into your eyes*
2 ***Baking soda*** - *A solution of baking soda and water can be used to neutralize corrosion*
3 ***Petroleum jelly*** - *A layer of this on the battery posts will help prevent corrosion*
4 ***Battery post/cable cleaner*** - *This wire brush cleaning tool will remove all traces of corrosion from the battery posts and cable clamps*
5 ***Treated felt washers*** - *Placing one of these on each post, directly under the cable clamps, will help prevent corrosion*
6 ***Puller*** - *Sometimes the cable clamps are very difficult to pull off the posts, even after the nut/bolt has been completely loosened. This tool pulls the clamp straight up and off the post without damage*
7 ***Battery post/cable cleaner*** - *Here is another cleaning tool that is a slightly different version of number 4 above, but it does the same thing*
8 ***Rubber gloves*** - *Another safety item to consider when servicing the battery; remember that's acid inside the battery*

CHECK AND MAINTENANCE

Refer to illustrations 7.1, 7.6a, 7.6b, 7.7a and 7.7b

1 A routine preventive maintenance program for the battery in your vehicle is the only way to ensure quick and reliable starts. But before performing any battery maintenance, make sure that you have the proper equipment necessary to work safely around the battery (see illustration).

2 There are also several precautions that should be taken whenever battery maintenance is performed. Before servicing the battery, always turn the engine and all accessories off and disconnect the cable from the negative terminal of the battery.

3 The battery produces hydrogen gas, which is both flammable and explosive. Never create a spark, smoke or light a match around the battery. Always charge the battery in a ventilated area.

4 Electrolyte contains poisonous and corrosive sulfuric acid. Do not allow it to get in your eyes, on your skin on your clothes. Never ingest it. Wear protective safety glasses when working near the battery. Keep children away from the battery.

5 Note the external condition of the battery. If the positive terminal and cable clamp on your vehicle's battery is equipped with a rubber protector, make sure that it's not torn or damaged. It should completely cover the terminal. Look for any corroded or loose connections, cracks in the case or cover or loose hold-down clamps. Also check the entire length of each cable for cracks and frayed conductors.

6 If corrosion, which looks like white, fluffy deposits (see illustration) is evident, particularly around the terminals, the battery should be removed for cleaning. Loosen the cable clamp bolts with a wrench, being careful to remove the ground cable first, and slide them off the terminals (see illustration). Then disconnect the hold-down clamp bolt and nut, remove the clamp and lift the battery from the engine compartment.

7 Clean the cable clamps thoroughly with a battery brush or a

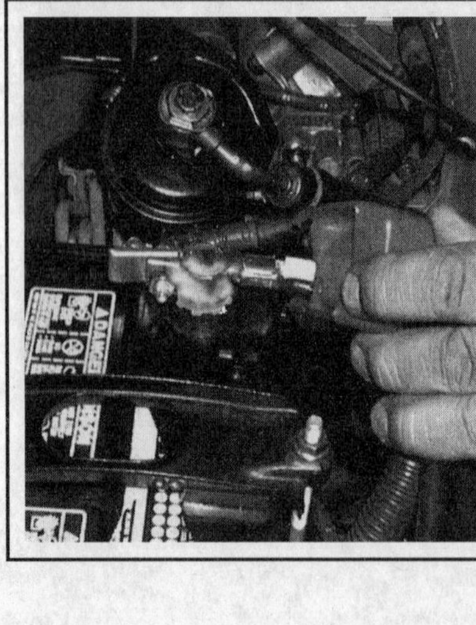

7.6a Battery terminal corrosion usually appears as light, fluffy powder

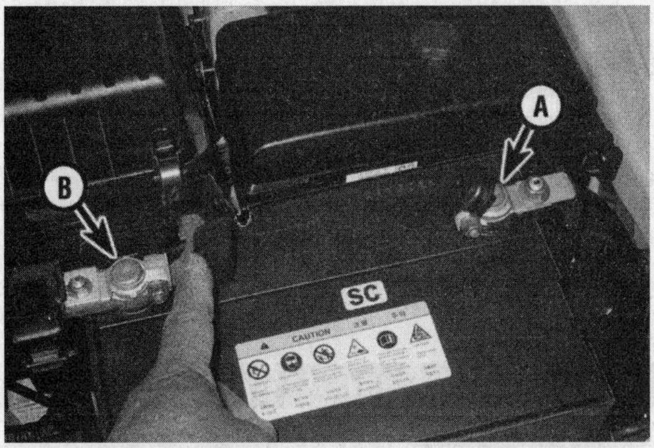

7.6b When disconnecting the battery, always disconnect the ground cable (A) first, then the positive cable (B). When reconnecting the battery, always connect the positive cable first, then the ground cable

7.7a When cleaning the cable clamps, all corrosion must be removed (the inside of the clamp is tapered to match the taper on the post, so don't remove too much material)

terminal cleaner and a solution of warm water and baking soda (see illustration). Wash the terminals and the top of the battery case with the same solution but make sure that the solution doesn't get into the battery. When cleaning the cables, terminals and battery top, wear safety goggles and rubber gloves to prevent any solution from coming in contact with your eyes or hands. Wear old clothes too - even diluted, sulfuric acid splashed onto clothes will burn holes in them. If the terminals have been extensively corroded, clean them up with a terminal cleaner (see illustration). Thoroughly wash all cleaned areas with plain water.

8 Make sure that the battery tray is in good condition and the hold-down clamp bolts are tight. If the battery is removed from the tray, make sure no parts remain in the bottom of the tray when the battery is reinstalled. When reinstalling the hold-down clamp bolts, do not overtighten them.

9 Any metal parts of the vehicle damaged by corrosion should be covered with a zinc-based primer, then painted.

10 Information on removing and installing the battery can be found in Chapter 5. Information on jump starting can be found at the front of this manual.

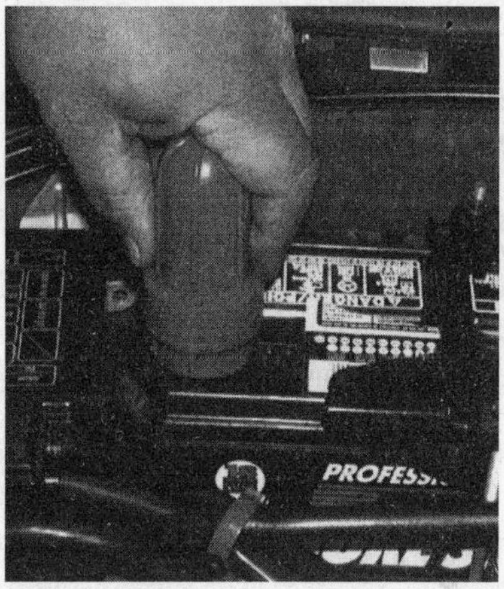

7.7b Regardless of the type of tool used to clean the battery posts, a clean, shiny surface should be the result

CHARGING

WARNING:

When batteries are being charged, hydrogen gas, which is very explosive and flammable, is produced. Do not smoke or allow open flames near a battery. Wear eye protection when near the battery during charging. Also, make sure the charger is unplugged before connecting or disconnecting the battery from the charger.

➡ Note: The manufacturer recommends the battery be removed from the vehicle for charging because the gas that escapes during this procedure can damage the paint. Fast charging with the battery cables connected can result in damage to the electrical system.

11 Slow-rate charging is the best way to restore a battery that's discharged to the point where it will not start the engine. It's also a good way to maintain the battery charge in a vehicle that's only driven a few miles between starts. Maintaining the battery charge is particularly important in the winter when the battery must work harder to start the engine and electrical accessories that drain the battery are in greater use.

12 It's best to use a one or two-amp battery charger (sometimes called a "trickle" charger). They are the safest and put the least strain on the battery. They are also the least expensive. For a faster charge, you can use a higher amperage charger, but don't use one rated more than 1/10th the amp/hour rating of the battery. Rapid boost charges that claim to restore the power of the battery in one to two hours are hardest on the battery and can damage batteries not in good condition. This type of charging should only be used in emergency situations.

13 The average time necessary to charge a battery should be listed in the instructions that come with the charger. As a general rule, a trickle charger will charge a battery in 12 to 16 hours.

14 Remove all the cell caps (if equipped) and cover the holes with a clean cloth to prevent spattering electrolyte. Disconnect the negative battery cable and hook the battery charger cable clamps up to the battery posts (positive to positive, negative to negative), then plug in the charger. Make sure it is set at 12-volts if it has a selector switch.

15 If you're using a charger with a rate higher than two amps, check the battery regularly during charging to make sure it doesn't overheat. If you're using a trickle charger, you can safely let the battery charge overnight after you've checked it regularly for the first couple of hours.

16 If the battery has removable cell caps, measure the specific gravity with a hydrometer every hour during the last few hours of the

charging cycle. Hydrometers are available inexpensively from auto parts stores - follow the instructions that come with the hydrometer. Consider the battery charged when there's no change in the specific gravity reading for two hours and the electrolyte in the cells is gassing (bubbling) freely. The specific gravity reading from each cell should be very close to the others. If not, the battery probably has a bad cell(s).

17 Some batteries with sealed tops have built-in hydrometers on the top that indicate the state of charge by the color displayed in the hydrometer window. Normally, a bright-colored hydrometer indicates a full charge and a dark hydrometer indicates the battery still needs charging.

18 If the battery has a sealed top and no built-in hydrometer, you can hook up a voltmeter across the battery terminals to check the charge. A fully charged battery should read 12.6 volts or higher after the surface charge has been removed.

19 Further information on the battery and jump starting can be found in Chapter 5 and at the front of this manual.

8 Tire rotation (every 5000 miles [8000 km] or 6 months)

Refer to illustration 8.2

1 The tires should be rotated at the specified intervals and whenever uneven wear is noticed. Since the vehicle will be raised and the tires removed anyway, check the brakes (see Section 12) at this time.

2 Radial tires must be rotated in a specific pattern (see illustration).

3 Refer to the information in *Jacking and towing* at the front of this manual for the proper procedures to follow when raising the vehicle and changing a tire. If the brakes are to be checked, do not apply the parking brake as stated. Make sure the tires are blocked to prevent the vehicle from rolling.

4 Preferably, the entire vehicle should be raised at the same time. This can be done on a hoist or by jacking up each corner and then lowering the vehicle onto jackstands placed under the frame rails. Always use four jackstands and make sure the vehicle is firmly supported.

5 After rotation, check and adjust the tire pressures as necessary and be sure to check the lug nut tightness.

6 For further information on the wheels and tires, refer to Chapter 10.

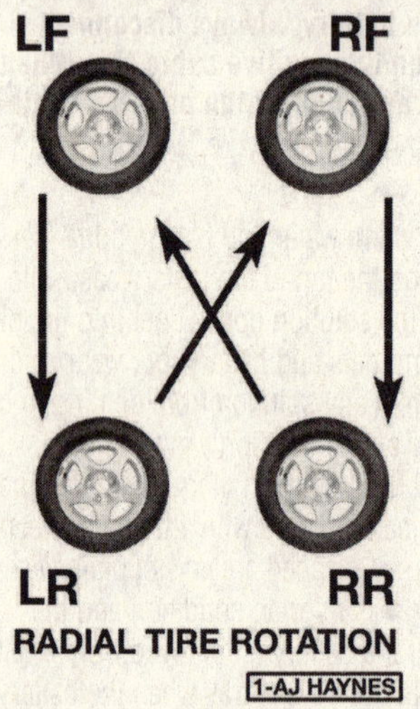

8.2 Recommended four-tire rotation pattern

9 Windshield wiper blade inspection and replacement (every 5000 miles [8000 km] or 6 months)

Refer to illustrations 9.5 and 9.6

1 The windshield wiper and blade assembly should be inspected periodically for damage, loose components and cracked or worn blade elements.

2 Road film can build up on the wiper blades and affect their efficiency, so they should be washed regularly with a mild detergent solution.

3 The action of the wiping mechanism can loosen bolts, nuts and fasteners, so they should be checked and tightened, as necessary, at the same time the wiper blades are checked.

4 If the wiper blade elements are cracked, worn or warped, or no longer clean adequately, they should be replaced with new ones.

5 Lift the arm assembly away from the glass for clearance, press

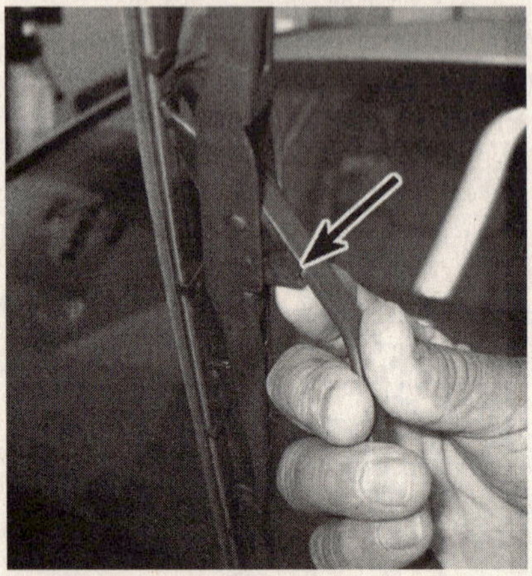

9.5 To release the blade holder, push the release pin and pull the wiper blade out of the arm

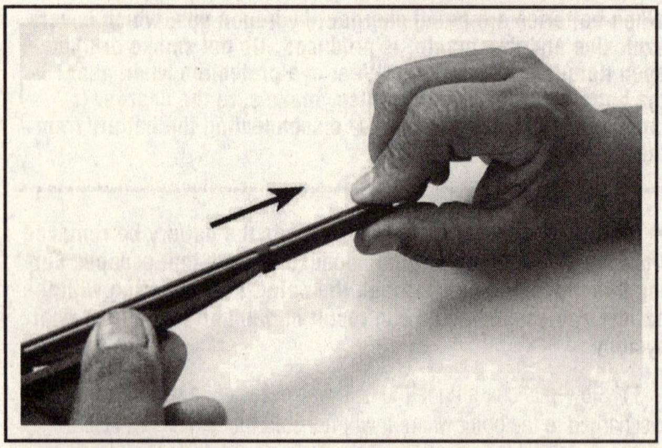

9.6 The rubber inserts can be replaced by sliding them out of the retainer

the release lever, then slide the wiper blade assembly out of the hook at the end of the arm (see illustration).

6 Wiper blade inserts can be put into the arm at this time. Simply pull the insert out of the arm and slide in a replacement (see illustration).

7 Attach the wiper blade to the arm. Connection can be confirmed by an audible click.

10 Underhood hose check and replacement (every 5000 miles [8000 km] or 6 months)

WARNING:

Replacement of air conditioning hoses must be left to a dealer service department or air conditioning shop that has the equipment to depressurize the system safely. Never remove air conditioning components or hoses until the system has been evacuated and the refrigerant recovered by a dealer service department or air conditioning shop.

GENERAL

1 High temperatures in the engine compartment can cause the deterioration of the rubber and plastic hoses used for engine, accessory and emission systems operation. Periodic inspection should be made for cracks, loose clamps, material hardening and leaks.

2 Information specific to the cooling system hoses can be found in Section 11.

3 Some, but not all, hoses are secured to the fittings with clamps. Where clamps are used, check to be sure they haven't lost their tension, allowing the hose to leak. If clamps aren't used, make sure the hose has not expanded and/or hardened where it slips over the fitting, allowing it to leak.

VACUUM HOSES

4 It's quite common for vacuum hoses, especially those in the emissions system, to be color coded or identified by colored stripes molded into them. Various systems require hoses with different wall thickness, collapse resistance and temperature resistance. When replacing hoses, be sure the new ones are made of the same material.

5 Often the only effective way to check a hose is to remove it completely from the vehicle. If more than one hose is removed, be sure to label the hoses and fittings to ensure correct installation.

6 When checking vacuum hoses, be sure to include any plastic T-fittings in the check. Inspect the fittings for cracks and the hose where it fits over the fitting for distortion, which could cause leakage.

7 A small piece of vacuum hose (1/4-inch inside diameter) can be used as a stethoscope to detect vacuum leaks. Hold one end of the hose to your ear and probe around vacuum hoses and fittings, listening for the hissing sound characteristic of a vacuum leak.

WARNING:

When probing with the vacuum hose stethoscope, be very careful not to come into contact with moving engine components such as the drivebelts, cooling fan, etc.

FUEL HOSE

WARNING:

Gasoline is extremely flammable, so take extra precautions when you work on any part of the fuel system. Don't smoke or allow open flames or bare light bulbs near the work area, and don't work in a garage where a gas-type appliance (such as a water heater or clothes dryer) is present. Since gasoline is carcinogenic, wear fuel resistant gloves when there's a possibility of being exposed to fuel, and, if you spill any fuel on your skin, rinse it off immediately with soap and water. Mop up any spills immediately and do not store fuel-soaked rags where they could ignite. The fuel system is under constant pressure, so, if any fuel lines are to be disconnected, the fuel pressure in the system must be relieved first. When you perform any kind of work on the fuel system, wear safety glasses and have a Class B type fire extinguisher on hand.

8 Check all rubber fuel lines for deterioration and chafing. Check especially for cracks in areas where the hose bends and just before fittings, such as where a hose attaches to the fuel filter.

9 High quality fuel line should be used for fuel line replacement. Never, under any circumstances, use unreinforced vacuum line, clear plastic tubing or water hose for fuel lines.

10 Spring-type clamps are commonly used on fuel lines. These clamps often lose their tension over a period of time, and can be sprung during removal. Replace all spring-type clamps with screw clamps whenever a hose is replaced.

METAL LINES

11 Sections of metal line are often used for fuel line between the fuel pump and fuel injection unit. Check carefully to be sure the line has not been bent or crimped and that cracks have not started in the line.

12 If a section of metal fuel line must be replaced, only seamless steel tubing should be used, since copper and aluminum tubing don't have the strength necessary to withstand normal engine vibration.

13 Check the metal brake lines where they enter the master cylinder and brake proportioning unit (if used) for cracks in the lines or loose fittings. Any sign of brake fluid leakage calls for an immediate thorough inspection of the brake system.

11 Cooling system check (every 5000 miles [8000 km] or 6 months)

➧ **Refer to illustration 11.4**

⁂ WARNING:

Most models use a cooling system with a pressure cap on the radiator and a coolant reservoir that does not hold pressure. However, some vehicles may have a coolant reservoir that uses a pressure cap and therefore can hold pressurized coolant. Always read the label on the cap and exercise caution when releasing a cooling system cap.

1 Many major engine failures can be attributed to a faulty cooling system. On vehicles with an automatic transaxle, the cooling system also cools the transaxle fluid and plays an important role in prolonging transaxle life.

2 The cooling system should be checked with the engine cold. Do this before the vehicle is driven for the day or after the engine has been shut off for at least three hours.

⁂ WARNING:

Never remove the cooling system pressure cap when the engine is running or has just been shut down, because the cooling system is hot. Escaping steam and scalding liquid could cause serious injury.

3 Remove the coolant reservoir cap by turning it to the left until it reaches a stop. If you hear a hissing sound (indicating there is pressure in the system), wait until it stops. Now press down on the cap with the palm of your hand and continue turning to the left until the cap can be removed. Thoroughly clean the cap, inside and out, with clean water. Also clean the filler neck on the tank. All traces of corrosion should be removed. The coolant inside should be relatively transparent. If it's rust colored, the system should be drained and refilled (see Section 26). If the coolant level isn't up to the proper level, add additional antifreeze/coolant mixture (see Section 4).

4 Carefully check the large upper and lower radiator hoses along with the smaller diameter heater hoses which run from the engine to the firewall. Inspect each hose along its entire length, replacing any hose that is cracked, swollen or shows signs of deterioration. Cracks may become more apparent if the hose is squeezed (see illustration). Regardless of condition, it's a good idea to replace hoses with new ones every two years.

5 Make sure that all hose connections are tight. A leak in the cooling system will usually show up as white or rust colored deposits on the areas adjoining the leak. If wire-type clamps are used at the ends of the hoses, it may be a good idea to replace them with more secure screw-type clamps.

6 Use compressed air or a soft brush to remove bugs, leaves, etc. from the front of the radiator or air conditioning condenser. Be careful not to damage the delicate cooling fins or cut yourself on them.

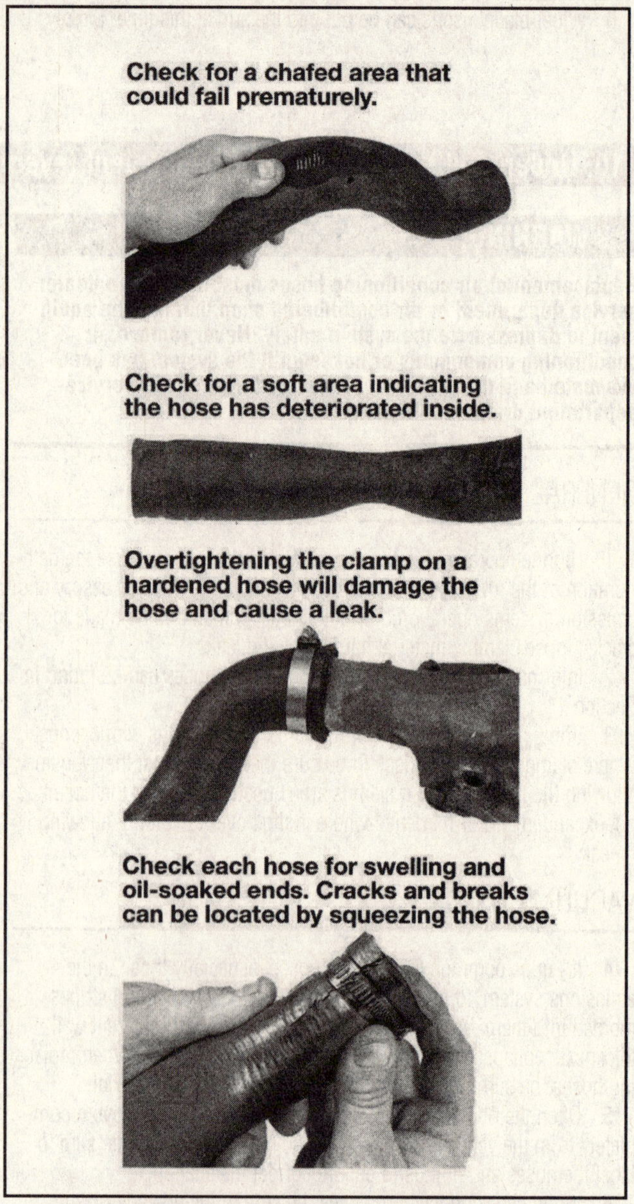

11.4 Hoses, like drivebelts, have a habit of failing at the worst possible time - to prevent the inconvenience of a blown radiator or heater hose, inspect them carefully as shown here

7 Every other inspection, or at the first indication of cooling system problems, have the cap and system pressure tested. If you don't have a pressure tester, most gas stations and garages will do this for a minimal charge.

12 Brake check (every 5000 miles [8000 km] or 6 months)

WARNING:

The dust created by the brake system is harmful to your health. Never blow it out with compressed air and don't inhale any of it. An approved filtering mask should be worn when working on the brakes. Do not, under any circumstances, use petroleum-based solvents to clean brake parts. Use brake system cleaner only!

Note: For detailed photographs of the brake system, refer to Chapter 9.

1 In addition to the specified intervals, the brakes should be inspected every time the wheels are removed or whenever a defect is suspected.

2 Any of the following symptoms could indicate a potential brake system defect: The vehicle pulls to one side when the brake pedal is depressed; the brakes make squealing or dragging noises when applied; brake pedal travel is excessive; the pedal pulsates; or brake fluid leaks, usually onto the inside of the tire or wheel.

3 Loosen the wheel lug nuts.

4 Raise the vehicle and place it securely on jackstands.

5 Remove the wheels (see *Jacking and towing* at the front of this book, or your owner's manual, if necessary).

DISC BRAKES

Refer to illustrations 12.7a and 12.7b

6 There are two pads (an outer and an inner) in each caliper. The pads are visible with the wheels removed.

7 Check the pad thickness by looking at each end of the caliper and through the inspection window in the caliper body (see illustrations). If the lining material is less than the thickness listed in this Chapter's Specifications, replace the pads.

Note: Keep in mind that the lining material is riveted or bonded to a metal backing plate and the metal portion is not included in this measurement.

8 If it is difficult to determine the exact thickness of the remaining pad material by the above method, or if you are at all concerned about the condition of the pads, remove the caliper(s), then remove the pads from the calipers for further inspection (see Chapter 9).

9 Once the pads are removed from the calipers, clean them with brake cleaner and re-measure them with a ruler or a vernier caliper.

10 Measure the disc thickness with a micrometer to make sure that it still has service life remaining. If any disc is thinner than the specified minimum thickness, replace it (see Chapter 9). Even if the disc has service life remaining, check its condition. Look for scoring, gouging and burned spots. If these conditions exist, remove the disc and have it resurfaced (see Chapter 9).

11 Before installing the wheels, check all brake lines and hoses for damage, wear, deformation, cracks, corrosion, leakage, bends and twists, particularly in the vicinity of the rubber hoses at the calipers. Check the clamps for tightness and the connections for leakage. Make sure that all hoses and lines are clear of sharp edges, moving parts and the exhaust system. If any of the above conditions are noted, repair, reroute or replace the lines and/or fittings as necessary (see Chapter 9).

REAR DRUM BRAKES

Refer to illustrations 12.15 and 12.17

12 On models with rear drum brakes, make sure the parking brake is off. Remove the two screws around the center of the drum (if installed), then tap on the outside of the drum with a rubber mallet to loosen it.

13 Remove the brake drums. If the drums do not pull off easily, apply some penetrating oil to the center of the hub, allow it to soak in, then tap around the center of the drum with a hammer. If it is still on solidly, tap around the outside edge of the drum from the backside.

14 With the drums removed, carefully clean the brake assembly with brake system cleaner.

WARNING:

Don't blow the dust out with compressed air and don't inhale any of it; it is harmful to your health.

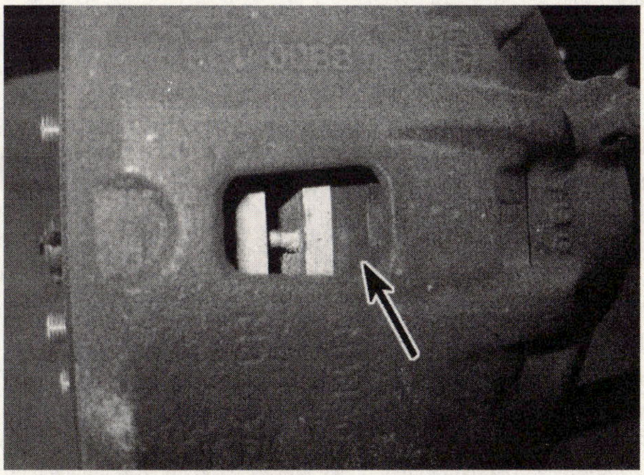

12.7a You'll find an inspection hole like this in each caliper through which you can view the inner brake pad lining

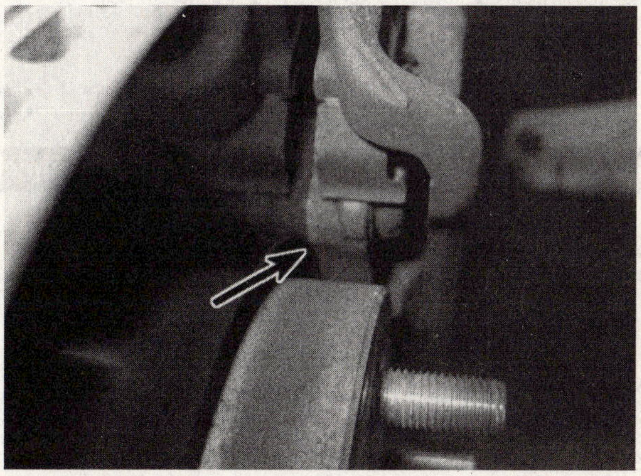

12.7b The outer pad is more easily checked at the edge of the caliper

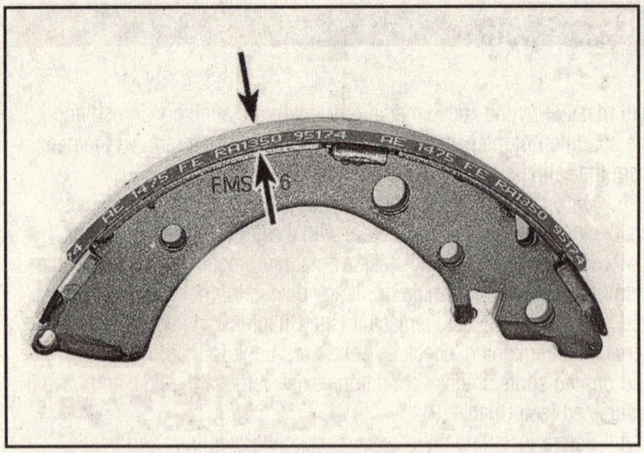

12.15 If the lining is bonded to the brake shoe, measure the lining thickness from the outer surface to the metal shoe, as shown here; if the lining is riveted to the shoe, measure from the lining outer surface to the rivet head

15 Note the thickness of the lining material on the leading and trailing brake shoes. If the material has worn away to within 1/16-inch of the recessed rivets or metal backing on bonded type shoes, the shoes should be replaced (see illustration). The shoes should also be replaced if they're cracked, glazed (shiny areas), or covered with brake fluid.

16 Make sure all the brake assembly springs are connected and in good condition.

17 Check the brake components for signs of fluid leakage. With your finger or a small screwdriver, carefully pry back the rubber cups on the wheel cylinder located at the top of the brake shoes (see illustration). Any leakage here is an indication that the wheel cylinders should be replaced immediately (see Chapter 9). Also, check all hoses and connections for signs of leakage.

18 Wipe the inside of the drum with a clean rag and denatured alcohol or brake cleaner. Again, be careful not to breathe the dust.

19 Check the inside of the drum for cracks, score marks, deep scratches and hard spots which will appear as small discolored areas. If imperfections cannot be removed with fine emery cloth, the drum must be taken to an automotive machine shop for resurfacing.

20 Repeat the procedure for the remaining wheel. If the inspection reveals that all parts are in good condition, reinstall the brake drums, install the wheels and lower the vehicle to the ground.

12.17 Check the wheel cylinder boots for leaking fluid indicating that the cylinder must be replaced or rebuilt

BRAKE BOOSTER CHECK

21 Sit in the driver's seat and perform the following sequence of tests.

22 With the brake fully depressed, start the engine - the pedal should move down a little when the engine starts.

23 With the engine running, depress the brake pedal several times - the travel distance should not change.

24 Depress the brake, stop the engine and hold the pedal in for about 30 seconds - the pedal should neither sink nor rise.

25 Restart the engine, run it for about a minute and turn it off. Then firmly depress the brake several times - the pedal travel should decrease with each application.

26 If your brakes do not operate as described, the brake booster has failed. Refer to Chapter 9 for the replacement procedure.

PARKING BRAKE

27 One method of checking the parking brake is to park the vehicle on a steep hill with the parking brake set and the transmission in Neutral (be sure to stay in the vehicle for this check). If the parking brake cannot prevent the vehicle from rolling, it's in need of attention (see Chapter 9).

13 Steering, suspension and driveaxle boot check (every 15,000 miles [24,000 km] or 18 months)

STEERING CHECK

➡ **Note: For detailed illustrations of the steering and suspension components, refer to Chapter 10.**

1 With the vehicle on the ground and the front wheels pointed straight ahead, rock the steering wheel gently back and forth. If freeplay is excessive, a front wheel bearing, main shaft yoke, intermediate shaft yoke, lower arm balljoint or steering system joint is worn or the steering gear is out of adjustment or broken. Steering wheel freeplay is the amount of travel (measured at the rim of the steering wheel) between the initial steering input and the point at which the front wheels begin to turn (indicated by slight resistance). Refer to Chapter 10 for the appropriate repair procedure.

2 Other symptoms, such as excessive vehicle body movement over rough roads, swaying (leaning) around corners and binding as the steering wheel is turned, may indicate faulty steering and/or suspension components.

SUSPENSION CHECK

➧ **Refer to illustrations 13.7 and 13.8**

3 Check the shock absorbers by pushing down and releasing the vehicle several times at each corner. If the vehicle does not come back to a level position within one or two bounces, the shocks/struts are worn and must be replaced. When bouncing the vehicle up and down, listen for squeaks and noises from the suspension components. Additional information on suspension components can be found in Chapter 10.

4 Raise the vehicle with a floor jack and support it securely on jackstands. See *Jacking and towing* at the front of this book for the proper jacking points.

5 Check the tires for irregular wear patterns and proper inflation. See Section 5 in this Chapter for information regarding tire wear and Chapter 10 for the wheel bearing replacement procedures.

6 Inspect the universal joint between the steering shaft and the steering gear housing. Check the steering gear housing for lubricant leakage or oozing. Make sure that the dust seals and boots are not damaged and that the boot clamps are not loose. Check the tie-rod ends for excessive play. Look for loose bolts, broken or disconnected parts and deteriorated rubber bushings on all suspension and steering components. While an assistant turns the steering wheel from side to side, check the steering components for free movement, chafing and binding. If the steering components do not seem to be reacting with the movement of the steering wheel, try to determine where the slack is located.

7 Check the balljoints for wear by trying to move each control arm up and down with a prybar (see illustration) to ensure that its balljoint has no play. If any balljoint does have play, replace it. See Chapter 10 for the front balljoint replacement procedure.

8 Inspect the balljoint boots for damage and leaking grease (see illustration). Replace the balljoints with new ones if they are damaged (see Chapter 10).

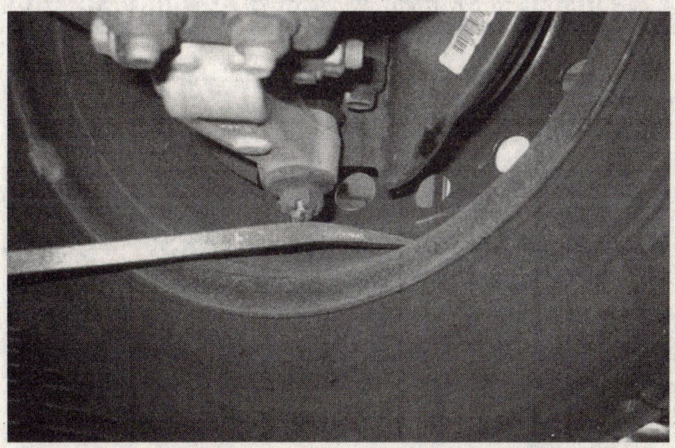

13.7 To check the balljoints, attempt to move the control arm up and down with a prybar to make sure there is no play in the balljoint (if there is, replace it)

DRIVEAXLE BOOT CHECK

➧ **Refer to illustration 13.10**

9 The driveaxle boots are very important because they prevent dirt, water and foreign material from entering and damaging the constant velocity (CV) joints.

10 Inspect the boots for tears and cracks as well as loose clamps (see illustration). If there is any evidence of cracks or leaking lubricant, they must be replaced as described in Chapter 8.

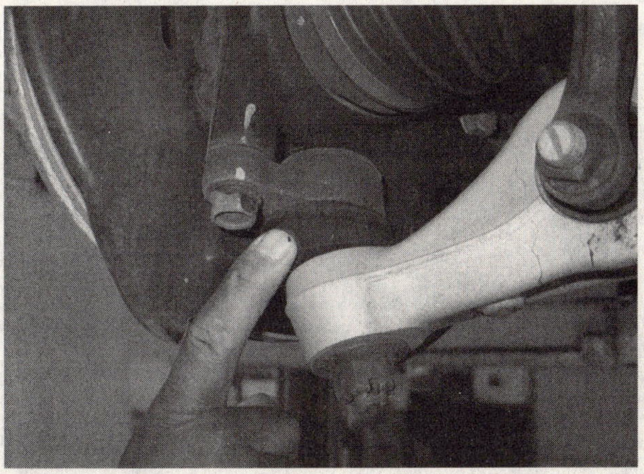

13.8 Push on the balljoint boot to check for tears and grease leaks

13.10 Flex the driveaxle boots by hand to check for tears, cracks and leaking grease

14 Exhaust system check (every 15,000 miles [24,000 km] or 18 months)

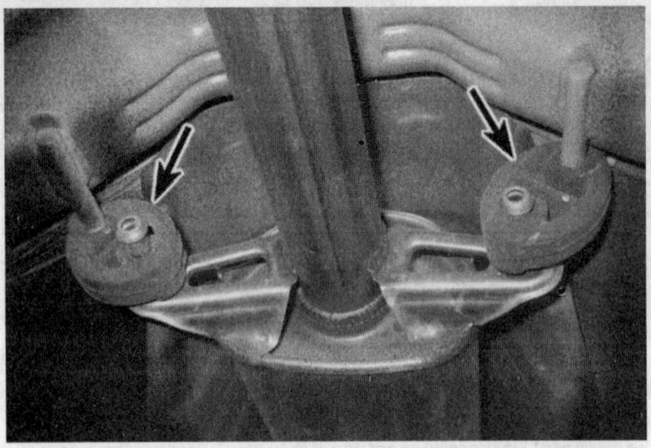

14.2 Check the exhaust system rubber hangers for damage

➧ **Refer to illustration 14.2**

1 With the engine cold (at least three hours after the vehicle has been driven), check the complete exhaust system from its starting point at the engine to the end of the tailpipe. Preferably this should be done on a hoist where unrestricted access is available.

2 Check the pipes and connections for evidence of leaks, severe corrosion or damage. Make sure that all brackets and hangers are in good condition and tight (see illustration).

3 At the same time, inspect the underside of the body for holes, corrosion, open seams, etc. that may allow exhaust gases to enter the passenger compartment. Seal all body openings with silicone or body putty.

4 Rattles and other noises can often be traced to the exhaust system, especially the mounts and hangers. Try to move the pipes, silencer and catalytic converter. If the components can come in contact with the body or suspension parts, secure the exhaust system with new mounts.

15 Air filter replacement (every 30,000 miles [48,000 km] or 36 months)

➧ **Refer to illustrations 15.1 and 15.2**

1 The air filter element is located inside the air filter housing, which is located on the left side of the engine compartment. To remove the air filter, release the clamps retaining the two halves of the air filter housing (see illustration). Disconnect the wiring from the mass airflow sensor (if necessary) to get enough clearance to raise the lid.

2 Lift the cover up and remove the air filter element (see illustration).

3 Inspect the outer surface of the filter element. If it is dirty, replace it. If it is only moderately dusty, it can be reused by blowing it clean from the back to the front surface with compressed air.

⁂ WARNING:

Always wear eye protection when using compressed air!

15.1 Release the spring clips securing the top part of the air filter housing

Because it is a pleated paper type filter, it cannot be washed or oiled. If it cannot be cleaned satisfactorily with compressed air, discard and replace it.

⁂ CAUTION:

Never drive the vehicle with the air filter removed. Excessive engine wear could result and backfiring could even cause a fire under the hood.

4 Clean any leaves and debris from the air filter housing.

5 Installation is the reverse of removal.

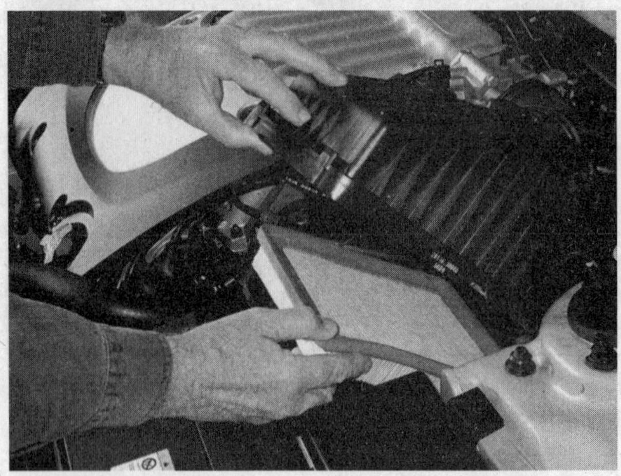

15.2 After releasing the spring clips, lift the cover up, remove the filter element and install the new one

16 Fuel system check (every 30,000 miles [48,000 km] or 36 months)

⁂ WARNING:

Gasoline is extremely flammable, so take extra precautions when you work on any part of the fuel system. Don't smoke or allow open flames or bare light bulbs near the work area, and don't work in a garage where a gas-type appliance (such as a water heater or clothes dryer) is present. Since gasoline is carcinogenic, wear fuel resistant gloves when there's a possibility of being exposed to fuel, and, if you spill any fuel on your skin, rinse it off immediately with soap and water. Mop up any spills immediately and do not store fuel-soaked rags where they could ignite. The fuel system is under constant pressure, so, if any fuel lines are to be disconnected, the fuel pressure in the system must be relieved first. When you perform any kind of work on the fuel system, wear safety glasses and have a Class B type fire extinguisher on hand.

1 If you smell fuel while driving or after the vehicle has been sitting in the sun, inspect the fuel system immediately.

2 Remove the fuel filler cap and inspect it for damage and corrosion. The gasket should have an unbroken sealing imprint. If the gasket is damaged or corroded, remove it and install a new one.

3 Inspect the fuel lines for cracks. Make sure that the threaded flare-nut type connectors which secure the metal fuel lines to the fuel injection system and the fittings on the in-line fuel filter are tight.

4 Since some components of the fuel system are underneath the vehicle, they can be inspected more easily with the vehicle raised on a hoist. If that's not possible, raise the vehicle and support it securely on jackstands.

5 With the vehicle raised and safely supported, inspect the fuel tank and filler neck for punctures, cracks and other damage. The connection between the filler neck and the tank is particularly critical. Sometimes a rubber filler neck will leak because of loose clamps or deteriorated rubber. These are problems a home mechanic can usually rectify.

⁂ WARNING:

Do not, under any circumstances, try to repair a fuel tank (except rubber components). A welding torch or any open flame can easily cause fuel vapors inside the tank to explode.

6 Carefully check all rubber hoses and metal lines leading away from the fuel tank. Check for loose connections, deteriorated hoses, crimped lines and other damage. Carefully inspect the lines from the tank to the fuel injection system. Repair or replace damaged sections as necessary (see Chapter 4).

17 Interior ventilation filter replacement (every 30,000 miles [48,000 km] or 36 months)

➧ Refer to illustrations 17.2 and 17.3

➡ Note: The interior ventilation filter (or, cabin air filter) cleans the air entering the passenger compartment. The following procedure is typical; the procedure for replacing the filter differs slightly depending on the model year.

1 Disengage the glove box (see Chapter 11) and allow it to drop down.

2 On 2001 through 2006 models, rotate the locking knob on the filter cover counterclockwise (see illustration), remove the cover and pull out the cabin air filter.

3 On 2006.5 and later models, pinch the release tabs or locking clips and pull out the cabin air filter (see illustration).

4 Installation is the reverse of removal.

17.2 On 2001 through 2006 models, rotate the lock counterclockwise to remove the filter

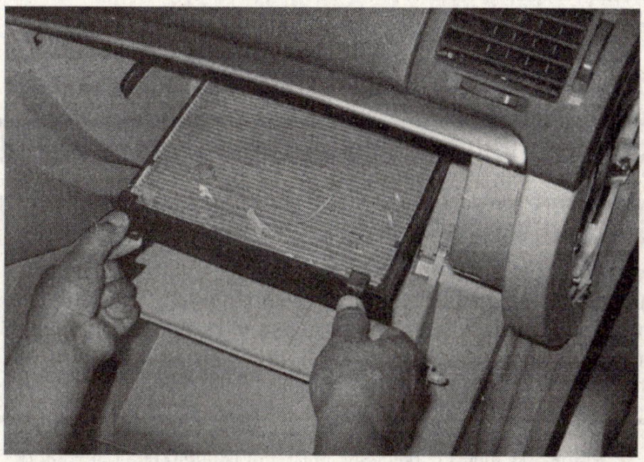

17.3 On 2006.5 and later models, detach the locking clips to remove the filter

18 Positive Crankcase Ventilation (PCV) valve check and replacement (every 30,000 miles [48,000 km] or 36 months)

Refer to illustrations 18.2a, 18.2b and 18.2c

1 On four-cylinder models, the PCV valve is located on the valve cover. On V6 models, it's located on the front valve cover.

2 Disconnect the hose, unscrew the PCV valve from the cover, then reconnect the hose (see illustrations).

Note: On some models there is a foam rubber silencer over the PCV valve that must be removed in order to unscrew the valve (see illustration).

3 With the engine idling at normal operating temperature, place your finger over the valve opening. If there's no vacuum at the valve, check for a plugged hose or valve. Replace any plugged or deteriorated hoses.

4 Turn off the engine. Remove the PCV valve from the hose. Blow through the valve from the valve cover (cylinder head) end. If air will not pass through the valve in this direction, replace it with a new one.

5 When purchasing a replacement PCV valve, make sure it's for your particular vehicle and engine size. Compare the old valve with the new one to make sure they're the same.

18.2a PCV valve location (four-cylinder engines)

18.2b PCV hose (A) and PCV valve (B) locations (V6 engines)

18.2c On some four-cylinder engines, remove the silencer from the PCV valve, then use a wrench to unscrew the valve

19 Brake fluid change (every 30,000 miles [48,000 km] or 36 months)

WARNING:

Brake fluid can harm your eyes and damage painted surfaces, so use extreme caution when handling or pouring it. Do not use brake fluid that has been standing open or is more than one year old. Brake fluid absorbs moisture from the air. Excess moisture can cause a dangerous loss of braking effectiveness.

1 At the specified intervals, the brake fluid should be drained and replaced. Since the brake fluid may drip or splash when pouring it, place plenty of rags around the master cylinder to protect any surrounding painted surfaces.

2 Before beginning work, purchase the specified brake fluid (see *Recommended lubricants and fluids* in this Chapter's Specifications).

3 Remove the cap from the master cylinder reservoir.

4 Using a hand-held suction pump or similar device, withdraw the fluid from the master cylinder reservoir.

5 Add new fluid to the master cylinder until it rises to the base of the filler neck.

6 Bleed the brake system as described in Chapter 9 at all four brakes until new and uncontaminated fluid is expelled from the bleeder screw. Be sure to maintain the fluid level in the master cylinder as you perform the bleeding process. If you allow the master cylinder to run dry, air will enter the system.

7 Refill the master cylinder with fluid and check the operation of the brakes. The pedal should feel solid when depressed, with no sponginess.

WARNING:

Do not operate the vehicle if you are in doubt about the effectiveness of the brake system.

20 Drivebelt check, adjustment and replacement (60,000 miles [96,000 km] or 72 months

CHECK

➧ Refer to illustrations 20.2 and 20.4

1 The drivebelt(s) are located at the front of the engine. The good condition and proper adjustment of the belts is critical to the operation of the engine. Because of their composition and the high stresses to which they are subjected, drivebelts stretch and deteriorate as they get older. They must therefore be periodically inspected.

2 With the engine off, open the hood and locate the drivebelts. With a flashlight, check each belt for separation of the adhesive rubber on both sides of the core, core separation from the belt side, a severed core, separation of the ribs from the adhesive rubber, cracking or separation of the ribs, and torn or worn ribs or cracks in the inner ridges of the ribs (see illustration).

3 Also check for fraying and glazing, which gives the belt a shiny appearance. Both sides of the belt should be inspected, which means you will have to twist the belt to check the underside. Use your fingers to feel the belt where you can't see it. If any of the above conditions are evident, replace the belt.

4 On 2001 through 2006 four-cylinder engines, the tension of each belt is checked by pushing on the belt at a distance halfway between the pulleys. Push firmly with your thumb and see how much the belt moves (deflects) (see illustration). The belt should deflect approximately 1/4-inch. All other models have a self-adjusting, spring-loaded tensioner.

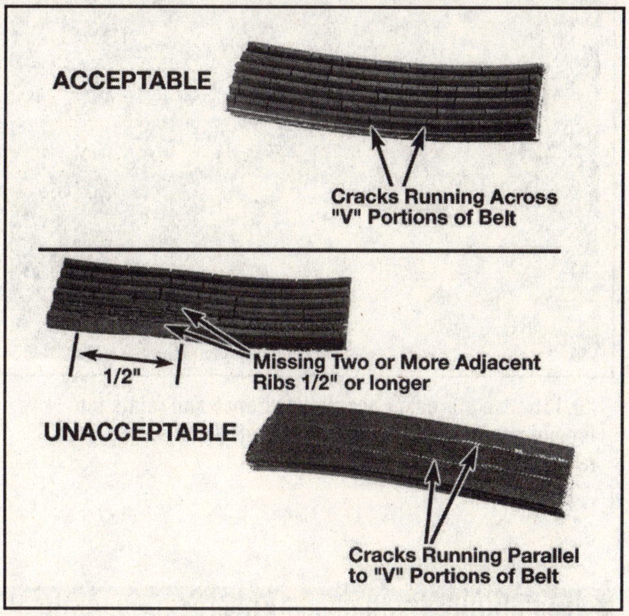

20.2 Check a multi-ribbed belt for signs like these - if the belt looks worn, replace it

ADJUSTMENT (2001 THROUGH 2006 FOUR-CYLINDER ENGINES)

➡ Note: 2006.5 and later four-cylinder and all V6 engines have self-adjusting belt tensioners.

Alternator belt

5 Loosen the lower alternator mounting bolt and the upper tension bolts.

6 Carefully tension the belt by prying on the alternator housing. Tighten the upper tension and lock bolts and the lower bolt.

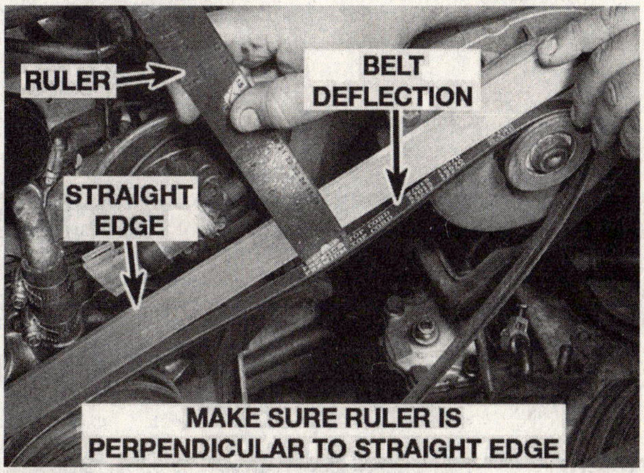

20.4 Measuring drivebelt deflection with a straightedge and ruler (models with adjustable belts)

Power steering pump and air conditioning compressor belts

7 Loosen the lock bolt on the belt tensioner assembly. Use the adjacent adjustment bolt to adjust the tension on the belt.

8 Tighten the tensioner lock bolt.

REPLACEMENT

9 Remove any interfering components such as engine covers and engine brackets.

Four-cylinder engines (2001 through 2006 models)

10 Release tension on the belt(s). Refer to the adjustment procedures above. Loosen the tension so that the belt(s) will slip off the pulleys.

2006.5 and later four-cylinder engines and all V6 engines

➧ Refer to illustrations 20.11a and 20.11b

11 These engines use a self-adjusting spring-loaded tensioner. Use

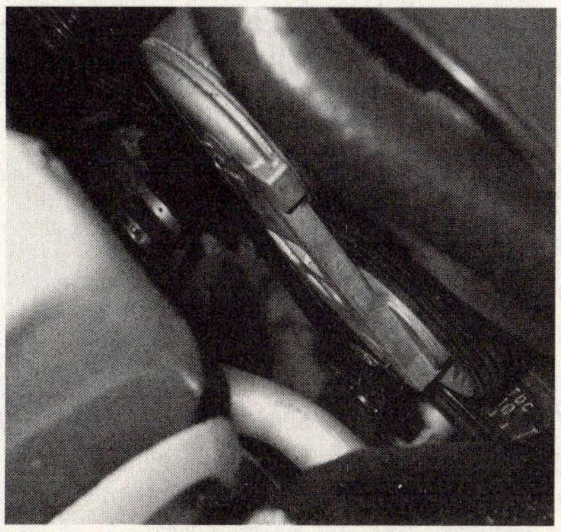

20.11a On engines with an automatic tensioner, put a wrench on the tensioner lug

20.11b Use a breaker bar on the wrench and rotate the tensioner clockwise to take tension off the drivebelt, then remove the belt

a breaker bar or a long-handle ratchet to rotate the tensioner and release tension on the belt (see illustrations). Slip the belt from the pulleys while the tension is released.

All engines

12 Take the old belt(s) to the parts store, if possible, in order to make a direct comparison for length, width and design.

13 After replacing the drivebelt, make sure that it fits properly in the ribbed grooves in the pulleys. It is essential that the belt be properly centered.

14 To replace a belt, follow the procedures for drivebelt adjustment, but slip the belt off the crankshaft pulley and remove it. Because belts tend to wear out more or less together, it is a good idea to replace both belts at the same time (on models so equipped). Mark each belt and its appropriate pulley groove so the replacement belts can be fitted in their proper positions.

15 On 2001 through 2006 four-cylinder engines, adjust the belt(s) in accordance with the procedures outlined earlier in this Section.

21 Fuel filter replacement (every 60,000 miles [96,000 km] or 72 months)

WARNING:

Gasoline is extremely flammable, so take extra precautions when you work on any part of the fuel system. Don't smoke or allow open flames or bare light bulbs near the work area, and don't work in a garage where a gas-type appliance (such as a water heater or clothes dryer) is present. Since gasoline is carcinogenic, wear fuel resistant gloves when there's a possibility of being exposed to fuel, and, if you spill any fuel on your skin, rinse it off immediately with soap and water. Mop up any spills immediately and do not store fuel-soaked rags where they could ignite. The fuel system is under constant pressure, so, if any fuel lines are to be disconnected, the fuel pressure in the system must be relieved first (see Chapter 4, Section 2). When you perform any kind of work on the fuel system, wear safety glasses and have a Class B type fire extinguisher on hand.

Note: This procedure applies only to 2001 through 2006 four-cylinder models and 2001 V6 models, which use an external fuel filter. On all other models, the fuel filter is an integral component of the fuel pump assembly.

1 Relieve the fuel system pressure (see Chapter 4, Section 2), then disconnect the cable from the negative terminal of the battery (see Chapter 5, Section 1).

2 Place rags or a drain pan under the fuel filter.

3 Raise the rear of the vehicle and support it securely on jackstands.

Note: The fuel filter is mounted near the left front corner of the fuel tank.

4 Loosen the fitting nuts on the fuel lines. Be sure to hold the fuel filter fittings with a wrench.

5 Remove the bolt securing the filter mounting strap, then remove the filter.

6 Installation is the reverse of the removal procedure. Use new sealing washers and tighten the fitting nuts to the torque listed in this Chapter's Specifications.

7 Reconnect the battery, turn the ignition key to the On position, then check for leaks.

22 Automatic transaxle fluid change (60,000 miles [96,000 km] or 72 months)

Refer to illustration 22.7

1 At the specified time intervals, the automatic transaxle and differential fluid should be drained and replaced.

Note: Although the manufacturer doesn't specify it, it is a good idea to replace the transaxle fluid filter periodically to remove accumulated dirt and metal particles.

2 Before beginning work, purchase the specified transaxle fluid (see *Recommended fluids and lubricants* in this Chapter's Specifications).

3 Other tools necessary for this job include jackstands to support the vehicle in a raised position, an appropriate wrench, a drain pan capable of holding at least eight pints, newspapers and clean rags.

4 The fluid should be drained immediately after the vehicle has been driven. Hot fluid is more effective than cold fluid at removing built up sediment.

WARNING:

Fluid temperature can exceed 350-degrees F in a hot transaxle. Wear protective gloves.

5 After the vehicle has been driven to warm up the fluid, raise it and place it on jackstands for access to the transaxle and differential drain plugs.

6 Move the necessary equipment under the vehicle, being careful not to touch any of the hot exhaust components.

7 Place the drain pan under the transaxle drain plug and remove the drain plug (see illustration). Once the fluid is drained, reinstall the drain plug and tighten it to the torque listed in this Chapter's Specifications.

8 Lower the vehicle.

9 Early-production 2001 models have a cartridge-type transmission fluid filter located on top of the transaxle case; remove the air filter housing for access (see Chapter 4). Using an oil filter wrench, unscrew the filter. Lubricate the O-ring of the new filter with clean transmission fluid, then install the new filter, tightening it hand-tight.

10 Add new fluid to the transaxle through the dipstick tube (see this Chapter's Specifications for the recommended fluid type and capacity). Use a funnel to prevent spills. It is best to add a little fluid at a time, continually checking the level with the dipstick (see Section 4).

⁂ CAUTION:

It's important not to overfill the transaxle.

11 Start the engine and shift into all positions from P through L, then shift into P and apply the parking brake.

12 With the engine idling, check the fluid level. Add fluid up to the Cool (or lower) level mark on the dipstick.

13 Drive the vehicle to warm up the transaxle to normal operating temperature, then recheck the fluid level.

22.7 Automatic transaxle drain plug

23 Manual transaxle lubricant change (60,000 miles [96,000 km] or 72 months)

➡ Note: This procedure applies only to vehicles that are used in rough service such as constant stop-and-go driving, towing, etc. Vehicles operated in typical conditions don't require manual transaxle lubricant changes as a part of normal maintenance.

1 Operate the vehicle until the transaxle is warmed up.

2 Raise the vehicle and support it securely on jackstands.

3 Remove the transaxle fill plug on the side of the case and verify that the lubricant is near the bottom of the hole. If it isn't, find the cause of the leakage. It is not normal for a manual transaxle to need refilling.

4 Place a drain pan under the transaxle. If the transaxle has a drain plug, remove it and allow the fluid to run into the pan. Reinstall the drain plug and tighten it securely. If there is no drain plug, use a suction gun fitted with a hose to remove the lubricant through the fill hole.

5 Add fresh lubricant through the fill hole until it starts to run out. Be sure to use the correct grade of lubricant (refer to the Specifications in this Chapter).

6 Replace the plug and lower the vehicle.

7 Dispose of the old lubricant in a responsible manner. Check with your local auto parts store, disposal facility or environmental agency to see if they will accept the oil for recycling. After the oil has cooled it can be drained into a container (capped plastic jugs, topped bottles, milk cartons, etc.) for transport to one of these disposal sites. Don't dispose of the oil by pouring it on the ground or down a drain!

8 Lower the vehicle, drive it, then check for leaks.

24 Timing belt replacement (2001 through 2006 four-cylinder and all V6 models) (60,000 miles [96,000 km] or 72 months)

➡ Note: 2006 and earlier four-cylinder and all V6 models use timing belts. Other models use timing chains that are not regularly serviced.

1 Refer to Chapter 2, Part A (four-cylinder engine) or Part B (V6 engines) for information on this procedure.

2 The timing belt should be inspected every 30,000 miles or whenever there is a possibility that oil leakage may have damaged it. Remove the upper timing belt cover and make sure that the belt is clean, oil-free and in good condition.

3 Any sign of oil leakage onto the timing belt must be investigated and repaired at once.

4 Even if the timing belt appears fine, it must be replaced at the proper interval to avoid the possibility of a breakdown and engine damage.

25 Valve clearance inspection and adjustment (2006.5 and later models) (60,000 miles [96,000 km] or 72 months)

1 Refer to Section 7 in Chapter 2A for four-cylinder engines, or Section 10 in Chapter 2B for V6 engines. The adjustment procedure outlines the steps necessary to record all of the valve clearances using feeler gauges. These figures can then be compared to the clearances listed in the Specifications in that Chapter.

2 If the clearances are out of specification, the valves should be adjusted to eliminate noise and poor performance if they're too loose, and possible engine damage if they're too tight.

3 The engine must be cool when the measurements are taken. Before you get started, be aware that the adjustment procedure involves buying new bucket-style lifters from a dealer.

26 Cooling system servicing (draining, flushing and refilling) (at 100,000 miles [160,000 km] or 120 months and every 50,000 miles [80,500 km] or 60 months thereafter)

⁂ WARNING:

Wait until the engine is completely cool before beginning this procedure.

⁂ WARNING:

Do not allow engine coolant (antifreeze) to come in contact with your skin or painted surfaces of the vehicle. Rinse off spills immediately with plenty of water. Antifreeze is highly toxic if ingested. Never leave antifreeze lying around in an open container or in puddles on the floor; children and pets are attracted by its sweet smell and may drink it. Check with local authorities on proper disposal methods for used antifreeze. Many communities have collection centers that will see that antifreeze is disposed of safely.

1 Periodically, the cooling system should be drained, flushed and refilled to replenish the antifreeze mixture and prevent formation of rust and corrosion, which can impair the performance of the cooling system and cause engine damage. When the cooling system is serviced, all hoses and the radiator cap should be checked and replaced if necessary.

DRAINING

➧ Refer to illustrations 26.4

2 Apply the parking brake and block the wheels. If the vehicle has just been driven, wait several hours to allow the engine to cool down before beginning this procedure.

3 Once the engine is completely cool, remove the coolant reservoir cap and the radiator cap.

4 Move a large container under the radiator drain to catch the coolant. Attach a hose to the drain fitting to direct the coolant into the container (some models are already equipped with a hose), then open the drain fitting (see illustration).

5 After the coolant stops flowing out of the radiator, move the container under the engine block drain plug(s). Loosen the plug(s) and allow the coolant in the block to drain. On four-cylinder models, the block drain plug is on the front side of the engine block. On V6 models, there's one on each side of the block.

6 While the coolant is draining, check the condition of the radiator hoses, heater hoses and clamps (refer to Section 11 if necessary).

7 Replace any damaged clamps or hoses (see Chapter 3).

26.4 Radiator drain plug

FLUSHING

➧ Refer to illustration 26.10

8 Once the system is completely drained, remove the thermostat from the engine (see Chapter 3). Then reinstall the thermostat housing temporarily without the thermostat. This will allow the system to be flushed.

9 Reinstall the engine block drain plug(s) and tighten the radiator drain plug. Turn the heating system controls to Hot, so that the heater core will be flushed at the same time as the rest of the cooling system.

10 Disconnect the upper radiator hose from the radiator. Place a garden hose in the upper radiator inlet, turn the water on and flush the system until the water runs clear out of the upper radiator hose (see illustration).

11 In severe cases of contamination or clogging of the radiator, remove the radiator (see Chapter 3) and have a radiator repair facility clean and repair it, if necessary. Many deposits can be removed by the chemical action of a cleaner available at auto parts stores. Follow the procedure outlined in the manufacturer's instructions.

➡ Note: When the coolant is regularly drained and the system refilled with the correct antifreeze/water mixture, there should be no need to use chemical cleaners or descalers.

12 After flushing, drain the radiator and remove the block drain plugs once again to drain the water from the system.

REFILLING

13 Close and tighten the radiator drain. Install and tighten the block drain plug(s). Reinstall the thermostat (see Chapter 3).

14 Place the heater temperature control in the maximum heat position.

15 Slowly add new coolant to the radiator until it's full. Add coolant to the reservoir up to the lower mark.

16 Install the radiator cap and run the engine in a well-ventilated area until the thermostat opens (coolant will begin flowing through the radiator and the upper radiator hose will become hot).

17 Turn the engine off and let it cool completely. Add more coolant mixture to bring the level back up to the lip on the radiator filler neck.

18 Squeeze the upper radiator hose to expel air, then add more coolant mixture if necessary. Fill the coolant reservoir with coolant/water. Reinstall the coolant reservoir cap.

19 Start the engine, allow it to reach normal operating temperature and check for leaks.

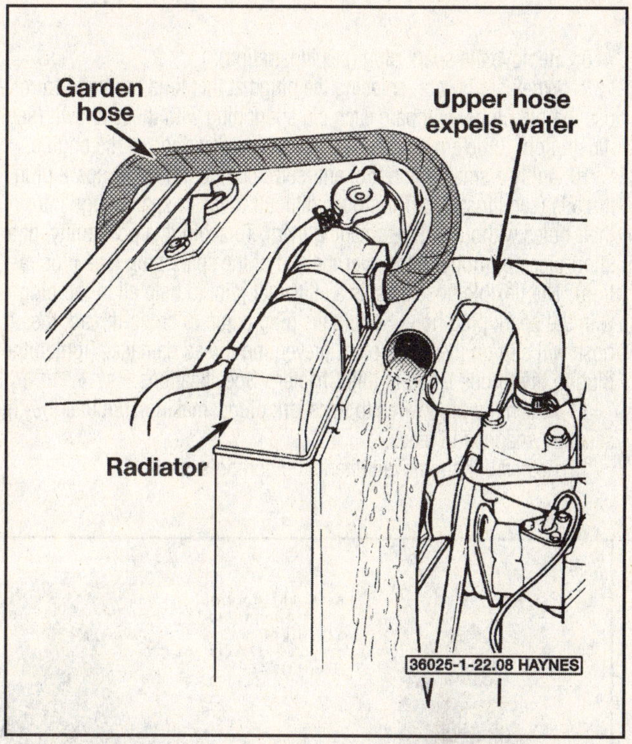

26.10 With the thermostat removed, disconnect the upper radiator hose and flush the radiator and engine block with a garden hose

27 Spark plug check and replacement (every 120,000 miles [193,000 km] or 144 months)

Refer to illustrations 27.1, 27.8, 27.9, 27.10a and 27.10b

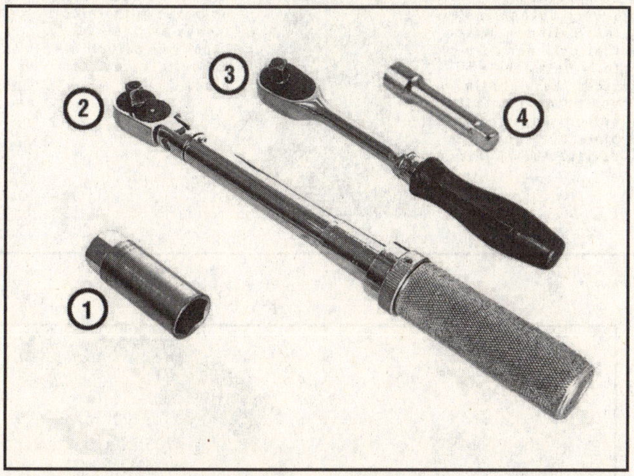

27.1 Tools required for changing spark plugs

1 **Spark plug socket** - *This will have special padding inside to protect the spark plug's porcelain insulator*
2 **Torque wrench** - *Although not mandatory, using this tool is the best way to ensure the plugs are tightened properly*
3 **Ratchet** - *Standard hand tool to fit the spark plug socket*
4 **Extension** - *Depending on model and accessories, you may need special extensions and universal joints to reach one or more of the plugs*

Note: Do not adjust the gap on platinum or iridium spark plugs. Using a gapping tool on them could damage the plating on the electrodes. These spark plugs are pre-gapped by the manufacturer.

1 Spark plug replacement requires a spark plug socket that fits onto a ratchet. This socket is lined with a rubber grommet to protect the porcelain insulator of the spark plug and to hold the plug while you insert it into the spark plug hole (see illustration).

2 If you are replacing the plugs, purchase the new plugs and replace each plug one at a time.

3 Inspect each of the new plugs for defects. If there are any signs of cracks in the porcelain insulator of a plug, don't use it.

4 Remove the engine cover(s) and disconnect any hoses or components that would interfere with access and move them out of the way.

5 On V6 engines, it will be necessary to remove the upper intake manifold to access the rear spark plugs. Refer to Chapter 2B for this procedure.

6 Some spark plugs have a conventional spark plug wire attached. On these, pull the spark plug wires from the spark plugs, grasping the wires by the boots, not the wire itself. On those that have a coil directly over the spark plugs, disconnect the coil wiring and unbolt and remove each coil (see Chapter 5).

7 If compressed air is available, blow any dirt or foreign material away from the spark plug area before proceeding.

WARNING:

Always wear eye protection when using compressed air!

8 Remove the spark plug (see illustration).

9 Whether you are replacing the plugs at this time or intend to re-use the old plugs, compare each old spark plug with those shown (see illustration) to determine the overall running condition of the engine.

10 Apply a small amount of anti-seize compound to the spark plug threads (see illustration). It's often difficult to insert spark plugs into their holes without cross-threading them. To avoid this possibility, fit a short piece of rubber hose over the end of the spark plug (see illustration). The flexible hose acts as a universal joint to help align the plug with the spark plug hole. Should the plug begin to cross-thread, the hose will slip on the spark plug, preventing thread damage. Tighten the plug to the torque listed in this Chapter's Specifications.

11 Attach the plug wires to the spark plugs, making sure that they're securely snapped in place.

12 Reinstall the removed interfering components.

27.8 Because they are deeply recessed, the proper spark plug socket and an extension will be required when removing and installing the spark plugs

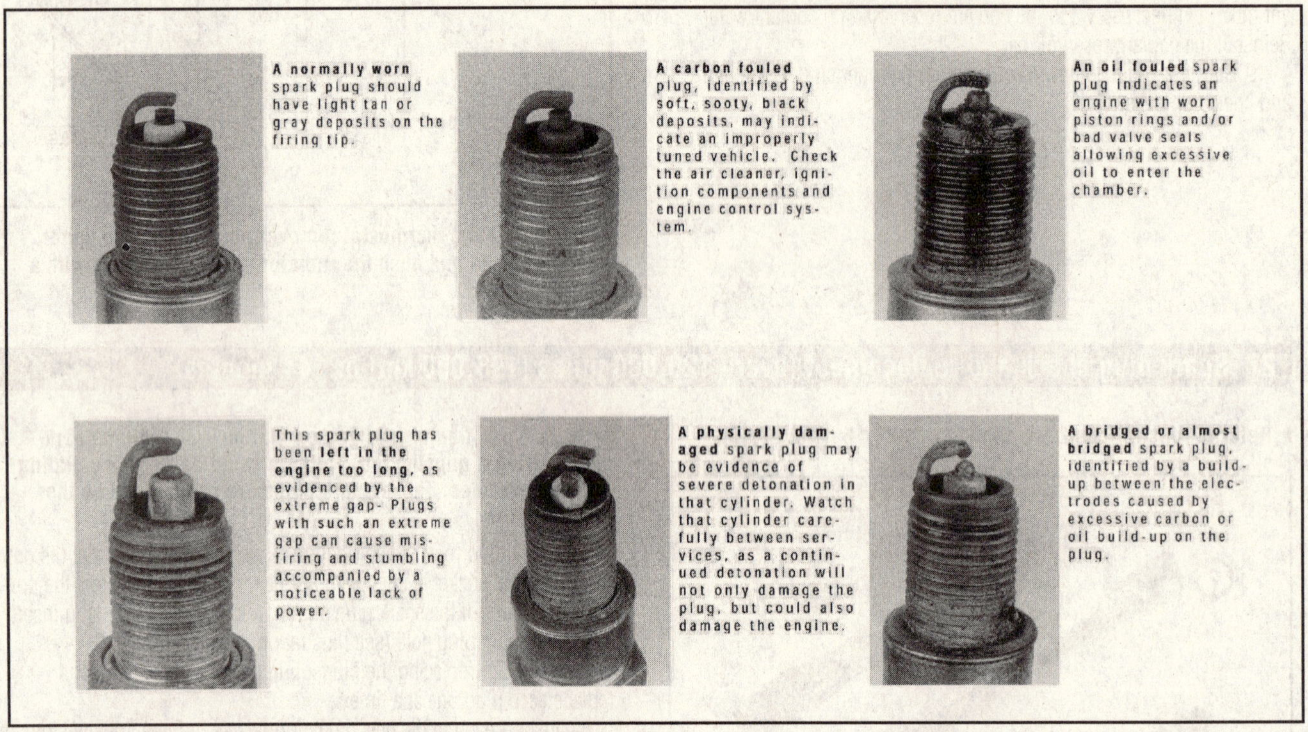

27.9 Inspect the spark plug to determine engine running conditions

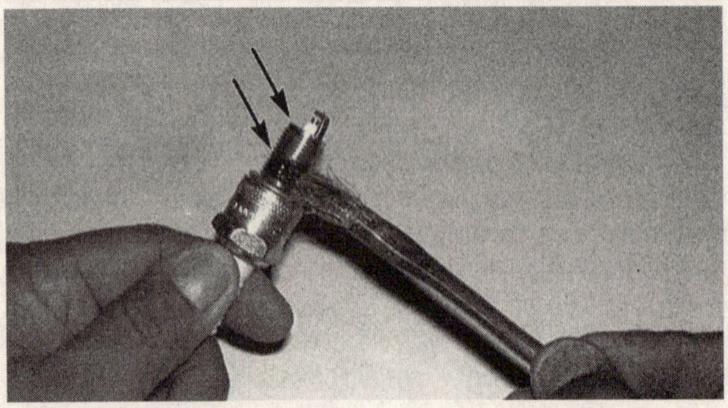

27.10a A light coat of anti-seize compound applied to the threads of the spark plugs will keep the threads in the cylinder head from being damaged the next time the plugs are removed

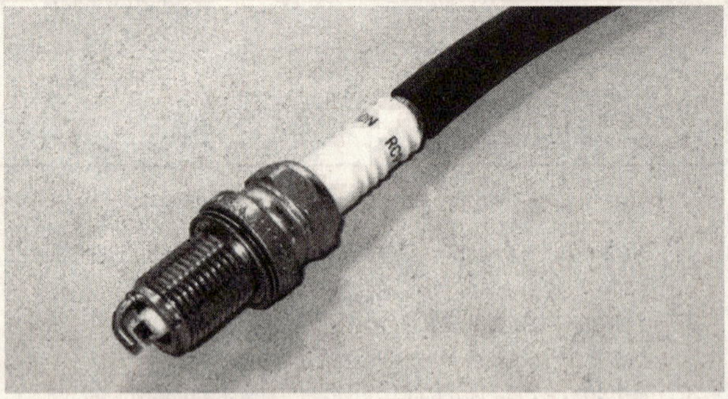

27.10b A length of rubber hose will aid in getting the spark plug threads started

28 Ignition system component check and replacement (every 120,000 miles [193,000 km] or 144 months)

➡ **Note: Some models don't use spark plug wires; instead they use an ignition coil mounted on each spark plug.**

1 The spark plug wires should be checked whenever new spark plugs are installed.

2 Begin this procedure by making a visual check of the spark plug wires while the engine is running. In a darkened garage (make sure there is adequate ventilation) start the engine and observe each plug wire. Be careful not to come into contact with any moving engine parts. If there is a break in the wire, you will see arcing or a small spark at the damaged area. If arcing is noticed, make a note to obtain new wires, then allow the engine to cool and check the ignition coil packs.

3 The spark plug wires should be inspected one at a time to prevent mixing up the order, which is essential for proper engine operation. Each original plug wire should be numbered to help identify its location. If the number is illegible, a piece of tape can be marked with the correct number and wrapped around the plug wire.

4 Disconnect the plug wire from the spark plug. Grasp the rubber boot, twist the boot half a turn and pull the boot free. Do not pull on the wire itself.

5 Check inside the boot for corrosion, which will look like a white crusty powder. Light corrosion can be removed with a small wire brush, but replace the wires if corrosion is heavy.

6 Push the wire and boot back onto the end of the spark plug. It should fit tightly onto the end of the plug. If it doesn't, remove the wire and use pliers to carefully crimp the metal connector inside the wire boot until the fit is snug.

7 Using a clean rag, wipe the entire length of the wire to remove built-up dirt and grease. Once the wire is clean, check for burns, cracks and other damage. Do not bend the wire sharply, because the conductor might break.

8 Disconnect the wire from the ignition coil pack. Pull only on the rubber boot. Check for corrosion and a tight fit. Reconnect the wire to the coil pack.

9 Inspect the remaining spark plug wires, making sure that each one is securely fastened at the coil pack and spark plug when the check is complete.

10 If new spark plug wires are required, purchase a set for your specific engine model. Remove and replace the wires one at a time to avoid mix-ups in the firing order.

11 Clean the coil pack(s) and spark plug wires (on models so equipped) with a dampened cloth and dry them thoroughly.

12 Inspect the coil pack for cracks, damage and carbon tracking. If damage exists, refer to Chapter 5 for the replacement procedure.

Specifications

Recommended lubricants and fluids

➡ Note: Listed here are manufacturer recommendations at the time this manual was written. Manufacturers occasionally upgrade their fluid and lubricant specifications, so check with your auto parts store for current recommendations.

Engine oil	
Type	API "certified for gasoline engines"
Viscosity	See accompanying chart
Coolant	Ethylene-glycol based for use with aluminum, 50/50 mix with water
Automatic transaxle	Diamond or SK SP-III automatic transmission fluid or equivalent
Manual transaxle	75W/85 gear lubricant or API GL-4 lubricant
Brake fluid type	DOT 3 or DOT 4 brake fluid
Clutch fluid type	DOT 3 or DOT 4 brake fluid
Power steering system fluid	PSF 3 power steering fluid

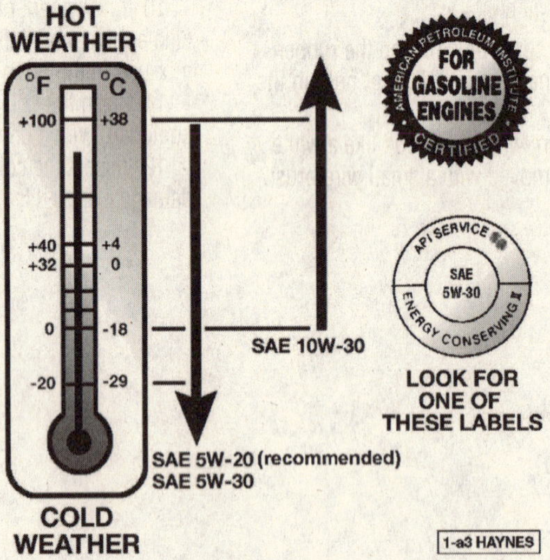

Engine oil viscosity chart

Capacities*

Engine oil (including filter)	
Four-cylinder engines	
2001 through 2006	4.5 quarts (4.3 liters)
2006.5 on	4.2 quarts (4.0 liters)
V6 engines	
2001 through 2006	5.1 quarts (4.8 liters)
2006.5 on	4.75 quarts (4.5 liters)
Coolant	
Four-cylinder models	6.9 quarts (6.5 liters)
V6 models	7.5 quarts (7.1 liters)
Automatic transaxle	
All models except 2006 and later V6 models	Up to 8.2 quarts (7.8 liters)**
2006 and later V6 models	Up to 10 quarts (9.5 liters)**
Manual transaxle (all models	2.3 quarts (2.15 liters)

**All capacities are approximate.*

**** Note: This is a dry-fill capacity. The best way to determine the amount of fluid to add during a routine fluid change is to measure the amount drained. When refilling, add that amount initially, then check the fluid level and add a little at a time, as necessary. It is important not to overfill the transaxle.**

Specifications

Ignition system

Spark plugs	
Type	
Four-cylinder engines	
2001 through 2006	NGK PRG5C-11, Champion RN10PYP4 or equivalent
2006.5	Denso SKI 6PR-A11 or equivalent
2007 and 2008	NGK 16PR-11, Champion RC 10YC4 or equivalent
2009 on	FK16HQR11
V6 engines	
2001 through 2006	NGK PFR5N-11, Champion PFR6N-11 or equivalent
2006.5 on	NGK ILFRSB11 or equivalent
Gap	0.039 to 0.043 inch (1.0 to 1.1 mm)
Engine firing order	
Four-cylinder engines	1-3-4-2
V6 engines	1-2-3-4-5-6

Cylinder numbering - four-cylinder engine

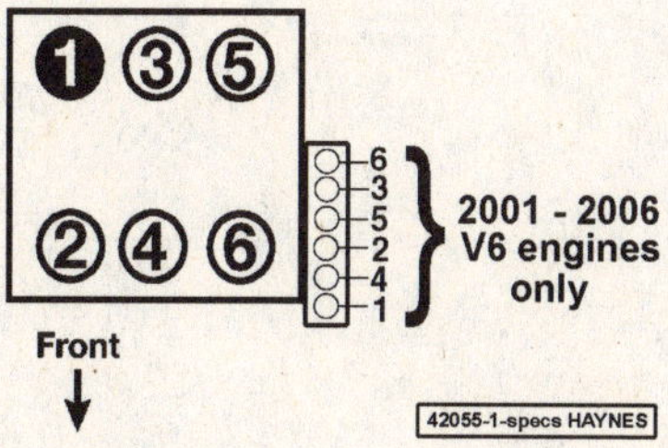

Cylinder numbering - V6 engines

Brakes

Minimum disc brake pad lining thickness (front and rear)	5/64 inch (1.98 mm)

Torque specifications

Torque specifications	Ft-lbs	Nm
Automatic transaxle drain plug		
2001 through 2006	24	32
2006.5 on	29 to 36	40 to 50
Engine oil pan drain plug	29 to 33	39 to 44
Spark plugs		
2001 through 2005	15 to 21	20 to 30
2006 on	N/A	
Wheel lug nuts	66 to 81	90 to 110

Notes

2A

FOUR-CYLINDER ENGINES

Section

1 General information
2 Repair operations possible with the engine in the vehicle
3 Top Dead Center (TDC) for number one piston - locating
4 Valve cover - removal and installation
5 Timing belts and sprockets (2001 through 2006 models) - removal, inspection and installation
6 Timing chain and sprockets (2006.5 and later models) - removal, inspection and installation
7 Camshafts and valvetrain - removal, inspection, installation and adjustment
8 Intake manifold - removal and installation
9 Exhaust manifold - removal and installation
10 Cylinder head - removal, inspection and installation
11 Crankshaft pulley/vibration damper - removal and installation
12 Oil seals - replacement
13 Oil pan - removal and installation
14 Oil pump - removal and installation
15 Flywheel/driveplate - removal and installation
16 Rear main oil seal - replacement
17 Powertrain mounts - check and replacement

Reference to other Chapters

Balance shaft - removal and installation - See Chapter 2C
CHECK ENGINE light on - See Chapter 6
Cylinder compression check - See Chapter 2C
Drivebelt - check, adjustment and replacement - See Chapter 1
Engine - removal and installation - See Chapter 2C
Engine oil and filter change - See Chapter 1
Engine overhaul - general information - See Chapter 2C
Spark plug replacement - See Chapter 1
Water pump - removal and installation - See Chapter 3

1 General information

This Part of Chapter 2 is devoted to in-vehicle repair procedures for the four-cylinder engine. Information concerning engine removal, installation and overhaul can be found in Part C of this Chapter.

The following repair procedures are based on the assumption that the engine is installed in the vehicle. If the engine has been removed from the vehicle and mounted on a stand, many of the steps outlined in this Part of Chapter 2 will not apply. The Specifications included in this Part of Chapter 2 apply only to the in-vehicle procedures contained in this Part.

The Sirius II engine used in 2001 through 2006 models incorporates a cast iron cylinder block. The aluminum cylinder head utilizes dual overhead camshafts (DOHC). The camshafts are driven from a single timing belt off the crankshaft. The Theta engine, introduced in 2006.5 models, is an all-aluminum design. It uses a timing chain rather than a belt and has variable intake camshaft timing

➡ Note: 2006 and 2006.5 models will both have a "6" in the tenth position of the VIN. To distinguish a 2006 model from a 2006.5 model, refer to the 8th position of the VIN (the engine code): A 2006 model will have a "6," while a 2006.5 will have a "3."

2 Repair operations possible with the engine in the vehicle

Many major repair operations can be accomplished without removing the engine from the vehicle.

Clean the engine compartment and the exterior of the engine with some type of degreaser before any work is done. It will make the job easier and help keep dirt out of the internal areas of the engine.

Depending on the components involved, it may be helpful to remove the hood to improve access to the engine as repairs are performed (refer to Chapter 11 if necessary). Cover the fenders to prevent damage to the paint. Special pads are available, but an old bedspread or blanket will also work.

If vacuum, exhaust, oil or coolant leaks develop, indicating a need for gasket or seal replacement, the repairs can generally be made with the engine in the vehicle. The intake and exhaust manifold gaskets, oil pan gasket, crankshaft oil seals, camshaft oil seals and cylinder head gasket are all accessible with the engine in place.

Exterior engine components, such as the intake and exhaust manifolds, the oil pan, the oil pump, the water pump, the starter motor, the alternator and the fuel system components can be removed for repair with the engine in place.

Since the cylinder head can be removed without pulling the engine, camshaft and valve component servicing can also be accomplished with the engine in the vehicle. Replacement of the timing belt or chain and sprockets is also possible with the engine in the vehicle.

3 Top Dead Center (TDC) for number one piston - locating

➧ Refer to illustrations 3.5 and 3.8

1 Top Dead Center (TDC) is the highest point in the cylinder that each piston reaches as it travels up the cylinder bore. Each piston reaches TDC on the compression stroke and again on the exhaust stroke, but TDC generally refers to piston position on the compression stroke.

2 Positioning the piston(s) at TDC is an essential part of certain procedures such as camshaft and timing belt/sprocket removal.

3 Before beginning this procedure, be sure to place the transmission in Neutral and apply the parking brake or block the rear wheels. Also, disable the fuel system (see Chapter 4, Section 2) and disable the ignition system by disconnecting the primary (low voltage) wires from the ignition coil(s) (see Chapter 5).

4 In order to bring any piston to TDC, the crankshaft must be turned using one of the methods outlined below. When looking at the front of the engine, normal crankshaft rotation is clockwise.

a) The preferred method is to turn the crankshaft with a socket and ratchet attached to the bolt threaded into the front of the crankshaft. Turn the bolt in a clockwise direction.

b) If an assistant is available to turn the ignition switch to the Start position in short bursts, you can get the piston close to TDC without a remote starter switch. Make sure your assistant is out of the vehicle, away from the ignition switch, then disconnect the cable from the negative terminal of the battery and use a socket and ratchet as described in Paragraph a) to complete the procedure.

5 Remove the spark plugs (see Chapter 1) and install a compression gauge in the number one spark plug hole. It should be a gauge with a screw-in fitting and a hose at least six inches long (see illustration).

6 Rotate the crankshaft using one of the methods described above while observing for pressure on the compression gauge. The moment the gauge shows pressure indicates that the number one cylinder has begun the compression stroke.

7 Once the compression stroke has begun, TDC for the compression stroke is reached by bringing the piston to the top of the cylinder.

3.5 A compression gauge can be used in the number one spark plug hole to assist in finding TDC

8 Continue turning the crankshaft until the timing marks on the crankshaft pulley and the front cover are aligned (see illustration).

➡ **Note: If there are no marks on the crankshaft pulley, align the marks on the camshaft pulleys with the marks on the valve cover (see Section 5).**

At this point, the number one cylinder is at TDC on the compression stroke. If the marks are aligned but there was no compression, the piston was on the exhaust stroke; continue rotating the crankshaft 360-degrees (one turn).

➡ **Note: If a compression gauge is not available, you can simply place a blunt object over the spark plug hole and listen for compression as the engine is rotated. Once compression at the No. 1 spark plug hole is noted, the remainder of the Step is the same.**

9 After the number one piston has been positioned at TDC on the compression stroke, TDC for any of the remaining cylinders can be located by turning the crankshaft 180-degrees and following the firing order (refer to the Specifications). For example, rotating the engine 180-degrees past TDC #1 will put the engine at TDC compression for cylinder #3.

3.8 Align the mark on the crankshaft pulley with the "0" mark on the front cover

4 Valve cover - removal and installation

REMOVAL

1 Disconnect the cable from the negative terminal of the battery (see Chapter 5).

2 Remove the engine cover, then remove the ignition coils (see Chapter 5).

3 Detach the PCV hose from the valve cover.

4 Disconnect any other interfering components. Be sure to label hoses and wires so you can connect them later with no confusion.

5 Remove the valve cover mounting fasteners (see illustrations 4.8a and 4.8b), then detach the valve cover and gasket from the cylinder head. If the valve cover is stuck to the cylinder head, bump the end with a wood block and a hammer to jar it loose. If that doesn't work, try to slip a flexible putty knife between the cylinder head and valve cover to break the seal.

INSTALLATION

➧ **Refer to illustrations 4.6a, 4.6b, 4.7, 4.8a and 4.8b**

6 Remove the valve cover gasket from the valve cover and clean the mating surfaces with brake system cleaner. Install a new rubber gasket, pressing it evenly into the grooves around the bottom of the valve cover (see illustration).

➡ **Note: Make sure the spark plug tube seals are in place on the bottom of the valve cover before reinstalling it (see illustration).**

The mating surfaces of the timing belt cover, the cylinder head and valve cover must be perfectly clean when the valve cover is installed. If there's residue or oil on the mating surfaces when the valve cover is installed, oil leaks may develop.

7 Apply RTV sealant around the semi-circular rubber rear seal,

4.6a Make sure that the new gasket is correctly inserted into the valve cover groove

4.6b There are rubber seals around the spark plug openings that should be replaced whenever the valve cover is removed

4.7 Apply a small dab of RTV sealant to the spots where the head and front cover meet in order to avoid oil seepage (2006.5 and later models)

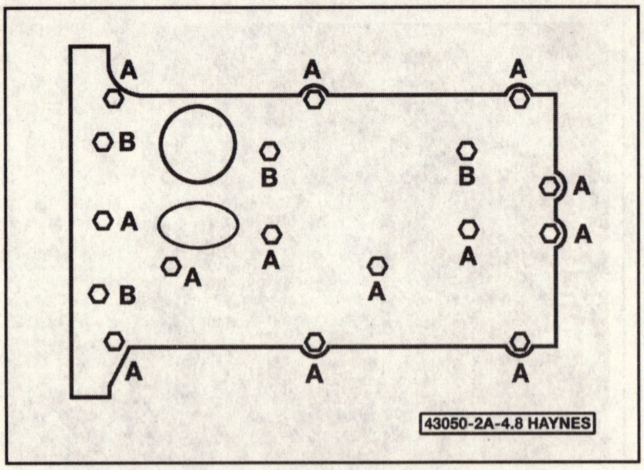

4.8a On 2006 and earlier models, the valve cover uses two types of bolts; refer to the Specifications for the correct torque for each

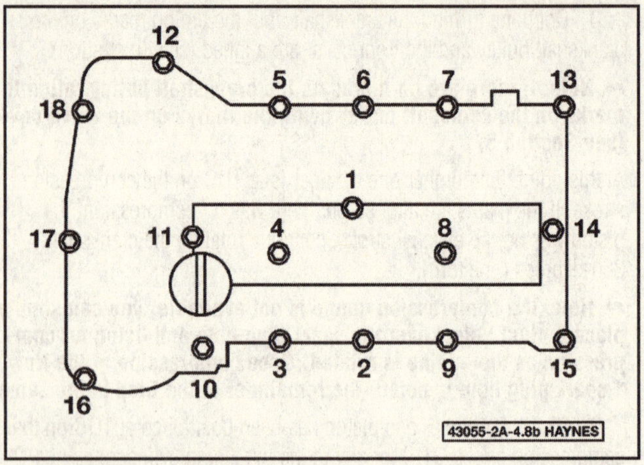

4.8b Valve cover bolt tightening sequence (2006.5 and later models)

and, on 2006.5 and later models, at the sharp corners of the timing belt cover-to-cylinder head joint (see illustration), then install the valve cover and fasteners.

8 Tighten the nuts/bolts to the torque listed in this Chapter's Specifications in three or four equal steps (see illustration). On 2006.5 and later models, be sure to use the correct tightening sequence (see illustration).

9 Reinstall the remaining parts, run the engine and check for oil leaks.

5 Timing belts and sprockets (2001 through 2006 models) - removal, inspection and installation

WARNING:

Wait until the engine is completely cool before beginning this procedure.

CAUTION:

The timing system is complex, and severe engine damage will occur if you make any mistakes. Do not attempt this procedure unless you are highly experienced with this type of repair. If you are at all unsure of your abilities, be sure to consult an expert. Double-check all your work and be sure everything is correct before you attempt to start the engine.

REMOVAL

Refer to illustrations 5.5 and 5.9

1 Detach the cable from the negative terminal of the battery (see Chapter 5). Position the number one piston at TDC on the compression stroke (see Section 3). The marks on the camshafts and the valve cover should be aligned. The dowels on the camshaft sprockets should be facing upward.

2 Remove the drivebelts (see Chapter 1) and the alternator (see Chapter 5).

3 Remove the valve cover (see Section 4).

4 Refer to Section 11 and remove the crankshaft pulley. Also remove the water pump pulley.

5 Remove the timing belt cover (see illustration).

6 Confirm that the engine is still at TDC on the compression stroke for cylinder number one.

Note: If you intend to reuse the timing belt, use white paint or chalk to make a mark indicating the front of the belt. If a used timing belt is reinstalled with the wear pattern in the opposite direction, noise and increased wear may occur.

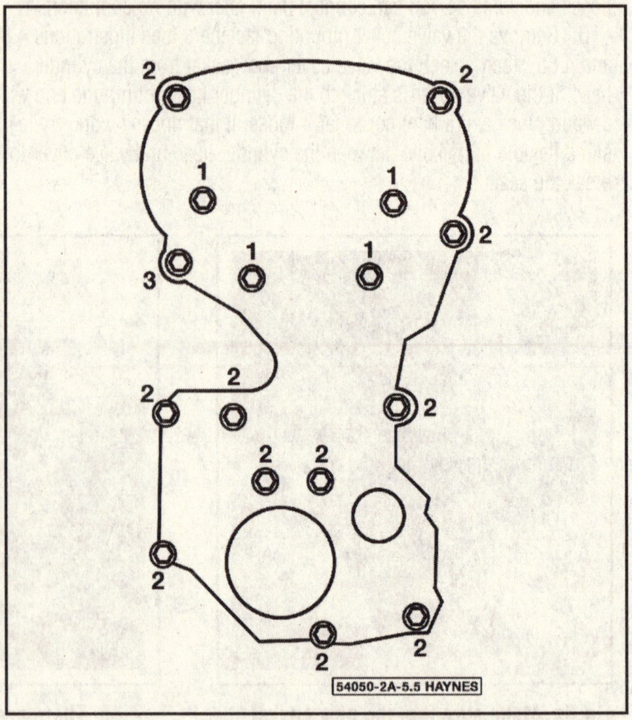

5.5 Timing belt cover bolt guide (2001 through 2006 models):

1 6 X 10 mm 2 6 X 25 mm 3 6 X 28 mm

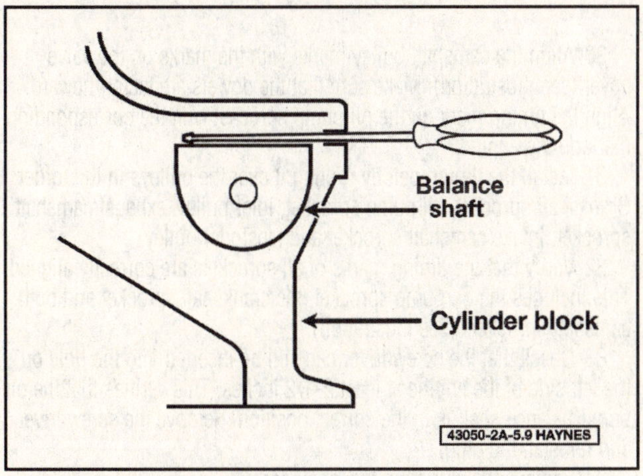

5.9 Remove the plug on the side of the block and insert a screwdriver to lock the balance shaft in position - it will engage with a flat area when it is properly aligned

7 Remove the timing belt tensioner, then the timing belt. Mark the pulley flange so it can be installed with the same side facing outward.

CAUTION:

If the crankshaft is rotated while the timing belt is removed, the pistons may contact the valves and bend them.

8 The camshaft sprockets can be removed at this time if necessary. To remove the camshaft sprockets, loosen the bolts while holding the lug on the camshaft with a wrench, on the hex portion of the camshaft only. Note the identification marks on the camshaft sprockets before removal, then remove the bolts. Pull the sprockets by hand until they slip off the dowels.

9 Remove the plug on the left (front) side of the block and insert a screwdriver into the hole (see illustration). This will lock the left balance shaft.

10 Remove the oil pump sprocket nut and lift off the sprocket.

11 Remove the plug from the right (rear) side of the block, then loosen the right balance shaft sprocket bolt using the same technique as in Step 9.

12 Remove the tensioner and the inner timing belt. Mark the pulley flange so it can be installed with the same side facing outward.

INSPECTION

13 Visually inspect all parts for wear and damage. Check the timing belt for any signs of wear; if there is any doubt, replace it now.

14 If the timing belt is to be replaced, replace the inner belt at the same time.

15 Check all pulleys for rough operation, grease leakage and damage. Check sprockets for cracks. Check the tensioner for leakage and wear. Replace all components as necessary.

INSTALLATION

Refer to illustrations 5.18, 5.30, 5.32 and 5.35

16 Install the inner crankshaft pulley if it was removed. Make sure to put the flange on the engine side of the belt, and with the sharp edge facing toward the rear of the engine, if you didn't mark it previously.

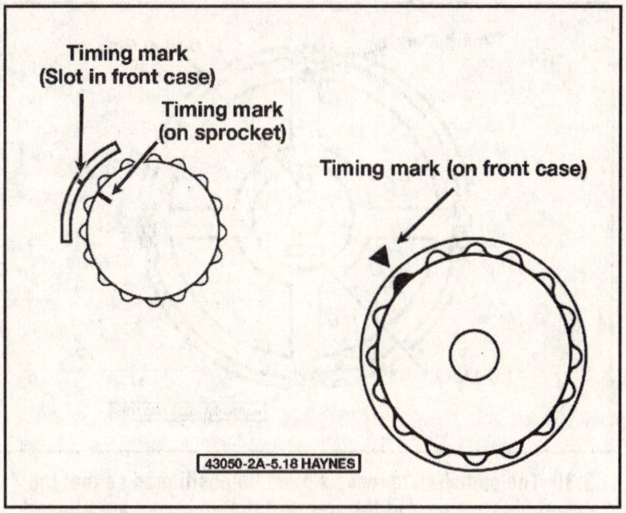

5.18 The sprockets of the inner belt have timing marks located at about the ten o'clock position

17 Install the spacer to the right balance shaft if it was removed. Apply oil to the outside of the spacer and be sure to place the chamfered end facing toward the engine. Place the right balance shaft sprocket onto the shaft and tighten the bolt by hand.

18 Align the timing slot on the front of the engine with the mark on the right balance shaft sprocket. Align the timing mark on the crankshaft sprocket with the mark on the front of the engine. Both marks are at approximately the ten o'clock position (see illustration).

19 Install the inner tensioner. The pulley should be on the left of the mounting bolt.

20 Check the timing marks for the right balance shaft as well as the crankshaft sprocket.

21 Lift the tensioner to tighten the tension side of the timing belt and tighten the bolt.

CAUTION:

Be careful to avoid turning the shaft as the bolt is tightened. This will cause the belt to become overly tight.

22 Confirm that all of the timing marks are still lined up.

23 Press in on the upper right side of the timing belt with your index finger. The belt should move no more than a quarter inch (7 mm).

24 Install the outer crankshaft sprocket and flange. Use the marks you made previously to avoid installing the flange backward. Tighten the sprocket bolt to the torque listed in this Chapter's Specifications.

25 Make sure the screwdriver is still inserted in the hole in the left side of the block (to hold the balance shaft from turning).

26 Install the oil pump sprocket and tighten the nut to the torque listed in this Chapter's Specifications.

27 Install the camshaft sprockets if they were removed and tighten the bolts to the torque listed in this Chapter's Specifications.

28 Place the tensioner in a vise with cushioned jaws. If there is a plug on the bottom of the tensioner, use a large washer under it. Compress the tensioner very slowly until you can insert a piece of wire in the small hole to lock the tensioner in the collapsed position.

29 Install the tensioner. Tighten the tensioner pulley bolt to the torque listed in this Chapter's Specifications.

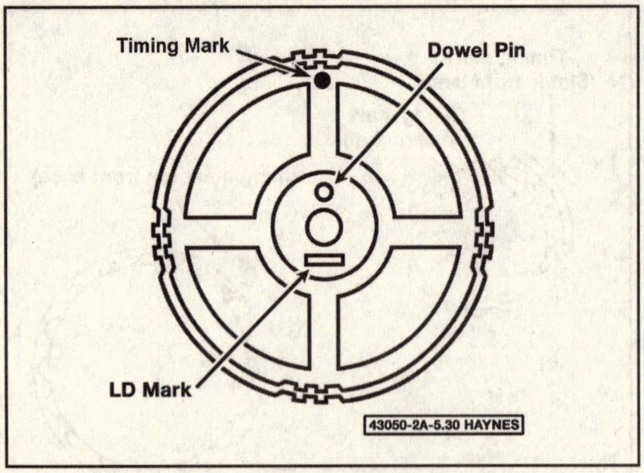

5.30 The camshaft sprockets must be positioned so that the dowel pins are up and the sprocket timing marks are aligned with the marks on the valve cover

30 Align the camshaft pulley marks with the marks on the valve cover (see illustration). Make sure that the dowels are facing upward. Align the timing mark on the oil pump sprocket with the corresponding mark on the engine.

31 Install the timing belt by routing it over the pulleys in this order: Crankshaft sprocket, oil pump sprocket, idler pulley, exhaust camshaft sprocket, intake camshaft sprocket and tensioner pulley.

32 Verify that the timing marks of all sprockets are correctly aligned. This includes the oil pump sprocket, the crankshaft sprocket and both camshaft sprockets (see illustration).

33 Check that the screwdriver can still be inserted into the hole on the left side of the engine at least 2-1/2 inches. This verifies that the oil pump/balance shaft is in the correct position. Remove the screwdriver and reinstall the plug.

34 Remove the wire from the tensioner.

35 Rotate the engine two turns by hand and let it sit for a few minutes.

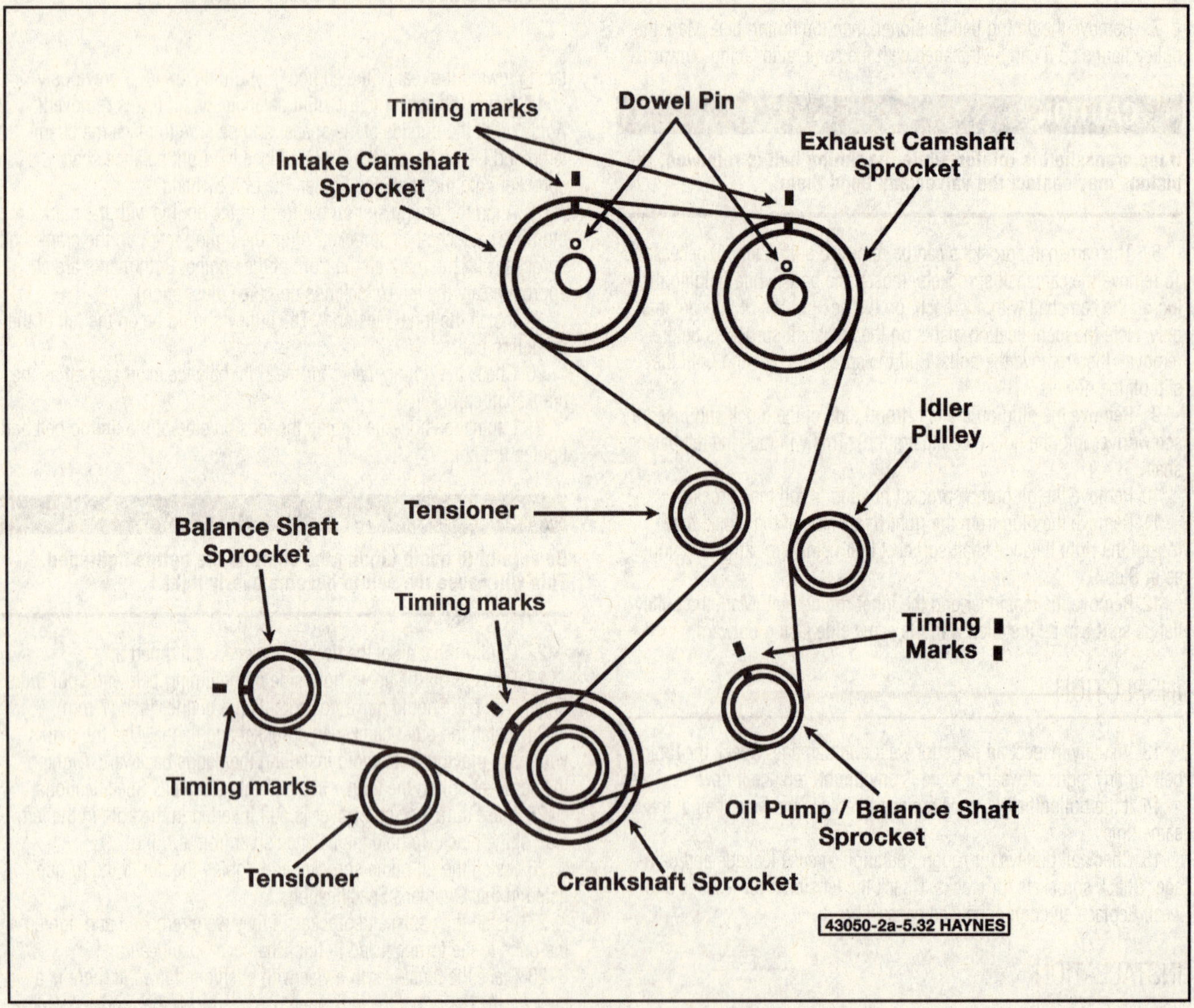

5.32 The outer timing belt is installed when the marks on all the sprockets are lined up properly; the oil pump sprocket, the camshaft sprockets and the crankshaft sprocket must all have their respective marks aligned

CAUTION:

If you feel any resistance, STOP! There is something wrong - most likely valves are contacting the pistons. You must find the problem before proceeding. Check your work and see if any updated repair information is available.

Check the protrusion of the tensioner plunger (see illustration). It should be within the Specifications shown in this Chapter. Verify that all sprockets are aligned correctly.

36 The remainder of the procedure is the reverse of disassembly.

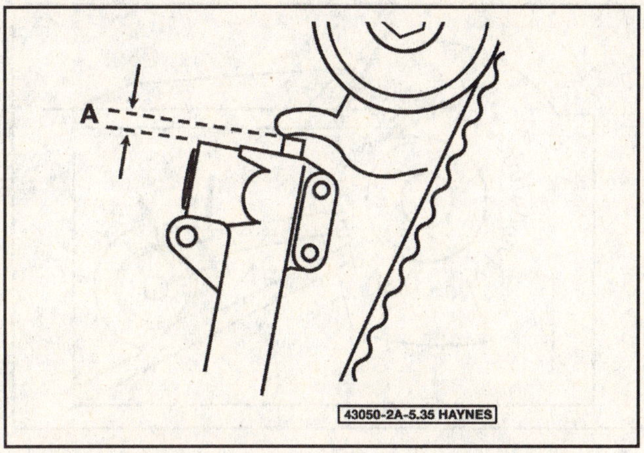

5.35 The tensioner plunger for the outer timing belt must protrude a specified distance (A) - rotate the engine and allow it to sit for a few minutes before measuring it

6 Timing chain and sprockets (2006.5 and later models) - removal, inspection and installation

WARNING:

Wait until the engine is completely cool before beginning this procedure.

CAUTION:

The timing system is complex, and severe engine damage will occur if you make any mistakes. Do not attempt this procedure unless you are highly experienced with this type of repair. If you are at all unsure of your abilities, be sure to consult an expert. Double-check all your work and be sure everything is correct before you attempt to start the engine.

REMOVAL

1 Disconnect the cable from the negative battery terminal (see Chapter 5).

2 Loosen the lug nuts on the right front wheel. Raise the vehicle and support it securely on jackstands. Remove the right front wheel.

3 Set the engine at TDC compression for cylinder number one (see Section 3).

4 Remove the right engine splash shield.

5 Place a floor jack and a block of wood under the oil pan. Raise it enough to take weight off of the engine mounts.

6 Remove the upper engine mount bracket.

7 Loosen the water pump pulley bolts.

8 Remove the drivebelt (see Chapter 1).

9 Remove the idler pulley.

10 Remove the drivebelt tensioner pulley assembly.

CAUTION:

The tensioner pulley bolt has a left-hand thread.

11 Remove the water pump pulley.

12 Refer to Section 11 and remove the crankshaft pulley.

➡ **Note: It will be necessary to hold the pulley from turning while removing the bolt. A strap wrench or chain wrench is a good tool for this.**

13 Remove the engine mount bracket from the front of the timing chain cover.

14 Refer to Section 4 and remove the valve cover.

15 Remove the lower bolts from the air conditioning compressor, then remove the compressor mounting bracket.

16 The engine must be supported in order to remove the jack from beneath the oil pan. The easiest way to do this is with an engine support fixture that mounts spanning the front fenders. If you don't have one of these tools and can't rent or borrow one, you will have to reposition the jack to a part of the lower engine assembly that provides clearance for work on the oil pan. After the engine is securely supported, refer to Section 13 and remove the oil pan.

17 Temporarily place the crankshaft pulley onto the crankshaft and verify that the engine is still at TDC. Remove the timing chain cover. Make notes of how the crankshaft key is aligned with the block mating surface of the front main bearing cap. It must remain in this exact position during the installation procedure. Also note how the TDC marks on the camshaft sprockets are aligned with the top surface of the cylinder head.

18 Compress the plunger of the timing chain tensioner, then put a small drill bit or other steel pin in the tensioner hole to secure it in the retracted position. Remove the tensioner.

19 Remove the timing chain tensioner arm and lift off the timing chain. The timing chain guide can now be removed, if necessary.

20 Remove the chain oiling nozzle and the crankshaft sprocket.

21 Compress the balance shaft chain tensioner and remove as in Step 18. Remove the chain tensioner.

22 Remove the balance shaft chain tensioner arm and guide.

23 Unbolt the balance shaft module and remove it along with the chain.

INSPECTION

24 Visually inspect all parts for wear and damage. Check the timing chain for any signs of wear; if there is any doubt, replace it now.

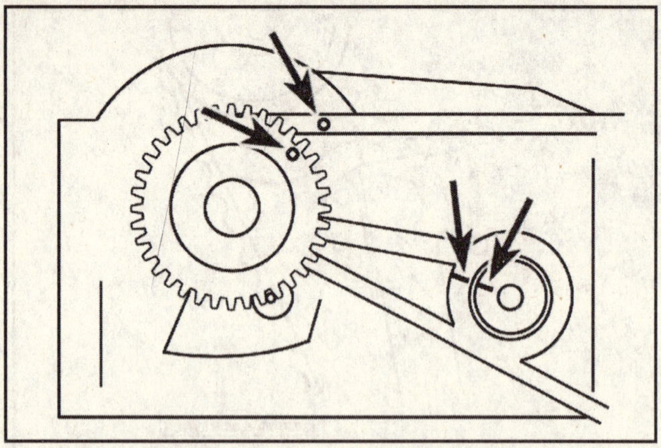

6.27 **Align these marks on the balancer shaft module before installing it along with the balance shaft chain**

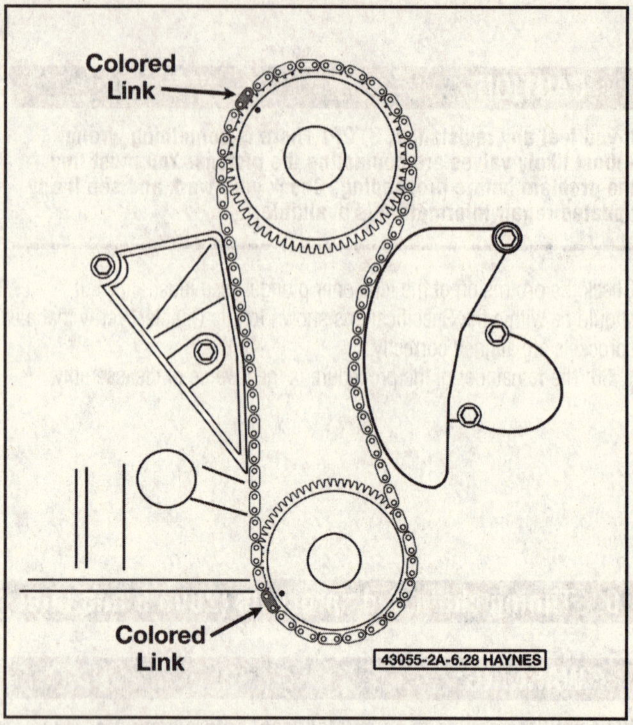

6.28 **The colored links on the balance shaft chain must align with the marks on the sprockets**

25 If the timing chain is to be replaced, replace the balance shaft chain at the same time.

26 Check all sprockets for rough operation, grease leakage and damage. Check sprockets for cracks. Check the tensioners for leakage and wear. Replace all components as necessary.

INSTALLATION

Refer to illustrations 6.27, 6.28, 6.32, 6.34 and 6.38

27 Refer to Step 17 and verify that the crankshaft hasn't turned. Align the marks on the balance shaft module with the cast marks on the housing (see illustration).

28 Align the colored link of the balance shaft chain with the mark on the balance shaft module sprocket, put the chain over the crankshaft sprocket and install the balance shaft module. Tighten the bolts to the torque listed in this Chapter's Specifications. The colored links of the chain must be aligned with the marks on the sprockets (see illustration).

29 Install the chain guide, the tensioner arm and the tensioner. Pull the pin from the tensioner to allow the rod to extend.

30 Again verify that the colored links and the timing marks are aligned properly.

31 Install the timing chain sprocket and the oil spray nozzle.

32 Check that the crankshaft key is aligned with the block-contact surface of the front main bearing cap as before. Verify that the marks on the camshaft sprockets are still aligned with the top surface of the cylinder head (see illustration).

33 Install the timing chain guide.

34 Put the timing chain on with the colored links aligned with the sprocket marks. The exhaust camshaft sprocket has a mark at eleven o'clock, the intake camshaft sprocket at one o'clock and the crankshaft sprocket at six o'clock (see illustration). The chain should go on the crankshaft first, followed by the guide, the intake camshaft, then the exhaust camshaft. There should be no slack in the chain between the sprockets.

35 Install the tensioner arm and the tensioner. Pull the pin from the tensioner.

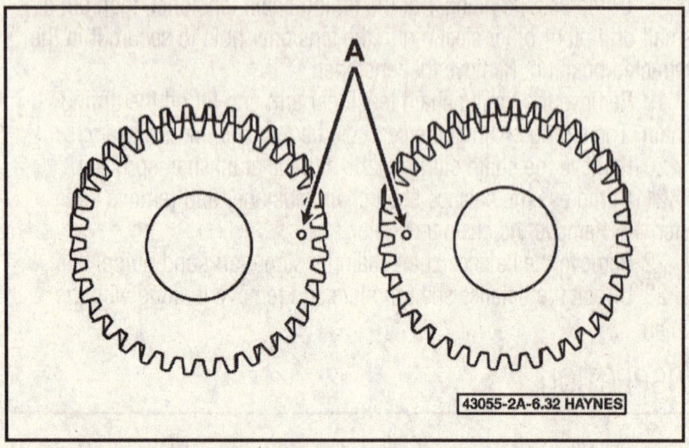

6.32 **The camshaft sprockets have marks (A) that must align with the top surface of the cylinder head**

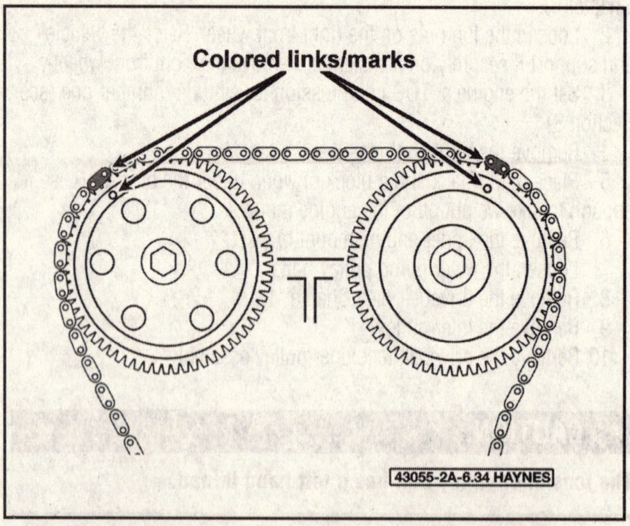

6.34 **Set the colored links of the timing chain directly on the camshaft sprocket marks and on the mark on the bottom of the crankshaft sprocket**

36 Rotate the crankshaft clockwise two complete turns by hand (use a socket and breaker bar on the crankshaft pulley center-bolt).

CAUTION:

If you feel any resistance, STOP! There is something wrong - most likely valves are contacting the pistons. You must find the problem before proceeding. Check your work and see if any updated repair information is available.

Verify that the camshaft sprocket TDC marks are aligned with each other and even with the top surface of the cylinder head as in Step 32.

37 Carefully clean all sealing surfaces of the timing cover and the engine using acetone or lacquer thinner. All sealing surfaces must be completely free of foreign material and grease. Remove the crankshaft oil seal at this time if you intend to replace it.

38 Apply a dab of RTV sealant to the two points where the block meets the cylinder head. Apply an even bead of the sealant around the entire timing chain cover and as shown (see illustration).

39 Set the timing chain cover in place, aligning its holes with the dowels on the block. Tighten all bolts to the torque listed in this Chapter's Specifications.

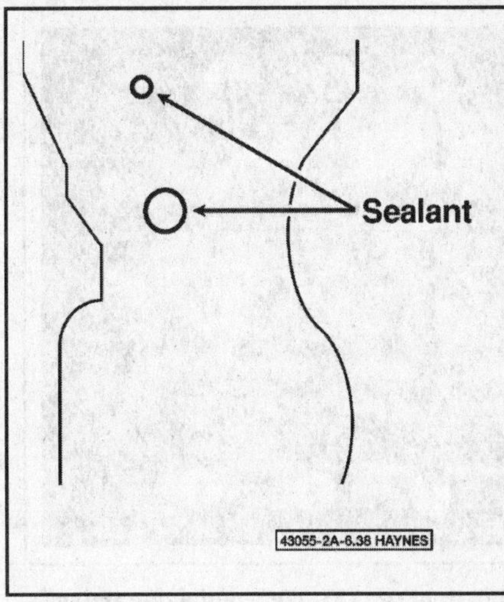

6.38 Apply a little RTV sealant to these areas as well as the outer edge of the timing chain cover

40 The crankshaft oil seal can now be installed. Tap it into place with a hammer and a block of wood after oiling the rubber lip.

41 The remainder of installation is the reverse of removal. Refer to the appropriate Sections for information on the individual components.

7 Camshafts and valvetrain - removal, inspection, adjustment and installation

Note: The camshafts should always be thoroughly inspected before installation and camshaft endplay should always be checked prior to camshaft removal (see Step 12).

REMOVAL

Refer to illustrations 7.9a and 7.9b

1 Disconnect the cable from the negative terminal of the battery (see Chapter 5).

2 Refer to Section 3 and place the engine on TDC for number 1 cylinder. Visually confirm the engine is at TDC on the compression stroke by verifying that the timing mark on the crankshaft pulley/vibration damper is aligned with the "0" mark on the timing belt cover and the camshaft sprocket TDC marks are aligned with the valve cover marks (2001 through 2006 models) or the top of the cylinder head (2006.5 and later models).

3 Remove the valve cover (see Section 4).

4 With the TDC marks aligned, apply a dab of paint to the timing belt (or chain) and the camshaft sprockets for alignment later.

5 On 2001 through 2006 models, refer to Section 5 and remove the timing belt from the camshaft sprockets. Put match marks on the sprockets and the belt so the original alignment will not be lost.

6 On 2006.5 and later models, refer to Section 6 and remove the timing chain.

7 Prevent the camshaft from turning by placing a wrench on the hexagonal portion of the camshaft, then loosen the camshaft sprocket bolts several turns. Don't allow the camshafts to turn while loosening the bolts. Remove the camshaft sprockets.

CAUTION:

Don't attempt to disassemble the variable valve timing assembly on the intake camshaft sprocket.

8 Measure the camshaft endplay as described in Step 12, then proceed to Step 9.

9 Remove the front camshaft bearing cap first. Loosen all other camshaft cap bolts in two or three steps in the recommended sequence (see illustration). Remove the caps and the camshafts from the cylinder head.

7.9a Keep every bearing cap in order as you remove it and make notes of the numbers and arrows on the caps

7.9b After removing the front cap (A), remove the remaining caps in the order shown

⁂ CAUTION:

Keep the caps in order. They must go back in the same location from which they were removed (see illustration). It is very important that the camshafts are returned to their original locations during installation.

10 Remove the lash adjusters and the rocker arms (2001 through 2006 models) or the lifters (2006.5 and later models).

⁂ CAUTION:

Keep the components in order. It is critical that they go back in the positions from which they were removed.

11 Inspect the camshafts, camshaft bearings, adjusters and rocker arms (if equipped) as described below. Also inspect the camshaft sprockets for wear on the teeth. Inspect the belts for cracks or excessive wear of the rollers, and for stretching. If any of the components show signs of excessive wear, they must be replaced.

INSPECTION

Refer to illustrations 7.12, 7.14 and 7.15

12 Before the camshafts are removed from the engine, check the camshaft endplay by placing a dial indicator with the stem in line with the camshaft and touching the snout (see illustration). Push the camshaft all the way to the rear and zero the dial indicator. Next, pry the camshaft to the front as far as possible and check the reading on the dial indicator. The distance it moves is the endplay. If the endplay for either camshaft is greater than the Specifications listed in this Chapter, the camshaft or the cylinder head (or both) may need to be replaced.

13 With the camshafts removed, visually check the camshaft bearing surfaces in the cylinder head for pitting, score marks, galling and abnormal wear. If the bearing surfaces are damaged, the cylinder head or the journal bearings of the camshafts may have to be replaced.

14 Measure the outside diameter of each camshaft bearing journal and record your measurements (see illustration). Compare them to the journal outside diameter specified in this Chapter, then measure the inside diameter of each corresponding camshaft bearing and record the measurements. Subtract each cam journal outside diameter from its respective cam bearing bore inside diameter to determine the oil clearance for each bearing. Compare the results to the specified journal-to-bearing clearance. If any of the measurements fall outside the standard specified wear limits in this Chapter, either the camshaft or the cylinder head, or both, must be replaced.

➡ Note: If precision measuring tools are not available, Plastigage may be used to determine the bearing journal oil clearance.

15 Using a micrometer, measure the height of each camshaft lobe (see illustration). Compare your measurements with this Chapter's Specifications. If the height for any one lobe is less than the specified minimum, replace the camshaft.

16 Check the camshaft runout by placing the camshaft back into the cylinder head and set up a dial indicator on the center journal. Zero the dial indicator. Turn the camshaft slowly and note the dial indicator readings. Runout should not exceed 0.0012 inch (0.03 mm). If the measured runout exceeds the specified runout, replace the camshaft.

17 On 2001 through 2006 models, inspect each hydraulic adjuster

7.12 Mount a dial indicator as shown to measure camshaft endplay - pry the camshaft forward and back and read the endplay on the dial

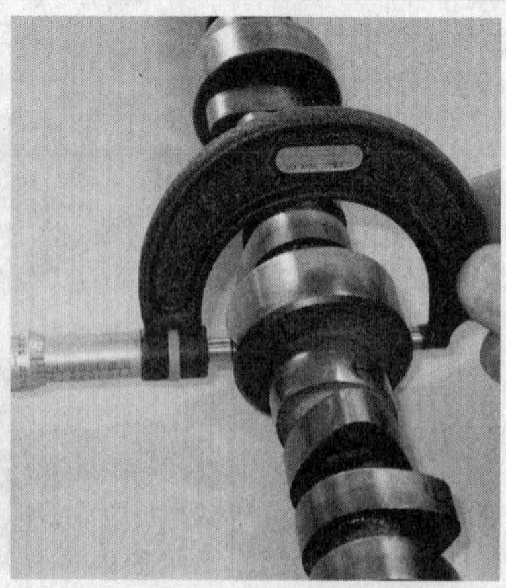

7.14 Measure each journal diameter with a micrometer - if any journal measures less than the specified limit, replace the camshaft

7.15 Measure the lobe heights on each camshaft - if any lobe height is less than the specified allowable minimum, replace that camshaft

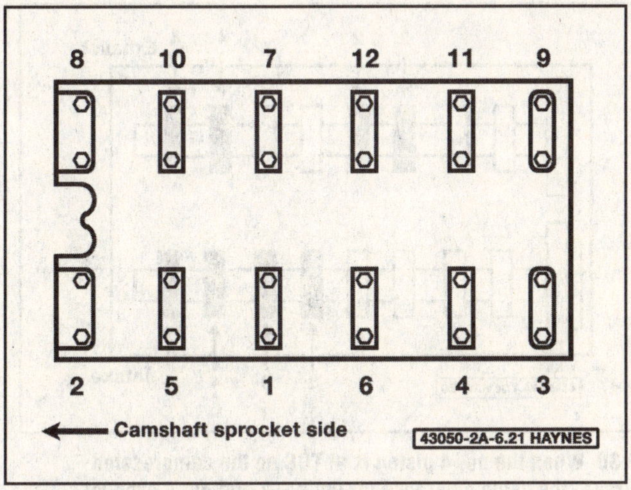

7.22a Camshaft bearing cap bolt TIGHTENING sequence for 2001 through 2006 models

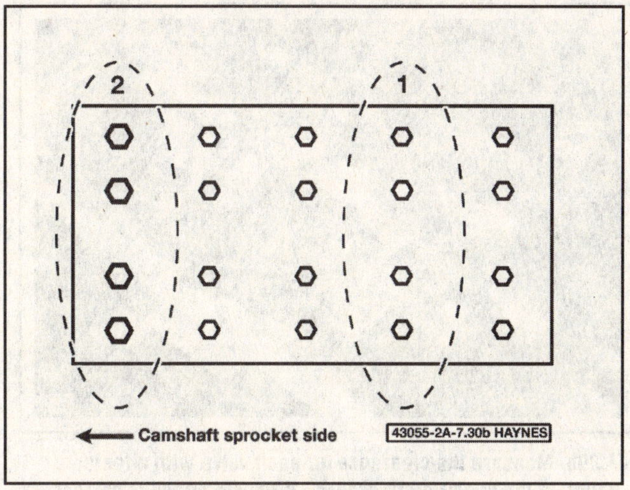

7.22b Camshaft bearing cap TIGHTENING sequence for 2006.5 and later models; evenly tighten the bolts in area 1, then the larger bolts in area 2 followed by the remaining bolts

for scuffing and score marks. Check each roller rocker for smooth bearing operation and damage to either end. On 2006.5 and later models, inspect each bucket-shaped lifter for wear and scuffing. Using a micrometer, measure the outside diameter of each lifter, comparing your readings with the values listed in this Chapter's Specifications.

INSTALLATION

➧ Refer to illustrations 7.22a and 7.22b

18 On 2001 through 2006 models, lubricate the lash adjusters with moly-based engine assembly lubricant and install them in their bores. Lubricate the rocker arms as well, then install them in their positions.

19 On 2006.5 and later models, lubricate the lifters with moly-based engine assembly lubricant and install them in their bores.

20 Apply moly-based engine assembly lubricant to the camshaft lobes and journals and install the camshaft into the cylinder head with the dowel pins facing upward. If the old camshafts are being used, make sure they're installed in the same location from which they came.

21 Install the bearing caps and bolts and tighten them hand tight. Each cap is marked with either an "I" or an "E," indicating if it is for the intake or exhaust side. They are also numbered (see illustration 7.9a).

22 Tighten the bearing cap bolts in several equal steps, to the torque listed in this Chapter's Specifications, using the proper tightening sequence (see illustrations).

23 On 2001 through 2006 models, if a camshaft oil seal needs to be replaced, do it at this time. Oil the outside of the seal and use a seal driver or large socket to drive the new seal into place until it is flush with the bearing cap.

24 On 2006.5 and later models, check the valve clearances and adjust them as necessary (see Steps 27 through 36).

25 Engage the camshaft sprocket teeth with the timing belt so that the match marks made during removal align with the upper timing marks on the sprockets. Position the sprockets over the dowels on the camshaft hubs and install the camshaft sprocket bolts finger tight. At this point, all of the sprocket paint marks should be lined up with the paint marks on the belt. Refer to Section 5 and verify that all of the sprockets are also aligned with their respective marks on the engine. Install the camshaft position sensor and its support, aligning the match marks previously made.

26 The remainder of installation is the reverse of removal (see Sections 4 and 5).

ADJUSTMENT (2006.5 AND LATER MODELS)

➧ Refer to illustrations 7.29a, 7.29b, 7.30 and 7.33

➡ Note: Valve clearance on 2001 through 2006 models is automatically achieved by hydraulic adjusters. 2006.5 and later models use bucket-style lifters that must be replaced with ones of the proper thickness in order to adjust clearance.

27 Refer to Section 4 and remove the valve cover (if not already done).

28 Refer to Section 3 and set number one cylinder to TDC on the compression stroke (if not already done).

29 Use a feeler gauge to measure the clearance between the camshaft lobes and the lifters indicated (see illustrations). These include all

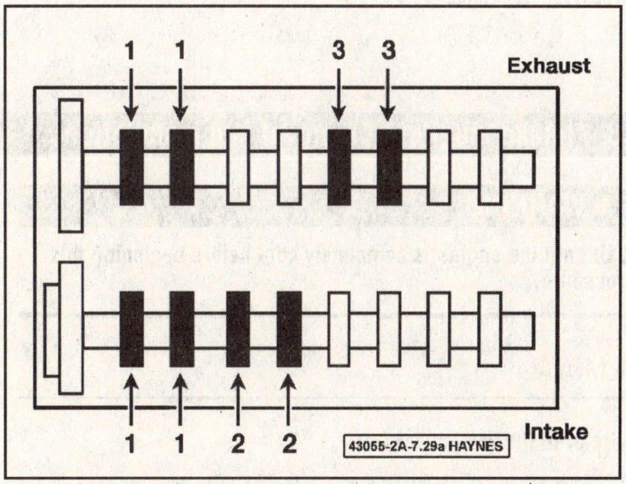

7.29a When the no. 1 piston is at TDC on the compression stroke, the valve clearance for the no. 1 and no. 3 cylinder exhaust valves and the no. 1 and no. 2 cylinder intake valves can be measured

7.29b Measure the clearance for each valve with a feeler gauge of the specified thickness - if the clearance is correct, you should feel a slight drag on the gauge as you pull it out

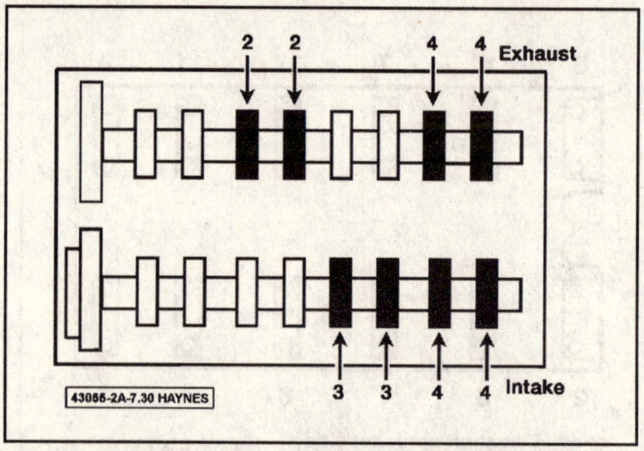

7.30 When the no. 4 piston is at TDC on the compression stroke, the valve clearance for the no. 2 and no. 4 exhaust valves and the no. 3 and no. 4 intake valves can be measured

valves for number one cylinder, the intake valves on cylinder number two and the exhaust valves on cylinder number three. Carefully record the figures.

30 Rotate the engine one turn clockwise and repeat the procedure on the remaining valves (see illustration).

31 If any clearances are outside of the limits shown in the Specifications in this Chapter, new lifters of the proper thickness will have to be installed in the location(s) with the incorrect clearance(s). To do so, proceed with the next Step.

32 Remove the camshaft(s).

33 Remove and measure the lifter (from the location with the incorrect clearance) with a micrometer (see illustration).

34 To calculate the correct thickness of a replacement lifter, use this formula:

N = T + (A - V)
N = Thickness of the new lifter
T = Thickness of the old lifter
A = Valve clearance measured
V = Valve clearance specified in this Chapter's Specifications

35 Purchase replacement lifters of the correct thicknesses from a dealer parts department.

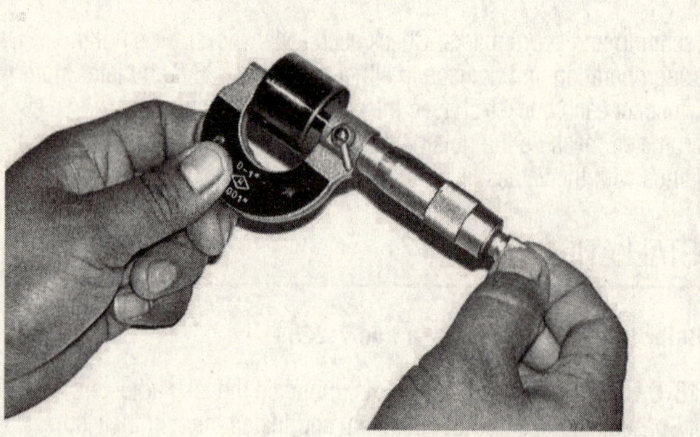

7.33 Measure the thickness of the lifter head with a micrometer

36 After installing the lifters and camshafts, check the clearances again and make sure they are within specification before installing the valve cover.

8 Intake manifold - removal and installation

WARNING:

Wait until the engine is completely cool before beginning this procedure.

REMOVAL

Refer to illustration 8.11

1 Relieve the fuel system pressure (see Chapter 4)

2 Disconnect the negative cable from the battery (see Chapter 5).

3 Remove the engine cover.

4 Remove the air intake duct assembly (see Chapter 4).

5 Remove the vent hose from the throttle body and disconnect the throttle cable.

6 Clamp off the coolant hoses connected to the throttle body, then disconnect them.

7 Disconnect all interfering wiring. These connections vary from year to year. Be sure to label each connector to eliminate confusion later.

8 Disconnect the brake booster hose and the PCV hose.

9 Refer to Chapter 4 and remove the fuel rail along with the injectors.

10 Remove the lower intake manifold brace. On 2006.5 and later models, remove the oil dipstick assembly.

11 Remove the intake manifold along with the throttle body (see illustration).

INSTALLATION

12 Clean the mating surfaces of the intake manifold and the cylinder head mounting surface with brake system cleaner.

13 Install the manifold and gasket on the cylinder head and install the mounting fasteners.

14 Tighten the manifold-to-cylinder head nuts/bolts in three or four equal steps to the torque listed in this Chapter's Specifications. Work from the middle bolts out to avoid flexing the manifold.

15 Install the remaining parts in the reverse order of removal. Check the coolant level, adding as necessary (see Chapter 1).

16 Run the engine and check for coolant and vacuum leaks.

17 Road test the vehicle and check for proper operation.

8.11 Intake manifold mounting bolt locations (2006.5 and later engines)

9 Exhaust manifold - removal and installation

WARNING:

The engine must be completely cool before beginning this procedure.

REMOVAL

Refer to illustrations 9.4 and 9.5

1 Disconnect the cable from the negative terminal of the battery (see Chapter 5).

2 Raise the front of the vehicle and support it securely on jackstands. Disconnect the wiring from the oxygen sensor only if it interferes with manifold removal.

3 Apply penetrating oil to the nuts and springs retaining the catalytic converter to the manifold. After the nuts have soaked, remove the nuts retaining the converter to the manifold. Separate the converter from the manifold, being careful not to damage the oxygen sensors. Remove the complete front muffler assembly on 2006.5 and later models.

4 Working in the engine compartment, remove the upper heat shield from the manifold (see illustration). On 2006.5 and later models, there is an exhaust manifold brace that must be unbolted from the manifold. Disconnect any other interfering brackets; these vary from vehicle to vehicle.

5 Remove the nuts and detach the manifold and gasket (see illustration).

INSTALLATION

6 Use a scraper to remove all traces of old gasket material and carbon deposits from the manifold and cylinder head mating surfaces. If the gasket shows signs of leaking, check the manifold for warpage with a straightedge and compare your readings with those listed in this Chapter's Specifications. If the manifold is warped, it must be resurfaced

9.4 The upper oxygen sensor must be removed from 2006.5 and later engines in order to remove the exhaust manifold heat shield

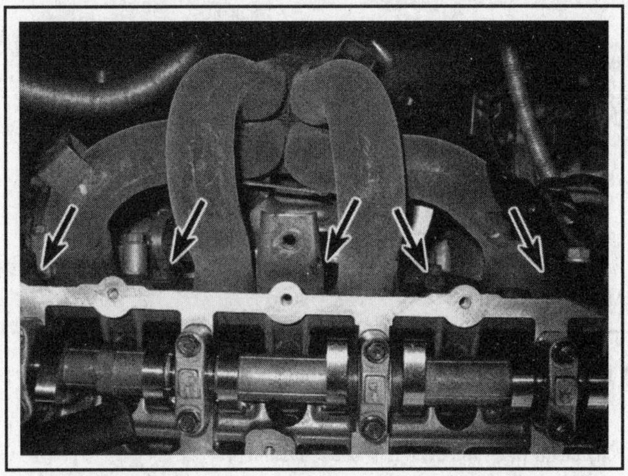

9.5 Access to the exhaust manifold nuts is limited in all models (not all nuts are visible here)

or replaced.

7 Position a new gasket over the cylinder head studs, noting any directional marks or arrows on the gasket that may be present.

8 Install the manifold and thread the mounting nuts into place.

9 Working from the center out, tighten the nuts/bolts to the torque listed in this Chapter's Specifications in three or four equal steps.

10 Reinstall the remaining parts in the reverse order of removal.

11 Run the engine and check for exhaust leaks.

10 Cylinder head - removal, inspection and installation

WARNING:

The engine must be completely cool before beginning this procedure.

CAUTION:

Replace all of the cylinder head bolts with new ones.

REMOVAL

1 Relieve the fuel system pressure (see Chapter 4), then disconnect the cable from the negative terminal of the battery (see Chapter 5).

2 Drain the engine coolant (see Chapter 1).

3 Remove the intake manifold (see Section 8) and the exhaust manifold (see Section 9).

4 Remove the camshafts (see Section 7).

5 Label and detach the electrical connections from the cylinder head.

6 Detach the coolant hoses from the cylinder head (see Chapter 3). The water temperature control unit attached to 2006 and later models may be removed at this time.

7 Loosen the cylinder head bolts in 1/4-turn increments until they can be removed by hand. Loosen the cylinder head bolts in the reverse order of the recommended tightening sequence (see illustration 10.21) to avoid warping or cracking the cylinder head.

8 With the help of an assistant, lift the cylinder head off the engine block. If it's stuck, very carefully pry up at the transaxle end, beyond the gasket surface.

9 Remove any remaining external components from the cylinder head to allow for thorough cleaning and inspection.

INSPECTION

10 Use a precision straightedge to check the gasket surfaces of each head. Try to insert a feeler gauge of the correct size between the straightedge and the head surface. If the clearance is more than that listed in this Chapter's Specifications, the head must be surfaced or replaced.

11 Also check the intake and exhaust manifold mating surfaces of the head for warpage.

12 Examine all areas of each head for signs of cracks and coolant leakage, especially around the valve seats.

INSTALLATION

Refer to illustration 10.21

13 The mating surfaces of the cylinder head and block must be perfectly clean when the cylinder head is installed.

14 Use a gasket scraper to remove all traces of carbon and old gasket material, then clean the mating surfaces with brake system cleaner. If there's oil on the mating surfaces when the cylinder head is installed, the gasket may not seal correctly and leaks could develop. When working on the block, stuff the cylinders with clean shop rags to keep out debris. Use a vacuum cleaner to remove material that falls into the cylinders.

CAUTION:

The cylinder head is made of aluminum. It is very easy to scratch it, so use care.

15 Check the block and cylinder head mating surfaces for nicks, deep scratches and other damage. If damage is slight, it can be removed with a file; if it's excessive, machining may be the only alternative.

16 Use a tap of the correct size to chase the threads in the cylinder head bolt holes, then clean the holes with compressed air - make sure that nothing remains in the holes.

WARNING:

Wear eye protection when using compressed air!

17 Install the components that were removed from the cylinder head.

18 Position the new gasket over the dowel pins in the block. Examine it carefully to verify that it is installed in the correct orientation.

19 Carefully set the cylinder head on the block without disturbing the gasket.

20 Before installing the NEW cylinder head bolts, apply a small amount of clean engine oil to the threads and under the bolt heads.

21 Install the bolts and tighten them finger tight. Following the recommended sequence (see illustration), tighten the bolts to the torque listed in this Chapter's Specifications.

22 The remaining installation steps are the reverse of removal.

23 Change the engine oil and filter (see Chapter 1).

24 Refill the cooling system (see Chapter 1), run the engine and check for leaks.

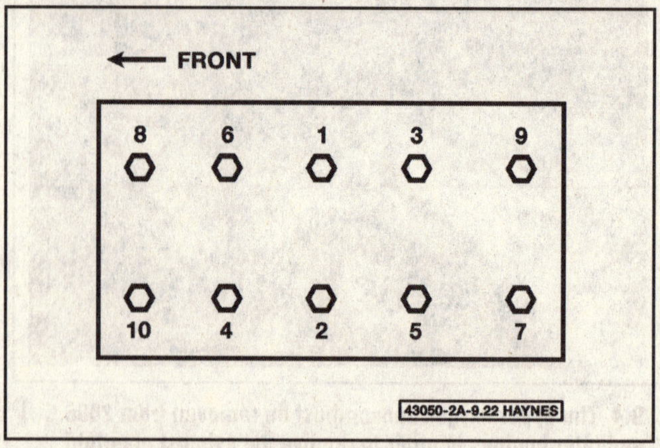

10.21 Cylinder head bolt TIGHTENING sequence

11 Crankshaft pulley/vibration damper - removal and installation

Refer to illustrations 11.3a, 11.3b and 11.5

Note: This procedure also applies to the V6 engines. However, if you are working on a V6 engine, be sure to use the bolt torque specification listed in Chapter 2B.

1 Disconnect the cable from the negative terminal of the battery (see Chapter 5).

2 Remove the drivebelt (see Chapter 1).

3 With the parking brake applied and the shifter in Park (automatic) or in gear (manual), loosen the lug nuts from the right front wheel, then raise the front of the vehicle and support it securely on jackstands. Remove the engine splash shield (see illustration), the front wheel and the splash shield from the right wheel well (see illustration).

4 Remove all other interfering components that are installed on your particular vehicle.

5 Remove the bolt from the front of the crankshaft (see illustration). A breaker bar will probably be necessary, since the bolt is very tight. Have an assistant lock the flywheel in place with a prybar inserted into the ring gear (it will be necessary to remove the flywheel/driveplate access cover).

6 Using a puller that grasps the crankshaft hub, remove the crankshaft pulley from the crankshaft.

CAUTION:

Do not use a jaw-type puller that grabs the outer portion of the damper - it will damage the pulley/damper assembly. Also, be sure to use the proper adapter to prevent damage to the end of the crankshaft.

Note: The pulley is sometimes removable by hand. Try to pull it straight off before attaching the puller.

11.3a Remove the lower engine splash shield . . .

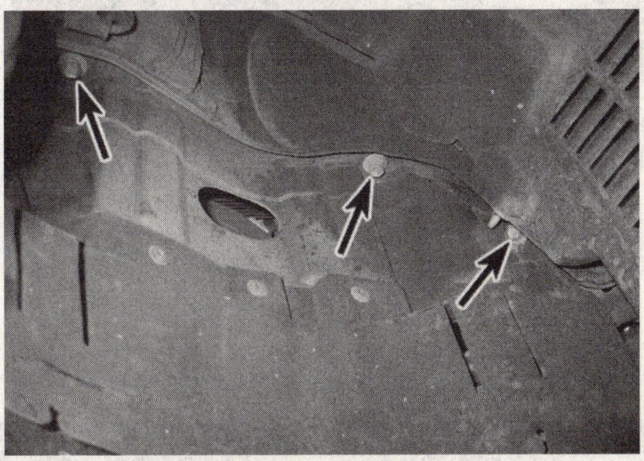

11.3b . . . and the inner fender splash shield from the right side

7 To install the crankshaft pulley, slide the pulley onto the crankshaft as far as it will slide on; if you were able to remove the pulley by hand, install the bolt and washer and tighten the bolt to the torque listed in this Chapter's Specifications. If a puller was required to remove the pulley, use a vibration damper installation tool to press the pulley onto the crankshaft, then install the bolt and washer and tighten the bolt to the torque listed in this Chapter's Specifications (or the 2B Specifications, if you're working on a V6). Note that the slot (keyway) in the hub must be aligned with the Woodruff key in the end of the crankshaft.

8 The remaining installation steps are the reverse of removal.

11.5 If you don't have an impact wrench, you'll have to lock the flywheel with a large screwdriver to prevent the crankshaft from turning when the bolt is loosened

12 Oil seals - replacement

CRANKSHAFT FRONT OIL SEAL

Refer to illustrations 12.2 and 12.3

1 Remove the crankshaft pulley (see Section 11). On 2001 through 2006 models, remove the timing belts and the crankshaft sprocket (see Section 5).

2 Note how the seal is installed - the new one must be installed to the same depth and facing the same way. Carefully pry the oil seal out of the cover with a seal puller or a large screwdriver (see illustration). Be very careful not to distort the cover or scratch the crankshaft! Wrap electrician's tape around the tip of the screwdriver to avoid damage to the crankshaft.

3 Apply clean engine oil or multi-purpose grease to the outer edge of the new seal, then install it in the cover with the lip (spring side) facing IN. Drive the seal into place with a seal driver or a large socket and a hammer (see illustration). Make sure the seal enters the bore squarely and stop when the front face is at the proper depth.

4 Lubricate the pulley hub with clean engine oil and reinstall the crankshaft pulley (see Section 11).

5 Install the crankshaft pulley retaining bolt and tighten it to the torque listed in this Chapter's Specifications as in Section 11.

6 The remainder of installation is the reverse of the removal.

12.2 Carefully pry the old seal out of the timing belt cover - don't damage the crankshaft in the process

CAMSHAFT OIL SEALS

Note: This procedure applies only to 2001 through 2006 models.

7 Remove the timing belt and camshaft sprockets (see Section 5).

8 Note how far the seals are installed in the bores and pry them out with a screwdriver wrapped with tape. Don't scratch the bore or the camshaft - either one can cause a leak.

9 Clean the bores. Coat the outer edge of the new seals with oil or grease. Also apply grease to the lips of the seals.

10 Using a seal driver or a socket with an outside diameter slightly smaller than the outer edge of the seal, carefully drive the new seals into place with a hammer. Make sure they're installed square and that they're driven in to the same depth as the originals.

11 Install all of the removed components, referring to the appropriate Sections in this Chapter to ensure that the belt and sprockets are correctly aligned. Clean all areas around the seals so you'll be able to detect any leaks later.

12 Operate the vehicle for a few days, then check for leaks.

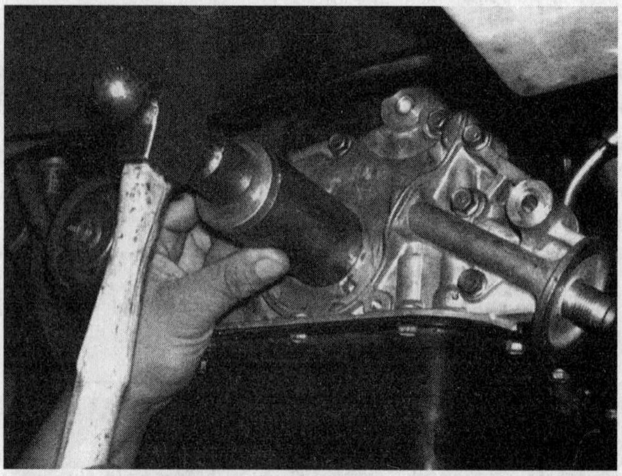

12.3 Drive the new seal into place with a seal driver or a large socket and hammer

13 Oil pan - removal and installation

REMOVAL

Refer to illustration 13.5

1 Disconnect the cable from the negative terminal of the battery (see Chapter 5).

2 Set the parking brake and block the rear wheels. Raise the front of the vehicle and support it securely on jackstands.

3 Remove the engine splash shield, if so equipped

4 Drain the engine oil and remove the oil filter (see Chapter 1).

Remove the oil dipstick.

5 Remove any interfering components. The oil pan has two parts: an upper cast aluminum section and a lower section made of stamped steel.

➡ **Note: The lower oil pan can be removed independently of the upper oil pan. Remove the lower oil pan now (see illustration).**

6 Remove the bolts and detach the upper oil pan. Note the locations of the different size bolts. If the pan is stuck, pry it loose very carefully with a small screwdriver or putty knife. Don't damage the sealing surfaces or oil leaks could develop.

INSTALLATION

7 Use a scraper to remove all traces of old sealant from the block and oil pan. Clean the mating surfaces with lacquer thinner or acetone.

8 Make sure the threaded bolt holes in the block are clean.

9 Check the oil pan flange for distortion, particularly around the bolt holes. Remove any nicks or burrs as necessary.

10 Apply a 3/16-inch wide bead of RTV sealant to the mating surface of the oil pan, following the groove but going to the inside where the bolt holes are located. Install the pan within 15 minutes.

11 Carefully position the upper oil pan on the engine block and install the oil pan-to-engine block bolts loosely.

12 Working from the center out, tighten the oil pan-to-engine block bolts to the torque listed in this Chapter's Specifications in three or four steps.

13 Install the lower oil pan, tightening the bolts evenly in several steps to the torque listed in this Chapter's Specifications. The remainder of installation is the reverse of removal.

14 Run the engine and check for oil pressure and leaks.

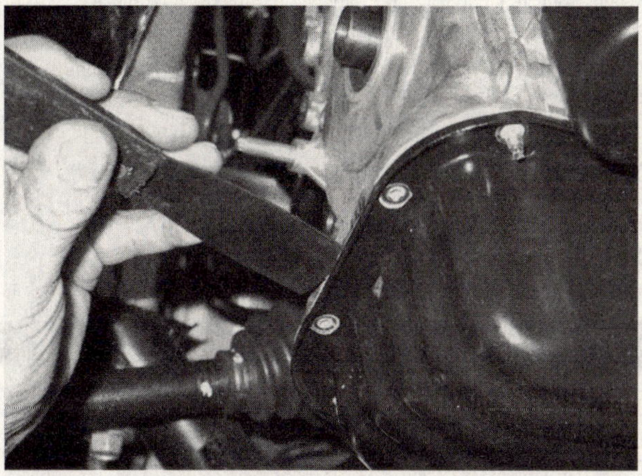

13.5 Pry the oil pan loose with a screwdriver or putty knife - be careful not to damage the mating surfaces of the pan and block or oil leaks may develop

14 Oil pump - removal and installation

2001 THROUGH 2006 MODELS

Removal

1 Refer to Section 5 and remove the timing belt.

2 Refer to Section 13 and remove the oil pan to remove the oil pickup and its gasket.

3 Remove the access plug on the left (front) side of the engine block and insert a screwdriver to lock the balance shaft into position (see illustration 5.9).

4 Remove the left (front) balance shaft and oil pump sprocket bolt.

5 Remove the front case/oil pump housing.

6 Remove the oil pump cover from the case and lift out the oil pump gears.

7 Use a scraper to remove all traces of sealant and old gasket material from the pump body and engine block, then clean the mating surfaces with brake system cleaner.

8 Inspect the oil pump for wear and damage. If the oil pump shows signs of wear or you're in doubt about its condition, it is best to simply replace it. The clearances can be measured using a feeler gauge. Compare your readings to those listed in this Chapter's Specifications.

Installation

9 Position the oil pump gears and align the two timing marks so they are facing each other.

10 Prime the pump by packing the voids between the gears with petroleum jelly.

11 Install new oil seals at this time, if necessary. Also be sure to use new gaskets. There is an O-ring in the front case that should also be replaced.

12 Tighten the bolts to the torque listed in this Chapter's Specifications in several steps. Follow a criss-cross pattern to avoid warping the body.

13 Tighten the lower drive sprocket retaining bolt to the torque listed in this Chapter's Specifications.

14 Reinstall the timing belts by referring to Section 5.

15 Add oil to the proper level, start the engine and check for oil pressure and leaks.

2006.5 AND LATER MODELS

16 The oil pump on these models is a part of the balance shaft module. Refer to Section 6 and remove the module as part of the timing chain removal procedure. The oil pump is not serviced separately; you must replace the entire module.

15 Flywheel/driveplate - removal and installation

REMOVAL

1 Disconnect the cable from the negative terminal of the battery (see Chapter 5).

2 Remove the transaxle (see Chapter 7). If the vehicle has a manual transaxle, refer to Chapter 8 and remove the clutch assembly.

3 Using a center punch or paint, apply alignment marks on the crankshaft flange and driveplate to ensure correct alignment on installation.

4 Remove the bolts retaining the driveplate to the crankshaft. Use a driveplate holding tool (available at auto parts stores) or wedge a screwdriver or prybar through one of the holes in the driveplate to keep it from turning while you loosen the bolts.

5 Remove the flywheel/driveplate, taking note of any spacers used and on which side of the driveplate they are installed.

INSTALLATION

6 Look for any fractures in the driveplate. Inspect it carefully for any other type of damage, especially on the ring gear teeth.

7 Position the driveplate on the crankshaft flange, aligning the marks made during removal. Align the bolt holes; note that some models may have a staggered bolt pattern to ensure correct installation.

8 Apply non-hardening thread locking compound to the threads of the bolts. Install the bolts and tighten them in a criss cross pattern to the torque listed in this Chapter's Specifications. Work up to the final torque in several steps.

9 Install the transaxle (see Chapter 7).

16 Rear main oil seal - replacement

1 Remove the transaxle (see Chapter 7).

2 Remove the driveplate or flywheel (see Section 15).

3 Pry the oil seal from the rear of the engine with a seal removal tool or a screwdriver. Be careful not to nick or scratch the crankshaft or the seal bore. Thoroughly clean the seal bore in the block with a shop towel. Remove all traces of oil and dirt.

4 Lubricate the outside diameter of the seal and install the seal over the end of the crankshaft. Make sure the lip of the seal points toward the engine. Preferably, a seal installation tool (available at most auto parts stores) should be used to press the new seal back into place.

➡ **Note: There is a small oil drain in the separator that must be in the lowest position.**

If the proper seal installation tool is unavailable, use a large socket and carefully drive the new seal squarely into the seal bore and flush with the edge of the engine block.

5 Install the driveplate or flywheel (see Section 15).

6 Install the transaxle (see Chapter 7).

17 Powertrain mounts - check and replacement

1 Powertrain mounts seldom require attention, but broken or deteriorated mounts should be replaced immediately or the added strain placed on driveline components may cause damage and wear.

CHECK

➧ **Refer to illustrations 17.4a, 17.4b, 17.4c and 17.4d**

2 During the check, the engine (or transaxle) must be raised slightly to remove the weight from the mounts.

3 Raise the vehicle and support it securely on jackstands, then remove the engine splash shield (if so equipped) and position a jack under the engine oil pan. Place a large block of wood between the jack and the oil pan, then carefully raise the engine just enough to take the weight off the mounts. Do not position the wood block under the oil drain plug.

⁂ WARNING:

DO NOT place any part of your body under the engine when only a jack supports it!

17.4a Typical right side engine mount

4 Check the mounts to see if the rubber is cracked, hardened or separated from the bushing in the center of the mount (see illustrations).

5 Check for relative movement between the mount brackets and the engine or frame (use a large screwdriver or prybar to attempt to move the mounts).

6 If movement is noted, lower the engine and tighten the mount fasteners.

REPLACEMENT

7 All engine mounts are replaced in the same manner. Use the jack to securely support the weight of the engine, then use it to remove all force from the mount in question.

8 Remove the bolts from both sides of the mount, then remove the mount.

9 Install the replacement mount and tighten all fasteners securely.

17.4b Typical upper transaxle mount

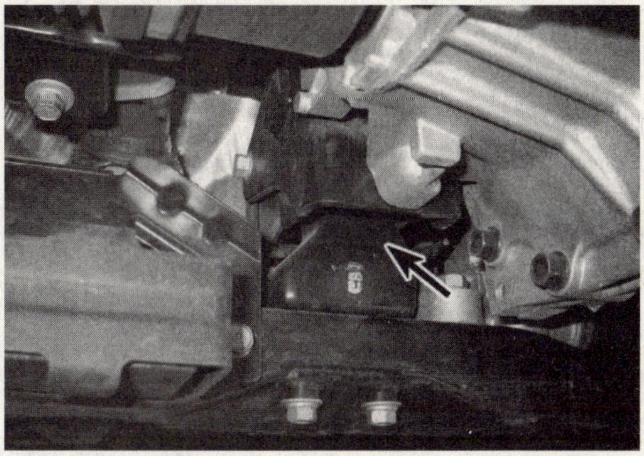

17.4c Typical upper rear transaxle mount

17.4d Typical lower front transaxle mount

Specifications

➡ **Note: 2006 and 2006.5 models will both have a "6" in the tenth position of the VIN. To distinguish a 2006 model from a 2006.5 model, refer to the 8th position of the VIN (the engine code): A 2006 model will have a "6," while a 2006.5 will have a "3."**

General

Engine type	Dual overhead camshaft
Engine identification	
2001 through 2006 models (iron block)	G4JS (Sirius II engine)
2006.5 and later models (aluminum block)	G4KC (Theta engine)
Displacement	
2001 through 2006 models	143.5 cubic inches (2.35 liters)
2006.5 and later models	143.9 cubic inches (2.36 liters)
Cylinder numbers (drivebelt end-to-transaxle end)	1-2-3-4
Firing order	1-3-4-2

Cylinder numbering

Cylinder head

Warpage limits	
Block surface	
2001 through 2006 models	0.008 inch (0.2 mm)
2006.5 and later models	0.002 inch (0.05 mm)
Manifold surfaces	
2001 through 2006 models	0.012 inch (0.3 mm)
2006.5 and later models	0.004 inch (0.1 mm)

Camshaft and lifters

Journal diameter	
2001 through 2006 models	1.02 inches (26 mm)
2006.5 and later models	
Intake	
#1 journal	1.181 inches (30 mm)
All others	0.945 inch (24 mm)
Exhaust	
#1 journal	1.575 inches (40 mm)
All other journals	0.945 inch (24 mm)
Bearing oil clearance	
2001 through 2006 models	0.002 to 0.003 inch (0.040 to 0.076 mm)
2006.5 and later models	
Intake	
#1 journal	0.0008 to 0.0022 inch (0.020 to 0.057 mm)
All other journals	0.0018 to 0.0032 inch (0.045 to 0.082 mm)
Exhaust	0.0018 to 0.0032 inch (0.045 to 0.082 mm)
Endplay	
2001 through 2006 models	0.004 to 0.006 inch (0.10 to 0.15 mm)
2006.5 and later models	0.004 to 0.009 inch (0.10 to 0.22 mm)
Cam lobe height (standard)	
2001 through 2006 models	
Intake camshaft	1.3974 inches (35.493 mm)
Exhaust camshaft	1.3904 inches (35.317 mm)
2006.5 and later models	
Intake camshaft	1.724 inches (43.80 mm)
Exhaust camshaft	1.772 inches (45.00 mm)

Camshaft and lifters (continued)

Cam lobe height wear limit	
2001 through 2006 models	
Intake	1.378 inches (34.99 mm)
Exhaust	1.371 inches (34.82 mm)
2006.5 and later models	Replace if less than standard
Valve clearance (2006.5 and later models)	
Standard	
Intake	0.007 to 0.009 inch (0.17 to 0.23 mm)
Exhaust	0.011 to 0.013 inch (0.27 to 0.33 mm)
Allowable limits	
Intake	0.004 to 0.012 inch (0.10 to 0.30 mm)
Exhaust	0.008 to 0.016 inch (0.20 to 0.40 mm)
Valve lifters (2006.5 and later models)	
Lifter diameter	1.258 to 1.259 inches (31.96 to 31.98 mm)
Lifter bore diameter	1.260 to 1.261 inches (32.00 to 32.03 mm)
Lifter to bore oil clearance	
Standard	0.0008 to 0.0024 inch (0.020 to 0.061 mm)
Limit	0.0028 inch (0.07 mm)

Oil pump

2001 through 2006 models	
Tip clearance wear limit	
Drive gear	0.010 inch (0.25 mm)
Driven gear	0.010 inch (0.25 mm)
Side clearance wear limit	
Drive gear	0.010 inch (0.25 mm)
Driven gear	0.010 inch (0.25 mm)

➡ **Note: The oil pump on 2006.5 and later models is part of the balance shaft module and is not separately serviceable.**

Timing belt (2001 through 2006 models)

Tensioner plunger protrusion, installed (dimension "A" in illustration 5.35)	0.22 to 0.35 inch (5.5 to 9 mm)

Torque specifications

➡ **Note: One foot-pound (ft-lb) of torque is equivalent to 12 inch-pounds (in-lbs) of torque. Torque values below approximately 15 foot-pounds are expressed in inch-pounds, because most foot-pound torque wrenches are not accurate at these smaller values.**

➡ **Note: 2006 and 2006.5 models will both have a "6" in the tenth position of the VIN. To distinguish a 2006 model from a 2006.5 model, refer to the 8th position of the VIN (the engine code): A 2006 model will have a "6," while a 2006.5 will have a "3."**

Torque specifications	Ft-lbs (unless otherwise indicated)	Nm
Balance shaft (2006.5 and later models)		
Balance shaft/oil pump module bolts		
Step 1	151 in-lbs	17
Step 2	Tighten an additional 60-degrees	
Step 3	Tighten an additional 60-degrees	
Chain tensioner arm bolt	84 to 108 in-lbs	10 to 12
Chain guide bolts	84 to 108 in-lbs	10 to 12
Chain tensioner bolts	84 to 108 in-lbs	10 to 12

Torque specifications	Ft-lbs (unless otherwise indicated)	Nm

➡ **Note: One foot-pound (ft-lb) of torque is equivalent to 12 inch-pounds (in-lbs) of torque. Torque values below approximately 15 foot-pounds are expressed in inch-pounds, because most foot-pound torque wrenches are not accurate at these smaller values.**

➡ **Note: 2006 and 2006.5 models will both have a "6" in the tenth position of the VIN. To distinguish a 2006 model from a 2006.5 model, refer to the 8th position of the VIN (the engine code): A 2006 model will have a "6," while a 2006.5 will have a "3."**

	Ft-lbs	Nm
Camshaft bearing cap bolts		
2001 through 2006 models	16	21
2006.5 and later models		
8 mm	20 to 23	27 to 31
6 mm	108 in-lbs	12
Camshaft sprocket bolt		
2001 through 2006 models	59 to 74	80 to 100
2006.5 and later models	40 to 47	54 to 64
Crankshaft pulley/vibration damper bolt		
2001 through 2006 models	118 to 125	160 to 170
2006.5 and later models	123 to 130	167 to 176
Cylinder head bolts (in sequence - see illustration 10.21)		
2001 through 2006 models		
Step 1	47	64
Step 2	Loosen all bolts completely	
Step 3	168 in-lbs	19
Step 4	Tighten an additional 90-degrees	
Step 5	Tighten an additional 90-degrees	
2006.5 and later models		
Step 1	25	34
Step 2	Tighten an additional 90-degrees	
Step 3	Tighten an additional 90-degrees	
Exhaust manifold nuts		
2001 through 2006 models		
Small	18 to 22	25 to 30
Large	26 to 40	35 to 55
2006.5 and later models	29 to 32	39 to 44
Front exhaust pipe-to-exhaust manifold nuts		
(2001 through 2006 models)	29 to 37	40 to 50
Flywheel or driveplate bolts		
2001 through 2006 models	96 to 103	130 to 140
2006.5 and later models	87 to 94	118 to 127
Intake manifold bolts		
2001 through 2006 models	132 to 168 in-lbs	15 to 19
2006.5 and later models	14 to 20	19 to 27
Intake manifold nuts		
2001 through 2006 models	22 to 31	30 to 42
2006.5 and later models	14 to 20	19 to 27
Oil pan bolts		
2001 through 2006 models		
(upper and lower pans)	84 to 108 in-lbs	10 to 12
2006.5 and later models		
6 mm bolts	84 to 108 in-lbs	10 to 12
8 mm bolts	20 to 22	27 to 30

Torque specifications

➡ Note: One foot-pound (ft-lb) of torque is equivalent to 12 inch-pounds (in-lbs) of torque. Torque values below approximately 15 foot-pounds are expressed in inch-pounds, because most foot-pound torque wrenches are not accurate at these smaller values.

➡ Note: 2006 and 2006.5 models will both have a "6" in the tenth position of the VIN. To distinguish a 2006 model from a 2006.5 model, refer to the 8th position of the VIN (the engine code): A 2006 model will have a "6," while a 2006.5 will have a "3."

Torque specifications	Ft-lbs (unless otherwise indicated)	Nm
Oil pump (2001 through 2006 models)*		
Cover bolts	132 to 156 in-lbs	15 to 18
Sprocket nut	37 to 44	50 to 60
Bolts	84 to 108 in-lbs	10 to 12
Timing belt (2001 through 2006 models)		
Cover bolts	52 to 84 in-lbs	6 to 10
Rear cover bolts	96 in-lbs	11
Tensioner pulley bolt	31 to 40	43 to 55
Timing chain (2006.5 and later models)		
6 mm cover bolts	72 to 84 in-lbs	8 to 10
8 mm cover bolts	4 to 17	19 to 23
Tensioner bolts	84 to 108 in-lbs	10 to 12
Tensioner arm bolt	84 to 108 in-lbs	10 to 12
Guide bolts	84 to 108 in-lbs	10 to 12
Valve cover fasteners		
2001 through 2006 models (see illustration 4.8a)		
"A" fasteners	52 to 84 in-lbs	6 to 10
"B" fasteners	36 to 48 in-lbs	4 to 5
2006.5 and later models (see illustration 4.8b)	72 to 84 in-lbs	8 to 10

*** Note: On 2006.5 and later models, the oil pump is an integral component of the balance shaft module and can't be separately serviced.**

Notes

2B

V6 ENGINES

Section

Reference to other Chapters

CHECK ENGINE light on - See Chapter 6
Crankshaft pulley - removal and installation - See Chapter 2A
Cylinder compression check - See Chapter 2C
Drivebelt check, adjustment and replacement - See Chapter 1
Engine - removal and installation - See Chapter 2C
Engine oil and filter change - See Chapter 1
Engine overhaul - general information - See Chapter 2C
Spark plug replacement - See Chapter 1
Water pump - removal and installation - See Chapter 3

1 General information

➡ **Note: 2006 and 2006.5 models will both have a "6" in the tenth position of the VIN. To distinguish a 2006 model from a 2006.5 model, refer to the 8th position of the VIN (the engine code): A 2006 model will have an "8," while a 2006.5 will have a "4."**

The DOHC (Dual OverHead Cam) 2.5L and 2.7L V6 engines have four valves per cylinder, aluminum cylinder heads and a two-piece oil pan.

This Part of Chapter 2 is devoted to in-vehicle repair procedures for the V6 engine. Information concerning engine removal and installation and engine overhaul can be found in Part C of this Chapter.

The following repair procedures are based on the assumption that the engine is installed in the vehicle. If the engine has been removed from the vehicle and mounted on a stand, many of the steps outlined in this Part of Chapter 2 will not apply.

2 Repair operations possible with the engine in the vehicle

Many major repair operations can be accomplished without removing the engine from the vehicle.

Clean the engine compartment and the exterior of the engine with some type of degreaser before any work is done. It will make the job easier and help keep dirt out of the internal areas of the engine.

Depending on the components involved, it may be helpful to remove the hood to improve access to the engine as repairs are performed (see Chapter 11 if necessary). Cover the fenders to prevent damage to the paint. Special pads are available, but an old bedspread or blanket will also work.

If vacuum, exhaust, oil or coolant leaks develop, indicating a need for gasket or seal replacement, the repairs can generally be made with the engine in the vehicle. The intake and exhaust manifold gaskets, oil pan gasket, crankshaft oil seals and cylinder head gaskets are all accessible with the engine in place.

Exterior engine components, such as the intake and exhaust manifolds, the oil pan, the oil pump, the water pump, the starter motor, the alternator, and the fuel system components can be removed for repair with the engine in place.

Since the cylinder heads can be removed without pulling the engine, valve component servicing can also be accomplished with the engine in the vehicle. Replacement of the camshafts, timing belt and sprockets is also possible with the engine in the vehicle.

3 Top Dead Center (TDC) for number one piston - locating

Refer to illustration 3.5

1 Top Dead Center (TDC) is the highest point in the cylinder that each piston reaches as it travels up the cylinder bore. Each piston reaches TDC on the compression stroke and again on the exhaust stroke, but TDC generally refers to piston position on the compression stroke.

2 Positioning the piston(s) at TDC is an essential part of certain procedures such as camshaft and timing belt/sprocket removal.

3 Before beginning this procedure, be sure to place the transaxle in Neutral and apply the parking brake or block the rear wheels. Disable the fuel pump (see Chapter 4, Section 2). Disable the ignition system by disconnecting the electrical connector(s) from the coil(s).

4 In order to bring any piston to TDC, the crankshaft must be turned using one of the methods outlined below. When looking at the front of the engine, normal crankshaft rotation is clockwise.

a) The preferred method is to turn the crankshaft clockwise with a socket and ratchet attached to the bolt threaded into the front of the crankshaft.

b) A remote starter switch, which may save some time, can also be used. Follow the instructions included with the switch. Once the piston is close to TDC, use a socket and ratchet as described in the previous paragraph.

c) If an assistant is available to turn the ignition switch to the Start position in short bursts, you can get the piston close to TDC without a remote starter switch. Make sure your assistant is out of the vehicle, away from the ignition switch, then use a socket and ratchet as described in Paragraph a) to complete the procedure.

5 Remove the spark plug and install a compression gauge in the number one spark plug hole. It should be a gauge with a screw-in fitting and a hose at least six inches long (see illustration).

3.5 A compression gauge can be used in the number one spark plug hole to assist in finding TDC

CAUTION:

It is possible to check the compression on cylinder number 1 on the V6 engine with the upper intake manifold and throttle body installed on the engine. The spark plugs can remain in the cylinder heads (except for number 1) if the ignition system and the fuel pump have been disabled.

6 Rotate the crankshaft using one of the methods described above while observing the compression gauge. When the compression stroke of the number one cylinder is reached, pressure will begin to show on the gauge; continue to rotate the crankshaft and align the notch on the crankshaft pulley with the 0 mark on the timing plate. If you go past the marks, release the gauge pressure and rotate the crankshaft around two more revolutions.

7 After the number one piston has been positioned at TDC on the compression stroke, TDC for the remaining cylinders can be located by turning the crankshaft 120-degrees (1/3-turn) at a time and following the firing order (see this Chapter's Specifications).

4 Valve covers - removal and installation

REMOVAL

Refer to illustrations 4.2 and 4.3

1 Disconnect the cable from the negative terminal of the battery (see Chapter 5).

2 Remove the engine cover (see illustration).

3 Remove the upper intake manifold (see Section 5) to remove the rear valve cover (see illustration).

4 Detach all of the engine wiring harnesses and pull them out of the way. There are also mounting brackets on most models that must be removed. Be sure to keep brackets and fasteners in order for reassembly.

5 Disconnect all interfering wiring and hoses. Be sure to label them as you go to prevent confusion later. Remove the spark plugs (see Chapter 1).

6 Remove the retaining bolts, then detach the cover(s). If a cover is stuck to the head, bump the end with a wood block and a hammer to jar it loose. If that doesn't work, try to slip a flexible putty knife between the head and cover to break the seal.

CAUTION:

Don't pry at the cover-to-head joint or damage to the sealing surfaces may occur, leading to oil leaks after the cover is reinstalled.

INSTALLATION

7 The mating surfaces of the cylinder head and cover must be clean when the cover is installed. Use a gasket scraper to remove all traces of sealant and old gasket material, then clean the mating surfaces with brake system cleaner. If there's residue or oil on the mating surfaces when the cover is installed, oil leaks may develop.

8 Install new spark plug tube seals.

9 Apply RTV sealant to the gasket/seal joints at the front and rear camshaft-to-head mounts and install the valve cover with a new gasket.

10 Tighten the bolts evenly, a little at a time, to the torque listed in this Chapter's Specifications.

11 Reinstall the remaining parts, run the engine and check for oil leaks.

4.2 Engine cover bolts

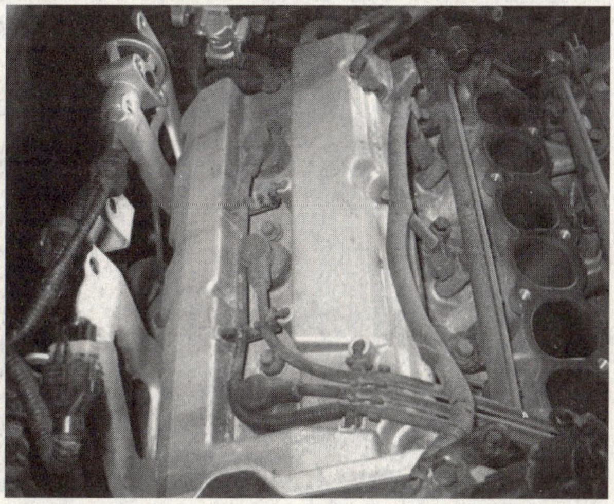

4.3 With the upper intake manifold removed, the rear valve cover is accessible

5 Intake manifold - removal and installation

WARNING:

Wait until the engine is completely cool before beginning this procedure.

REMOVAL

1 Relieve the fuel system pressure (see Chapter 4), then disconnect the cable from the negative terminal of the battery (see Chapter 5).

2 Remove the engine cover and the air intake duct assembly (see Chapter 4).

Upper intake manifold

Refer to illustration 5.6

3 Disconnect the PCV hose.

4 Disconnect the ground strap, the electrical connectors and the vacuum lines from the upper intake manifold. Label each connector using tape and a marker to ensure correct reassembly. Pull the wiring harnesses aside. The wiring and hoses vary from model to model - make sure that all interfering hoses and harnesses have been labeled, disconnected and pulled out of the way.

5 Disconnect the hoses and wires from the throttle body (see Chapter 4).

Note: Clamp off the coolant hoses before detaching them, or plug them as soon as they are detached. Be prepared for coolant spillage.

6 Unbolt the upper intake manifold brace(s) at the back of the upper intake manifold assembly (see illustration). Also remove the bolts from the EGR valve at the rear of the intake manifold and pull the EGR valve away.

7 There are other brackets that must be removed whose locations vary from year to year. Be sure to keep them in order with the correct fasteners as you remove them.

8 Remove the bolts mounting the upper intake manifold to the lower intake manifold, following the reverse of the tightening sequence (see illustration 5.17).

9 Separate the upper intake manifold from the lower intake manifold.

Lower intake manifold

10 Drain the cooling system (see Chapter 1).

11 Disconnect the electrical connectors from the fuel injectors (see Chapter 4). Also detach the fuel line from the fuel rail (see Chapter 4).

Note: The intake manifold can be removed with the injectors and fuel rails in place or removed, depending on the work to be done.

Pull the wiring harness aside.

12 Disconnect any remaining components from the lower manifold.

13 Remove the mounting bolts following the reverse of the tightening sequence (see illustration 5.16), then detach the lower intake manifold from the engine. If the manifold is stuck, don't pry between the gasket mating surfaces or damage may result.

14 Check the manifold's surface with a precision straightedge and compare your readings with those listed in this Chapter's Specifications. If it's excessively deformed, it must be replaced.

INSTALLATION

Refer to illustrations 5.16 and 5.17

15 Use a scraper to remove all traces of old gasket material and sealant from the lower intake manifold and cylinder heads, then clean the mating surfaces with brake system cleaner.

16 Install new gaskets, then position the lower intake manifold on the engine. Make sure the gaskets haven't shifted, and install the bolts. Tighten the bolts in three or four equal steps to the torque listed in this Chapter's Specifications. Tighten the bolts in the correct sequence (see illustration).

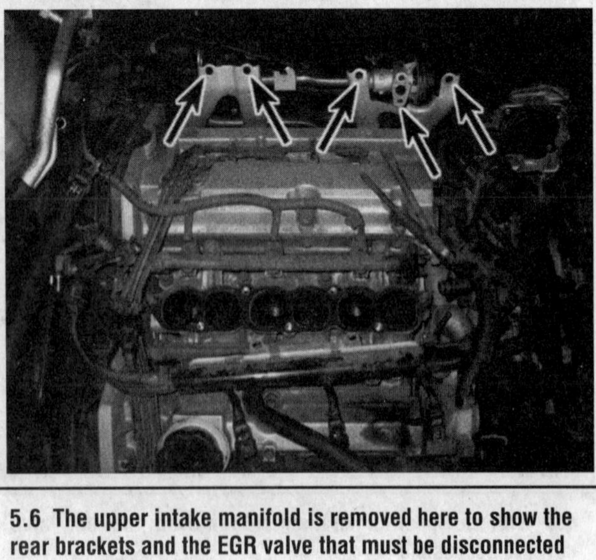

5.6 The upper intake manifold is removed here to show the rear brackets and the EGR valve that must be disconnected

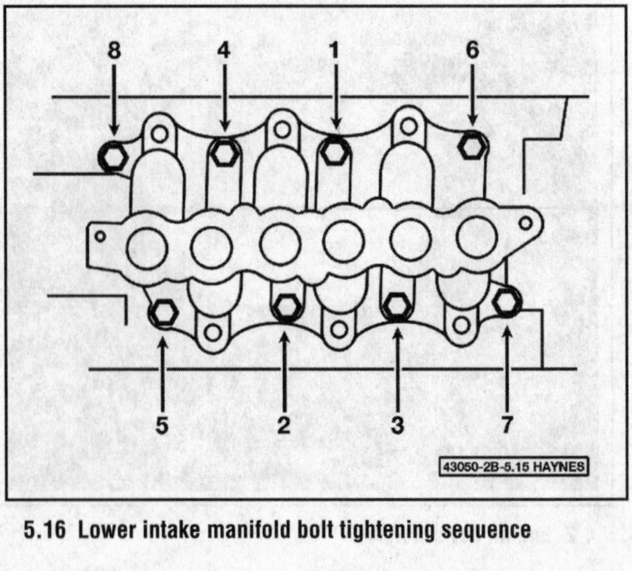

5.16 Lower intake manifold bolt tightening sequence

17 Install a new gasket between the lower intake manifold and the upper intake manifold. Place the upper intake manifold on the lower intake manifold. Install the bolts and tighten them, in the proper sequence (see illustration), to the torque listed in this Chapter's Specifications.

18 Refill the cooling system (see Chapter 1). If the lower intake manifold was removed, change the engine oil and filter (see Chapter 1). Run the engine and check for fuel, vacuum and coolant leaks.

5.17 Typical upper intake manifold bolt TIGHTENING sequence

6 Exhaust manifold/catalytic converter assemblies - removal and installation

Refer to illustrations 6.4 and 6.7

WARNING:

The engine must be completely cool before beginning this procedure.

1 Disconnect the cable from the negative terminal of the battery (see Chapter 5).

2 Spray penetrating oil on the exhaust manifold fasteners and allow it to soak in.

3 Raise the front of the vehicle and support it securely on jackstands, then remove the engine lower splash shield.

4 Disconnect or remove the heated oxygen sensors from the manifold(s) (see Chapter 6) (see illustration).

5 Remove the bolts and the heat shield over the exhaust manifold.

6 Remove the exhaust manifold brace, if equipped.

7 Remove the fasteners retaining the exhaust pipe(s) to the exhaust manifold(s) or catalytic converter(s) (see illustration).

8 Unbolt the exhaust manifold(s) from the cylinder head(s), working from the ends toward the middle. Slip the manifold(s) off the mounting studs.

9 Carefully inspect the manifold(s) and fasteners for cracks and damage.

10 Use a scraper to remove all traces of old gasket material and carbon deposits from the manifold and cylinder head mating surfaces. If the gasket was leaking, check the manifold for warpage on the cylinder head mounting surface by placing a straightedge over the surface and trying to insert a feeler gauge. If the clearance exceeds the limit listed in this Chapter's Specifications, have the manifold resurfaced at an automotive machine shop.

11 Position a new gasket over the cylinder head studs.

12 Install the manifold(s) and thread the mounting nuts into place.

13 Working from the center out, tighten the nuts to the torque listed in this Chapter's Specifications in three or four equal steps.

14 Reinstall the remaining parts in the reverse order of removal. Use new gaskets when connecting the exhaust pipes.

15 Run the engine and check for exhaust leaks.

6.4 There is an oxygen sensor immediately before and after each catalytic converter (downstream sensor shown)

6.7 Front exhaust pipe fasteners and rubber hangers (2001 through 2006 models)

7 Timing belt and sprockets - removal, inspection and installation

⁂ CAUTION:

The timing system is complex, and severe engine damage will occur if you make any mistakes. Do not attempt this procedure unless you are highly experienced with this type of repair. If you are at all unsure of your abilities, be sure to consult an expert. Double-check all your work and be sure everything is correct before you attempt to start the engine.

REMOVAL

Refer to illustration 7.9

1 Disconnect the cable from the negative terminal of the battery (see Chapter 5).

7.9 If the camshaft sprockets are to be removed, hold the hex portion of the camshaft with a wrench while removing the sprocket bolt

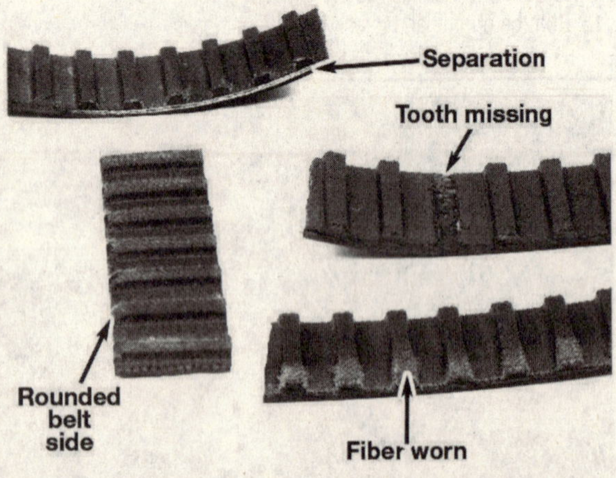

7.10 Check the timing belt for cracked or missing teeth - if the belt is cracked or worn, also check the sprockets and pulleys for nicks or burrs - wear on one side of the belt indicates sprocket misalignment problems

2 Remove the engine cover.

3 Remove the drivebelt (see Chapter 1).

4 Remove the pulleys from the power steering pump, the idler, the belt tensioner and the crankshaft (see Chapter 2A).

5 Remove both timing belt covers.

6 Set the engine at TDC on the number one cylinder (see Section 3). Make absolutely sure that all of the timing marks are aligned.

7 If you intend to reuse the belt, mark it with an arrow indicating direction of travel and put match marks from the belt to the sprockets so it can be realigned easily.

8 Remove the timing belt tensioner, then remove the timing belt.

9 The camshaft sprockets can be removed now (see illustration). Remove the valve covers and hold the hex area of the camshaft securely with a wrench while removing the bolts.

INSPECTION

Refer to illustrations 7.10 and 7.12

10 Check the belt for the presence of oil or dirt, and inspect for visible defects (see illustration).

11 Check the belt tensioner for visible oil leakage. If there's only a faint trace of oil on the pushrod side, the tensioner seal is in satisfactory condition.

12 Hold the tensioner in both hands and push it forcefully against an immovable object (see illustration). If the pushrod moves, replace the tensioner.

13 Check that the idler pulleys turn smoothly.

INSTALLATION

Refer to illustrations 7.18 and 7.20

14 Remove all dirt, oil and grease from the timing belt area at the front of the engine.

15 Install the camshaft sprockets (if removed) on the camshaft. Align the pin hole in the sprocket with the pin in the end of the camshaft.

16 Install the camshaft sprocket bolts and tighten them to the torque listed in this Chapter's Specifications.

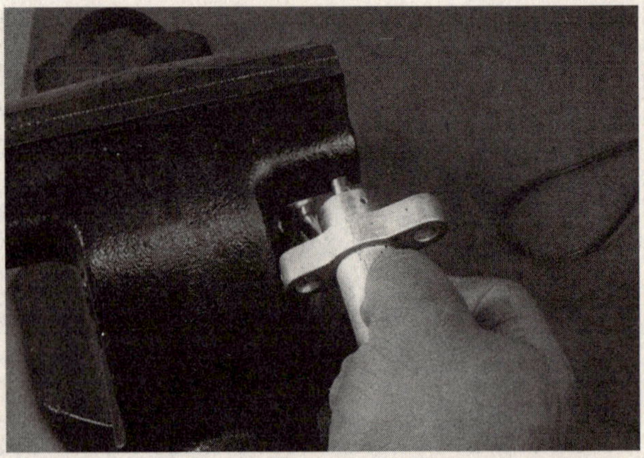

7.12 Check the tensioner for signs of leakage and test for leakdown by forcing it against an immovable object

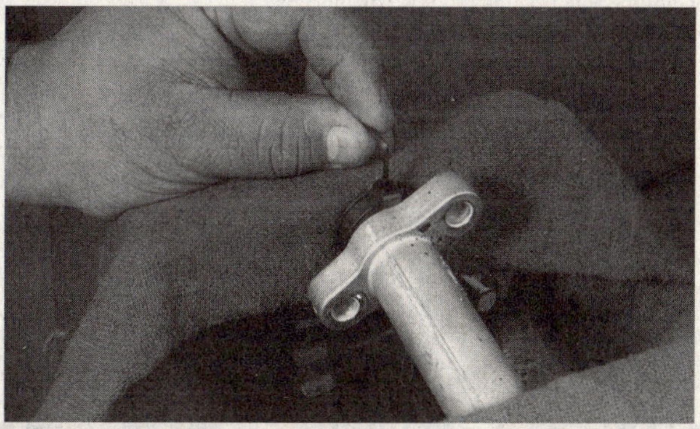

7.18 Restrain the tensioner pushrod by compressing the unit in a vise and inserting a pin approximately 0.060-inch (1.5 mm) in diameter

17 Carefully align all of the camshaft sprocket marks with the marks on the engine.

18 Using a press or vise, compress the timing belt tensioner pushrod extremely slowly. Insert a metal pin, drill bit or Allen wrench through the holes in the pushrod and housing. Remove the tensioner from the press or vise (see illustration).

19 Install the timing belt tensioner and tighten the bolts to the torque listed in this Chapter's Specifications.

20 Align all of the timing marks and place the timing belt around the sprockets and pulleys in this order (see illustration):

Crankshaft
Idler
Front (left) camshaft
Water pump
Rear (right) camshaft
Tensioner

21 Again verify that all timing marks are aligned, then pull the pin from the tensioner, allowing it to snap into position.

22 Using a socket and breaker bar on the crankshaft pulley bolt, turn the crankshaft slowly (clockwise) through two complete revolutions (720-degrees) by hand (use a socket and breaker bar on the crankshaft pulley center-bolt).

CAUTION:

If you feel any resistance, STOP! There is something wrong - most likely valves are contacting the pistons. You must find the problem before proceeding. Check your work and see if any updated repair information is available.

Recheck the timing marks.

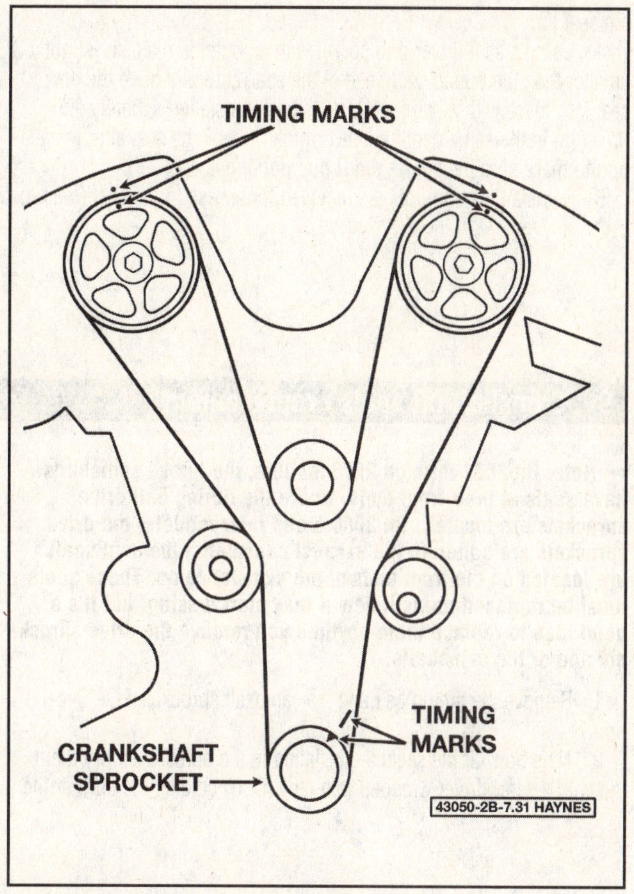

7.20 Timing belt alignment marks

CAUTION:

If the timing marks are not aligned exactly as shown in illustration 7.20, repeat the timing belt installation procedure. DO NOT start the engine until you're absolutely certain that the timing belt is installed correctly. Serious and costly engine damage could occur if the belt is installed incorrectly. Stop turning the crankshaft immediately if you feel solid resistance; the valves could be contacting the pistons.

23 Let the engine sit for five minutes at TDC, then check the protrusion of the tensioner rod. Compare your measurement to that listed in this Chapter's Specifications. If it isn't correct, replace the tensioner or determine if there's another problem.

24 Reinstall the remaining parts in the reverse order of removal.

8 Crankshaft oil seals - replacement

FRONT CRANKSHAFT OIL SEAL

1 Remove the timing belt and crankshaft sprocket (see Section 7). Slip off the sensor ring and the spacer behind it.

2 Carefully pry the seal out with a screwdriver or seal removal tool. If you use a screwdriver, wrap tape around the tip - don't scratch the housing bore or damage the crankshaft (if the crankshaft is damaged, the new seal will end up leaking).

3 Clean the bore in the engine and coat the outer edge of the new seal with engine oil or multi-purpose grease. Apply the same grease to

the seal lip.

4 Using a seal driver or a socket with an outside diameter slightly smaller than the outside diameter of the seal, carefully drive the new seal into place with a hammer. Make sure it's installed squarely and driven in to the same depth as the original. Check the seal after installation to make sure the spring didn't pop out of place.

5 Reinstall the components removed for access to the seal (refer to the appropriate Sections in this Chapter).

6 Run the engine and check for oil leaks at the front seal.

REAR CRANKSHAFT REAR OIL SEAL

7 Refer to Chapter 2A, Section 16.

9 Camshaft oil seals - replacement

➡ Note: On 2001 through 2006 models, the intake camshafts have seals at their front ends, where the timing belt drive sprockets are located. On 2006.5 and later models, the drive sprockets are bolted to the exhaust camshafts; the cam seals are located on the front ends of the exhaust cams. These seals must be replaced immediately if they start leaking, but it's a good idea to replace them anytime you remove the drive sprockets and/or the camshafts.

1 Remove the timing belt and the camshaft sprockets (see Section 7).

2 Note how far the seals are installed in the bores, then pry them out with a screwdriver wrapped with tape. Don't scratch the bore or the camshaft - either one can cause a leak.

3 Clean the bores. Coat the outer edge of the new seals with oil or grease. Also apply grease to the lips of the seals.

4 Using a seal driver or a socket with an outside diameter slightly smaller than the outer edge of the seal, carefully drive the new seals into place with a hammer. Make sure they're installed square and that they're driven in to the same depth as the originals.

5 Install all of the removed components, referring to the appropriate Sections in this Chapter to ensure that the belt and sprockets are correctly aligned. Clean carefully around the seals so you'll be able to detect any leaks later.

6 Operate the vehicle for a few days, then check for leaks.

10 Camshafts and lifters - removal, inspection, installation and adjustment

REMOVAL

⁂ CAUTION:

Don't try to disassemble the VVT (variable valve timing) assembly on the intake camshaft sprockets on engines so equipped. This assembly must be removed and installed intact. To remove the sprocket and VVT assembly, simply remove the center bolt from the end of the camshaft.

1 Remove the valve covers (see Section 4).

2 Position the engine at TDC (see Section 3), then remove the timing belt (see Section 7).

3 The following steps apply to the removal of each of the four camshafts. Make sure the cam timing marks on the sprockets and engine are in alignment.

4 The camshafts are not interchangeable. Mark them clearly to avoid confusion later.

5 Loosen the camshaft bearing cap bolts in 1/4-turn increments until they can be removed by hand. Start with the outer caps and work inward.

6 The bearing caps are marked I and E (for intake and exhaust), and should already be numbered; mark the caps with your own numbers if necessary. Remove the bearing caps and gently lift out the camshafts.

➡ Note: The camshafts in each head must be removed together because they are connected by a timing chain.

7 Store the bearing caps in the correct order. If necessary, the lifters can now be removed. Be sure to store all components in order so they can be reinstalled in their original locations.

INSPECTION

8 Refer to Chapter 2, Part A for camshaft, lifter and related component inspection procedures. Be sure to use the Specifications in this Part of Chapter 2 for the V6 engines.

INSTALLATION

➧ Refer to illustration 10.11

9 Apply camshaft installation lubricant to the camshaft lobes and bearing journals.

10 Install the lash adjusters in their original positions.

11 Install the timing chains around the sprockets of each pair of camshafts and set them in their journals. Make sure that the timing marks on the sprockets are aligned with the marks on the timing chains (see illustration).

12 Install the bearing caps in numerical order with the arrows pointing toward the drivebelt end of the engine.

13 Tighten the bearing cap bolts in 1/4-turn increments to the torque listed in this Chapter's Specifications. Start with the center cap and work your way out to the ends.

14 Install new camshaft oil seals (see Section 9).

15 The remainder of the installation is the reverse of removal. Be sure to verify that all timing marks are aligned (see Section 7).

CAUTION:

Major engine damage can occur if all the timing marks are not aligned.

16 Run the engine, then check for leaks and proper operation. If the hydraulic valve adjusters have been somewhat drained, it may take several minutes for valvetrain noise to disappear.

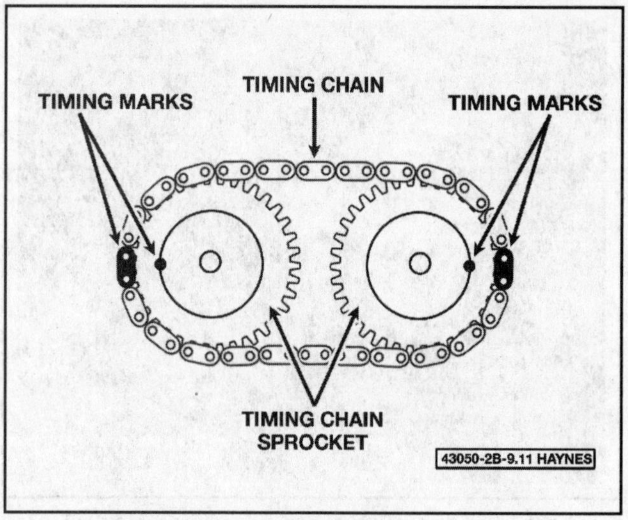

10.11 Camshaft sprocket/timing chain alignment marks

11 Cylinder heads - removal, inspection and installation

WARNING:

Wait until the engine is completely cool before beginning this procedure.

CAUTION:

Replace the cylinder head bolts with new ones.

REMOVAL

1 Remove the engine cover, if equipped.

2 Relieve the fuel system pressure (see Chapter 4), then disconnect the cable from the negative terminal of the battery (see Chapter 5). On 2006.5 and later models, disconnect both battery cables.

3 Drain the cooling system, including the engine block (see Chapter 1). Remove the upper radiator hose. On 2006.5 and later models, remove the lower radiator hose as well.

4 Remove the air intake duct (see Chapter 4, Section 9). On 2006.5 and later models, remove the air filter housing as well.

5 On 2006.5 and later models, remove the fresh air inlet duct (see Chapter 4) and remove the battery (see Chapter 5).

6 On 2001 through 2006 models, disconnect the spark plug wires and remove the ignition coils (see Chapter 5). If you're going to be sending the head(s) to a machine shop for overhaul, remove the spark plugs too. On 2006.5 and later models, remove the ignition coils (see Chapter 5).

7 Disconnect the fuel lines and remove the fuel rail and fuel injectors (see Chapter 4).

8 Remove the upper and lower intake manifolds (see Section 5).

9 Remove the timing belt (see Section 7).

10 Disconnect all remaining sensors and hoses that interfere with valve cover and cylinder head removal.

11 Remove the valve covers (see Section 4.

12 Remove the exhaust manifold(s) (see Section 6).

13 Remove the camshafts (see Section 10).

14 Loosen the cylinder head bolts in 1/4-turn increments until they can be removed by hand, along with their hardened washers. Follow the reverse order of the recommended tightening sequence (see illustration 11.27).

15 Lift the cylinder head off the engine block. If the head is stuck, place a wood block against it and strike the wood with a hammer.

CAUTION:

Don't pry between the head and block. The gasket surfaces may be damaged and leaks could result.

Set the cylinder head on wood blocks to prevent damage to the sealing surfaces.

16 Repeat the procedure for the other head if necessary.

INSPECTION

17 Use a precision straightedge to check the gasket surfaces of each head. Try to insert a feeler gauge of the maximum specified size between the straightedge and the head surface. If the clearance is more than that listed in this Chapter's Specifications, the head must be resurfaced or replaced. Check the intake and exhaust manifold surfaces as well as the block surface.

18 Examine all areas of each head for signs of cracks and coolant leakage, especially around the valve seats.

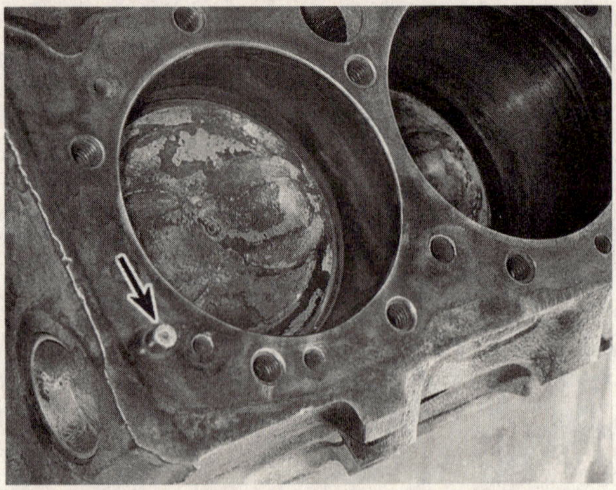

11.23 **Be sure the new head gaskets are positioned right side up (check all holes and coolant passages for correct alignment) and over the block dowels**

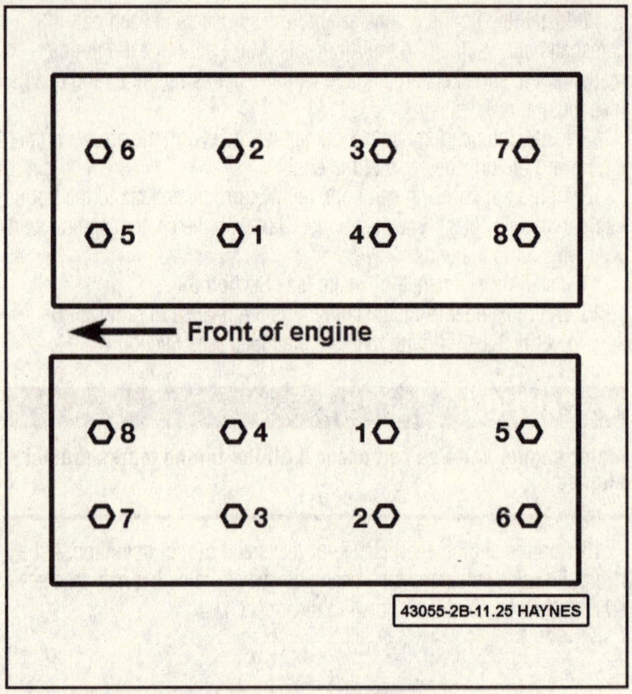

11.27 Cylinder head bolt TIGHTENING sequence

INSTALLATION

Refer to illustrations 11.23 and 11.27

19 The mating surfaces of the cylinder heads and block must be perfectly clean when the heads are installed.

20 Use a gasket scraper to remove all traces of carbon and old gasket material, then clean the mating surfaces with brake system cleaner. If there's oil on the mating surfaces when the head is installed, the gasket may not seal correctly and leaks could develop. When working on the block, stuff the cylinders with clean shop rags to keep out debris. Use a vacuum cleaner to remove material that falls into the cylinders.

21 Check the block and head mating surfaces for nicks, deep scratches and other damage. If damage is slight, it can be removed with a file; if it's excessive, machining may be the only alternative.

22 Use a tap of the correct size to chase the threads in the cylinder head bolt holes, then clean the holes with compressed air - make sure that nothing remains in the holes.

WARNING:

Wear eye protection when using compressed air!

23 Position the new gaskets over the dowel pins in the block (see illustration). The side of the gasket with the identification mark must face upward.

24 Apply a small dab of RTV sealant to the end of each leg of the gaskets.

25 Carefully set the head on the block without disturbing the gasket.

26 Before installing the NEW head bolts, apply a small amount of clean engine oil to the threads and the underside of the bolt heads.

27 Install the bolts and tighten them finger tight. Following the recommended sequence, tighten the bolts to the torque listed in this Chapter's Specifications (see illustration). If you don't have a torque angle gauge attachment, simply apply a paint mark to the socket you will be using to act as a reference point.

28 The remainder of installation is the reverse of removal.

29 Refill the cooling system, then change the oil and oil filter (see Chapter 1).

30 Run the engine and check for leaks.

12 Oil pan - removal and installation

Note: The oil pan is a two-part assembly, with an aluminum casting attached to the cylinder block and transaxle, and a lower stamped-steel pan section at the bottom.

LOWER OIL PAN

Removal

Refer to illustration 12.5

1 Disconnect the cable from the negative terminal of the battery (see Chapter 5).

2 Raise the vehicle and support it securely on jackstands

3 Remove the engine splash shields.

4 Drain the engine oil.

5 Remove the bolts and detach the lower steel pan (see illustration). If it's stuck, pry it loose very carefully with a small screwdriver or putty knife. Don't damage the mating surfaces of the pan, or oil leaks could develop. Don't pry too much in one area, as you can bend the pan flange. Instead, drive in a putty knife and hammer it around the perimeter of the oil pan to break the seal.

Installation

➧ **Refer to illustration 12.11**

6 Use a scraper to remove all traces of old sealant from the block and oil pan. Clean the mating surfaces with lacquer thinner or acetone.

7 Make sure the threaded bolt holes in the block are clean.

8 Check the flange of the steel pan section for distortion, particularly around the bolt holes. If necessary, place the pan on a wood block and use a hammer to flatten and restore the gasket surface.

9 Clean the mating surfaces of the engine block and aluminum upper oil pan section, being careful not to gouge the soft metal, which could lead to leaks. Use brake system cleaner to remove all traces of oil.

10 Apply a continuous 1/8-inch bead of RTV sealant to the pan.

11 Install the pan within five minutes and tighten the bolts, a little at a time and in the correct sequence (see illustration) to the torque listed in this Chapter's Specifications. Allow the sealant to set for at least two hours before adding new oil and a new oil filter (see Chapter 1).

UPPER OIL PAN

Removal

12 Refer to Step 1 and remove the lower oil pan. Remove the oil filter.

13 Disconnect the exhaust pipe from both exhaust manifolds.

➡ **Note: This isn't necessary on some models, as the exhaust doesn't interfere with oil pan removal.**

14 Disconnect the oxygen sensors (if necessary) and support the pipe temporarily. Unbolt the pipe at the rear, disconnect it from the hangers and remove it from the vehicle.

15 Remove any other interfering components. These components vary by year and model; be sure you have enough clearance for oil pan removal.

16 Remove the lower baffle and the oil pump strainer/pickup.

17 Remove the upper oil pan fasteners including the ones inside of the pan, and those that secure it to the transaxle.

18 Remove the upper oil pan by tapping it loose with a plastic hammer.

12.5 There are two oil pans: a lower stamped steel pan (A) and an upper cast aluminum pan (B)

Installation

➧ **Refer to illustration 12.22**

19 Clean all sealing surfaces thoroughly with brake system cleaner to remove all traces of oil.

20 Inspect the oil pump pick-up/strainer assembly for cracks and a blocked strainer. Clean the pickup with solvent or thinner and install it now, using a new gasket. Tighten the fasteners to the torque listed in this Chapter's Specifications.

21 Apply a 3/16-inch wide bead of RTV sealant to the aluminum pan section.

➡ **Note: The pan must be installed within five minutes after the sealant has been applied.**

22 Carefully position the pan on the engine block and install the bolts, tightening them to the torque listed in this Chapter's Specifications in three or four steps. Follow the tightening sequence shown (see illustration).

23 The remainder of installation is the reverse of removal. Allow the sealant to set for at least two hours before adding new oil and a new oil filter.

24 Run the engine and check for oil pressure and leaks.

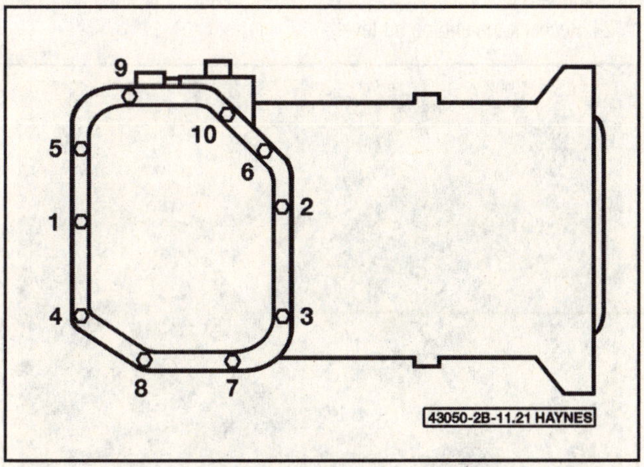

12.11 Lower oil pan bolt TIGHTENING sequence

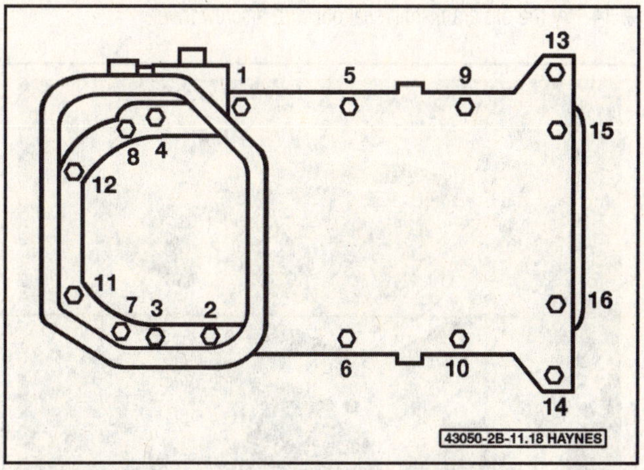

12.22 Upper oil pan bolt TIGHTENING sequence

13 Oil pump - removal, inspection and installation

REMOVAL

1 Disconnect the cable from the negative battery terminal (see Chapter 5).
2 Remove the timing belt (see Section 7).
3 Remove the oil filter.
4 Remove the oil filter bracket and its gasket.
5 Remove the crankshaft sprocket.
6 Remove the oil pressure relief plug, the spring and the valve plunger.
7 Remove the oil pump case from the front of the engine.
8 Remove the cover from the oil pump and lift out the inner and outer gears.
9 Lift the cover off and remove the pump rotors.
10 Use a scraper to remove all traces of sealant and old gasket material from the pump body and engine block, then clean the mating surfaces with brake system cleaner.

INSPECTION

Refer to illustrations 13.13a, 13.13b and 13.13c

11 Clean all components with solvent, then inspect them for wear and damage.
12 Check the oil pressure relief valve sliding surface and valve spring. If either the spring or the valve is damaged, they must be replaced as a set.
13 Check the clearance of the following components with a feeler gauge and compare the measurements to this Chapter's Specifications (see illustrations):

a) Driven rotor-to-oil pump body clearance
b) Rotor side clearance
c) Rotor tip clearance

INSTALLATION

14 Pry the old crankshaft seal out with a screwdriver.

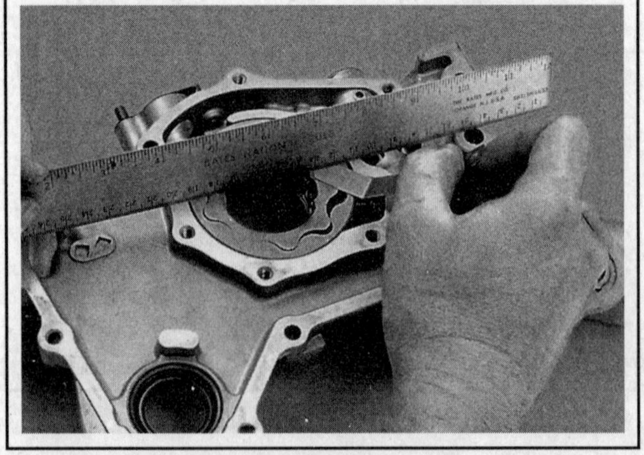

13.13b Measure the rotor side clearance with a precision straightedge and feeler gauge

13.13a Measure the driven rotor-to-body clearance with a feeler gauge

15 Apply multi-purpose grease or engine oil to the outer edge of the new seal and carefully drive it into place with a seal driver and a hammer. Also apply multi-purpose grease to the seal lip.
16 Place the drive and driven rotors into the pump body.
17 Pack the pump cavities with petroleum jelly and install the cover using either a new gasket or RTV sealant. Tighten the screws securely following a criss-cross pattern to the torque listed in this Chapter's Specifications.
18 Lubricate the oil pressure relief valve with engine oil and install the valve components in the pump body.
19 Use brake cleaner and a clean rag to remove all traces of oil from the case gasket surfaces.
20 Install the oil pump case with a new gasket. Install the mounting bolts and tighten them to the torque listed in this Chapter's Specifications in a criss-cross pattern.
21 Using a new gasket, install the oil pick-up tube and tighten the fasteners to the torque listed in this Chapter's Specifications.
22 Reinstall the remaining parts in the reverse order of removal.
23 Add oil (see Chapter 1), start the engine and check for oil pressure and leaks.
24 Recheck the engine oil level.

13.13c Measure the rotor tip clearance with a feeler gauge - note the rotor marks are facing out (when the pump body cover is installed, the marks will be against the cover)

14 Flywheel/driveplate - removal and installation

Refer to Chapter 2, Part A for this procedure, but be sure to use the torque specifications in this Part of Chapter 2 for the V6 engine. On automatic transaxle vehicles, there is an adapter plate used on the rear of the driveplate.

15 Powertrain mounts - check and replacement

Refer to Chapter 2, Part A; the V6 engine mounts are slightly different in ways that don't significantly affect the check and replacement procedures.

Specifications

➡ **Note: 2006 and 2006.5 models will both have a "6" in the tenth position of the VIN. To distinguish a 2006 model from a 2006.5 model, refer to the 8th position of the VIN (the engine code): A 2006 model will have an "8," while a 2006.5 will have a "4."**

General

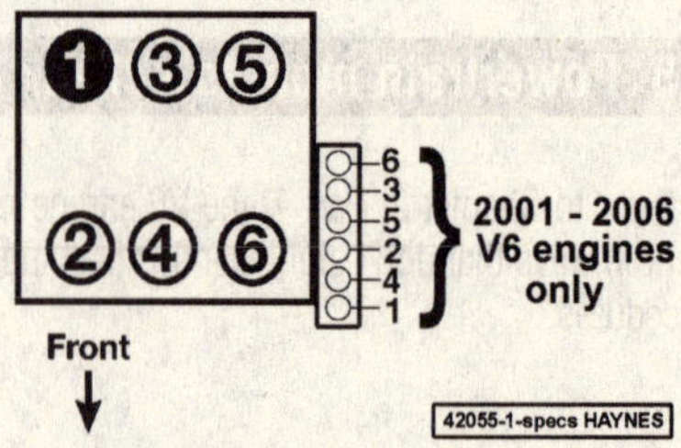

Cylinder numbering

Engine identification	
2001 models	G6BW (2.5L Delta engine)
2002 through 2006 models	G6BA (2.7L Delta engine)
2006.5 and later models	G6EA (2.7L Mu engine)
Displacement	
2001 models	152 cubic inches (2493 cc)
2002 and later models	162 cubic inches (2656 cc)
Cylinder numbers (timing belt or chain end-to-transaxle end)	
Right (firewall) side	1-3-5
Left (radiator) side	2-4-6
Firing order	1-2-3-4-5-6

Cylinder head

Warpage limits	
Block surface	0.002 inch (0.05 mm)
Intake surface	0.006 inch (0.15 mm)
Exhaust surface	0.006 inch (0.15 mm)

Camshafts and lifters

2001 through 2006 models	
Bearing journal diameter	1.022 to 1.023 inches (25.96 to 25.98 mm)
Bearing oil clearance	0.0007 to 0.0024 inch (0.02 to 0.06 mm)
Lobe height minimum allowable	1.7303 to 1.7382 inches (43.95 to 44.15 mm)
Endplay (limit)	0.004 to 0.006 inch (0.1 to 0.15 mm)
2006.5 and later models	
Bearing journal diameter	1.1009 to 1.1016 inches (27.964 to 27.980 mm)
Bearing oil clearance	0.0008 to 0.0022 inch (0.020 to 0.057 mm)
Lobe height minimum allowable	1.7520 inches (44.5 mm)
Endplay (limit)	0.0039 to 0.0079 inch (0.1 to 0.2 mm)
Valve clearance	
Intake	
Standard	0.006 to 0.009 inch (0.17 to 0.23 mm)
Service limit	0.004 to 0.0118 inch (0.10 to 0.30 mm)
Exhaust	
Standard	0.0106 to 0.0129 inch (0.27 to 0.33 mm)
Service limit	0.008 to 0.0157 inch (0.20 to 0.40 mm)
Valve lifters	
Lifter diameter	1.1797 to 1.1803 inches (29.964 to 29.980 mm)
Lifter bore diameter	1.1811 to 1.1821 inches (30.0 to 30.025 mm)
Lifter-to-bore clearance	
Standard	0.0008 to 0.0024 inch (0.020 to 0.061 mm)
Service limit	0.0027 inch (0.07 mm)

Specifications

➡ **Note: 2006 and 2006.5 models will both have a "6" in the tenth position of the VIN. To distinguish a 2006 model from a 2006.5 model, refer to the 8th position of the VIN (the engine code): A 2006 model will have an "8," while a 2006.5 will have a "4."**

Intake manifold

Surface warpage limit	0.008 inch (0.2 mm)

Exhaust manifold

Surface warpage limit	0.012 inch (0.3 mm)

Oil pump

Driven rotor-to-pump body clearance	0.004 to 0.007 inch (0.10 to 0.18 mm)
Rotor side clearance	0.0016 to 0.0037 inch (0.040 to 0.095 mm)
Rotor tip clearance	0.0024 to 0.0071 inch (0.06 to 0.18 mm)

Timing belt tensioner

Tensioner rod extended length*	
2001 through 2006 models	0.24 to 0.32 inch (6.1 to 8.1 mm)
2006.5 and later models	0.20 to 0.28 inch (5 to 7 mm)

*** Note: Turn the crankshaft two revolutions, then wait five minutes before measuring the tensioner rod.**

Torque specifications

➡ **Note: One foot-pound (ft-lb) of torque is equivalent to 12 inch-pounds (in-lbs) of torque. Torque values below approximately 15 ft-lbs are expressed in inch-pounds, since most foot-pound torque wrenches are not accurate at these smaller values.**

➡ **Note: 2006 and 2006.5 models will both have a "6" in the tenth position of the VIN. To distinguish a 2006 model from a 2006.5 model, refer to the 8th position of the VIN (the engine code): A 2006 model will have an "8," while a 2006.5 will have a "4."**

Torque specifications	Ft-lbs (unless otherwise indicated)	Nm
Crankshaft pulley bolt		
2001 through 2006 models	133 to 140	180 to 190
2006.5 and later models	123 to 130	167 to 176
Camshaft bearing cap bolts		
2001 through 2006 models	120 to 132 in-lbs	14 to 15
2006.5 and later models		
6 X 38 bolts	96 to 108 in-lbs	11 to 12
8 X 38 bolts	16 to 19	21 to 25
Camshaft sprocket bolts	66 to 81	90 to 110
Cylinder head bolts (in sequence - see illustration 11.27)		
Step 1	18	25
Step 2	Tighten an additional 60 degrees	
Step 3	Tighten an additional 45 degrees	
Exhaust manifold nuts		
2001 through 2006 models	18 to 22	25 to 30
2006.5 and later models	21 to 25	29 to 34
Flywheel/driveplate bolts	54 to 56	73 to 76
Intake manifold bolts		
2001 through 2006 models		
Upper manifold	132 to 168 in-lbs	15 to 19
Lower manifold	15	20
2006.5 and later models (bolts and nuts)	14 to 17	19 to 24

Torque specifications	Ft-lbs (unless otherwise indicated)	Nm

➡ **Note: One foot-pound (ft-lb) of torque is equivalent to 12 inch-pounds (in-lbs) of torque. Torque values below approximately 15 ft-lbs are expressed in inch-pounds, since most foot-pound torque wrenches are not accurate at these smaller values.**

➡ **Note: 2006 and 2006.5 models will both have a "6" in the tenth position of the VIN. To distinguish a 2006 model from a 2006.5 model, refer to the 8th position of the VIN (the engine code): A 2006 model will have an "8," while a 2006.5 will have a "4."**

Torque specifications	Ft-lbs (unless otherwise indicated)	Nm
Oil pan bolts		
Upper oil pan		
Bolts 1 through 15 (see illustration 12.22)	14 to 20	19 to 28
Bolts 16 and 17 (see illustration 12.22)	48 to 60 in-lbs	5 to 7
Oil pan-to-transaxle bolts	22 to 31	30 to 42
Lower oil pan bolts (see illustration 12.11)	84 to 108 in-lbs	10 to 12
Oil pressure switch	72 to 108 in-lbs	8 to 12
Oil pump		
Oil pump case bolt	106 to 133 in-lbs	12 to 15
Oil pump cover screw	71 to 106 in-lbs	8 to 12
Oil pump pressure relief valve plug	29 to 36	39 to 49
Oil pump pick-up tube mounting bolts	11 to 16	15 to 22
Timing belt		
Timing belt automatic tensioner fixed bolt	15 to 20	20 to 27
Timing belt automatic tensioner arm bolt	25 to 40	34 to 54
Timing belt idler pulley bolt	36 to 43	49 to 59
Timing belt tensioner pulley bolt	11 to 16	15 to 22
Rear main oil seal retainer mounting bolts	84 to 108 in-lbs	10 to 12
Valve cover bolts	44 to 53 in-lbs	5 to 6

Notes

Notes

2C

GENERAL ENGINE OVERHAUL PROCEDURES

Section

Reference to other Chapters

CHECK ENGINE light on - See Chapter 6

1 General information - engine overhaul

Refer to illustrations 1.1, 1.2, 1.3, 1.4, 1.5 and 1.6

Included in this portion of Chapter 2 are general information and diagnostic testing procedures for determining the overall mechanical condition of your engine.

The information ranges from advice concerning preparation for an overhaul and the purchase of replacement parts and/or components to detailed, step-by-step procedures covering removal and installation.

The following Sections have been written to help you determine whether your engine needs to be overhauled and how to remove and install it once you've determined it needs to be rebuilt. For information concerning in-vehicle engine repair, see Chapter 2A or 2B.

The Specifiations included in this Part are general in nature and include only those necessary for testing the oil pressure, checking the engine compression, and bottom-end torque specifications. Refer to Chapter 2A or 2B for additional Specifications.

It's not always easy to determine when, or if, an engine should be completely overhauled, because a number of factors must be considered.

High mileage is not necessarily an indication that an overhaul is needed, while low mileage doesn't preclude the need for an overhaul. Frequency of servicing is probably the most important consideration. An engine that's had regular and frequent oil and filter changes, as well as other required maintenance, will most likely give many thousands of miles of reliable service. Conversely, a neglected engine may require an overhaul very early in its service life.

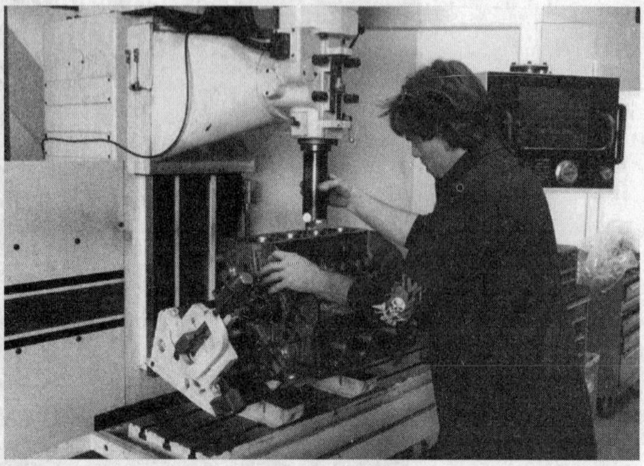

1.1 An engine block being bored. An engine rebuilder will use special machinery to recondition the cylinder bores

Excessive oil consumption is an indication that piston rings, valve seals and/or valve guides are in need of attention. Make sure that oil leaks aren't responsible before deciding that the rings and/or guides are bad. Perform a cylinder compression check to determine the extent of the work required (see Section 3). Also check the vacuum readings under various conditions (see Section 4).

Check the oil pressure with a gauge installed in place of the oil pressure sending unit and compare it to this Chapter's Specifications (see Section 2). If it's extremely low, the bearings and/or oil pump are probably worn out.

Loss of power, rough running, knocking or metallic engine noises, excessive valve train noise and high fuel consumption rates may also point to the need for an overhaul, especially if they're all present at the same time. If a complete tune-up doesn't remedy the situation, major mechanical work is the only solution.

An engine overhaul involves restoring the internal parts to the specifications of a new engine. During an overhaul, the piston rings are replaced and the cylinder walls are reconditioned (rebored and/or honed) (see illustrations 1.1 and 1.2). If a rebore is done by an automotive machine shop, new oversize pistons will also be installed. The main bearings and connecting rod bearings are generally replaced with new ones and, if necessary, the crankshaft may be reground to restore the journals (see illustration 1.3). Generally, the valves are serviced as well, since they're usually in less-than-perfect condition at this point. While the engine is being overhauled, other components, such as the starter and alternator, can be rebuilt as well. The end result should be a like-new engine that will give many trouble-free miles.

➡ Note: Critical cooling system components such as the hoses, drivebelts, thermostat and water pump should be replaced with new parts when an engine is overhauled. The radiator should be checked carefully to ensure that it isn't clogged or leaking (see Chapter 3). If you purchase a rebuilt engine or short block, some

1.2 If the cylinders are bored, the machine shop will normally hone the engine on a machine like this

1.3 A crankshaft having a main bearing journal ground

1.4 A machinist checks for a bent connecting rod, using specialized equipment

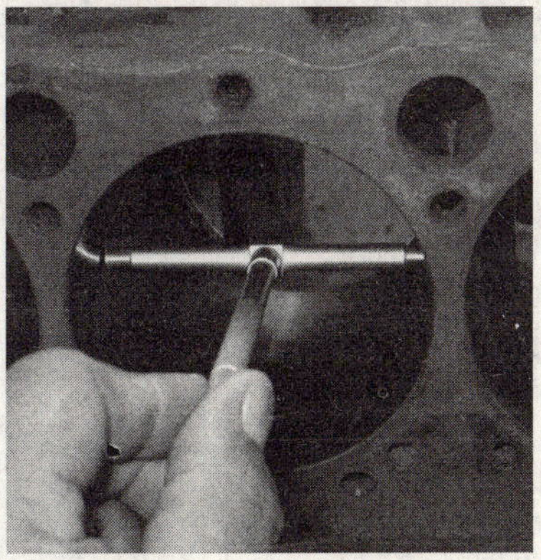

1.5 A bore gauge being used to check the main bearing bore

1.6 Uneven piston wear like this indicates a bent connecting rod

rebuilders will not warranty their engines unless the radiator has been professionally flushed. Also, we don't recommend overhauling the oil pump - always install a new one when an engine is rebuilt.

Overhauling the internal components on today's engines is a difficult and time-consuming task that requires a significant amount of specialty tools and is best left to a professional engine rebuilder (see illustrations 1.4, 1.5 and 1.6). A competent engine rebuilder will handle the inspection of your old parts and offer advice concerning the reconditioning or replacement of the original engine. Never purchase parts or have machine work done on other components until the block has been thoroughly inspected by a professional machine shop. As a general rule, time is the primary cost of an overhaul, especially since the vehicle may be tied up for a minimum of two weeks or more. Be aware that some engine builders only have the capability to rebuild the engine you bring them while other rebuilders have a large inventory of rebuilt exchange engines in stock. Also be aware that many machine shops could take as much as two weeks time to completely rebuild your engine depending on shop workload. Sometimes it makes more sense to simply exchange your engine for another engine that's already rebuilt to save time.

2 Oil pressure check

➧ Refer to illustration 2.3

1 Low engine oil pressure can be a sign of an engine in need of rebuilding. A low oil pressure indicator (often called an "idiot light") is not a test of the oiling system. Such indicators only come on when the oil pressure is dangerously low. Even a factory oil pressure gauge in the instrument panel is only a relative indication, although much better for driver information than a warning light. A better test is with a mechanical (not electrical) oil pressure gauge.

2 Locate the oil pressure sending unit; typically they can be found on the side of the block (front or rear) or near the oil filter housing.

3 Unscrew and remove the oil pressure sending unit, then screw in the hose for your oil pressure gauge (see illustration). If necessary, install an adapter fitting. Use Teflon tape or thread sealant on the threads of the adapter and/or the fitting on the end of your gauge's hose.

4 Check the oil pressure with the engine running (normal operating temperature) at idle, and compare it to this Chapter's Specifications. If it's extremely low, the bearings and/or oil pump are probably worn out.

2.3 The oil pressure can be checked by removing the sending unit and installing a pressure gauge in its place (typical)

3 Cylinder compression check

Refer to illustration 3.6

1 A compression check will tell you what mechanical condition the upper end of your engine (pistons, rings, valves, head gaskets) is in. Specifically, it can tell you if the compression is down due to leakage caused by worn piston rings, defective valves and seats or a blown head gasket.

Note: The engine must be at normal operating temperature and the battery must be fully charged for this check.

2 Begin by cleaning the area around the spark plugs before you remove them (compressed air should be used, if available). The idea is to prevent dirt from getting into the cylinders as the compression check is being done.

3 Disable the fuel pump circuit (see Chapter 4, Section 2).

4 Remove all of the spark plugs from the engine (see Chapter 1). On 2006 and earlier V6 models with a coil pack, disconnect the primary (low voltage) electrical connector(s) from the ignition coil to disable the ignition system. On all other models the ignition system is disabled when the spark plugs are removed, since the coil-over-plug type ignition coils have also been removed.

5 Block the throttle wide open.

6 Install a compression gauge in the spark plug hole (see illustration).

7 Crank the engine over at least seven compression strokes and watch the gauge. The compression should build up quickly in a healthy engine. Low compression on the first stroke, followed by gradually increasing pressure on successive strokes, indicates worn piston rings. A low compression reading on the first stroke, which doesn't build up during successive strokes, indicates leaking valves or a blown head gasket (a cracked head could also be the cause). Deposits on the undersides of the valve heads can also cause low compression. Record the highest gauge reading obtained.

8 Repeat the procedure for the remaining cylinders and compare the results to this Chapter's Specifications.

9 Add some engine oil (about three squirts from a plunger-type oil can) to each cylinder, through the spark plug hole, and repeat the test.

10 If the compression increases after the oil is added, the piston rings are definitely worn. If the compression doesn't increase significantly, the leakage is occurring at the valves or head gasket. Leakage past the valves may be caused by burned valve seats and/or faces or warped, cracked or bent valves.

3.6 Use a compression gauge with a threaded fitting for the spark plug hole, not the type that requires hand pressure to maintain the seal - be sure to open the throttle valve as far as possible during the test

11 If two adjacent cylinders have equally very low compression, there's a strong possibility that the head gasket between them is blown. The appearance of coolant in the combustion chambers or the crankcase would verify this condition.

12 If one cylinder is slightly lower than the others, and the engine has a slightly rough idle, a worn lobe on the camshaft could be the cause.

13 If the compression is unusually high, the combustion chambers are probably coated with carbon deposits. If that's the case, the cylinder head(s) should be removed and decarbonized.

14 If compression is way down or varies greatly between cylinders, it would be a good idea to have a leak-down test performed by an automotive repair shop. This test will pinpoint exactly where the leakage is occurring and how severe it is.

4 Vacuum gauge diagnostic checks

Refer to illustrations 4.4 and 4.6

1 A vacuum gauge provides inexpensive but valuable information about what is going on in the engine. You can check for worn rings or cylinder walls, leaking head or intake manifold gaskets, restricted exhaust, stuck or burned valves, weak valve springs, improper ignition or valve timing and ignition problems.

2 Unfortunately, vacuum gauge readings are easy to misinterpret, so they should be used in conjunction with other tests to confirm the diagnosis.

3 Both the absolute readings and the rate of needle movement are important for accurate interpretation. Most gauges measure vacuum in inches of mercury (in-Hg). The following references to vacuum assume the diagnosis is being performed at sea level. As elevation increases (or atmospheric pressure decreases), the reading will decrease. For every 1,000-foot increase in elevation above approximately 2000 feet, the gauge readings will decrease about one inch of mercury.

4 Connect the vacuum gauge directly to the intake manifold vacuum, not to ported (throttle body) vacuum (see illustration). Be sure no hoses are left disconnected during the test or false readings will result.

5 Before you begin the test, allow the engine to warm up completely. Block the wheels and set the parking brake. With the transmission in Park, start the engine and allow it to run at normal idle speed.

WARNING:

Keep your hands and the vacuum gauge clear of the fans and drivebelts.

6 Read the vacuum gauge; an average, healthy engine should normally produce about 17 to 22 in-Hg with a fairly steady needle (see illustration). Refer to the following vacuum gauge readings and what they indicate about the engine's condition:

7 A low steady reading usually indicates a leaking gasket between the intake manifold and cylinder head(s) or throttle body, a leaky vac-

uum hose, late ignition timing or incorrect camshaft timing. Check ignition timing with a timing light and eliminate all other possible causes, utilizing the tests provided in this Chapter before you remove the timing belt cover to check the timing marks.

8 If the reading is three to eight inches below normal and it fluctuates at that low reading, suspect an intake manifold gasket leak at an intake port or a faulty fuel injector.

9 If the needle has regular drops of about two-to-four inches at a steady rate, the valves are probably leaking. Perform a compression check or leak-down test to confirm this.

10 An irregular drop or down-flick of the needle can be caused by a sticking valve or an ignition misfire. Perform a compression check or leak-down test and read the spark plugs.

11 A rapid vibration of about four in-Hg variation at idle combined with exhaust smoke indicates worn valve guides. Perform a leak-down test to confirm this. If the rapid vibration occurs with an increase in engine speed, check for a leaking intake manifold gasket or head gasket, weak valve springs, burned valves or ignition misfire.

12 A slight fluctuation, say one inch up and down, may mean ignition problems. Check all the usual tune-up items and, if necessary, run the engine on an ignition analyzer.

13 If there is a large fluctuation, perform a compression or leak-down test to look for a weak or dead cylinder or a blown head gasket.

14 If the needle moves slowly through a wide range, check for a clogged PCV system, incorrect idle fuel mixture, throttle body or intake manifold gasket leaks.

15 Check for a slow return after revving the engine by quickly snapping the throttle open until the engine reaches about 2,500 rpm and let it shut. Normally the reading should drop to near zero, rise above normal idle reading (about 5 in-Hg over) and then return to the previous idle reading. If the vacuum returns slowly and doesn't peak when the throttle is snapped shut, the rings may be worn. If there is a long delay, look for a restricted exhaust system (often the muffler or catalytic converter). An easy way to check this is to temporarily disconnect the exhaust ahead of the suspected part and redo the test.

4.4 A simple vacuum gauge can be handy in diagnosing engine condition and performance. Connect it to an intake manifold vacuum source, not a ported (throttle body) source

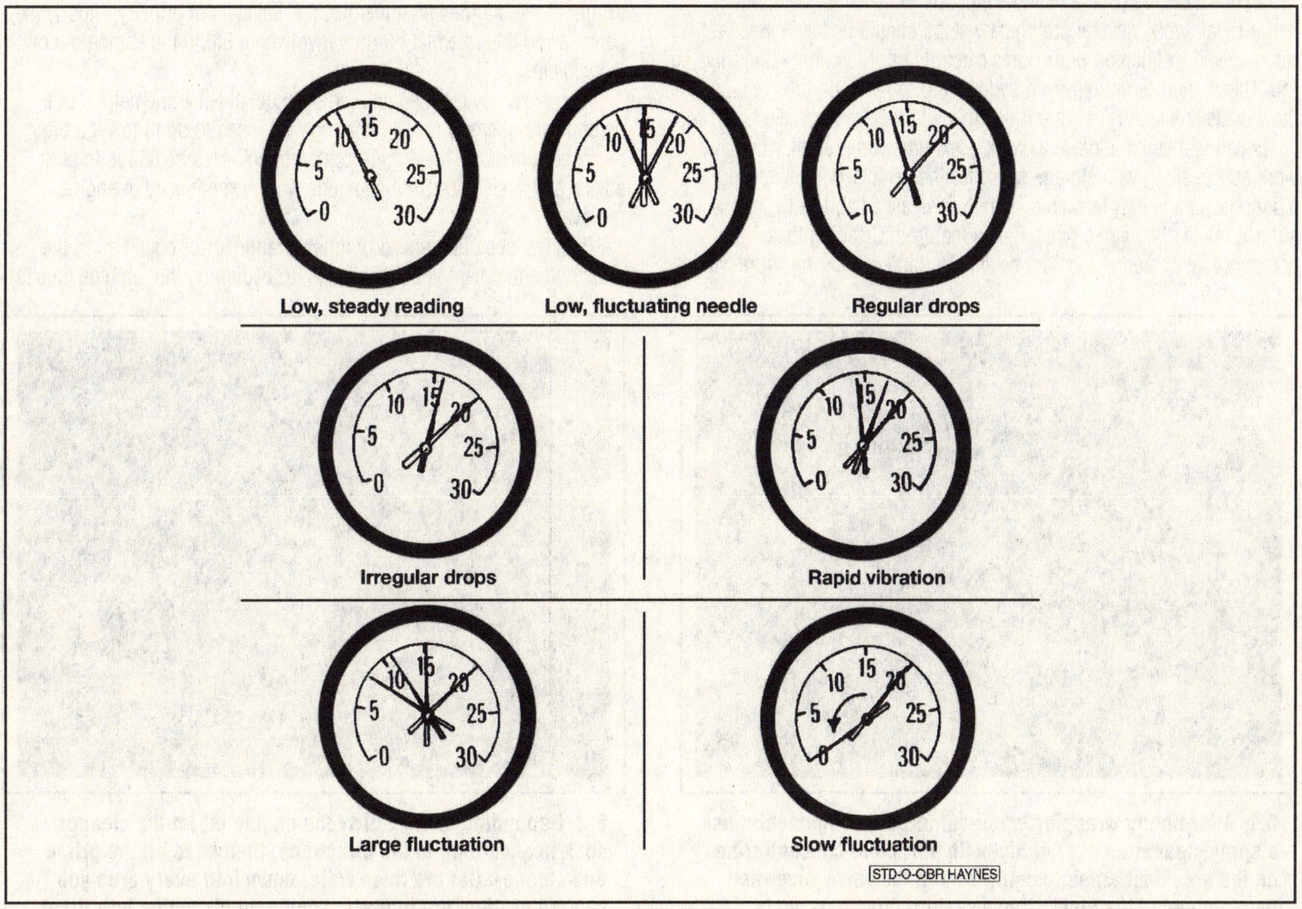

4.6 Typical vacuum gauge readings

5 Engine rebuilding alternatives

The do-it-yourselfer is faced with a number of options when purchasing a rebuilt engine. The major considerations are cost, warranty, parts availability and the time required for the rebuilder to complete the project. The decision to replace the engine block, piston/connecting rod assemblies and crankshaft depends on the final inspection results of your engine. Only then can you make a cost effective decision whether to have your engine overhauled or simply purchase an exchange engine for your vehicle.

Some of the rebuilding alternatives include:

Individual parts - If the inspection procedures reveal that the engine block and most engine components are in reusable condition, purchasing individual parts and having a rebuilder rebuild your engine may be the most economical alternative. The block, crankshaft and piston/connecting rod assemblies should all be inspected carefully by a machine shop first.

Short block - A short block consists of an engine block with a crankshaft and piston/connecting rod assemblies already installed. All new bearings are incorporated and all clearances will be correct. The existing camshafts, valve train components, cylinder head and external parts can be bolted to the short block with little or no machine shop work necessary.

Long block - A long block consists of a short block plus an oil pump, oil pan, cylinder head, valve cover, camshaft and valve train components, timing sprockets and belt or gears and timing cover. All components are installed with new bearings, seals and gaskets incorporated throughout. The installation of manifolds and external parts is all that's necessary.

Low mileage used engines - Some companies now offer low mileage used engines that are a very cost effective way to get your vehicle up and running again. These engines often come from vehicles that have been in totaled in accidents or come from other countries that have a higher vehicle turn over rate. A low mileage used engine also usually has a similar warranty like the newly remanufactured engines.

Give careful thought to which alternative is best for you and discuss the situation with local automotive machine shops, auto parts dealers and experienced rebuilders before ordering or purchasing replacement parts.

6 Engine removal - methods and precautions

Refer to illustrations 6.1, 6.2, 6.3 and 6.4

If you've decided that an engine must be removed for overhaul or major repair work, several preliminary steps should be taken. Read all removal and installation procedures carefully prior to committing this job. These engines are removed by lowering to the floor, then raising the vehicle sufficiently to slide it out; this will require a vehicle hoist.

Locating a suitable place to work is extremely important. Adequate work space, along with storage space for the vehicle, will be needed. If a shop or garage isn't available, at the very least a flat, level, clean work surface made of concrete or asphalt is required. Cleaning the engine compartment and engine before beginning the removal procedure will help keep tools clean and organized (see illustrations 6.1 and 6.2).

Make sure the lifting equipment is rated in excess of the combined weight of the engine and transmission. Safety is of primary importance, considering the potential hazards involved in lifting the engine out of the vehicle.

If you're a novice at engine removal, get at least one helper. One person cannot easily do all the things you need to do to lower a big heavy engine out of the engine compartment. Also helpful is to seek advice and assistance from someone who's experienced in engine removal.

Plan the operation ahead of time. Arrange for or obtain all of the tools and equipment you'll need prior to beginning the job (see illustra-

6.1 After tightly wrapping water-vulnerable components, use a spray cleaner on everything, with particular concentration on the greasiest areas, usually around the valve cover and lower edges of the block. If one section dries out, apply more cleaner

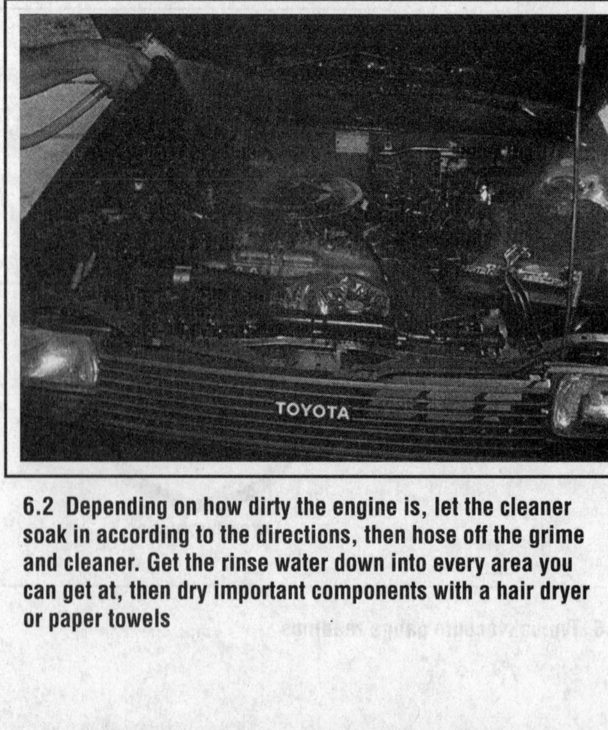

6.2 Depending on how dirty the engine is, let the cleaner soak in according to the directions, then hose off the grime and cleaner. Get the rinse water down into every area you can get at, then dry important components with a hair dryer or paper towels

6.3 Get an engine hoist that's strong enough to easily lift your engine in and out of the engine compartment; an adapter, like the one shown here, can be used to change the angle of the engine as it's being removed or installed

6.4 Get an engine stand sturdy enough to firmly support the engine while you're working on it. Stay away from three-wheeled models - they have a tendency to tip over more easily, so get a four-wheeled unit

tions 6.3 and 6.4). Some of the equipment necessary to perform engine removal and installation safely and with relative ease are a heavy duty floor jack, complete sets of wrenches and sockets as described in the front of this manual, wooden blocks, plenty of rags and cleaning solvent for mopping up spilled oil, coolant and gasoline. If the hoist must be rented, make sure that you arrange for it in advance and have everything disconnected and/or removed before bringing the hoist home. This will save you money and time.

Plan for the vehicle to be out of use for quite a while. A machine shop can do the work that is beyond the scope of the home mechanic. Machine shops often have a busy schedule, so before removing the engine, consult the shop for an estimate of how long it will take to rebuild or repair the components that may need work.

7 Engine - removal and installation

WARNING:

The engine must be completely cool before beginning this procedure.

Note: Engine removal on these vehicles is a difficult job, especially for the do-it-yourself mechanic working at home. Because of the vehicle's design, the engine and transaxle have to be removed as a unit from the bottom of the vehicle, not the top. With a floor jack and jackstands, the vehicle can't be raised high enough or supported safely enough for the engine/transaxle assembly to slide out from underneath. The manufacturer recommends that removal of the engine/transaxle assembly only be performed with the use of a frame-contact type vehicle hoist.

REMOVAL

Refer to illustrations 7.4, 7.18 and 7.21

1 Have the air conditioning system discharged by an authorized shop. Park the vehicle on a frame-contact type vehicle hoist, then engage the arms of the hoist with the jacking points of the vehicle. Raise the hoist arms until they contact the vehicle, but not so much that the wheels come off the ground. Loosen the front wheel lug nuts and the driveaxle/hub nuts.

2 Relieve the fuel system pressure and remove the air cleaner housing and duct (see Chapter 4).

3 Remove the battery and battery tray (see Chapter 5). Remove the air inlet assembly and air filter housing (see Chapter 4).

4 Clearly label and disconnect all vacuum lines, emissions hoses, electrical connectors and ground straps connecting the engine and

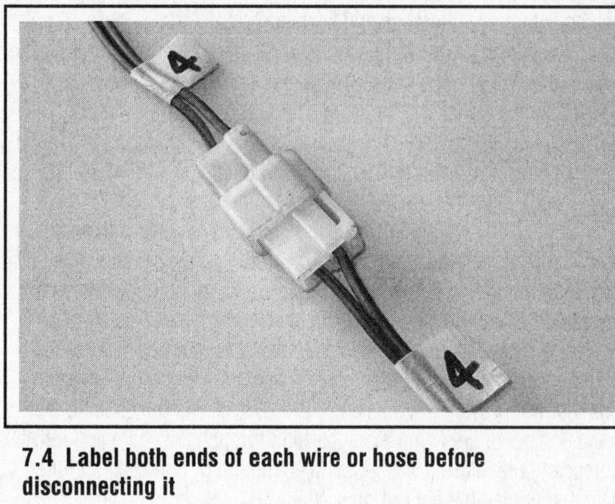

7.4 Label both ends of each wire or hose before disconnecting it

7.18 Location of the engine lifting brackets (four-cylinder engine shown)

transaxle to the vehicle. Masking tape and/or a touch up paint applicator work well for marking items (see illustration). Take instant photos or sketch the locations of components and brackets, if necessary.

5 Remove the lower engine splash shield and drain the coolant, transaxle fluid and the engine oil (see Chapter 1).

6 Disconnect the cooler hoses from the automatic transaxle. Plug the hose ends to prevent leakage and contamination. Disconnect the speedometer cable.

7 Refer to Chapter 3 and remove the engine cooling fan and radiator.

8 Disconnect both heater hoses from the engine.

9 Disconnect the accelerator cable (on models so equipped).

10 Disconnect the fuel line(s) at the fuel rail (see Chapter 4).

11 If you're working on an early model with a manual transaxle, remove the clutch release cylinder and support it out of the way with a piece of wire. Don't disconnect the hose from the release cylinder.

⁂ CAUTION:

Do not depress the clutch pedal while the release cylinder is removed.

12 Detach the shift cable(s) from the transaxle.

13 Disconnect the power steering hoses from the pump. Plug the hose ends to prevent leakage and contamination.

14 Disconnect the steering shaft U-joint after pulling back the plastic cover and making match marks with dabs of paint (see Chapter 10).

15 Raise the vehicle on the hoist and remove the front wheels.

16 Remove the driveaxles (see Chapter 8). On 2006.5 and later models, disconnect the stabilizer bar links from the bar (see Chapter 10).

17 Remove the entire front section of the exhaust system.

18 Support the engine/transaxle assembly from above with an engine hoist. Attach the hoist chain to the lifting brackets (see illustration). If no lifting brackets or hooks are present, lifting hooks may be available from your local auto parts store or dealer parts department. If not, you will have to fasten the chain to some substantial parts of the engine - ones that are strong enough to take the weight, but in locations that will provide good balance. If you're attaching a chain to a stud on the engine, or are using a bolt passing through the chain and into a threaded hole, place a washer between the nut or bolt head and the chain and tighten the nut or bolt securely.

7.21 Subframe mounting bolts

⁂ WARNING:

Do not place any part of your body under the engine/transaxle when it's supported only by a hoist or other lifting device.

Take up the slack until there is slight tension on the hoist. Position the chain on the hoist so it balances the engine and the transaxle level with the vehicle.

➡ **Note: Depending on the design of the engine hoist, it may be helpful to position the hoist from the side of the vehicle, so that when the engine/transaxle assembly is lowered, it will fit between the legs of the hoist.**

➡ **Note: The chain or sling must be long enough to allow the engine hoist to lower the engine/transaxle assembly to the ground, without letting the hoist arm contact the vehicle.**

19 Working in the engine compartment, remove the transaxle mounting bracket. Also remove the engine mount bracket from the right end (passenger's side) of the engine.

20 Recheck to be sure nothing is still connecting the engine or transaxle to the vehicle. Disconnect and label anything still remaining.

21 Support the subframe with a pair of floor jacks (one on each side). Remove the subframe mounting bolts (see illustration). Remove the two lower brackets that attach the engine and transaxle to the subframe. On early models, remove the crossmember stud locknut. Lower the subframe from the vehicle and remove it.

22 Lower the engine and transaxle assembly with the hoist until it is on the floor.

23 Once the engine/transaxle assembly is on the floor, disconnect the engine hoist and raise the vehicle until it clears the engine/transaxle assembly.

24 Reconnect the belt or sling to support the engine and transaxle.

25 Raise the engine/transaxle assembly, then support the engine with blocks of wood or floor jack, while leaving the chain or sling attached. Support the transaxle with another floor jack, preferably one with a transaxle jack head adapter. Be very careful to ensure that the components are supported securely so they won't topple off their supports during disconnection.

26 Remove the transaxle-to-engine bolts and separate the transaxle from the engine.

27 Reconnect the lifting chain to the engine, then raise the engine and attach it to an engine stand.

INSTALLATION

28 Installation is the reverse of removal, noting the following points:

a) *Check the engine/transaxle mounts. If they're worn or damaged, replace them.*
b) *Attach the transaxle to the engine following the procedure described in Chapter 7.*
c) *When installing the subframe, tighten the subframe mounting bolts to the torque listed in the Chapter 10 Specifications.*
d) *Tighten all steering and suspension fasteners to the torque listed in the Chapter 10 Specifications. After lowering the vehicle, tighten the driveaxle/hub nuts to the torque listed in the Chapter 8 Specifications. Tighten the wheel lug nuts to the torque listed in the Chapter 1 Specifications.*
e) *Refill the engine coolant, oil, power steering and transaxle fluids (see Chapter 1).*
f) *Reconnect the battery (see Chapter 5, Section 1).*
g) *Run the engine and check for proper operation and leaks. Shut off the engine and recheck fluid levels.*
h) *Have the air conditioning system recharged by the shop that discharged it.*

8 Engine overhaul - disassembly sequence

1 It's much easier to disassemble the engine if it's mounted on a portable engine stand. A stand can often be rented quite cheaply from an equipment rental yard. Before the engine is mounted on a stand, the driveplate should be removed from the engine.

2 If a stand isn't available, it's possible to remove the external engine components with it blocked up on the floor. Be extra careful not to tip or drop the engine when working without a stand.

3 If you're going to obtain a rebuilt engine, all external components must come off first, to be transferred to the replacement engine. These components include:

Driveplate
Ignition system components
Emissions-related components
Engine mounts and mount brackets
Fuel injection components
Intake/exhaust manifolds
Oil filter
Thermostat and housing assembly
Water pump

➡ **Note: When removing the external components from the engine, pay close attention to details that may be helpful or important during installation. Note the installed position of gaskets, seals, spacers, pins, brackets, washers, bolts and other small items.**

4 If you're going to obtain a short block (assembled engine block, crankshaft, pistons and connecting rods), then you should remove the timing belt, cylinder head, oil pan, oil pump pick-up tube, oil pump and water pump from your engine so that you can turn in your old short block to the rebuilder as a core. See *Engine rebuilding alternatives* for additional information regarding the different possibilities to be considered.

9 Balance shafts (2001 through 2006 four-cylinder models) - removal and installation

➡ **Note: This procedure assumes that the engine has been removed from the vehicle and the driveplate, timing belt and oil pan have also been removed (see Chapter 2A).**

➡ **Note: 2006.5 and later engines use a balance shaft module that incorporates the oil pump. Refer to Chapter 2A, Section 6 for information on removing and installing the oil pump and balance shaft module on these engines.**

REMOVAL

1 The balance shafts are located in the lower section of the engine block. The right balance shaft is driven from the crankshaft by its own small inner belt, which has its own tensioner. The left balance shaft is connected to the rear of the oil pump that is driven by the main timing belt. The shafts counterbalance moving masses within the engine and result in an engine with less vibration.

2 Remove the timing belt and tensioner from the engine block (see Chapter 2A). Remove the inner timing belt and its tensioner.

3 Remove the oil pump (see Chapter 2A).

4 Remove both balance shafts by sliding them straight out the front of the block. Take care to avoid damaging the balance shaft bearings.

CLEANING AND INSPECTION

5 Clean all components with solvent and dry thoroughly. Inspect all components for damage and wear. Pay close attention to the belt, sprocket teeth and the bearing surfaces of the balance shafts. Replace defective parts as necessary.

INSTALLATION

6 Lubricate the balance shafts with clean engine oil. Install the balance shafts into the lower block.

7 The remainder of installation is the reverse of removal. When installing the belts, be sure all of the timing marks are aligned properly (see Chapter 2A).

10 Pistons and connecting rods - removal and installation

REMOVAL

Refer to illustrations 10.1, 10.3 and 10.4

Note: Prior to removing the piston/connecting rod assemblies, remove the cylinder head, oil pan, and the upper (aluminum) oil pan (see Chapter 2A or 2B). Also, on four-cylinder engines, remove the balance shafts or the balance shaft module (see Section 9).

1 Use your fingernail to feel if a ridge has formed at the upper limit of ring travel (about 1/4-inch down from the top of each cylinder). If carbon deposits or cylinder wear have produced ridges, they must be completely removed with a special tool (see illustration). Follow the manufacturer's instructions provided with the tool. Failure to remove the ridges before attempting to remove the piston/connecting rod assemblies may result in piston breakage.

2 After the cylinder ridges have been removed, turn the engine so the crankshaft is facing up. Remove the upper oil pan and baffle, or the main bearing cap bridge, as applicable.

3 Before the pistons and connecting rods are removed, check the connecting rod endplay with feeler gauges. Slide them between the first connecting rod and the crankshaft throw until the play is removed (see illustration). Repeat this procedure for each connecting rod. The endplay is equal to the thickness of the feeler gauge(s). Check with an automotive machine shop for the endplay service limit. If the play exceeds the service limit, new connecting rods will be required. If new rods (or a new crankshaft) are installed, the endplay may fall under the minimum allowable clearance. If it does, the rods will have to be machined to restore it. If necessary, consult an automotive machine shop for advice.

4 Check the connecting rods and caps for identification marks (see illustration). If they aren't plainly marked, use a small center-punch to make the appropriate number of indentations on each rod and cap (1, 2, 3, etc., depending on the cylinder they're associated with).

5 Loosen each of the connecting rod cap bolts or nuts 1/2-turn at a time until they can be removed by hand. Remove the number one connecting rod cap and bearing insert. Don't drop the bearing insert out of the cap.

6 Push the connecting rod/piston assembly out through the top of the engine. Use a wooden or plastic hammer handle to push on the upper bearing surface in the connecting rod. Be careful to avoid scratching the crankshaft bearing journals with the rod bolts.

10.1 Before you try to remove the pistons, use a ridge reamer to remove the raised material (ridge) from the top of the cylinders

Note: On engines that use connecting rod cap nuts, slip a short section of rubber hose over the rod bolts before pushing the piston/rod assemblies out to make sure the crankshaft isn't damaged.

7 If resistance is felt, double-check to make sure that the entire ridge was removed from the cylinder.

8 Repeat the procedure for the remaining cylinders.

9 After removal, reassemble the connecting rod caps and bearing inserts in their respective connecting rods and install the cap bolts or nuts finger tight. Leaving the old bearing inserts in place until reassembly will help prevent the connecting rod bearing surfaces from being accidentally nicked or gouged.

10 The pistons and connecting rods are now ready for inspection and overhaul at an automotive machine shop.

10.3 Checking the connecting rod endplay (side clearance)

10.4 If the connecting rods and caps are not marked, use permanent ink or paint to mark the caps to the rods by cylinder number

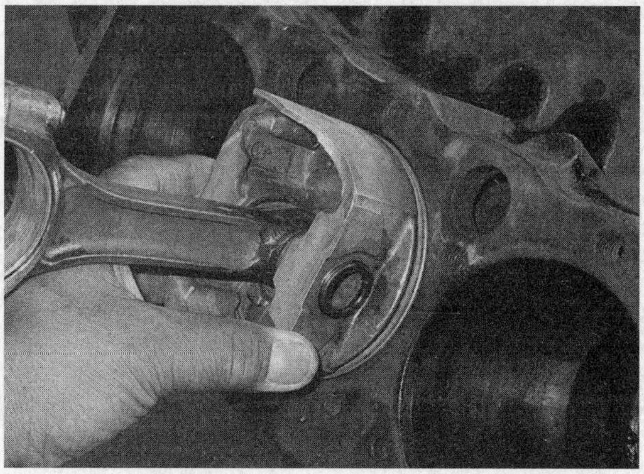

10.13 Install the piston ring into the cylinder, then push it down into position using a piston so the ring will be square in the cylinder

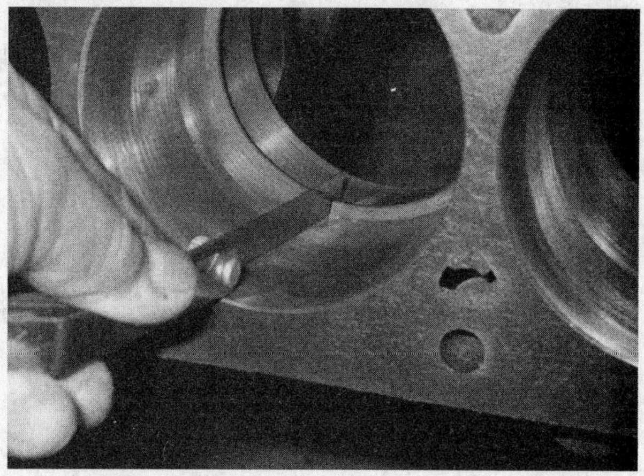

10.14 With the ring square in the cylinder, measure the ring end gap with a feeler gauge

PISTON RING INSTALLATION

➧ Refer to illustrations 10.13, 10.14, 10.15, 10.19a, 10.19b and 10.22

11 Before installing the new piston rings, the ring end gaps must be checked. It's assumed that the piston ring side clearance has been checked and verified correct.

➡ Note: Pistons and rods can only be installed after the crankshaft has been installed (see Section 11).

12 Lay out the piston/connecting rod assemblies and the new ring sets, so the ring sets will be matched with the same piston and cylinder during the end gap measurement and engine assembly.

13 Insert the top (number one) ring into the first cylinder and square it up with the cylinder walls by pushing it in with the top of the piston (see illustration). The ring should be near the bottom of the cylinder, at the lower limit of ring travel.

14 To measure the end gap, slip feeler gauges between the ends of the ring until a gauge equal to the gap width is found (see illustration). The feeler gauge should slide between the ring ends with a slight amount of drag. Check with an automotive machine shop for the correct end gap for your engine. If the gap is larger or smaller than specified, double-check to make sure you have the correct rings before proceeding.

15 If the gap is too small, it must be enlarged or the ring ends may come in contact with each other during engine operation, which can cause serious damage to the engine. The end gap can be increased by filing the ring ends very carefully with a fine file. Mount the file in a vise equipped with soft jaws, slip the ring over the file with the ends contacting the file face and slowly move the ring to remove material from the ends. When performing this operation, file only by pushing the ring from the outside end of the file towards the vise (see illustration).

16 Excess end gap isn't critical unless it's greater than approximately 0.030-inch. Again, double-check to make sure you have the correct ring type.

17 Repeat the procedure for each ring that will be installed in the first cylinder and for each ring in the remaining cylinders. Remember to keep rings, pistons and cylinders matched up.

18 Once the ring end gaps have been checked/corrected, the rings can be installed on the pistons.

19 The oil control ring (lowest one on the piston) is usually installed first. It's composed of three separate components. Slip the spacer/expander into the groove (see illustration). If an anti-rotation tang is

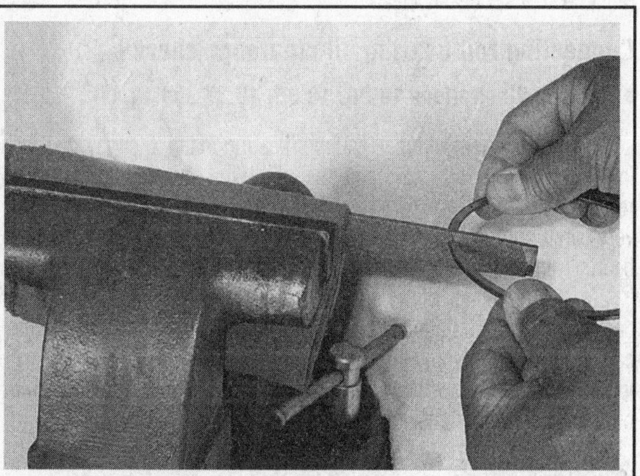

10.15 If the ring end gap is too small, clamp a file in a vise as shown and file the piston ring ends - be sure to file the ends squarely and finish by removing all raised material or burrs with a fine stone

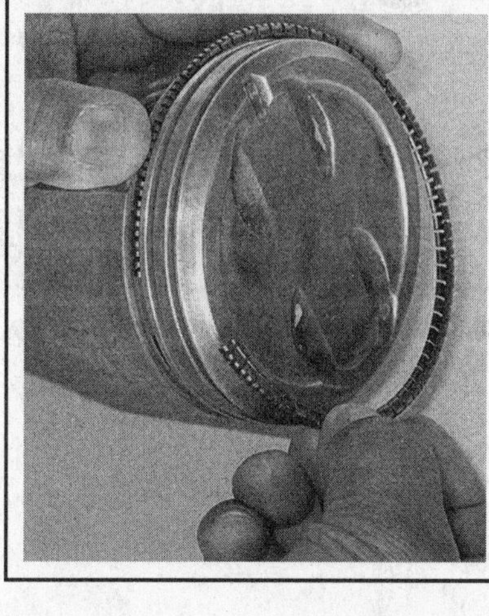

10.19a Installing the spacer/expander in the oil ring groove

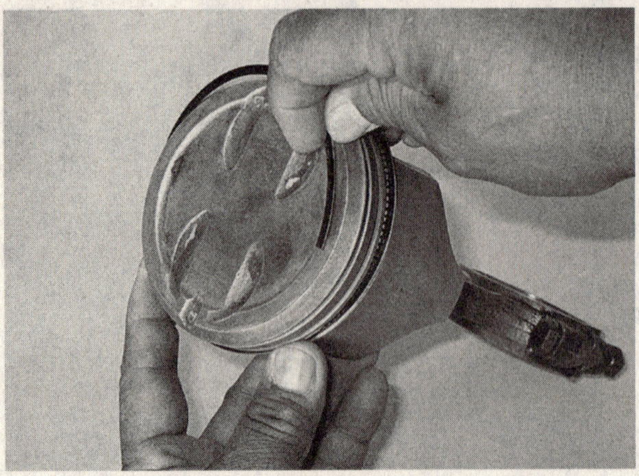

10.19b DO NOT use a piston ring installation tool when installing the oil control side rails

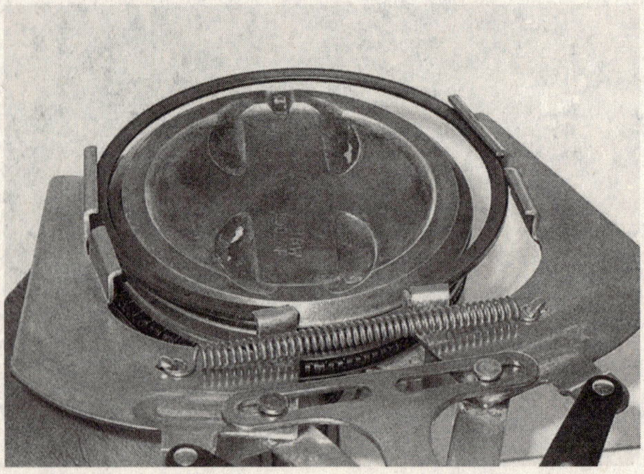

10.22 Use a piston ring installation tool to install the number 2 and the number 1 (top) rings - be sure the directional mark on the piston ring(s) is facing toward the top of the piston

used, make sure it's inserted into the drilled hole in the ring groove. Next, install the upper side rail in the same manner (see illustration). Don't use a piston ring installation tool on the oil ring side rails, as they may be damaged. Instead, place one end of the side rail into the groove between the spacer/expander and the ring land, hold it firmly in place and slide a finger around the piston while pushing the rail into the groove. Finally, install the lower side rail.

20 After the three oil ring components have been installed, check to make sure that both the upper and lower side rails can be rotated smoothly inside the ring grooves.

21 The number two (middle) ring is installed next. It's usually stamped with a mark that must face up, toward the top of the piston. Do not mix up the top and middle rings, as they have different cross-sections.

➡ Note: Always follow the instructions printed on the ring package or box - different manufacturers may require different approaches.

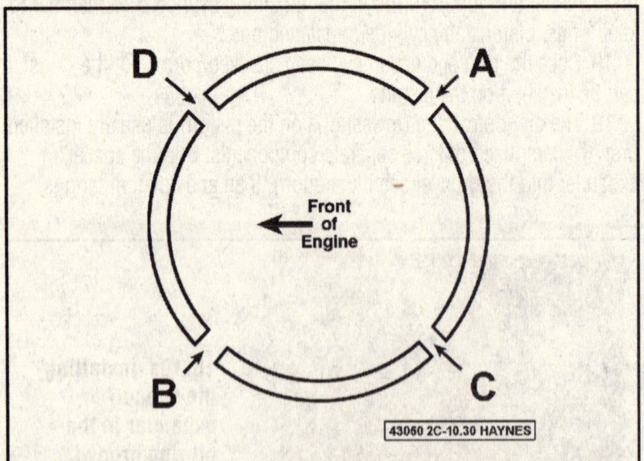

10.30 Position the piston ring end gaps as shown here before installing the piston/connecting rod assemblies into the engine

A Top compression ring gap
B Second compression ring and oil ring spacer gap
C Upper oil ring side rail gap
D Lower oil ring side rail gap

22 Use a piston ring installation tool and make sure the identification mark is facing the top of the piston, then slip the ring into the middle groove on the piston (see illustration). Don't expand the ring any more than necessary to slide it over the piston.

23 Install the number one (top) ring in the same manner. Make sure the mark is facing up. Be careful not to confuse the number one and number two rings.

24 Repeat the procedure for the remaining pistons and rings.

INSTALLATION

25 Before installing the piston/connecting rod assemblies, the cylinder walls must be perfectly clean, the top edge of each cylinder bore must be chamfered, and the crankshaft must be in place.

26 Remove the cap from the end of the number one connecting rod (refer to the marks made during removal - the bearing locating tangs must be together).

27 Remove the original bearing inserts and wipe the bearing surfaces of the connecting rod and cap with a clean, lint-free cloth. They must be kept spotlessly clean.

Connecting rod bearing oil clearance check

➧ Refer to illustrations 10.30, 10.35, 10.37 and 10.41

28 Clean the rear of the new upper bearing insert, then lay it in place in the connecting rod. Make sure the tab on the bearing fits into the recess in the rod. Don't hammer the bearing insert into place and be very careful not to nick or gouge the bearing face. Don't lubricate the bearing at this time.

29 Clean the back of the other bearing insert and install it in the rod cap. Again, make sure the tab on the bearing fits into the recess in the cap, and don't apply any lubricant. It's critically important that the mating surfaces of the bearing and connecting rod are perfectly clean and oil free when they're assembled.

30 Position the piston ring gaps around the piston as shown (see illustration).

31 Lubricate the piston and rings with clean engine oil and attach a piston ring compressor to the piston. Leave the skirt protruding about 1/4-inch to guide the piston into the cylinder. The rings must be compressed until they're flush with the piston.

10.35 Use a plastic or wooden hammer handle to push the piston into the cylinder

➡ **Note: On engines that use connecting rod cap nuts, slip pieces of rubber hose about 6 inches long over each rod bolt. These will guide the connecting rod into position and keep the rod bolts from damaging the crankshaft.**

32 Rotate the crankshaft until the number one connecting rod journal is at BDC (bottom dead center) and apply a liberal coat of engine oil to the cylinder walls.

33 With the mark on top of the piston facing the front (timing belt or chain end) of the engine, gently insert the piston/connecting rod assembly into the number one cylinder bore and rest the bottom edge of the ring compressor on the engine block.

➡ **Note: The connecting rod also has a mark on it that must face the correct direction.**

34 Tap the top edge of the ring compressor to make sure it's contacting the block around its entire circumference.

35 Gently tap on the top of the piston with the end of a hammer handle (see illustration) while guiding the end of the connecting rod into place on the crankshaft journal. The piston rings may try to pop out of the ring compressor just before entering the cylinder bore, so keep some downward pressure on the ring compressor. Work slowly, and if any resistance is felt as the piston enters the cylinder, stop immediately. Find out what's hanging up and fix it before proceeding. Do not, for any reason, force the piston into the cylinder - you might break a ring and/or the piston.

36 Once the piston/connecting rod assembly is installed, the connecting rod bearing oil clearance must be checked before the rod cap is permanently installed.

37 Cut a piece of the appropriate size Plastigage slightly shorter than the width of the connecting rod bearing and lay it in place on the number one connecting rod journal, parallel with the journal axis (see illustration).

38 Clean the connecting rod cap bearing face and install the rod cap. Make sure the mating mark on the cap is on the same side as the mark on the connecting rod.

39 Install the old rod bolts and tighten them to the torque listed in this Chapter's Specifications in two steps.

➡ **Note: Use a thin-wall socket to avoid erroneous torque readings that can result if the socket is wedged between the rod cap and the bolt. If the socket tends to wedge itself between the fastener and the cap, lift up on it slightly until it no longer contacts the cap. DO NOT rotate the crankshaft at any time during this operation.**

10.37 Place Plastigage on each connecting rod bearing journal parallel to the crankshaft centerline

40 Remove the fasteners and detach the rod cap, being very careful not to disturb the Plastigage.

41 Compare the width of the crushed Plastigage to the scale printed on the Plastigage envelope to obtain the oil clearance (see illustration). The connecting rod oil clearance is usually about 0.001 to 0.002 inch. Consult an automotive machine shop for the clearance specified for the rod bearings on your engine.

42 If the clearance is not as specified, the bearing inserts may be the wrong size (which means different ones will be required). Before deciding that different inserts are needed, make sure that no dirt or oil was between the bearing inserts and the connecting rod or cap when the clearance was measured. Also, recheck the journal diameter. If the Plastigage was wider at one end than the other, the journal may be tapered. If the clearance still exceeds the limit specified, the bearing will have to be replaced with an undersize bearing.

⁂ CAUTION:

When installing a new crankshaft always use a standard size bearing.

10.41 Use the scale on the Plastigage package to determine the bearing oil clearance - be sure to measure the widest part of the Plastigage and use the correct scale; it comes with both standard and metric scales

ENGINE BEARING ANALYSIS

Debris

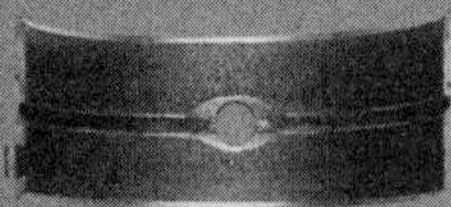

Babbitt bearing embedded with debris from machinings

Microscopic detail of debris

Microscopic detail of gouges

Overplated copper alloy bearing gouged by cast iron debris

Aluminum bearing embedded with glass beads

Microscopic detail of glass beads

Damaged lining caused by dirt left on the bearing back

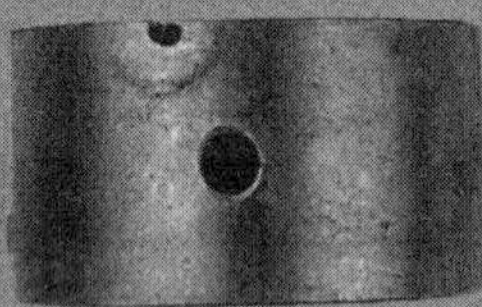

Misassembly

Result of a lower half assembled as an upper - blocking the oil flow

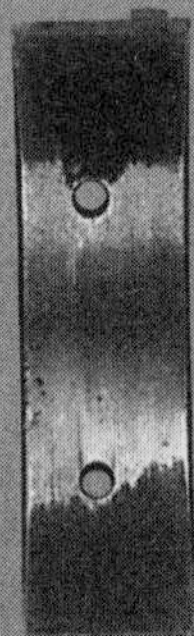

Excessive oil clearance is indicated by a short contact arc

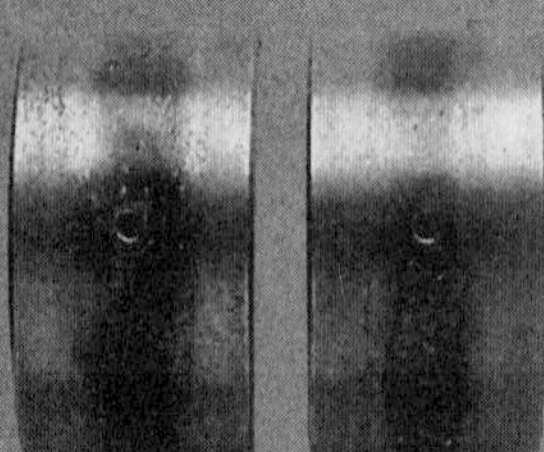

Polished and oil-stained backs are a result of a poor fit in the housing bore

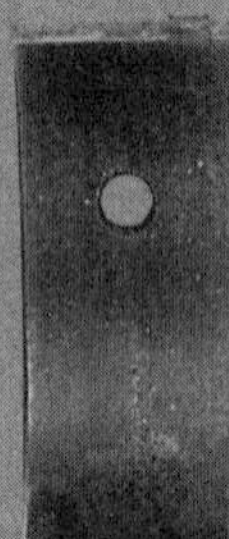

Result of a wrong, reversed, or shifted cap

Overloading

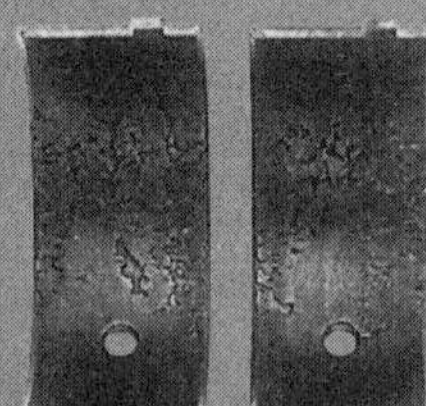

Damage from excessive idling which resulted in an oil film unable to support the load imposed

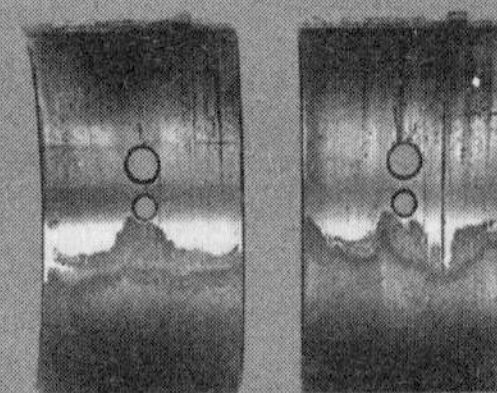

Damaged upper connecting rod bearings caused by engine lugging; the lower main bearings (not shown) were similarly affected

The damage shown in these upper and lower connecting rod bearings was caused by engine operation at a higher-than-rated speed under load

Misalignment

A warped crankshaft caused this pattern of severe wear in the center, diminishing toward the ends

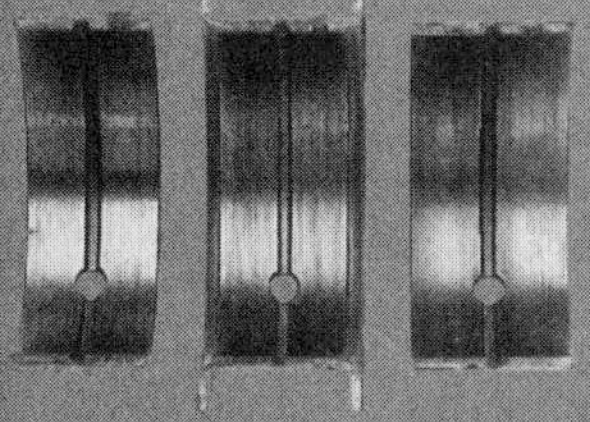

A poorly finished crankshaft caused the equally spaced scoring shown

A tapered housing bore caused the damage along one edge of this pair

A bent connecting rod led to the damage in the "V" pattern

Lubrication

Result of dry start: The bearings on the left, farthest from the oil pump, show more damage

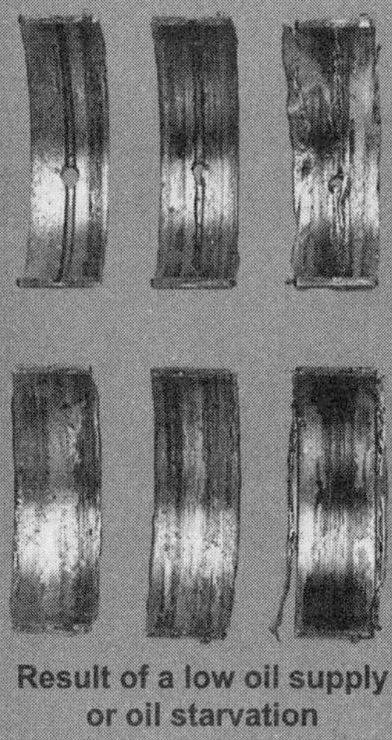

Result of a low oil supply or oil starvation

Severe wear as a result of inadequate oil clearance

Corrosion

Microscopic detail of corrosion

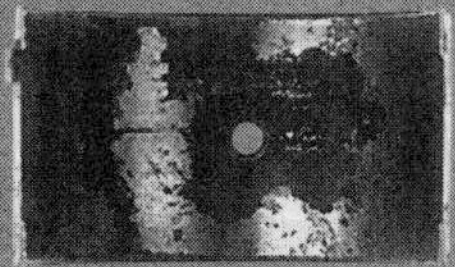

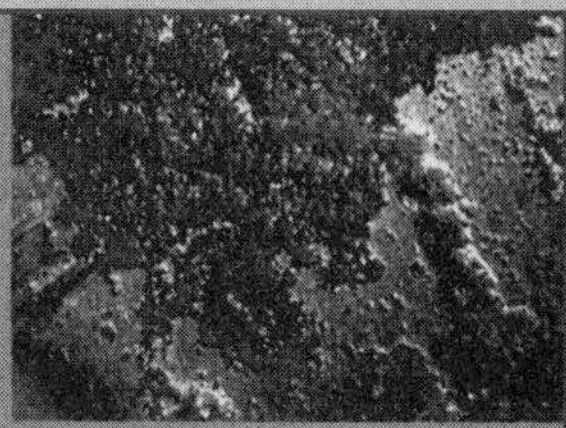

Corrosion is an acid attack on the bearing lining generally caused by inadequate maintenance, extremely hot or cold operation, or inferior oils or fuels

Microscopic detail of cavitation

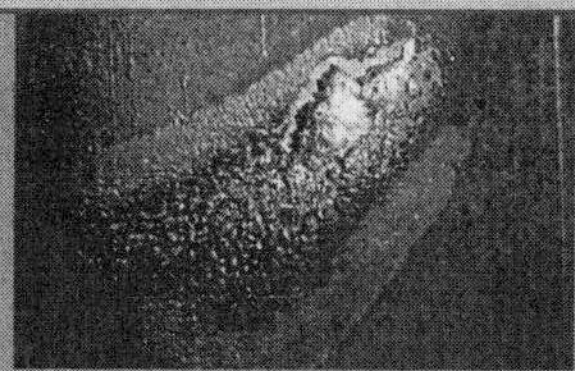

Example of cavitation - a surface erosion caused by pressure changes in the oil film

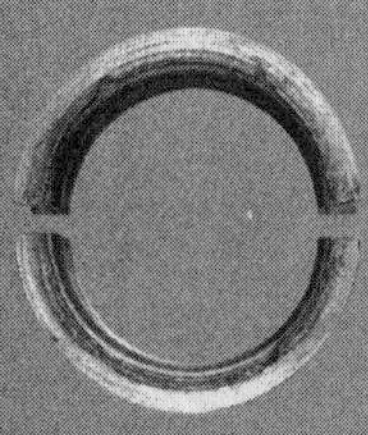

Damage from excessive thrust or insufficient axial clearance

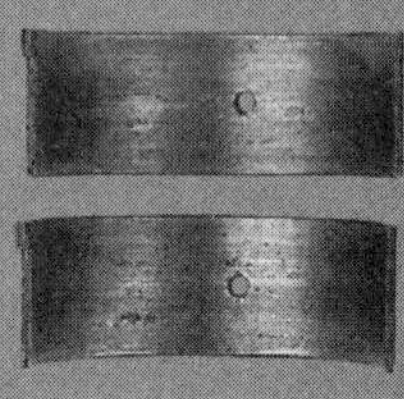

Bearing affected by oil dilution caused by excessive blow-by or a rich mixture

Final installation

43 Carefully scrape all traces of the Plastigage material off the rod journal and/or bearing face. Be very careful not to scratch the bearing - use your fingernail or the edge of a plastic card.

44 Make sure the bearing faces are perfectly clean, then apply a uniform layer of clean moly-base grease or engine assembly lube to both of them. You'll have to push the piston into the cylinder to expose the face of the bearing insert in the connecting rod.

45 Slide the connecting rod back into place on the journal, install the rod cap and NEW bolts, tightening them to the torque listed in this Chapter's Specifications in two steps.

46 Repeat the entire procedure for the remaining pistons/connecting rods.

47 The important points to remember are:

a) Keep the back sides of the bearing inserts and the insides of the connecting rods and caps perfectly clean when assembling them.
b) Make sure you have the correct piston/rod assembly for each cylinder.
c) The mark on the piston must face the front (timing belt end) of the engine.
d) Lubricate the cylinder vwalls liberally with clean oil.
e) Lubricate the bearing faces when installing the rod caps after the oil clearance has been checked.

48 After all the piston/connecting rod assemblies have been correctly installed, rotate the crankshaft a number of times by hand to check for any obvious binding.

49 As a final step, check the connecting rod endplay again. If it was correct before disassembly and the original crankshaft and rods were reinstalled, it should still be correct. If new rods or a new crankshaft were installed, the endplay may be inadequate. If so, the rods will have to be removed and taken to an automotive machine shop for resizing.

11 Crankshaft - removal and installation

REMOVAL

Refer to illustrations 11.1 and 11.3

Note: The crankshaft can be removed only after the engine has been removed from the vehicle. It's assumed that the flywheel/driveplate, crankshaft pulley, timing belt or chain, oil pan, oil pump body, oil filter and piston/connecting rod assemblies have already been removed. The rear main oil seal retainer must be unbolted and separated from the block before proceeding with crankshaft removal.

1 Before the crankshaft is removed, measure the endplay. Mount a dial indicator with the indicator in line with the crankshaft and touching the end of the crankshaft (see illustration).

2 Pry the crankshaft all the way to the rear and zero the dial indicator. Next, pry the crankshaft to the front as far as possible and check the reading on the dial indicator. The distance traveled is the endplay. A typical crankshaft endplay will fall between 0.003 to 0.010-inch. If it's greater than that, check the crankshaft thrust surfaces for wear after it's removed. If no wear is evident, new main bearings should correct the endplay.

3 If a dial indicator isn't available, feeler gauges can be used. Gently pry the crankshaft all the way to the front of the engine. Slip feeler gauges between the crankshaft and the front face of the thrust bearing or washer to determine the clearance (see illustration).

4 Loosen the main bearing cap bolts 1/4-turn at a time each, until they can be removed by hand. On 2.7L V6 engines, loosen the bolts in the reverse order of the tightening sequence (see illustration 11.19).

5 Gently tap the main bearing caps with a soft-face hammer. Pull the main bearing cap straight up and off the cylinder block. Try not to drop the bearing inserts if they come out with the cap.

Note: The 2.7L V6 engine uses a main bearing cap support that must be removed prior to removing the main caps.

6 Carefully lift the crankshaft out of the engine. It may be a good idea to have an assistant available, since the crankshaft is quite heavy

11.1 Checking crankshaft endplay with a dial indicator

11.3 Checking crankshaft endplay with feeler gauges at the thrust bearing journal

11.17 Place the Plastigage onto the crankshaft bearing journal as shown

and awkward to handle. With the bearing inserts in place inside the engine block and main bearing caps, reinstall the main bearing caps onto the engine block and tighten the bolts finger tight. Make sure you install the main bearing cap(s) with the arrow facing the front end of the engine.

INSTALLATION - MAIN BEARING OIL CLEARANCE CHECK

➧ Refer to illustrations 11.17, 11.19 and 11.21

7 Crankshaft installation is the first step in engine reassembly. It's assumed at this point that the engine block and crankshaft have been cleaned, inspected and repaired or reconditioned.

8 Position the engine block with the bottom facing up.

9 Remove the bolts and lift off the main bearing cap(s).

➡ Note: The main bearing cap bolts must be replaced with new ones, but save the old ones for the main bearing oil clearance check. The new bolts will be used for final assembly.

10 If they're still in place, remove the original bearing inserts from the block and from the main bearing caps. Wipe the bearing surfaces of the block and main bearing caps with a clean, lint-free cloth. They must be kept spotlessly clean. This is critical for determining the correct bearing oil clearance.

11 Without mixing them up, clean the backs of the new upper main bearing inserts (with grooves and oil holes) and lay one in each main bearing saddle in the block. Each upper bearing has an oil groove and oil hole in it.

⁂ CAUTION:

The oil holes in the block must line up with the oil holes in the upper bearing inserts.

Install the thrust washers with the grooved side facing out. Clean the back sides of the lower main bearing inserts (without grooves) and lay them in the corresponding caps. Make sure the tab on the bearing insert fits into the recess in the block or main bearing cap.

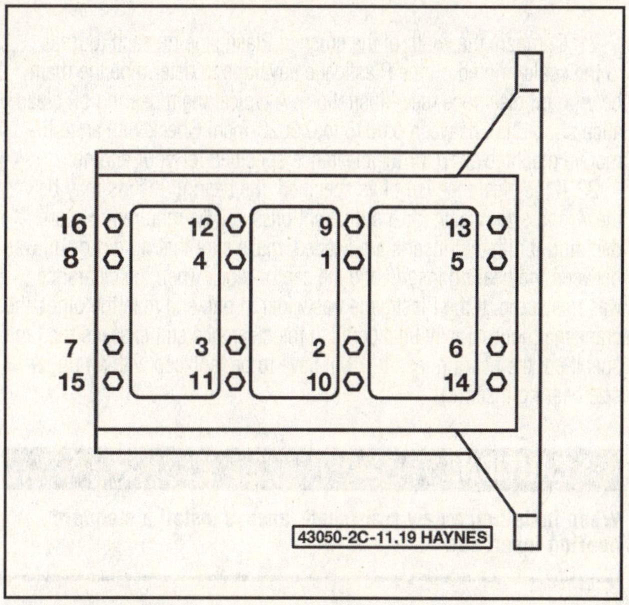

11.19 Main bearing cap bolt tightening sequence - 2.7L V6 engine

⁂ CAUTION:

Do not hammer the bearing insert into place and don't nick or gouge the bearing faces. DO NOT apply any lubrication at this time.

12 Clean the faces of the bearing inserts in the block and the crankshaft main bearing journals with a clean, lint-free cloth.

13 Check or clean the oil holes in the crankshaft, as any dirt here can go only one way - straight through the new bearings.

14 Once you're certain the crankshaft is clean, carefully lay it in position in the cylinder block.

15 Before the crankshaft can be permanently installed, the main bearing oil clearance must be checked.

16 Cut several strips of the appropriate size of Plastigage (they must be slightly shorter than the width of the main bearing journal).

17 Place one piece on each crankshaft main bearing journal, parallel with the journal axis (see illustration).

18 Clean the faces of the bearing inserts in the main bearing caps. Hold the bearing inserts in place and install the caps onto the crankshaft and cylinder block. DO NOT disturb the Plastigage. Make sure you install the main bearing cap with the arrow facing the front of the engine.

19 Apply clean engine oil to the bolt threads prior to installation, then install the bolts finger-tight.

➡ Note: Use the old main bearing cap bolts for the oil clearance check.

If you're working on a 2.7L V6 engine, tighten the bolts in the proper sequence (see illustration). On other models, tighten the bolts evenly. Progressing in two steps, to the torque listed in this Chapter's Specifications. DO NOT rotate the crankshaft at any time during this operation.

20 Remove the bolts in the reverse order of the tightening sequence and carefully lift the main bearing cap straight up and off the block. Do not disturb the Plastigage or rotate the crankshaft. If the main bearing cap is difficult to remove, tap it gently from side-to-side with a soft-face hammer to loosen it.

21 Compare the width of the crushed Plastigage on each journal to the scale printed on the Plastigage envelope to determine the main bearing oil clearance (see illustration). A typical main bearing oil clearance should fall between 0.0015 to 0.0023-inch. Check with an automotive machine shop for the clearance specified for your engine.

22 If the clearance is not as specified, the bearing inserts may be the wrong size (which means different ones will be required). Before deciding if different inserts are needed, make sure that no dirt or oil was between the bearing inserts and the cap or block when the clearance was measured. If the Plastigage was wider at one end than the other, the crankshaft journal may be tapered. If the clearance still exceeds the limit specified, the bearing insert(s) will have to be replaced with an undersize bearing insert(s).

⁂ CAUTION:

When installing a new crankshaft, always install a standard bearing insert set.

23 Carefully scrape all traces of the Plastigage material off the main bearing journals and/or the bearing insert faces. Be sure to remove all residue from the oil holes. Use your fingernail or the edge of a plastic card - don't nick or scratch the bearing faces.

FINAL INSTALLATION

24 Carefully lift the crankshaft out of the cylinder block.

25 Clean the bearing insert faces in the cylinder block, then apply a thin, uniform layer of moly-base grease or engine assembly lube to each of the bearing surfaces. Be sure to coat the thrust faces as well as the journal face of the thrust bearing.

➡ Note: The thrust bearings are installed in the no. 3 main cap/saddle position (counting from the front) on all engines covered by this manual.

26 Make sure the crankshaft journals are clean, then lay the crankshaft back in place in the cylinder block.

27 Clean the bearing insert faces and apply the same lubricant to them.

28 Hold the bearing inserts in place and install the main bearing caps on the crankshaft and cylinder block. Tap the bearing caps into place with a brass punch or a soft-face hammer. On early V6 engines, install the bearing support.

29 Apply clean engine oil to the bolt threads, wipe off any excess oil and install the bolts finger-tight.

11.21 Use the scale on the Plastigage package to determine the bearing oil clearance - be sure to measure the widest part of the Plastigage and use the correct scale; it comes with both standard and metric scales

⁂ CAUTION:

The main bearing cap bolts must be replaced with new ones at this stage.

30 Tighten the main bearing cap bolts, in sequence (see illustration 11.19), to 10 or 12 foot-pounds.

➡ Note: If there is no specific sequence given for your engine, start with the center bolts and work back-and-forth toward each end.

31 Push the crankshaft forward using a screwdriver or prybar to seat the thrust bearing. Once the crankshaft is pushed fully forward to seat the thrust bearing, leave the screwdriver in position so that force stays on the crankshaft until after all main bearing cap bolts have been tightened.

32 Tighten the main bearing cap bolts in two steps (and in sequence on 2.7L V6 engines - see illustration 11.19) and to the torque and angle listed in this Chapter's Specifications.

33 Recheck crankshaft endplay with a feeler gauge or a dial indicator. The endplay should be correct if the crankshaft thrust faces aren't worn or damaged and if new bearings have been installed.

34 Rotate the crankshaft a number of times by hand to check for any obvious binding. It should rotate with a running torque of 50 in-lbs or less. If the running torque is too high, correct the problem at this time.

35 Install a new rear main oil seal (see Chapter 2A or 2B).

12 Engine overhaul - reassembly sequence

1 Before beginning engine reassembly, make sure you have all the necessary new parts, gaskets and seals as well as the following items on hand:

Common hand tools
A 1/2-inch drive torque wrench
New engine oil
Gasket sealant
Thread locking compound

2 If you obtained a short block, it will be necessary to install the cylinder head, the oil pump and pick-up tube, the oil pan, the water pump, the timing belt and timing cover, and the valve cover (see Chapter 2A or 2B). In order to save time and avoid problems, the external components must be installed in the following general order:

Thermostat and housing cover
Water pump
Intake and exhaust manifolds
Fuel injection components
Emission control components
Spark plugs
Ignition coils
Oil filter
Engine mounts and mount brackets
Flywheel and clutch (manual transaxle)
Driveplate (automatic transaxle)

13 Initial start-up and break-in after overhaul

✲✲ WARNING:

Have a fire extinguisher handy when starting the engine for the first time.

1 Once the engine has been installed in the vehicle, double-check the engine oil and coolant levels.

2 With the spark plugs out of the engine and the ignition system and fuel pump disabled (see Section 3 to disable the ignition system and Chapter 4, Section 2 to disable the fuel pump), crank the engine until oil pressure registers on the gauge or the light goes out.

3 Install the spark plugs and ignition coils and restore the fuel pump and ignition functions.

4 Start the engine. It may take a few moments for the fuel system to build up pressure, but the engine should start without a great deal of effort.

5 After the engine starts, it should be allowed to warm up to normal operating temperature. While the engine is warming up, make a thorough check for fuel, oil and coolant leaks.

6 Shut the engine off and recheck the engine oil and coolant levels.

7 Drive the vehicle to an area with minimum traffic, accelerate from 30 to 50 mph, and then allow the vehicle to slow to 30 mph with the throttle closed. Repeat the procedure 10 or 12 times. This will load the piston rings and cause them to seat properly against the cylinder walls. Check again for oil and coolant leaks.

8 Drive the vehicle gently for the first 500 miles (no sustained high speeds) and keep a constant check on the oil level. It is not unusual for an engine to use oil during the break-in period.

9 At approximately 500 to 600 miles, change the oil and filter.

10 For the next few hundred miles, drive the vehicle normally. Do not pamper it or abuse it.

11 After 2,000 miles, change the oil and filter again and consider the engine broken in.

COMMON ENGINE OVERHAUL TERMS

B

Backlash - The amount of play between two parts. Usually refers to how much one gear can be moved back and forth without moving the gear with which it's meshed.

Bearing Caps - The caps held in place by nuts or bolts which, in turn, hold the bearing surface. This space is for lubricating oil to enter.

Bearing clearance - The amount of space left between shaft and bearing surface. This space is for lubricating oil to enter.

Bearing crush - The additional height which is purposely manufactured into each bearing half to ensure complete contact of the bearing back with the housing bore when the engine is assembled.

Bearing knock - The noise created by movement of a part in a loose or worn bearing.

Blueprinting - Dismantling an engine and reassembling it to EXACT specifications.

Bore - An engine cylinder, or any cylindrical hole; also used to describe the process of enlarging or accurately refinishing a hole with a cutting tool, as to bore an engine cylinder. The bore size is the diameter of the hole.

Boring - Renewing the cylinders by cutting them out to a specified size. A boring bar is used to make the cut.

Bottom end - A term which refers collectively to the engine block, crankshaft, main bearings and the big ends of the connecting rods.

Break-in - The period of operation between installation of new or rebuilt parts and time in which parts are worn to the correct fit. Driving at reduced and varying speed for a specified mileage to permit parts to wear to the correct fit.

Bushing - A one-piece sleeve placed in a bore to serve as a bearing surface for shaft, piston pin, etc. Usually replaceable.

C

Camshaft - The shaft in the engine, on which a series of lobes are located for operating the valve mechanisms. The camshaft is driven by gears or sprockets and a timing chain. Usually referred to simply as the cam.

Carbon - Hard, or soft, black deposits found in combustion chamber, on plugs, under rings, on and under valve heads.

Cast iron - An alloy of iron and more than two percent carbon, used for engine blocks and heads because it's relatively inexpensive and easy to mold into complex shapes.

Chamfer - To bevel across (or a bevel on) the sharp edge of an object.

Chase - To repair damaged threads with a tap or die.

Combustion chamber - The space between the piston and the cylinder head, with the piston at top dead center, in which air-fuel mixture is burned.

Compression ratio - The relationship between cylinder volume (clearance volume) when the piston is at top dead center and cylinder volume when the piston is at bottom dead center.

Connecting rod - The rod that connects the crank on the crankshaft with the piston. Sometimes called a con rod.

Connecting rod cap - The part of the connecting rod assembly that attaches the rod to the crankpin.

Core plug - Soft metal plug used to plug the casting holes for the coolant passages in the block.

Crankcase - The lower part of the engine in which the crankshaft rotates; includes the lower section of the cylinder block and the oil pan.

Crank kit - A reground or reconditioned crankshaft and new main and connecting rod bearings.

Crankpin - The part of a crankshaft to which a connecting rod is attached.

Crankshaft - The main rotating member, or shaft, running the length of the crankcase, with offset throws to which the connecting rods are attached; changes the reciprocating motion of the pistons into rotating motion.

Cylinder sleeve - A replaceable sleeve, or liner, pressed into the cylinder block to form the cylinder bore.

D

Deburring - Removing the burrs (rough edges or areas) from a bearing.

Deglazer - A tool, rotated by an electric motor, used to remove glaze from cylinder walls so a new set of rings will seat.

E

Endplay - The amount of lengthwise movement between two parts. As applied to a crankshaft, the distance that the crankshaft can move forward and back in the cylinder block.

F

Face - A machinist's term that refers to removing metal from the end of a shaft or the face of a larger part, such as a flywheel.

Fatigue - A breakdown of material through a large number of loading and unloading cycles. The first signs are cracks followed shortly by breaks.

Feeler gauge - A thin strip of hardened steel, ground to an exact thickness, used to check clearances between parts.

Free height - The unloaded length or height of a spring.

Freeplay - The looseness in a linkage, or an assembly of parts, between the initial application of force and actual movement. Usually perceived as slop or slight delay.

Freeze plug - See Core plug.

G

Gallery - A large passage in the block that forms a reservoir for engine oil pressure.

Glaze - The very smooth, glassy finish that develops on cylinder walls while an engine is in service.

H

Heli-Coil - A rethreading device used when threads are worn or damaged. The device is installed in a retapped hole to reduce the thread size to the original size.

I

Installed height - The spring's measured length or height, as installed on the cylinder head. Installed height is measured from the spring seat to the underside of the spring retainer.

J

Journal - The surface of a rotating shaft which turns in a bearing.

K

Keeper - The split lock that holds the valve spring retainer in position on the valve stem.

Key - A small piece of metal inserted into matching grooves machined into two parts fitted together - such as a gear pressed onto a shaft - which prevents slippage between the two parts.

Knock - The heavy metallic engine sound, produced in the combustion chamber as a result of abnormal combustion - usually detonation. Knock is usually caused by a loose or worn bearing. Also referred to as detonation, pinging and spark knock. Connecting rod or main bearing knocks are created by too much oil clearance or insufficient lubrication.

L

Lands - The portions of metal between the piston ring grooves.

Lapping the valves - Grinding a valve face and its seat together with lapping compound.

Lash - The amount of free motion in a gear train, between gears, or in a mechanical assembly, that occurs before movement can begin. Usually refers to the lash in a valve train.

Lifter - The part that rides against the cam to transfer motion to the rest of the valve train.

M

Machining - The process of using a machine to remove metal from a metal part.

Main bearings - The plain, or babbit, bearings that support the crankshaft.

Main bearing caps - The cast iron caps, bolted to the bottom of the block, that support the main bearings.

O

O.D. - Outside diameter.

Oil gallery - A pipe or drilled passageway in the engine used to carry engine oil from one area to another.

Oil ring - The lower ring, or rings, of a piston; designed to prevent excessive amounts of oil from working up the cylinder walls and into the combustion chamber. Also called an oil-control ring.

Oil seal - A seal which keeps oil from leaking out of a compartment. Usually refers to a dynamic seal around a rotating shaft or other moving part.

O-ring - A type of sealing ring made of a special rubberlike material; in use, the O-ring is compressed into a groove to provide the sealing action.

Overhaul - To completely disassemble a unit, clean and inspect all parts, reassemble it with the original or new parts and make all adjustments necessary for proper operation.

P

Pilot bearing - A small bearing installed in the center of the flywheel (or the rear end of the crankshaft) to support the front end of the input shaft of the transmission.

Pip mark - A little dot or indentation which indicates the top side of a compression ring.

Piston - The cylindrical part, attached to the connecting rod, that moves up and down in the cylinder as the crankshaft rotates. When the fuel charge is fired, the piston transfers the force of the explosion to the connecting rod, then to the crankshaft.

Piston pin (or wrist pin) - The cylindrical and usually hollow steel pin that passes through the piston. The piston pin fastens the piston to the upper end of the connecting rod.

Piston ring - The split ring fitted to the groove in a piston. The ring contacts the sides of the ring groove and also rubs against the cylinder wall, thus sealing space between piston and wall. There are two types of rings: Compression rings seal the compression pressure in the combustion chamber; oil rings scrape excessive oil off the cylinder wall.

Piston ring groove - The slots or grooves cut in piston heads to hold piston rings in position.

Piston skirt - The portion of the piston below the rings and the piston pin hole.

Plastigage - A thin strip of plastic thread, available in different sizes, used for measuring clearances. For example, a strip of plastigage is laid across a bearing journal and mashed as parts are assembled. Then parts are disassembled and the width of the strip is measured to determine clearance between journal and bearing. Commonly used to measure crankshaft main-bearing and connecting rod bearing clearances.

Press-fit - A tight fit between two parts that requires pressure to force the parts together. Also referred to as drive, or force, fit.

Prussian blue - A blue pigment; in solution, useful in determining the area of contact between two surfaces. Prussian blue is commonly used to determine the width and location of the contact area between the valve face and the valve seat.

R

Race (bearing) - The inner or outer ring that provides a contact surface for balls or rollers in bearing.

Ream - To size, enlarge or smooth a hole by using a round cutting tool with fluted edges.

Ring job - The process of reconditioning the cylinders and installing new rings.

Runout - Wobble. The amount a shaft rotates out-of-true.

S

Saddle - The upper main bearing seat.

Scored - Scratched or grooved, as a cylinder wall may be scored by abrasive particles moved up and down by the piston rings.

Scuffing - A type of wear in which there's a transfer of material between parts moving against each other; shows up as pits or grooves in the mating surfaces.

Seat - The surface upon which another part rests or seats. For example, the valve seat is the matched surface upon which the valve face rests. Also used to refer to wearing into a good fit; for example, piston rings seat after a few miles of driving.

Short block - An engine block complete with crankshaft and piston and, usually, camshaft assemblies.

Static balance - The balance of an object while it's stationary.

Step - The wear on the lower portion of a ring land caused by excessive side and back-clearance. The height of the step indicates the ring's extra side clearance and the length of the step projecting from the back wall of the groove represents the ring's back clearance.

Stroke - The distance the piston moves when traveling from top dead center to bottom dead center, or from bottom dead center to top dead center.

Stud - A metal rod with threads on both ends.

T

Tang - A lip on the end of a plain bearing used to align the bearing during assembly.

Tap - To cut threads in a hole. Also refers to the fluted tool used to cut threads.

Taper - A gradual reduction in the width of a shaft or hole; in an engine cylinder, taper usually takes the form of uneven wear, more pronounced at the top than at the bottom.

Throws - The offset portions of the crankshaft to which the connecting rods are affixed.

Thrust bearing - The main bearing that has thrust faces to prevent excessive endplay, or forward and backward movement of the crankshaft.

Thrust washer - A bronze or hardened steel washer placed between two moving parts. The washer prevents longitudinal movement and provides a bearing surface for thrust surfaces of parts.

Tolerance - The amount of variation permitted from an exact size of measurement. Actual amount from smallest acceptable dimension to largest acceptable dimension.

U

Umbrella - An oil deflector placed near the valve tip to throw oil from the valve stem area.

Undercut - A machined groove below the normal surface.

Undersize bearings - Smaller diameter bearings used with re-ground crankshaft journals.

V

Valve grinding - Refacing a valve in a valve-refacing machine.

Valve train - The valve-operating mechanism of an engine; includes all components from the camshaft to the valve.

Vibration damper - A cylindrical weight attached to the front of the crankshaft to minimize torsional vibration (the twist-untwist actions of the crankshaft caused by the cylinder firing impulses). Also called a harmonic balancer.

W

Water jacket - The spaces around the cylinders, between the inner and outer shells of the cylinder block or head, through which coolant circulates.

Web - A supporting structure across a cavity..

Woodruff key - A key with a radiused backside (viewed from the side).

Specifications

General

Displacement	
Four-cylinder engines	144 cubic inches (2,351 cc)
V6 engines	
2001 models	152 cubic inches (2,493 cc)
2002 and later models	162 cubic inches (2,656 cc)
Minimum compression pressure (all models)	140 psi
Variation between cylinders (all models)	14 psi
Minimum oil pressure, engine warm	
Four-cylinder engines	
2001 through 2007 models	11.6 psi (80 kPa) at idle
2008 and 2009 models	24 psi (166 kPa) at 1000 rpm
2010 and later models	21.3 psi (147 kPa) at 1000 rpm
V6 engines	
2001 through 2006 models	7.3 psi (50 kPa) at idle
2006.5 and later models	18.77 psi (130 kPa) at 1000 rpm
Connecting rod side clearance (all engines)	
Standard	0.004 to 0.010 inch (0.10 to 0.25 mm)
Limit	0.016 inch (0.4 mm)

Torque specifications

➡ Note: One foot-pound (ft-lb) of torque is equivalent to 12 inch-pounds (in-lbs) of torque. Torque values below approximately 15 foot-pounds are expressed in inch-pounds, because most foot-pound torque wrenches are not accurate at these smaller values.

Torque specifications	Ft-lbs (unless otherwise indicated)	Nm
Connecting rod bearing cap bolts (all engines)		
Step 1	15	20
Step 2	Tighten an additional 90-degrees	
Main bearing cap bolts*		
Four-cylinder engines		
2001 through 2006 models		
Step 1	18	25
Step 2	Tighten an additional 90-degrees	
2006.5 and later models		
Step 1	22	30
Step 2	Tighten an additional 120-degrees	
V6 engines		
2001 and 2002 models		
Step 1	18	25
Step 2	Tighten an additional 90-degrees	
2003 through 2006 models		
M10 bolts		
Step 1	24	33
Step 2	Tighten an additional 90-degrees	
M7 bolts		
Step 1	15	19
Step 2	Tighten an additional 90-degrees	

*** Always replace the main bearing cap bolts with new ones at final assembly.**

Torque specifications	Ft-lbs (unless otherwise indicated)	Nm

➡ Note: One foot-pound (ft-lb) of torque is equivalent to 12 inch-pounds (in-lbs) of torque. Torque values below approximately 15 foot-pounds are expressed in inch-pounds, because most foot-pound torque wrenches are not accurate at these smaller values.

Main bearing cap bolts (continued)*		
2006.5 and later models		
M10 bolts		
Step 1	22	30
Step 2	Tighten an additional 90-degrees	
M8 bolts		
Step 1	132 in-lbs	15
Step 2	Tighten an additional 90-degrees	

*** Always replace the main bearing cap bolts with new ones at final assembly.**

Notes

3

COOLING, HEATING AND AIR CONDITIONING SYSTEMS

Section

1 General information

ENGINE COOLING SYSTEM

➧ **Refer to illustrations 1.1 and 1.2**

All vehicles covered by this manual employ a pressurized engine cooling system with thermostatically controlled coolant circulation (see illustration). An impeller-type water pump mounted on the front of the block pumps coolant through the engine. The coolant flows around each cylinder and toward the rear of the engine. Cast-in coolant passages direct coolant around the intake and exhaust ports, near the spark plug areas and over the exhaust valve guides.

A wax pellet-type thermostat is located in the thermostat housing (see illustration). During warm up, the closed thermostat prevents coolant from circulating through the radiator. When the engine reaches normal operating temperature, the thermostat opens and allows hot coolant to travel through the radiator, where it is cooled before returning to the engine.

The radiator is sealed by a pressure cap. This raises the boiling point of the coolant, and this higher boiling point increases the efficiency of the radiator. If the system pressure exceeds the cap's pressure relief value, then the excess pressure in the system forces the spring-loaded valve in the cap off its seat and allows the coolant to escape through the overflow tube and into the coolant reservoir. When the system cools, the coolant is drawn from the reservoir back into the radiator. This type of system is known as a closed design because coolant that escapes past the pressure cap is saved and reused.

The coolant reservoir serves as both the point at which fresh coolant is added to the cooling system to maintain the proper fluid level and as a holding tank for heated coolant.

1.1 Typical cooling system component locations

1 Coolant reservoir
2 Radiator cap
3 Upper radiator hose
4 Cooling fans
5 Radiator
6 Fuse and relay box

HEATING SYSTEM

The heating system consists of a blower fan and heater core located within the heater box, the inlet and outlet hoses connecting the heater core to the engine cooling system and the heater/air conditioning control head on the dashboard. Hot engine coolant is circulated through the heater core. When the heater mode is activated, a flap door opens to expose the heater box to the passenger compartment. A fan switch on the control head activates the blower motor, which forces air through the core, heating the air.

AIR CONDITIONING SYSTEM

The air conditioning system consists of a condenser mounted in front of the radiator, an evaporator mounted adjacent to the heater core under the dashboard, a compressor mounted on the engine, a receiver-drier which contains a high pressure relief valve and the plumbing connecting all of the above.

A blower fan forces the warmer air of the passenger compartment through the evaporator core (sort of a radiator-in-reverse), transferring the heat from the air to the refrigerant. The liquid refrigerant boils off into low-pressure vapor, taking the heat with it when it leaves the evaporator. The compressor keeps refrigerant circulating through the system, pumping the warmed coolant through the condenser where it is cooled and then circulated back to the evaporator.

Some models are equipped with an optional automatic temperature control air conditioning system. With this system, the driver selects the desired interior temperature with the controls, similar to setting the temperature on a home heating/cooling thermostat, and the system automatically adds the right blend of cool or warm air to maintain this temperature. The system has sensors that detect both the interior and outside temperature.

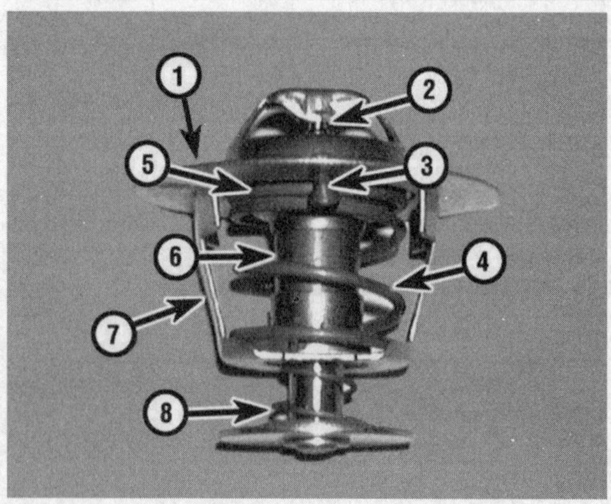

1.2 A typical thermostat

1 Flange
2 Piston
3 Jiggle valve
4 Main coil spring
5 Valve seat
6 Valve
7 Frame
8 Secondary coil spring

2 Antifreeze - general information

Refer to illustration 2.4

WARNING:

Do not allow antifreeze to come in contact with your skin or painted surfaces of the vehicle. Rinse off spills immediately with plenty of water. Antifreeze is highly toxic if ingested. Never leave antifreeze lying around in an open container or in puddles on the floor; children and pets are attracted by its sweet smell and may drink it. Check with local authorities on disposing of used antifreeze. Many communities have collection centers that will see that antifreeze is disposed of safely. Never dump used antifreeze on the ground or into drains.

Note: Non-toxic coolant is available at local auto parts stores. Although the coolant is non-toxic when fresh, proper disposal of used coolant is still required.

The cooling system should be filled with a water/ethylene-glycol based antifreeze solution, which will prevent freezing down to at least -20 degrees F, or lower if local climate requires it. It also provides protection against corrosion and increases the coolant boiling point.

The cooling system should be drained, flushed and refilled at least every other year (see Chapter 1). The use of antifreeze solutions for periods of longer than two years is likely to cause damage and encourage the formation of rust and scale in the system. If your tap water is hard (it contains a lot of dissolved minerals), use distilled water with the antifreeze.

Before adding antifreeze to the system, check all hose connections, because antifreeze tends to leak through very minute openings. Engines do not normally consume coolant. Therefore, if the level goes down, find the cause and correct it.

2.4 An inexpensive hydrometer can be used to test the condition of your coolant

The exact mixture of antifreeze-to-water that you should use depends on the relative weather conditions. The mixture should contain at least 40-percent antifreeze, but should never contain more than 70-percent antifreeze. Consult the mixture ratio chart on the antifreeze container before adding coolant. Hydrometers are available at most auto parts stores to test the ratio of antifreeze to water (see illustration). Use antifreeze that meets the vehicle manufacturer's specifications.

3 Thermostat - check and replacement

WARNING:

Do not attempt to remove the surge tank cap, coolant or thermostat until the engine has cooled completely.

CAUTION:

Do not drive the vehicle without a thermostat. The computer will stay in open loop and emissions and fuel economy will suffer.

GENERAL CHECK

1 Before assuming the thermostat is responsible for a cooling system problem, check the coolant level (see Chapter 1), drivebelt tension (see Chapter 1) and temperature gauge (or light) operation.

2 If the engine takes a long time to warm up (as indicated by the temperature gauge or heater operation), the thermostat is probably stuck open. Replace the thermostat with a new one.

3 If the engine runs hot, use your hand to check the temperature of the outlet radiator hose. If the hose is not hot, but the engine is, the thermostat is probably stuck in the closed position, preventing the coolant inside the engine from escaping to the radiator. Replace the thermostat.

4 If the outlet radiator hose is hot, it means that the coolant is flowing and the thermostat is open. Consult the *Troubleshooting* Section at the front of this manual for further diagnosis.

THERMOSTAT TEST

5 A more thorough test of the thermostat can only be made when it is removed from the vehicle (see below). If the thermostat remains in the open position at room temperature, it is faulty and must be replaced.

6 To test it fully, suspend the (closed) thermostat on a length of string or wire in a container of cold water, with a thermometer (cooking type that reads beyond 212-degrees F). A clear Pyrex cooking container is easiest to use.

7 Heat the water on a stove while observing the temperature and the

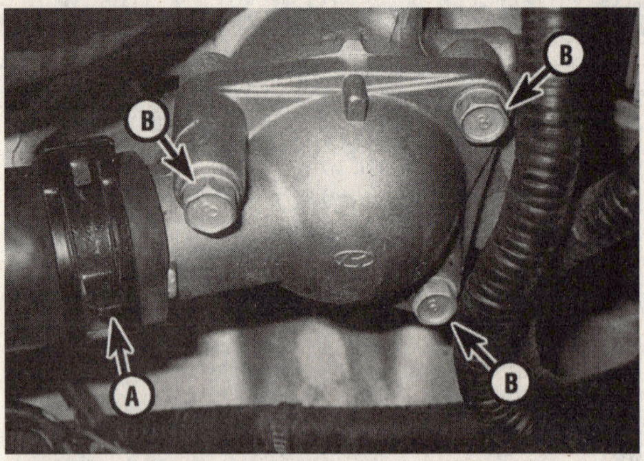

3.11 To remove the thermostat housing cover, loosen the hose clamp (A), disconnect the hose, remove the cover bolts (B) and pull off the cover

thermostat. Neither should contact the sides of the container.

8 Note the temperature when the thermostat begins to open and when it is fully open. Compare the temperatures to the Specifications in this Chapter. The number stamped into the thermostat is generally the fully-open temperature.

3.15 Note the position of the thermostat - the jiggle pin should be installed at the highest point

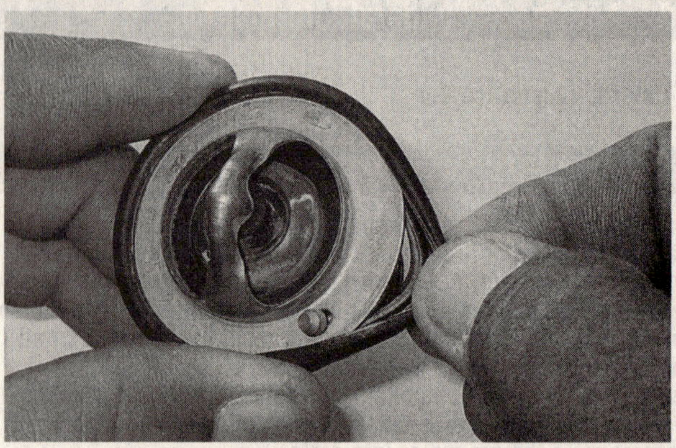

3.14 The thermostat seal fits around the edge of the thermostat

9 If the thermostat doesn't open and close as specified, or sticks in any position, replace it.

REPLACEMENT

➧ Refer to illustrations 3.11, 3.14 and 3.15

10 Drain the cooling system (see Chapter 1).

11 Follow the radiator hose to the thermostat housing cover and disconnect the hose (see illustration).

12 Remove the thermostat housing cover mounting fasteners and remove it from the cylinder block. Be prepared for some coolant to spill as the gasket seal is broken.

13 Remove the thermostat, noting the direction in which it was installed in the housing, and thoroughly clean the sealing surfaces.

14 Install a new gasket onto the thermostat. Make sure it is evenly fitted all the way around (see illustration).

15 Install the thermostat with the jiggle pin at the highest point (see illustration).

16 Install the housing cover and the cover bolts and tighten the bolts to the torque listed in this Chapter's Specifications.

17 The remainder of installation is the reverse of removal.

18 Refill the cooling system (see Chapter 1). Run the engine and check for leaks and proper operation.

4 Engine cooling fans - removal and installation

⁂ WARNING:

Do not start this procedure until the engine is completely cool.

ENGINE COOLING FAN

➧ Refer to illustrations 4.2, 4.3a, 4.3b, 4.4, 4.5 and 4.6

1 Disconnect the cable from the negative terminal of the battery (see Chapter 5).

2 On 2006.5 and later models, remove the air intake duct (see illustration).

3 Disconnect the electrical connector (see illustration), then remove the fan/shroud mounting fasteners (see illustration).

4 Lift out the fan assembly (see illustration).

5 Hold the fan blades and remove the fan retaining nut or clip (see illustration). Remove the fan blade.

6 Remove the fan motor from the fan shroud (see illustration).

7 Installation is the reverse of removal.

4.2 Remove the fasteners securing the air intake duct (2006.5 and later models)

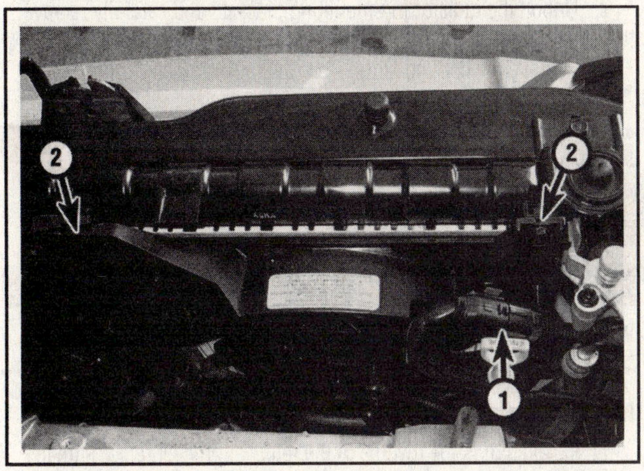

4.3b Typical fan assembly details (right fan assembly):

1 *Right fan electrical connector*
2 *Shroud mounting bolts*

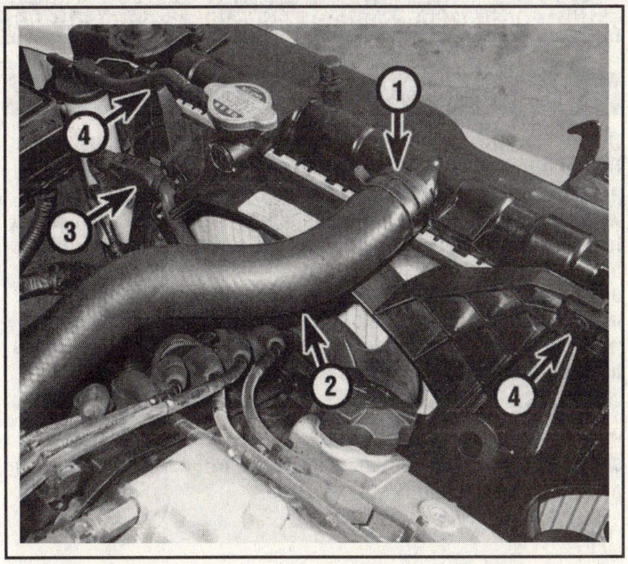

4.3a Typical fan assembly details (left fan assembly):

1 *Radiator hose clamp*
2 *Upper radiator hose*
3 *Left fan electrical connector*
4 *Shroud mounting bolts*

CONDENSER COOLING FAN (2006 AND EARLIER MODELS)

8 Disconnect the cable from the negative terminal of the battery (see Chapter 5).

9 Disconnect the electrical connector, then remove the fan/shroud mounting fasteners.

10 Lift out the fan assembly.

11 Installation is the reverse of removal.

4.4 After removing the upper mounting bolts, the fan and shroud can be lifted out (2006.5 and later model shown)

4.5 The fan blade is secured to the motor with a nut or clip; there may be ball bearings pressed into the rim of the assembly - don't remove them (they are for balancing)

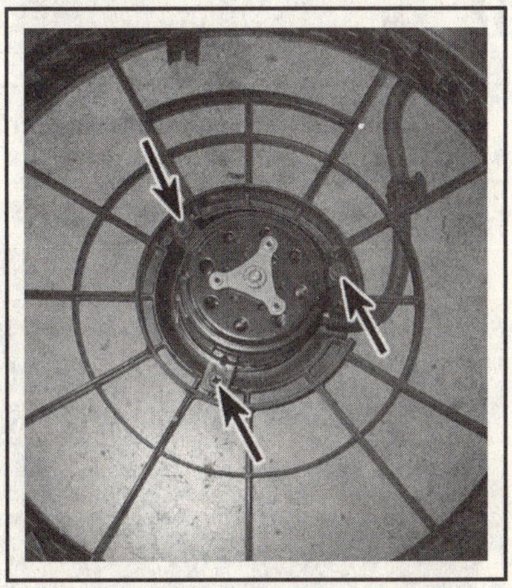

4.6 Remove the fasteners securing the fan motor to the fan shroud

5 Radiator and coolant reservoir - removal and installation

WARNING:

Do not start this procedure until the engine is completely cool. Do not allow antifreeze to come in contact with your skin or painted surfaces of the vehicle. Rinse off spills immediately with plenty of water. Antifreeze is highly toxic if ingested. Never leave antifreeze lying around in an open container or in puddles on the floor; children and pets are attracted by its sweet smell and may drink it. Check with local authorities on disposing of used antifreeze. Many communities have collection centers, which will see that antifreeze is disposed of safely. Never dump used antifreeze on the ground or into drains.

➡ **Note: Non-toxic coolant is available at local auto parts stores. Although the coolant is non-toxic when fresh, proper disposal of used coolant is still required.**

RADIATOR

Removal

➧ **Refer to illustrations 5.6, 5.7a and 5.7b**

1 Disconnect the negative battery cable (see Chapter 5).

2 Remove the engine splash shield(s) from beneath the radiator and any covers for the engine, if equipped (see Chapter 2).

3 Disconnect the wiring to the fan motor(s).

4 Drain the cooling system (see Chapter 1). On 2006.5 and later models, remove the air inlet duct (see illustration 4.2).

5 Detach the upper and lower radiator hoses from the radiator and the reservoir hose from the radiator filler neck. Be sure to mark the exact positions of the hoses and clamps with a dab of white paint or something similar.

6 On vehicles equipped with automatic transaxles, disconnect the transaxle oil cooler hoses from the cooler lines (see illustration). Place a drip pan to catch the fluid and cap the fittings to prevent leakage and contamination.

➡ **Note: If you are replacing the radiator, be sure to remove the cooler lines from the old radiator and transfer them to the new one.**

7 Unbolt the radiator top mounting brackets and carefully remove the radiator and fan(s) as an assembly (see illustrations).

8 Remove the cooling fan(s) from the radiator (see Section 4).

9 With the radiator removed, it can be inspected for leaks, damage and internal blockage. If in need of repairs, have a professional radiator shop perform the work, as special techniques are required.

10 Bugs and dirt can be cleaned from the radiator with compressed air and a soft brush. Don't bend the cooling fins as this is done.

WARNING:

Wear eye protection.

Installation

11 Installation is the reverse of the removal procedure. Be sure the rubber mounts are correctly in place.

12 After installation, fill the cooling system with the proper mixture of antifreeze and water. Refer to Chapter 1 if necessary.

13 Start the engine and check for leaks. Allow the engine to reach normal operating temperature, indicated by the upper radiator hose becoming hot. Recheck the coolant level and add more if required.

14 Be sure to check the automatic transaxle fluid level and add fluid as needed (see Chapter 1).

5.6 Disconnect the cooler line hoses from the radiator

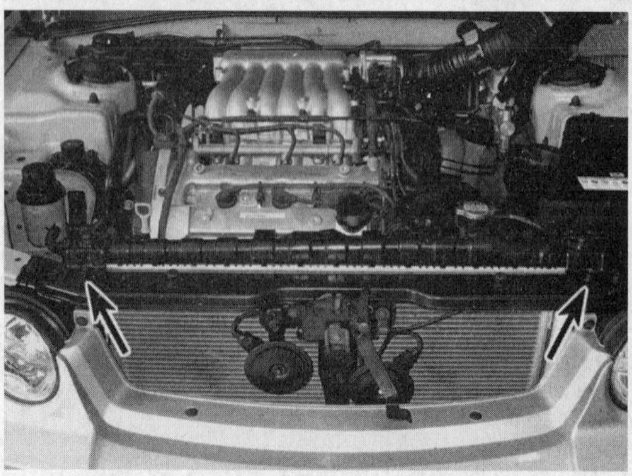

5.7a Upper radiator fasteners (2001 through 2006 models)

5.7b Remove the fasteners securing the radiator mounting brackets (typical 2006.5 and later model shown)

COOLANT RESERVOIR

Refer to illustration 5.15

15 On 2001 through 2006 models, the coolant reservoir is located to the left of the radiator and underneath the battery tray. On 2006.5 and later models, the coolant reservoir is fastened to the fenderwell (see illustration).

16 Use a small clamp to pinch the hose connecting the reservoir to the radiator. Place a drain pan under the reservoir, then disconnect the hose.

17 On 2001 through 2006 models, remove the battery (see Chapter 5) and the battery tray.

18 Remove the mounting fasteners and lift out the reservoir.

19 Pour any remaining coolant into the container. Wash out and inspect the reservoir for cracks and chafing. If it's damaged, replace it.

20 Installation is the reverse of removal. Refill the reservoir to the lower level line.

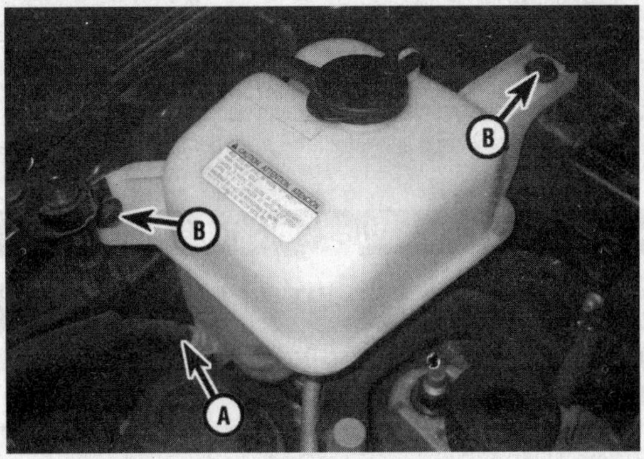

5.15 Coolant reservoir details (2006.5 and later model shown)

A Radiator-to-coolant reservoir hose
B Coolant reservoir mounting fasteners

6 Water pump - check

1 A failure in the water pump can cause serious engine damage due to overheating.

2 Water pumps are equipped with weep or vent holes. If a failure occurs in the pump seal, coolant will leak from this hole.

3 The water pumps on V6 models and 2006 and earlier four-cylinder models are located behind the timing belt covers. If you suspect water pump leakage, remove this cover (see Chapter 2A or 2B).

4 In most cases, it will be necessary to use a flashlight to find the hole in the water pump by looking through the space behind the pulley, just below the water pump shaft. A slight gray discoloration around the weep hole is normal, while dark brown stains indicate a problem.

5 If the water pump shaft bearings fail, there may be a howling sound at the front of the engine while it is running. Bearing wear can be felt if the water pump pulley can be rocked up and down. Do not mistake drivebelt slippage, which causes a squealing sound, for water pump failure. This can occur on engines with adjustable drivebelts. Spray automotive drivebelt dressing on the belts to eliminate the belt as a possible cause of the noise.

7 Water pump - removal and installation

WARNING:

Do not start this procedure until the engine is completely cool. Do not allow antifreeze to come in contact with your skin or painted surfaces of the vehicle. Rinse off spills immediately with plenty of water. Antifreeze is highly toxic if ingested. Never leave antifreeze lying around in an open container or in puddles on the floor; children and pets are attracted by its sweet smell and may drink it. Check with local authorities on disposing of used antifreeze. Many communities have collection centers, which will see that antifreeze is disposed of safely. Never dump used antifreeze on the ground or into drains.

Note: Non-toxic coolant is available at local auto parts stores. Although the coolant is non-toxic when fresh, proper disposal of used coolant is still required.

Note: 2006 and 2006.5 models will both have a "6" in the tenth position of the VIN. To distinguish a 2006 model from a 2006.5 model, refer to the 8th position of the VIN (the engine code): A 2006 model will have a "6" (four-cylinder) or "8" (V6), while a 2006.5 will have a "3" (four-cylinder) or "4" (V6).

1 Disconnect the negative battery cable (see Chapter 5) and drain the cooling system (see Chapter 1).

2006 AND EARLIER MODELS

2 Remove the timing belt (see Chapter 2A or 2B).

Note: Now is a good time to replace the timing belt if it's fairly old. Refer to Chapter 1 for timing belt replacement intervals.

3 If you are working on a four-cylinder model, remove the water pump pulley using a strap wrench or pin spanner wrench to hold the pulley while you loosen the bolts.

4 Remove the water pump fasteners. On four-cylinder engines, remove the alternator brace.

5 Pry the water pump off. If necessary, tap the pump loose with a soft-face hammer.

2006.5 AND LATER FOUR-CYLINDER MODELS

6 Loosen the water pump pulley bolts. Remove the drivebelt (see Chapter 1).

7 Remove the exhaust manifold (see Chapter 2A).

8 Remove the water pump pulley.

9 Remove the water inlet pipe nut.

10 Remove the water pump fasteners and pry the water pump off. If necessary, tap the pump loose with a soft-face hammer.

ALL MODELS

11 To install, clean the water pump and block of any old gasket material or sealant, then clean with brake system cleaner.

12 Install a new gasket and install the water pump. Install the water pump bolts and nuts and tighten them to the torque listed in this Chapter's Specifications.

13 Install the remaining parts in the reverse order of removal.

14 Refill the cooling system (see Chapter 1), then run the engine and check for leaks and proper operation.

8 Coolant temperature indicator - check

⁂ WARNING:

Wait until the engine is completely cool before beginning this procedure.

1 The coolant temperature indicator system consists of a temperature gauge on the dash and a sensor mounted on the engine. On all models, the Engine Coolant Temperature sensor gives information to the Powertrain Control Module (PCM) that then controls the coolant temperature gauge in addition to controlling engine operation. Refer to Chapter 6 for more information on this sensor.

2 If an overheating indication has occurred, first check the coolant level in the system (see Chapter 1) and that the coolant mixture is correct (see Section 2). Also, refer to the *Troubleshooting* Section at the beginning of this book before assuming that the temperature indicator is faulty.

3 Start the engine and warm it up for 10 minutes. If the temperature gauge has not moved from the C position, check the wiring harness connections going to the instrument cluster.

9 Blower motor - removal and installation

9.3 On 2001 through 2006 models, disengage the clips on this trim panel and pull it down

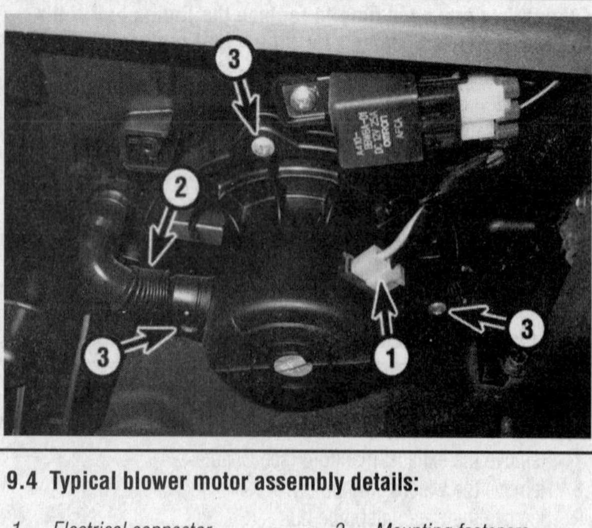

9.4 Typical blower motor assembly details:

1 *Electrical connector*
2 *Air duct*
3 *Mounting fasteners*

➧ **Refer to illustrations 9.3, 9.4 and 9.5**

⁂ WARNING:

The models covered by this manual are equipped with Supplemental Restraint Systems (SRS), more commonly known as airbags. Always disarm the airbag system before working in the vicinity of any airbag system component to avoid the possibility of accidental deployment of the airbag, which could cause personal injury (see Chapter 12).

1 Disconnect the cable from the negative terminal of the battery (see Chapter 5).

2 The blower unit is located under the dash, ahead of the glove box.

3 Remove the trim panel below the glove box (see illustration).

4 Disconnect the electrical connector from the blower motor (see illustration), remove the duct, remove the blower mounting bolts and remove the blower motor.

5 If the motor is being replaced, transfer the fan to the new motor prior to installation (see illustration).

6 Installation is the reverse of removal. Check for proper operation.

9.5 Use pliers to release and remove this clip, then lift the blower fan off the motor shaft

10 Heater and air conditioning control assembly - removal and installation

WARNING:

The models covered by this manual are equipped with Supplemental Restraint Systems (SRS), more commonly known as airbags. Always disarm the airbag system before working in the vicinity of any airbag system component to avoid the possibility of accidental deployment of the airbag, which could cause personal injury (see Chapter 12).

1 Disconnect the negative cable from the battery (see Chapter 5).
2 Remove the center trim panel (see Chapter 11).
3 Remove the screws that secure the heater and air conditioning control assembly to the center trim panel and remove the control unit.
4 Installation is the reverse of removal. Run the engine and check for proper functioning of the heater and air conditioning.

11 Heater core - removal and installation

Refer to illustrations 11.6, 11.7 and 11.8

WARNING:

The models covered by this manual are equipped with Supplemental Restraint Systems (SRS), more commonly known as airbags. Always disarm the airbag system before working in the vicinity of any airbag system component to avoid the possibility of accidental deployment of the airbag, which could cause personal injury (see Chapter 12).

WARNING:

Do not allow antifreeze to come in contact with your skin or painted surfaces of the vehicle. Rinse off spills immediately with plenty of water. Antifreeze is highly toxic if ingested. Never leave antifreeze lying around in an open container or in puddles on the floor; children and pets are attracted by its sweet smell and may drink it. Check with local authorities on disposing of used antifreeze. Many communities have collection centers that will see that antifreeze is disposed of safely. Never dump used antifreeze on the ground or into drains.

WARNING:

Wait until the engine is completely cool before beginning this procedure.

11.6 Remove the fasteners from both ends of the instrument panel support beam (right end shown)

Note: Non-toxic coolant is available at local auto parts stores. Although the coolant is non-toxic when fresh, proper disposal of used coolant is still required.

Note: Removal of the heater core is a difficult procedure for the home mechanic. There are numerous fasteners involved, some of which can be difficult to access. We recommend that you have considerable mechanical experience before performing a heater core replacement.

1 Take the vehicle to a dealer service department or automotive air conditioning shop and have the air conditioning system discharged and the refrigerant recovered.
2 Disconnect the cable from the negative terminal of the battery (see Chapter 5).
3 Drain the cooling system (see Chapter 1).
4 The procedure for removal of the heater core involves removal of the heater/evaporator housing, which requires complete removal of the instrument panel and its support beam. Remove the instrument panel assembly (see Chapter 11).
5 Detach the electrical harnesses clipped to the instrument panel support beam.
6 Remove the instrument panel support beam mounting bolts and pull the bar away from the firewall (see illustration).

Note: Take your time and don't use excessive force - there may be some fasteners that were overlooked.

7 Remove the plastic cover and disconnect the air conditioner lines at the firewall (see illustration). Seal the openings to prevent contamination.

11.7 Remove this nut to remove the cover for the firewall connection of the air conditioning system refrigerant lines

11.8 Disconnect the heater hoses at the firewall

8 Disconnect the heater hoses at the firewall (see illustration).

9 Disconnect any remaining wiring harnesses from the heater unit.

10 Remove the mounting fasteners from the unit. Carefully pull it rearward until the tubes are free of the firewall openings.

11 Remove the heater core cover, then carefully slide the heater core out of the heater unit. Be careful of damaging the tubes as you slide them out.

12 Installation is the reverse order of removal. Use new O-rings to seal the evaporator refrigerant connections. Make sure all of the instrument panel support beam mounting fasteners are tightened securely before installing the instrument panel.

13 Refill the cooling system (see Chapter 1). Have the air conditioning system serviced at the station that discharged it.

12 Air conditioning and heating system - check and maintenance

AIR CONDITIONING SYSTEM

WARNING:

The air conditioning system is under high pressure. Do not loosen any hose fittings or remove any components until the system has been discharged. Air conditioning refrigerant must be properly discharged into an EPA-approved recovery/recycling unit by a dealer service department or an automotive air conditioning repair facility. Always wear eye protection when disconnecting air conditioning system fittings.

1 The following maintenance checks should be performed on a regular basis to ensure that the air conditioner continues to operate at peak efficiency.

a) *Inspect the condition of the compressor drivebelt. If it is worn or deteriorated, replace it (see Chapter 1).*
b) *Check the drivebelt tension (see Chapter 1).*
c) *Inspect the system hoses. Look for cracks, bubbles, hardening and deterioration. Inspect the hoses and all fittings for oil bubbles or seepage. If there is any evidence of wear, damage or leakage, replace the hose(s).*
d) *Inspect the condenser fins for leaves, bugs and any other foreign material that may have embedded itself in the fins. Use a fin comb or compressed air to remove debris from the condenser.*
e) *Make sure the system has the correct refrigerant charge.*

2 It's a good idea to operate the system for about ten minutes at least once a month. This is particularly important during the winter months because long-term non-use can cause hardening, and subsequent failure, of the seals.

3 Because of the complexity of the air conditioning system and the special equipment necessary to service it, in-depth troubleshooting and repairs are beyond the scope of this manual. However, simple component replacement procedures are provided in this Chapter.

4 The most common cause of poor cooling is simply a low system refrigerant charge. If a noticeable drop in system cooling ability occurs, one of the following quick checks will help you determine whether the refrigerant level is low.

CHECK

Refer to illustration 12.8

5 Warm the engine up to normal operating temperature.

6 Place the air conditioning temperature selector at the coldest setting and put the blower at the highest setting. Open the doors (to make sure the air conditioning system doesn't cycle off as soon as it cools the passenger compartment).

7 After the system reaches operating temperature, feel the two pipes connected to the evaporator at the firewall.

8 The pipe (thinner tubing) leading from the condenser outlet to the evaporator should be cold, and the evaporator outlet line (the thicker tubing that leads back to the compressor) should be slightly colder (3 to 10 degrees F). If the evaporator outlet is considerably warmer than the inlet, the system needs a charge. Insert a thermometer in the center air distribution duct (see illustration) while operating the air conditioning system - the temperature of the output air should be 35 to 40 degrees F below the ambient air temperature (down to approximately

12.8 Place an accurate thermometer in the center dash vent, turn the air conditioning on and check the output temperature; on hot days, the system performance will be much lower than otherwise, but there should be about a 30-degree drop in temperature

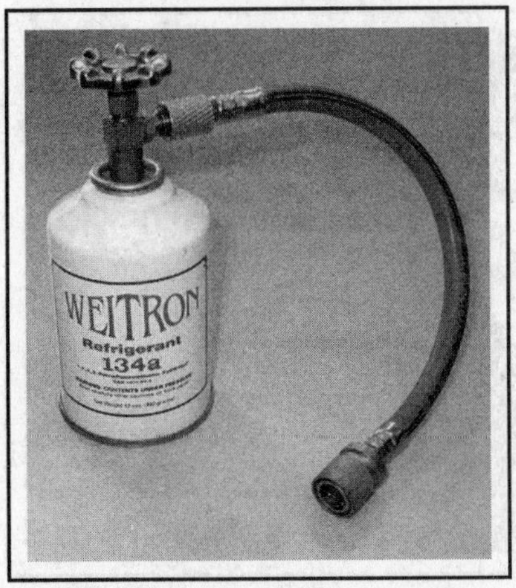

12.9 A basic charging kit for R-134a systems is available at most auto parts stores - it must say R-134a (not R-12) and so must the can of refrigerant

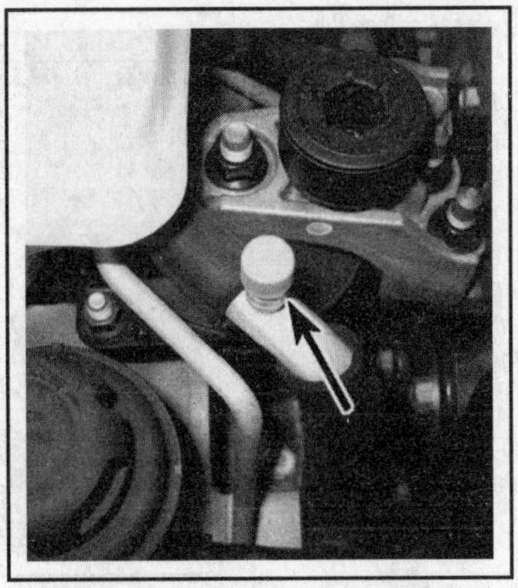

12.12a The low pressure fitting cap is clearly marked "L," and is on the larger of the two lines

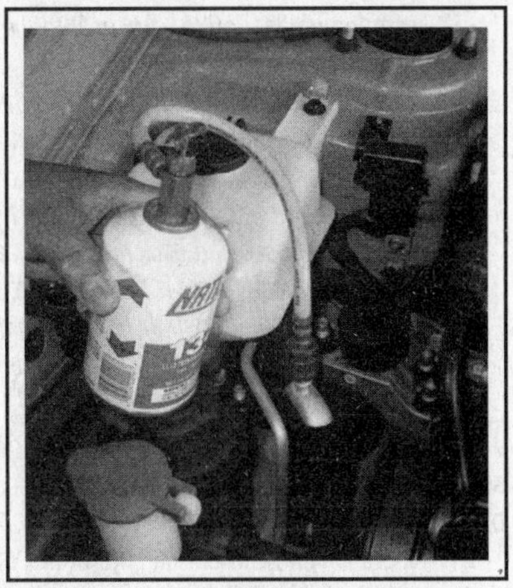

12.12b Add R-134a only to the low side port - the procedure is easier if you wrap the can with a warm, wet towel to prevent icing

40 degrees F). If the ambient (outside) air temperature is very high, say 110-degrees F, the duct air temperature may be as high as 60 degrees F, but generally the air conditioning is 35 to 40 degrees F cooler than the ambient air. If the air isn't as cold as it used to be, the system probably needs a charge. Further inspection or testing of the system is beyond the scope of the home mechanic and should be left to a professional.

ADDING REFRIGERANT

➧ Refer to illustrations 12.9, 12.12a and 12.12b

➡ Note: All models covered by this manual use the refrigerant R-134a. When recharging or replacing air conditioning components, use only refrigerant, refrigerant oil and seals compatible with this system. The seals and compressor oil used with older, conventional R-12 refrigerant are not compatible with the components in this system.

9 Buy an automotive charging kit at an auto parts store. A charging kit includes a can of R-134a refrigerant, a tap valve and a short section of hose that can be attached between the tap valve and the system low side service valve (see illustration).

10 Connect the charging kit by following the manufacturer's instructions.

11 Back off the valve handle on the charging kit and screw the kit onto the refrigerant can, first making sure that the O-ring or rubber seal inside the threaded portion of the kit is in place.

⁂ WARNING:

Wear protective eyewear when dealing with pressurized refrigerant cans.

12 Remove the dust cap from the low-side charging port and attach the quick-connect fitting on the kit hose (see illustrations).

⁂ WARNING:

DO NOT hook the charging kit hose to the system high side! The fittings on the charging kit are designed to fit *only* on the low side of the system.

13 Warm the engine to normal operating temperature and turn on the air conditioning. Keep the charging kit hose away from the fan and other moving parts. In some cases, if the refrigerant charge is low enough, the air conditioning system pressure switch may prevent the compressor from operating.

➡ Note: The charging process requires that the compressor be running. If the clutch cycles off, you can switch the A/C controls to High and leave the vehicle's doors open to keep the clutch on the compressor working.

14 Turn the valve handle on the kit until the stem pierces the can, then back the handle out to release the refrigerant. You should be able to hear the rush of gas.

15 Add refrigerant to the low side of the system until both the outlet and the evaporator inlet pipe feel about the same temperature. Allow stabilization time between each addition.

⁂ CAUTION:

Never add more than one can of refrigerant to the system. If more refrigerant than that is required, the system should be evacuated and leak tested.

The can may tend to frost up, slowing the procedure. Wet a shop towel with hot water and wrap it around the bottom of the can to keep it from frosting.

16 Put your thermometer back in the center register and check that the output air is getting colder.

17 When the can is empty, turn the valve handle to the closed position and release the connection from the low-side port. Reinstall the dust cap.

18 Remove the charging kit from the can and store the kit for future use with the piercing valve in the UP position, to prevent inadvertently piercing the can on the next use.

HEATING SYSTEMS

19 If the air coming out of the heater vents isn't hot, the problem could stem from any of the following causes:

a) *The thermostat is stuck open, preventing the engine coolant from warming up enough to carry heat to the heater core. Replace the thermostat (see Section 3).*

b) *A heater hose is blocked, preventing the flow of coolant through the heater core. Feel both heater hoses at the firewall. They should be hot. If one of them is cold, there is an obstruction in one of the hoses or in the heater core, or the heater control valve is shut. Detach the hoses and back flush the heater core with a water hose. If the heater core is clear but circulation is impeded, remove the two hoses and flush them out with a garden hose.*

c) *If flushing fails to remove the blockage from the heater core, the core must be replaced (see Section 11).*

20 If the blower motor speed does not correspond to the setting selected on the blower switch, the problem could be a bad fuse, circuit, blower relay, speed switch or blower resistor.

21 If there isn't any air coming out of the vents:

a) *Turn the ignition ON and activate the fan control. Place your ear at the heating/air conditioning register (vent) and listen. Most motors are audible. Can you hear the motor running?*

b) *If you can't (and have already verified that the blower switch and the blower motor resistor are good), the blower motor itself is probably bad (see Section 9).*

22 If the carpet under the heater core is damp, or if antifreeze vapor or steam is coming through the vents, the heater core is leaking. Remove it (see Section 11) and install a new unit (most radiator shops will not repair a leaking heater core).

23 Inspect the drain hose from the heater/evaporator, which exits the body under the floor. If there is a humid mist coming from the system ducts, this hose may be plugged with leaves or road debris.

ELIMINATING AIR CONDITIONING ODORS

Refer to illustration 12.27

24 Unpleasant odors that often develop in air conditioning systems are caused by the growth of a fungus, usually on the surface of the evaporator core. The warm, humid environment there is a perfect breeding ground for mildew to develop.

25 The evaporator core on most vehicles is difficult to access, and factory dealerships have a lengthy, expensive process for eliminating the fungus by opening up the evaporator case and using a powerful disinfectant and rinse on the core until the fungus is gone. You can service your own system at home, but it takes something much stronger than basic household germ-killers or deodorizers.

12.27 Remove the cabin air filter, then insert the disinfectant spray nozzle

26 Aerosol disinfectants for automotive air-conditioning systems are available in most auto parts stores, but remember when shopping for them that the most effective treatments are also the most expensive. The basic procedure for using these sprays is to start by running the system in the RECIRC mode for ten minutes with the blower on its highest speed. Use the highest heat mode to dry out the system and keep the compressor from engaging by disconnecting the wiring connector at the compressor (see Section 14).

27 The disinfectant can usually comes with a long spray hose. Remove the interior ventilation filter (see Chapter 1), point the nozzle inside the hole, with the blower fan running, and spray according to the manufacturer's recommendations (see illustration).

28 Once the evaporator has been cleaned, the best way to prevent the mildew from coming back again is to make sure your evaporator housing drain tube is clear and to run the defrost cycle briefly to dry the evaporator out after a long drive with the air conditioning on.

13 Air conditioning receiver/drier - removal and installation

WARNING:

The air conditioning system is under high pressure. Do not loosen any hose fittings or remove any components until the system has been discharged. Air conditioning refrigerant must be properly discharged into an EPA-approved recovery/recycling unit by a dealer service department or an automotive air conditioning repair facility. Always wear eye protection when disconnecting air conditioning system fittings.

Note: Early models use a receiver/drier that is replaceable. All later vehicles have a receiver/drier that's a part of the condenser and is not serviceable by itself.

1 Have the refrigerant discharged by a certified air conditioning technician.

2 Disconnect the negative battery cable (see Chapter 5).

EARLY MODELS WITH SEPARATE RECEIVER/DRIER

3 The receiver/drier is attached to the end of the condenser. Refer to Section 15 for information about access to this assembly.

4 Disconnect the tube from each end of the receiver/drier. Seal the ends immediately to prevent contamination.

5 Remove the receiver/drier from the end of the condenser.

6 Add 40 cc of refrigerant oil to the system, then mount the new receiver/drier to the condenser.

7 Replace the O-rings on the tubes with new ones, lubricate them with R-134a-compatible oil and tighten the nuts securely.

LATER MODELS WITH RECEIVER/DRIER AN INTEGRAL COMPONENT OF THE CONDENSER ASSEMBLY

▸ Refer to illustration 13.9

8 Remove the condenser from the vehicle (see Section 15).

9 Using an Allen wrench, detach the bottom cap and remove the desiccant from the receiver/drier with a pair of needle-nose pliers (see illustration).

10 Use new O-rings and a new bottom cap when installing the new desiccant and tighten the bottom cap to the torque listed in this Chapter's Specifications. Be sure to lubricate the O-rings with R-134a-compatible refrigerant oil.

ALL MODELS

11 Installation is the reverse of removal.

12 Have the system evacuated, charged and leak tested by the shop that discharged it.

13.9 After the system has been discharged and the condenser removed from the vehicle, remove the bottom cap from the receiver/drier and pull out the desiccant

14 Air conditioning compressor - removal and installation

▸ Refer to illustrations 14.5a, 14.5b and 14.5c

✻✻ WARNING:

The air conditioning system is under high pressure. Do not loosen any hose fittings or remove any components until the system has been discharged. Air conditioning refrigerant must be properly discharged into an EPA-approved recovery/recycling unit by a dealer service department or an automotive air conditioning repair facility. Always wear eye protection when disconnecting air conditioning system fittings.

✻✻ CAUTION:

The receiver/drier should be serviced or replaced whenever the compressor is replaced.

1 Have the refrigerant discharged by an automotive air conditioning technician.

2 Disconnect the negative cable from the battery (see Chapter 5).

3 Raise the vehicle and support it securely on jackstands.

4 Remove the drivebelt from the compressor (see Chapter 1).

5 Disconnect the electrical connector and the refrigerant lines. Seal

14.5a The air conditioning compressor is mounted on the front side of the block (four-cylinder engine shown)

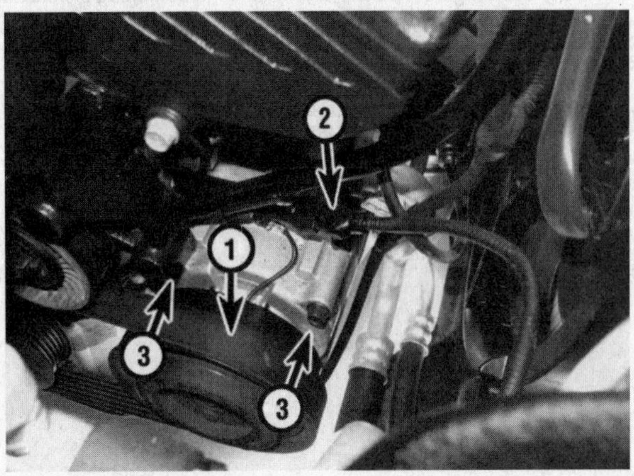

14.5b Typical air conditioning compressor assembly details (V6 model shown):

1 Drivebelt
2 Electrical connector
3 Upper mounting bolts.

the ends to prevent contamination. Unbolt the compressor and lower it from the vehicle (see illustrations).

6 If a new or rebuilt compressor is being installed, follow the directions that came with the compressor regarding adding oil to the proper level prior to installation.

7 Installation is the reverse of removal. Replace any O-rings with new ones specifically made for the purpose and lubricate them with refrigerant oil. Tighten the mounting bolts evenly in several passes to avoid stressing the compressor case.

8 Have the system evacuated, recharged and leak tested by the shop that discharged it.

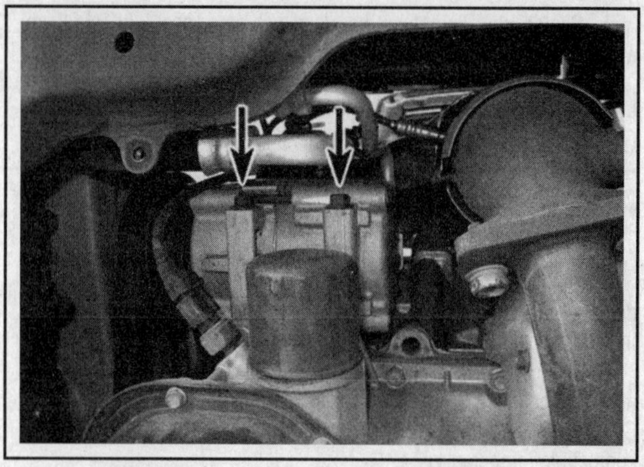

14.5c Compressor lower mounting bolts (V6 model shown)

15 Air conditioning condenser - removal and installation

➧ **Refer to illustration 15.6**

✲✲ WARNING:

The air conditioning system is under high pressure. Do not loosen any hose fittings or remove any components until the system has been discharged. Air conditioning refrigerant must be properly discharged into an EPA-approved recovery/recycling unit by a dealer service department or an automotive air conditioning repair facility. Always wear eye protection when disconnecting air conditioning system fittings.

✲✲ CAUTION:

On early models, the receiver/drier should be replaced whenever the condenser is replaced. On later models, it is a component of the condenser assembly.

1 Have the refrigerant discharged by an air conditioning technician.

2 Disconnect the cable from the negative battery terminal (see Chapter 5).

3 On 2006.5 and later models, remove the air intake duct (see illustration 4.2).

4 Remove the upper radiator brackets (see Section 5). Pull the radiator rearward for access to the condenser.

5 Disconnect the inlet and outlet fittings. Cap the open fittings immediately to keep moisture and dirt out of the system.

6 Remove the mounting fasteners. Push the radiator back toward the engine, then push the condenser rearward until it's free of the radiator support and can be pulled up and out of the vehicle (see illustration).

7 Install the condenser, brackets and bolts, making sure the rubber cushions fit on the mounting points properly.

8 Reconnect the refrigerant lines, using new O-rings.

9 Reinstall the remaining parts in the reverse order of removal.

10 Have the system evacuated, charged and leak tested by the shop that discharged it.

15.6 Push the radiator back toward the engine (A), then push the condenser rearward (B) until it's free of the radiator support and can be pulled up and out of the vehicle.

Torque specifications	Ft-lbs (unless otherwise indicated)	Nm

➡ Note: One foot-pound (ft-lb) of torque is equivalent to 12 inch-pounds (in-lbs) of torque. Torque values below approximately 15 foot-pounds are expressed in inch-pounds, because most foot-pound torque wrenches are not accurate at these smaller values.

Torque specifications	Ft-lbs (unless otherwise indicated)	Nm
Receiver/drier Allen plug	15 to 18	20 to 24
Thermostat housing bolts		
Four-cylinder engines	132 in-lbs	15
V6 engines	144 to 168 in-lbs	16 to 19
Water pump bolts		
Four-cylinder engines	15 to 20	20 to 27
V6 engines	11 to 16	15 to 22

Notes

4 FUEL AND EXHAUST SYSTEMS

Reference to other Chapters

Air filter replacement - See Chapter 1
CHECK ENGINE light on - See Chapter 6
Exhaust system check - See Chapter 1
Fuel system check - See Chapter 1
Underhood hose check and replacement - See Chapter 1

1 General information

The fuel system consists of the fuel tank, the electric in-tank fuel pump, the fuel pressure regulator, the fuel rail, the fuel injectors and the fuel lines connecting the pump to the fuel rail. The injectors are energized by the Powertrain Control Module (PCM). The fuel system electrical circuits are protected by the EFI fuse and the circuit opening relay (fuel pump relay). The air intake system consists of the air filter housing, the air intake duct, the throttle body and the intake manifold (the intake manifold is covered in Chapter 2). The fuel pressure regulator and the fuel filter are parts of the fuel pump assembly on 2006 and later models.

ELECTRONIC FUEL INJECTION (EFI) SYSTEM

The manufacturer refers to the fuel injection systems used on these vehicles as Electronic Fuel Injection (EFI). The system uses timed impulses to inject the fuel directly into the intake port of each cylinder. The Powertrain Control Module (PCM) controls the injectors. The PCM monitors various engine parameters and delivers the exact amount of fuel required into the intake ports. The throttle body controls the amount of air drawn into the engine.

FUEL PUMP AND LINES

Fuel is circulated from the in-tank fuel pump to the fuel rail through fuel lines running along the underside of the vehicle. Various sections of the fuel line are either rigid metal or nylon, or flexible fuel hose. The various sections of the fuel hose are connected by quick-connect fittings. An electric fuel pump/fuel level sending unit is located inside the fuel tank.

The circuit opening relay (fuel pump relay) is equipped with a primary and secondary voltage circuit. The primary circuit is controlled by the PCM and the secondary circuit is linked directly to the relay from the ignition switch. With the ignition switch ON (engine not running), the PCM will ground the relay for two seconds. During cranking, the PCM grounds the fuel pump relay as long as the Camshaft Position (CMP) sensor sends its position signal. If there are no reference pulses, the fuel pump will shut off after two seconds.

EXHAUST SYSTEM

The exhaust system consists of the exhaust manifold(s), the exhaust pipe(s), the catalytic converters, mufflers, and a tail pipe. On all models, there are multiple catalytic converters, an upstream catalyst just below each exhaust manifold and a downstream catalyst underneath the vehicle.

2 Fuel pressure relief procedure

⁂ WARNING:

Gasoline is extremely flammable, so take extra precautions when you work on any part of the fuel system. Don't smoke or allow open flames or bare light bulbs near the work area, and don't work in a garage where a gas-type appliance (such as a water heater or clothes dryer) is present. Since gasoline is carcinogenic, wear fuel resistant gloves when there's a possibility of being exposed to fuel, and, if you spill any fuel on your skin, rinse it off immediately with soap and water. Mop up any spills immediately and do not store fuel-soaked rags where they could ignite. The fuel system is under constant pressure, so, if any fuel lines are to be disconnected, the fuel pressure in the system must be relieved first. When you perform any kind of work on the fuel system, wear safety glasses and have a Class B type fire extinguisher on hand.

1 Remove the gas cap to release any pressure in the fuel tank.
2 Remove the rear seat cushion (see Chapter 11).
3 Remove the fuel pump/sending unit floor service hole cover (see Section 5).
4 Disconnect the fuel pump electrical connector.
5 Start the engine and allow it to run until it stops, then turn the ignition key to OFF.
6 Disconnect the cable from the negative battery terminal before working on the fuel system (see Chapter 5).
7 The fuel system pressure is now relieved, and you can now safely open fuel line fittings anywhere in the system. But even though there is no longer any pressure in the system, it's still a good idea to wrap a shop rag around a fitting before opening it to soak up any fuel that leaks out.

3 Fuel pump/fuel pressure - check

⁂ WARNING:

Gasoline is extremely flammable, so take extra precautions when you work on any part of the fuel system. See the *Warning* in Section 2.

➡ Note: 2006 and 2006.5 models will both have a "6" in the tenth position of the VIN. To distinguish a 2006 model from a 2006.5 model, refer to the 8th position of the VIN (the engine code): A 2006 model will have a "6" (four-cylinder) or "8" (V6), while a 2006.5 will have a "3" (four-cylinder) or "4" (V6).

GENERAL CHECKS

1 Make sure that there is adequate fuel in the fuel tank.
2 Verify the fuel pump actually runs. Have an assistant turn the ignition switch to ON - you should hear a brief whirring noise for about two seconds as the pump comes on and pressurizes the system.

➡ Note: The fuel pump is easy to hear through the fuel filler neck.

If the fuel pump makes no sound, check the EFI fuse and the circuit opening or fuel pump relay, both of which are located in the fuse and

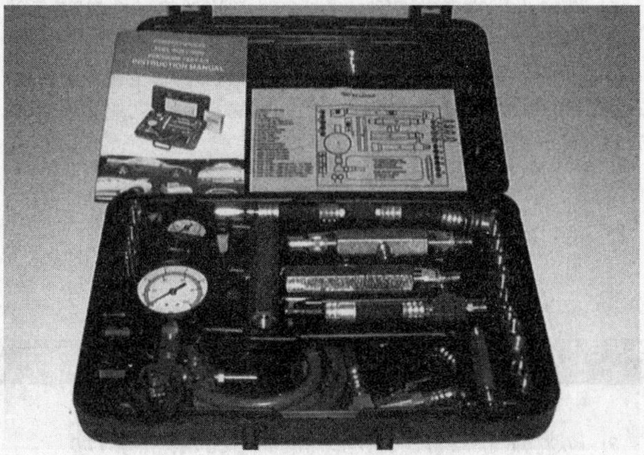

3.4 This fuel pressure testing kit contains all the necessary fittings and adapters, along with the fuel pressure gauge, to test most automotive fuel systems

3.5 Connect the pressure gauge to the hose you've spliced into the fuel supply line

relay box. If the fuse and relay are OK, check the wiring back to the fuel pump. If voltage is present at the fuel pump electrical connector for a couple of seconds when the ignition key is turned on (or when the engine is cranking), the fuel pump is defective. If no voltage is present, the PCM might be defective. Have the vehicle checked at a dealer service department.

FUEL PUMP PRESSURE CHECK

➧ **Refer to illustrations 3.4 and 3.5**

3 Relieve the fuel system pressure (see Section 2).

4 To test the fuel pressure, you will need a fuel pressure gauge capable of measuring the fuel pressure in the range listed in this Chapter's Specifications, and you'll need a T-fitting that fits the inside diameter of the fuel hoses. Fuel pressure gauge kits (see illustration) are available at many auto parts stores and specialty tool suppliers.

5 Disconnect the fuel supply line from the fuel rail, then hook up your fuel pressure test rig between the fuel supply line and the fuel rail. Make sure that the clamps are tight on the hoses (see illustration).

WARNING:

This procedure requires some ingenuity in assembling the necessary fittings. Although it is only a temporary connection, make sure that the fittings won't leak or blow off when pressure is applied.

RETURN-TYPE FUEL SYSTEMS (2001 THROUGH 2006 MODELS)

6 Turn off all accessories and turn the ignition switch key to ON. The fuel pump should run for about two seconds to pressurize the system. Note the reading on the gauge. After the pump stops running, the pressure should hold steady.

7 Start the engine, allow it to warm up to its normal operating temperature, then measure the fuel pressure and compare your readings to the system pressure listed in this Chapter's Specifications.

a) *If the pressure is high, disconnect the vacuum hose from the fuel pressure regulator and connect a vacuum gauge to the hose. Make sure there is 12 in-Hg or more vacuum present at the hose. If there isn't, check the hose for a restriction or leak.*
b) *If there is adequate vacuum to the regulator but the pressure is high, check for a restricted fuel return hose or line. If the return hose and line are clear, replace the pressure regulator.*
c) *If the pressure is low, pinch the fuel return hose. If the pressure goes up, replace the fuel pressure regulator. If the pressure does not increase, replace the fuel filter (see Chapter 1) and recheck the pressure. If it's still low, check the fuel supply hose and line for a restriction. If there is no restriction, replace the fuel pump (see Section 6).*

➡ **Note: As the fuel pump is removed, check the inlet strainer on the bottom of the pump for clogging.**

d) *Another possible cause of low fuel pressure is a leaking fuel injector, but that would most likely set a trouble code and turn on the CHECK ENGINE light (because the fuel mixture would be too rich).*

8 To check the operation of the fuel pressure regulator, disconnect the vacuum hose from the regulator with the engine idling and watch the fuel pressure gauge - the fuel pressure should increase 3 to 10 psi as soon as the hose is disconnected. If it doesn't, check for vacuum at the hose (see Step 7a). If vacuum is present, replace the fuel pressure regulator.

9 Turn the key off and observe the pressure for five minutes. If the pressure drops substantially, then there is either a leaking injector or a faulty check valve in the fuel pump.

10 Relieve the system fuel pressure (see Section 2), then disconnect the cable from the negative battery terminal (see Chapter 5). Remove the fuel pressure gauge and test hoses, then reconnect the fuel supply hose to the fuel rail. Reconnect the cable to the negative battery terminal (see Chapter 5), then start the engine and check for leaks.

RETURNLESS FUEL SYSTEMS (2006.5 AND LATER MODELS)

11 Start the engine and let it warm up until it's idling at its normal operating temperature, then measure the fuel pressure and compare your reading to the fuel pressure listed in this Chapter's Specifications.

a) *If the indicated fuel pressure is low, inspect the fuel supply hose and line for an obstruction. If the hose and line are clear, the fault could be in the fuel filter. The fuel filter is part of the fuel pump assembly. Replace the fuel pump/regulator/filter, then recheck the fuel pressure.*

➡ **Note: At the time of writing, neither the fuel filter nor the pressure regulator was available separately. Check with your local auto parts store or dealer parts department to see if the filter or pressure regulator can be purchased separately.**

b) If the indicated fuel pressure is high, replace the fuel pump/fuel pressure regulator.

12 After the test is complete, relieve the system fuel pressure (see Section 2), then disconnect the cable from the negative battery terminal (see Chapter 5).

13 Remove the fuel pressure gauge.

14 Reconnect the cable to the negative battery terminal.

15 Start the engine and check for fuel leaks.

4 Fuel lines and fittings - general information

⁂ WARNING:

Gasoline is extremely flammable, so take extra precautions when you work on any part of the fuel system. See the *Warning* in Section 2.

FUEL LINES

1 Before servicing fuel lines or fittings, relieve the fuel pressure (see Section 2) and disconnect the cable from the negative battery terminal (see Chapter 5).

2 The fuel line extends from the fuel tank to the engine compartment. The fuel line is secured to the underbody with plastic clips. Inspect these clips and the fuel line whenever you're working under the vehicle.

3 Look for leaks, kinks and dents in the fuel line. If you find any sign of damage, replace the fuel line immediately. Make sure that the metal fuel lines don't chafe against the pan or against any under-vehicle components. There must be a minimum of 1/4-inch clearance around the metal fuel lines to prevent chafing.

4 Some of the fuel line clips are bolted to the underside of the vehicle. To detach a bolted clip, simply remove the retaining bolt. Most of the clips, however, are pushed onto threaded studs welded to the pan. This type of clip is secured to the stud by ratchet teeth that grip the threads on the stud.

5 To install a new fuel line clip:

a) Push the fuel and EVAP lines into their guides in the clip.
b) Align the clip with the threaded stud.
c) Push the clip onto the threaded stud until it seats firmly against the underside of the vehicle.

6 If you're replacing a damaged metal fuel line, replace the damaged line with factory replacement metal fuel line tubing or use equivalent grade steel tubing that meets the manufacturer's specifications. An unapproved line might fail when subjected to the high pressure of the fuel system. Don't use copper or aluminum tubing to replace steel tubing. These materials cannot withstand normal vehicle vibration.

7 Some fuel lines use banjo fittings with banjo bolts and sealing washers. Replace the two sealing washers every time that you open one of these fittings.

FUEL HOSES

⁂ WARNING:

Use only original equipment replacement hoses or their equivalent. Unapproved hoses might fail when pressurized.

8 Never route flexible fuel hose within four inches of any part of the exhaust system or within ten inches of the catalytic converter. Rubber hoses must never be allowed to chafe against the frame. A minimum of 1/4-inch clearance must be maintained around a hose to prevent contact with the frame.

NYLON FUEL LINES

9 Some fuel lines are nylon, and use quick-connect fittings to connect them to the fuel pump, metal fuel lines and the fuel rail. These nylon fuel lines and quick-connect fittings cannot be serviced separately from one another. If any part of one of these lines or fittings is damaged, replace the entire assembly. Do not attempt to repair them.

10 Read through the following procedure for disconnecting and reconnecting a quick-connect fitting before trying to disconnect it.

QUICK-CONNECT FITTINGS

Button-type quick-connects

➧ **Refer to illustrations 4.11, 4.12 and 4.13**

11 Some button-type quick-connect fittings are protected by a plastic cover (see illustration) that surrounds the fitting on three sides. To remove the cover, simply pull it off.

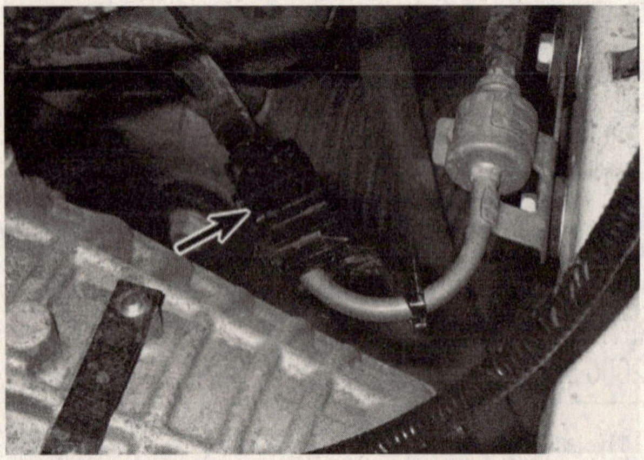

4.11 To remove the protective cover from the quick-connect fitting, simply push it off to the side

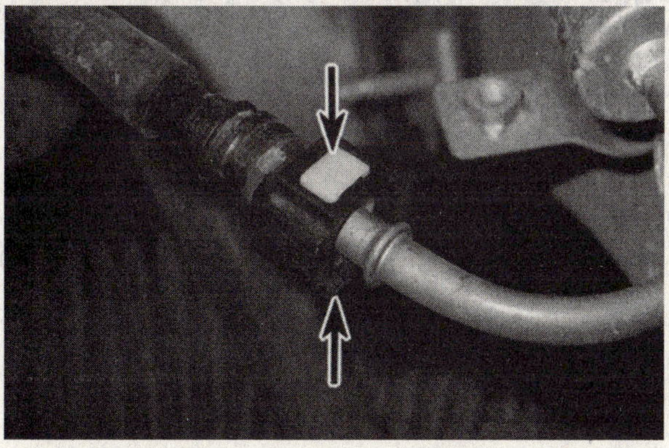

4.12 To disconnect a quick-connect fitting, depress the two buttons on opposite sides of the fitting, then pull the fitting off the end of the fuel line

4.13 Inspect the O-ring inside the quick-connect fitting. If it's damaged, replace it

12 To disconnect a button-type quick-connect fitting, depress the two buttons on either side of the fitting and pull the fitting off the fuel line (see illustration).

13 Inspect the condition of the O-ring inside the fitting (see illustration). If it's damaged, replace it.

14 Installation is the reverse of removal. To reconnect a button-type quick-connect fitting, push it onto the fuel line until both retaining pawls lock with a clicking sound.

15 Before installing the plastic cover over the fitting, reconnect the cable to the negative battery terminal, start the engine and check for leaks.

Clamp-type quick-connects

Refer to illustrations 4.16a and 4.16b

16 To unlock the clamp, press the locking tab and turn the clamp clockwise to unlock the fitting (see illustrations).

17 Pull the two halves of the fitting apart.

18 Installation is the reverse of removal. Make sure that the raised ridge on the fuel line clicks into the fitting.

19 To verify that the fitting is securely connected, try to pull the two sides of the fitting apart.

20 Reconnect the cable to the negative battery terminal, start the engine and check for leaks.

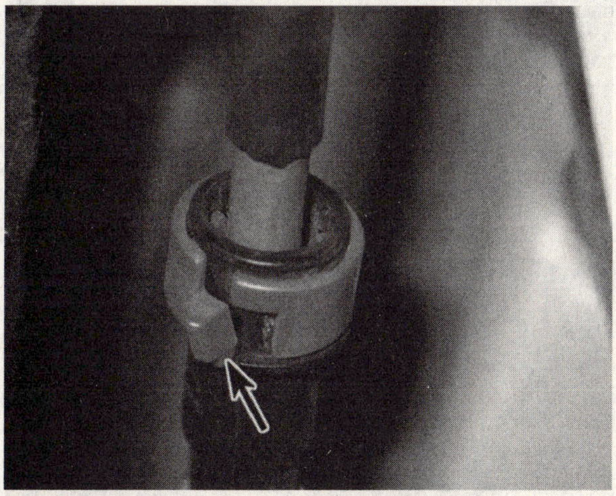

4.16a To unlock a clamp-type quick-connect fitting, push this locking tab to unlock the clamp . . .

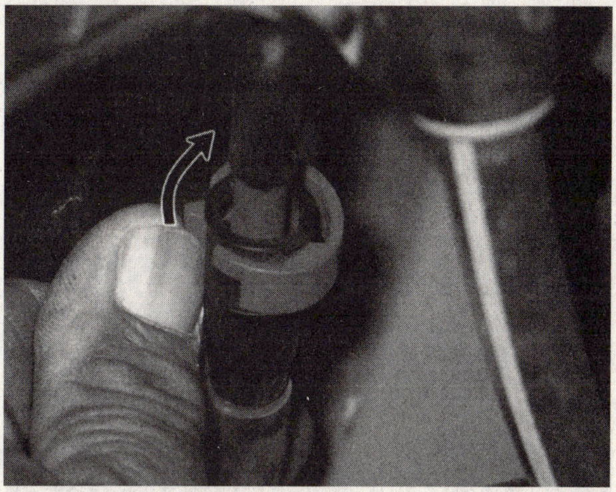

4.16b . . . then rotate the clamp in a clockwise direction to unlock the fitting

5 Fuel pump/fuel level sending unit - removal and installation

Refer to illustrations 5.2a, 5.2b, 5.5a and 5.5b

WARNING:

Gasoline is extremely flammable, so take extra precautions when you work on any part of the fuel system. See the *Warning* in Section 2.

1 On 2001 through 2006 models, the fuel pump module is located at the rear of the fuel tank under the vehicle (raise the vehicle and support it securely on jackstands). On 2006.5 and later models, it's located under a cover in the trunk floor.

2 Remove the cover and disconnect the fuel pump electrical connector (see illustrations).

3 Relieve the fuel system pressure (see Section 2) and remove the fuel tank cap.

4 Disconnect the cable from the negative battery terminal (see Chapter 5).

5 Disconnect the fuel lines from the top of the fuel pump unit (see illustrations).

6 Remove the retaining bolts from the fuel pump/fuel level sending unit mounting flange.

7 Carefully lift the fuel pump/fuel level sending unit assembly from the fuel tank.

8 Inspect the fuel pump inlet strainer for contamination. If it's dirty, try cleaning the strainer with some clean solvent and an old toothbrush. If the strainer is too dirty to be cleaned while it's installed, remove it from the fuel pump/fuel level sending unit (see Section 6) and try cleaning it again. If you still can't clean it adequately, replace it.

9 Installation is the reverse of removal.

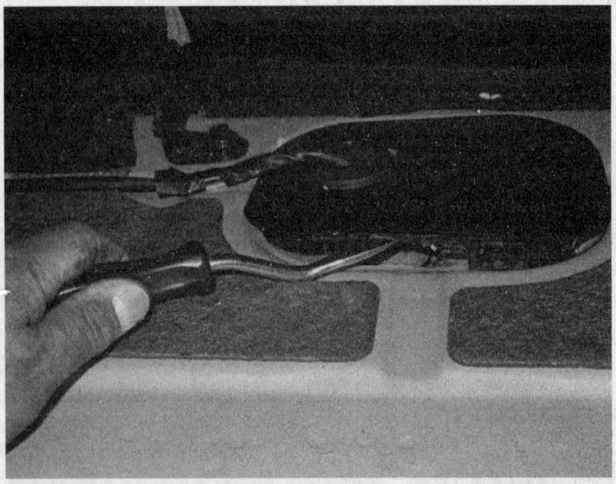

5.2a On 2006.5 and later models, the fuel pump/fuel level sending unit is located under a small cover in the forward part of the trunk floor. To remove the cover, pry it loose from the floor

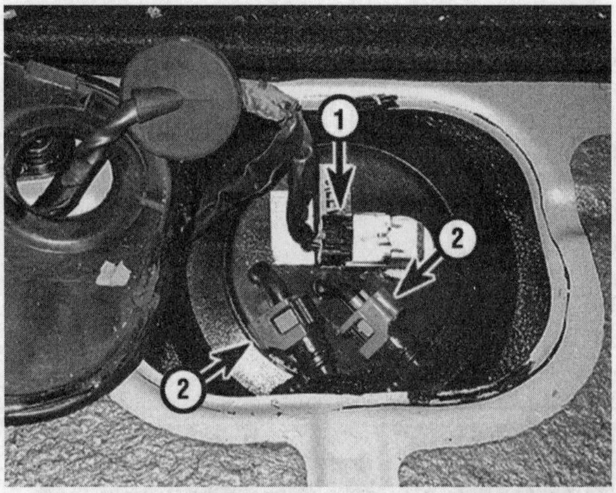

5.2b Typical fuel pump/fuel level sending unit electrical connector (1) and quick-connect fittings (2) (2006.5 and later models)

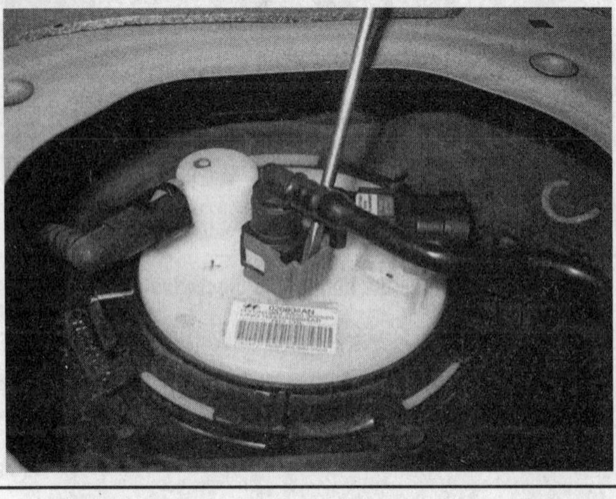

5.5a The locking clip on 2006.5 and later models must be released in order to remove the fuel line

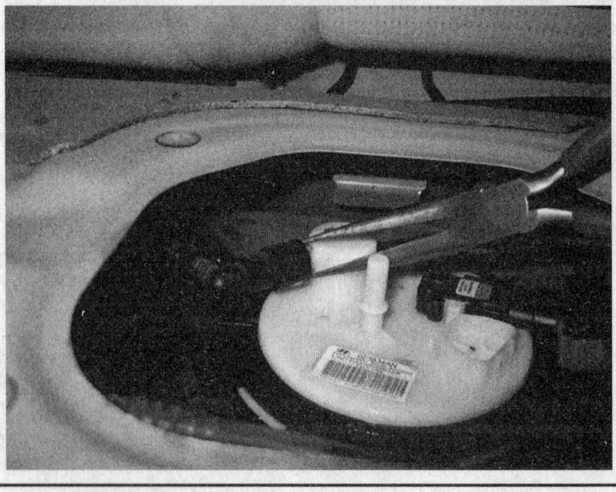

5.5b Needle-nose pliers work well for releasing the locking clips on fuel vapor lines

6 Fuel pump/fuel level sending unit - component replacement

⁂ WARNING:

Gasoline is extremely flammable, so take extra precautions when you work on any part of the fuel system. See the *Warning* in Section 2.

➡ Note: Once you have removed the fuel pump/fuel level sending unit from the fuel tank, you can replace the entire assembly, or you can disassemble it and replace the fuel inlet strainer, the fuel pump or the fuel level sending unit.

1 Remove the fuel pump/fuel level sending unit assembly from the fuel tank (see Section 5).

2 Drain any residual gasoline from the fuel pump/fuel level sending unit, then place the fuel pump/fuel level sending unit on a clean workbench. Make sure that the work area is well ventilated, because there will be gasoline evaporating from the pump/sending unit for a while.

3 Check the filter for clogging. If in doubt, replace it.

4 The fuel level sending unit can be replaced on 2001 through 2006 models. Unclip it from the main assembly. Other components such as the pressure regulator and the pump may be serviceable with individual aftermarket parts available from a local parts store.

5 Reassembly is the reverse of disassembly.

6 Install the fuel pump/fuel level sending unit in the fuel tank (see Section 5).

7 Fuel tank - removal and installation

➧ Refer to illustrations 7.6 and 7.7

⁂ WARNING:

Gasoline is extremely flammable, so take extra precautions when you work on any part of the fuel system. See the *Warning* in Section 2.

1 Relieve the fuel system pressure (see Section 2). Remove the fuel filler cap to relieve fuel tank pressure.

2 Disconnect the cable from the negative battery terminal (see Chapter 5).

3 Disconnect the wiring and hoses from the fuel pump/fuel level sending unit assembly (see Section 5).

4 Remove the drain plug and drain the fuel into an approved container. On later models that don't have a drain fitting, siphon the fuel into an approved container using a hand pump siphon. These are available at most auto parts stores.

⁂ WARNING:

Never start the siphoning action by mouth!

5 Raise the vehicle and place it securely on jackstands. Support the fuel tank.

6 Disconnect the fuel tank filler neck hose and the EVAP system breather and air filter hoses (see illustration).

7 Remove the nuts from the tank retaining straps and lower the straps (see illustration).

8 Lower the tank just enough to inspect the top of the tank, then disconnect any electrical harnesses and/or fuel or EVAP hoses that are connected to the tank.

9 Carefully lower the tank to the ground.

10 Installation is the reverse of removal. Be sure to tighten the fuel tank strap bolts securely.

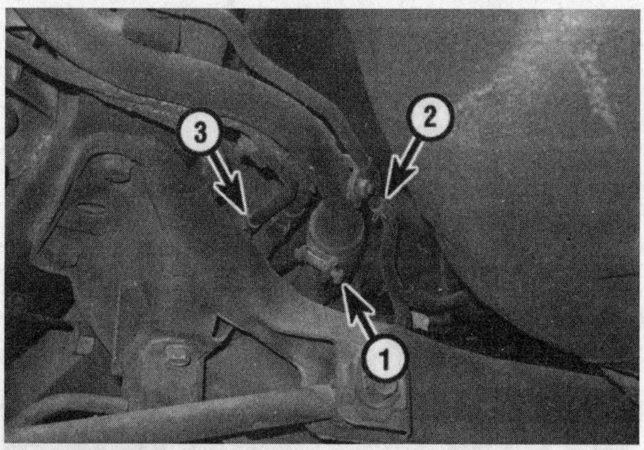

7.6 Typical fuel tank and EVAP system hoses (2006 model shown):

1 Fuel tank filler neck hose clamp
2 Fuel tank EVAP system breather hose clamp
3 Fuel tank EVAP system air filter hose

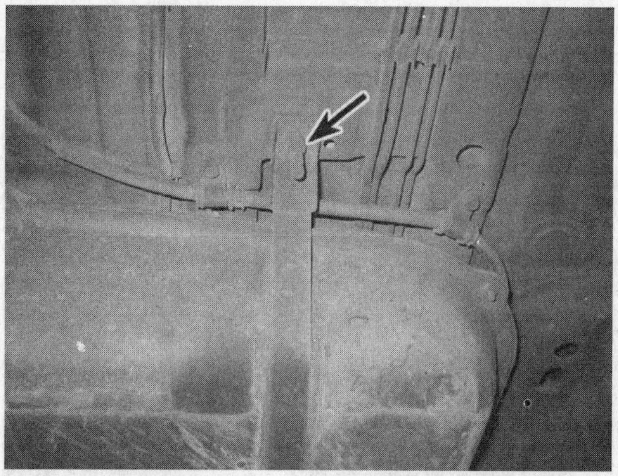

7.7 Remove the nuts from the fuel tank retaining straps

8 Fuel tank cleaning and repair - general information

1 Any repairs to the fuel tank or filler neck should be done by a professional with experience in this critical and potentially dangerous work. Even after cleaning and flushing of the fuel system, explosive fumes can remain and ignite during repair of the tank.

2 If the fuel tank is removed from the vehicle, it should not be placed in an area where sparks or open flames could ignite the fumes coming out of the tank. Be especially careful inside garages where a gas-type appliance is located, because it could cause an explosion.

9 Air filter housing - removal and installation

9.2 Air intake duct details (early 2006 V6 model shown):

1 *Mass Air Flow (MAF) sensor electrical connector*
2 *Throttle Position (TP) sensor electrical connector*
3 *PCV fresh air inlet hose*
4 *Air intake duct hose clamps*

AIR INTAKE DUCT

Refer to illustration 9.2

1 Remove the engine cover (see "Intake manifold - removal and installation" in Chapter 2).

2 Disconnect the electrical connector at the Mass Airflow (MAF) sensor, then disconnect the electrical connector from the Throttle Position (TP) sensor (V6 models). Disconnect the PCV fresh air inlet hose from the duct (see illustration).

3 Loosen the hose clamps at both ends of the air intake duct and remove the duct.

4 If you're replacing the air intake duct, remove the MAF sensor (see Chapter 6) and install it on the new intake duct.

5 Installation is the reverse of removal.

AIR FILTER HOUSING

Refer to illustrations 9.8a and 9.8b

6 Remove the air intake duct (see Steps 1 through 3).

7 Remove the air filter housing cover and remove the filter element (see Chapter 1).

8 Remove the air filter housing mounting bolts (see illustrations).

9 Remove the air filter housing.

10 Installation is the reverse of removal.

9.8a Front and rear air filter housing mounting bolts (early 2006 model shown)

9.8b Use a socket with an extension to remove the left filter housing mounting bolt (early 2006 model shown)

10 Accelerator cable - removal and installation

Refer to illustrations 10.2 and 10.4

Note: All 2001 through 2006 models are equipped with an accelerator cable (and a cruise control cable). Other models have no accelerator cable (or cruise control cable); throttle operation (and cruise control) is controlled electronically by the Powertrain Control Module (PCM), which uses data from the Accelerator Pedal Position (APP) sensor (see Chapter 6) to control the position of the throttle plate inside the throttle body.

1 Remove the engine cover, if applicable.

2 Disengage the accelerator cable from the throttle lever (see illustration).

3 Trace the accelerator cable back to the firewall, note the routing of the cable and detach all cable clips and guides.

4 Inside the vehicle, disengage the cable from the accelerator pedal (see illustration).

5 Remove the bolts and detach the cable from the firewall. Pull the cable through the firewall from the engine compartment side.

6 Installation is the reverse of removal. Apply a dab of white grease to the fitting at the accelerator pedal end of the cable.

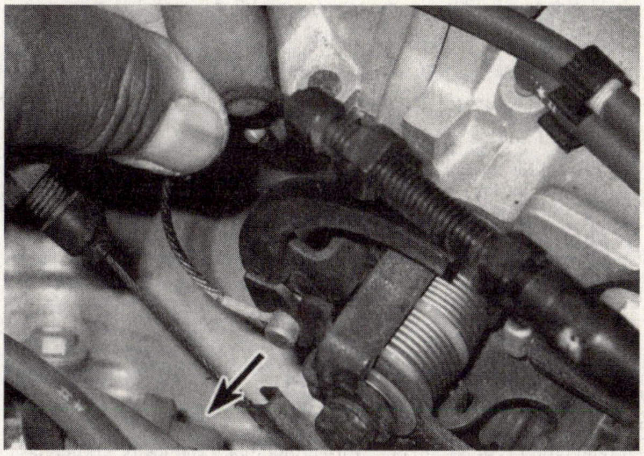

10.2 To disconnect the accelerator cable from the throttle cam, align the cable with the slot in the side of the cam, then slide the cable end plug out of the cam

10.4 To disconnect the cable from the accelerator pedal, pull the cable end (A) out of the pedal, then guide the cable out the slot on the left (B)

11 Electronic Fuel Injection (EFI) system - general information

The EFI system consists of the fuel tank, the electric in-tank fuel pump, the fuel filter, the fuel pressure regulator, the EFI main relay, the circuit opening relay (fuel pump relay), the fuel rail and the fuel injectors. The induction system consists of the air filter housing, the air intake duct and the throttle body. The throttle body on 2001 through 2006 models is a conventional, cable-operated unit. 2006.5 and later models use an electronic throttle body that doesn't have a mechanical connection to the accelerator pedal. The EFI system is divided into three sub-systems: the air intake system, the electronic control system and the fuel delivery system.

AIR INTAKE SYSTEM

The air intake system consists of the air filter housing, the air intake duct, the resonator, the throttle body and the intake manifold. The resonator has oddly shaped appendages clamped to the air intake duct. They function as accumulators, or reservoirs, that help to quiet the flow of air through the air intake duct. The replacement procedures for all of these components are covered in this Chapter except the intake manifolds, which are covered in Chapter 2A or 2B.

The throttle body on all models is a conventional single-barrel design. The lower portion of the throttle body is heated by engine coolant to prevent icing in cold weather. The Throttle Position (TP) sensor is attached to the throttle shaft to monitor changes in the throttle opening. For information about the TP sensor, refer to Chapter 6.

2001 through 2006 models

When the engine is idling, the air/fuel ratio is controlled by the Idle Speed Control (ISC) system. The ISC system consists of the Engine Coolant Temperature (ECT) sensor, the Intake Air Temperature (IAT) sensor, the Throttle Position (TP) sensor, the Mass Air Flow (MAF) sensor, various other sensors, the Powertrain Control Module (PCM) and the ISC valve. The ISC valve is activated by the PCM under certain conditions, such as cold temperature during cranking, or loads imposed on the engine by power steering demand at low vehicle speeds or by turning on the air conditioning. The ISC valve regulates the amount of airflow bypassing the throttle plate and into the intake manifold. For more information about the ISC valve and the ISC system, refer to Chapter 6.

2006.5 and later models

The throttle on these models is electrically controlled by the PCM in response to signals from the accelerator position sensor as well as other sensors. The electronic throttle motor is mounted on the rear of the throttle body; the throttle position sensor and idle switch are on the front. The air/fuel ratio is controlled as with the two other engines.

ELECTRONIC CONTROL SYSTEM

The information sensors, Powertrain Control Module (PCM) and output actuators, and the various emission control systems employed on these vehicles, are described in Chapter 6.

FUEL DELIVERY SYSTEM

The fuel delivery system consists of the fuel pump, the fuel pressure regulator, the fuel filter, the fuel lines, the fuel rail and the fuel injectors. The in-tank fuel pump is an electric in-line type. Fuel is drawn through an inlet filter into the pump, passes through the fuel filter and is delivered to the injectors.

The injectors are solenoid-actuated, constant stroke, pintle types consisting of a solenoid, plunger, needle valve and housing. When current is applied to the solenoid coil, the needle valve is raised off its seat and pressurized fuel squirts out of the injector body through the nozzle. The injection quantity is determined by the pulse width (the length of time that the pintle valve is open), which is controlled by the length of time during which current is supplied to the solenoid coil.

The EFI main relay, located in the instrument panel relay/fuse box, supplies power to the fuel pump relay (circuit opening relay) from the ignition key. The PCM controls the grounding signal to the fuel pump in response to the starting and camshaft position signals at start-up.

12 Fuel injection system - check

Refer to illustrations 12.7, 12.8 and 12.9

WARNING:

Gasoline is extremely flammable, so take extra precautions when you work on any part of the fuel system. See the *Warning* in Section 2.

1 Check all electrical connectors, especially ground connections, for the system. Loose connectors and poor grounds can cause many engine control system problems.

2 Verify that the battery is fully charged, because the Powertrain Control Module (PCM) and sensors cannot operate properly without an adequate voltage supply.

12.7 Using a stethoscope, listen to each fuel injector and verify that it's making a clicking sound when the engine is running

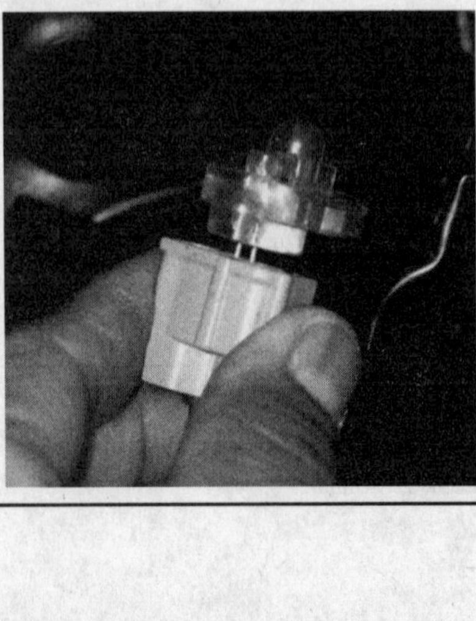

12.8 Plug the noid light into the electrical connector for the inoperative fuel injector and see if it blinks with the engine running

3 Refer to Chapter 1 and check the air filter element. A dirty or partially blocked filter will reduce performance.

4 Check fuel pump operation (see Section 3). If the fuel pump fuse is blown, replace it and see if it blows again. If it does, look for a short in the wiring harness to the fuel pump.

5 Inspect the vacuum hoses connected to the intake manifold for damage, deterioration and leakage.

6 Remove the air intake duct from the throttle body and check for dirt, carbon, varnish, or other residue in the throttle body, particularly around the throttle plate. If it's dirty, refer to Chapter 6 and troubleshoot the PCV and EGR systems for the cause of excessive varnish buildup.

7 With the engine running, place an automotive stethoscope against each injector, one at a time, and listen for a clicking sound that indicates operation (see illustration). If you don't have a stethoscope, you can place the tip of a long screwdriver against the injector and listen through the handle.

8 If an injector does not seem to be operating electrically (not clicking), purchase a special injector test light (sometimes called a 'noid light - short for solenoid) and install it into the injector wiring harness connector (see illustration). Start the engine and see if the 'noid light flashes. If it does, the injector is receiving proper voltage. If it doesn't flash, further diagnosis is necessary. You might want to have it checked by a dealership service department or other qualified repair shop.

9 With the engine off and the fuel injector electrical connectors disconnected, measure the resistance of each injector with an ohmmeter (see illustration). If any injector differs from the average of the others by more than 15-percent, replace it.

10 Refer to Chapter 6 for other system checks.

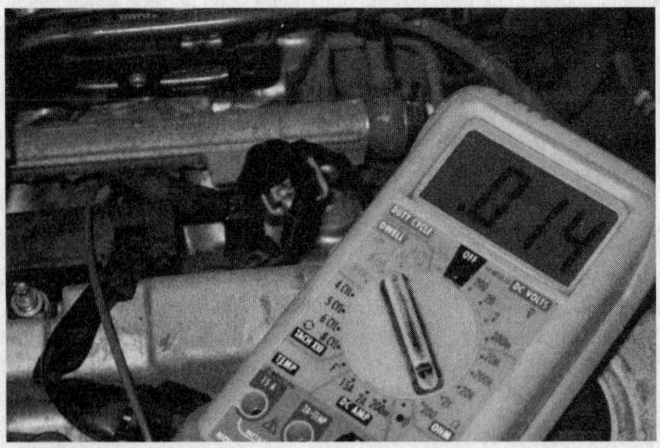

12.9 Turn the mode knob on your multimeter to the appropriate resistance range, touch the probes of the meter to the two terminals on each injector and measure the resistance, which should be within the range listed in this Chapter's Specifications

13 Throttle body - check, removal and installation

CHECK

Refer to illustration 13.2

1 If equipped, verify that the throttle cable operates smoothly.

2 Remove the air intake duct from the throttle body and check for carbon and residue build-up. If it is dirty, clean it with aerosol carburetor/throttle body cleaner (make sure the can specifically states that it is safe with oxygen sensor systems and catalytic converters) and a toothbrush (see illustration).

CAUTION:

Do not clean the Throttle Position (TP) sensor or the Idle Speed Actuator (ISA) valve with the solvent.

REMOVAL AND INSTALLATION

Refer to illustrations 13.5 and 13.9

WARNING:

Wait until the engine is completely cool before beginning this procedure.

3 Disconnect the cable from the negative battery terminal (see Chapter 5).

4 Remove the air intake duct (see Section 9).

5 Disconnect the electrical connector from the Throttle Position (TP) sensor on 2001 through 2006 models. On later models, disconnect the electrical connector (see illustration) from the electronic throttle body.

6 On models so equipped, disconnect the accelerator and cruise control cables from the throttle body (see Section 10).

13.5 Electrical connector (typical 2006.5 and later electronic throttle body)

13.2 With the engine off, use aerosol carburetor cleaner, a toothbrush and a shop rag to clean the throttle body bore. Open the throttle plate so you can clean behind it. Make sure the carb cleaner is safe for use with catalytic converters and oxygen sensors

7 Clearly label any vacuum lines connected to the throttle body, then disconnect them.

8 Clamp off and disconnect the coolant hoses to the throttle body to minimize coolant loss.

9 Remove the throttle body mounting fasteners (see illustration) and remove the throttle body.

10 Disconnect the coolant hoses from the throttle body.

11 Remove and discard the old throttle body gasket.

12 Installation is the reverse of removal. Be sure to tighten the throttle body mounting fasteners to the torque listed in this Chapter's Specifications. Check the coolant level and add as necessary (see Chapter 1).

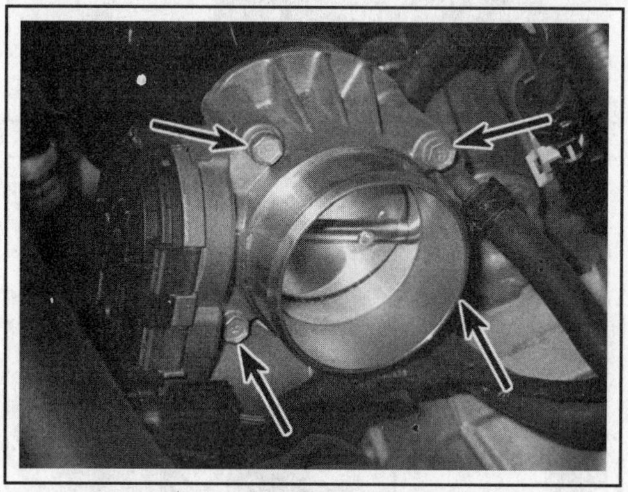

13.9 Throttle body mounting bolts (2006.5 and later four-cylinder unit shown)

14 Fuel rail and injectors - removal and installation

Refer to illustrations 14.6a, 14.6b, 14.7, 14.9 and 14.10

WARNING:

Gasoline is extremely flammable, so take extra precautions when you work on any part of the fuel system. See the *Warning* in Section 2.

Note: We recommend replacing all injector O-rings even when only one injector O-ring or seal is leaking. On most fuel rails, you have to remove the entire assembly anyway, so replace all of the O-rings/seals to avoid having to remove the fuel rail later.

1 Relieve the fuel pressure (see Section 2).

2 Disconnect the cable from the negative battery terminal (see Chapter 5).

3 Remove the engine cover, if equipped.

4 Remove the air intake duct (see Section 9).

5 On V6 models, refer to Chapter 2B and remove the upper intake manifold.

6 Disconnect the electrical connectors from the fuel injectors (see illustration), unbolt the harness and set the injector harness aside (see illustration).

7 Remove the fuel rail mounting bolts (see illustration).

8 Remove the fuel rail and the fuel injectors as a single assembly.

14.6b Injector assembly detail - arrow indicates retaining clip that secures the injector to the fuel rail

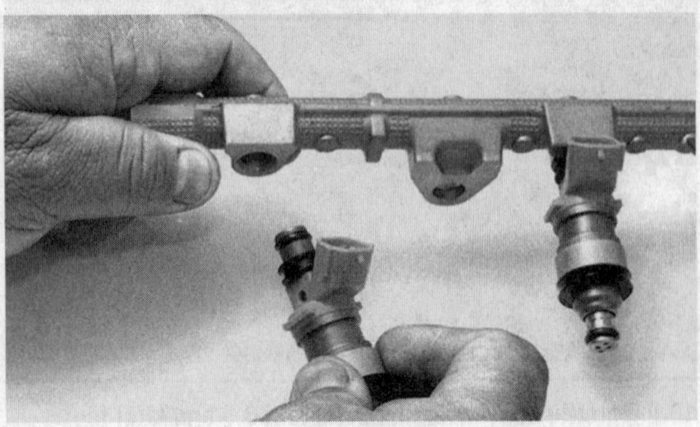

14.9 To remove each fuel injector from the fuel rail, simultaneously twist and pull it out after first removing the retaining clip

9 Remove the fuel injectors from the fuel rail (see illustration).

10 If you intend to re-use the same injectors, replace the grommets and O-rings (see illustration).

11 Installation is the reverse of removal. Be sure to use new injector O-rings and tighten the fuel rail mounting bolts to the torque listed in this Chapter's Specifications.

14.6a Some injector electrical connectors have a locking device that must be released; then use pliers to pull the connector from the injector

14.7 Typical fuel rail mounting bolts

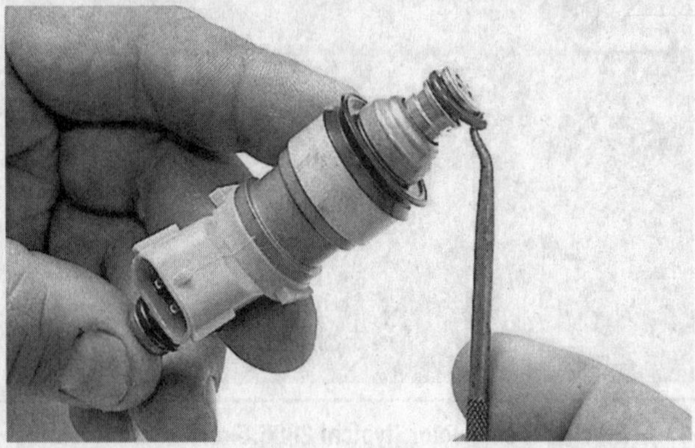

14.10 If you plan to reinstall the original injectors, remove and discard the old O-rings and grommets and replace them with new ones

15 Fuel pressure regulator - replacement

RETURN-TYPE FUEL SYSTEMS (2001 THROUGH 2006 MODELS)

1 Relieve the fuel system pressure (see Section 2).
2 Disconnect the cable from the negative terminal of the battery.
3 Disconnect the vacuum hose from the fuel pressure regulator.
4 Detach the fuel return line from the regulator.
5 Remove the two bolts and detach the fuel pressure regulator from the fuel rail.
6 If you're installing the same regulator, check the condition of the O-ring, replacing it if necessary.
7 Installation is the reverse of the removal procedure.

RETURNLESS FUEL SYSTEMS (2006.5 AND LATER MODELS)

8 The fuel pressure regulator is a part of the fuel pump assembly. This includes the pump, the fuel level sender, the filter and the pressure regulator.
9 At the time of writing, the fuel pressure regulator was not available separately, necessitating replacement of the entire fuel pump assembly. Check with your local auto parts store or dealer parts department to see if the pressure regulator can currently be purchased separately.

16 Exhaust system servicing - general information

➧ Refer to illustration 16.1

⁂ WARNING:

Inspect and repair exhaust system components only after the system components have cooled down.

1 The exhaust system consists of the exhaust manifold(s), the catalytic converters, the muffler, the tailpipe and the exhaust pipes that connect these components together, as well as the brackets, hangers and clamps that support and secure these components. The exhaust system is attached to the body with mounting brackets and rubber hangers (see illustration). If any of these parts are damaged or deteriorated, excessive noise and vibration will be transmitted to the body. The exhaust system is divided into various sections, which are bolted together. Some of these sections consist of several components welded together into one assembly. For example, the center part of the exhaust system, which is also the longest single section, includes the downstream catalytic converter and the pre-muffler. If either of these components is damaged, you will have to replace the entire assembly, or have the old catalyst or muffler cut off and a new unit welded in. You'll also have to remove the center exhaust pipe assembly in order to remove the fuel tank.
2 Conducting regular inspections of the exhaust system will keep it safe and quiet. Look for damaged or bent parts, open seams, holes, loose connections, excessive corrosion or other damage that could allow exhaust fumes to enter the vehicle. Do not repair deteriorated exhaust system components - replace them.
3 If the exhaust system components are extremely corroded or rusted together, they will probably have to be cut from the exhaust system. The convenient way to accomplish this is to have a muffler repair shop remove the corroded sections with a cutting torch. If, however, you want to save money by doing it yourself and you don't have an oxy/acetylene welding outfit with a cutting torch, simply cut off the old components with a hacksaw. If you have compressed air, you can also use special pneumatic cutting chisels. If you do decide to tackle the job at home, be sure to wear eye protection to protect your eyes from metal chips, and wear work gloves to protect your hands.
4 Here are some simple guidelines to apply when repairing the exhaust system:

a) *Work from the back to the front when removing exhaust system components.*
b) *Apply penetrating oil to the exhaust system component fasteners to make them easier to remove.*
c) *Use new gaskets, hangers and clamps when installing exhaust system components. Unless the fasteners are in good condition, it's also a good idea to replace them as well. Even if you're successful in unscrewing rusted fasteners, they will be even more difficult to unscrew the next time that you need to do so, and they might break the next time that they're loosened or tightened.*
d) *Apply anti-seize compound to the threads of all exhaust system fasteners during reassembly. Be sure to allow sufficient clearance between newly installed parts and all points on the underbody to avoid overheating the floor pan and possibly damaging the interior carpet and insulation. Pay particularly close attention to the catalytic converter and its heat shield.*

⁂ WARNING:

The catalytic converter operates at very high temperatures and takes a long time to cool. Wait until it's completely cool before attempting to remove the converter. Failure to do so could result in serious burns.

16.1 The rubber exhaust system hangers can deteriorate and break - they should be checked periodically

Specifications

➡ Note: 2006 and 2006.5 models will both have a "6" in the tenth position of the VIN. To distinguish a 2006 model from a 2006.5 model, refer to the 8th position of the VIN (the engine code): A 2006 model will have a "6" (four-cylinder) or "8" (V6), while a 2006.5 will have a "3" (four-cylinder) or "4" (V6).

General

Fuel system pressure	
2001 through 2006 models	
With pressure regulator vacuum hose connected, at idle	Approximately 38 psi (262 kPa)
With pressure regulator vacuum hose disconnected	47 to 50 psi (324 to 345 kPa)
2006.5 and later models	50 to 52 psi (345 to 358 kPa)
Fuel injector resistance (approximate)	13 to 16 ohms

Torque specifications

➡ Note: One foot-pound (ft-lb) of torque is equivalent to 12 inch-pounds (in-lbs) of torque. Torque values below approximately 15 foot-pounds are expressed in inch-pounds, because most foot-pound torque wrenches are not accurate at these smaller values.

Torque specifications	Ft-lbs (unless otherwise indicated)	Nm
Fuel rail mounting bolts or nuts		
2001 through 2006 models	84 to 132 in-lbs	10 to 15
2006.5 and later models	15 to 18	20 to 25
Throttle body mounting bolts/nuts	132 to 168 in-lbs	15 to 19

5 ENGINE ELECTRICAL SYSTEMS

Section

Reference to other Chapters

Battery check, maintenance and charging - See Chapter 1
CHECK ENGINE light on - See Chapter 6
Drivebelt check, adjustment and replacement - See Chapter 1
Spark plug replacement - See Chapter 1
Spark plug wire check and replacement - See Chapter 1

1 General information, precautions and battery disconnection

The engine electrical systems include all ignition, charging and starting components. Because of their engine-related functions, these components are discussed separately from body electrical devices such as the lights, the instruments, etc. (which are included in Chapter 12).

PRECAUTIONS

Always observe the following precautions when working on the electrical system:

a) *Be extremely careful when servicing engine electrical components. They are easily damaged if checked, connected or handled improperly.*
b) *Never leave the ignition switched on for long periods of time when the engine is not running.*
c) *Never disconnect the battery cables while the engine is running.*
d) *Maintain correct polarity when connecting battery cables from another vehicle during jump starting - see the "Booster battery (jump) starting" Section at the front of this manual.*
e) *Always disconnect the negative battery cable from the battery before working on the electrical system, but read the following battery disconnection procedure first.*

It's also a good idea to review the safety-related information regarding the engine electrical systems located in the "Safety first!" Section at the front of this manual, before beginning any operation included in this Chapter.

BATTERY DISCONNECTION

Several systems - such as the alarm system, radio, power door locks or power windows - require continuous battery power, either to ensure their continued operation or to maintain control unit memory, such as the Powertrain Control Module (PCM), which will be lost if the battery is disconnected. Therefore, whenever the battery is to be disconnected, first note the following to ensure that there are no unforeseen consequences of this action:

a) *The engine management system's PCM will eventually lose some data stored in its memory when the battery is disconnected. This could include idling and operating values, detected fault codes and the system monitors required for emissions testing. Whenever the battery is disconnected, the computer may require a certain period of time to re-learn the operating values.*
b) *On any vehicle with power door locks, it is a wise precaution to remove the key from the ignition and to keep it with you, so that it does not get locked inside if the power door locks should engage accidentally when the battery is reconnected!*

Devices known as "memory-savers" can be used to avoid some of the above problems. Typically, a memory-saver is plugged into the cigarette lighter and connected to another voltage source. The vehicle battery is then disconnected from the electrical system, and the memory-saver provides current levels sufficient to maintain audio unit security codes and PCM memory values, and to power always-on circuits such as the clock and radio memory, all the while isolating the battery in the event that a short-circuit occurs while servicing the vehicle.

**** WARNING:**

Some of these devices allow a considerable amount of current to pass, which can mean that many of the vehicle's systems are still operational when the main battery is disconnected. So if you're using a memory-saver, make sure that a circuit is actually open before touching it.

**** WARNING:**

If you're working around an airbag, disconnect the battery and do not use a memory saver. If you use a memory-saver device to keep up power while working around an airbag, remember that the airbag is capable of accidental deployment.

The battery on all models is located in the engine compartment. To disconnect the battery for service procedures requiring power to be cut from the vehicle, loosen the negative cable clamp nut and detach the negative cable from the negative battery post. Isolate the cable end to prevent it from accidentally coming into contact with the battery post.

2 Battery - emergency jump starting

Refer to the *Booster battery (jump) starting* procedure at the front of this manual.

3 Battery - check and replacement

CHECK

➧ Refer to illustrations 3.2 and 3.3

1 Disconnect the negative battery cable, then the positive cable from the battery.

2 Check the battery state of charge. Perform an open voltage circuit test using a digital voltmeter (see illustration).

➡ Note: The battery's surface charge must be removed before accurate voltage measurements can be made. Turn on the high beams for ten seconds, then turn them off, and let the vehicle stand for two minutes.

With the engine and all accessories turned off, touch the negative probe of the voltmeter to the negative terminal of the battery and the positive probe to the positive terminal of the battery. The battery voltage should be about 12.6 to 12.9 volts. If the battery is less than the specified voltage, charge the battery before proceeding to the next test. Do not proceed with the battery load test unless the battery charge is correct.

3 Perform a battery load test. An accurate check of the battery condition can only be performed with a load tester (available at most auto parts stores). This test evaluates the ability of the battery to operate the starter and other accessories during periods of heavy load (current draw). Connect a battery load-testing tool to the terminals (see illustration). Load test the battery according to the tool manufacturer's instructions. Observe that the battery voltage does not drop below 9.6 volts. If the battery condition is weak or defective, the tool will indicate this condition immediately.

➡ Note: Cold temperatures will cause the minimum voltage reading to drop slightly. Follow the chart given in the tool manufacturer's instructions to compensate for cold climates. Minimum load voltage for freezing temperatures (32-degrees F) should be approximately 9.1 volts.

REPLACEMENT

➧ Refer to illustrations 3.4 and 3.5

4 Disconnect the negative cable, then the positive cable from the battery (see illustration).

5 Remove the battery hold-down clamp (see illustration).

6 Lift out the battery. Be careful - it's heavy.

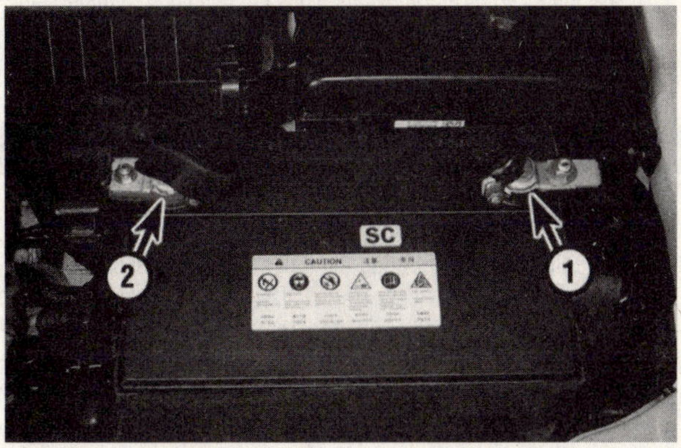

3.4 Disconnect the cable from the negative battery terminal first (1), then disconnect the cable from the positive terminal (2)

3.2 To test the open circuit voltage of the battery, touch the black probe of the voltmeter to the negative terminal and the red probe to the positive terminal of the battery. A fully charged battery should read between 12.6 and 12.9 volts, depending on the ambient temperature

3.3 Some battery load testers are equipped with an ammeter that enables you to dial in the battery load. Less expensive testers only have a load switch and voltmeter (shown)

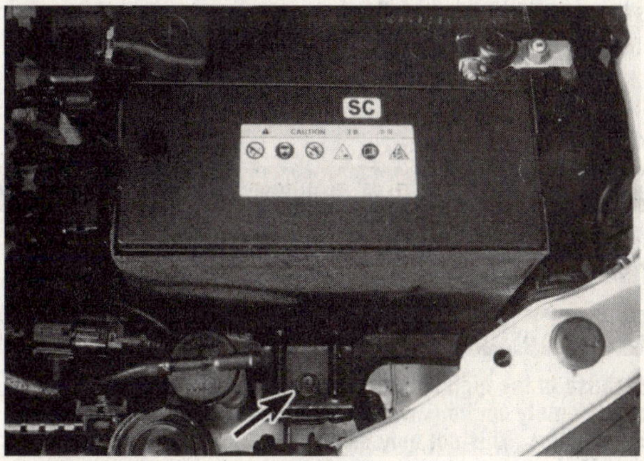

3.5 The battery is secured on its tray by a clamp at the base; check it for acid corrosion and replace damaged components

➡ **Note: Battery straps and handlers are available at most auto parts stores for a reasonable price. They make it easier to remove and carry the battery.**

7 While the battery is out, remove the battery tray and inspect it for corrosion.

8 If there's corrosion on the battery tray, wash the tray thoroughly in clean water. If the tray is cracked or damaged, replace it.

9 If you are replacing the battery, make sure you get one that's identical, with the same dimensions, amperage rating, cold cranking rating, etc.

10 Installation is the reverse of removal.

4 Battery cables - check and replacement

1 Periodically, inspect the entire length of each battery cable for damage, cracked or burned insulation and corrosion. Poor battery cable connections can cause starting problems.

2 Inspect the cable-to-terminal connections at the ends of the cables for cracks, loose wire strands and corrosion (see Chapter 1). The presence of white, fluffy deposits under the insulation at the cable terminal connection are a sign that the cable is corroded and should be replaced. Check the terminals for distortion, missing mounting bolts and corrosion.

3 When removing the cables, always disconnect the negative cable first and hook it up last or you might accidentally short the battery with the tool that you're using to loosen the cable clamps. Even if only the positive cable is being replaced, be sure to disconnect the negative cable from the battery first.

4 Disconnect the old cables from the battery, then trace each of them to their opposite ends and detach them from the starter solenoid and ground terminals. Note the routing of each cable to ensure correct installation.

5 If you are replacing either or both of the old cables, take them with you when buying new cables. It is vitally important that you replace the cables with identical parts. Cables have characteristics that make them easy to identify. Positive cables are usually red and larger in cross-section; ground cables are usually black and smaller in cross section.

6 Clean the threads of the solenoid or ground connection with a wire brush to remove rust and corrosion. Apply a light coat of battery terminal corrosion inhibitor, or petroleum jelly, to the threads to prevent future corrosion.

7 Attach the cable to the solenoid or ground connection and tighten the mounting nut/bolt securely.

8 Before connecting a new cable to the battery, make sure that it reaches the battery post without having to be stretched.

9 Connect the positive cable first, followed by the negative cable.

5 Ignition system - general information and precautions

1 All models covered by this manual are equipped with a computer-controlled electronic ignition system. The ignition system includes the Camshaft Position (CMP) sensor, the Crankshaft Position (CKP) sensor, the Powertrain Control Module (PCM), and the spark plugs; there is no distributor. Various other sensors influence the ignition timing. 2001 through 2006 V6 engines use a conventional coil pack that fires the spark plugs via six spark plug wires. On 2001 through 2006 four-cylinder engines, there are coils on only two cylinders. Each of these coils has a spark plug wire attached that also fires another spark plug simultaneously. This is called a "waste spark" system. The cylinder that is being fired while on its exhaust stroke consumes very little spark energy. All other engines use a coil-on-plug system.

2 When working on the ignition system, take the following precautions:

a) Do not keep the ignition switch on for more than 10 seconds if the engine will not start.

b) Always connect a tachometer in accordance with the manufacturer's instructions. Some tachometers may be incompatible with this ignition system. Consult an auto parts counterperson before buying a tachometer for use with this vehicle.

c) Never allow the ignition coil terminals to touch ground. Grounding the coil could result in damage to the igniter and/or the ignition coil.

d) Do not disconnect the battery when the engine is running.

6 Ignition system - check

➧ **Refer to illustration 6.2**

⁂ WARNING:

Because of the high voltage generated by the ignition system, be extremely cautious when servicing or checking ignition components. This not only includes the ignition coils and spark plugs but test equipment as well.

1 Relieve the fuel system pressure (see Chapter 4). Keep the fuel system disabled while performing the ignition system checks.

2 If the engine turns over but won't start, disconnect an ignition coil (or spark plug wire) from its corresponding spark plug (see Section 7) and attach it to a calibrated ignition tester (see illustration). Calibrated ignition testers are available at most auto parts stores.

3 Crank the engine and watch the tester to see if the tester body flashes, or if bright blue, well-defined sparks occur (depending on the

type of tester you're using).

4 If the tester body flashes (or if sparks occur), sufficient voltage is reaching the spark plug to fire it. Repeat this test at each spark plug to verify that all the ignition coils are functioning. If there is no spark at a plug, the ignition coil for that plug is probably bad. However, the plug itself might be fouled, so remove and check the plug as described in Chapter 1. If a number of plugs are fouled, it's a good idea to install a set of new spark plugs so that the plug gaps are uniform and the electrodes are all in the same condition.

5 Use a code-reading tool or a scan tool to check for any stored Diagnostic Trouble Codes (DTCs) related to the ignition system, the Camshaft Position (CMP) sensor, the Crankshaft Position (CKP) sensor, other sensors or and/or the Powertrain Control Module (PCM).

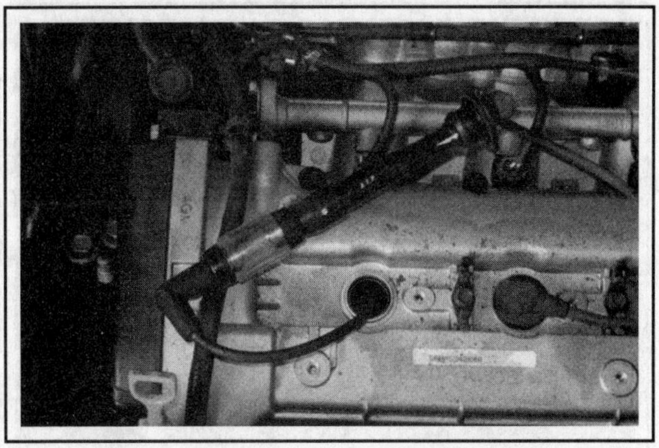

6.2 To use this type of calibrated ignition tester, unbolt and remove the ignition coil (then reconnect the electrical connector), plug the tester into the boot at the lower end of the coil, clip the tester to a convenient ground and crank the engine. If there's enough power to fire the plug, the tester body will flash

7 Ignition coils - check and replacement

CHECK

2001 through 2006 models

Four-cylinder engines

Refer to illustration 7.2

1 Remove the coils from the engine.

2 Connect an ohmmeter between the two secondary terminals of each coil and write down your readings (see illustration). This is the secondary resistance value.

3 If any reading differs substantially from that listed in this Chapter's Specifications, replace that coil.

4 Use jumper wires to connect two 1.5-volt batteries in series to make a 3-volt power supply.

5 Connect the negative end of the power supply to the middle terminal of the three-wire coil wiring connector.

6 Connect an ohmmeter between the number two and three terminals. Take a reading. There should be nearly infinite resistance.

7 Now connect the positive end of the power supply to terminal one and again read the resistance. It should now be close to the figure listed in this Chapter's Specifications.

8 If any of the above readings vary substantially, replace the coil.

V6 engines

Refer to illustration 7.12

9 Disconnect the spark plug wires from the coil pack. Also disconnect the primary wiring connector.

10 Connect an ohmmeter between the first two spark plug terminals on the coil. This is the secondary resistance. Compare your reading with this Chapter's Specifications. If it's substantially out of range, replace the coil.

11 Repeat this procedure for the middle two terminals, then the last two.

12 Connect the ohmmeter between terminals 1 and 2 of the wiring connector (see illustration). This is the primary resistance for cylinders 3 and 6. Compare your reading with this Chapter's Specifications. If it's

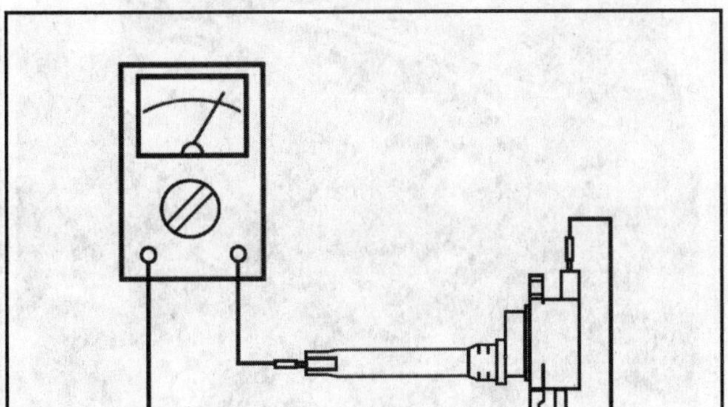

7.2 On four-cylinder engines, connect the ohmmeter between the spark plug terminal and spark plug wire terminal to check the secondary resistance (2001 through 2006 models)

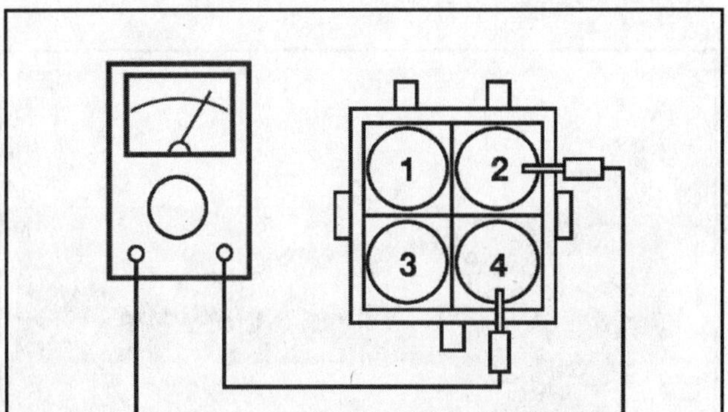

7.12 On 2.5L and 2.7L V6 engines, unplug the wiring harness from the coil pack and probe terminals 1 and 2, 2 and 4, then 2 and 3, with an ohmmeter (2001 through 2006 models)

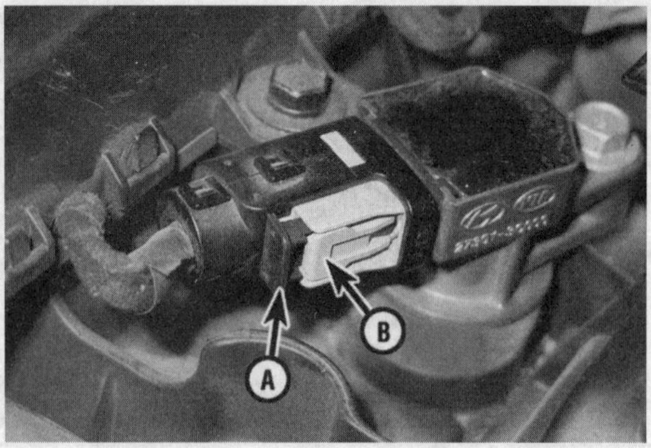

7.21a To disconnect the electrical connector from an ignition coil, slide the lock (A) out of the connector, then depress the tab (B) and pull the connector off the coil

7.21b Ignition coil bolt locations (2006.5 and later four-cylinder engines)

substantially out of range, replace the coil.

13 Repeat this procedure between terminals 2 and 4. This will give the primary resistance for cylinders 1 and 4. Repeat it again between terminals 2 and 3. This will give the primary resistance for cylinders 2 and 5.

2006.5 and later models

14 Remove the coils from the engine (see Steps 21 through 23).

15 Connect an ohmmeter between the two primary (low voltage) terminals of each coil and write down the readings.

16 Compare your readings with this Chapter's Specifications. If any coil differs greatly from the specifications, replace it. Modest variations (up to plus or minus 15-percent) are normal.

17 The manufacturer does not furnish secondary resistance values for these coils.

18 If you're in doubt about a coil, try swapping it to another cylinder. If a PCM trouble code indicated a misfire on the old cylinder, the problem will transfer to the new cylinder if the coil is bad.

REPLACEMENT

19 Disconnect the cable from the negative battery terminal (see Sections 1 and 3).

20 Remove the engine cover.

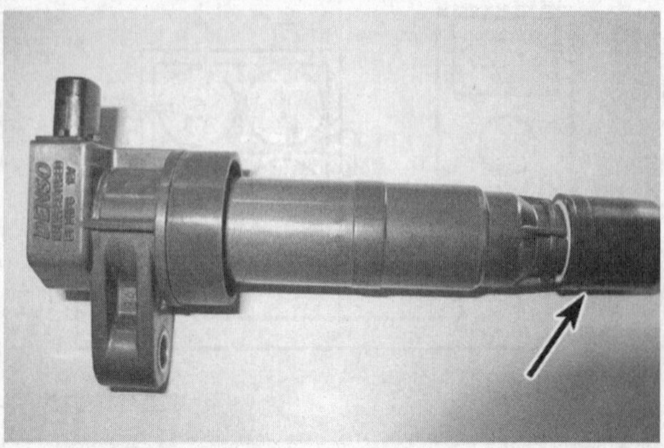

7.23 Make sure the rubber boot of each coil isn't deteriorated (all four-cylinder, and 2006.5 and later V6 models)

All four-cylinder, and 2006.5 and later V6 models

➧ Refer to illustrations 7.21a, 7.21b and 7.23

21 Disconnect the electrical connector from the ignition coils, then remove the mounting bolts (see illustrations).

22 On 2001 through 2006 four-cylinder models, disconnect the spark plug wire. Pull on the boot only - not on the wire.

23 Pull the coil straight up and out of the valve cover (see illustration).

24 Installation is the reverse of removal.

2001 through 2006 V6 models

➧ Refer to illustration 7.27

25 The coil pack on these engines is mounted at the left end of the front cylinder head.

26 Mark the positions of the spark plug wires, then detach them from the coil pack.

27 Disconnect the electrical connector from the ignition coil, then remove the mounting bolts (see illustration).

28 Lift the coil pack from the cylinder head.

29 Installation is the reverse of removal.

7.27 Ignition coil pack details (2001 through 2006 V6 models):

1 *Electrical connector*
2 *Coil pack mounting bracket bolts (underneath bracket at indicated locations, bolts not visible in this photo)*

8 Charging system - general information and precautions

The charging system includes the alternator with an internal voltage regulator, the discharge warning light, the battery, a fusible link and the wiring between all the components. The charging system supplies electrical power for the ignition system, the lights, the radio, etc. The alternator is driven by a drivebelt at the front of the engine. The voltage regulator limits the alternator's voltage to a preset value to prevent power surges and circuit overloads during peak voltage output.

The discharge warning light on the instrument cluster should come on when the ignition key is turned to START, then it should go off immediately. If it remains on, or if it comes on during vehicle operation, there is a malfunction in the charging system.

The charging system doesn't ordinarily require periodic maintenance. However, the drivebelt, battery and wires and connections should be inspected at the intervals outlined in Chapter 1. Be very careful when making electrical circuit connections to a vehicle equipped with an alternator and note the following:

- a) *When reconnecting wires to the alternator from the battery, note the polarity.*
- b) *Before using arc-welding equipment to repair any part of the vehicle, disconnect the wires from the alternator and the battery terminals.*
- c) *Never start the engine with a battery charger connected.*
- d) *Always disconnect both battery leads before using a battery charger.*
- e) *The alternator is driven by an engine drivebelt that could cause serious injury if your hand, hair or clothes become entangled in it with the engine running.*
- f) *Because the alternator is connected directly to the battery, it could arc or cause a fire if overloaded or shorted out.*
- g) *Wrap a plastic bag over the alternator and secure it with rubber bands before steam cleaning the engine.*

9 Charging system - check

Refer to illustration 9.3

1 If a malfunction occurs in the charging circuit, do not immediately assume that the alternator is causing the problem. First, check the following items:

- a) *Make sure the battery cable clamps are clean and tightly secured to the battery terminals.*
- b) *Test the condition of the battery (see Section 3). If it does not pass all the tests, replace it.*
- c) *Check the external alternator wiring and connections.*
- d) *Check the drivebelt condition and tension (see Chapter 1).*
- e) *Check the alternator mounting bolts for tightness.*
- f) *Run the engine and check the alternator for abnormal noise.*
- g) *Check the fusible link (see Chapter 12). If it's burned, determine the cause and repair the circuit.*
- h) *Check the discharge warning indicator light on the instrument cluster. It should illuminate when the ignition key is turned to ON (engine not running). If it doesn't, check the circuit between the alternator and the discharge warning indicator light (see the Wiring Diagrams at the end of Chapter 12).*
- i) *Check the fuses that are in series with the charging system circuit (see the Wiring Diagrams at the end of Chapter 12).*

2 With the ignition key off, check the battery voltage with no accessories operating. It should be approximately 12.6 to 12.9 volts (see illustration 3.2). It may be slightly higher if the engine had been operating within the last hour.

3 Connect an ammeter to the charging system following the tool manufacturer's instructions. Start the engine, and check the battery voltage and amperage. It should now be approximately 13.2 to 14.8 volts (see illustration).

4 Load the battery by turning on the high beam headlights and the air conditioning system and place the blower fan on HIGH. Raise the engine speed to 2,000 rpm and check the voltage and amperage. If the charging system is working properly the voltage should stay above 13.5 volts and the amperage should be 30 amps or more (depending on the condition of the battery, it could be less than 30 amps).

9.3 To check charging voltage, connect a voltmeter to the battery terminals and check the battery voltage with the engine running

5 If the voltage rises above 15.0 volts in either test, the regulator is defective and the alternator should be replaced.

6 If the indicated voltage reading is less than the specified charge voltage, the alternator is probably defective. Have the charging system checked at a dealer service department or other properly equipped repair facility.

Note: Many auto parts stores will bench test an alternator off the vehicle. Ask your local auto parts store about their policy (many will perform this service free of charge).

10 Alternator - removal and installation

REMOVAL

1 Disconnect the cable from the negative battery terminal (see Section 1).

2001 through 2006 four-cylinder models

2 Disconnect the electrical connectors from the alternator.

3 Loosen the lock bolt on the upper alternator adjusting mount and the lower mount bolt.

4 Turn the adjusting bolt counterclockwise to release tension on the drivebelt.

5 Remove the drivebelt.

6 Remove the two alternator mounting bolts and remove the alternator.

All other models

Refer to illustrations 10.8a and 10.8b

7 Remove the drivebelt (see Chapter 1).

Note: Access is very limited on these models. It will be necessary to remove various components including the lower engine splash shield to gain access. These components vary from model to model.

8 Disconnect the electrical connectors from the alternator (see illustrations).

9 Remove the alternator mounting fasteners and remove the alternator.

INSTALLATION

10 If you're replacing the alternator, take the old alternator with you when purchasing a replacement unit. Make sure that the new/rebuilt unit is identical to the old alternator. Look at the terminals - they should be the same in number, size and locations as the terminals on the old alternator. Finally, look at the identification markings - they will be stamped in the housing or printed on a tag or plaque affixed to the housing. Make sure that these numbers are the same on both alternators.

11 If the replacement alternator doesn't have a pulley installed, you may have to switch the pulley from the old unit to the replacement unit. When buying a new or rebuilt alternator, ask about the shop's policy regarding pulley swapping. Some shops will perform this service for free.

12 Installation is the reverse of removal. Adjust the drivebelt tension on 2005 and earlier 2.4L four-cylinder models only (see Chapter 1). Check the charging voltage to verify that the alternator is operating correctly (see Section 9).

10.8a Alternator electrical connectors (2006.5 and later four-cylinder models)

10.8b Alternator electrical connectors (2006.5 and later V6 models)

11 Starting system - general information and precautions

The starting system consists of the battery, the starter motor, the starter solenoid and the electrical circuit connecting the components. The solenoid is mounted directly on the starter motor. The solenoid/starter motor assembly is installed on the upper part of the transaxle bellhousing.

When the ignition key is turned to the START position, the starter solenoid is actuated through the starter control circuit. The starter solenoid then connects the battery to the starter. The battery supplies the electrical energy to the starter motor, which does the actual work of cranking the engine.

Always observe the following precautions when working on the starting system:

a) *Excessive cranking of the starter motor can overheat it and cause serious damage. Never operate the starter motor for more than 15 seconds at a time without pausing to allow it to cool for at least two minutes.*

b) *The starter is connected directly to the battery and could arc or cause a fire if mishandled, overloaded or short-circuited.*

c) *Always detach the cable from the negative terminal of the battery before working on the starting system.*

12 Starter motor and circuit - check

Refer to illustrations 12.3 and 12.4

1 If a malfunction occurs in the starting circuit, do not immediately assume that the starter is causing the problem. First, check the following items:

a) Make sure the battery cable clamps, where they connect to the battery, are clean and tight.
b) Check the condition of the battery cables (see Section 4). Replace any defective battery cables with new parts.
c) Test the condition of the battery (see Section 3). If it does not pass all the tests, replace it with a new battery.
d) Check the starter solenoid wiring and connections. Refer to the wiring diagrams at the end of Chapter 12.
e) Check the starter mounting bolts for tightness.
f) Check the fusible link (see Chapter 12). If it's burned, determine the cause and repair the circuit.
g) Check the operation of the Park/Neutral switch. Make sure the shift lever is in PARK or NEUTRAL. Refer to Chapter 7 for the Park/Neutral switch check and adjustment procedure. Refer to Chapter 12 wiring diagrams, if necessary, when performing circuit checks. These systems must operate correctly to provide battery voltage to the ignition solenoid.
h) Check the operation of the starter relay. The starter relay is located in the fuse/relay box inside the engine compartment. Refer to Chapter 12 for the relay testing procedure.

2 If the starter does not actuate when the ignition switch is turned to the start position, check for battery voltage to the solenoid. This will determine if the solenoid is receiving the correct voltage signal from the ignition switch. Connect a test light or voltmeter to the starter solenoid positive terminal and while an assistant turns the ignition switch to the start position. If voltage is not available, refer to the wiring diagrams in Chapter 12 and check all the fuses and relays in series with the starting system. If voltage is available but the starter motor does not operate, remove the starter (see Section 13) and bench test it (see Step 4).

3 If the starter turns over slowly, check the starter cranking voltage and the current draw from the battery. This test must be performed with the starter assembly on the engine. Crank the engine over (for 10 seconds or less) and observe the battery voltage. It should not drop below 8.0 volts on manual transaxle models or 8.5 volts on automatic transaxle models. Also, observe the current draw using an ammeter (see illustration). It should not exceed 400 amps or drop below 250 amps. If the starter motor cranking amp values are not within the correct range, replace it with a new unit. There are several conditions that may affect the starter cranking potential. The battery must be in good condition and the battery cold-cranking rating must not be under-rated for the particular application. Be sure to check the battery specifications carefully. The battery terminals and cables must be clean and not corroded. Also, in cases of extreme cold temperatures, make sure the battery and/or engine block is warmed before performing the tests.

4 If the starter receives voltage but does not activate, remove and check the starter/solenoid assembly on the bench (see illustration). Most likely the solenoid is defective. In some rare cases, the engine may be seized, so be sure to try and rotate the crankshaft pulley (see Chapter 2A or 2B) before proceeding. With the starter/solenoid assembly mounted in a vise on the bench, install one jumper cable from the negative battery terminal to the body of the starter. Install the other jumper cable from the positive battery terminal to the B+ terminal on the starter. Install a starter switch and apply battery voltage to the solenoid S terminal (for 10 seconds or less) and see if the solenoid plunger, shift lever and overrunning clutch extends and rotates the pinion drive. If the pinion drive extends but does not rotate, the solenoid is operating but the starter motor is defective. If there is no movement but the solenoid clicks, the solenoid and/or the starter motor is defective. If the solenoid plunger extends and rotates the pinion drive, the starter/solenoid assembly is working properly.

12.3 To use an inductive ammeter, simply hold the ammeter over the positive or negative cable (whichever is more accessible)

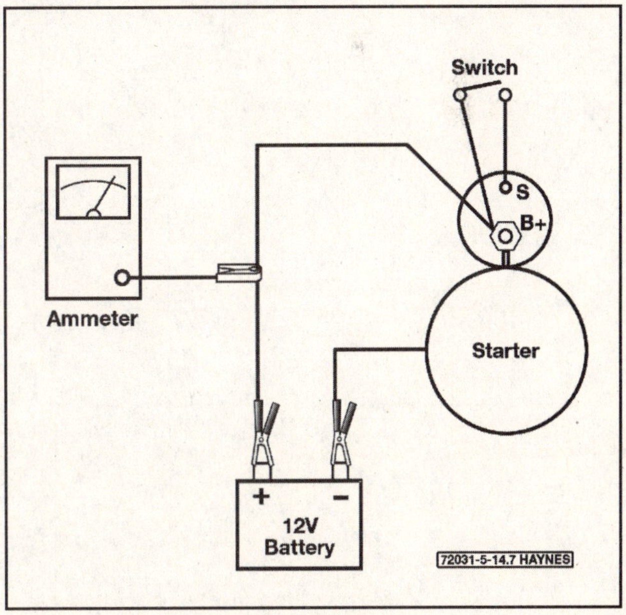

12.4 Starter motor bench testing details

13 Starter motor - removal and installation

Refer to illustrations 13.3, 13.5a and 13.5b

1 Disconnect the cable from the negative terminal of the battery.

2 Remove the lower engine splash shield, if so equipped. Detach the electrical connectors from the starter/solenoid assembly.

3 Remove the starter heat shield (see illustration), if so equipped.

4 On 2001 through 2006 models, disconnect the speedometer cable and the transaxle shifter cable.

5 Remove the starter motor mounting fasteners and remove the starter (see illustrations).

6 Installation is the reverse of removal.

13.3 Typical heat shield (early 2006 V6 engine shown)

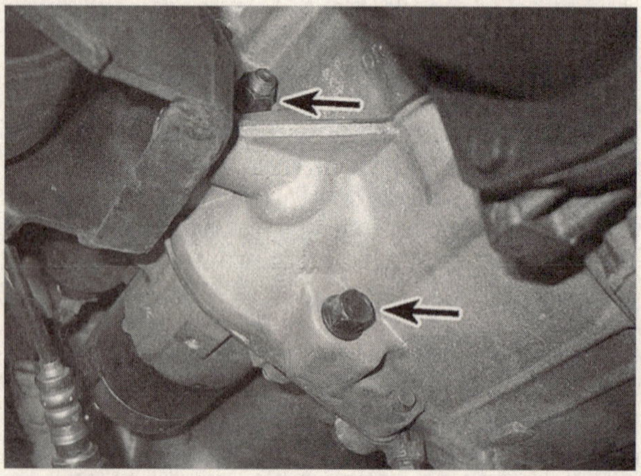

13.5a Starter mounting fasteners (four-cylinder engines)

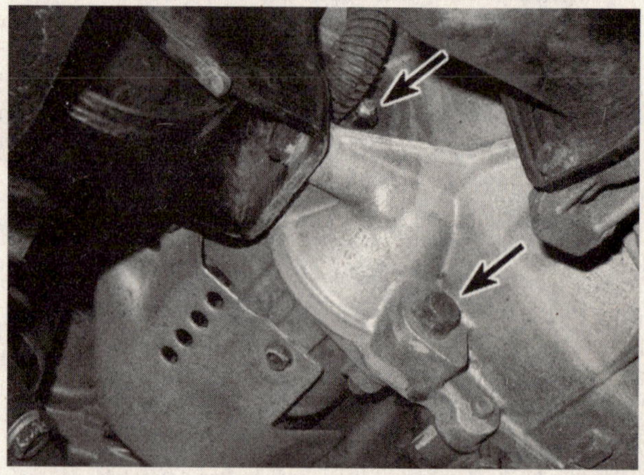

13.5b Starter mounting fasteners (V6 engines)

Specifications

Charging system

Battery voltage	12.6 to 12.9 volts
Charging voltage	14.0 to 15.0 volts

Ignition system

Ignition coil resistance (approximate)	
2001 through 2006 models	
Four-cylinder engines	
Primary	0.8 ohms
Secondary*	11,000 to 23,000 ohms
V6 engines	
Primary	0.66 to 0.82 ohms
Secondary	11,300 to 15,300 ohms
2006.5 and later models	
Primary	0.55 to 0.68 ohms
Secondary	Not available

** These coils vary in resistance. Any coil that differs from the others installed on that engine by more than 15-percent should be replaced.*

Notes

6

EMISSIONS AND ENGINE CONTROL SYSTEMS

Section

1 General information

➧ Refer to illustrations 1.6a and 1.6b

To prevent pollution of the atmosphere from incompletely burned and evaporating gases, and to maintain good driveability and fuel economy, a number of emission control systems are incorporated. They include the:

Catalytic converter
Electronic Throttle Control System
Evaporative Emissions Control (EVAP) system
Exhaust Gas Recirculation (EGR) system
Positive Crankcase Ventilation (PCV) system
Electronic Fuel Injection (EFI) system

The Sections in this Chapter include general descriptions, general inspection procedures within the scope of the home mechanic and component replacement procedures, where possible, for the components used in each of the systems listed above. You'll also find a general description of each information sensor and output actuator used in the engine management system, including its function and location, and a brief description of how it works (see Section 2). We have also included replacement procedures for all sensors and actuators.

Before assuming that an emissions control system is malfunctioning, check the fuel and ignition systems carefully. Diagnosis of many emission control devices requires specialized tools, equipment and training. If a service procedure is beyond the scope of this book, or your ability, consult a dealer service department or other repair shop. But keep in mind that the most frequent cause of emissions problems is simply a loose connector, a broken wire or a disconnected vacuum hose, so always check the hoses, wiring and connections first.

Emission control systems are not, however, particularly difficult to maintain and repair. You can quickly and easily perform many checks and do most of the regular maintenance at home with common tune-up and hand tools.

➡ Note: Because of a Federally mandated warranty that covers the emissions control system components, check with your dealer about warranty coverage before working on any emissions-related systems. Once the warranty has expired, you may wish to perform some of the component checks and/or replacement procedures in this Chapter to save money.

Pay close attention to any special precautions outlined in this Chapter. It should be noted that the illustrations of the various systems might not exactly match the system installed on your vehicle because of changes made by the manufacturer during production or from year-to-year.

A Vehicle Emissions Control Information (VECI) label is attached to the hood. This label contains important emissions specifications and adjustment information (see illustration) with emissions components identified. When servicing the engine or emissions systems, always refer to the VECI label and the vacuum hose routing diagram on your vehicle for up-to-date information (see illustration).

➡ Note: 2006 and 2006.5 models will both have a "6" in the tenth position of the VIN. To distinguish a 2006 model from a 2006.5 model, refer to the 8th position of the VIN (the engine code): A 2006 model will have a "6" (four-cylinder) or "8" (V6), while a 2006.5 will have a "3" (four-cylinder) or "4" (V6).

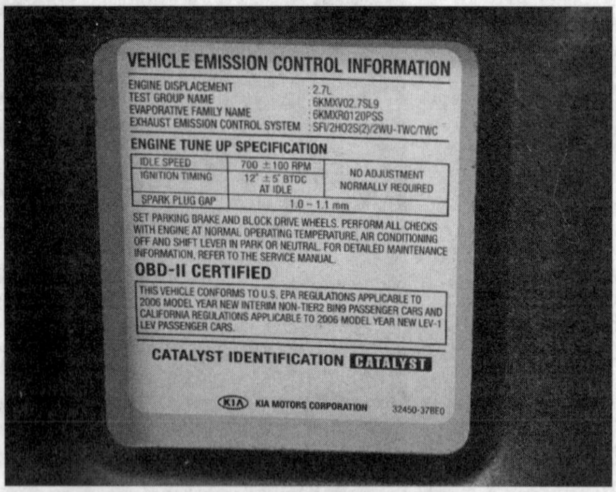

1.6a The VECI label contains such essential information as the types of emission control systems installed on the engine and certain tune-up specifications

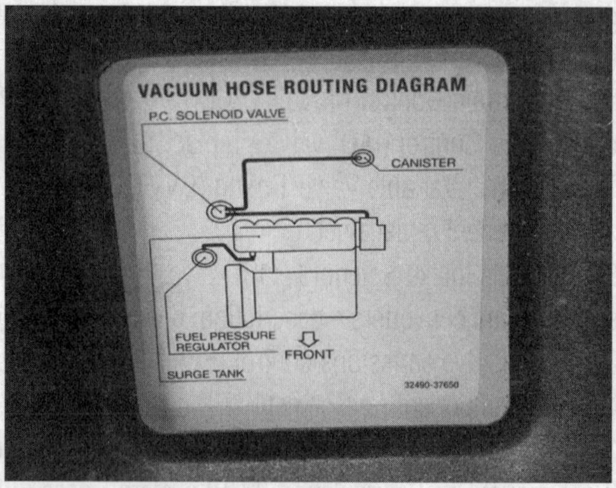

1.6b There's also a vacuum hose routing diagram on the underside of the hood

2 On Board Diagnostic (OBD) system and trouble codes

SCAN TOOL INFORMATION

Refer to illustrations 2.1 and 2.2

1 Hand-held scanners are handy for analyzing the engine management systems used on late-model vehicles. Because extracting the Diagnostic Trouble Codes (DTCs) from an engine management system is now the first step in troubleshooting many computer-controlled systems and components, even the most basic generic code readers are capable of accessing a computer's DTCs (see illustration). More powerful scan tools can also perform many of the diagnostics once associated with expensive factory scan tools. If you're planning to obtain a generic scan tool for your vehicle, make sure that it's compatible with OBD-II systems. If you don't plan to purchase a code reader or scan tool and don't have access to one, you can have the codes extracted by a dealer service department or by an independent repair shop. Some auto parts stores also provide this service.

2 With the advent of the Federally mandated emission control system known as On-Board Diagnostics-II (OBD-II), specially designed scanners were developed. Several tool manufacturers have released OBD-II scan tools for the home mechanic (see illustration).

OBD-II SYSTEM GENERAL DESCRIPTION

3 All models are equipped with the second generation On-Board Diagnostic (OBD-II) system. The OBD-II system includes a computer known as the Powertrain Control Module (PCM), information sensors that monitor various functions of the engine and send data to the PCM, and output actuators that carry out the PCM's various control commands. The OBD-II system also incorporates a series of diagnostic monitors that detect and identify fuel injection and emission control system faults and store the information in the computer memory. The system also tests sensors and output actuators, diagnoses drive cycles, freezes data and clears codes.

4 This powerful diagnostic computer must be accessed with an OBD-II scan tool and the 16 pin Data Link Connector (DLC) located under the driver's dash area. The PCM is the brain of the electronically controlled fuel and emissions system. It receives data from a number of sensors and other electronic components (switches, relays, etc.). Based on the information it receives, the PCM generates output signals to control various relays, solenoids (fuel injectors) and other actuators. The PCM is specifically calibrated to optimize the emissions, fuel economy and driveability of the vehicle.

5 It isn't a good idea to attempt diagnosis or replacement of the PCM or emission control components at home while the vehicle is under warranty. Because of a Federally mandated warranty which covers the emissions system components and because any owner-induced damage to the PCM, the sensors and/or the control devices may void this warranty. Take the vehicle to a dealer service department if the PCM or a system component malfunctions.

INFORMATION SENSORS

6 **Accelerator Pedal Position (APP) sensor** - 2006.5 and later models covered by this manual are equipped with an electronically operated throttle. This system uses an electronic throttle body instead

2.1 Simple code readers are an economical way to extract trouble codes when the CHECK ENGINE light comes on

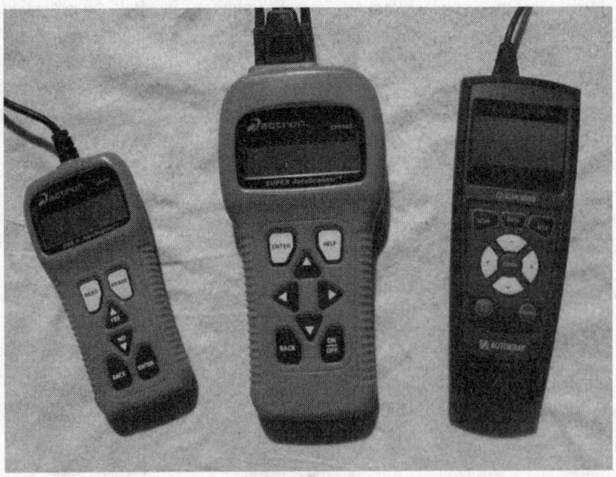

2.2 Hand-held scan tools like these can extract computer codes and also perform diagnostics

Information Sensors

Accelerator Pedal Position (APP) sensor - as you press the accelerator pedal, the APP sensor alters its voltage signal to the PCM in proportion to the angle of the pedal, and the PCM commands a motor inside the throttle body to open or close the throttle plate accordingly

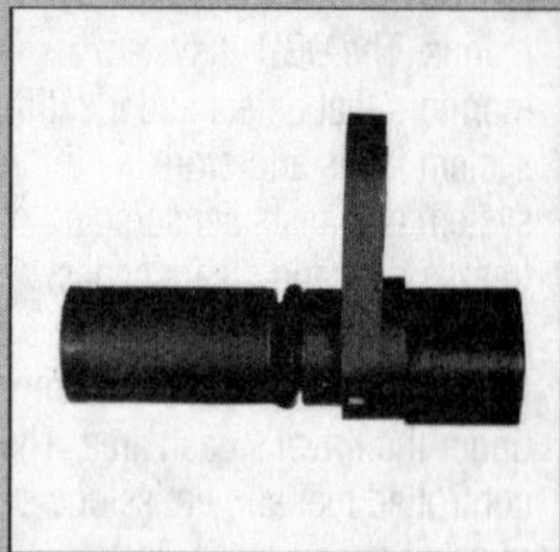

Camshaft Position (CMP) sensor - produces a signal that the PCM uses to identify the number 1 cylinder and to time the firing sequence of the fuel injectors

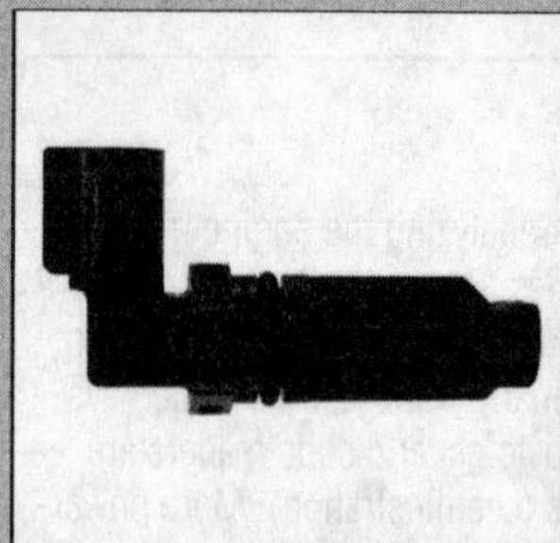

Crankshaft Position (CKP) sensor - produces a signal that the PCM uses to calculate engine speed and crankshaft position, which enables it to synchronize ignition timing with fuel injector timing, and to detect misfires

Engine Coolant Temperature (ECT) sensor - a thermistor (temperature-sensitive variable resistor) that sends a voltage signal to the PCM, which uses this data to determine the temperature of the engine coolant

Fuel tank pressure sensor - measures the fuel tank pressure and controls fuel tank pressure by signaling the EVAP system to purge the fuel tank vapors when the pressure becomes excessive

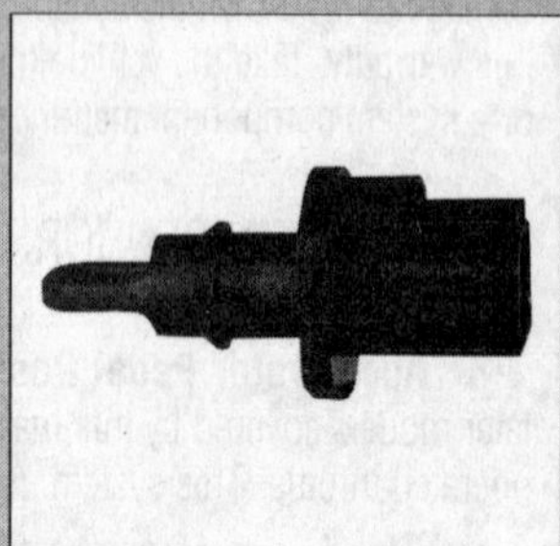

Intake Air Temperature (IAT) sensor - monitors the temperature of the air entering the engine and sends a signal to the PCM to determine injector pulse-width (the duration of each injector's on-time) and to adjust spark timing (to prevent spark knock)

Knock sensor - a piezoelectric crystal that oscillates in proportion to engine vibration which produces a voltage output that is monitored by the PCM. This retards the ignition timing when the oscillation exceeds a certain threshold

Manifold Absolute Pressure (MAP) sensor - monitors the pressure or vacuum inside the intake manifold. The PCM uses this data to determine engine load so that it can alter the ignition advance and fuel enrichment

Mass Air Flow (MAF) sensor - measures the amount of intake air drawn into the engine. It uses a hot-wire sensing element to measure the amount of air entering the engine

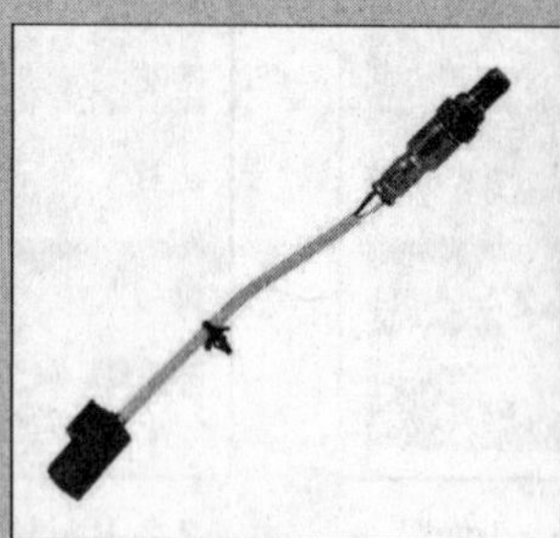

Oxygen sensors - generates a small variable voltage signal in proportion to the difference between the oxygen content in the exhaust stream and the oxygen content in the ambient air. The PCM uses this information to maintain the proper air/fuel ratio. A second oxygen sensor monitors the efficiency of the catalytic converter

Throttle Position (TP) sensor - a potentiometer that generates a voltage signal that varies in relation to the opening angle of the throttle plate inside the throttle body. Works with the PCM and other sensors to calculate injector pulse width (the duration of each injector's on-time)

Photos courtesy of Wells Manufacturing, except APP and MAF sensors.

of a conventional cable-operated throttle body. The Powertrain Control Module (PCM) controls the position of the throttle plate with a solenoid that's located in the throttle body. The PCM's commands are based on the inputs that it receives from the APP sensor, which is located on the accelerator pedal. Its electrical output signal, which is proportional to the angle of the accelerator pedal, is used by the system to determine the corresponding opening angle of the throttle plate inside the throttle body.

7 **Camshaft Position (CMP) sensor** - A CMP sensor monitors the position of the camshaft and tells the Powertrain Control Module (PCM) when the piston in the No. 1 cylinder is on its compression stroke. The PCM uses the CMP sensor signal to synchronize the firing of the fuel injectors. On four-cylinder engines, the sensor is located on the driver's-side end of the cylinder head. V6 engines use two CMP sensors, both mounted on the driver's end of the cylinder heads.

The CMP sensor generates a signal pulse each time that a boss on the timing rotor passes by the sensor. The PCM uses these voltage outputs to determine the position of the intake camshaft.

8 **Crankshaft Position (CKP) sensor** - Like the CMP sensor, the CKP sensor generates a signal pulse each time that a boss on the timing rotor passes by the sensor. It is mounted at the driver's end of the engine on most models. On 2001 through 2006 four-cylinder models, it's mounted near the crankshaft under the timing belt cover. On all other models, it's mounted near the driver's side of the engine near the flywheel, toward the rear of the engine. The CKP sensor is the primary sensor that provides ignition information to the PCM. The PCM uses the CKP sensor to determine crankshaft position (which piston will be at TDC next) and crank speed (rpm), both of which it needs to synchronize the ignition system.

9 **Engine Coolant Temperature (ECT) sensor** - The ECT sensor measures the temperature of the engine coolant. The ECT sensor is a thermistor; its resistance decreases as the temperature increases, and its resistance increases as the temperature decreases. This type of thermistor is also referred to as a Negative Temperature Coefficient (NTC) thermistor. This variable resistance produces an analogous voltage drop across the sensor terminals, thus providing an electrical signal to the PCM that accurately reflects the engine coolant temperature.

The ECT sensor is a critical sensor because it tells the PCM when the engine is warmed up sufficiently to go into closed loop operation. Once the engine is in closed loop, the PCM also uses the ECT sensor to control fuel injector pulse width and ignition timing. It also uses the ECT sensor signal to determine when to purge the EVAP system.

It is mounted at the driver's end of the engine on all models, near the thermostat housing.

10 **Fuel tank pressure sensor (FTPS)** - The vapor pressure sensor, which is a component of the Evaporative Emission Control (EVAP) system, monitors the pressure inside the fuel tank and sends a signal to the Powertrain Control Module (PCM). When the pressure exceeds the upper threshold, the PCM commands the canister closed valve to send the excessive vapors to the EVAP canister. The vapor pressure sensor is located on top of the fuel tank.

11 **Intake Air Temperature (IAT) sensor** - The IAT sensor is used by the PCM to calculate air density, which is one of the variables that it must know in order to calculate injector pulse width and adjust ignition timing (to prevent spark knock when air intake temperature is high). Like the ECT sensor, the IAT sensor is a Negative Temperature Coefficient (NTC) type thermistor, whose resistance decreases as the temperature increases. The IAT sensor is an integral component of the Mass Air Flow (MAF) sensor, which is located on the air inlet duct. For more information about the MAF sensor, see paragraph 14.

12 **Knock sensor** - The knock sensor monitors engine vibration caused by detonation. Basically, a knock sensor converts engine vibration to an electrical signal. When the knock sensor detects a knock in one of the cylinders, it signals the PCM so that the PCM can retard ignition timing accordingly. The knock sensor contains a piezoelectric material, a certain type of piezoresistive crystal that has the ability to produce a voltage when subjected to a mechanical stress. The piezoelectric crystal in the knock sensor vibrates constantly and produces an output signal that's proportional to the intensity of the vibration. As the intensity of the vibration increases, so does the voltage of the output signal. When the intensity of the crystal's vibration reaches a specified threshold, the PCM stores that value in its memory and retards ignition timing in all cylinders (the PCM does not selectively retard timing only at the affected cylinder). The PCM doesn't respond to the knock sensor's input when the engine is idling; it only responds when the engine reaches a specified speed.

On 2001 through through 2006 models, the knock sensor is at the front side of the engine block. On 2006.5 and later four-cylinder engines, the sensor connector is near the thermostat housing. Trace the wiring from this point to locate the sensor. On 2006.5 and later V6 engines, the two knock sensors are under the lower intake manifold in the valley of the block (the intake manifold must be removed to access them).

13 **Manifold Absolute Pressure (MAP) sensor** - This sensor is used only on 2001 through 2006 four-cylinder models and 2006.5 and later V6 models. Its purpose is to provide the PCM with information regarding the amount of vacuum in the intake manifold. The MAP sensor converts the vacuum into a voltage signal that varies with the vacuum. The PCM uses this signal to calculate the load on the engine so it can calculate the correct amount of spark advance and the air/fuel ratio. The MAP sensor is attached to the intake manifold by a vacuum hose at the center rear of the engine compartment.

14 **Mass Air Flow/Intake Air Temperature (MAF/IAT) sensor** - The MAF sensor is the principal means by which the PCM monitors intake airflow. It uses a hot-film sensing element to measure the amount of air entering the engine. Air passing over the hot film causes it to cool down. The hot film's temperature is maintained at a preset level above the ambient temperature by electrical current supplied to the wire and controlled by the PCM. The current required to maintain the specified constant temperature value is used by the PCM as an indicator of airflow.

The functions of the MAF and the Intake Air Temperature (IAT) sensors are combined into one assembly on all models. For more information about the IAT sensor, see paragraph 11. The MAF/IAT sensor is located in the air intake duct.

15 **CVVT Oil Temperature (OTS) sensor** - This sensor is used on 2006.5 and later models. These engines have variable camshaft timing that is operated by engine oil pressure. This system is dependent on the temperature of the engine oil for proper operation. The OTS gives the PCM continuous information on this parameter. On four-cylinder engines, it's mounted at the top passenger side of the engine. On V6 models, it's at the driver's side rear of the engine.

16 **Oxygen sensors** - Oxygen sensors generate a voltage signal that varies in accordance with the amount of oxygen in the exhaust stream. The PCM uses the data from the upstream oxygen sensor to calculate the injector pulse width. The downstream oxygen sensor monitors the oxygen content of the exhaust gases as they exit the catalytic converters. This information is used by the PCM to predict catalyst deterioration and/or failure. One job of the catalytic converter is to store excess oxygen. As long as the catalyst is functioning correctly, the downstream sensor should show little activity because there should be little oxygen exiting the catalyst. But as the catalyst deteriorates, its

ability to store oxygen is compromised. When the output signal from the downstream sensor starts to look like the output signal from the upstream sensor, the PCM stores a DTC and turns on the MIL to let you know that it's time to replace the catalyst.

On all models there are two oxygen sensors at each exhaust manifold; one immediately before and one after the catalytic converter.

17 **Power Steering Pressure (PSP) sensor** - The PSP sensor monitors the hydraulic pressure of the power steering fluid in the power steering system. The PSP sensor provides a voltage input to the PCM that varies in accordance with changes in the hydraulic pressure. The PCM uses the input signal from the PSP sensor to elevate the idle speed when the engine is already under some other load, such as the air conditioning compressor, while maneuvering the vehicle at low speed, such as parking or stop-and-go driving. The PSP sensor is located near the power steering pump.

18 **Throttle Position (TP) sensor** - The TP sensor, which is located on the throttle body, is a rotary potentiometer, which is a type of variable resistor that produces a variable voltage signal in proportion to the opening angle of the throttle plate. The PCM sends 5 volts to the TP sensor. As the plate opens and closes, the resistance of the TP sensor changes with it, altering the signal back to the PCM. The output voltage of the TP sensor is about 0.6 volt at idle (closed throttle plate) to 4.8 volts at wide-open throttle. This variable signal enables the PCM to calculate the position (opening angle) of the throttle plate. The PCM uses the TP sensor input, along with other sensor inputs, to adjust fuel injector pulse-width and ignition timing.

19 **Transmission Range (TR) sensor** - Like the Park/Neutral Position (PNP) switch that it replaces, the TR sensor prevents you from starting the engine unless the automatic transaxle is in Park or Neutral, and it activates the back-up lights when you put the shift lever in Reverse. Unlike a PNP or inhibitor switch, however, the TR sensor also tells the PCM what range the transaxle is in. The PCM uses this information to determine what gear the transaxle *should* be in based on the load, engine speed, vehicle speed, etc. and to determine when to upshift and downshift the transaxle. The TR sensor is mounted on the transaxle.

20 **Transmission speed sensors** - There are two speed sensors on all transaxles covered by this manual: the **Input Turbine Speed Sensor**, or **Input Shaft RPM Sensor,** and the **Counter Gear Speed Sensor,** or **Counter Gear RPM Sensor.** The speed sensors are variable reluctance (pick-up coil) type sensors that generate an analog (sine wave) signal pulse each time that a boss on a timing rotor passes by the sensor. Both sensors are located on top of the transaxle. The PCM uses the signal from the Input Turbine Speed Sensor to monitor input turbine or input shaft speed. And it uses the signal from the Counter Gear Speed Sensor to monitor counter gear or output shaft speed. The PCM constantly compares these two speeds to its map (program) for the transaxle in order to determine shift scheduling, Torque Converter Clutch (TCC) engagement scheduling and optimal hydraulic pressure for various hydraulically-controlled components inside the transaxle. Both of the speed sensors are located inside of the transaxle.

21 **Vapor pressure sensor** - The vapor pressure sensor is a component of the Evaporative Emission Control (EVAP) system. It's located on top of the fuel tank. The vapor pressure sensor monitors the pressure of fuel vapors inside the tank. When the vapor pressure exceeds the upper threshold, the vapor pressure sensor signals the PCM, which opens the Vacuum Switching Valve (VSV) for the pressure switching valve, allowing the fuel vapors to migrate to the EVAP canister, where they are stored until they're purged.

POWERTRAIN CONTROL MODULE (PCM)

22 Based on the information that it receives from the information sensors described above, the PCM adjusts fuel injector pulse width, idle speed, ignition spark advance, ignition coil dwell, EVAP canister purge operation and many other things. It does so by controlling the *output actuators.* The following list provides a brief description of the function, location and operation of each of the important output actuators.

OUTPUT ACTUATORS

23 **Canister closed valve (CCV)** - The canister closed valve is a part of the Evaporative Emissions Control (EVAP) system. The canister closed valve opens and closes the EVAP system's fresh air line (between the air filter housing and the EVAP canister) in response to signals from the Powertrain Control Module (PCM). When commanded by the PCM, the canister closed valve also closes the EVAP canister for monitor testing. It's mounted near the fuel tank.

24 **Purge control solenoid valve (PCSV)** - The canister purge valve is a component of the Evaporative Emission Control (EVAP) system. When the engine is cold or still warming up, no captive fuel vapors are allowed to escape from the EVAP canister. After the engine is warmed up, the PCM energizes the canister purge valve, which regulates the flow of these vapors from the canister to the intake manifold. The rate of vapor flow is regulated by the purge valve in response to commands from the PCM, which controls the duty cycle of the valve. It's mounted near the driver's side of the engine compartment. For more information about the EVAP system, see Section 20.

25 **Electronic Throttle Body** - 2006.5 and later models are equipped with the electronic throttle control system. These vehicles do not have a conventional accelerator cable-actuated throttle body. Instead, they use an electronic throttle body that is controlled by the Powertrain Control Module (PCM). The throttle plate inside the throttle body is opened and closed by a PCM-controlled throttle motor. There is no cruise control cable and no Idle Air Control (IAC) valve. Cruise control and idle speed are handled electronically by the PCM. The electronic throttle body still has a Throttle Position (TP) sensor. The PCM determines the correct throttle plate angle by processing the input signal from the Accelerator Pedal Position (APP) sensor (see *Accelerator Pedal Position sensor* in paragraph 6).

26 **Fuel injectors** - The PCM activates the fuel injectors. The PCM also controls the injector pulse width, which is the interval of time during which each injector is open. The pulse width of an injector (measured in milliseconds) determines the amount of fuel delivered. For more information on the fuel system and the fuel injectors, including injector replacement, refer to Chapter 4.

27 **Fuel pump relay** - When grounded by the PCM, the fuel pump relay provides battery voltage to the fuel pump (and to other fuel system components). The location of this relay may change depending on model and year, so if you can't find it, refer to the fuse and relay guide in your owner's manual.

28 **Idle Air Control (IAC) valve** - The PCM-controlled IAC valve, which is located on the throttle body on 2001 through 2006 models, regulates the flow of air that bypasses the throttle plate when the engine is idling. The PCM opens and closes the IAC valve in response to loads - air conditioning and power steering loads, for example - to keep the engine idle speed at its target rpm. The IAC valve also increases the idle speed during the early stages of the warm-up period and functions as a

dashpot when the throttle plate is abruptly closed during sudden deceleration conditions. There is no IAC valve on 2006.5 and later models because the electronic throttle body does not require an IAC valve to control idle speed.

29 **Ignition coil(s)** - 2001 through 2006 four-cylinder models use a modified coil-on-plug system in which half of the cylinders use an ignition coil mounted directly to the spark plug. These coils have spark plug wires that attach to the other cylinders. Each coil therefore ignites two cylinders at the same time. This is called a "waste spark" system since one cylinder receives a spark that is wasted on its exhaust stroke. 2001 through 2006 V6 engines use a three-coil pack mounted to the side of the engine that fires all six cylinders via spark plug wires using the same waste-spark principle. There is no separate ignition control module. The Powertrain Control Module (PCM) handles this function. 2006.5 and later models have individual coils for each cylinder. For more information about the ignition coils, refer to Chapter 5.

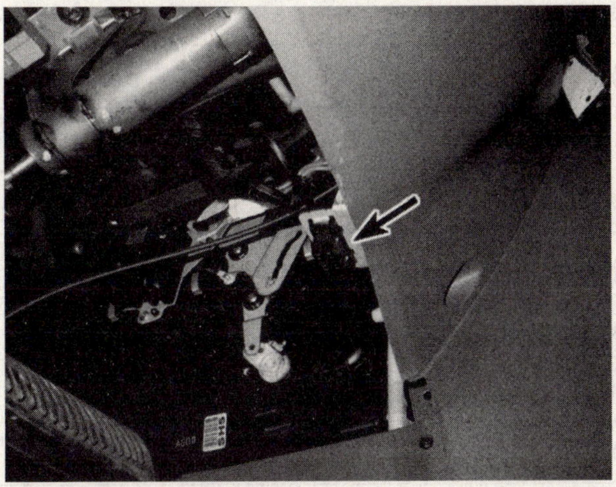

2.33 The 16-pin Data Link Connector (DLC) is located under the left end of the dash

30 **CVVT Oil Control Valve(s) (OCV)** - 2006.5 and later engines have CVVT (variable camshaft timing). The camshaft(s) are advanced or retarded based on instructions from the PCM. The PCM instructs the oil control valve(s) to modulate the amount of oil going to the camshaft phasers. The phasers (mounted at the chain ends of the camshafts) then rotate the camshafts.

31 **Variable Intake Solenoid (VIS) valve** - This system is used only on 2006.5 and later V6 models. The PCM instructs the VIS to open at high engine speed to increase the volume of the intake manifold. This increases horsepower and torque while not adversely affecting low speed operation. The actuator is located at the rear passenger side of the engine compartment and is connected to the valve by a hose.

OBTAINING TROUBLE CODES

➧ Refer to illustration 2.33

32 The PCM illuminates the CHECK ENGINE light (also called the Malfunction Indicator Light) on the dash if it recognizes a component fault for two consecutive drive cycles. It will continue to turn on the light until the PCM does not detect any malfunction for three or more consecutive drive cycles.

33 To extract the Diagnostic Trouble Codes (DTCs), you will need an OBD-II scan tool (see illustration 2.2). Plug the scan tool into the PCM's data link connector, which is located under the left side of the dash (see illustration).

34 Plug the scan tool into the 16-pin data link connector (DLC), and follow the instructions included with the scan tool to extract all the diagnostic codes.

DIAGNOSTIC TROUBLE CODES

Trouble code	Code identification
P0011	"A" Camshaft position - timing over-advanced (Bank 1)
P0012	"A" Camshaft position - timing over-retarded (Bank 1)
P0014	"B" Camshaft position - timing over-retarded (Bank 1)
P0016	Crankshaft position/camshaft position, Bank 1, Sensor A - correlation
P0017	Crankshaft position/camshaft position, Bank 1, Sensor B - correlation
P0018	Crankshaft position/camshaft position, Bank 2, Sensor A - correlation
P0021	Intake camshaft position timing - over-advanced (Bank 2)
P0022	Intake camshaft position timing - over-retarded (Bank 2)

DIAGNOSTIC TROUBLE CODES (CONTINUED)

Trouble code	Code identification
P0026	Intake Valve Control Solenoid - circuit, range performance (Bank 1)
P0028	Intake Valve Control Solenoid - circuit, range performance (Bank 2)
P0030	Oxygen sensor heater control circuit (Bank 1, Sensor 1)
P0031	Oxygen sensor heater control circuit, low voltage (Bank 1, Sensor 1)
P0032	Oxygen sensor heater control circuit, high voltage (Bank 1, Sensor 1)
P0036	Oxygen sensor heater control circuit (Bank 1, Sensor 2)
P0037	Oxygen sensor heater control circuit, low voltage (Bank 1, Sensor 2)
P0038	Oxygen sensor heater control circuit, high voltage (Bank 1, Sensor 2)
P0050	Oxygen sensor heater control circuit (Bank 2, Sensor 1)
P0051	Oxygen sensor heater control circuit low (Bank 2, Sensor 1)
P0052	Oxygen sensor heater control circuit high (Bank 2, Sensor 1)
P0056	Oxygen sensor heater control circuit (Bank 2, Sensor 2)
P0057	Oxygen sensor heater control circuit low (Bank 2, Sensor 2)
P0058	Oxygen sensor heater control circuit high (Bank 2, Sensor 2)
P0076	Intake valve control solenoid circuit low (Bank 1)
P0077	Intake valve control solenoid circuit high (Bank 1)
P0079	Exhaust valve control solenoid circuit low (Bank 1)
P0080	Exhaust valve control solenoid circuit high (Bank 1)
P0082	Intake valve control solenoid circuit low (Bank 2)
P0083	Intake valve control solenoid circuit high (Bank 2)
P0100	Mass Air Flow (MAF) or Volume Air Flow Sensor circuit malfunction
P0101	Mass Air Flow (MAF) or Volume Air Flow Sensor, range or performance problem
P0102	Mass Air Flow (MAF) or Volume Air Flow Sensor, low input voltage
P0103	Mass Air Flow (MAF) or Volume Air Flow Sensor, high input voltage
P0105	Manifold Absolute Pressure (MAP) or barometric pressure circuit problem

Trouble code	Code identification
P0106	Manifold Absolute Pressure (MAP) or barometric pressure circuit, range or performance problem
P0107	Manifold Absolute Pressure (MAP) or barometric pressure circuit, low input
P0108	Manifold Absolute Pressure (MAP) or barometric pressure circuit, high input
P0109	Manifold Absolute Pressure (MAP) or barometric pressure circuit, Intermittent
P0110	Intake Air Temperature (IAT) sensor, circuit fault
P0111	Intake Air Temperature (IAT) sensor circuit, range or performance problem
P0112	Intake Air Temperature (IAT) sensor circuit, low input voltage
P0113	Intake Air Temperature (IAT) sensor circuit, high input voltage
P0115	Engine Coolant Temperature (ECT) circuit
P0116	Engine Coolant Temperature (ECT) sensor, range or performance problem
P0117	Engine Coolant Temperature (ECT) sensor circuit, low input voltage
P0118	Engine Coolant Temperature (ECT) sensor circuit, high input voltage
P0119	Engine Coolant Temperature (ECT) circuit, Intermittent
P0120	Throttle Position (TP) sensor or Accelerator Pedal Position (APP) Sensor circuit malfunction
P0121	Throttle Position (TP) sensor or Accelerator Pedal Position (APP) Sensor circuit, range or performance problem
P0122	Throttle Position (TP) sensor or Accelerator Pedal Position (APP) Sensor circuit, low input voltage
P0123	Throttle Position (TP) sensor or Accelerator Pedal Position (APP) Sensor circuit, high input voltage
P0125	Insufficient coolant temperature for closed loop fuel control
P0128	Coolant thermostat (coolant temperature below thermostat regulating temperature)
P0130	Oxygen sensor circuit malfunction (Bank 1, Sensor 1)
P0131	Oxygen sensor circuit, low voltage (Bank 1, Sensor 1)
P0132	Oxygen sensor circuit, high voltage (Bank 1, Sensor 1)
P0133	Oxygen sensor circuit, slow response (Bank 1, Sensor 1)
P0134	Oxygen sensor circuit - no activity detected (Bank 1, Sensor 1)
P0135	Oxygen sensor heater circuit - malfunction (Bank 1, Sensor 1)
P0136	Oxygen sensor circuit fault (Bank 1, Sensor 2)

DIAGNOSTIC TROUBLE CODES (CONTINUED)

Trouble code	Code identification
P0137	Oxygen sensor circuit, low voltage (Bank 1, Sensor 2)
P0138	Oxygen sensor circuit, high voltage (Bank 1, Sensor 2)
P0139	Oxygen sensor circuit, slow response (Bank 1, Sensor 2)
P0140	Oxygen sensor circuit - no activity detected (Bank 1, Sensor 2)
P0141	Oxygen sensor heater circuit malfunction (Bank 1, Sensor 2)
P0150	Oxygen sensor circuit malfunction (Bank 2, Sensor 1)
P0151	Oxygen sensor circuit, low voltage (Bank 2, Sensor 1)
P0152	Oxygen sensor circuit, high voltage (Bank 2, Sensor 1)
P0153	Oxygen sensor circuit, slow response (Bank 2, Sensor 1)
P0154	Oxygen sensor circuit - no activity detected (Bank 2, Sensor 1)
P0155	Oxygen sensor heater circuit malfunction (Bank 2, Sensor 1)
P0156	Oxygen sensor circuit fault (Bank 2, Sensor 2)
P0157	Oxygen sensor circuit, low voltage (Bank 2, Sensor 2)
P0158	Oxygen sensor circuit, high voltage (Bank 2, Sensor 2)
P0159	Oxygen sensor circuit, slow response (Bank 2, Sensor 2)
P0160	Oxygen sensor circuit - no activity detected (Bank 2, Sensor 2)
P0161	Oxygen sensor heater circuit malfunction (Bank 2, Sensor 2)
P0170	Fuel trim malfunction (Bank 1)
P0171	Fuel injection system, fuel trim too lean (Bank 1)
P0172	Fuel injection system fuel trim too rich (Bank 1)
P0173	Fuel trim malfunction (Bank 2)
P0174	Fuel injection system fuel trim too lean (Bank 2)
P0175	Fuel injection system fuel trim too rich (Bank 2)
P0181	Fuel temperature sensor circuit A, range or performance

Trouble code	Code identification
P0182	Fuel temperature sensor circuit A, low input
P0183	Fuel temperature sensor circuit A, high input
P0196	Engine oil temperature sensor circuit, range or performance problem
P0197	Engine oil temperature sensor circuit, low input
P0198	Engine oil temperature sensor circuit, high input
P0201	Injector circuit open - cylinder number 1
P0202	Injector circuit open - cylinder number 2
P0203	Injector circuit open - cylinder number 3
P0204	Injector circuit open - cylinder number 4
P0205	Injector circuit open - cylinder number 5
P0206	Injector circuit open - cylinder number 6
P0217	Engine overheating condition
P0221	Throttle position or pedal position sensor/switch B, range or performance problem
P0222	Throttle position or pedal position sensor/switch B circuit, low input
P0223	Throttle position or pedal position sensor/switch B circuit, high input
P0230	Fuel pump primary circuit malfunction
P0261	Cylinder no. 1 injector circuit, low
P0262	Cylinder no. 1 injector circuit, high
P0264	Cylinder no. 2 injector circuit, low
P0265	Cylinder no. 2 injector circuit, high
P0267	Cylinder no. 3 injector circuit, low
P0268	Cylinder no. 3 injector circuit, high
P0270	Cylinder no. 4 injector circuit, low
P0271	Cylinder no. 4 injector circuit, high
P0273	Cylinder no. 5 injector circuit, low

DIAGNOSTIC TROUBLE CODES (CONTINUED)

Trouble code	Code identification
P0274	Cylinder no. 5 injector circuit, high
P0276	Cylinder no. 6 injector circuit, low
P0277	Cylinder no. 6 injector circuit, high
P0300	Random or multiple cylinder misfire detected
P0301	Cylinder no. 1 misfire detected
P0302	Cylinder no. 2 misfire detected
P0303	Cylinder no. 3 misfire detected
P0304	Cylinder no. 4 misfire detected
P0305	Cylinder no. 5 misfire detected
P0306	Cylinder no. 6 misfire detected
P0315	Crankshaft position system - variation not learned
P0320	Ignition distributor engine speed input circuit
P0325	Knock sensor no. 1 circuit malfunction (Bank 1 or single Sensor)
P0326	Knock sensor no. 1 circuit, range or performance problem (Bank 1 or single Sensor)
P0330	Knock sensor no. 2 circuit malfunction (Bank 2)
P0331	Knock sensor no. 2 circuit, range or performance problem (Bank 2)
P0335	Crankshaft position sensor "A" circuit malfunction
P0336	Crankshaft position sensor A circuit - range or performance problem
P0337	Crankshaft position sensor A circuit - low input
P0338	Crankshaft position sensor A circuit - high input
P0340	Camshaft position sensor "A" circuit malfunction (Bank 1)
P0341	Camshaft position sensor "A", circuit - range or performance problem
P0342	Camshaft position sensor "A", circuit - low input

Trouble code	Code identification
P0343	Camshaft position sensor "A", circuit - high input
P0346	Camshaft position sensor "A", range/performance problem (Bank 2)
P0350	Ignition coil primary sensor circuit malfunction
P0351	Ignition coil A primary or secondary circuit malfunction
P0352	Ignition coil B primary or secondary circuit malfunction
P0353	Ignition coil C primary or secondary circuit malfunction
P0354	Ignition coil D primary or secondary circuit malfunction
P0355	Ignition coil E primary or secondary circuit malfunction
P0356	Ignition coil F primary or secondary circuit malfunction
P0365	Camshaft position sensor "B" circuit malfunction (Bank 1)
P0366	Camshaft position sensor "B", circuit - range or performance problem
P0401	Exhaust gas recirculation flow insufficient
P0403	Exhaust gas recirculation control circuit problem
P0420	Catalyst system efficiency below threshold (Bank 1)
P0421	Warm-up catalyst system efficiency below threshold (Bank 1)
P0430	Catalyst system efficiency below threshold (Bank 2)
P0441	Evaporative Emission Control (EVAP) system, incorrect purge flow
P0442	Evaporative Emission Control (EVAP) system malfunction or small leak detected
P0443	Evaporative Emission Control (EVAP) system, open purge control valve circuit or small leak detected
P0444	Evaporative Emission Control (EVAP) system, purge control valve circuit
P0445	Evaporative Emission Control (EVAP) system, short in purge control valve circuit
P0446	Evaporative Emission Control (EVAP) system, vent control circuit
P0447	Evaporative Emission Control (EVAP) system, open vent control circuit
P0448	Evaporative Emission Control (EVAP) system, shorted vent control circuit
P0449	Evaporative Emission Control (EVAP) system, vent valve/solenoid circuit malfunction

DIAGNOSTIC TROUBLE CODES (CONTINUED)

Trouble code	Code identification
P0451	Evaporative Emission Control (EVAP) system, pressure sensor range or performance problem
P0452	Evaporative Emission Control (EVAP) system, pressure sensor/switch, low input voltage
P0453	Evaporative Emission Control (EVAP) system, pressure sensor/switch, high input voltage
P0454	Evaporative Emission Control (EVAP) system, pressure sensor intermittent
P0455	Evaporative Emission Control (EVAP) system, large leak detected
P0456	Evaporative Emission Control (EVAP) system, small leak detected
P0460	Fuel level sensor circuit problem detected
P0461	Fuel level sensor circuit, range or performance problem
P0462	Fuel level sensor circuit, low input
P0463	Fuel level sensor circuit, high input
P0464	Fuel level sensor circuit, intermittent
P0480	Cooling fan no. 1, control circuit malfunction
P0481	Cooling fan no. 2, control circuit malfunction
P0489	Exhaust Gas Recirculation (EGR) control circuit - low voltage
P0490	Exhaust Gas Recirculation (EGR) control circuit - high voltage
P050B	Cold start ignition timing performance problem
P0500	Vehicle speed sensor - malfunction
P0501	Vehicle speed sensor, range or performance problem
P0504	Brake switch A/B correlation
P0506	Idle control system, rpm lower than expected
P0507	Idle control system, rpm higher than expected
P0532	A/C refrigerant pressure sensor, low input
P0533	A/C refrigerant pressure sensor, high input
P0551	Power steering pressure sensor circuit, range or performance problem

Trouble code	Code identification
P0560	System voltage problem
P0562	System voltage low
P0563	System voltage high
P0564	Cruise control multi-function input A circuit
P0565	Cruise control ON signal
P0566	Cruise control CANCEL signal
P0567	Cruise control RESUME signal
P0568	Cruise control SET signal
P0571	Cruise control/brake switch A, circuit malfunction
P0600	Serial communication link malfunction
P0601	Internal control module or EEPROM, memory check sum error
P0602	Internal control module or EEPROM, programming error
P0604	Internal control module random access memory (RAM) error
P0605	Internal control module or EEPROM, read only memory (ROM) error
P0606	PCM failure; SELF TEST failed
P061B	Internal control module torque calculation performance error
P0625	Generator field terminal - circuit low
P0626	Generator field terminal - circuit high
P0630	VIN not programmed or mismatch - PCM
P0638	Throttle actuator control range/performance
P0641	Sensor reference voltage A - circuit open
P0642	Sensor reference voltage A - circuit low
P0643	Sensor reference voltage A - circuit high
P0646	A/C clutch relay control circuit low
P0647	A/C clutch relay control circuit high
P0650	Malfunction indicator lamp (MIL), control circuit malfunction

DIAGNOSTIC TROUBLE CODES (CONTINUED)

Trouble code	Code identification
P0651	Sensor reference voltage B - circuit open
P0652	Sensor reference voltage B - circuit low
P0653	Sensor reference voltage B - circuit high
P0660	Intake manifold tuning valve control circuit (Bank 1)
P0661	Intake manifold tuning valve control circuit - low (Bank 1)
P0662	Intake manifold tuning valve control circuit - high (Bank 1)
P0663	Intake manifold tuning valve control circuit (Bank 2)
P0685	PCM power relay, control - circuit open
P0698	Sensor reference voltage C - circuit low
P0699	Sensor reference voltage C - circuit high
P06A4	Sensor reference voltage D - circuit low
P06A5	Sensor reference voltage D - circuit high
P0700	Transmission control system malfunction

3 Accelerator Pedal Position (APP) sensor - replacement

3.3 APP sensor electrical connector (A) and pedal mounting nuts

Refer to illustration 3.3

Note: This procedure applies to 2006.5 and later models only. Earlier models use a cable connection between the pedal and the throttle body.

1 Disconnect the cable from the negative battery terminal (see Chapter 5).

2 Move the driver's seat to the full rearward position. The APP sensor is attached to the accelerator pedal.

3 Depress the tab and unplug the APP sensor electrical connector (see illustration).

4 Remove the nuts and detach the accelerator pedal/sensor assembly from the firewall.

5 Installation is the reverse of removal.

4 Camshaft Position (CMP) sensor - replacement

Refer to illustrations 4.3a and 4.3b

Note: The CMP sensor is located on the driver's end of the cylinder head.

1 Disconnect the cable from the negative battery terminal (see Chapter 5).

2 Remove the air intake duct, if necessary, to provide more room to work (see *Air filter housing - removal and installation* in Chapter 4).

3 Disconnect the electrical connector from the CMP sensor (see illustrations).

4 Remove the CMP sensor mounting bolt(s) and remove the sensor.

5 If you're going to install the same sensor, check the condition of the O-ring. Replace the O-ring if it's damaged.

6 Installation is the reverse of removal.

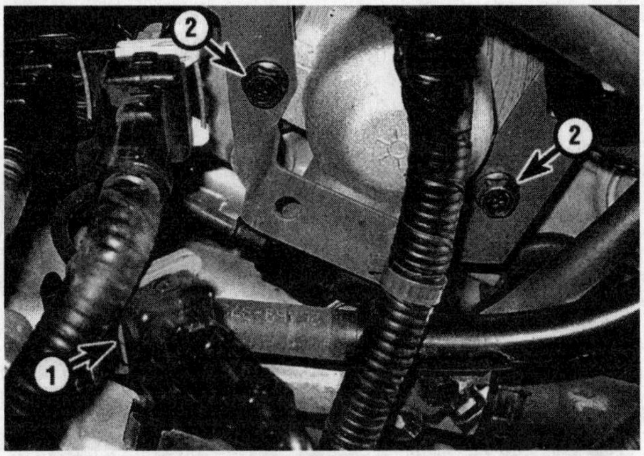

4.3a CMP sensor electrical connector (1) and mounting bolts (2) (2001 through 2006 V6 engines)

4.3b On 2006.5 and later four-cylinder engines, the CMP sensor is mounted on the left end of the cylinder head

5 Crankshaft Position (CKP) sensor - replacement

2001 THROUGH 2006 FOUR-CYLINDER MODELS

Note: The CKP sensor is located on the right (passenger's) end of the engine, behind the timing belt cover, next to the crankshaft sprocket.

1 Disconnect the cable from the negative battery terminal (see Chapter 5).
2 Remove the lower timing belt cover (see Chapter 2A).
3 Disconnect the sensor wiring harness.
4 Remove the two mounting bolts and lift the sensor off.
5 Installation is the reverse of removal.

2006.5 FOUR-CYLINDER MODELS AND ALL V6 MODELS

Refer to illustration 5.7

Note: The CKP sensor on four-cylinder engines is located at the front of the engine block, below the left end of the cylinder head. On V6 engines it's located on the front of the engine block, below the left end of the exhaust manifold.

6 Remove any components that are in the way.

7 Using a mirror and a flashlight locate the CKP sensor (see illustration).

8 Trace the CKP sensor wiring harness to its electrical connector and disconnect the connector.

9 Remove the CKP sensor mounting bolt and remove the CKP sensor.

10 Installation is the reverse of removal. If you're going to install the same sensor, make sure the O-ring is in good condition.

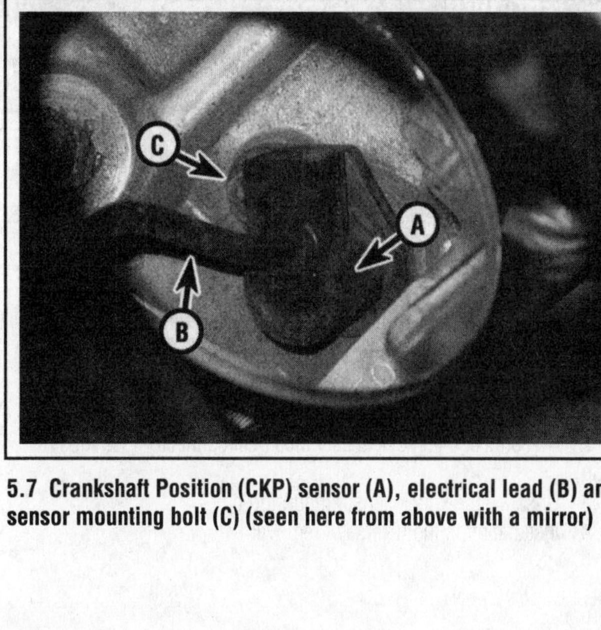

5.7 Crankshaft Position (CKP) sensor (A), electrical lead (B) and sensor mounting bolt (C) (seen here from above with a mirror)

6 Engine Coolant Temperature (ECT) sensor - replacement

Refer to illustrations 6.2a and 6.2b

WARNING:

Wait until the engine is completely cool before beginning this procedure.

CAUTION:

Handle the ECT sensor with care. Damage to the ECT sensor will affect the operation of the entire fuel injection system.

Note: The ECT sensor is located at the left (driver's) end of the engine, on or near the thermostat housing.

1 Disconnect the cable from the negative battery terminal (see Chapter 5). Partially drain the cooling system (see Chapter 1).

2 Disconnect the electrical connector from the ECT sensor (see illustrations).

3 Unscrew the ECT sensor from the coolant passage.

4 Don't seal the threads of the new ECT sensor with Teflon tape, as this will interfere with the grounding of the sensor. Apply a small amount of liquid sealer to the threads before installation.

5 Installation is the reverse of removal. Be sure to tighten the ECT sensor securely.

6 Refill the cooling system (see Chapter 1).

6.2a Location of the Engine Coolant Temperature (ECT) sensor (2006.5 and later four-cylinder engines)

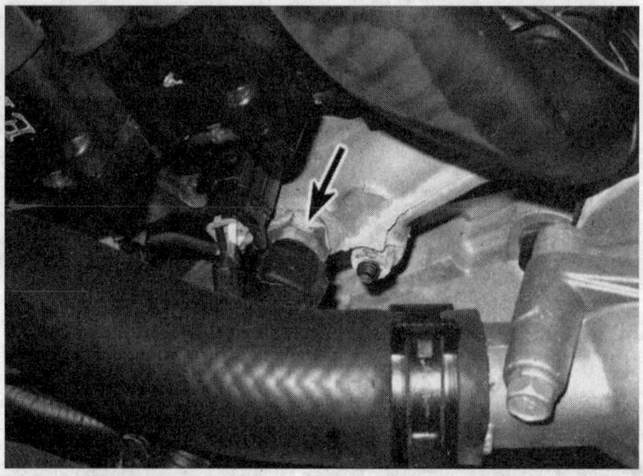

6.2b Location of the Engine Coolant Temperature (ECT) sensor (V6 engines)

7 Knock sensor - replacement

WARNING:

Wait until the engine is completely cool before beginning this procedure.

FOUR-CYLINDER MODELS AND 2001 THROUGH 2006 V6 MODELS

Refer to illustration 7.2

Note: The knock sensor is located on the front side of the engine block.

1 Disconnect the cable from the negative battery terminal (see Chapter 5).

2 Disconnect the knock sensor electrical connector (see illustration).

3 Unscrew the knock sensor mounting bolt.

4 Installation is the reverse of removal.

7.2 Knock sensor location (below the no. 4 intake manifold runner) (2006.5 and later four-cylinder engines)

2006.5 AND LATER V6 MODELS

➡ Note: The knock sensors are located in the valley between the cylinder heads. To access them, the intake manifold must be removed.

5 Disconnect the cable from the negative battery terminal (see Chapter 5).

6 Remove the upper and lower intake manifolds (see Chapter 2B).

7 Disconnect the electrical connector(s) from the knock sensor(s).

8 Disconnect the wiring harness retainers from the engine block.

9 Unscrew the sensor mounting bolt(s) and remove the sensor(s).

10 Installation is the reverse of removal.

8 Mass Air Flow/Intake Air Temperature (MAF/IAT) sensor - replacement

➧ Refer to illustration 8.2

➡ Note: The MAF/IAT sensor is located in the air inlet duct between the air cleaner assembly and the throttle body.

1 Disconnect the cable from the negative battery terminal (see Chapter 5).

2 Disconnect the electrical connector from the MAF sensor (see illustration).

3 Loosen the hose clamps and remove the MAF sensor from the air intake ducts. Handle the sensor carefully.

4 Installation is the reverse of removal.

8.2 Mass Air Flow/Intake Air Temperature (MAF/IAT) sensor details (2001 through 2006 V6 engines,other units similar):

1 Electrical connector
2 Hose clamps

9 Oxygen sensors - general information and replacement

GENERAL INFORMATION

1 Use special care when servicing an oxygen sensor:

a) Oxygen sensors have a permanently attached pigtail and electrical connector that can't be removed from the sensor. Damage to or removal of the pigtail or the electrical connector will ruin the sensor.
b) Keep grease, dirt and other contaminants away from the electrical connector and the oxygen sensor.
c) Do not use cleaning solvents of any kind on an oxygen sensor.
d) Do not drop or roughly handle an oxygen sensor.

REPLACEMENT

➧ Refer to illustrations 9.2, 9.6a and 9.6b

➡ Note: Because it is installed in the exhaust manifold or catalytic converter, both of which contract when cool, an oxygen sensor might be very difficult to loosen when the engine is cold. Rather than risk damage to the sensor, start and run the engine for a minute or two, then shut it off. Be careful not to burn yourself during the following procedure.

2 The sensors (see illustration) are located at each primary catalytic converter near the exhaust manifolds. There is also a rear sensor in the exhaust pipe beneath the vehicle.

9.2 Oxygen sensor locations - V6 engine (2001 through 2006 engines; 2006.5 and later engines similar):

1 Upstream sensor (front cylinder head)
2 Downstream sensor (front cylinder head)
3 Upstream sensor (rear cylinder head)
4 Downstream sensor (rear cylinder head)

9.6a The oxygen sensors are easier to remove with a specialty socket

9.6b Some oxygen sensors that are mounted through heat shields have a large flange. To remove this kind of sensor, an oxygen sensor socket is required

3 If you're working on the rear sensor, raise the vehicle and support it securely on jackstands. This may ease things even if you're removing a front lower sensor.

4 Remove any interfering components to provide wrench access to the sensor. These components vary greatly depending on your model year and the options installed.

5 Disconnect the sensor pigtail and release the wiring from any retainers.

6 Unscrew the sensor (see illustrations).

➡ Note: Special oxygen sensor sockets are available at most auto parts stores. Be careful to avoid damaging the hex on the sensor.

7 Installation is the reverse of removal. Be sure to coat the threads of the oxygen sensor with anti-seize compound and tighten it to the torque listed in this Chapter's Specifications.

10 Power Steering Pressure (PSP) sensor - replacement

Refer to illustrations 10.2a and 10.2b

WARNING:

Wait until the power steering fluid has cooled completely before beginning this procedure.

➡ Note: The sensor is installed either in the pump or in the fluid line near the pump.

1 Disconnect the cable from the negative battery terminal (see Chapter 5).

2 Locate the PSP sensor, then disconnect the sensor electrical connector (see illustrations).

3 Place a drain pan or rags under the sensor, then unscrew the PSP sensor. Be prepared for some power steering fluid to leak out.

4 Installation is the reverse of removal. Check the power steering fluid level (see Chapter 1) and add fluid as necessary

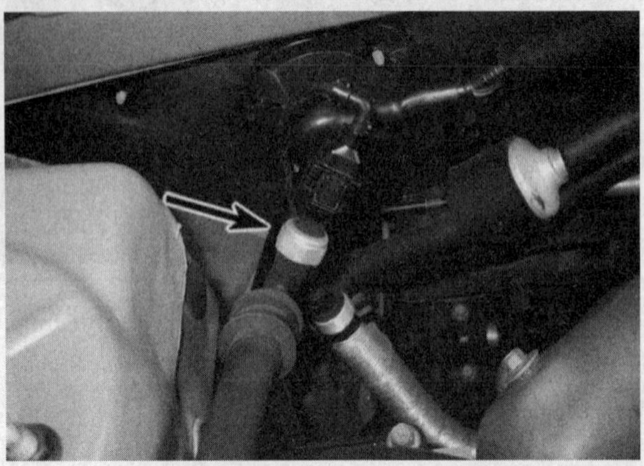

10.2a The power steering pressure switch is installed in the fluid line on some models . . .

10.2b . . . on others it's on the pump itself

11 Throttle Position (TP) sensor - replacement and adjustment

WARNING:

Wait until the engine has cooled completely before beginning this procedure.

Note: The TP sensor is located on the throttle body. It is a serviceable part only on 2001 through 2006 models. On 2006.5 and later models, it is a part of the electronic throttle control module.

REPLACEMENT

Refer to illustration 11.3

1 Disconnect the cable from the negative battery terminal (see Chapter 5).

2 Remove the engine cover, if necessary (see "Intake manifold - removal and installation" in Chapter 2).

3 Disconnect the TP sensor electrical connector (see illustration).

4 Mark the position of the sensor if you plan to reinstall the same one.

5 Remove the TP sensor mounting screws and remove the sensor from the throttle body.

6 Install the sensor and rotate it until the mounting holes in the TP sensor are aligned with the mounting holes in the throttle body. Install the screws and align the marks (if you're installing the same sensor), then tighten the screws securely. If you're installing a new sensor, proceed to adjust the sensor as follows.

7 Installation is otherwise the reverse of removal.

ADJUSTMENT

Refer to illustration 11.8

Note: Use only a high-impedance digital voltmeter for this procedure.

Four-cylinder engines

8 Using a high-impedance digital voltmeter, backprobe terminals 1 and 3 of the TP sensor electrical connector (see illustration). It will be necessary to use straight-pins, or pierce the wire with pins and connect the leads to them (although the latter method isn't recommended if at all possible). It may also be necessary to separate the clamshell halves of the connector to allow the connector to be backprobed.

9 Turn the ignition key to the On position.

10 With the throttle fully closed, note the value on the voltmeter; it should be 300 to 900 millivolts (mV).

11 Slowly open the throttle. The voltage should increase evenly and without drop-offs to about 4.5 volts

12 If the sensor voltage doesn't fall within the specified range, loosen the TP sensor mounting screws and turn the sensor one way or the other until it does, then tighten the screws securely.

V6 engines

13 Unplug the electrical connector from the TP sensor.

14 Insert a 0.025-inch (0.65 mm) thick feeler gauge between the throttle lever and its stop.

15 Connect an ohmmeter between terminals 1 and 2 of the TP sensor. Loosen the TP sensor mounting screws and turn the sensor fully counterclockwise. Make sure continuity registers on the meter.

16 Turn the sensor clockwise slowly until there is no continuity, then tighten the screws. Reconnect the electrical connector.

17 Using a high-impedance digital voltmeter, backprobe terminals 1 and 3 of the TP sensor electrical connector (see illustration 11.8). It will be necessary to use straight-pins, or pierce the wire with pins and connect the leads to them (although the latter method isn't recommended if at all possible). It may also be necessary to separate the clamshell halves of the connector to allow the connector to be backprobed.

18 Turn the ignition key to the On position. The sensor output voltage should be 250 to 800 millivolts (mV). If not, repeat the adjustment procedure.

19 If the output voltage still doesn't fall within the specified range, the TP sensor is probably bad.

11.3 Typical Throttle Position sensor electrical connector (1) and mounting bolts (2) (2001 through 2006 engines, others similar)

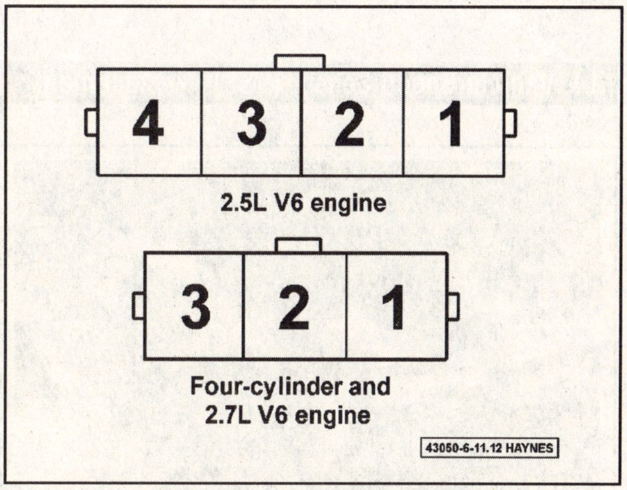

11.8 TP sensor terminal designations

12 Transmission Range (TR) sensor - replacement

REMOVAL

Refer to illustration 12.2

Note: The TR sensor is located on the top of the transaxle, where the shift cable connects.

1 Disconnect the cable from the negative battery terminal (see Chapter 5). Remove the air filter housing (see Chapter 4).

2 Disconnect the electrical connector from the TR sensor (see illustration).

12.2 Remove the air cleaner housing and the battery tray for access to the transmission range sensor

3 Remove the nut that secures the shift control cable to the control shaft lever and disconnect the cable from the lever.

4 Remove the nut and washer that secures the control shaft lever to the manual valve shaft and remove the control shaft lever from the manual valve shaft.

5 Remove the TR sensor mounting bolts and remove the TR sensor.

INSTALLATION AND ADJUSTMENT

6 To install the TR sensor, slide it onto the manual valve shaft, then loosely install the mounting bolts.

7 Install the lever on the manual valve shaft. Install the nut and tighten it securely. Turn the lever through the gears - it will click as it changes to the next gear - until it stops at Park, then turn it two clicks. It's now in the Neutral position.

8 Connect the cable to the manual valve shaft and install the nut, but don't tighten it yet.

9 Align the holes on the manual lever and the sensor; use an appropriately sized drill bit to insert into the holes to ensure alignment, turning the sensor as necessary. When alignment is achieved, tighten the sensor mounting screws securely, being careful to avoid moving the sensor.

10 The remainder of installation is the reverse of removal.

11 Tighten the cable nut and check that the transmission and indicator operate properly. Make sure the engine only starts in Park and Neutral, and make sure the back-up lights come on when the shifter is placed in Reverse.

13 Manifold Absolute Pressure (MAP) sensor - replacement

Note: On 2001 through 2006 four-cylinder engines, this sensor is attached to the rear of the upper intake manifold. On 2006.5 and later V6 engines, it is located at the rear of the engine; it's connected to the upper intake manifold by a vacuum hose. 2001 through 2006 V6 engines and 2006.5 and later four-cylinder engines do not use a MAP sensor.

1 Disconnect the cable from the negative battery terminal (see Chapter 5).

2 Disconnect the vacuum hose from the sensor, if equipped.

3 Remove the mounting screw(s) and detach the sensor.

4 Installation is the reverse of removal.

14 Vehicle Speed Sensor (VSS) - replacement

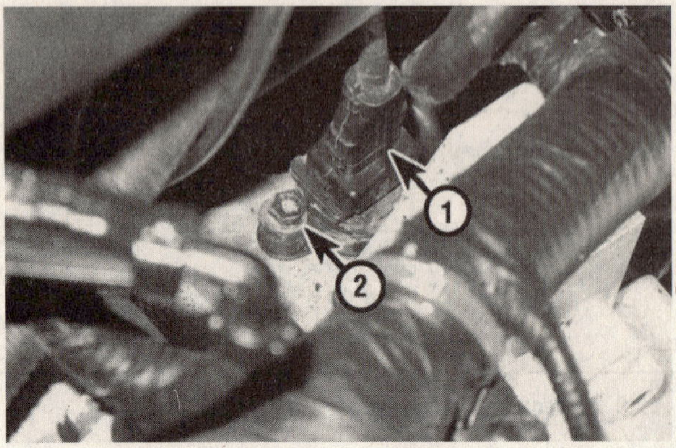

14.2 Typical VSS electrical connector (1) and mounting bolt (2) locations

Refer to illustration 14.2

Note: The VSS is located behind the engine, on top of the transaxle, near the inner CV joint for the right driveaxle assembly.

1 Depending on the year and model, some components may need to be disconnected or removed to access the VSS.

2 Using a flashlight, locate the VSS (see illustration).

3 Disconnect the VSS electrical connector.

4 Remove the VSS mounting bolt and remove the VSS.

5 Installation is the reverse of removal. Be sure to use a new O-ring and tighten the VSS mounting bolt securely.

15 Powertrain Control Module (PCM) - removal and installation

CAUTION:

To avoid electrostatic discharge damage to the PCM, handle the PCM only by its case. Do not touch the electrical terminals during removal and installation. If available, ground yourself to the vehicle with an anti-static ground strap, available at computer supply stores, and use a special anti-static pad to store the PCM on once it is removed.

Note: If a Diagnostic Trouble Code (DTC) indicating a problem with the PCM is ever set, have the PCM replaced by a dealer. A new PCM must be reprogrammed with a factory scan tool by a dealership service department, so even if you were to replace the old PCM with a new unit, it wouldn't work until the vehicle was towed to a dealer for programming.

1 Disconnect the cable from the negative terminal of the battery (see Chapter 5).

2001 THROUGH 2006 MODELS

Note: The PCM on these models is located under the center of the instrument panel, forward of the center console, on top of the tunnel.

2 Remove the right-side trim panel that's forward of the center console and under the instrument panel (see "Dashboard trim panels - removal and installation" in Chapter 11).

3 Disconnect the electrical connectors from the PCM.

4 Unscrew the mounting fasteners and remove the PCM.

5 Installation is the reverse of removal.

2006.5 AND LATER MODELS

Refer to illustration 15.6

Note: The PCM on these models is located on the back of the air filter housing.

6 Disconnect the electrical connectors from the PCM (see illustration).

7 Remove the mounting fasteners and carefully detach the PCM from the air filter housing.

8 Installation is the reverse of removal.

15.6 Flip open the locking levers, then unplug the electrical connectors from the PCM

16 Idle Air Control (IAC) valve - replacement

Refer to illustration 16.3

Note: The IAC is valve is used on 2001 through 2006 engines. The IAC valve is located on the underside of the throttle body on four-cylinder engines and on the side of the throttle body (near the TP sensor) on V6 engines.

1 Disconnect the cable from the negative battery terminal (see Chapter 5).

2 On four-cylinder engines, remove the throttle body (see Chapter 4).

3 Disconnect the electrical connector from the IAC valve (see illustration).

4 Remove the IAC valve mounting fasteners and remove the IAC valve. Remove and discard the old IAC valve gasket.

5 Installation is the reverse of removal. Be sure to use a new gasket and tighten the IAC valve mounting fasteners securely.

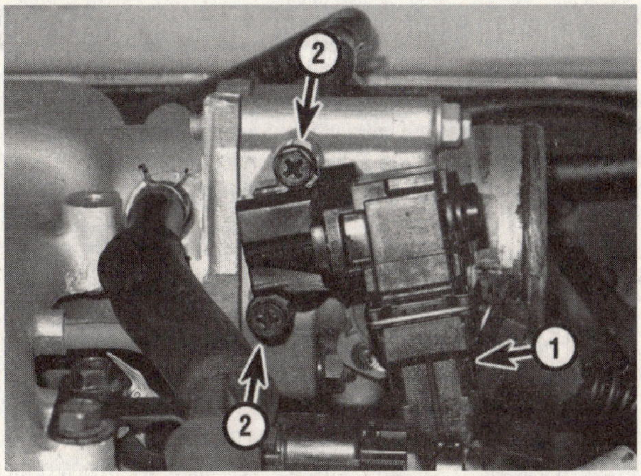

16.3 IAC valve electrical connector (1) and mounting bolt (2) locations

17 Camshaft Variable Valve Timing (CVVT) system - component replacement

Refer to illustration 17.3

WARNING:

Wait until the engine has cooled completely before beginning this procedure.

Note: The CVVT system is used on 2006.5 and later models. The oil temperature sensor and oil control valve are at the left (driver's) end of each cylinder head on V6 models and at the right (passenger's) end of the cylinder head on four-cylinder engines.

1 Disconnect the cable from the negative battery terminal (see Chapter 5).

2 Remove the upper engine cover.

3 Locate the oil temperature sensor or oil control valve and disconnect the wiring harness from it (see illustration).

4 Place rags under the sensor or valve to minimize oil leakage.

5 Carefully clean around the sensor or valve to avoid dropping bits of debris into the opening.

6 Unscrew the sensor or valve.

7 Installation is the reverse of removal.

Note: On V6 engines, the oil control valves are color-coded. The valve for the rear cylinder bank is gray, and the valve for the front cylinder bank is black. They are not interchangeable.

17.3 Camshaft variable valve timing components (2006.5 and later four-cylinder engines)

A Oil temperature sensor *B Oil control valve*

18 Variable Intake Solenoid (VIS) valve - replacement

Note: The VIS valve is only used on 2006.5 and later V6 engines. The valve is mounted near the passenger end of the rear cylinder head. A vacuum hose connects it to the intake manifold.

1 Disconnect the cable from the negative battery terminal (see Chapter 5).

2 Remove the upper engine cover.

3 Locate the sensor and disconnect the wiring harness from it.

4 Disconnect the vacuum hose and remove the mounting screws. Detach the valve.

5 Installation is the reverse of removal.

19 Catalytic converters - description, check and component replacement

Note: Because of a Federally mandated extended warranty which covers emissions-related components such as the catalytic converter, check with a dealer service department before replacing the converter at your own expense.

GENERAL DESCRIPTION

1 The catalytic converter is an emission control device installed in the exhaust system that reduces pollutants from the exhaust gas stream. There are two types of converters: The oxidation catalyst reduces the levels of hydrocarbon (HC) and carbon monoxide (CO) by adding oxygen to the exhaust stream to produce water vapor (H2O) and carbon dioxide (CO2). The reduction catalyst lowers the levels of oxides of nitrogen (NOx) by removing oxygen from the exhaust gases to produce nitrogen (N) and oxygen. These two types of catalysts are combined into a three-way catalyst that reduces all three pollutants.

2 The amount of oxygen entering the catalyst is critical to its operation, because without oxygen it cannot convert harmful pollutants into harmless compounds. The catalyst is most efficient at capturing and storing oxygen when it converts the exhaust gases of an intake charge that's mixed at the ideal (stoichiometric) air/fuel ratio of 14.7:1. If the air/fuel ratio is leaner than stoichiometric for an extended period of time, the catalyst will store even more oxygen. But if the air/fuel ratio is richer than stoichiometric for any length of time, the oxygen content in the catalyst can become totally depleted. If this condition occurs, the catalyst will not convert anything!

3 Because the catalyst's ability to store oxygen is such an important factor in its operation, it can also be considered a factor in the catalyst's eventual inability to do its job. The PCM monitors the oxygen content going into and coming out of the catalyst by comparing the voltage signals from the upstream and downstream oxygen sensors. When the catalyst is functioning correctly, there is very little oxygen to monitor at the outlet end of the catalyst because it's capturing, storing and releasing oxygen as needed to convert HC, CO and NOx into more benign substances. If the catalyst isn't doing its job, the downstream oxygen sensor tells the PCM that the oxygen content in the catalyzed exhaust gases is going up. When the amount of oxygen exiting the catalyst reaches a specified threshold, the PCM stores a Diagnostic Trouble Code (DTC) and turns on the Malfunction Indicator Light (MIL), also known as the CHECK ENGINE light.

CHECK

4 The test equipment for a catalytic converter is expensive and highly sophisticated. If you suspect that the converter on your vehicle is malfunctioning, take it to a dealer or authorized emissions inspection facility for diagnosis and repair.

5 Whenever the vehicle is raised for servicing of underbody components, check the converter for leaks, corrosion, dents and other damage. Check the welds/flange bolts that attach the front and rear ends of the converter to the exhaust system. If damage is discovered, the converter should be replaced.

6 Although catalytic converters don't break too often, they can become plugged. The easiest way to check for a restricted converter is to use a vacuum gauge to diagnose the effect of a blocked exhaust on intake vacuum.

a) *Connect a vacuum gauge to an intake manifold vacuum source (see Chapter 2C).*
b) *Warm the engine to operating temperature, place the transaxle in Park (automatic) or Neutral (manual) and apply the parking brake.*
c) *Note and record the vacuum reading at idle.*
d) *Quickly open the throttle to near full throttle and release it shut. Note and record the vacuum reading.*
e) *Perform the test three more times, recording the reading after each test.*
f) *If the reading after the fourth test is more than one in-Hg lower than the reading recorded at idle, the exhaust system may be restricted (the catalytic converter could be plugged or an exhaust pipe or muffler could be restricted).*

REPLACEMENT

**** WARNING:**

Do NOT service a catalytic converter until it has completely cooled down.

Manifold catalytic converters

2001 through 2006 four-cylinder models

➡ Note: On these models, the exhaust manifold catalytic converters are located directly below the exhaust manifolds, to which they're bolted.

7 Raise the vehicle and support it securely on jackstands.

8 Unbolt the exhaust pipe from the bottom of the catalytic converter.

9 Disconnect the rubber exhaust pipe supports under the vehicle and carefully lower the front of the pipe as much as possible for access to the catalytic converters.

10 Disconnect the oxygen sensor wiring harnesses from the catalytic converter.

11 Unbolt the converter from the exhaust manifold and remove it from beneath the vehicle.

All other models

12 On these models, the primary catalytic converters are integral parts of the exhaust manifolds. See Chapter 2B for the procedure.

Undercar catalytic converter

➧ Refer to illustration 19.15

➡ Note: The downstream catalytic converter is located underneath the vehicle, between the flange at the rear end of the front exhaust pipe and the muffler, to which it's connected by a short pipe. These catalytic converters are usually replaced at muffler shops that are equipped with the proper welding equipment. If you wish to replace the catalytic converter without welding, it will be necessary to replace the section of exhaust pipe that includes the converter from flange to flange.

13 Raise the front of the vehicle and place it securely on jackstands.

14 Support the catalytic converter with a floor jack.

15 Remove the bolts from the flanges at each end of the catalytic converter (see illustration).

16 Disconnect the flanges and remove any gaskets.

17 Lower the converter from the vehicle.

19.15 A typical downstream catalytic converter; the upstream converters are located at the exhaust manifolds

20 Evaporative emissions control (EVAP) system - description and component replacement

DESCRIPTION

1 The Evaporative Emissions Control (EVAP) system absorbs fuel vapors (unburned hydrocarbons) and, during engine operation, releases them into the intake manifold, from which they're drawn into the intake ports where they mix with the incoming air-fuel mixture. The EVAP system consists of the fuel tank filler neck cap, the EVAP canister, the vapor pressure sensor, the canister closed valve, the two-way valve and the purge valve. Everything except the purge valve is located underneath the vehicle.

2 Modern EVAP systems are quite complex, but basically, here's how they work: When the gasoline inside the fuel tank warms up on a hot day, it evaporates and produces fuel vapors. These vapors, which are raw unburned hydrocarbons, elevate the pressure inside the sealed

fuel tank. If there were no way to vent them somewhere, the fuel tank would eventually spring a leak. The vapor pressure sensor monitors the pressure inside the tank and keeps the Powertrain Control Module (PCM) informed. The fuel tank vapors enter the canister by flowing through a two-way valve. The canister stores these vapors until the PCM energizes the purge control solenoid valve, which opens and purges the EVAP system, allowing intake manifold vacuum to pull the vapors from the canister into the intake manifold.

3 The vapor pressure sensor is located on top of the fuel tank. The vapor pressure sensor monitors the pressure of fuel vapors inside the tank.

4 After the engine is warmed up (165 degrees F), the PCM puts the system into closed loop operation. Then it energizes the canister purge control solenoid valve, which regulates the flow of vapors from the canister to the intake manifold. The rate of vapor flow is regulated by the purge valve in response to commands from the PCM, which controls the duty cycle of the valve. This means that the valve's opening can be controlled to a fine degree (it's not just open or closed) in order to regulate the volume of the purged vapors in an appropriate way so that the air/fuel mixture doesn't become too rich. On all models, the canister purge control solenoid valve is located in the engine compartment.

5 When the EVAP system is being purged and stored vapors are being drawn from the canister by intake manifold vacuum, a vacuum condition would quickly result inside the canister and the fuel tank if they were not vented to atmospheric pressure. So during purging, atmospheric air is drawn through the fresh air line, into the canister. The canister closed valve opens and closes the EVAP system's fresh air line in response to signals from the Powertrain Control Module (PCM). When commanded by the PCM, the canister closed valve also closes the fresh air line to the EVAP canister for monitor testing. The canister closed valve is located on the canister.

The EVAP system monitor

6 The EVAP system diagnostic monitor is an OBD-II test that the PCM runs to check the EVAP system and the fuel tank for leaks. Before the monitor sequence begins, several things must happen. First, you must start the engine. If the engine is cold, the engine coolant temperature and the intake air temperature are about the same. The PCM watches the progress of the warm-up sequence closely. Once the oxygen sensors and the catalysts have warmed up enough for the PCM to put the system into closed loop operation, the PCM initiates the EVAP purge sequence. The purge valve opens, the canister closed valve opens and the EVAP canister's contents are purged (drawn into the intake manifold). During a fast-idle warm-up, intake vacuum is high and the extra-rich mixture caused by purging the vapors stored inside the EVAP canister actually helps to smooth out the idle.

7 During purging, the pressure inside the EVAP system is neutral because the opened canister closed valve allows atmospheric pressure to be drawn into the canister as vapors are drawn from the canister into the intake manifold. During this initial period of operation, the PCM is also monitoring the fuel tank pressure with the vapor pressure sensor. As soon as the purge sequence is complete, the PCM closes the canister closed valve. When the canister closed valve is first closed, the pressure switching valve and the purge valve are still open, so a (relative) vacuum develops inside the purge line from the air intake to the canister and to the EVAP line from the canister to the fuel tank. The PCM then closes the purge valve to produce a (relative) vacuum in the line between the tank and the purge valve. Then it monitors any change in pressure (through the vapor pressure sensor) to check for EVAP system leaks. If there's a leak, the Malfunction Indicator Light (MIL) or Check Engine light comes on and the PCM stores a Diagnostic Trouble Code (DTC) that indicates a malfunction in the EVAP system (see Section 2).

8 At a certain point in the monitoring sequence the PCM closes the canister closed valve which causes a pressure drop in the EVAP system. The PCM keeps the purge valve open until the pressure inside the EVAP system drops to a specified threshold, at which point the PCM closes the purge valve. If the pressure doesn't drop, or drops too much, the PCM turns on the MIL or Check Engine light and stores a DTC (see Section 2) that indicates an incorrect purge flow in the EVAP system.

9 Then the PCM monitors the operation of the canister closed valve and the venting (air inlet) function of the system. When vapor pressure rises to a specified threshold, the PCM opens the canister closed valve. The pressure inside the system goes up quickly because of the air drawn into the system. If the PCM detects no increase in pressure or if the pressure is below the specified increase, the PCM concludes that either the canister closed valve is malfunctioning or there's a restriction somewhere in the venting and, again, stores a DTC (see Section 2) and turns on the MIL or Check Engine light.

10 Finally, the PCM closes the pressure switching valve, which prevents atmospheric air from entering the fuel tank side of the system. When the pressure switching valve is operating correctly, this should produce a slight pressure rise inside the tank (because the fuel inside the tank is still slowly getting warmer). But if there's no change in pressure, the PCM concludes that the pressure switching valve isn't closing and, again, stores a DTC (see Section 2) and turns on the MIL or Check Engine light. The monitoring sequence is now completed. The PCM immediately repeats the entire sequence again, conditions permitting, and continues to do so as long as the engine is operating in closed loop.

REPLACEMENT

⁂ WARNING:

Gasoline and gasoline vapor is extremely flammable, so take extra precautions when you work on any part of the fuel system or EVAP system. Don't smoke or allow open flames or bare light bulbs near the work area, and don't work in a garage where a gas-type appliance (such as a water heater or clothes dryer) is present. Since gasoline is carcinogenic, wear fuel-resistant gloves when there's a possibility of being exposed to fuel, and, if you spill any fuel on your skin, rinse it off immediately with soap and water. Mop up any spills immediately and do not store fuel-soaked rags where they could ignite. When you perform any kind of work on the fuel system, wear safety glasses and have a Class B type fire extinguisher on hand.

Purge control solenoid valve

➧ Refer to illustrations 20.13a and 20.13b

11 Disconnect the cable from the negative battery terminal (see Chapter 5).

12 Remove the engine cover, if applicable (see "Intake manifold - removal and installation" in Chapter 2).

20.13a Purge control valve (2006.5 and later four-cylinder models)

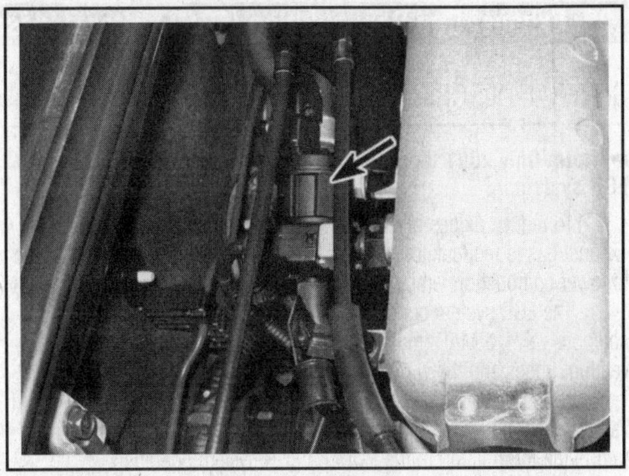

20.13b Purge control valve (2001 through 2006 V6 models)

13 Disconnect the electrical connector from the purge valve (see illustrations).

14 Disconnect the vacuum hoses from the purge valve.

15 Remove the purge valve mounting fasteners and remove the purge valve.

16 Installation is the reverse of removal.

EVAP canister

Refer to illustration 20.19

Note: The EVAP canister is mounted under the vehicle, near the fuel tank.

17 Disconnect the cable from the negative battery terminal (see Chapter 5).

18 Raise the rear of the vehicle and support it securely on jackstands.

19 Remove the protective cover from the EVAP canister assembly, if so equipped (see illustration).

20 Clearly label, then disconnect the hoses from the canister.

21 Disconnect the electrical connector from the EVAP canister.

22 Remove the EVAP canister mounting bracket bolts and remove the EVAP canister and mounting bracket as a single assembly.

23 Installation is the reverse of removal.

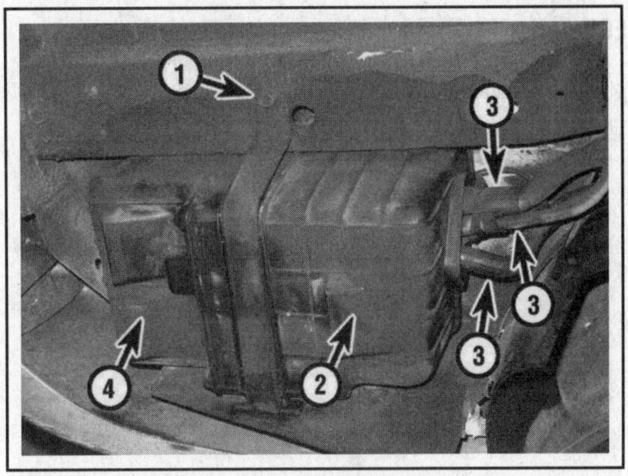

20.19 Typical EVAP canister details (2001 through 2006 models)

1. *Cover retaining strap bolt*
2. *Cover*
3. *EVAP hoses (label clearly before disconnecting)*
4. *EVAP canister (mounting bracket bolts not visible in this photo)*

21 Positive Crankcase Ventilation (PCV) system - general information

1 The Positive Crankcase Ventilation (PCV) system reduces hydrocarbon emissions by directing blow-by gases and crankcase vapors into the intake manifold, where they're mixed with intake air before being drawn into the combustion chambers, where they're consumed along with the air/fuel mixture. The PCV system does this by circulating fresh air from the air filter housing through a series of hoses into the crankcase, where the fresh air mixes with blow-by gases before being drawn from the crankcase by intake vacuum, through the PCV valve then into the intake manifold.

2 During idle and part-throttle conditions, intake manifold vacuum is high. Blow-by gases and crankcase vapors flow from the crankcase through the PCV valve and the crankcase ventilation hose (also known as the PCV hose) into the intake manifold. The strong intake manifold vacuum also pulls fresh air from the air intake duct or the air filter housing through the fresh air inlet hose into the crankcase.

3 There is no scheduled maintenance interval for the PCV valve or the PCV system hoses, but over time the PCV system might become less efficient as an oily residue of sludge builds up inside the PCV valve and the hoses. One symptom of a clogged PCV system is leaking engine seals. When crankcase vapors can't escape, pressure builds inside the bottom end and eventually causes engine seals to leak. Anytime that you're changing the oil filter, air filter, fuel filter, spark plugs, etc. it's a good idea to pull off the PCV hoses and inspect them. If the hoses are clogged, remove them and clean them out. If they're cracked, torn or deteriorated, replace them.

4 Checking and replacement of the PCV valve are covered in Chapter 1. It is mounted to the valve cover on all models.

22 Exhaust Gas Recirculation (EGR) system - description and component replacement

GENERAL DESCRIPTION

➡ **Note: Only 2001 through 2006 four-cylinder models use an EGR system.**

1 To reduce oxides of nitrogen (NOx) emissions, some of the exhaust gas is recirculated through the EGR valve to the intake manifold to lower combustion temperatures.

2 The EGR system consists of an EGR valve, an EGR vacuum solenoid valve, a MAP (manifold absolute pressure) sensor, the PCM, vacuum hoses and the wiring harnesses. The position of the EGR valve is controlled by vacuum. The vacuum is modulated by the EGR solenoid valve, which in turn is controlled by the PCM. The MAP sensor is used to provide information to the PCM for EGR system operation.

REPLACEMENT

EGR valve

3 Remove the engine cover and gain access to the EGR valve. It is identifiable by the large diaphragm housing with the vacuum hose attached near the throttle body.

4 Disconnect the vacuum hose.

5 Remove the mounting bolts and lift the EGR valve off.

6 Check the EGR valve for sticking and heavy carbon deposits. They can sometimes be cleaned of carbon, but if it's excessive, it must be replaced.

7 Installation is the reverse of removal. Be sure to use a new gasket, and to clean the mounting surfaces thoroughly.

EGR vacuum solenoid valve

8 The EGR vacuum solenoid valve is connected to the EGR valve by a vacuum hose. There is also a vacuum hose connecting it to an engine vacuum source. It's on the top of the engine near the valve cover.

9 Disconnect the wiring harness from the valve.

10 Disconnect both vacuum hoses from the valve. Label them if there is any chance they could be confused later.

11 Remove the mounting bolts and take off the solenoid valve.

12 Installation is the reverse of removal.

EGR MAP sensor

13 The MAP sensor is connected directly to the intake manifold. Its only function is to supply information to the PCM for proper operation of the EGR system. It is not used as a sensor for general engine performance. It's located at the rear side of the intake manifold.

14 Disconnect the wiring/vacuum hose connections from the valve.

15 Remove the mounting screws and lift off the sensor.

16 Installation is the reverse of removal.

Torque specifications	Ft-lbs	Nm
Oxygen sensors	35	47

7A

MANUAL TRANSAXLE

Section

1 General information

The vehicles covered by this manual are equipped with either a 5-speed manual or an automatic transaxle. This Part of Chapter 7 contains information on the manual transaxle. Service procedures for the automatic transaxle are contained in Part B.

The transaxle is contained in a cast-aluminum alloy casing bolted to the engine's rear end, and consists of the gearbox and final drive differential. The transaxle unit type is stamped on a plate attached to the transaxle.

TRANSAXLE OVERHAUL

Because of the complexity of the assembly, possible unavailability of replacement parts and special tools necessary, internal repair procedures for the transaxle are not recommended for the home mechanic. The bulk of the information in this Chapter is devoted to removal and installation procedures.

2 Shift lever - removal and installation

1 Apply the parking brake. Place the shift lever in Neutral. Unscrew and remove the shift lever knob.

2 Remove the center console assembly (see Chapter 11).

3 Use pliers to remove the shift cable pins and clips, then pull the cable housing retaining clips out of the shifter base and move the cables aside.

4 Remove the shifter assembly mounting fasteners, then remove the shifter assembly.

5 Installation is the reverse of removal.

3 Shift cables - removal and installation

1 Apply the parking brake. Place the shift lever in Neutral. Unscrew and remove the shift lever knob.

2 Remove the center console assembly (see Chapter 11).

3 Use pliers to remove the pins from the ends of the shift cables.

4 Pull the cable housing retaining clips out of the shifter base.

5 Locate the shift cables at the transaxle and pull their retaining clips out. Mark one of the cables to avoid confusing them later.

6 Pull the clips out of the transaxle ends of the shift cables.

7 Feed the cables through the firewall grommet to remove them.

➡ **Note: On some later models, it may be necessary to remove the two fasteners under the dash that secure the grommet to the firewall.**

8 Check the end bushings for any signs of looseness or damage before replacing the cables.

9 Installation is the reverse of removal.

4 Driveaxle oil seals - replacement

4.4 Insert the tip of a large screwdriver or prybar behind the oil seal and very carefully pry the seal out

➧ **Refer to illustrations 4.4 and 4.6**

1 Oil leaks frequently occur due to wear of the driveaxle oil seals. Replacement of these seals is relatively easy, since the repair can be performed without removing the transaxle from the vehicle.

2 Driveaxle oil seals are located at the sides of the transaxle/transfer case, where the driveaxles are attached. If leakage at the seal is suspected, raise the vehicle and support it securely on jackstands. If the seal is leaking, lubricant will be found on the sides of the transaxle below the seals.

3 Refer to Chapter 8 and remove the driveaxles.

4 Use a screwdriver or prybar to carefully pry the oil seal out of the transaxle bore (see illustration).

5 If the oil seal cannot be removed with a screwdriver or prybar, a special oil seal removal tool (available at auto parts stores) will be required.

6 Using a large section of pipe or a large deep socket (slightly smaller than the outside diameter of the seal) as a drift, install the new oil seal. Drive it into the bore squarely and make sure it's completely seated (see illustration). Coat the seal lip with transaxle lubricant.

7 Install the driveaxle(s). Be careful not to damage the lip of the new seal.

8 Fill the transaxle with the correct lubricant until it runs out of the inspection hole (see Chapter 1).

4.6 Using a seal driver or large socket, drive the new seal squarely into the bore

5 Transaxle mount - replacement

1 Insert a large screwdriver or prybar between the mount and the transaxle and pry up.

2 The transaxle should not move excessively away from the mount. If it does, replace the mount.

3 There are two lower mounts (one each at the front and rear of the transaxle) and an upper mount assembly.

4 Support the transaxle from below with a jack, remove the nuts and bolts and remove the mount. It may be necessary to raise the transaxle slightly to provide enough clearance to remove the mount.

5 Installation is the reverse of removal.

➡ **Note: Install all of the mount fasteners before tightening any of them.**

6 Manual transaxle - removal and installation

➡ **Note: 2006 and 2006.5 models will both have a "6" in the tenth position of the VIN. To distinguish a 2006 model from a 2006.5 model, refer to the 8th position of the VIN (the engine code): A 2006 model will have a "6" (four-cylinder) or "8" (V6), while a 2006.5 will have a "3" (four-cylinder) or "4" (V6).**

REMOVAL

1 Loosen the front wheel lug nuts and the driveaxle/hub nuts.

2 Disconnect the cable from the negative battery terminal (see Chapter 5).

3 Refer to Chapter 4 and remove the entire air cleaner assembly along with the intake duct.

4 Disconnect the wiring from the back-up light switch.

5 Disconnect the speedometer connection at the transaxle.

2006 and earlier models

6 Disconnect the clutch fluid line from its retainer and unbolt the slave cylinder. Disconnect the clutch release lever from the release fork/transaxle.

⁂ CAUTION:

The clutch release lever on the bellhousing must be disconnected from the transaxle before attempting to separate the transaxle from the engine, because the release bearing is secured to the clutch by a snap-ring and to the release fork by clips. The transaxle will seem to be stuck to the engine if the clutch release mechanism is not disconnected.

2006.5 and later models

➡ **Note: These models have concentric slave cylinders and self-adjusting clutches.**

7 Disconnect the brake fluid line from the transaxle by first removing the end clip with pliers.

All models

8 Disconnect both transaxle shift cables. Unbolt the starter and secure it out of the way with wire.

9 Remove the top transaxle mounting bolts.

10 Support the transaxle-end of the engine securely from above with

a fixture that mounts between the fenders. These can be rented at most rental yards if you don't own one.

11 Make sure the weight is removed from the transaxle, then remove the main transaxle mount.

12 Raise the vehicle and support it securely on jackstands. Make sure that there is plenty of room to slide the transaxle out from under the vehicle. Remove both driveaxles and disconnect the stabilizer bar links (see Chapter 8).

13 Drain the transaxle lubricant (see Chapter 1).

14 Disconnect the steering intermediate shaft U-joint (see Chapter 10, Section 19).

15 Disconnect the power steering fluid hoses and the electronic power steering wiring, if equipped.

16 Remove the front section of the exhaust pipe that's under the transaxle.

17 Make sure that the engine is solidly supported by the fixture. Remove the subframe mounting bolts and lift the subframe clear with the help of an assistant.

18 Remove the transaxle mounting bracket and the front and rear lower roll stopper mounts.

19 Put a transmission jack (or a floor jack with an appropriate saddle) under the transaxle. Safety chains will help steady the transaxle on the jack.

20 Remove the remaining transaxle-to-engine bolts. Check to make certain that all connections between the transaxle and the vehicle are disconnected.

21 With the help of an assistant, pull the transaxle away from the engine and slowly lower it to the ground, checking that it's not catching on other components as you do so.

22 Pull the transaxle out from beneath the vehicle, remove it from the jack and set it where it can't roll over and become damaged.

INSTALLATION

23 Lightly lubricate the release bearing contact sleeve and install the release bearing onto the fork and the input shaft.

24 Install the release lever to the fork.

25 Lubricate the input shaft with a light coat of high-temperature grease. With the transaxle secured to the jack, raise it into position behind the engine and carefully slide it forward, engaging the input shaft with the clutch. Do not use excessive force to install the transaxle - if the input shaft won't slide into place, readjust the angle of the transaxle or turn the input shaft so the splines engage properly with the clutch.

26 Once the transaxle is snug against the engine, install the transaxle-to-engine bolts and tighten them securely.

⁂ CAUTION:

Don't use the bolts to force the transaxle and engine together. Don't tighten the roll-stopper bolts to the point where they bend the steel ears. This will cause idle vibrations.

27 Push the release lever away from the slave cylinder about 16-degrees. There should be a click as the release bearing snaps into position on the clutch. The release lever should now have about 3-degrees of travel in its operation

⁂ CAUTION:

If there is more than 3-degrees of travel or if there was no click heard, you must remove the transaxle and find out why the bearing didn't snap onto the clutch cover.

28 The remainder of installation is the reverse of removal, but note the following points:

a) *Tighten the suspension mounting bolts to the torque values listed in the Chapter 10 Specifications.*
b) *Tighten the driveaxle/hub nuts to the torque value listed in the Chapter 8 Specifications.*
c) *Tighten the starter mounting bolts to the torque value listed in the Chapter 5 Specifications.*
d) *Tighten the wheel lug nuts to the torque listed in the Chapter 1 Specifications.*
e) *Fill the transaxle with the correct type and amount of transaxle fluid as described in Chapter 1.*

7 Manual transaxle overhaul - general information

1 Overhauling a manual transaxle is a difficult job for the do-it-yourselfer. It involves the disassembly and reassembly of many small parts. Numerous clearances must be precisely measured and, if necessary, changed with select-fit spacers and snap-rings. As a result, if transaxle problems arise, it can be removed and installed by a competent do-it-yourselfer, but overhaul should be left to a transmission repair shop. Rebuilt transaxles may be available - check with your dealer parts department and auto parts stores. At any rate, the time and money involved in an overhaul is almost sure to exceed the cost of a rebuilt unit.

2 Nevertheless, it's not impossible for an inexperienced mechanic to rebuild a transaxle if the special tools are available and the job is done in a deliberate step-by-step manner so nothing is overlooked.

3 The tools necessary for an overhaul include internal and external snap-ring pliers, a bearing puller, a slide hammer, a set of pin punches, a dial indicator and possibly a hydraulic press. In addition, a large, sturdy workbench and a vise or transaxle stand will be required.

4 During disassembly of the transaxle, make careful notes of how each piece comes off, where it fits in relation to other pieces and what holds it in place.

5 Before taking the transaxle apart for repair, it will help if you have some idea what area of the transaxle is malfunctioning. Certain problems can be closely tied to specific areas in the transaxle, which can make component examination and replacement easier. Refer to the *Troubleshooting* Section at the front of this manual for information regarding possible sources of trouble.

Specifications

General

Transaxle oil type	See Chapter 1
Transaxle oil capacity	See Chapter 1

Torque specifications	Ft-lbs	Nm
Front roll stopper bracket-to-subframe bolts	44 to 59	60 to 80
Rear roll stopper bracket-to-subframe bolts	36 to 47	50 to 65
Roll stopper insulator bolt and nut	36 to 47	50 to 65
Roll stopper bracket-to-transaxle bolts	44 to 59	60 to 80
Transaxle mounting bracket bolts	44 to 59	60 to 80
Transaxle mounting insulator bolt	65 to 80	90 to 110
Subframe-to-body mounting bolts	74 to 88	100 to 120

Notes

7B

AUTOMATIC TRANSAXLE

Section

Reference to other Chapters

Driveaxle oil seals - replacement - See Chapter 7A

1 General information

All information on the automatic transaxle is included in this Part of Chapter 7. Information for the manual transaxle can be found in Part A of this Chapter.

Because of the complexity of the automatic transaxles and the specialized equipment necessary to perform most service operations, this Chapter contains only those procedures related to general diagnosis, routine maintenance, adjustment and removal and installation.

If the transaxle requires major repair work, it should be left to a dealer service department or an automotive or transmission repair shop. However, once properly diagnosed, you can remove and install the transaxle yourself and save the expense, even if the repair work is done by a transmission shop.

2 Diagnosis - general

1 Automatic transaxle malfunctions may be caused by five general conditions:

a) Poor engine performance
b) Improper adjustments
c) Hydraulic malfunctions
d) Mechanical malfunctions
e) Malfunctions in the computer or its signal network

2 Diagnosis of these problems should always begin with a check of the easily repaired items: fluid level and condition (see Chapter 1), shift cable adjustment and shift lever installation. Next, perform a road test to determine if the problem has been corrected or if more diagnosis is necessary. If the problem persists after the preliminary tests and corrections are completed, additional diagnosis should be performed by a dealer service department or other qualified transmission repair shop. Refer to the *Troubleshooting* Section at the front of this manual for information on symptoms of transaxle problems.

PRELIMINARY CHECKS

3 Drive the vehicle to warm the transaxle to normal operating temperature.

4 Check the fluid level as described in Chapter 1:

a) If the fluid level is unusually low, add enough fluid to bring the level within the designated area of the dipstick, then check for external leaks (see following).
b) If the fluid level is abnormally high, drain off the excess, then check the drained fluid for contamination by coolant. The presence of engine coolant in the automatic transmission fluid indicates that a failure has occurred in the internal radiator oil cooler walls that separate the coolant from the transmission fluid (see Chapter 3).
c) If the fluid is foaming, drain it and refill the transaxle, then check for coolant in the fluid, or a high fluid level.

5 Check the engine idle speed.

➡ Note: If the engine is malfunctioning, do not proceed with the preliminary checks until it has been repaired and runs normally.

6 Check and adjust the shift cable, if necessary (see Section 4).

7 If hard shifting is experienced, inspect the shift cable under the steering column and at the manual lever on the transaxle (see Section 4).

FLUID LEAK DIAGNOSIS

8 Most fluid leaks are easy to locate visually. Repair usually consists of replacing a seal or gasket. If a leak is difficult to find, the following procedure may help.

9 Identify the fluid. Make sure it's transmission fluid and not engine oil or brake fluid (automatic transmission fluid is a deep red color).

10 Try to pinpoint the source of the leak. Drive the vehicle several miles, and then park it over a large sheet of cardboard. After a minute or two, you should be able to locate the leak by determining the source of the fluid dripping onto the cardboard.

11 Make a careful visual inspection of the suspected component and the area immediately around it. Pay particular attention to gasket mating surfaces. A mirror is often helpful for finding leaks in areas that are hard to see.

12 If the leak still cannot be found, clean the suspected area thoroughly with a degreaser or solvent, then dry it thoroughly.

13 Drive the vehicle for several miles at normal operating temperature and varying speeds. After driving the vehicle, visually inspect the suspected component again.

14 Once the leak has been located, the cause must be determined before it can be properly repaired. If a gasket is replaced but the sealing flange is bent, the new gasket will not stop the leak. The bent flange must be straightened.

15 Before attempting to repair a leak, check to make sure that the following conditions are corrected or they may cause another leak.

➡ Note: Some of the following conditions cannot be fixed without highly specialized tools and expertise. Such problems must be referred to a qualified transmission shop or a dealer service department.

Gasket leaks

16 Check the pan periodically. Make sure the bolts are tight, no bolts are missing, the gasket is in good condition and the pan is flat (dents in the pan may indicate damage to the valve body inside).

17 If the pan gasket is leaking, the fluid level or the fluid pressure may be too high, the vent may be plugged, the pan bolts may be too tight, the pan sealing flange may be warped, the sealing surface of the transaxle housing may be damaged, the gasket may be damaged or the transaxle casting may be cracked or porous. If sealant instead of gasket material has been used to form a seal between the pan and the transaxle housing, it may be the wrong type of sealant.

Seal leaks

18 If a transaxle seal is leaking, the fluid level or pressure may be too high, the vent may be plugged, the seal bore may be damaged, the seal itself may be damaged or improperly installed, the surface of the shaft protruding through the seal may be damaged or a loose bearing may be causing excessive shaft movement.

19 Make sure the dipstick tube seal is in good condition and the tube is properly seated. Periodically check the area around the sensors for leakage. If transmission fluid is evident, check the seals for damage.

Case leaks

20 If the case itself appears to be leaking, the casting is porous and will have to be repaired or replaced.

21 Make sure the oil cooler hose fittings are tight and in good condition.

Fluid comes out vent pipe or fill tube

22 If this condition occurs, the possible causes are: the transaxle is overfilled, there is coolant in the fluid, the case is porous, the dipstick is incorrect, the vent is plugged or the drain-back holes are plugged.

3 Shift lever - replacement

WARNING:

These models are equipped with a Supplemental Restraint System (SRS), more commonly known as airbags. Always disable the airbag system before working in the vicinity of any airbag system component to avoid the possibility of accidental deployment of the airbag(s), which could cause personal injury (see Chapter 12).

WARNING:

Do not use a memory saving device to preserve the PCM or radio memory when working on or near airbag system components.

Note: 2006 and 2006.5 models will both have a "6" in the tenth position of the VIN. To distinguish a 2006 model from a 2006.5 model, refer to the 8th position of the VIN (the engine code): A 2006 model will have a "6" (four-cylinder) or "8" (V6), while a 2006.5 will have a "3" (four-cylinder) or "4" (V6).

1 Disconnect the cable from the negative battery terminal (see Chapter 5).

2001 THROUGH 2006 MODELS

2 Refer to Chapter 11 and remove the center console.

3 Disconnect the shift cable from the shifter.

4 Disconnect the shift lock cable as well as the key lock cable.

5 Disconnect the lamp wiring connector.

6 Remove the two screws from the front of the shift knob. Remove the shift knob, paying attention to the direction of the push button and the spring behind it.

7 Remove the shift position indicator if necessary.

8 Unbolt the shifter assembly and remove it. Installation is the reverse of removal.

2006.5 AND LATER MODELS

Refer to illustrations 3.9, 3.11 and 3.12

9 Remove the shift knob (see illustration).

10 Remove the center console (see Chapter 11).

11 Disconnect the electrical wiring from the shift assembly (see illustration).

12 Disconnect the shift cable (see illustration).

13 Unbolt and remove the shifter assembly.

14 Installation is the reverse of removal.

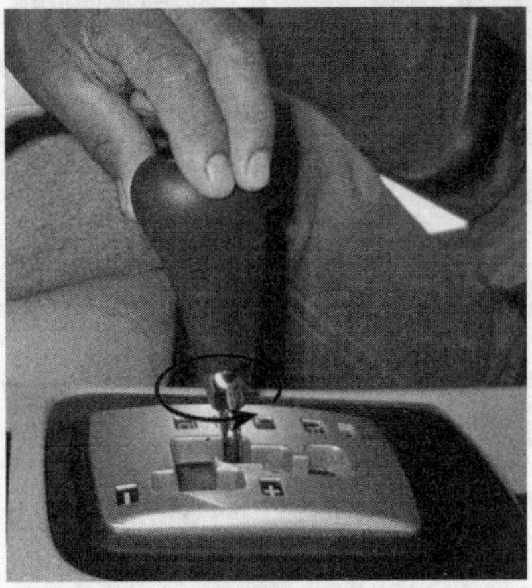

3.9 Unscrew the shift knob

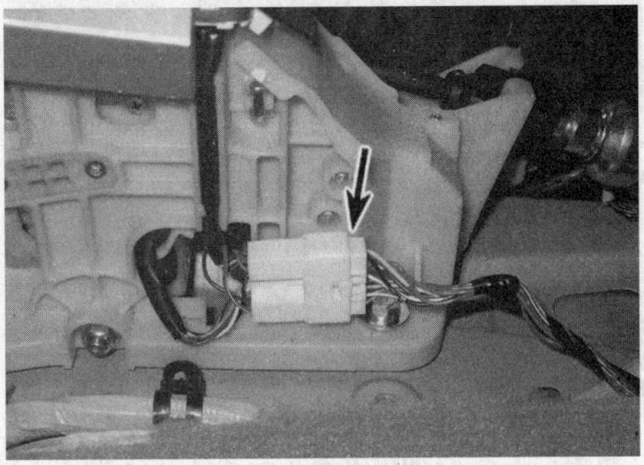

3.11 Disconnect the electrical connector for the shifter

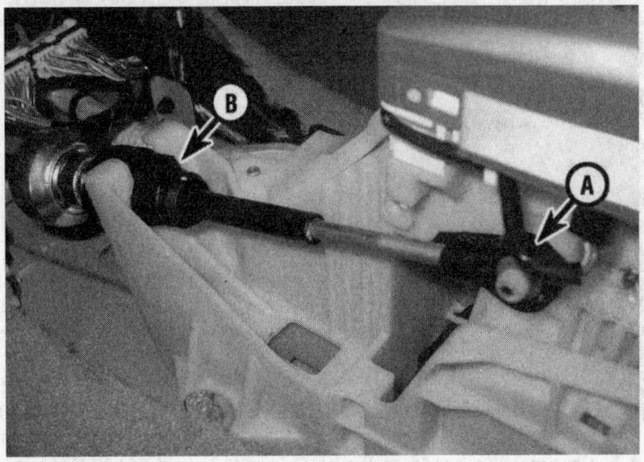

3.12 Carefully pry off the end of the shift cable from the lever (A), then squeeze these two tabs to release the shift cable from its bracket (B)

4 Shift and interlock cables - replacement and adjustment

SHIFT CABLE REPLACEMENT

Refer to illustrations 4.3a, 4.3b and 4.6

1 Disconnect the cable from the negative battery terminal (see Chapter 5).

2 Disassemble the shifter assembly enough to get access to the end of the shift cable.

3 On 2006 and earlier models, remove the retaining pin from the end of the cable and disconnect/remove the clip that secures the cable housing to the shifter bracket (see illustrations). If you're working on a 2006.5 and later model, refer to illustration 3.12.

4 Feed the cable through the instrument panel area and through the grommet in the firewall.

5 Disconnect the cable from retainers and interfering components.

6 Disconnect the cable from the lever at the transaxle and remove it from the vehicle (see illustration).

7 Installation is the reverse of removal. Be certain to adjust the new cable after installation.

ADJUSTMENT

Shift cable

8 Refer to Chapter 6 to adjust the Transmission Range sensor.

9 Put the shifter and the transaxle into the Neutral position with the cable disconnected from the transaxle lever.

10 Adjust the cable so that it can be connected to the transaxle lever when the lever is gently pushed toward it.

11 Check for proper operation in all ranges. Verify that the engine will start only in Park and Reverse.

Interlock cables

Refer to illustration 4.12

12 Remove the console cover if it hasn't been removed already (see illustration). Loosen the screws securing the interlock cables to the shifter bracket.

13 Shift the lever into the Park position. Verify that the key is in the Off position.

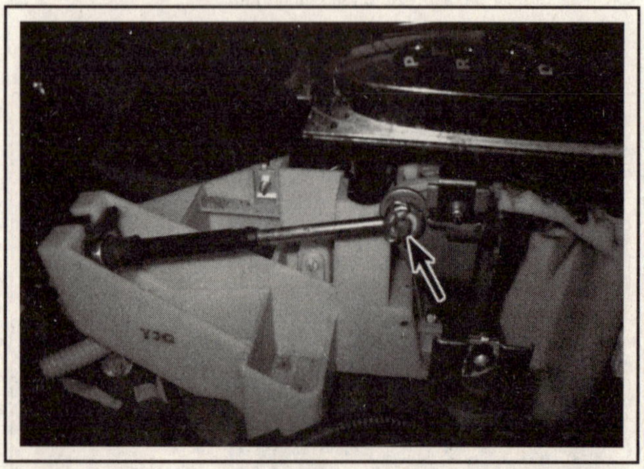

4.3a On 2006 and earlier models, remove the retaining pin from the end of the cable. . .

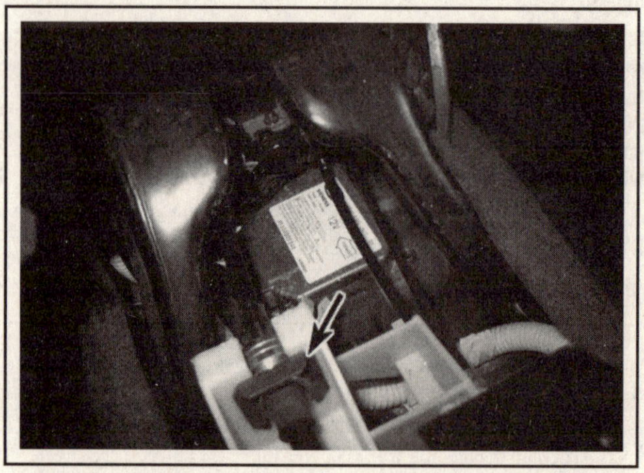

4.3b . . . then remove the retainer with pliers to release the shift cable from the lever bracket

4.6 Remove the nut from the shift lever (A) and the C-clip from the bracket (B) and detach the shift cable

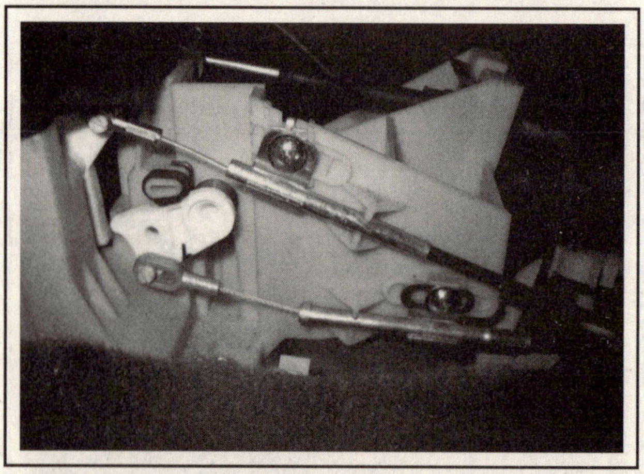

4.12 The interlock cables attach to the right side of the shifter - if one is disconnected or misadjusted, it might be possible to shift out of Park without turning the key On and pressing the brake pedal

14 Make sure that the key lock cable cam is placed in the correct position by the detent pin. The key lock cable is connected to the key cylinder.

15 Make sure that the shift lock cable cam is in the correct position. The shift lock cable is attached to the brake pedal assembly.

16 Gently push the lower shift lock cable away from the shifter and tighten the self-tapping screw.

17 Gently pull the upper key lock cable toward the shifter and tighten the self-tapping screw.

18 After installing any remaining components, apply the parking brake and operate the vehicle in each gear position to verify the adjustment is correct. Verify that the vehicle can't be shifted out of Park unless the key is On and the brake pedal is depressed. Check that the key can't be turned to the Lock position unless the shifter is in Park.

5 Automatic transaxle - removal and installation

REMOVAL

Refer to illustrations 5.10, 5.13 and 5.15

1 Remove the battery (see Chapter 5).

2 Drain the fluid from the transaxle (see Chapter 1).

3 Refer to Chapter 4 and remove the entire air cleaner assembly including the air duct. On 2006.5 and later four-cylinder models, remove the PCM (see Chapter 6).

4 Disconnect the wiring harnesses from the speedometer sensor, Transmission Range sensor, solenoid connector and the oil temperature sensor.

5 Disconnect the transmission fluid cooler hoses and seal their ends to prevent leakage and contamination.

6 Disconnect the shift control cable.

7 Disconnect the steering shaft from the steering gear. Make sure to mark the parts so they can be installed in the same positions.

8 Disconnect both power steering hoses and seal their ends.

9 Support the engine securely from above with a fixture that mounts between the fenders. These can be rented at most rental yards if you don't own one.

10 Remove the upper transaxle mounting bolt (see illustration).

11 Loosen the front wheel lug nuts and the driveaxle/hub nuts. Raise the vehicle and support it securely on jackstands. Remove the driveaxles (see Chapter 8). After the driveaxles have been removed, temporarily reattach the steering knuckles to the suspension.

12 Remove the inspection plate, then remove the torque converter-to-driveplate fasteners. This will involve rotating the engine for access to all of the bolts. Have an assistant do this with a ratchet and socket on the end of the crankshaft. This will also hold the engine from rotating as the bolts are loosened. Mark the position of the torque converter on the driveplate with a dab of paint.

13 Remove the transaxle mounting bracket and the front and rear lower roll stopper mounts (see illustration).

14 Remove the front section of the exhaust system.

5.10 The upper transaxle mount carries much of the weight of the engine and transaxle - the assembly must be securely supported before it can be removed, then remove the mounting bolt

5.13 Remove both the front and rear roll stopper transaxle mounts after you've securely supported the engine/transaxle assembly from above

15 Make sure that the engine is solidly supported by the fixture. Detach the control arms from the steering knuckles and the stabilizer bar links from the control arms. Support the subframe with two floor jacks (one on each side). Remove the subframe mounting bolts and lower the subframe, steering gear and control arms with the help of an assistant (see illustration), then remove it out from under the vehicle.

16 Put a transmission jack (or a floor jack with an appropriate saddle) under the transaxle. Safety chains will help steady the transaxle on the jack.

17 Remove the remaining transaxle-to-engine bolts. Check to make certain that all connections between the transaxle and the vehicle are disconnected.

18 Move the transaxle to the rear to disengage it from the engine block dowel pins and make sure the torque converter is detached from the driveplate. Lower the transaxle with the jack. Clamp a pair of locking pliers on the bellhousing case. The pliers will prevent the torque converter from falling out while you're removing the transaxle.

19 Pull the transaxle out from beneath the vehicle, remove it from the jack and set it where it can't roll over and become damaged.

INSTALLATION

20 Installation of the transaxle is a reversal of the removal procedure, but note the following points:

a) *As the torque converter is reinstalled, ensure that the drive tangs at the center of the torque converter hub engage with the recesses in the automatic transaxle fluid pump inner gear. This can be confirmed by turning the torque converter while pushing it towards the transaxle. If it isn't fully engaged, it will clunk into place.*
b) *When installing the transaxle, make sure the matchmarks you made on the torque converter and driveplate line up.*
c) *Install all of the driveplate-to-torque converter fasteners before tightening any of them.*
d) *Tighten the transaxle mounting bolts securely.*
e) *Tighten the subframe mounting bolts to the torque listed in this Chapters Specifications.*
f) *Tighten the driveaxle/hub nuts to the torque value listed in the Chapter 8 Specifications.*
g) *Tighten the wheel lug nuts to the torque listed in the Chapter 1 Specifications.*
h) *Fill the transaxle with the correct type and amount of automatic transmission fluid as described in Chapter 1.*
i) *On completion, adjust the shift cable (see Section 4) and Transmission Range sensor (see Chapter 6).*

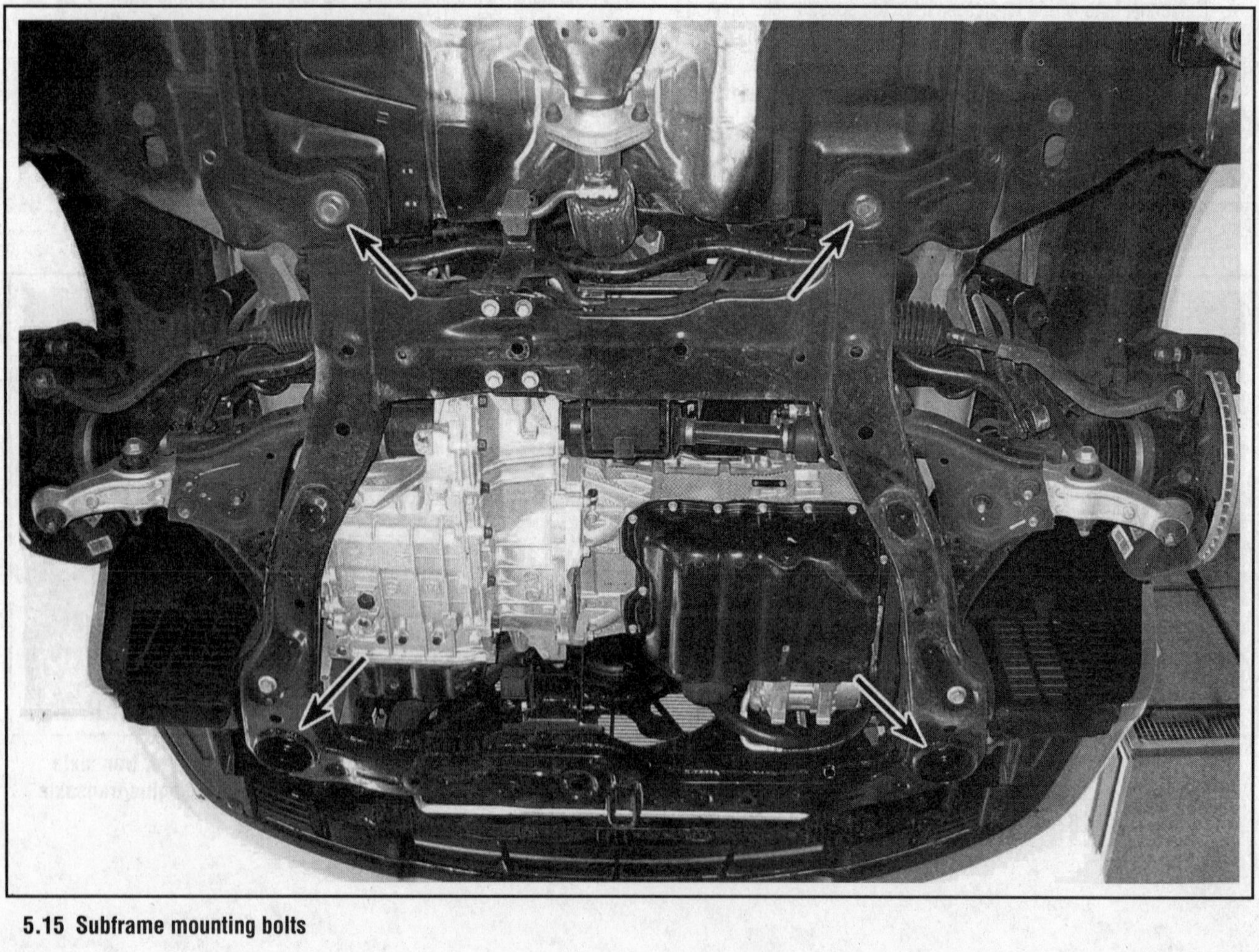

5.15 Subframe mounting bolts

6 Automatic transaxle overhaul - general information

In the event of a problem occurring, it will be necessary to establish whether the fault is electrical, mechanical or hydraulic in nature, before repair work can be contemplated. Diagnosis requires detailed knowledge of the transaxle's operation and construction, as well as access to specialized test equipment, and so is deemed to be beyond the scope of this manual. It is therefore essential that problems with the automatic transaxle be referred to a dealer service department or other qualified repair facility for assessment.

Note that a faulty transaxle should not be removed before the vehicle has been diagnosed by a knowledgeable technician equipped with the proper tools, as troubleshooting must be performed with the transaxle installed in the vehicle.

Specifications

General

Fluid type and capacity	See Chapter 1

Torque specifications

Torque specifications	Ft-lbs	Nm
Front roll stopper bracket-to-subframe bolts	43 to 58	60 to 80
Front roll stopper insulator bolt and nut	36 to 47	50 to 65
Rear roll stopper bracket-to-transaxle bolts	43 to 58	60 to 80
Subframe-to-body mounting bolts	74 to 88	100 to 120
Transaxle-to-mounting bracket bolts	43 to 58	60 to 80

8

CLUTCH AND DRIVELINE

Section

1 General information

The information in this Chapter deals with the components from the rear of the engine to the wheels, except for the transaxle, which is dealt with in the previous Chapter. For the purposes of this Chapter, these components are grouped into two categories - clutch and driveaxles. Separate Sections within this Chapter offer general descriptions and checking procedures for components in each of the two groups.

Since nearly all the procedures covered in this Chapter involve working under the vehicle, make sure it's securely supported on sturdy jackstands or on a hoist where the vehicle can be easily raised and lowered.

2 Clutch - description and check

1 All vehicles with a manual transaxle use a single dry plate, diaphragm spring type clutch. The clutch disc has a splined hub, which allows it to slide along the splines of the transaxle input shaft. The clutch and pressure plate are held in contact by spring pressure exerted by the diaphragm in the pressure plate.

2 The clutch release system is operated by hydraulic pressure. The hydraulic release system consists of the clutch pedal, a master cylinder and fluid reservoir, the hydraulic line, a release (or slave) cylinder that actuates the clutch release lever, the fork and the clutch release (or throwout) bearing.

3 When pressure is applied to the clutch pedal to release the clutch, hydraulic pressure is exerted against the outer end of the clutch release lever. As the lever pivots, the shaft fingers push against the release bearing. The bearing pushes against the fingers of the diaphragm spring of the pressure plate assembly, which in turn releases the clutch plate.

4 Terminology can be a problem when discussing the clutch components, because common names are in some cases different from those used by the manufacturer. For example, the driven plate is also called the clutch plate or disc, the clutch release bearing is sometimes called a throwout bearing, the release cylinder is sometimes called the operating or slave cylinder.

5 Other than to replace components with obvious damage, some preliminary checks should be performed to diagnose clutch problems.

a) The first check should be of the fluid level in the clutch master cylinder. If the fluid level is excessively low, add fluid as necessary and inspect the hydraulic system for leaks (fluid level will actually rise as the clutch wears).

b) To check clutch spin down time, run the engine at normal idle speed with the shifter in Neutral (clutch pedal up - engaged). Disengage the clutch (pedal down), wait several seconds and shift into Reverse. No grinding noise should be heard. A grinding noise would most likely indicate a problem in the pressure plate or the clutch disc.

c) To check for complete clutch release, run the engine (with the parking brake applied to prevent movement) and hold the clutch pedal approximately 1/2 inch from the floor. Shift between First gear and Reverse several times. If the shift is hard or grinds, component failure is indicated. Check the release cylinder pushrod travel. With the clutch pedal depressed completely, the release cylinder pushrod should extend substantially. If it doesn't, check the fluid level in the clutch master cylinder (see Chapter 1).

d) Visually inspect the pivot bushing at the top of the clutch pedal to make sure there is no binding or excessive play.

e) Crawl under the vehicle and make sure the clutch release lever is solidly mounted on the ball stud.

3 Clutch release system components - removal and installation

MASTER CYLINDER

1 Drain the clutch fluid through the bleeder screw. Be sure to catch the fluid in a container or with rags to prevent it from contacting painted surfaces.

2 Working under the instrument panel, disconnect the clutch pushrod from the pedal by removing the cotter pin, washer and the clevis pin.

3 Disconnect the clutch tubing from the clutch master cylinder.

4 Remove the master cylinder mounting bolts and lift it off.

➡ Note: If you need to remove the clutch fluid tube or hose, hold the hose nut with a wrench while you turn the flare nut on the tube using a flare nut wrench.

5 Installation is the reverse of removal. Bleed the system (see Section 4)

RELEASE CYLINDER

2001 through 2006 models

6 Raise the vehicle and support it securely on jackstands.

7 Disconnect the clutch fluid hose from the release cylinder and drain the system into a container.

8 Remove the cotter pin from the clevis pin at the end of the shaft. Slide out the clevis pin.

9 Remove the mounting bolts and remove the release cylinder.

10 Installation is the reverse of removal. Replace the copper washers on the hose banjo fitting with new ones.

11 Bleed the system (see Section 4).

2006.5 and later models

12 These vehicles use a concentric release cylinder that is a part of the release bearing assembly. You must first remove the transaxle in order to access and service the release cylinder.

4 Clutch hydraulic system - bleeding

1 The hydraulic system should be bled of all air whenever any part of the system has been removed, or if the fluid level has been allowed to fall so low that air has been drawn into the master cylinder. The procedure is very similar to bleeding a brake system.

2 Fill the master cylinder with new brake fluid conforming to DOT 3 specifications.

CAUTION:

Do not re-use any of the fluid coming from the system during the bleeding operation or use fluid that has been inside an open container for an extended period of time.

3 Raise the vehicle and place it securely on jackstands to gain access to the release cylinder, which is located on the left side of the clutch housing.

4 Remove the dust cap that fits over the bleeder valve and push a length of plastic hose over the valve. Place the other end of the hose into a clear container with about two inches of brake fluid in it. The hose end must be submerged in the fluid.

5 Have an assistant depress the clutch pedal and hold it. Open the bleeder valve on the release cylinder, allowing fluid to flow through the hose. Close the bleeder valve when fluid stops flowing from the hose. Once closed, have your assistant release the pedal.

6 Continue this process until all air is evacuated from the system, indicated by a full, solid stream of fluid being ejected from the bleeder valve each time, and no air bubbles in the hose or container. Keep a close watch on the fluid level inside the clutch master cylinder reservoir; if the level drops too low, air will be sucked back into the system and the process will have to be started all over again.

7 Install the dust cap and lower the vehicle. Check carefully for proper operation before placing the vehicle in normal service.

5 Clutch components - removal, inspection and installation

WARNING:

Dust produced by clutch wear and deposited on clutch components is hazardous to your health. DO NOT blow it out with compressed air and DO NOT inhale it. DO NOT use gasoline or petroleum-based solvents to remove clutch dust. Brake system cleaner should be used to flush the dust into a drain pan. After the clutch components are wiped clean with a rag, dispose of the contaminated rags and cleaner in a covered, marked container.

REMOVAL

Refer to illustration 5.7

1 Access to clutch components is normally accomplished by removing the transaxle from the vehicle. If, of course, the engine is being removed for major overhaul, then check the clutch for wear and replace worn components as necessary. However, the relatively low cost of the clutch components compared to the time and trouble spent gaining access to them warrants their replacement any time the engine or transaxle is removed, unless they are nearly new. The following procedures are based on the assumption that the engine will stay in place.

2 Refer to Chapter 7, Part A and remove the transaxle from the vehicle. Support the engine while the transaxle is out. Preferably, an engine hoist or support fixture should be used to support it from above. However, if a jack is used under the engine, make sure a piece of wood is between the jack and the oil pan to spread the load.

CAUTION:

The oil pump pickup is located very close to the bottom of the pan. If the pan is bent, engine oil starvation could occur.

3 The clutch fork can remain attached to the bellhousing.

2001 through 2006 models

4 Turn the release bearing to bring the opening of its snap-ring into view.

5 Put snap-ring pliers under the wave washer and engage the snap-ring.

6 Push down on the release bearing and open the snap-ring. Remove the release bearing.

All models

7 Inspect the flywheel and clutch for indexing marks (see illustration). If they can't be found, scribe marks yourself so the pressure plate and flywheel will be in the same alignment during installation (if you're not replacing them).

8 Insert a clutch alignment tool through the disc and into the pilot bushing to support the disc.

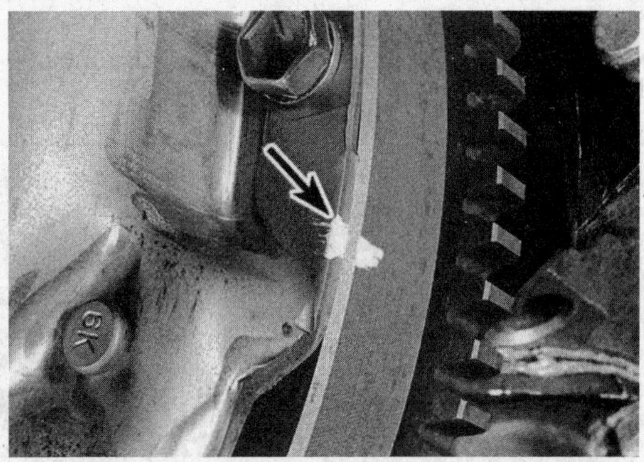

5.7 Be sure to mark the pressure plate and flywheel in order to ensure proper alignment during installation (this won't be necessary if a new pressure plate is to be installed)

5.11 **Check the flywheel for cracks, hot spots and other obvious defects - slight imperfections can be removed by a machine shop**

9 Turn each pressure plate bolt only 1/4 turn at a time to loosen the pressure plate-to-flywheel bolts. Work in a criss-cross pattern until all spring force is relieved. Hold the pressure plate securely and completely remove the bolts, followed by the pressure plate and clutch disc.

INSPECTION

➧ **Refer to illustrations 5.11, 5.13, 5.15a and 5.15b**

10 When a problem occurs in the clutch, it can usually be attributed to wear of the driven plate assembly (clutch disc). However, all components should be checked at this time.

11 Inspect the flywheel for cracks, heat checking, grooves and other obvious defects (see illustration). If the imperfections are small, a machine shop can machine the surface flat and smooth. This is highly recommended regardless of the surface appearance. Refer to Chapter 2 for the flywheel removal and installation procedures.

12 Inspect the pilot bushing (see Section 7).

13 Inspect the lining of the clutch disc (see illustration). There should be at least 1/16 inch of lining above the rivet heads. Check for loose rivets, cracks, distortion, broken springs and other obvious damage. As mentioned above, the clutch disc is routinely replaced, so if in doubt about the condition, replace it with a new one.

➡ **Note: Replace the pressure plate at the same time if you decide to replace the disc.**

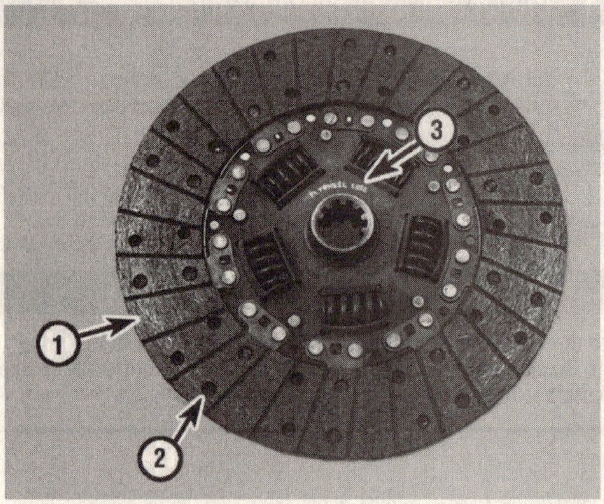

5.13 The clutch plate

1 ***Lining*** *- This will wear down in use*
2 ***Rivets*** *- These secure the lining and will damage the flywheel if allowed to contact the surfaces*
3 ***Markings*** *- "Flywheel side" or something similar*

14 The release bearing should also be replaced along with the clutch disc (see Section 6).

15 Check the machined surfaces and the spring fingers of the pressure plate (see illustrations). If the surface is grooved or otherwise damaged, replace it. Also check for obvious damage, distortion, cracking, etc. Light glazing can be removed with sandpaper or emery cloth. If a new pressure plate is required, new and rebuilt units are available.

➡ **Note: Replace the disc at the same time if you decide to replace the pressure plate.**

INSTALLATION

➧ **Refer to illustration 5.18**

16 Clean the flywheel and pressure plate machined surfaces with brake system cleaner. It's important that no oil or grease is on these surfaces or the lining of the clutch disc. Handle the parts only with clean hands.

17 Position the disc onto the flywheel with the side marked "flywheel" against the flywheel. On some clutches there is a "TB" mark that

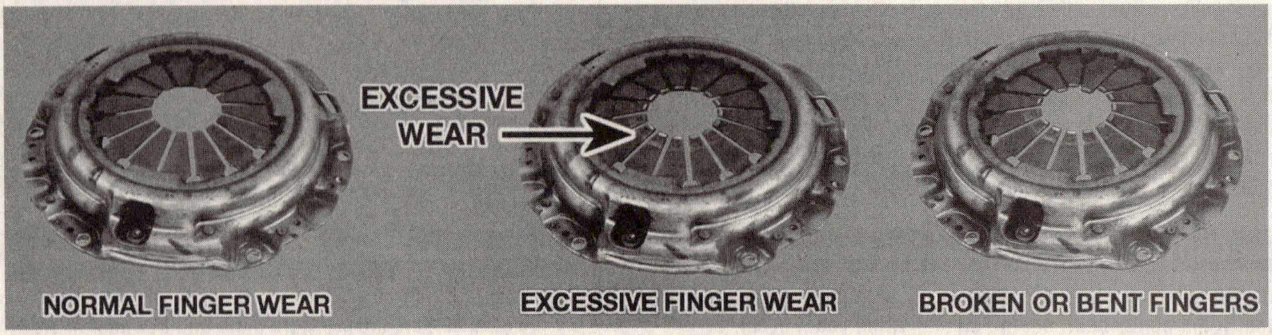

5.15a Replace the pressure plate if excessive wear is noted

5.15b Examine the pressure plate for scoring marks, cracks and evidence of overheating

faces the transaxle. If there are no marks, install the clutch disc with the springs facing the transaxle. They normally interfere with the flywheel bolts.

18 Secure the disc with the alignment tool (see illustration). Make sure the tool engages the pilot bushing.

19 Put the pressure plate into place, aligning the marks you previously made if you're not replacing it. Install the bolts and tighten them finger tight.

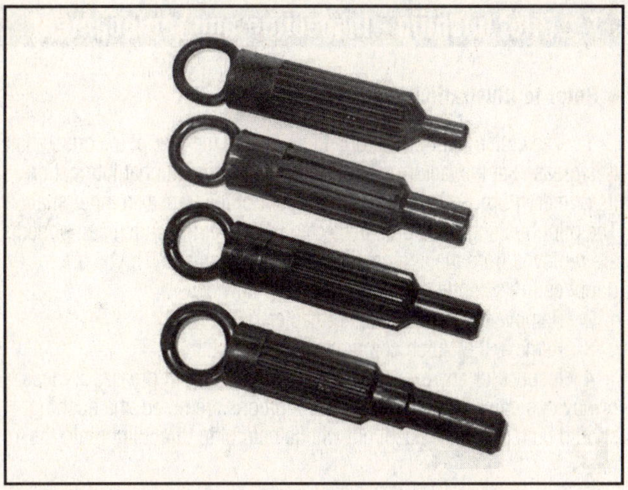

5.18 Center the clutch disc using an alignment tool

20 Tighten the bolts a little at a time, working in a criss-cross pattern to prevent distorting the cover. After all of the bolts are snug, tighten them to the torque listed in this Chapter's Specifications. Remove the alignment tool.

21 Refer to Section 6 for information on the proper installation of the release bearing.

22 The remainder of installation is the reverse of removal.

6 Clutch release bearing - removal, inspection and installation

WARNING:

Dust produced by clutch wear and deposited on clutch components is hazardous to your health. DO NOT blow it out with compressed air and DO NOT inhale it. DO NOT use gasoline or petroleum-based solvents to remove clutch dust. Brake system cleaner should be used to flush the dust into a drain pan. After the clutch components are wiped clean with a rag, dispose of the contaminated rags and cleaner in a covered, marked container.

REMOVAL

1 Refer to Chapter 7A and remove the transaxle from the vehicle.

2 Refer to Section 5 for information on disengaging the release bearing from the pressure plate on 2001 through 2005 models.

INSPECTION

3 Hold the center of the bearing and apply force while rotating the outer portion. If the bearing doesn't operate smoothly or if it's noisy, replace it with a new one. Wipe the bearing with a clean rag and inspect if for damage, wear and cracks. Don't immerse it in solvent - it's sealed for life and to do so would ruin it. Also check the release fork for wear on the fingertips, cracks and other damage.

4 Check the snap-ring for proper retention.

INSTALLATION

5 Apply a small amount of high-temperature grease to the inside of the release bearing and to the area where the fork fingers contact it.

6 Install the bearing onto the input shaft of the transaxle, engaging it with the fork fingers. Apply a small amount of grease to the surface of the input shaft over which the bearing slides.

2001 through 2006 models

7 Raise the transaxle into position next to the engine.

8 Install the release lever on the fork shaft and connect it to the release cylinder with the clevis pin and cotter pin.

9 Refer to Chapter 7A and bolt the transaxle to the engine.

10 Push the release lever away from the release cylinder about 16 degrees. There should be a click from the snap-ring as the assembly snaps into place. If it doesn't snap into position, start over again.

➡ **Note: The release lever is only supposed to move a maximum of 3 degrees in normal operation. If it moves more, then the bearing is not engaged properly on the pressure plate. Try pushing the lever forward again.**

11 The rest of the installation is the reverse of removal.

2006.5 and later models

12 Assemble the release bearing and the transaxle to the engine in the conventional manner. Installation is the reverse of removal.

7 Pilot bushing - inspection and replacement

➧ Refer to illustrations 7.5 and 7.6

1 The clutch pilot bushing is pressed into the rear of the crankshaft. It is greased at the factory and does not require additional lubrication. Its primary purpose is to support the front of the transaxle input shaft. The pilot bushing should be inspected whenever the clutch components are removed from the engine. Due to its inaccessibility, if you are in doubt as to its condition, replace it with a new one.

2 Remove the transaxle (see Chapter 7 Part A).

3 Remove the clutch components (see Section 5).

4 Inspect for any excessive wear, scoring, lack of grease, dryness or obvious damage. If any of these conditions are noted, the bushing should be replaced. A flashlight will be helpful to direct light into the recess.

5 Removal can be accomplished with a slide hammer fitted with a puller attachment (see illustration), which are available at most auto parts stores or equipment rental yards.

6 To install the new bushing, lightly lubricate the outside surface with multi-purpose grease, and then drive it into the recess with a hammer and bearing/bushing driver (see illustration). If you don't have a bearing driver, carefully tap it into place with a hammer and a socket.

⁂ CAUTION:

Be careful not to let the bushing become cocked in the bore.

7 Install the clutch components, transaxle and all other components removed previously, tightening all fasteners properly.

7.5 A small slide-hammer puller is handy for removing the pilot bushing

7.6 The pilot bushing can be driven in with an appropriately sized socket

8 Clutch pedal position switch - check and replacement

CHECK

1 The clutch pedal position switch, which is part of the starter relay circuit, is mounted at the top of the clutch pedal. The switch closes the starter relay circuit only when the clutch pedal is depressed.

2 To test the switch, verify that the engine will not crank over when the clutch pedal is in the released position and that it does crank over when the pedal is depressed.

3 If the engine can be started without depressing the clutch pedal, replace the switch.

REPLACEMENT

4 Slide the driver's seat fully rearward and access the pivot at the top of the clutch pedal.

5 Disconnect the wiring harness from the switch.

6 Make a mental note of the switch's adjustment, then remove it.

7 Installation is the reverse of removal. Position the new switch in the same adjustment range as the original one.

8 Test the new switch (see Step 2).

9 Driveaxles - removal and installation

REMOVAL

Refer to illustrations 9.1, 9.6, 9.7 and 9.8

1 Remove the wheel cover or hubcap. Remove the cotter pin and break the driveaxle/hub nut loose (see illustration). Loosen the wheel lug nuts.

2 Raise the vehicle and support it securely on jackstands. Remove the wheel.

3 Drain the transaxle lubricant or place rags under the transaxle end of the driveaxle (see Chapter 1).

4 Disconnect the wheel speed sensor from its bracket. Disconnect the brake hose assembly from the bracket.

5 Disconnect the outer tie-rod end from the steering knuckle (see Chapter 10).

6 Remove the two bolts from the lower balljoint (see illustration).

7 Swing the knuckle/hub assembly out (away from the vehicle) until the end of the driveaxle is free of the hub (see illustration).

Note: If the driveaxle splines stick in the hub, tap on the end of the driveaxle with a plastic hammer.

Support the outer end of the driveaxle with a piece of wire to avoid unnecessary strain on the inner CV joint.

8 Using a large screwdriver or prybar positioned between the CV joint housing and the transaxle (left driveaxle) or center bearing support bracket (right driveaxle), carefully pry the inner end of the driveaxle from the transaxle (see illustration) or center bearing support bracket. Support the CV joints and carefully remove the driveaxle from the vehicle.

Intermediate shaft removal

Refer to illustration 9.10

9 Remove the right driveaxle assembly (see Steps 1 through 8).

9.1 Loosen the driveaxle/hub nut with a long breaker bar

9.6 The lower balljoints can be disconnected from the knuckles by removing two bolts - there's no need to separate the pivot joint

9.7 Pull the knuckle outward until the driveaxle slips out of its bearing - don't allow it to fall as you do so

9.8 To separate the inner end of the driveaxle from the transaxle, pry on the CV joint housing like this with a large screwdriver or prybar - you may need to give the prybar a sharp rap with a brass hammer

9.10 Intermediate shaft bearing bracket bolts

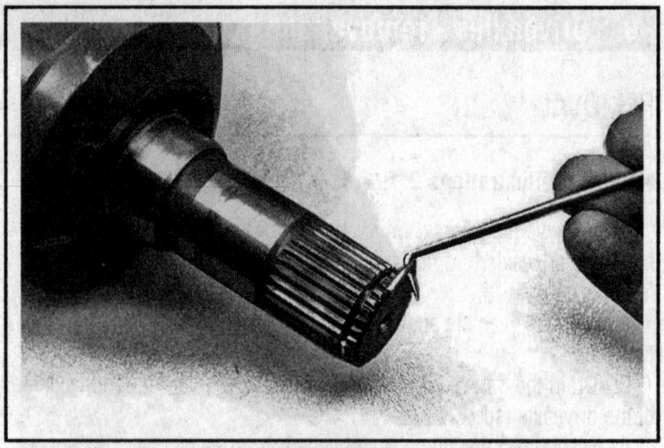

9.15a Pry the old spring clip from the inner end of the driveaxle with a small screwdriver or awl

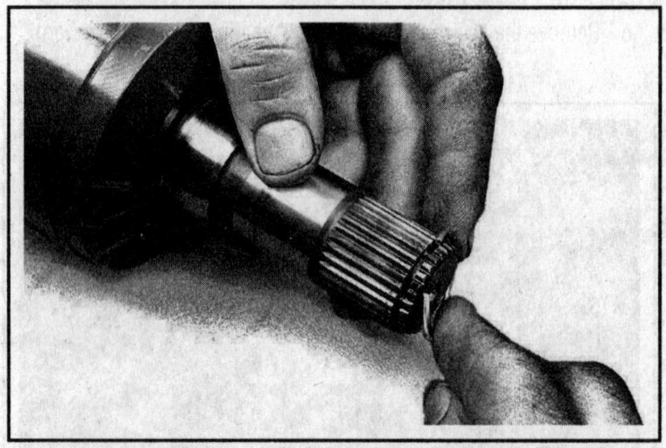

9.15b To install the new spring clip, start one end in the groove and work the clip over the shaft end, into the groove

10 Remove the center bearing support bracket bolts (see illustration).

11 Pull the intermediate shaft assembly from the transaxle.

12 Inspect the center bearing for scoring and discoloration, then rotate the intermediate shaft and verify that the bearing operates smoothly.

13 If the center bearing is scored, discolored or turns roughly, have it replaced by an automotive machine shop.

INSTALLATION

Refer to illustrations 9.15a and 9.15b

14 Install the intermediate shaft if it was removed.

15 Pry the old spring clip from the inner end of the driveaxle and install a new one (see illustrations). Lubricate the differential or intermediate shaft seal with multi-purpose grease and raise the driveaxle into position while supporting the CV joints.

16 Insert the splined end of the inner CV joint or the intermediate shaft into the differential side gear and make sure the spring clip locks in its groove.

Note: When installing the driveaxle, make sure the gap in the spring clip is facing down (this will allow it to compress and engage with its groove more easily).

17 Apply a light coat of multi-purpose grease to the outer CV joint splines, pull out on the strut/steering knuckle assembly and install the stub axle into the hub.

18 Reconnect the balljoint to the lower control arm and tighten the nuts (see the torque specifications in Chapter 10).

19 Install the driveaxle/hub nut with the convex side of the washer facing out. Tighten the hub nut securely, but don't try to tighten it to the actual torque specification until you've lowered the vehicle to the ground.

20 Grasp the inner CV joint housing (not the driveaxle) and pull out to make sure the driveaxle has seated securely in the transaxle.

21 Install the wheel and lug nuts, then lower the vehicle.

22 Tighten the lug nuts to the torque listed in the Chapter 1 Specifications. Tighten the driveaxle/hub nut to the torque listed in this Chapter's Specifications. Install a new cotter pin.

23 Refill the transaxle with the recommended type and amount of lubricant (see Chapter 1).

10 Driveaxle boot - replacement

DISASSEMBLY

➧ **Refer to illustrations 10.3, 10.4a, 10.4b, 10.6 and 10.7**

➡ **Note: If the CV joint boots must be replaced, explore all options before beginning the job. Complete rebuilt driveaxles are available on an exchange basis, which eliminates much time and work. Whichever route you choose to take, check on the cost and availability of parts before disassembling the vehicle.**

➡ **Note: Some auto parts stores carry split type replacement boots, which can be installed without removing the driveaxle from the vehicle. This is a convenient alternative; however, the driveaxle should be removed and the CV joint disassembled and cleaned to ensure the joint is free from contaminants such as moisture and dirt which will accelerate CV joint wear. Do NOT disassemble the outboard CV joints. All outer joints are Birfield joints. Inner joints may be tripod, U-type tripod or double offset joints.**

➡ **Note: The procedure shown here is of a tripod-type inner joint. The basic cleaning and checking procedure is the same for all joints.**

1 Remove the driveaxle (see Section 9).

2 Mount the driveaxle in a vise with wood lined jaws (to prevent damage to the axleshaft). Check the CV joint for excessive play in the radial direction, which indicates worn parts. Check for smooth operation throughout the full range of motion for each CV joint. If a boot is torn, disassemble the joint, clean the components and inspect for damage due to loss of lubrication and possible contamination by foreign matter.

3 Using a small screwdriver, pry the retaining tabs of the clamps up to loosen them and slide them off (see illustration).

4 Using a screwdriver, carefully pry up on the edge of the outer boot and push it away from the CV joint. Old and worn boots can be cut off. Pull the inner CV joint boot back from the housing and slide the housing off the joint; on double-offset type joints, a wire ring retainer must be removed first (see illustrations).

5 Mark the tripod and axleshaft to ensure that they are reassembled properly.

6 Remove the tripod joint snap-ring with a pair of snap-ring pliers (see illustration).

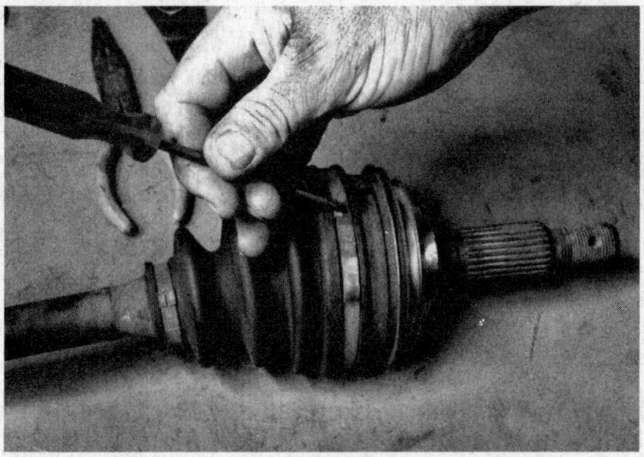

10.3 Lift the tabs on the boot clamps with a small screwdriver, then open the clamps

10.4a On tripod-type joints, remove the boot from the inner CV joint and slide the joint housing from the tripod

10.4b On double-offset type joints, remove the wire retainer, then pull the housing off

10.6 Remove the snap-ring with a pair of snap-ring pliers

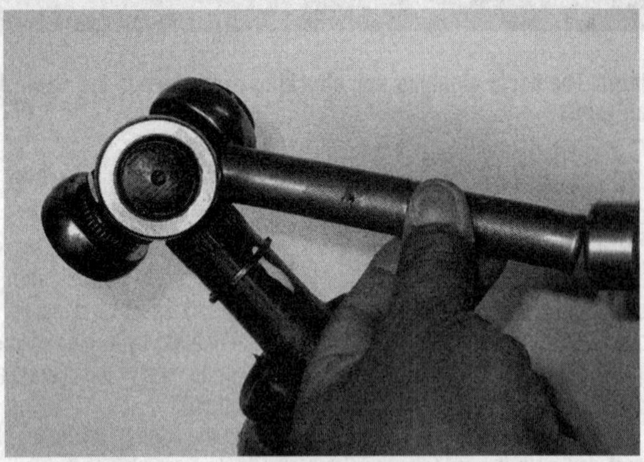

10.7 Drive the tripod joint from the driveaxle with a brass punch and hammer; be careful not to damage the bearing surfaces or the splines on the shaft

7 Use a hammer and a brass punch to drive the tripod joint from the driveaxle (see illustration).

8 If you haven't already cut them off, remove both boots.

Note: Do NOT disassemble the outboard CV joint.

10.10b Install the tripod with the recessed portion of the splines facing the axleshaft

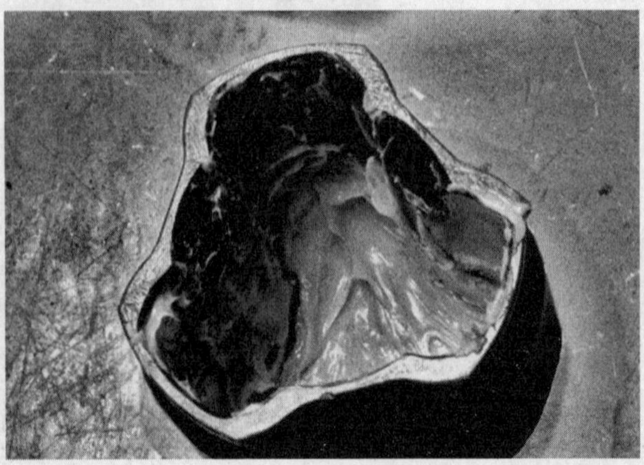

10.10c Place grease at the bottom of the CV joint housing

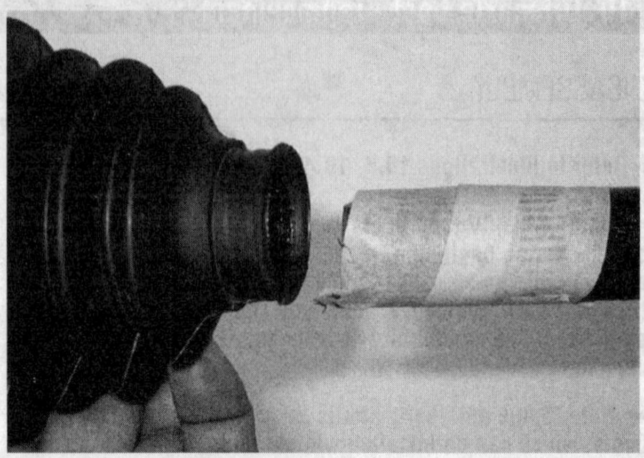

10.10a Wrap the splined area of the axleshaft with tape to prevent damage to the boots when installing them

CHECK

9 Thoroughly clean all components with solvent - including the outer CV joint assembly - until the old CV joint grease is completely removed. Inspect the bearing surfaces of the inner tripods and housings for cracks, pitting, scoring and other signs of wear. It's not possible to inspect the bearing surfaces of the inner and outer races of the outer CV joint, but you can at least check the surfaces of the ball bearings themselves. If they're in good shape, so are the races; if they're not, neither are the races. If the inner CV joint is worn, you can buy a new inner CV joint and install it on the old axleshaft; if the outer CV joint is worn, you'll have to purchase a new outer CV joint and axleshaft (they're sold pre-assembled).

REASSEMBLY

Refer to illustrations 10.10a, 10.10b, 10.10c, 10.10d, 10.12a, 10.12b, 10.12c and 10.12d

10 Wrap the splines on the inner end of the axleshaft with electrical

10.10d Install the boot clamps onto the axleshaft, then insert the tripod (or double-offset joint) into the housing, followed by the rest of the grease

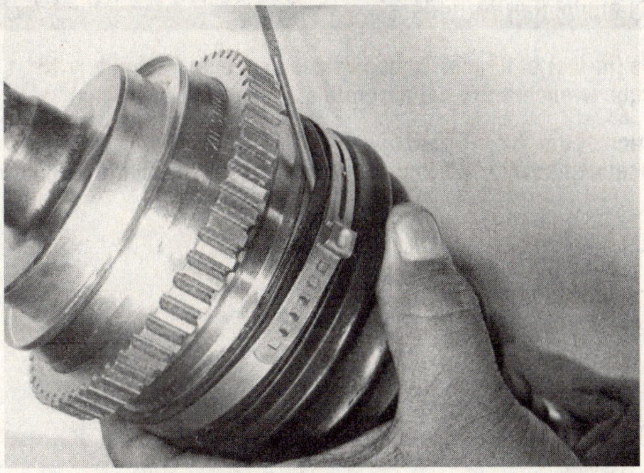

10.12a Equalize the pressure inside the boot by inserting a small, dull screwdriver between the boot and the outer race

10.12b To install the new clamps, bend the tang down . . .

or duct tape to protect the boots from the sharp edges of the splines. Slide the clamps and boot(s) onto the axleshaft, then place the tripod or double-offset on the shaft. Apply grease to the tripod assembly and inside the housing. Insert the tripod into the housing and pack the remainder of the grease around the tripod (see illustrations). If you're working on a double-offset joint, install the wire retainer.

11 Slide the boot into place, making sure both ends seat in their grooves. Adjust the length of the driveaxle, positioning it midway through its travel.

12 Equalize the pressure in the boot, then tighten and secure the boot clamps (see illustrations).

13 Install the driveaxle assembly (see Section 9).

10.12c . . . then tap the tabs over to hold it in place

10.12d If your replacement boot came with crimp-type clamps, a special tool such as this one (available at most auto parts stores) will be required to tighten them properly

Torque specifications	Ft-lbs (unless otherwise indicated)	Nm

➡ Note: One foot-pound (ft-lb) of torque is equivalent to 12 inch-pounds (in-lbs) of torque. Torque values below approximately 15 foot-pounds are expressed in inch-pounds, because most foot-pound torque wrenches are not accurate at these smaller values.

➡ Note: 2006 and 2006.5 models will both have a "6" in the tenth position of the VIN. To distinguish a 2006 model from a 2006.5 model, refer to the 8th position of the VIN (the engine code): A 2006 model will have a "6" (four-cylinder) or "8" (V6), while a 2006.5 will have a "3" (four-cylinder) or "4" (V6).

Clutch cover-to-flywheel bolts		
2006 and earlier models (except 2006.5 models)		
Conventional flywheel	132 to 192 in-lbs	15 to 22
Dual-mass flywheel	15 to 20	20 to 27
2006.5 and later models	108 to 132 in-lbs	12 to 15
Driveaxle/hub nut	148 to 206	200 to 280

9

BRAKES

Section

1 General information

The vehicles covered by this manual are equipped with hydraulically operated front and rear brake systems. The front brakes are disc type and the rear brakes are disc or drum type. Both the front and rear brakes are self adjusting. The disc brakes automatically compensate for pad wear, while the drum brakes incorporate an adjustment mechanism that is activated as the parking brake is applied.

HYDRAULIC SYSTEM

The hydraulic system consists of two separate circuits. The master cylinder has separate reservoirs for the two circuits, and, in the event of a leak or failure in one hydraulic circuit, the other circuit will remain operative.

POWER BRAKE BOOSTER

The power brake booster utilizes engine manifold vacuum and atmospheric pressure to provide assistance to the hydraulically operated brakes. The booster is mounted on the firewall in the engine compartment.

PARKING BRAKE

The parking brake operates the rear brakes only, through cable actuation. It's activated by a lever mounted in the center console.

SERVICE

After completing any operation involving disassembly of any part of the brake system, always test-drive the vehicle to check for proper braking performance before resuming normal driving. When testing the brakes, perform the tests on a clean, dry, flat surface. Conditions other than these can lead to inaccurate test results.

Test the brakes at various speeds with both light and heavy pedal force. The vehicle should stop evenly without pulling to one side or the other. Avoid locking the brakes, because this slides the tires and diminishes braking efficiency and control of the vehicle.

Tires, vehicle load and wheel alignment are factors that also affect braking performance.

PRECAUTIONS

There are some general cautions and warnings involving the brake system on this vehicle:

a) *Use only brake fluid conforming to DOT 3 or DOT 4 specifications.*
b) *The brake pads and linings contain fibers that are hazardous to your health if inhaled. Whenever you work on brake system components, clean all parts with brake system cleaner. Do not allow the fine dust to become airborne. Also, wear an approved filtering mask.*
c) *Safety should be paramount whenever any servicing of the brake components is performed. Do not use parts or fasteners that are not in perfect condition, and be sure that all clearances and torque specifications are adhered to. If you are at all unsure about a certain procedure, seek professional advice. Upon completion of any brake system work, test the brakes carefully in a controlled area before putting the vehicle into normal service. If a problem is suspected in the brake system, don't drive the vehicle until it's fixed.*
d) *Clean up any spilled brake fluid immediately and wash the area with large amounts of water. This is especially true for any finished, painted or plastic surfaces.*

2 Anti-lock Brake System (ABS) - general information

1 The Anti-lock Brake System (ABS) is designed to maintain vehicle steerability, directional stability and optimum deceleration under severe braking conditions and on most road surfaces. It does so by monitoring the rotational speed of each wheel and controlling the brake line pressure to each wheel during braking. This prevents the wheel from locking up. The ABS system is primarily designed to prevent wheel lockup during heavy braking, but the information provided by the wheel speed sensors of the ABS system is shared with several optional systems that can use the data to control vehicle handling.

2.2 Typical ABS actuator location - near the master cylinder

COMPONENTS

Hydraulic electronic control unit

➧ Refer to illustration 2.2

2 The actuator assembly is mounted in the engine compartment. It consists of an electric hydraulic pump and solenoid valves (see illustration).

a) *The electric pump provides hydraulic pressure to charge the reservoirs in the actuator, which supplies pressure to the braking system. The pump and reservoirs are housed in the actuator assembly.*
b) *The solenoid valves modulate brake line pressure during ABS operation.*

2.5 Front wheel speed sensor mounting bolt

2.6 The rear wheel speed sensor is bolted to the rear suspension hub carrier

3 The ABS computer is mounted in the control unit and is the brain for the ABS system. The function of the computer is to accept and process information received from the wheel speed sensors to control the hydraulic line pressure, avoiding wheel lock up. The computer also constantly monitors the system, even under normal driving conditions, to find faults within the system.

Speed sensors

➧ Refer to illustrations 2.5 and 2.6

4 These sensors are located at each wheel and generate small electrical pulsations when the toothed sensor rings are turning, sending a signal to the electronic controller indicating wheel rotational speed.

5 The front speed sensors are mounted to the front steering knuckles in close relationship to the toothed sensor rings, which are integral with the front driveaxle outer CV joints (see illustration).

6 The rear wheel sensors are bolted to the rear suspension hub carriers (see illustration). The sensor rings are integrated with the rear hub assemblies.

DIAGNOSIS AND REPAIR

7 If a dashboard warning light comes on and stays on while the vehicle is in operation, the ABS system requires attention. Although special electronic ABS diagnostic testing tools are necessary to properly diagnose the system, you can perform a few preliminary checks before taking the vehicle to a dealer service department.

a) Check the brake fluid level in the reservoir.
b) Verify that the computer electrical connectors are securely connected.
c) Check the electrical connectors at the hydraulic control unit.
d) Check the fuses.
e) Follow the wiring harness to each wheel and verify that all connections are secure and that the wiring is undamaged.

8 If the above preliminary checks do not rectify the problem, the vehicle should be diagnosed by a dealer service department or other qualified repair shop. Due to the complexity of this system, all actual repair work must be done by a qualified automotive technician.

⁂ WARNING:

Do NOT try to repair an ABS wiring harness. The ABS system is sensitive to even the smallest changes in resistance. Repairing the harness could alter resistance values and cause the system to malfunction. If the ABS wiring harness is damaged in any way, it must be replaced.

⁂ CAUTION:

Make sure the ignition is turned off before unplugging or reattaching any electrical connections.

WHEEL SPEED SENSOR - REMOVAL AND INSTALLATION

9 Loosen the wheel lug nuts, raise the vehicle and support it securely on jackstands. Remove the wheel

10 Make sure the ignition key is turned to the Off position.

11 Trace the wiring back from the sensor, detaching all brackets and clips while noting its correct routing, then disconnect the electrical connector.

12 Remove the mounting bolt and carefully pull the sensor out from the knuckle or trailing arm.

13 Installation is the reverse of the removal procedure. Tighten the mounting fastener securely.

14 Install the wheel and lug nuts, tightening them securely. Lower the vehicle and tighten the lug nuts to the torque listed in the Chapter 1 Specifications.

3 Disc brake pads - replacement

Refer to illustrations 3.5, 3.6a through 3.6n and 3.7a through 3.7m

WARNING:

Disc brake pads must be replaced on both front or rear wheels at the same time - never replace the pads on only one wheel. Also, the dust created by the brake system is harmful to your health. Never blow it out with compressed air and don't inhale any of it. An approved filtering mask should be worn when working on the brakes. Do not, under any circumstances, use petroleum-based solvents to clean brake parts. Use brake system cleaner only!

1 Remove the cap from the brake fluid reservoir.

2 Loosen the wheel lug nuts, raise the front or rear of the vehicle and support it securely on jackstands. Block the wheels at the opposite end.

3 Remove the wheels. Work on one brake assembly at a time, using the assembled brake for reference if necessary.

4 Inspect the brake disc carefully as outlined in Section 5. If machining is necessary, follow the information in that Section to remove the disc, at which time the pads can be removed as well.

5 Push the piston back into its bore to provide room for the new brake pads. A C-clamp can be used to accomplish this (see illustration). As the piston is depressed to the bottom of the caliper bore, the fluid in the master cylinder will rise. Make sure that it doesn't overflow. If necessary, siphon off some of the fluid.

6 If you're replacing the front brake pads, follow the accompanying photos, beginning with illustration 3.6a. Be sure to stay in order and read the caption under each illustration.

7 If you're replacing the rear brake pads, wash the brake assembly (see illustration 3.6a), then follow the accompanying photos, beginning with illustration 3.7a. Be sure to stay in order and read the caption

3.5 Before removing the caliper, slowly depress the piston in the caliper bore by using a large C-clamp between the outer brake pad and the back of the caliper

3.6a Always wash the brakes with brake cleaner before disassembling anything; don't use compressed air

3.6b For brake pad replacement, remove the caliper bolts but do not let the caliper hang by the brake hose

3.6c Lift the caliper free . . .

under each illustration.

8 When reinstalling the caliper, be sure to tighten the mounting bolts to the torque listed in this Chapter's Specifications. After the job has been completed, firmly depress the brake pedal a few times to bring the pads into contact with the disc. Check the level of the brake fluid, adding some if necessary. Check the operation of the brakes carefully before placing the vehicle into normal service.

3.6d . . . and hang it with a piece of wire

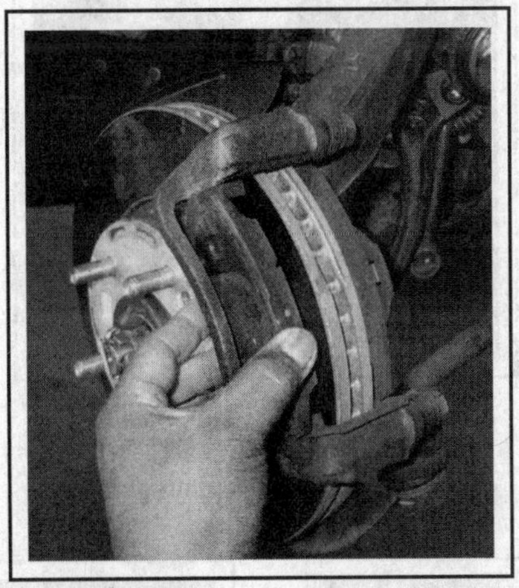

3.6e Remove the outer pad . . .

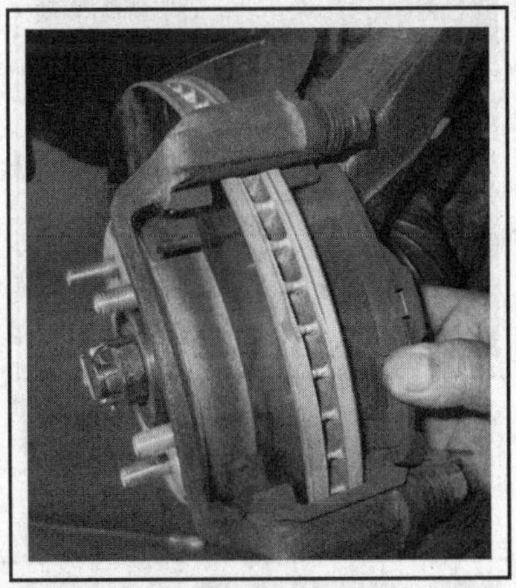

3.6f . . . and the inner pad

3.6g Remove the upper and lower pad support plates; make sure they are a tight fit and aren't worn. If necessary, replace them

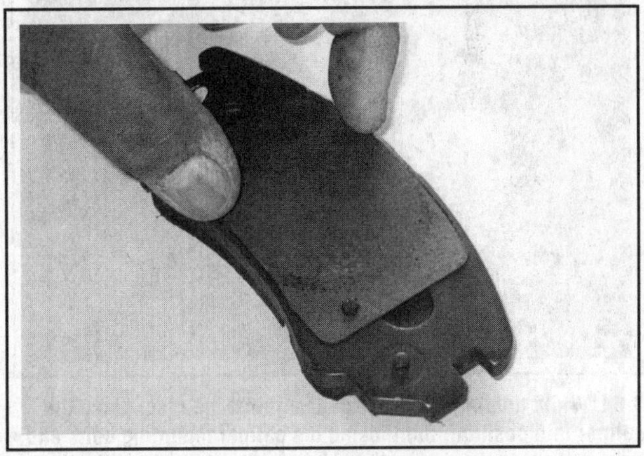

3.6h Transfer or replace any pad attachments

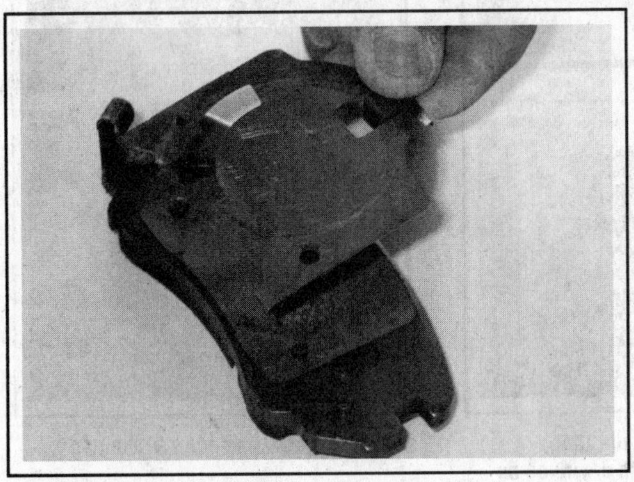

3.6i Also transfer the shims

3.6j Pull out the upper and lower sliding pins and clean them. Apply a coat of high-temperature grease to the pins and reinstall them. Be careful not to damage the pin boots; replace any boots that are worn or damaged

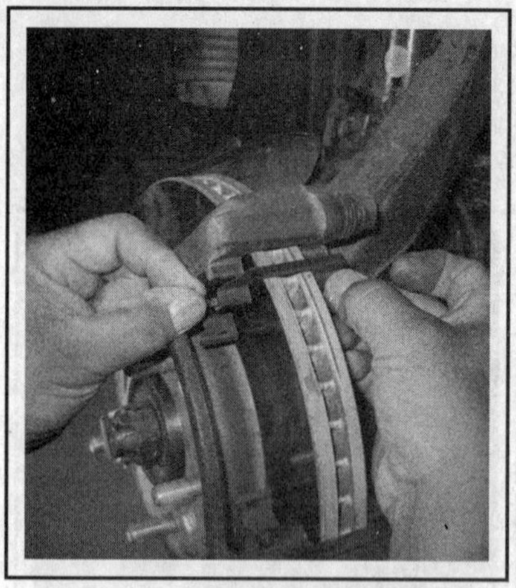

3.6k Install the pad support plates

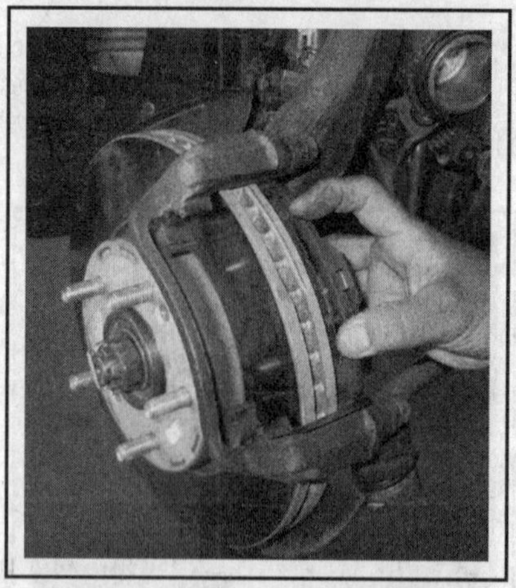

3.6l Install the inner pad, making sure that the ends are seated correctly on the pad support plates

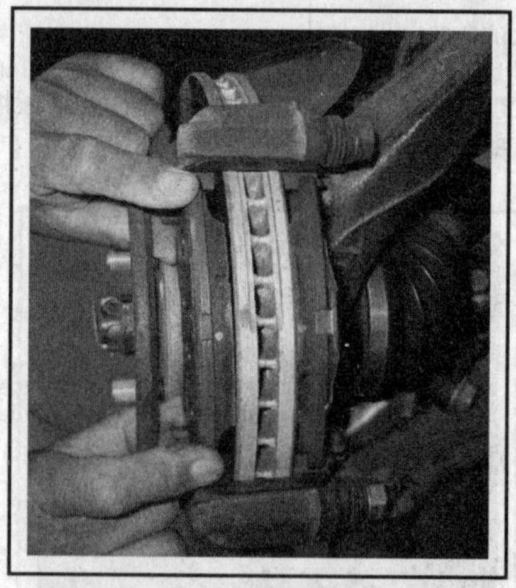

3.6m Install the outer pad, also making sure that the ends are seated correctly on the pad support plates

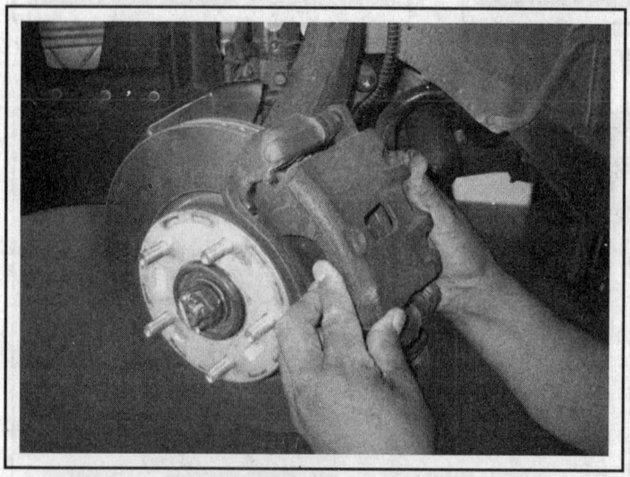

3.6n While holding the brake pads against the disc, place the caliper into position, then install the caliper mounting bolts and tighten them to the torque listed in this Chapter's Specifications

3.7a Before removing the caliper, slowly depress the piston in the caliper bore by using a large C-clamp between the outer brake pad and the back of the caliper

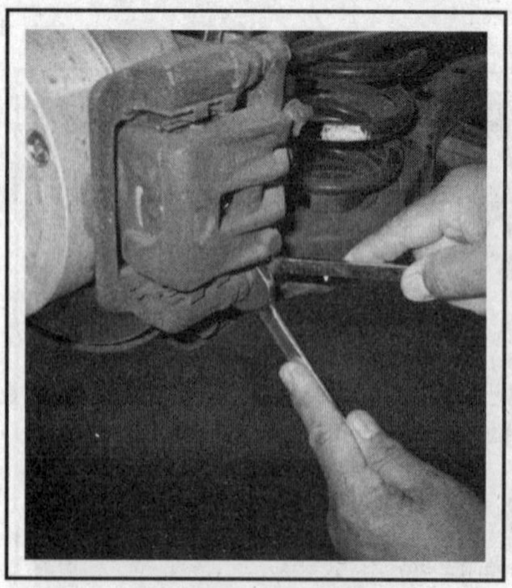

3.7b Remove the lower caliper mounting bolt and loosen the upper one

3.7c Pivot the caliper up, then support the caliper with a wire so as not to stress the brake hose

3.7d Remove the outer brake pad . . .

3.7e . . . and the inner brake pad

3.7f Remove the lower plate and thoroughly clean it and the mounting areas

3.7g Remove the upper pad support plate; make sure it's a tight fit and isn't worn. If necessary, replace them both

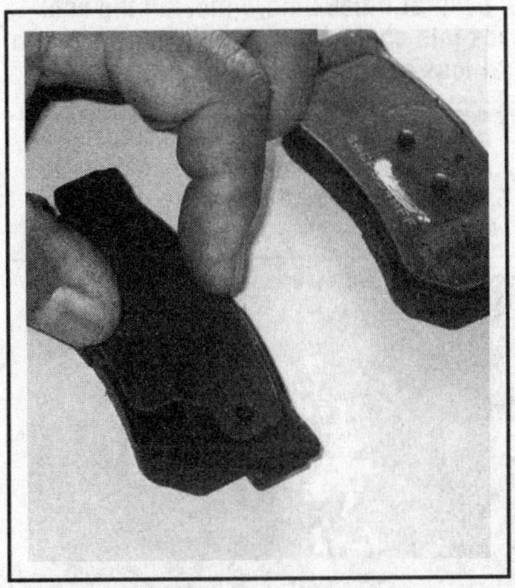

3.7h Transfer or replace any attachments

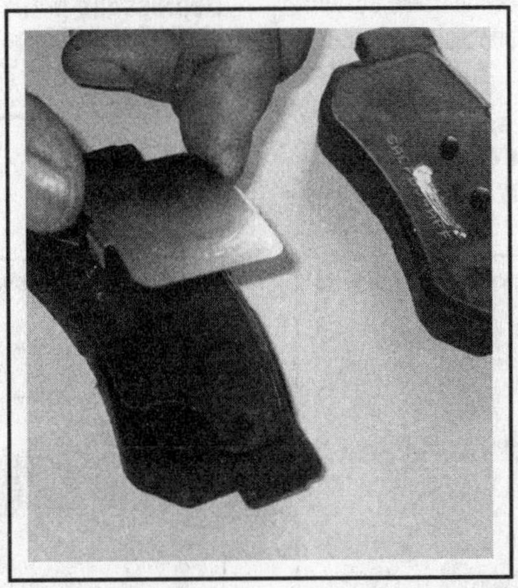

3.7i Install the pad shims onto the new pads

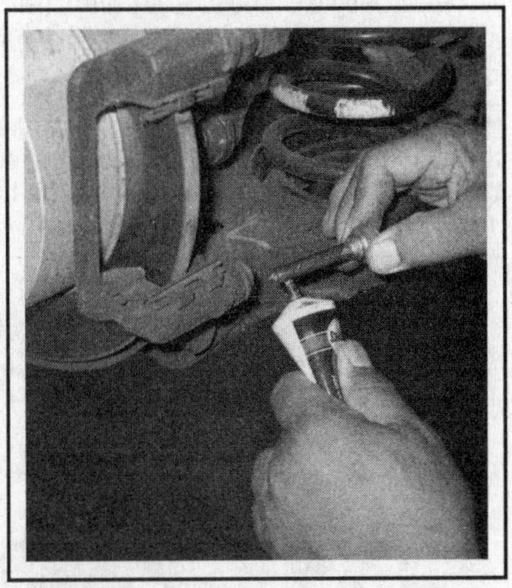

3.7j Pull out the sliding pins, clean them, then apply a coat of high-temperature grease to the pins and install them. Replace any boots that are worn or damaged

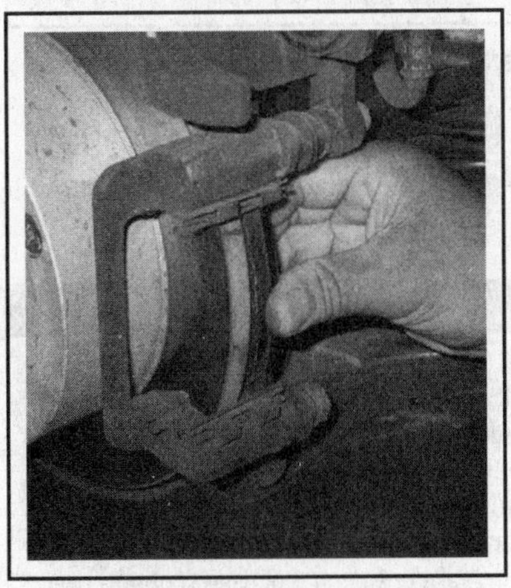

3.7k Install the new inner pad

3.7l Install the new lower pad

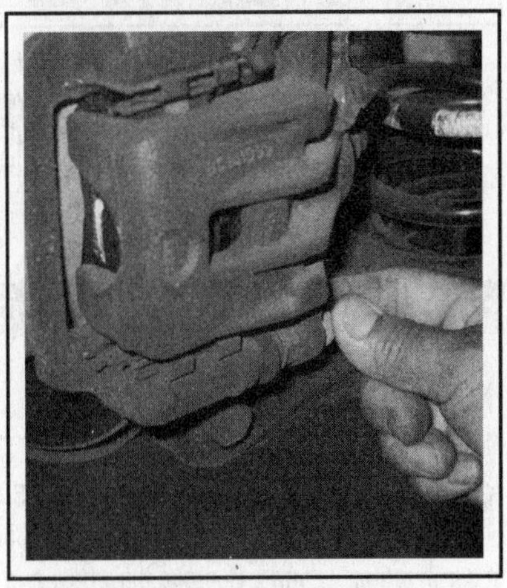

3.7m Swing the caliper back into place, install the bolt and tighten both to the torque listed in this Chapter's Specifications

4 Disc brake caliper - removal and installation

⁂ WARNING:

Dust created by the brake system is harmful to your health. Never blow it out with compressed air and don't inhale any of it. An approved filtering mask should be worn when working on the brakes. Do not, under any circumstances, use petroleum-based solvents to clean brake parts. Use brake system cleaner only!

➡ Note: Always replace the calipers in pairs - never replace just one of them.

REMOVAL

➧ Refer to illustrations 4.2 and 4.3

1 Loosen the wheel lug nuts, raise the vehicle and support it securely on jackstands. Remove the wheels

2 Remove the brake hose banjo bolt and disconnect the hose from the caliper. Plug the hose to keep contaminants out of the brake system and to prevent losing any more brake fluid than is necessary (see illustration).

➡ Note: If you're just removing the caliper for access to other components, don't detach the hose, but be sure to support the caliper with a piece of wire - don't let it hang by the hose.

3 Remove the caliper mounting bolts (see illustration).

4 Remove the caliper. If necessary, remove the caliper bracket from the steering knuckle or rear knuckle.

INSTALLATION

5 Install the caliper by reversing the removal procedure. Tighten the caliper mounting bolts (and bracket bolts, if removed) to the torque listed in this Chapter's Specifications. Install **new** sealing washers on both sides of the brake hose banjo fitting, then tighten the banjo bolt to the torque listed in this Chapter's Specifications.

6 Bleed the brake system (see Section 9).

7 Install the wheels and lug nuts. Lower the vehicle and tighten the lug nuts to the torque listed in the Chapter 1 Specifications.

⁂ WARNING:

Depress the brake pedal several times before moving the vehicle to bring the brake pads into contact with the discs. Failure to do so will cause an initial loss of braking.

Check the operation of the brakes carefully before driving the vehicle.

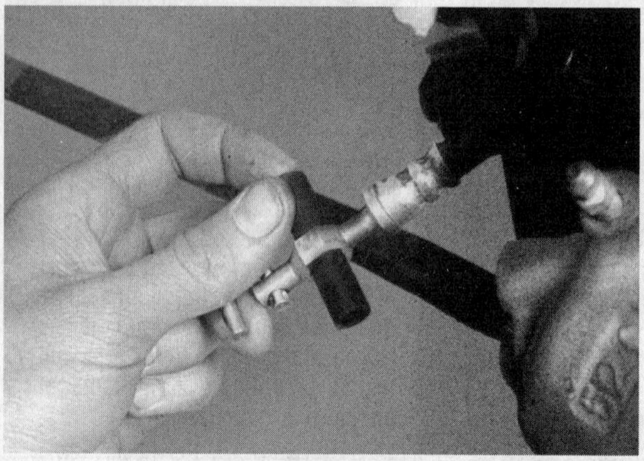

4.2 Using a piece of rubber hose of the appropriate size, plug the brake line banjo fitting to prevent brake fluid from leaking out and to prevent dirt and moisture from contaminating the fluid in the hose

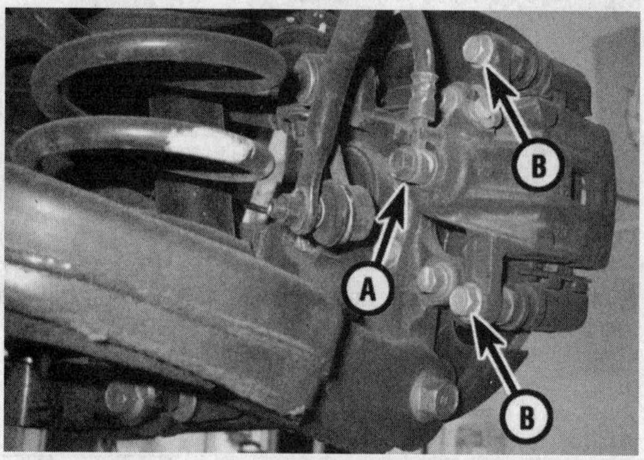

4.3 Rear brake caliper mounting details - the front caliper details are similar

A Brake hose banjo fitting bolt
B Caliper mounting bolts

5 Brake disc - inspection, removal and installation

INSPECTION

➧ Refer to illustrations 5.3, 5.4a, 5.4b, 5.5a and 5.5b

1 Loosen the wheel lug nuts, raise the vehicle and support it securely on jackstands. Remove the wheel and install the lug nuts to hold the disc in place. If the rear brake disc is being worked on, release the parking brake

2 Remove the brake caliper as outlined in Section 4. It isn't necessary to disconnect the brake hose. After removing the caliper bolts, suspend the caliper out of the way with a piece of wire (see illustration 3.6d). Remove the caliper bracket bolts and remove the bracket.

3 Visually inspect the disc surface for score marks and other damage. Light scratches and shallow grooves are normal after use and may not always be detrimental to brake operation, but deep scoring - over 0.039-inch (1.0 mm) - requires disc removal and refinishing by an automotive machine shop. Be sure to check both sides of the disc (see illustration). If pulsating has been noticed during application of the

5.3 The brake pads on this vehicle were obviously neglected, as they wore down completely and cut deep grooves into the disc - wear this severe means the disc must be replaced

5.4a Use a dial indicator to check disc runout; if the reading exceeds the maximum allowable runout limit, the disc will have to be machined or replaced

brakes, suspect disc runout.

4 To check disc runout, place a dial indicator at a point about 1/2-inch from the outer edge of the disc (see illustration). Set the indicator to zero and turn the disc. The indicator reading should not exceed the specified allowable runout limit. If it does, the disc should be refinished by an automotive machine shop.

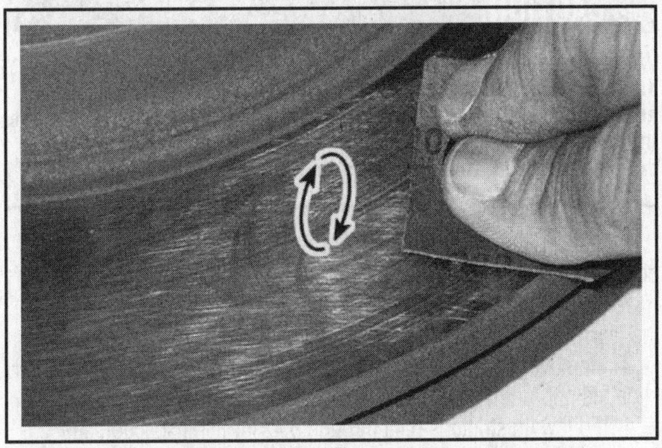

5.4b Using a swirling motion, remove the glaze from the disc surface with sandpaper or emery cloth

➡ **Note: Professionals recommend resurfacing the discs whenever the pads are replaced regardless of the dial indicator reading, as this will impart a smooth finish and ensure a perfectly flat surface, eliminating any brake pedal pulsation or other undesirable symptoms. At the very least, if you elect not to have the discs resurfaced, remove the glaze from the surface with sandpaper or emery cloth using a swirling motion (see illustration).**

5 It's absolutely critical that the disc not be machined to a thickness under the specified minimum allowable refinish thickness. The minimum wear (or discard) thickness is cast into the inside of the disc (see illustration). The disc thickness can be checked with a micrometer (see illustration).

REMOVAL

➧ **Refer to illustrations 5.7a and 5.7b**

6 Remove the lug nuts that were installed to hold the disc in place.

7 Remove the Phillips-head screws from the disc and slide the disc off the hub. If the rear disc won't come off, it may be interfering with the parking brake shoes; remove the plug (see illustration) and rotate the

5.5a The minimum wear dimension is cast into the rear of the disc (typical)

5.5b Use a micrometer to measure disc thickness

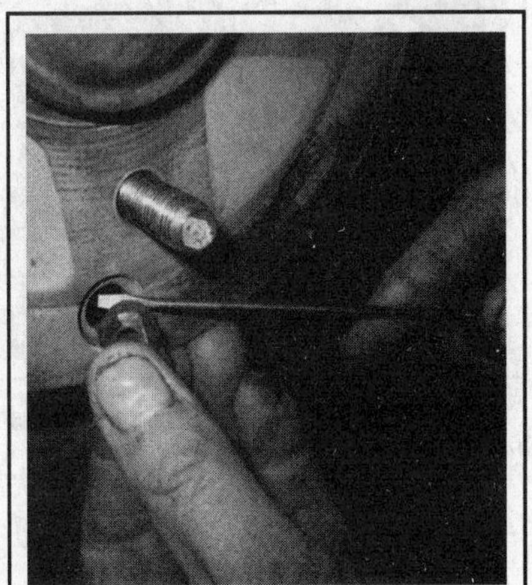

5.7a If the rear disc is difficult to remove, remove this plug . . .

5.7b . . . insert a screwdriver through the hole (the hole must be at the 11 o'clock position) and rotate the adjuster to back the parking brake shoes away from the drum surface in the disc

adjuster to back the parking brake shoes away from the drum surface within the disc (see illustration).

INSTALLATION

8 Place the disc in position over the threaded studs.

9 Install the caliper, tightening the bolts to the torque listed in this Chapter's Specifications. Bleeding won't be necessary unless the brake hose was disconnected from the caliper.

10 If you're installing a rear disc, adjust the parking brake shoes as described in Section 10.

11 Install the wheel and lug nuts. Lower the vehicle and tighten the lug nuts to the torque listed in the Chapter 1 Specifications.

WARNING:

Depress the brake pedal several times before moving the vehicle to bring the brake pads into contact with the discs. To do so will cause an initial loss of braking.

Check the operation of the brakes carefully before driving the vehicle.

6 Drum brake shoes - replacement

➧ Refer to illustrations 6.4a through 6.4z and 6.6

WARNING:

Drum brake shoes must be replaced on both wheels at the same time - never replace the shoes on only one wheel. Also, the dust created by the brake system is harmful to your health. Never blow it out with compressed air and don't inhale any of it. An approved filtering mask should be worn when working on the brakes. Do not, under any circumstances, use petroleum-based solvents to clean brake parts. Use brake system cleaner only!

6.4a Details of the rear drum brake assembly

1 *Wheel cylinder*
2 *Shoe return spring*
3 *Adjuster screw assembly*
4 *Parking brake lever*
5 *Trailing brake shoe*
6 *Parking brake cable*
7 *Shoe return spring*
8 *Leading brake shoe*
9 *Adjuster spring*
10 *Hold-down spring*
11 *Adjuster lever pawl*

CAUTION:

Whenever the brake shoes are replaced, the return and hold-down springs should also be replaced. Due to the continuous heating/cooling cycle that the springs are subjected to, they lose their tension over a period of time and may allow the shoes to drag on the drum and wear at a much faster rate than normal.

1 Loosen the wheel lug nuts, raise the rear of the vehicle and support it securely on jackstands.

2 Block the front wheels to keep the vehicle from rolling. Remove the rear wheels. Release the parking brake.

3 Remove the rear wheel bearing cap, spindle nut and washer, then slide the hub/drum assembly straight off the spindle (see Chapter 10).

4 Follow illustrations 6.4a through 6.4z for the inspection and

6.4b Before removing anything, clean the brake assembly with brake cleaner and allow it to dry - position a drain pan under the brake assembly to catch the residue - DO NOT USE COMPRESSED AIR TO BLOW BRAKE DUST OFF THE PARTS!

6.4c Unhook the adjuster spring . . .

6.4d . . . then remove the adjuster lever pawl

6.4e Unhook the upper return spring from the brake shoes

6.4f Unhook the lower return spring from the brake shoes

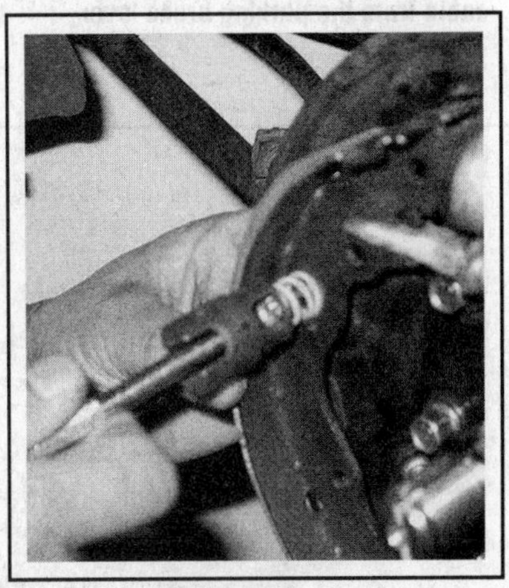

6.4g Push down on the hold-down spring, then turn it 90-degrees to align its slot with the blade on the pin, then remove the spring

replacement of the brake shoes. Be sure to stay in order and read the caption under each illustration. All four rear brake shoes must be replaced at the same time, but to avoid mixing up parts, work on only one brake assembly at a time.

5 Before reinstalling the drum, make sure the brake shoes are retracted to allow easy installation of the drum.

6.4h Lift off the leading brake shoe

6.4i Remove the adjuster screw assembly

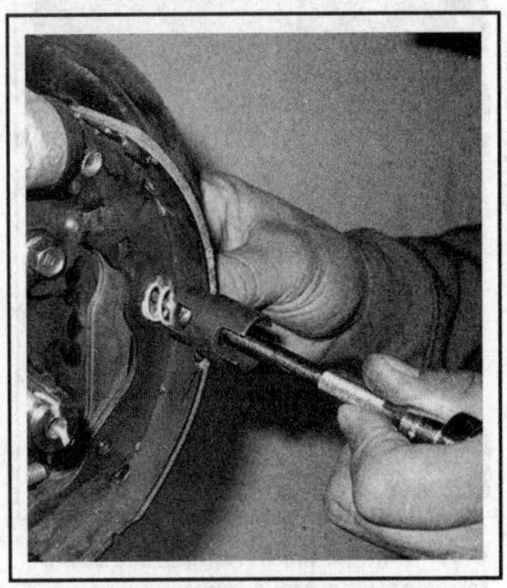

6.4j Remove the hold-down spring from the trailing brake shoe . . .

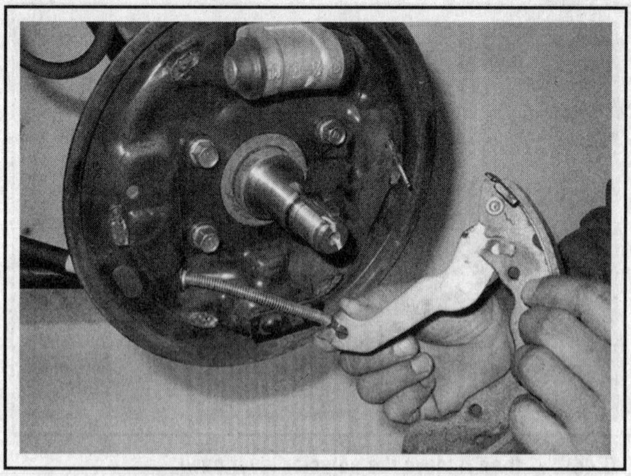

6.4k . . . then remove the shoe and detach the parking brake cable from the parking brake lever

6.4l Lubricate the brake shoe contact areas on the backing plate with high-temperature grease

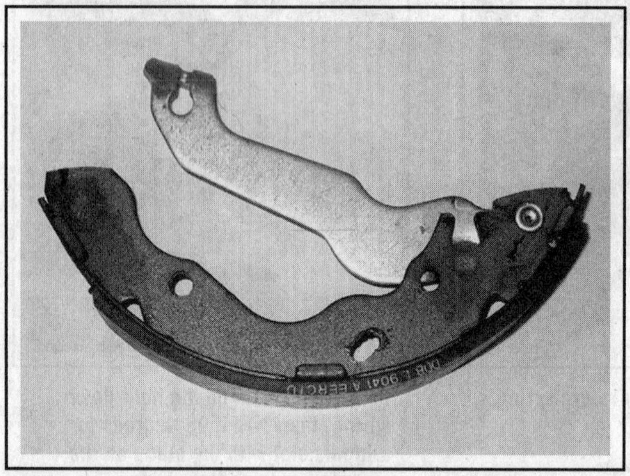

6.4m The parking brake lever and the trailing shoe are one assembly - don't try to separate them

6.4n Install the hold-down pins into the backing plate

6.4o Connect the parking brake cable to the parking brake lever

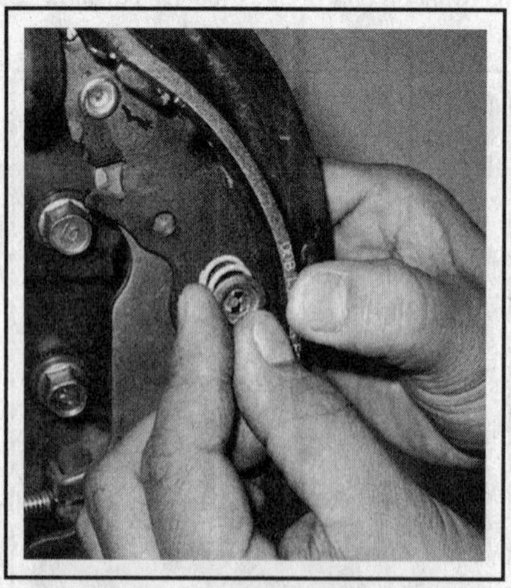

6.4p Place the trailing shoe and hold-down spring assembly in position

6.4q Install the trailing shoe hold-down spring with the tool

6.4r Connect the lower return spring to the brake shoes

6.4s Install the leading shoe onto the backing plate, making sure it engages correctly with the wheel cylinder . . .

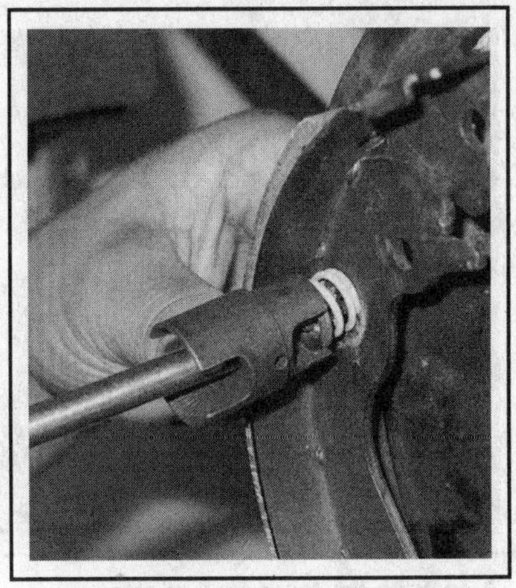

6.4t . . . and install the hold-down spring

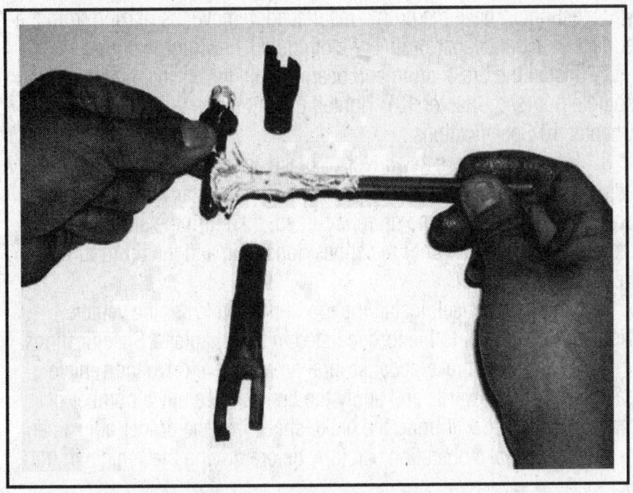

6.4u Prior to installing the adjuster screw assembly, lubricate the threads with high-temperature grease

6.4v Install the adjuster screw assembly

6.4w Connect the upper return spring to the brake shoes

6.4x Place the adjuster lever pawl in position

6.4y With the lever pawl in place . . .

6.4z . . . install the adjuster spring

6 Prior to reinstalling, the drum should be checked for cracks, score marks, deep scratches and hard spots, which will appear as small, discolored areas. If the hard spots cannot be removed with fine emery cloth or if any of the other conditions listed above exist, the drum must be taken to an automotive machine shop to have it machined.

➡ **Note: Professionals recommend resurfacing the drums whenever a brake job is done. Resurfacing will eliminate the possibility of out-of-round drums.**

6.6 The maximum allowable diameter is cast into the drum (typical)

If the drums are worn so much that they can't be resurfaced without exceeding the maximum allowable diameter (stamped into the drum) (see illustration), then new ones will be required. At the very least, if you elect not to have the drums resurfaced, remove the glazing from the surface with sandpaper or emery cloth using a swirling motion.

7 Install the brake drum and bearing unit, the washer and a new spindle nut (see Chapter 10). Tighten the nut to the torque listed in the Chapter 10 Specifications.

8 Insert a narrow screwdriver or brake adjusting tool through the adjustment hole in the backing plate and turn the star wheel until the brakes drag slightly as the drum is turned, then turn the star wheel in the opposite direction until the shoes don't drag and the drum turns freely.

9 Mount the wheel, install the lug nuts, then lower the vehicle. Tighten the lug nuts to the torque listed in the Chapter 1 Specifications.

10 Depress the brake pedal several times. Then, drive the vehicle backwards and forwards and apply the brakes forcefully a number of times. This action will bring the brake shoes into the proper adjustment.

11 Check brake operation carefully before driving the vehicle in traffic.

WARNING:

Do not operate the vehicle if you are in doubt about the effectiveness of the brake system.

7 Master cylinder - removal and installation

REMOVAL

➡ **Refer to illustration 7.3**

CAUTION:

Brake fluid will damage paint or finished surfaces. Cover all body parts and be careful not to spill fluid during this procedure. Clean up any spilled brake fluid immediately and wash the area with large amounts of water.

1 Remove the air filter housing and the air intake duct (see Chapter 4).

2 Remove as much fluid as possible from the reservoir with a syringe.

3 Unplug the electrical connector for the brake fluid level warning switch (see illustration).

4 Place rags under the fittings and prepare caps or plastic bags to cover the ends of the lines once they're disconnected.

5 Loosen the fittings at the ends of the brake lines where they enter the master cylinder. To prevent rounding off the flats, use a flare-nut

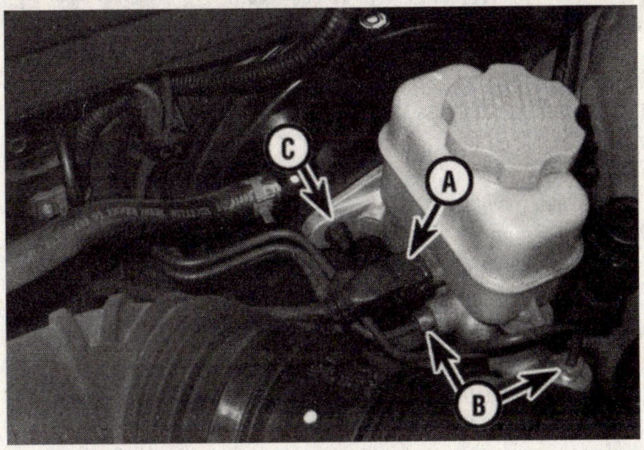

7.3 Master cylinder mounting details

A Electrical connector
B Hydraulic line fittings
C Mounting nut (one of two shown)

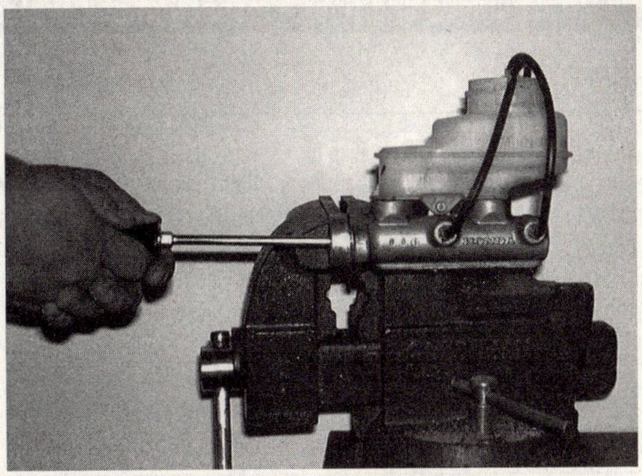

7.9 The best way to bleed air from the master cylinder before installing it on the vehicle is with a pair of bleed tubes (typical)

wrench, which wraps around the fitting hex.

6 Carefully move the brake lines away from the master cylinder and plug the ends to prevent contamination.

7 Remove the nuts attaching the master cylinder to the power booster. Pull the master cylinder off the studs to remove it. Again, be careful not to spill fluid or bend the brake lines as this is done.

➡ **Note: If necessary, remove brake lines going to the ABS actuator from the master cylinder if they cannot be moved aside without damaging them.**

INSTALLATION

➧ Refer to illustration 7.9

8 Bench bleed the new master cylinder before installing it. Because it will be necessary to depress the master cylinder piston and, at the same time, control flow from the brake line outlets, it is recommended that the master cylinder be mounted in a vise.

9 Attach a pair of master cylinder bleeder tubes to the outlet ports of the master cylinder (see illustration). On models with an auxiliary type reservoir, place the bleeder tubes into the small tank mounted on the master cylinder.

10 Fill the reservoir with brake fluid of the recommended type (see Chapter 1).

11 Slowly push the pistons into the master cylinder (a large Phillips screwdriver can be used for this) - air will be expelled from the pressure chambers and into the reservoir. Because the tubes are submerged in fluid, air can't be drawn back into the master cylinder when you release the pistons.

12 Repeat the procedure until no more air bubbles are present.

13 Remove the bleed tubes, one at a time, and install plugs in the open ports to prevent fluid leakage and air from entering.

14 Install the reservoir cover, then install the master cylinder over the studs on the power brake booster and tighten the attaching nuts only finger tight at this time.

15 Thread the brake line fittings into the master cylinder. Since the master cylinder is still a bit loose, it can be moved slightly in order for the fittings to thread in easily. Do not strip the threads as the fittings are tightened.

16 Tighten the mounting nuts to the torque listed in this Chapter's Specifications, then tighten the brake line fittings securely.

17 Fill the master cylinder reservoir with fluid, then bleed the master cylinder and the brake system as described in Section 9. To bleed the cylinder on the vehicle, have an assistant pump the brake pedal several times slowly, then hold the pedal to the floor. Loosen the fitting nut to allow air and fluid to escape. Repeat this procedure on both fittings until the fluid is clear of air bubbles.

⁂ CAUTION:

Have plenty of rags on hand to catch the fluid - brake fluid will ruin painted surfaces.

18 If it was necessary to remove the master cylinder-to-ABS actuator brake lines, also bleed the lines at the ABS control unit.

19 The remainder of installation is the reverse of removal. Test the operation of the brake system carefully before placing the vehicle into normal service.

⁂ WARNING:

Do not operate the vehicle if you are in doubt about the effectiveness of the brake system. On models equipped with ABS, it is possible for air to become trapped in the anti-lock brake system hydraulic control unit, so, if the pedal continues to feel spongy after repeated bleedings or the BRAKE or ANTI-LOCK light stays on, have the vehicle towed to a dealer service department or other qualified shop to be bled with the aid of a scan tool.

8 Brake hoses and lines - inspection and replacement

INSPECTION

1 About every six months, with the vehicle raised and supported securely on jackstands, the rubber hoses which connect the steel brake lines with the front and rear brake assemblies should be inspected for cracks, chafing of the outer cover, leaks, blisters and other damage. These are important and vulnerable parts of the brake system and inspection should be complete. A light and mirror will be helpful for a thorough check. If a hose exhibits any of the above conditions, replace it with a new one.

REPLACEMENT

Front brake hose

➧ Refer to illustrations 8.3 and 8.4

2 Loosen the wheel lug nuts, raise the vehicle and support it securely on jackstands. Remove the wheel.

3 At the frame bracket, unscrew the brake line fitting from the hose (see illustration). Use a flare-nut wrench to prevent rounding off the corners.

4 Remove the U-clip from the female fitting at the bracket with a pair of pliers (see illustration), then pass the hose through the bracket.

5 At the caliper end of the hose, remove the banjo-fitting bolt, then separate the hose from the caliper. Note that there are two copper sealing washers on each side of the fitting - they should be replaced with new ones during installation.

6 Remove the fastener from the strut bracket and detach the hose from it.

7 To install the hose, pass the caliper fitting end through the strut bracket, then connect the fitting to the caliper with the banjo bolt and new sealing washers. Make sure the locating lug on the fitting is engaged with the hole in the caliper, then tighten the bolt to the torque listed in this Chapter's Specifications.

8 Push the metal support into the strut bracket and install the U-clip. Make sure the hose isn't twisted between the caliper and the strut bracket.

9 Route the hose into the frame bracket, again making sure it isn't twisted, then connect the brake line fitting, starting the threads by hand. Install the clip and E-ring, if equipped, then tighten the fitting securely.

10 Bleed the caliper (see Section 9).

11 Install the wheel and lug nuts, lower the vehicle and tighten the lug nuts to the torque listed in the Chapter 1 Specifications.

Rear brake hoses

12 Perform Steps 2, 3 and 4 above, then repeat Steps 3 and 4 at the other end of the hose. Be sure to bleed the caliper (see Section 9).

Metal brake lines

13 When replacing brake lines, be sure to use the correct parts. Don't use copper tubing for any brake system components. Purchase genuine steel brake lines from a dealer or auto parts store.

14 Prefabricated brake line, with the tube ends already flared and fittings installed, is available at auto parts stores and dealer parts departments.

15 When installing the new line, make sure it's securely supported in the brackets and has plenty of clearance between moving or hot components.

16 After installation, check the master cylinder fluid level and add fluid as necessary. Bleed the brake system (see Section 9) and test the brakes carefully before driving the vehicle in traffic.

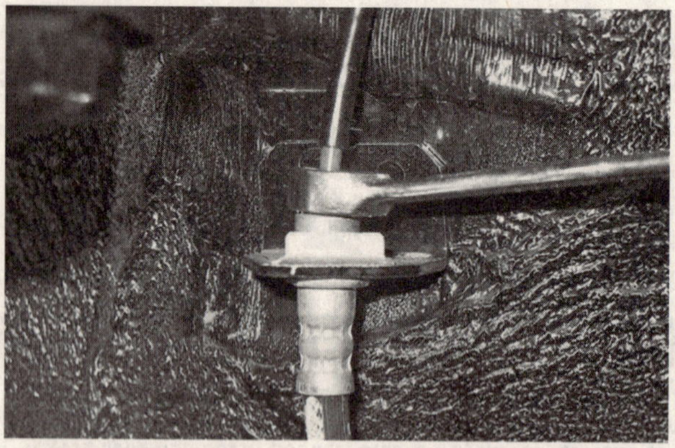

8.3 Unscrew the brake line threaded fitting with a flare-nut wrench to protect the fitting corners from being rounded off

8.4 Remove the brake hose-to-bracket U-clip with a pair of pliers

9 Brake hydraulic system - bleeding

Refer to illustration 9.8

WARNING:

Wear eye protection when bleeding the brake system. If the fluid comes in contact with your eyes, immediately rinse them with water and seek medical attention.

Note: Bleeding the hydraulic system is necessary to remove any air that manages to find its way into the system when it's opened during removal and installation of a hose, line, caliper or master cylinder.

1 You'll probably have to bleed the system at all four brakes if air has entered it due to low fluid level, or if the brake lines have been disconnected at the master cylinder.

2 If a brake line was disconnected only at a wheel, then only that caliper must be bled.

3 If a brake line is disconnected at a fitting located between the master cylinder and any of the brakes, that part of the system served by the disconnected line must be bled.

4 Remove any residual vacuum from the brake power booster by applying the brake several times with the engine off.

5 Remove the master cylinder reservoir cover and fill the reservoir with brake fluid. Reinstall the cover.

Note: Check the fluid level often during the bleeding operation and add fluid as necessary to prevent the fluid level from falling low enough to allow air bubbles into the master cylinder.

6 Have an assistant on hand, as well as a supply of new brake fluid, a clear container partially filled with clean brake fluid, a length of tubing to fit over the bleeder valve and a wrench to open and close the bleeder valve.

7 Beginning at the right rear wheel, loosen the bleeder valve slightly, then tighten it to a point where it's snug but can still be loosened quickly and easily.

8 Place one end of the tubing over the bleeder valve and submerge the other end in brake fluid in the container (see illustration).

9 Have the assistant depress the brake pedal slowly, then hold the pedal down firmly.

10 While the pedal is held down, open the bleeder valve just enough to allow a flow of fluid to leave the valve. Watch for air bubbles to exit the submerged end of the tube. When the fluid flow slows after a couple of seconds, close the valve and have your assistant release the pedal.

11 Repeat Steps 9 and 10 until no more air is seen leaving the tube, then tighten the bleeder valve and proceed to the left front wheel, the left rear wheel and the right front wheel, in that order, and perform the same procedure. Be sure to check the fluid in the master cylinder reservoir frequently.

9.8 When bleeding the brakes, a hose is connected to the bleeder valve at the caliper or wheel cylinder, then submerged in brake fluid. Air will be seen as bubbles in the tube and container. All air must be expelled before moving to the next wheel

12 Never use old brake fluid. It contains moisture that will deteriorate the brake system components.

13 Refill the master cylinder with fluid at the end of the operation.

14 Check the operation of the brakes. The pedal should feel solid when depressed, with no sponginess. If necessary, repeat the entire process.

WARNING:

Do not operate the vehicle if you are in doubt about the effectiveness of the brake system. It's possible for air to become trapped in the ABS hydraulic control unit. If the pedal continues to feel spongy after repeated bleedings or the BRAKE or ANTI-LOCK light stays on, have the vehicle towed to a dealer service department or other qualified shop to be bled with the aid of a scan tool.

10 Power brake booster - check, removal and installation

OPERATING CHECK

1 Depress the brake pedal several times with the engine off and make sure there's no change in the pedal reserve distance.

2 Depress the pedal and start the engine. If the pedal goes down slightly, operation is normal.

AIRTIGHTNESS CHECK

3 Start the engine and turn it off after one or two minutes. Depress the brake pedal slowly several times. If the pedal depresses less each time, the booster is airtight.

4 Depress the brake pedal while the engine is running, then stop the engine with the pedal depressed. If there's no change in the pedal reserve travel after holding the pedal for 30 seconds, the booster is airtight.

REMOVAL

Refer to illustration 10.9

5 Power brake booster units shouldn't be disassembled. They require special tools not normally found in most automotive repair stations or shops. They're fairly complex and, because of their critical relationship to brake performance, should be replaced with new or rebuilt ones.

10.9 Power brake booster mounting nuts

6 Remove the brake master cylinder (see Section 7). To provide room for booster removal, some models may require that the brake lines that cross in front of the master cylinder be removed entirely (at both ends), and not just disconnected from the master cylinder. Other brake lines that cross in front of the brake booster can be separated from the firewall and carefully moved aside.

7 Carefully disconnect the vacuum hose from the brake booster.

8 Remove the brake pedal return spring near the top of the brake pedal. Remove the clevis pin retaining clip with pliers and pull out the pin.

9 Remove the four fasteners holding the brake booster to the firewall (see illustration). Slide the booster straight out from the firewall until the studs clear the holes.

INSTALLATION

10 Installation procedures are basically the reverse of removal. Tighten the booster mounting nuts to the torque listed in this Chapter's Specifications.

11 After the final installation of the master cylinder and brake hoses and lines, the brake pedal height and freeplay must be adjusted and the system must be bled. See the appropriate Sections of this Chapter for those procedures.

11 Parking brake shoes - inspection and replacement

Refer to illustrations 11.4a through 11.4u, 11.5a through 11.5o, 11.7a and 11.7b

WARNING:

Dust created by the brake system is hazardous to your health. Never blow it out with compressed air and don't inhale any of it. An approved filtering mask should be worn when working on the brakes. Do not, under any circumstances, use petroleum-based solvents to clean brake parts. Use brake system cleaner only!

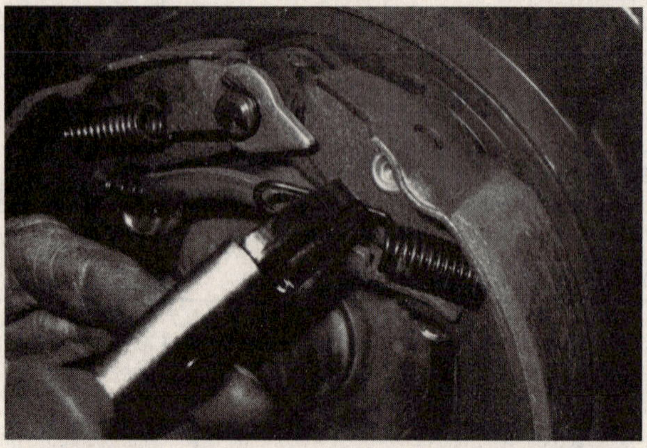

11.4a Remove the upper return springs (2001 through 2006 models)

WARNING:

Parking brake shoes must be replaced on both wheels at the same time - never replace the shoes on only one wheel.

Note: This procedure applies only to vehicles equipped with rear disc brakes. The main drum brake shoes operate as the parking brake shoes on drum brake-equipped vehicles.

1 Remove the rear brake discs (see Section 5).

2 Inspect the thickness of the lining material on the shoes. If the lining has worn down to 1/32-inch or less, the shoes must be replaced.

3 Remove the hub and bearing assembly (see Chapter 10).

Note: It is possible to perform the shoe replacement procedure without removing the hub and bearing assembly, although working room is very limited.

4 On 2001 through 2006 models, wash off the brake parts with brake system cleaner, then follow the accompanying illustrations for the brake shoe replacement procedure (see illustrations 11.4a through 11.4u). Be sure to stay in order and read the caption under each illustration.

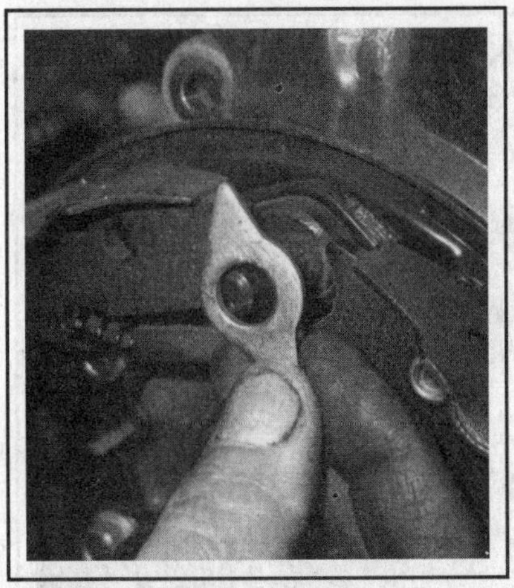

11.4b Lift off the retainer plate

11.4c Spread the shoes and remove the strut

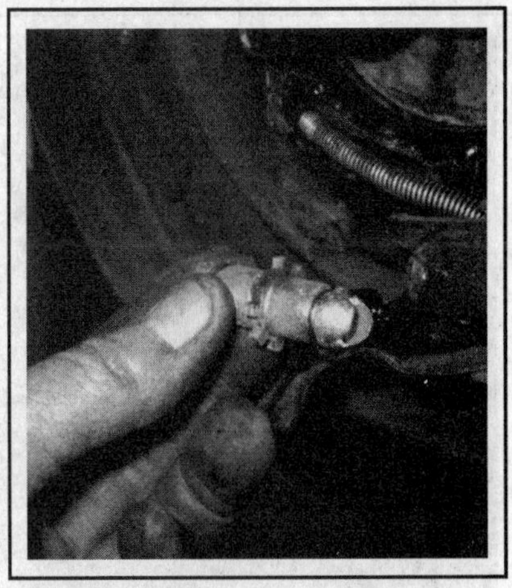

11.4d Remove the star-wheel mechanism, noting which end is facing forward

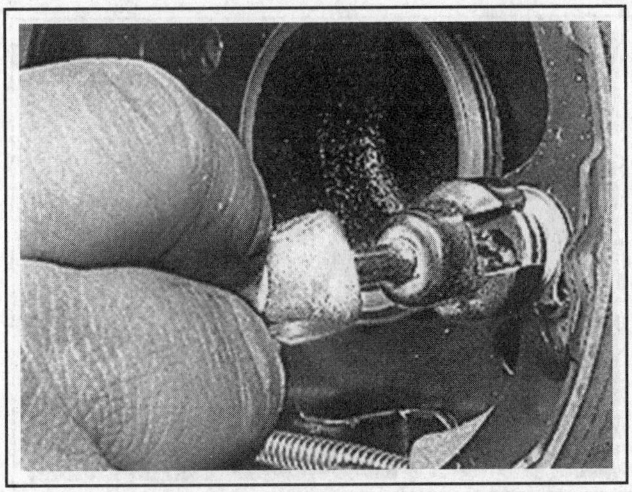

11.4e Remove the shoe hold-down springs and retainers

11.4f Remove the lower spring

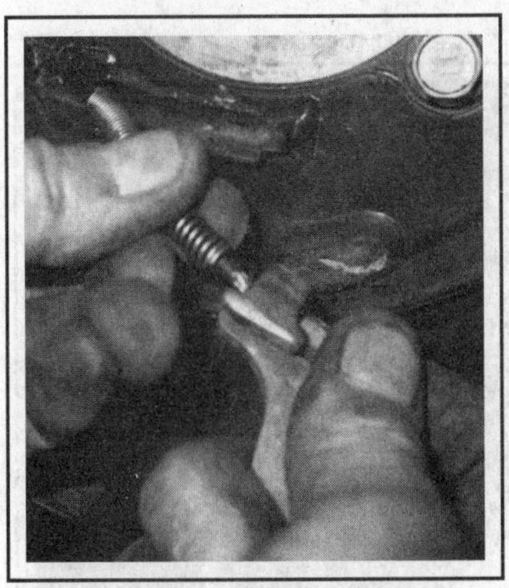

11.4g Disconnect the shoe from the parking brake cable and set all the components aside for cleaning

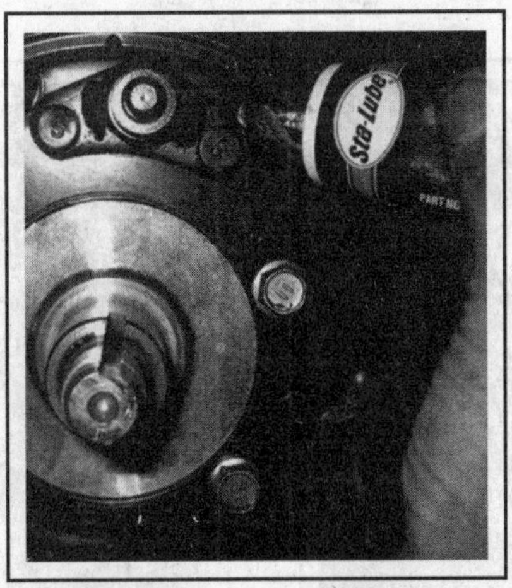

11.4h Apply brake lubricant to the backing plates at the raised areas that support the shoes

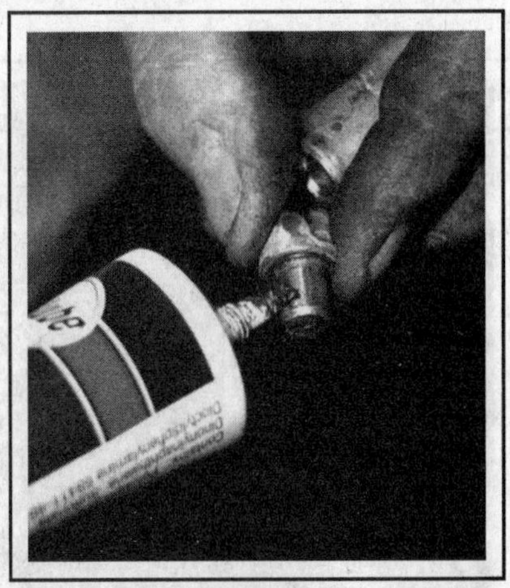

11.4i Lightly lubricate the star-wheel threads and friction plate

11.4j Install the front shoe . . .

11.4k . . . followed by its hold-down spring and retainer

11.4l Install the rear shoe, hold-down spring and retainer

11.4m Install the star-wheel with the threaded end facing forward

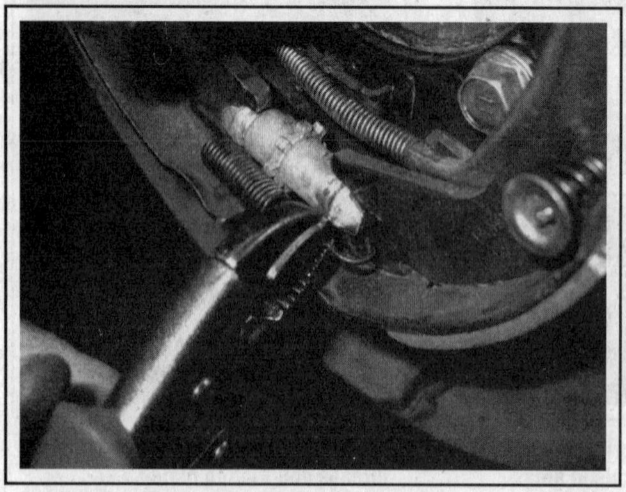

11.4n Install the lower spring

11.4o Install the strut with its spring on the forward end

11.4p Install the upper retainer

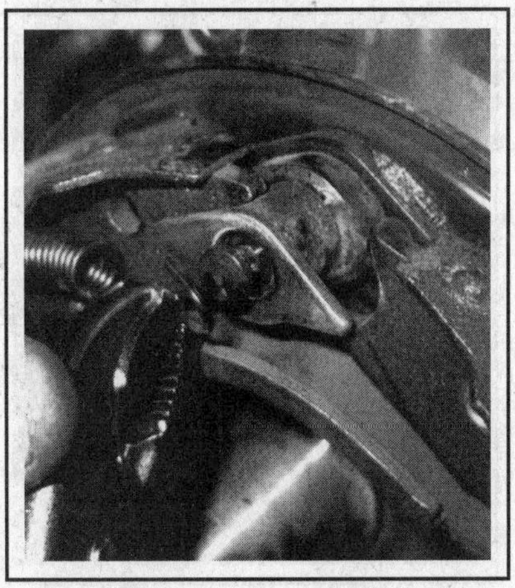

11.4q Install the front spring . . .

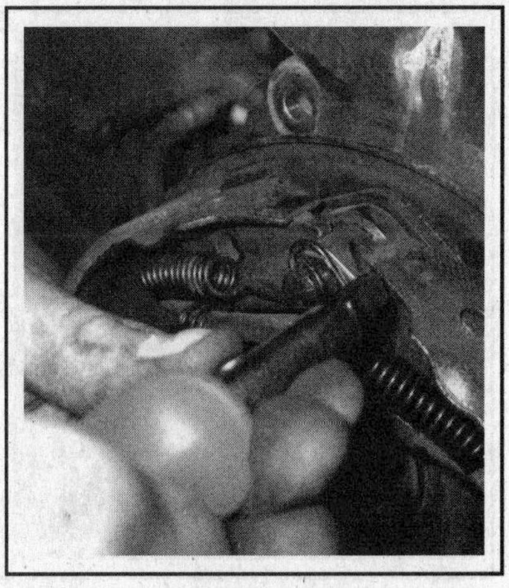

11.4r . . . and the rear spring

11.4s The upper section should now look like this

11.4t This is how the complete parking brake assembly should look when you're done!

5 On 2006.5 and later models, wash off the brake parts with brake system cleaner, then follow the accompanying illustrations for the brake shoe replacement procedure (see illustrations 11.5a through 11.5o). Be sure to stay in order and read the caption under each illustration.

11.4u Tighten the hub nut to the torque listed in this Chapter's Specifications, then stake the nut to the spindle. It might be necessary to shorten the adjuster to install the brake rotor

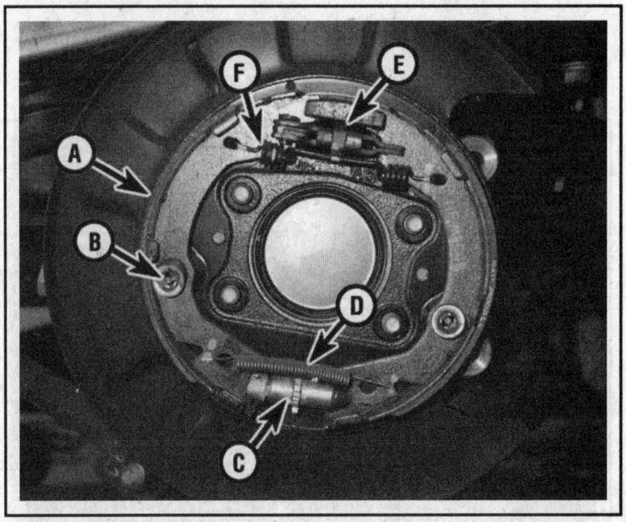

11.5a Details of the parking brake shoe assembly (2006.5 and later models)

A Parking brake shoe
B Hold-down spring
C Star-wheel adjuster assembly
D Lower return spring
E Strut
F Upper return spring

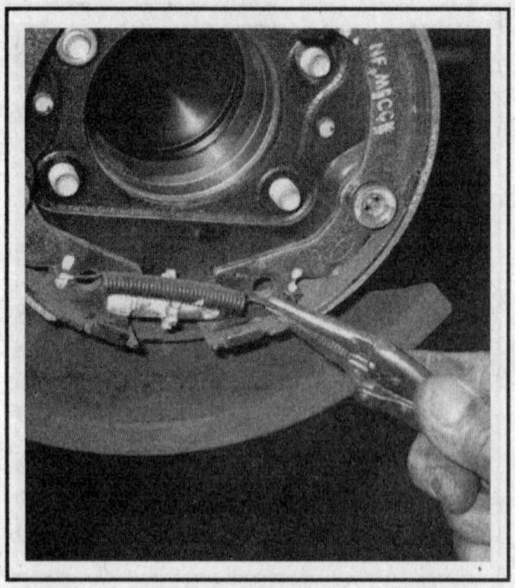

11.5b Remove the lower return spring

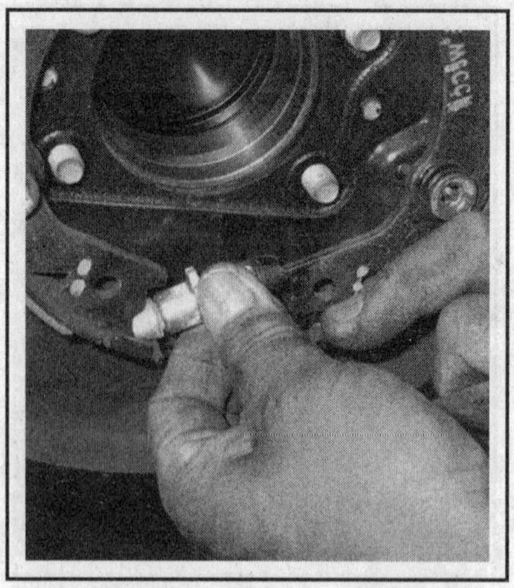

11.5c Lift out the star-wheel adjuster mechanism, noting which way it's facing

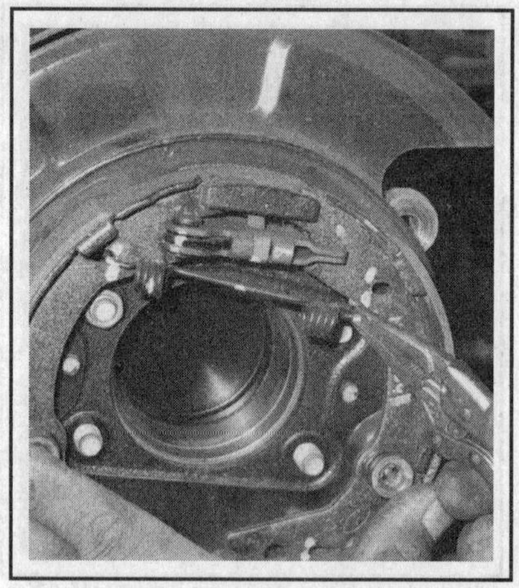

11.5d Remove the upper return spring

11.5e Release the front hold-down spring and lift off the front shoe

11.5f Remove the rear shoe assembly in the same way

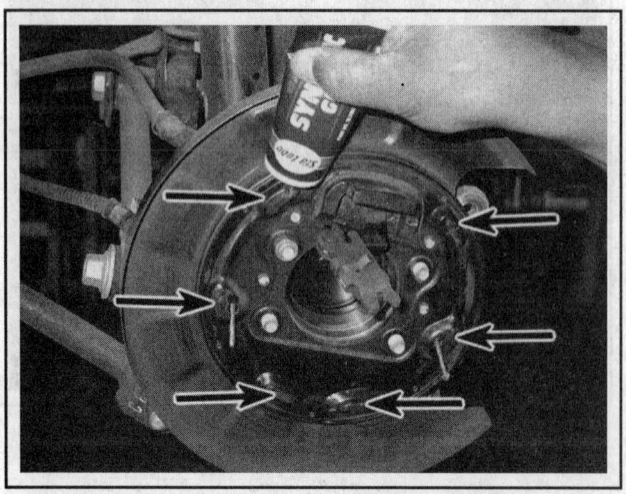

11.5g Thoroughly clean the backing plate and lightly lubricate the contact surfaces with high-temperature grease

11.5h Fit the new rear shoe to the backing plate . . .

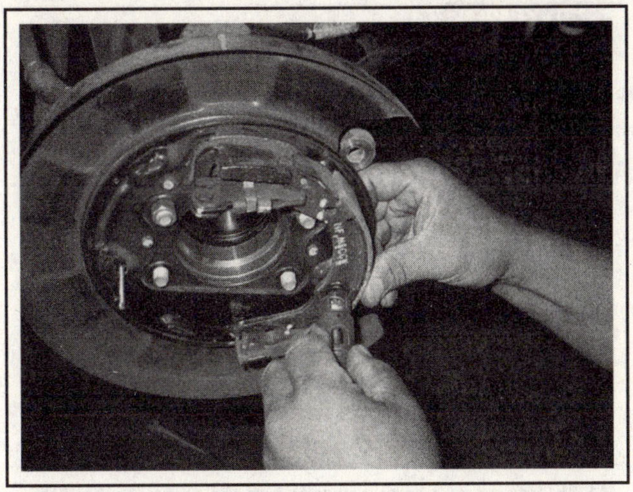

11.5i . . . and install the hold-down retainer

11.5j Install the new front shoe in the same way . . .

11.5k . . . and install its hold-down

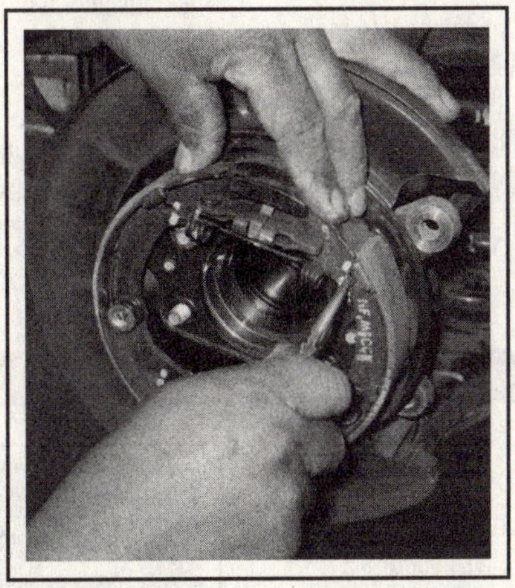

11.5l Install the upper return spring

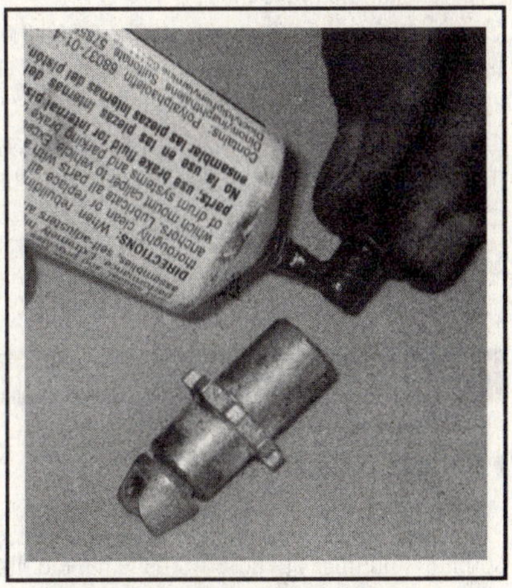

11.5m Clean the adjuster and lightly lubricate it with high-temperature grease

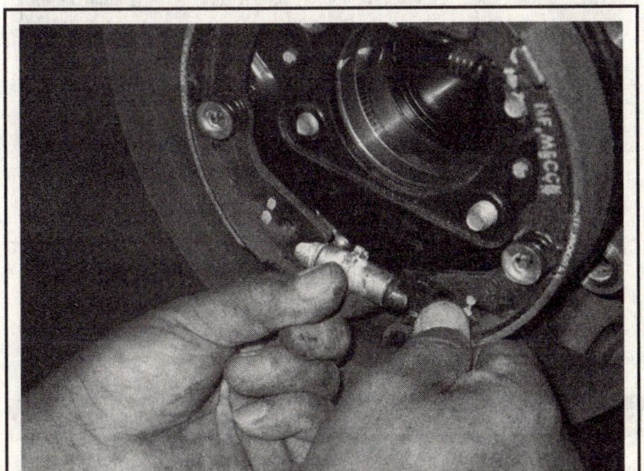

11.5n Install the adjuster in its original orientation

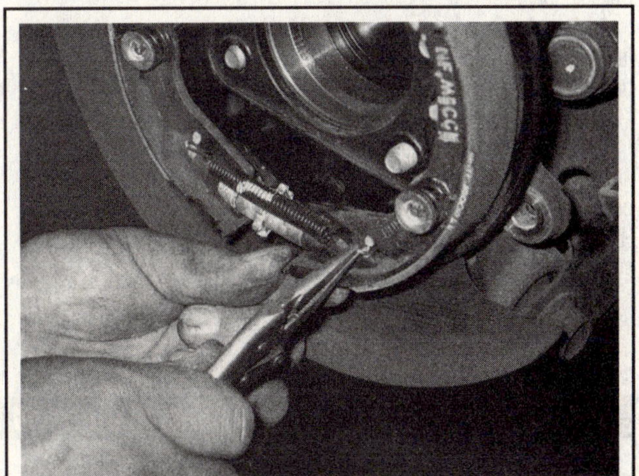

11.5o Install the lower return spring and rotate the adjuster so the drum/hub assembly will have enough clearance for installation

11.7a Remove the rubber plug from the star-wheel adjuster access hole

11.7b Use a small screwdriver to turn the adjuster wheel to give the correct adjustment (refer to the text)

6 Install the brake disc.

7 Remove the hole plugs from the brake discs. Adjust the parking brake shoe clearance by turning the adjuster star wheel with a brake adjusting tool or screwdriver until the shoes contact the discs and the discs can't be turned (see illustrations). Back off the adjusters five notches, then install the hole plugs. There must be no drag as the disc is turned.

8 Install the brake caliper (see Section 4). Be sure to tighten the bolts to the torque listed in this Chapter's Specifications.

9 Install the wheel and tighten the lug nuts to the torque specified in Chapter 1.

10 Set the parking brake with about 45 pounds of force and count the number of clicks that it travels. It should be about five clicks - if it's not, adjust the parking brake as described in Section 12.

12 Parking brake - adjustment

Refer to illustration 12.5

1 Pull the parking brake lever with about 45 pounds of force and count the number of clicks from the handle. It should take about six clicks to apply the parking brake. It should be locked at eight clicks. If it travels less than five clicks, there's a chance the parking brake might not be releasing completely. If it travels more than eight clicks, the parking brake may not hold adequately on an incline, allowing the car to roll. Release the lever.

2 Raise the rear of the vehicle and support it securely on jackstands. Be sure to block the front wheels. The parking brake should be released.

3 Refer to Step 7 in Section 11 to adjust the parking brake shoes.

4 Remove the console cover (see Chapter 11).

5 Adjust the nut on the end of the cable rod to get the correct number of clicks when operating the parking brake lever (see illustration).

6 With the lever released, move the rear wheels by hand to make sure that the parking brake isn't dragging.

7 Reinstall the console cover and lower the vehicle.

12.5 The parking brake adjusting nut is inside the center console

13 Brake light switch - removal, installation and adjustment

REMOVAL AND INSTALLATION

Refer to illustration 13.1

1 The brake light switch is located on a bracket at the top of the brake pedal (see illustration).

2 Disconnect the wiring harness at the brake light switch.

3 Loosen the locknut and unscrew the switch from the pedal bracket.

4 Installation is the reverse of removal.

13.1 The brake light switch is located on a bracket near the top of the brake pedal. Loosen the locknut and unscrew the switch from its bracket

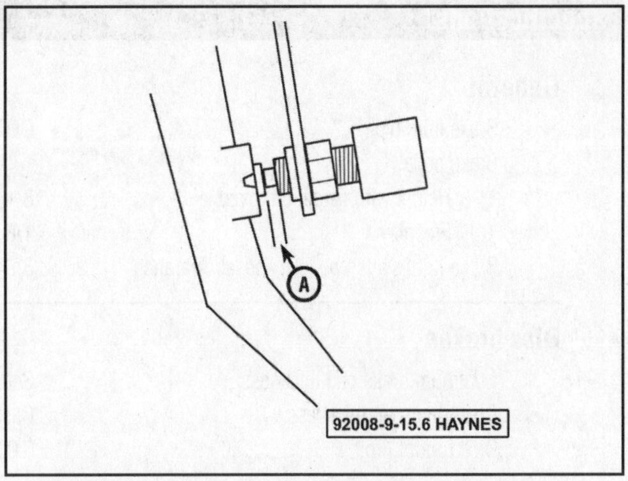

13.6 To adjust the brake light switch, loosen the locknut and rotate the switch until the plunger distance (A) is within the range listed in this Chapter's Specifications, then tighten the locknut

ADJUSTMENT

Refer to illustration 13.6

5 Check and, if necessary, adjust brake pedal height (see Section 14).

6 Loosen the switch locknut, adjust the switch so that the pedal has freeplay as listed in this Chapter's Specifications (see Section 14) (see illustration).

7 Plug the electrical connector into the switch. Make sure the brake lights come on when the brake pedal is depressed and go off when the pedal is released. If not, repeat the adjustment procedure until the brake lights function properly.

8 Check and, if necessary, adjust brake pedal freeplay (see Section 14).

14 Brake pedal - adjustment

PEDAL HEIGHT

Refer to illustration 14.1

1 The height of the brake pedal is the distance the pedal sits off the floor. If the pedal height is not within Specifications, it must be adjusted (see illustration).

2 To adjust the brake pedal, loosen the locknut and back the pushrod out for clearance. Turn the pushrod to adjust the pedal height in the middle of the specified range, then retighten the locknut.

3 At the brake pedal, loosen the locknut on the brake switch and retract the switch. Before measuring the brake pedal height, make sure the pedal is in the fully-returned position. Measure the pedal height and adjust it, if necessary (see Step 2). To get an accurate measurement, the carpet must be pulled back.

4 Adjust the brake pedal switch by turning it clockwise until the switch body just contacts the pedal arm, then rotate it counterclockwise to gain the clearance in this Chapter's Specifications, and tighten the switch locknut.

PEDAL FREEPLAY

5 The freeplay is the pedal slack, or the distance the pedal can be depressed before it begins to have any effect on the brake system. If the pedal freeplay is not within the specified range, it must be adjusted.

6 To adjust the pedal freeplay, loosen the brake pedal switch. Adjust it to get the freeplay to the specified range, then retighten the locknut.

7 Before adjusting brake pedal freeplay, depress the brake pedal several times (with the engine off). Measure the freeplay and adjust it, if necessary. Loosen the locknut on the pushrod, then back off the pushrod to adjust the pedal freeplay to the specified range and retighten the locknut.

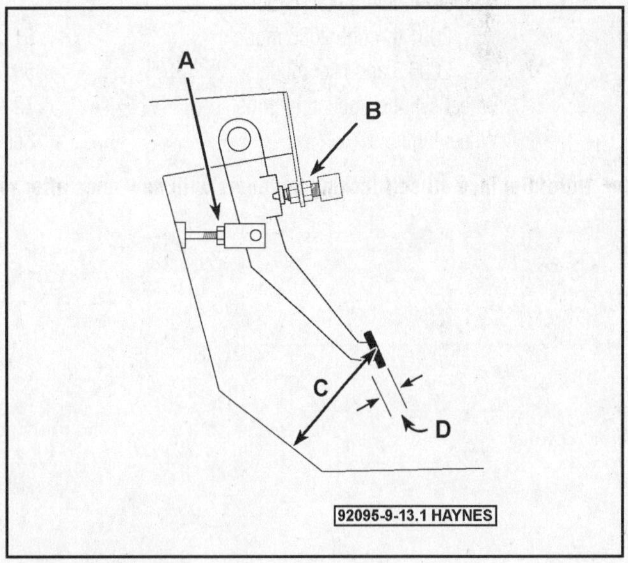

14.1 Brake pedal height and freeplay measuring and adjustment points

A Clevis locknut
B Brake light switch adjusting nut/locknut
C Pedal height measurement point (to steel floor)
D Freeplay measurement point

Specifications

General

Brake fluid type	DOT 3 or DOT 4
Brake pedal	
Height with carpet removed	8.19 to 8.21 inches (208 to 213 mm)
Freeplay	1/8 to 5/16 inch (3 to 8 mm)
Brake light switch body-to-pedal clearance	3/64 to 1/8 inch (1 to 3 mm)

Disc brakes

Minimum brake pad thickness	See Chapter 1
Disc minimum thickness	Cast into disc
Disc runout limit	0.0016 inch (0.04 mm)

Drum brakes

Maximum drum diameter	Cast into drum
Shoe lining minimum thickness	See Chapter 1

Parking brake shoe minimum thickness — 1/32-inch (0.8 mm)

Torque specifications

➡ Note: One foot-pound (ft-lb) of torque is equivalent to 12 inch-pounds (in-lbs) of torque. Torque values below approximately 15 foot-pounds are expressed in inch-pounds, because most foot-pound torque wrenches are not accurate at these smaller values.

Torque specifications	Ft-lbs (unless otherwise indicated)	Nm
Master cylinder-to-booster nuts	72 to 108 in-lbs	8 to 12
Booster mounting nuts	120 to 144 in-lbs	13 to 16
Brake hose banjo fitting bolt	18 to 22	25 to 30
Caliper guide rod (mounting) bolts	16 to 24	22 to 32
Caliper mounting bracket bolts		
2001 through 2006 models	51 to 63	69 to 85
2006.5 and later models	58 to 72	79 to 98
Wheel cylinder mounting bolts	72 to 96 in-lbs	8 to 11
Wheel lug nuts	See Chapter 1	

➡ Note: Replace all self-locking fasteners with new ones after removing them.

10

SUSPENSION AND STEERING SYSTEMS

Section

Reference to other Chapters

Power steering fluid level check - See Chapter 1
Steering and suspension check - See Chapter 1
Tire and tire pressure checks - See Chapter 1
Tire rotation - See Chapter 1

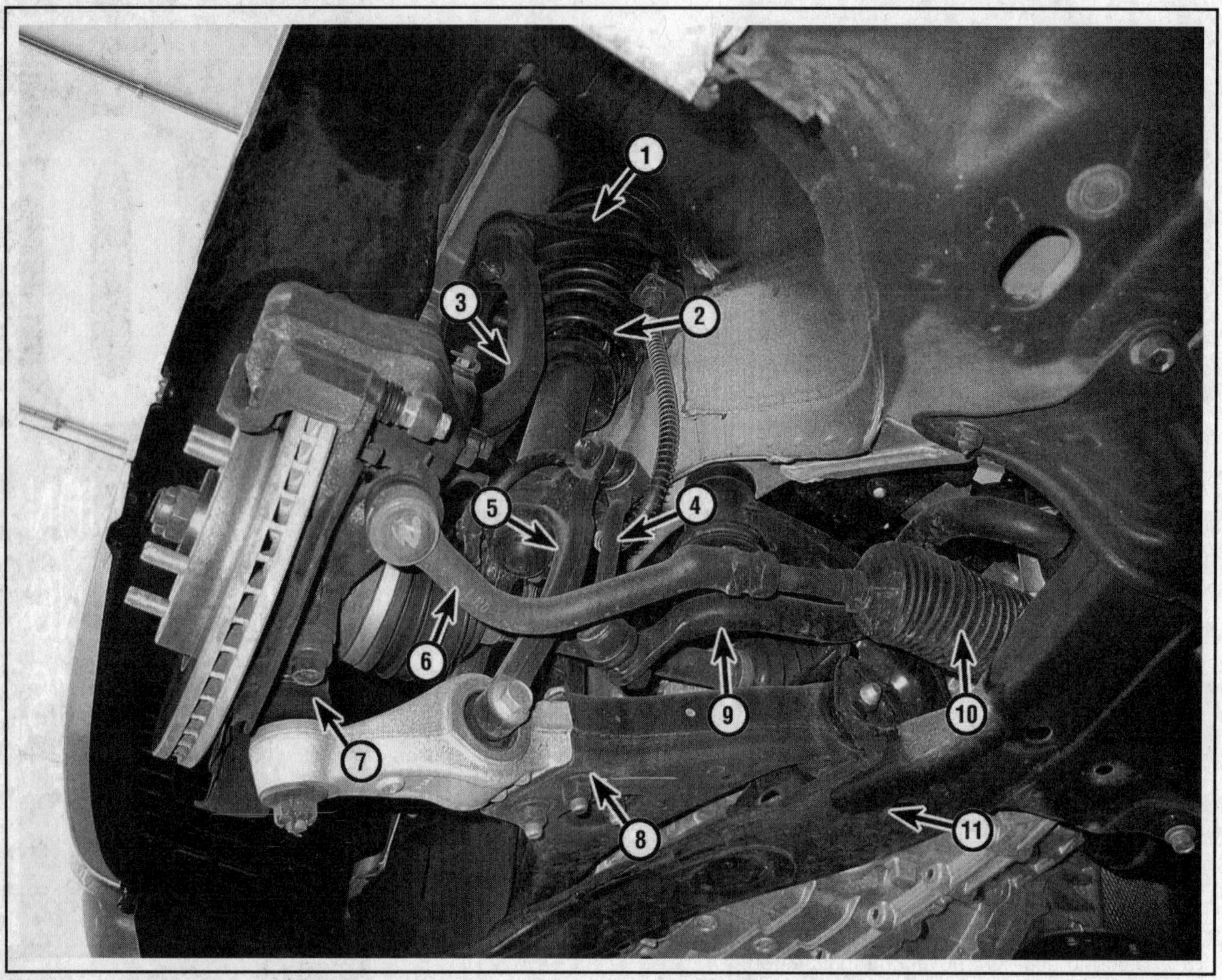

1.1 Front suspension and steering components (2006 and earlier models) - left side shown

1 *Upper control arm*
2 *Shock absorber/coil spring*
3 *Steering knuckle*
4 *Stabilizer bar link*
5 *Shock absorber fork*
6 *Tie-rod end*
7 *Lower balljoint*
8 *Lower control arm*
9 *Stabilizer bar*
10 *Steering gear boot*
11 *Subframe*

1 General information

Refer to illustrations 1.1, 1.2a and 1.2b

Front suspension is independent, with coil-over shock absorbers used on 2006 and earlier models, and strut/coil spring assemblies on 2006.5 and later models.

Note: 2006 and 2006.5 models will both have a "6" in the tenth position of the VIN. To distinguish a 2006 model from a 2006.5 model, refer to the 8th position of the VIN (the engine code): A 2006 model will have a "6" (four-cylinder) or "8" (V6), while a 2006.5 will have a "3" (four-cylinder) or "4" (V6).

Rear suspension is independent as well, with coil-over shock absorbers used on 2006 and earlier models and conventional shock absorbers and coil springs on 2006.5 and later models.

The power-assisted rack-and-pinion steering gear, which is located behind the engine/transaxe assembly, is mounted on the front subframe. The steering gear actuates the tie-rods, which are attached to the steering knuckles. The steering column is designed to collapse in the event of an accident.

1.2a Rear suspension components (2006 and earlier models):

1 Upper control arm	*4 Stabilizer bar link rod*	*7 Balljoint*
2 Carrier assembly (knuckle)	*5 Rear stabilizer bar*	*8 Center arm*
3 Trailing arm	*6 Rear shock absorber/coil spring assembly*	*9 Assist arm*

Frequently, when working on the suspension or steering system components, you may come across fasteners that seem impossible to loosen. These fasteners on the underside of the vehicle are continually subjected to water, road grime, mud, etc., and can become rusted or frozen, making them extremely difficult to remove. In order to unscrew these stubborn fasteners without damaging them (or other components), be sure to use lots of penetrating oil and allow it to soak in for a while. Using a wire brush to clean exposed threads will also ease removal of the nut or bolt and prevent damage to the threads. Sometimes a sharp blow with a hammer and punch will break the bond between nut and bolt threads, but care must be taken to prevent the punch from slipping off the fastener and ruining the threads. Heating the stuck fastener and surrounding area with a torch sometimes helps too, but isn't recommended because of the obvious dangers associated with fire. Long breaker bars and extension, or cheater, pipes will increase leverage, but never use an extension pipe on a ratchet - the ratcheting mechanism could be damaged. Sometimes tightening the nut or bolt first will help to break it loose. Fasteners that require drastic measures to remove should always be replaced with new ones.

Since most of the procedures dealt with in this Chapter involve jacking up the vehicle and working underneath it, a good pair of jackstands will be needed. A hydraulic floor jack is the preferred type of jack to lift the vehicle, and it can also be used to support certain components during various operations.

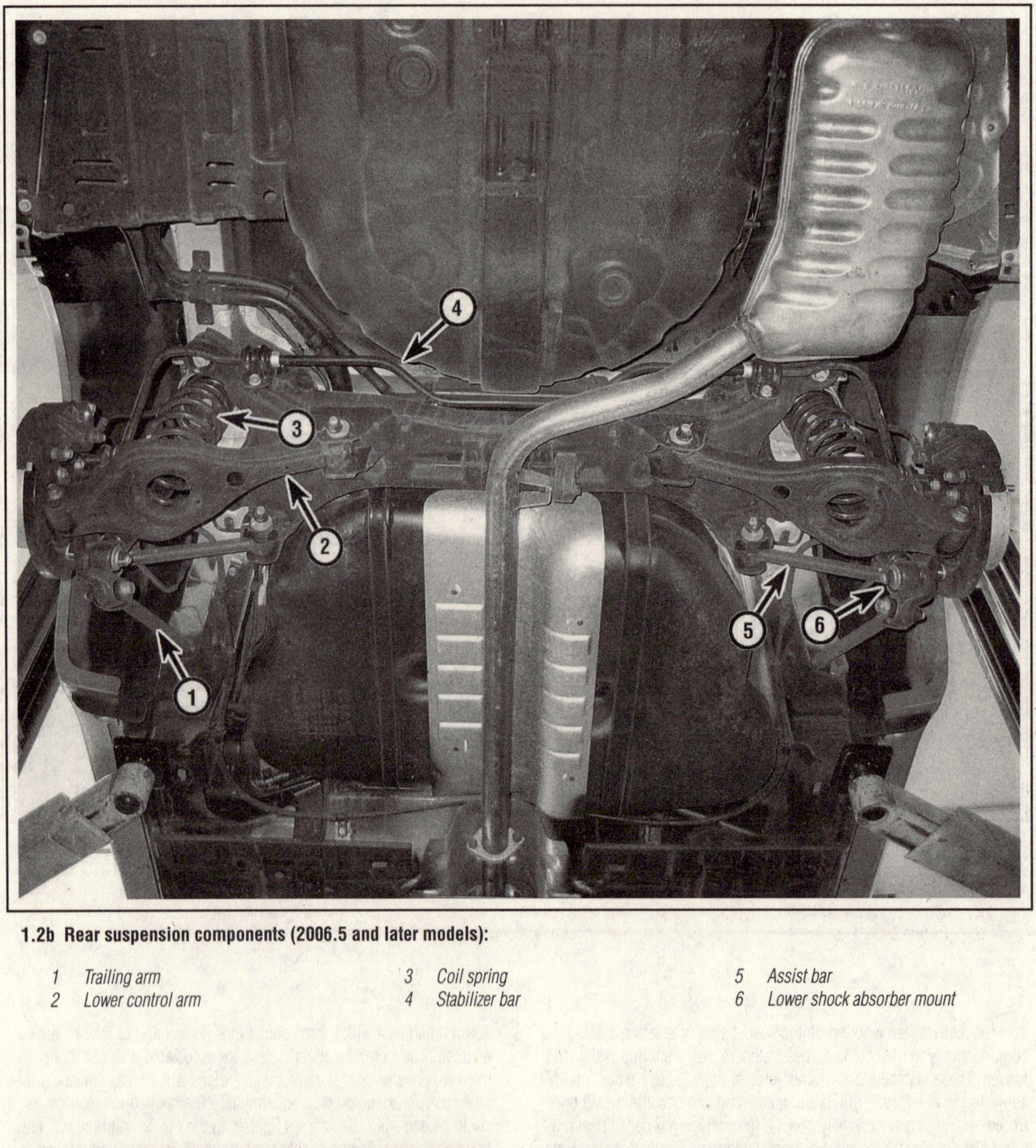

1.2b Rear suspension components (2006.5 and later models):

1 *Trailing arm*
2 *Lower control arm*
3 *Coil spring*
4 *Stabilizer bar*
5 *Assist bar*
6 *Lower shock absorber mount*

⁂ WARNING:

Never, under any circumstances, rely on a jack to support the vehicle while working on it. Whenever any of the suspension or steering fasteners are loosened or removed they must be inspected and, if necessary, replaced with new ones of the same part number or of original equipment quality and design. Torque specifications must be followed for proper reassembly and component retention. Never attempt to heat or straighten any suspension or steering components. Instead, replace any bent or damaged part with a new one.

2 Stabilizer bar, bushings and links (front) - removal and installation

Refer to illustrations 2.3 and 2.5

Note: If a stabilizer bar becomes damaged, it is most likely the result of an accident that was severe enough to damage other major components (such as the subframe itself). Damage this severe will require the services of an auto body shop.

1 Loosen the front wheel lug nuts, then raise the front of the vehicle and support it securely on jackstands.

2 Remove the front wheels.

3 Disconnect the stabilizer bar links from the bar or the lower control arms (see illustration).

4 On 2006.5 and later models, place a floor jack under the rear of the subframe. Remove the two rear subframe mounting bolts and lower the subframe slightly for clearance.

5 Detach both stabilizer bar bushing retainers from the subframe (see illustration).

6 While the stabilizer bar is detached, slide off the retainer bushings and inspect them. If they're cracked, worn or deteriorated, replace them. Also inspect the stabilizer bar links for loose ballstuds.

7 Clean the bushing area of the stabilizer bar with a stiff wire brush to remove any rust or dirt.

8 Lubricate the inside and outside of the new bushings with vegetable oil (used in cooking) to simplify reassembly.

CAUTION:

Don't use petroleum or mineral-based lubricants or brake fluid - they will lead to deterioration of the bushings.

9 Install the retainers and bolts, tightening the bolts to the torque listed in this Chapter's Specifications.

10 Install the links, tightening the link nuts to the torque listed in this Chapter's Specifications.

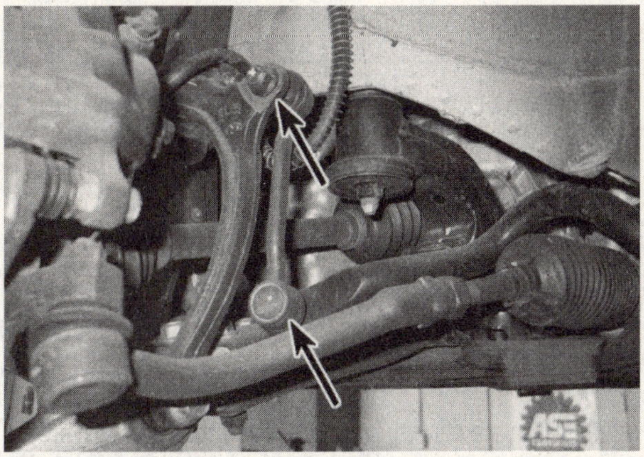

2.3 Stabilizer bar link mounting nuts (lower nut not visible here)

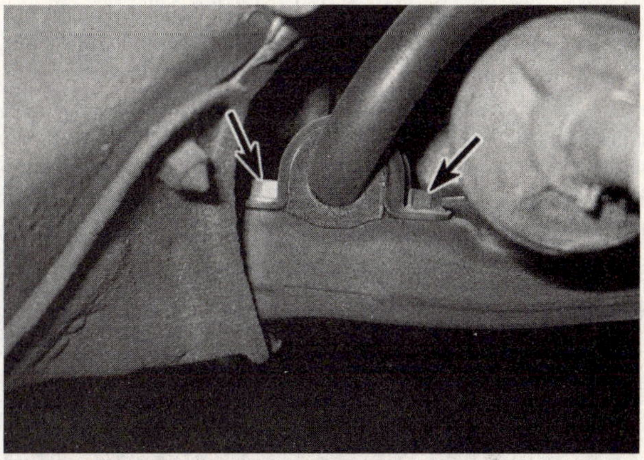

2.5 Stabilizer bar bushing retainer bolts

3 Shock absorber/coil spring assembly (front) - removal, inspection and installation

REMOVAL

Refer to illustrations 3.2, 3.4, 3.5 and 3.7

1 Loosen the wheel lug nuts, raise the vehicle and support it securely on jackstands. Remove the wheel. Support the lower control arm with a floor jack.

2 Remove the brake hose bracket from the shock absorber fork (see illustration). Disconnect the ABS wheel speed sensor wiring bracket if it interferes on your model.

3 On 2006.5 and later models, disconnect the stabilizer bar link from the shock absorber fork (see Section 2).

3.2 Unbolt the brake hose bracket and wheel speed sensor bracket from the shock absorber fork

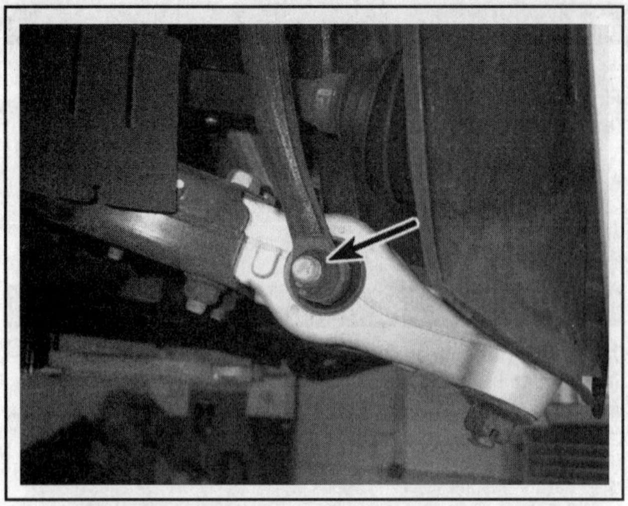

3.4 The lower end of the suspension fork attaches to the lower control arm with this bolt and nut

3.5 The upper end of the fork connects to the bottom of the shock absorber/spring assembly and is retained by this pinch bolt

4 Remove the fork-to-lower control arm bolt (see illustration).

5 Loosen the pinch bolt at the top of the fork and then remove the fork (see illustration).

6 If the shock absorber is to be disassembled, loosen, but do not remove, the damper shaft nut (in the center of the upper mount).

7 Support the shock and spring assembly with one hand (or have an assistant hold it) and remove the three shock absorber-to-shock tower nuts in the engine compartment (see illustration). Remove the assembly out from the fenderwell.

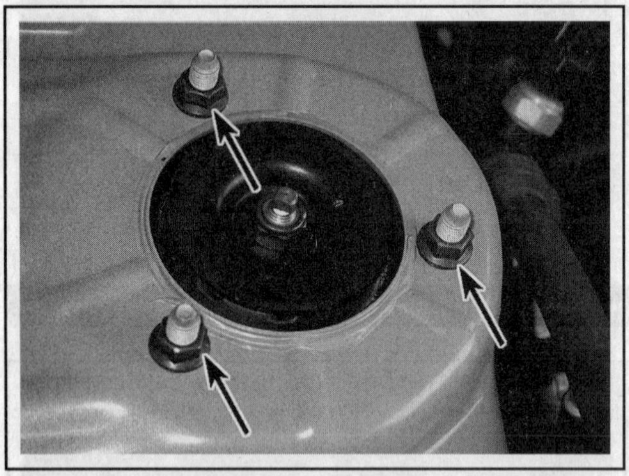

3.7 Remove the shock absorber upper mounting nuts.

⁂ WARNING:

Don't remove the nut in the center. If you plan on disassembling the shock absorber/coil spring unit, you may loosen it to make removal easier later

INSPECTION

8 Check the shock absorber body for leaking fluid, dents, cracks and other obvious damage that would warrant repair or replacement.

9 Check the coil spring for chips or cracks in the spring coating (this can cause premature spring failure due to corrosion). Inspect the spring seat for cuts, hardness and general deterioration.

10 If any undesirable conditions exist, proceed to the disassembly procedure (see Section 4).

INSTALLATION

11 Guide the assembly up into the fenderwell and insert the upper mounting studs through the holes in the shock tower. Once the studs protrude from the shock tower, install the nuts so the shock absorber assembly won't fall back through. This is most easily accomplished with the help of an assistant, as the unit is quite heavy and awkward.

12 Install the fork to the lower part of the shock absorber and the lower control arm. Tighten all fasteners to the torques listed in this Chapter's Specifications.

⁂ CAUTION:

Before tightening the shock absorber fork-to-lower control arm fasteners, raise the outer end of the lower control arm with a floor jack to simulate normal ride height.

13 Reattach the brake hose bracket and ABS wheel speed sensor bracket.

14 Install the wheel and lug nuts, then lower the vehicle and tighten the lug nuts to the torque listed in the Chapter 1 Specifications.

4 Shock absorbers/coil springs (front) - replacement

1 If the shocks or coil springs exhibit the telltale signs of wear (leaking fluid, loss of damping capability, chipped, sagging or cracked coil springs), explore all options before beginning any work. The shock absorber assemblies are not serviceable and must be replaced if a problem develops. Whichever route you choose to take, check on the cost and availability of parts before disassembling your vehicle.

WARNING:

Disassembling a coil-over shock absorber is potentially dangerous and utmost attention must be directed to the job, or serious injury may result. Use only a high-quality spring compressor and carefully follow the manufacturer's instructions furnished with the tool. After removing the coil spring from the shock absorber assembly, set it aside in a safe, isolated area.

DISASSEMBLY

Refer to illustrations 4.3, 4.4, 4.5, 4.6 and 4.7

2 Remove the shock absorber and spring assembly (see Section 3). Mount the assembly in a vise. Line the vise jaws with wood or rags to prevent damage to the unit and don't tighten the vise excessively.

3 Following the tool manufacturer's instructions, install the spring compressor (which can be obtained at most auto parts stores or equipment yards on a daily rental basis) on the spring and compress it sufficiently to relieve all force from the upper spring seat (see illustration). This can be verified by wiggling the spring.

4 Unscrew the damper shaft nut (see illustration).

5 Remove the nut and upper support components (see illustration). Keep all of the parts in order. Check the rubber portion of the suspension support for cracking and general deterioration. If there is any separation of the rubber, replace it.

6 Remove the upper spring seat from the damper shaft (see illustration). Check the spring seat for cracking and hardness; replace it if necessary. Remove the upper insulator.

7 Carefully lift the compressed spring from the assembly (see illustration) and set it in a safe place.

4.3 Install the spring compressor in accordance with the tool manufacturer's instructions and compress the spring until all pressure is relieved from the upper spring seat

4.4 Remove the damper shaft nut

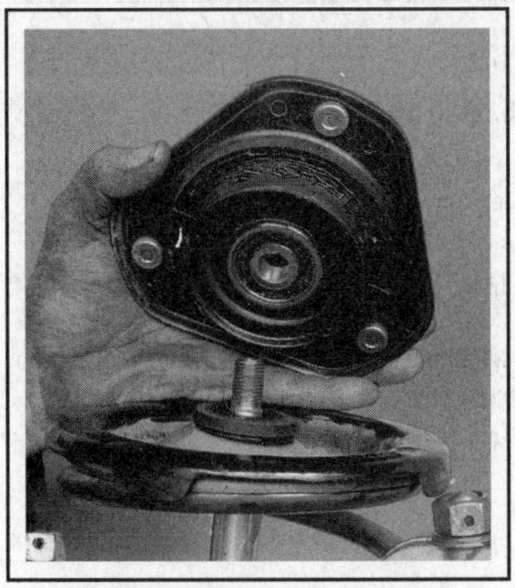

4.5 Lift the suspension support off the damper shaft

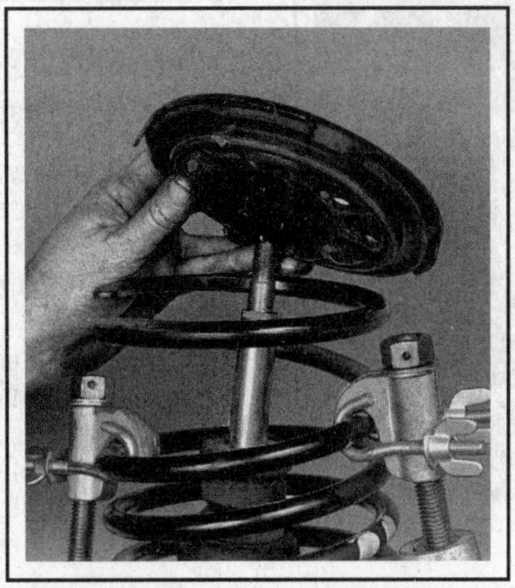

4.6 Remove the spring seat from the damper shaft

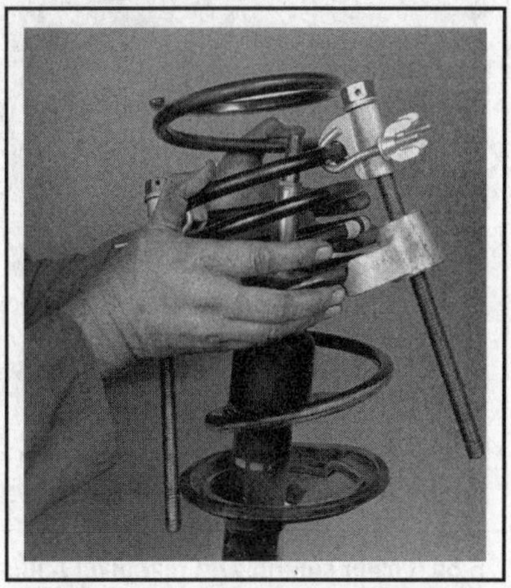

4.7 Remove the compressed spring assembly - keep the ends of the spring pointed away from your body

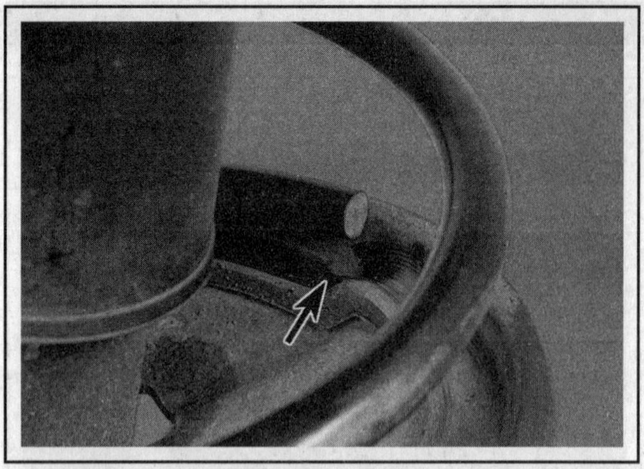

4.11 When installing the spring, make sure the end fits into the recessed portion of the lower seat

4.12 The flats on the damper shaft must match up with the flats in the spring seat

WARNING:

Never place your head near the end of the spring!

8 Slide the rubber bumper off the damper shaft.

9 Check the lower insulator for wear, cracking and hardness and replace it if necessary.

REASSEMBLY

Refer to illustrations 4.11 and 4.12

10 If the lower insulator is being replaced, set it into position with the dropped portion seated in the lowest part of the seat. Extend the damper rod to its full length and install the rubber bumper.

11 Carefully place the coil spring onto the lower insulator, with the end of the spring resting in the lowest part of the insulator (see illustration). The paint marks should face the outside of the vehicle.

12 Install the upper insulator on the spring. Install the spring seat, making sure that the flats in the hole in the seat match up with the flats on the damper shaft (see illustration).

13 Install the damper nut and tighten it to the torque listed in this Chapter's Specifications. Don't allow the holes in the spring seats to become misaligned. Remove the spring compressor tool.

14 Install the shock absorber/spring assembly.

5 Control arms (front) - removal and installation

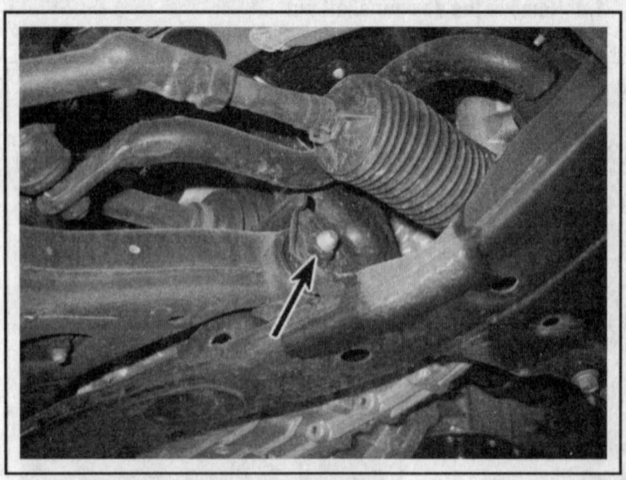

5.5a Lower control arm rear pivot bolt/nut

REMOVAL

Lower control arms

Refer to illustrations 5.5a, 5.5b and 5.6

1 Loosen the wheel lug nuts on the side to be dismantled, raise the front of the vehicle, support it securely on jackstands and remove the wheel.

2 Detach the lower balljoint from the control arm (see illustration 6.3).

3 Remove the bolt from the lower part of the shock absorber fork to disconnect it from the lower control arm (see illustration 3.4).

4 On 2001 through 2006 models, disconnect the stabilizer bar link from the lower control arm.

5 Remove the lower control arm mounting bolts (see illustrations).

6 Remove the control arm.

5.5b Lower control arm front mounting bolt

5.6 The lower control arm is made of two parts - these bolts attach the two pieces

➡ **Note: The two-piece lower front control arm can be further disassembled if required (see illustration).**

Upper control arms

➧ **Refer to illustrations 5.8 and 5.12**

7 Loosen the wheel lug nuts on the side to be dismantled, raise the front of the vehicle, support it securely on jackstands and remove the wheel.

8 Remove the lock pin (or cotter pin) and loosen the nut on the upper balljoint a few turns, but don't remove it completely (see illustration).

➡ **Note: Loosening the nut (without removing it) will prevent the balljoint and control arm from separating violently.**

9 Attach a balljoint/tie-rod end removal tool to the balljoint (see illustration 6.5). These tools are available at auto parts stores and rental yards. A pickle fork-type tool can also be used, but only if the balljoint is to be replaced, as it will damage the rubber boot.

10 Tighten the tool to break the balljoint free of the steering knuckle, then remove the nut and separate the balljoint/upper control arm from the steering knuckle.

11 On 2006.5 and later models, refer to Section 3 and remove the shock absorber/spring assembly for access to the control arm mounting bolts.

12 On 2001 through 2006 models, open the hood and remove the upper control arm mount nuts. On 2006.5 and later models, remove the two control arm pivot bolts (see illustration). Remove the control arm. On 2001 through 2006 models, the pivot bolts can now be removed and the mounts separated from the arm, if desired.

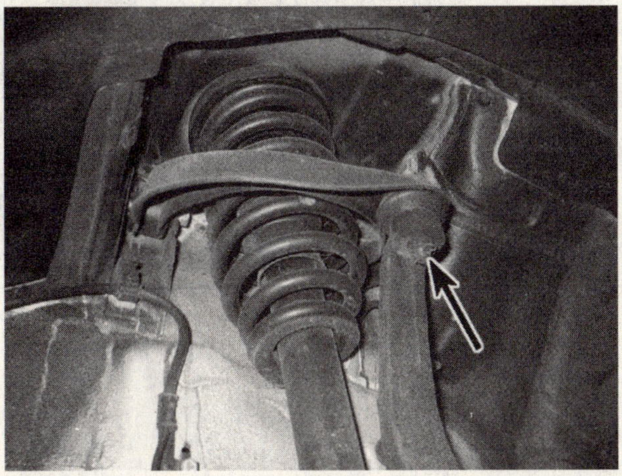

5.8 Remove the lock pin or cotter pin from the ballstud, then loosen the nut

5.12 Locations of the upper control arm pivot bolts (the shock absorber/coil spring unit must be removed to unscrew them)

INSTALLATION

13 Installation is the reverse of removal. Be sure to tighten all fasteners to the torque listed in this Chapter's Specifications, and use a new cotter pin.

➡ Note: Before tightening the rear pivot bolt nut on 2006.5 and later models, raise the outer end of the control arm with a floor jack to simulate normal ride height.

➡ Note: The balljoints on some models use traditional cotter pins which must be replaced with new ones during installation. Other models use spring-steel lock pins; these can be re-used if they are in good condition.

14 Install the wheel and lug nuts, lower the vehicle and tighten the lug nuts to the torque listed in the Chapter 1 Specifications.

15 It's a good idea to have the front wheel alignment checked, and if necessary, adjusted after this job has been performed.

6 Balljoints - replacement

LOWER

Refer to illustrations 6.3 and 6.5

1 Loosen the wheel lug nuts on the side to be dismantled, raise the front of the vehicle, support it securely on jackstands and remove the wheel.

2 Place a floor jack under the lower control arm to support it.

3 Remove the cotter pin and loosen the nut on the lower balljoint a few turns (see illustration).

➡ Note: Loosening the nut (without removing it) will prevent the balljoint and control arm from separating violently.

6.3 Lower balljoint details

A Balljoint-to-control arm nut (and cotter pin)
B Balljoint-to-steering knuckle bolts

4 Unbolt the lower balljoint from the steering knuckle.

5 Attach a balljoint/tie-rod end removal tool to the balljoint (see illustration). These tools are available at auto parts stores and rental yards. A pickle fork-type tool can also be used but only if the balljoint is to be replaced, as it will damage the rubber boot.

6 Tighten the tool to break the balljoint free of the lower control arm.

7 Remove the nut and detach the balljoint from the control arm.

8 Installation is the reverse of removal. Tighten all fasteners to the torque values listed in this Chapter's Specifications.

UPPER

9 If the balljoint has excessive play, the entire upper control arm must be replaced; at the time of writing, the balljoint was not available separately.

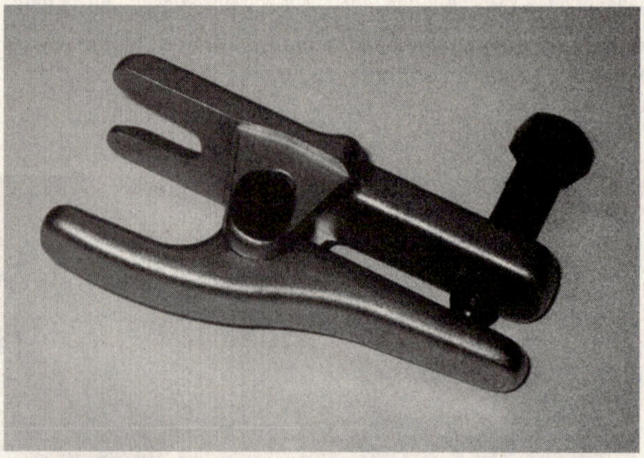

6.5 A balljoint separator tool like this one is available at most automotive parts stores and will not damage the balljoint boot when used correctly

7 Steering knuckle and hub - removal and installation

WARNING:

Dust created by the brake system is harmful to your health. Never blow it out with compressed air and don't inhale any of it. Do not, under any circumstances, use petroleum-based solvents to clean brake parts. Use brake system cleaner only.

REMOVAL

1 Loosen the driveaxle/hub nut (see Chapter 8). Loosen the wheel lug nuts, raise the vehicle and support it securely on jackstands. Remove the wheel.

2 Remove the wheel speed sensor from the knuckle and remove

the brake disc from the hub (see Chapter 9). Be sure to hang the caliper with a piece of wire.

3 Remove the driveaxle/hub nut. Tap the driveaxle in with a plastic hammer to loosen it from the splines.

4 Separate the tie-rod end from the steering knuckle arm (see Section 17).

5 Unbolt the lower balljoint from the steering knuckle (see illustration 6.3).

6 Disconnect the upper balljoint from the knuckle (see Section 5).

7 Push the driveaxle from the hub as described in Chapter 8 and remove the knuckle. Support the end of the driveaxle with a piece of wire.

INSTALLATION

8 Guide the knuckle and hub assembly into position, inserting the driveaxle into the hub.

9 Attach the upper balljoint to the knuckle (see Section 5).

10 Install the lower balljoint (see Section 6).

11 Attach the tie-rod to the steering knuckle arm (see Section 17). Tighten the balljoint nuts and the tie-rod nut to the torques listed in this Chapter's Specifications. Replace all cotter pins with new ones.

➡ **Note: The balljoints on some models use spring-steel lock pins; unlike cotter pins which must be bent (and sometimes cut) after insertion, these can be re-used if they are in good condition.**

12 Place the brake disc on the hub and install the caliper and wheel speed sensor as outlined in Chapter 9.

13 Install the driveaxle/hub nut and tighten it securely (final tightening will be carried out when the vehicle is lowered).

14 Install the wheel and lug nuts, lower the vehicle and tighten the lug nuts to the torque listed in the Chapter 1 Specifications.

15 Tighten the driveaxle/hub nut to the torque listed in the Chapter 8 Specifications (see Chapter 8).

8 Hub and bearing assembly (front) - removal and installation

Due to the special tools and expertise required to press the hub and bearing from the steering knuckle, this job should be left to a professional shop. However, the steering knuckle and hub may be removed and the assembly taken to a dealer service department or other qualified repair shop. See Section 7 for the steering knuckle and hub removal procedure.

9 Stabilizer bar and bushings (rear) - removal and installation

➧ **Refer to illustrations 9.3a, 9.3b and 9.4**

1 Loosen the rear wheel lug nuts for one wheel. Raise the rear of the vehicle and support it securely on jackstands. Remove one rear wheel.

2 Disconnect the exhaust system hangers if needed to provide clearance.

3 Disconnect the stabilizer bar links from the bar (see illustrations).

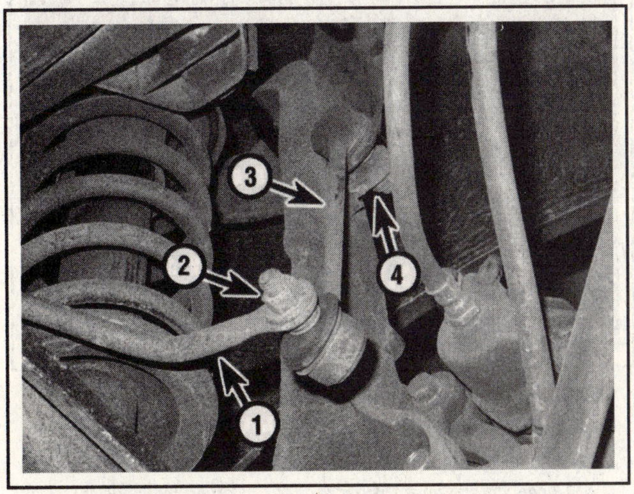

9.3a Rear stabilizer bar details (2001 through 2006 models):

1 *Stabilizer bar*
2 *Stabilizer-to-link rod nut*
3 *Link rod*
4 *Link rod-to-carrier nut*

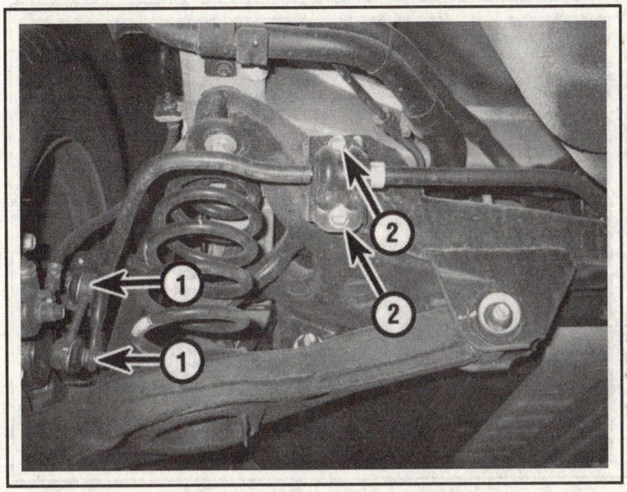

9.3b Rear stabilizer bar details (2006.5 and later models):

1 *Link nuts*
2 *Bushing retainer bolts*

9.4 Rear stabilizer bar bushing retainer bolts (2001 through 2006 models; later models, see illustration 9.3b)

4 Unbolt the stabilizer bar bushing retainers (see illustration).

5 The stabilizer bar can now be removed from the vehicle. Remove the bushings from the stabilizer bar, noting their positions.

6 Check the bushings for wear, hardness, distortion, cracking and other signs of deterioration, replacing them if necessary. Check the stabilizer bar links for loose ballstuds.

7 Using a wire brush, clean the areas of the bar where the bushings ride. Lubricate the inside and outside of the new bushings with vegetable oil (used in cooking).

CAUTION:

Don't use petroleum or mineral-based lubricants or brake fluid - they will lead to deterioration of the bushings.

8 Installation is the reverse of removal.

10 Shock absorbers (rear) - removal and installation

1 Raise the rear of the vehicle and support it securely on jackstands placed under the body jacking points.

2 Support the outer end of the lower control arm with a floor jack to prevent it from dropping when the shock absorber is disconnected.

2001 THROUGH 2006 MODELS

Refer to illustrations 10.3 and 10.4

Note: These models use coil-over shock absorber assemblies.

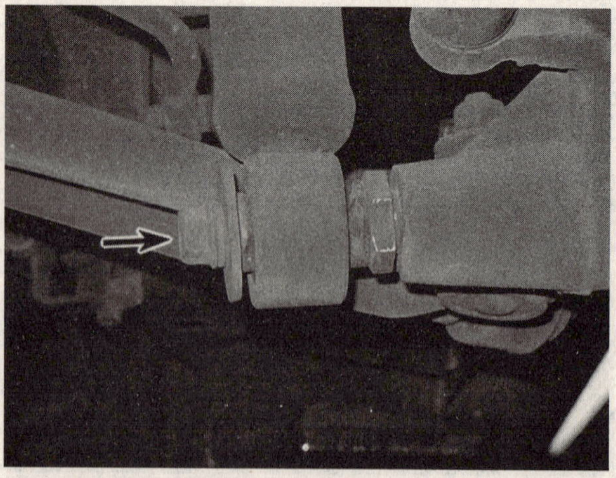

10.3 Rear shock absorber lower mounting bolt (2001 through 2006 models)

3 Remove the bolt from the lower end of the shock absorber (see illustration).

4 Unbolt the upper control arm from the carrier (knuckle) (see illustration).

5 Remove the bolts from the upper shock mounting bracket and lift the assembly out of the vehicle.

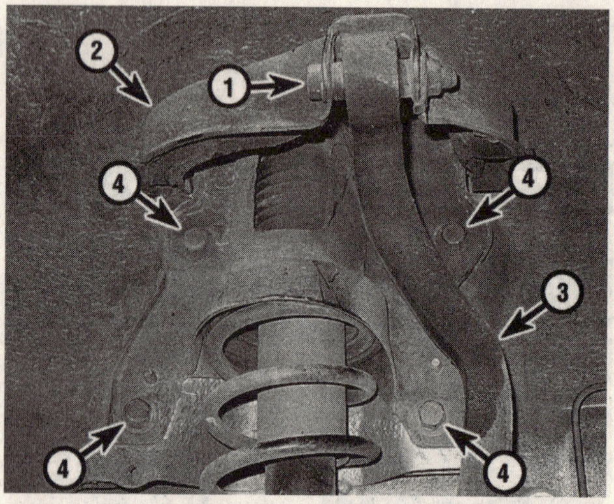

10.4 Rear shock absorber upper mounting details (2001 through 2006 models):

1 *Upper control arm-to-carrier bolt*
2 *Upper control arm*
3 *Carrier (rear knuckle)*
4 *Rear shock absorber upper mounting bracket bolts*

10.6 Rear shock absorber lower mounting bolt/nut (2006.5 and later models)

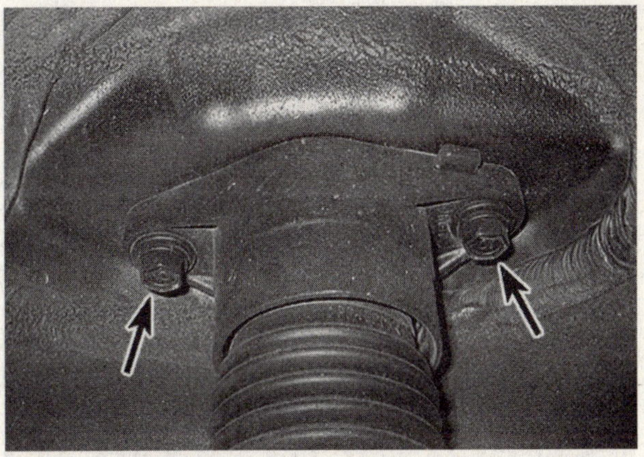

10.7 Rear shock absorber upper mounting bolts (2006.5 and later models)

2006.5 AND LATER MODELS

➧ **Refer to illustrations 10.6 and 10.7**

6 Remove the bolt from the lower end of the shock absorber (see illustration).

7 Unbolt the upper end of the shock absorber and remove it (see illustration).

ALL MODELS

8 Refer to Section 11 for information about disassembling the shock absorber/coil spring assembly.

9 Installation is the reverse of removal. Tighten the fasteners to the torque values listed in this Chapter's Specifications.

11 Coil springs (rear) - removal and installation

2001 THROUGH 2006 MODELS

Removal

WARNING:

Disassembling a coil-over shock absorber is potentially dangerous and utmost attention must be directed to the job, or serious injury may result. Use only a high-quality spring compressor and carefully follow the manufacturer's instructions furnished with the tool. After removing the coil spring from the shock absorber assembly, set it aside in a safe, isolated area.

➡ **Note: The coil springs on these vehicles are part of an assembly that includes the shock absorbers.**

1 Refer to Section 10 and remove the shock absorber/coil spring assembly from the vehicle.

2 Mount the assembly in a vise. Line the vise jaws with wood or rags to prevent damage to the unit and don't tighten the vise excessively.

3 Following the tool manufacturer's instructions, install a spring compressor (which can be obtained at most auto parts stores or equipment yards on a daily rental basis) on the spring and compress it sufficiently to relieve all force from the upper spring seat. This can be verified by wiggling the spring.

4 Unscrew the damper shaft nut. It will be necessary to hold the end of the shaft with locking pliers while turning the nut.

5 Remove the nut, mounting bracket, dust cover and spring seat. Keep all of the parts in order.

6 Carefully lift the compressed spring from the assembly and set it in a safe place.

WARNING:

Never place your head near the end of the spring!

7 Slide the rubber bumper off the damper shaft, if equipped.

8 Check the lower insulator for wear, cracking and hardness and replace it if necessary.

Installation

9 Carefully place the coil spring onto the lower insulator, with the end of the spring resting in the lowest part of the insulator (see illustration 4.11).

10 Install the upper insulator on the spring. Install the spring seat, making sure that is oriented correctly.

11 Install the damper nut and tighten it to the torque listed in this Chapter's Specifications. Don't allow the holes in the spring seats to become misaligned. Remove the spring compressor tool.

12 Install the shock absorber/spring assembly.

11.17 Lower control arm-to-hub carrier bolt (2006.5 and later models)

2006.5 AND LATER MODELS

Refer to illustration 11.17

13 Loosen the rear wheel lug nuts. Raise the vehicle and support it securely on jackstands.

14 Remove the wheel.

15 Place a floor jack under the outer part of the lower control arm to prevent movement when the shock absorber is disconnected.

16 Disconnect the lower end of the shock absorber from the hub carrier (see illustration 10.3).

17 Disconnect the outer end of the lower control arm from the hub carrier (see illustration).

18 Very slowly and carefully lower the jack until the spring can be removed from its seats. Pull the spring free.

19 Installation is the reverse of removal. Before tightening the lower control arm-to-hub carrier bolt/nut, raise the outer end of the lower control arm with a floor jack to simulate normal ride height.

12 Suspension arms (rear) - removal and installation

Refer to illustration 12.1

Note: When installing any rear suspension arms, tighten all the bolts hand-tight only, move the suspension to its normal ride-height angle and position (a floor jack can be used to do this), then fully tighten the bolts.

1 Loosen the rear wheel lug nuts, raise the rear of the vehicle and support it securely on jackstands. Remove the rear wheel for better access to the control arms; see illustration 1.2a (2001 through 2006 models) or the accompanying illustration (2006.5 and later models).

UPPER ARM

2001 through 2006 models

Refer to illustration 12.2

2 Unbolt the outer end of the control arm from the hub assembly (see illustration).

3 Remove the pivot bolts from the inner end of the control arm and lift it out.

4 Installation is the reverse of removal.

5 It's a good idea to have the rear wheel alignment checked and, if necessary, adjusted.

2006.5 and later models

6 Disconnect the parking brake cable, the brake fluid hose and the wheel speed sensor from the suspension.

7 Support the rear hub carrier with a floor jack, then disconnect the lower end of the shock absorber.

8 Disconnect the rear end of the trailing arm by removing its pivot bolt.

9 Remove the rear exhaust system section, including the muffler.

10 Support the entire rear crossmember with a floor jack. A floor jack with a transmission jack head adapter will work even better.

11 Remove the four crossmember bolts.

12 Remove the cotter pin and loosen the nut on the upper balljoint a

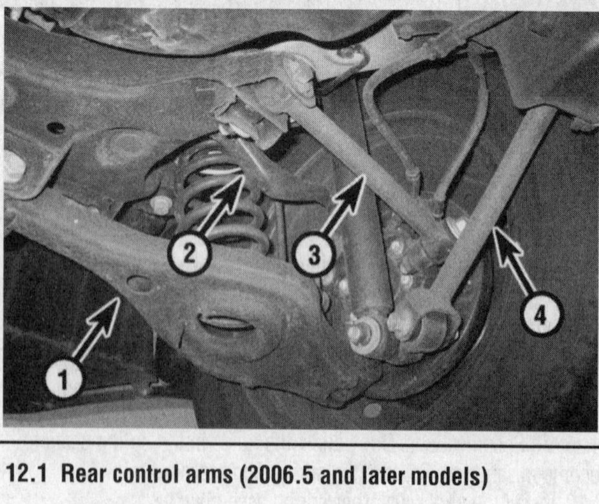

12.1 Rear control arms (2006.5 and later models)

1 Lower control arm
2 Upper control arm
3 Assist arm
4 Trailing arm

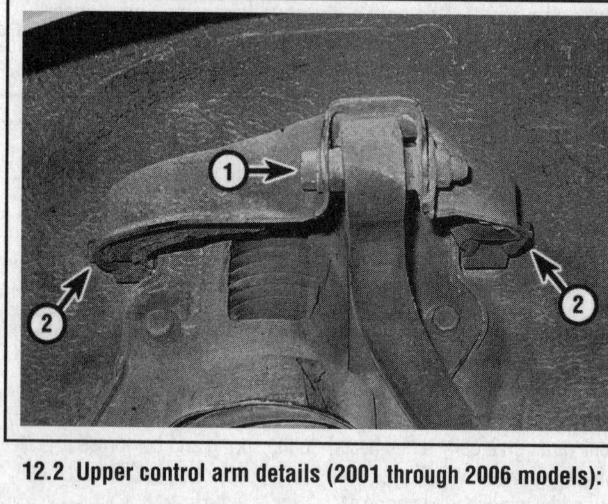

12.2 Upper control arm details (2001 through 2006 models):

1 Control arm-to-carrier bolt
2 Control arm pivot bolts

few turns.

13 Attach a balljoint/tie-rod end removal tool to the upper balljoint (see illustration 6.5). These tools are available at auto parts stores and rental yards. Tighten the tool to break the balljoint free. Remove the nut and detach the balljoint from the hub carrier.

14 Lower the rear crossmember using the floor jack for access to the upper control arm pivot bolts/nuts.

15 Remove the pivot bolts/nuts and lift out the upper control arm.

16 Installation is the reverse of removal. It's a good idea to have the rear wheel alignment checked and, if necessary, adjusted.

LOWER ARM

2001 through 2006 models

➧ Refer to illustration 12.17

17 Attach a balljoint/tie-rod end removal tool to the lower balljoint (see illustration). These tools are available at auto parts stores and rental yards.

18 Tighten the tool to break the balljoint free of the lower control arm.

19 Pull the control arm and balljoint out of the hub carrier.

20 Remove the pivot bolt from the inner end of the arm and remove the arm from the vehicle.

21 Installation is the reverse of removal. Have the rear wheel alignment checked and, if necessary, adjusted.

2006.5 and later models

➧ Refer to illustration 12.23

22 Refer to Section 11 and remove the coil spring assembly.

23 Mark the position of the camber adjuster to the subframe (see illustration). Remove the pivot bolts from each end of the lower control arm, then lift the arm out.

24 Installation is the reverse of removal. Have the rear wheel alignment checked and, if necessary, adjusted.

12.23 Mark the camber adjusters to the subframe before disassembling them so they can be installed in exactly the same position

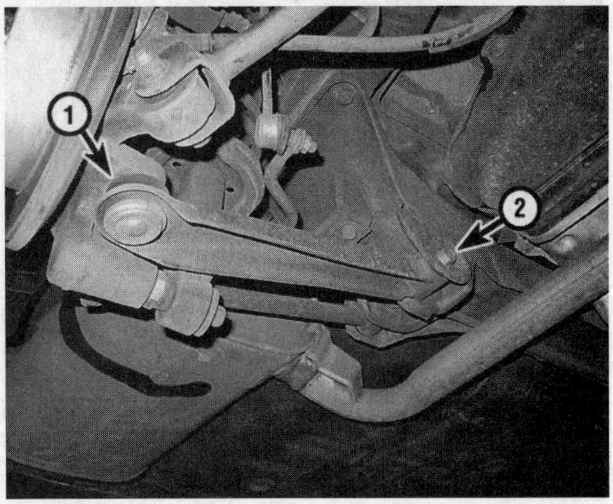

12.17 Rear lower suspension arm details (2001 through 2006 models):

1 *Lower arm-to-carrier balljoint*
2 *Lower arm pivot bolt*

TRAILING ARM

➧ Refer to illustration 12.26

25 Mark the position of the camber adjuster to the subframe (see illustration 12.23).

26 Remove the pivot bolts from each end of the trailing arm (see illustration) and remove the arm.

27 Installation is the reverse of removal. Have the rear wheel alignment checked and, if necessary, adjusted.

12.26 Typical trailing arm details (2001 through 2006 shown, others similar):

1 *Trailing arm-to-carrier bolt/nut*
2 *Trailing arm pivot bolt (not visible in this photo)*

12.28 **Typical assist arm details (2006.5 and later shown, other similar):**

1 *Assist arm-to-carrier bolt/nut*
2 *Assist arm pivot/camber adjustment bolt*

ASSIST ARM

Refer to illustration 12.28

28 Remove the pivot bolt from each end of the assist arm and lift it out (see illustration).

29 Installation is the reverse of removal. Have the rear wheel alignment checked and, if necessary, adjusted.

13 Hub and bearing assembly (rear) - removal and installation

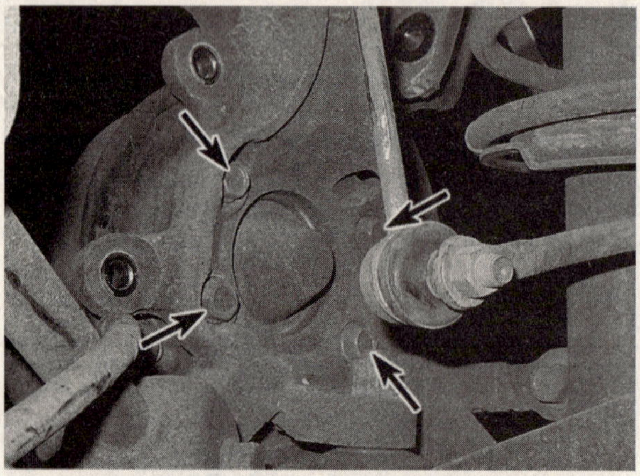

13.6 **Rear hub and bearing assembly mounting bolts**

Refer to illustration 13.6

1 Loosen the rear wheel lug nuts.

2 Raise the vehicle and support it securely on jackstands. Release the parking brake.

3 Remove the rear wheel.

4 Disconnect the wheel speed sensor from the hub carrier.

5 Refer to Chapter 9 and remove the brake disc.

6 Remove the four rear hub mounting bolts (see illustration) and detach the hub assembly from the hub carrier.

7 Further disassembly of the hub requires a large puller and a hydraulic press. It is recommended that the unit be taken to an automotive shop experienced in this work.

8 Installation is the reverse of removal. Be sure to put the part of the outer bearing support with the round protrusion facing upward, and tighten the mounting fasteners to the torque listed in this Chapter's Specifications. If you removed the main nut, be sure to stake the nut to the spindle after tightening it.

14 Steering system - general information

All models are equipped with rack-and-pinion steering. The steering gear is bolted to the subframe and operates the steering knuckles via tie-rods. The inner ends of the tie-rods are protected by rubber boots that should be inspected periodically for secure attachment, tears and leaking lubricant.

The power assist system consists of a belt-driven pump and the associated lines and hoses. The fluid level in the power steering pump reservoir should be checked periodically (see Chapter 1). Some vehicles are equipped with electronic power steering. On these vehicles, the power steering pump receives input from the vehicle speed sensor in order to vary the amount of pressure/assist it provides.

The steering wheel operates the steering shaft, which actuates the steering gear through universal joints. Looseness in the steering can be caused by wear in the steering shaft universal joints, the steering gear, the tie-rod ends and loose retaining bolts.

15 Steering wheel - removal and installation

WARNING:

The models covered by this manual are equipped with Supplemental Restraint Systems (SRS), more commonly known as airbags. Always disable the airbag system before working in the vicinity of any airbag system component to avoid the possibility of accidental deployment of the airbag(s), which could cause personal injury (see Chapter 12).

REMOVAL

➧ Refer to illustrations 15.2, 15.3, 15.4, 15.5 and 15.6

1 Turn the steering wheel so that the wheels are pointing straight ahead. Turn the ignition key to Off, then disconnect the cable from the negative terminal of the battery (see Chapter 5, Section 1).

2 On 2001 through 2006 models, remove the plastic covers on the sides of the steering wheel. On all models, remove the airbag module retaining screws (see illustration).

3 Carefully pull off the airbag module (see illustration).

4 Disconnect the electrical connectors (see illustration) and place the airbag in a safe location with the pad facing up.

5 Make match marks on the steering shaft and the hub so the steering wheel can be reinstalled in exactly the same position (see illustration). Remove the nut.

6 Disconnect any horn wiring (see illustration).

7 Try to remove the steering wheel by shaking the rim back and forth manually. If this fails, attach a steering wheel puller.

15.2 The screws retaining the airbag module have Torx heads

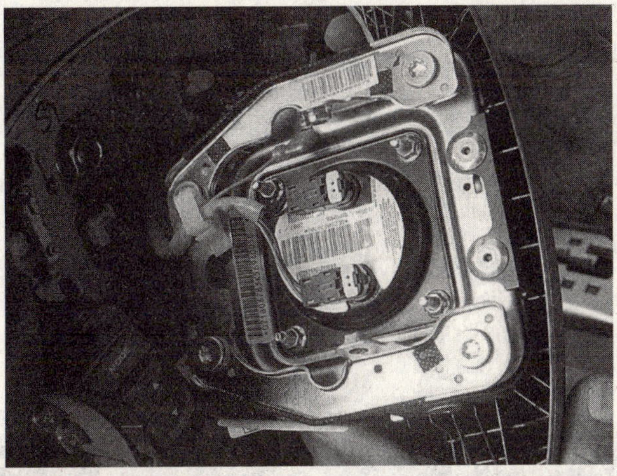

15.3 Lift the airbag module from the steering wheel, but be careful to avoid pulling on the wiring

15.4 The airbag electrical connectors have safety latches that must be released prior to disconnecting them

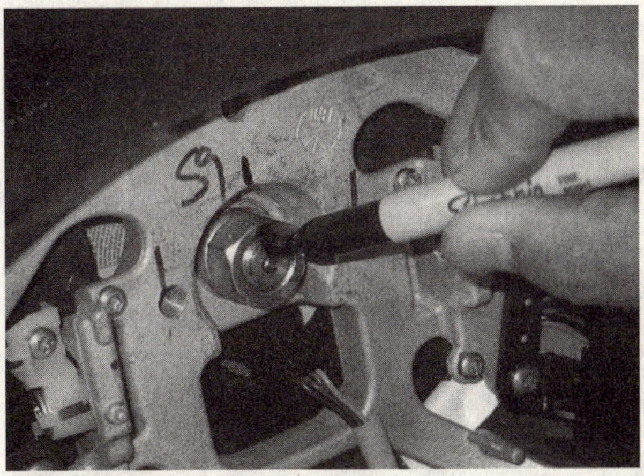

15.5 The steering shaft and the steering wheel must have match marks made so they can be assembled in the same orientation

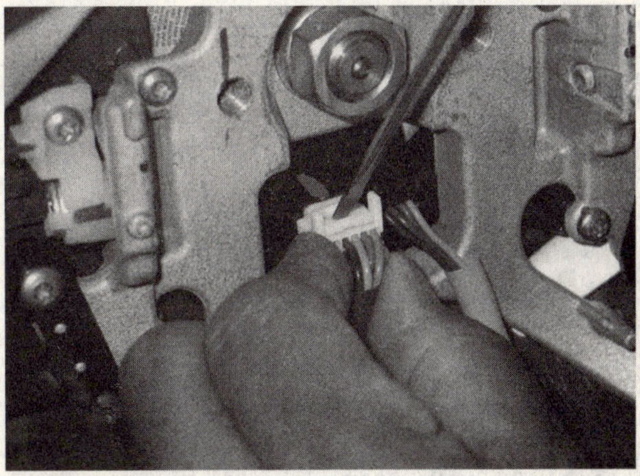

15.6 Disconnect all remaining wiring; all airbag wiring is covered with bright yellow sheathing

CAUTION:

Don't use a hammer in any way on the steering wheel or column.

8 Lift the wheel from the column while carefully threading the wires through it.

INSTALLATION

9 Make sure that the front wheels are facing straight ahead. If the clockspring has turned and is not centered, turn the hub in either direction until it stops (don't apply too much force). Now, rotate the hub in the other direction, counting the number of turns it takes to reach the opposite stop. Divide that number by two, then turn the hub back that many turns, approximately, until the neutral position indicator is aligned with its corresponding mark.

10 To install the wheel, align the mark on the steering wheel hub with the mark on the shaft and slip the wheel onto the shaft. Install the nut and tighten it to the torque listed in this Chapter's Specifications.

11 Plug in the electrical connectors for the airbag module and any other connectors. Make sure the module connector locks are pushed back into position.

12 Install the airbag module and tighten the retaining screws to the torque listed in this Chapter's Specifications.

13 Connect the negative battery cable (see Chapter 5, Section 1).

16 Steering column - removal and installation

REMOVAL

Refer to illustrations 16.6 and 16.8

1 Park the vehicle with the wheels pointing straight ahead. Disconnect the cable from the negative terminal of the battery.

2 Remove the steering wheel (see Section 15), then turn the ignition key to the LOCK position to prevent the steering shaft from turning.

CAUTION:

If this is not done, the airbag clockspring could be damaged.

3 Remove the steering column upper and lower covers (see Chapter 11).

4 Remove the driver's knee bolster (see Chapter 11, Section 24). Also remove the metal reinforcement behind it.

5 Remove the multi-function switch (see Chapter 12).

6 Mark the position of the lower universal joint at the steering gear pinion shaft, then remove the pinch bolt from the universal joint (see illustration).

7 On 2006.5 and later models, remove the shaft dust cover bolts from inside the vehicle.

8 Remove the mounting nuts and bolts (see illustration), then remove the steering column, separating it from the U-joint.

INSTALLATION

9 Guide the steering column into position, connect the intermediate shaft, then install the mounting nuts and U-joint pinch bolt, but don't tighten them yet.

10 Tighten the column mounting nuts to the torque listed in this Chapter's Specifications.

11 Tightening the pinch bolt to the torque listed in this Chapter's Specifications.

12 The remainder of installation is the reverse of removal.

WARNING:

Make sure the airbag clockspring is still in its centered position. If it isn't, refer to Section 15.

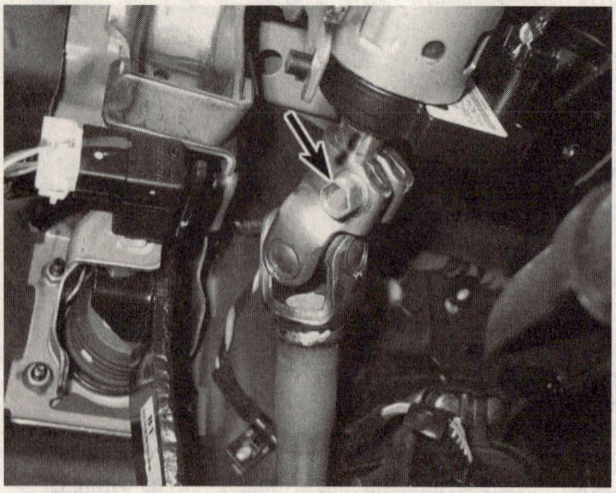

16.6 Steering column U-joint pinch bolt

16.8 Steering column mounting fasteners

17 Tie-rod ends - removal and installation

REMOVAL

Refer to illustrations 17.2a, 17.2b and 17.4

1 Loosen the wheel lug nuts. Raise the front of the vehicle, support it securely on jackstands, block the rear wheels and set the parking brake. Remove the front wheel.

2 Hold the tie-rod with a wrench and loosen the jam nut enough to mark the position of the tie-rod end in relation to the threads (see illustrations).

3 Remove the cotter pin and loosen the nut on the tie-rod end stud.

4 Disconnect the tie-rod from the steering knuckle arm with a puller (see illustration). Remove the nut and separate the tie-rod.

5 Unscrew the tie-rod end from the tie-rod.

INSTALLATION

6 Thread the tie-rod end on to the marked position and insert the tie-rod stud into the steering knuckle arm. Install the castle nut on the stud and tighten it to the torque listed in this Chapter's Specifications. Install a new cotter pin.

7 Tighten the jam nut securely.

8 Install the wheel and lug nuts. Lower the vehicle and tighten the lug nuts to the torque listed in the Chapter 1 Specifications.

9 Have the alignment checked and, if necessary, adjusted.

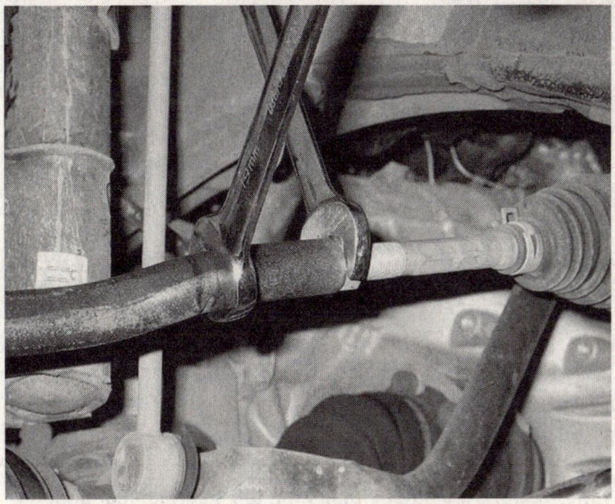

17.2a Hold the tie-rod end with a wrench and break the jam nut loose with another wrench

17.2b Back off the jam nut and mark the exposed threads to ensure that the new tie-rod end is threaded on the same number of turns

17.4 A balljoint separator like this can be used without removing the caliper lower mounting bolt for clearance

18 Steering gear boots - replacement

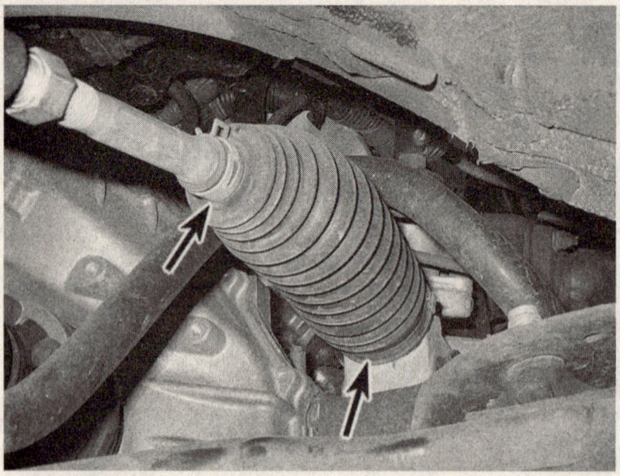

18.3 Remove the outer clamp from the steering gear boot with a pair of pliers; the inner clamp must be cut or pried off

➧ Refer to illustration 18.3

1 Loosen the lug nuts, raise the vehicle and support it securely on jackstands. Remove the wheel.

2 Remove the tie-rod end and jam nut (see Section 17).

3 Remove the steering gear boot clamps and slide off the boot (see illustration).

4 Before installing the new boot, wrap the threads and serrations on the end of the steering rod with a layer of tape so the small end of the new boot isn't damaged.

5 Slide the new boot into position on the steering gear until it seats in the groove in the steering rod, and install new clamps.

6 Remove the tape and install the tie-rod end (see Section 17).

7 Install the wheel and lug nuts. Lower the vehicle and tighten the lug nuts to the torque listed in the Chapter 1 Specifications.

8 Have the alignment checked by a dealer service department or an alignment shop.

19 Steering gear - removal and installation

✲✲ WARNING:

Make sure the steering shaft is not turned while the steering gear is removed or you could damage the clockspring for the airbag system. To prevent the shaft from turning, place the ignition key in the lock position or thread the seat belt through the steering wheel and clip it into place.

REMOVAL

➧ Refer to illustration 19.3

1 Park the vehicle with the front wheels pointing straight ahead. Loosen the front wheel lug nuts, raise the front of the vehicle and support it securely on jackstands. Apply the parking brake and remove the wheels. Remove the engine under-covers on models so equipped.

2 Place a drain pan under the steering gear. Detach the power steering pressure and return lines and cap the ends to prevent excessive fluid loss and contamination.

✲✲ CAUTION:

Use a flare-nut wrench for detaching the lines from the steering gear or the fittings could be severely damaged.

3 Mark the relationship of the intermediate shaft to the steering shaft U-joint and remove the pinch bolt (see illustration).

4 Separate the tie-rod ends from the steering knuckle arms (see Section 17).

5 Remove the front section of the exhaust system.

6 Support the engine from above with an engine support fixture or an engine hoist. Disconnect the front and rear engine roll-stopper mounts.

✲✲ WARNING:

DO NOT place any part of your body under the engine when it's supported only by a hoist or other lifting device.

7 Using two floor jacks, support the subframe. Position one jack on each side of the subframe, midway between the front and rear mounting points.

8 Remove all of the mounting bolts of the front subframe (see Section 22) and lower it for access to the steering gear mounting bolts. Separate the intermediate shaft U-joint from the steering gear input shaft as this is done.

9 Disconnect the pressure and return lines from the steering gear.

10 Remove the steering gear mounting bolts.

11 Maneuver the steering gear down and out.

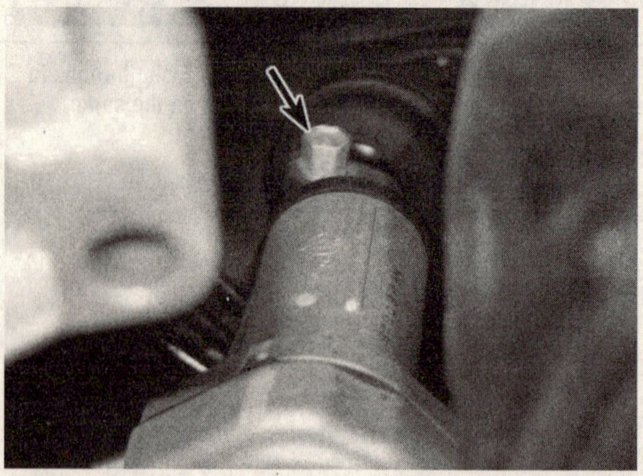

19.3 Intermediate shaft-to-steering gear input shaft pinch bolt

12 Check the steering gear mounting bushings for excessive wear or deterioration, replacing them if necessary.

INSTALLATION

13 If you're installing a new steering gear, center the pinion in the center of its travel by counting the number of turns lock to lock and setting the pinion midway.

14 Mount the steering gear to the subframe, install the mounting bolts and nuts and tighten them to the torque listed in this Chapter's Specifications.

15 Connect the power steering pressure and return hoses to the steering gear.

16 Raise the subframe into position and connect the intermediate shaft U-joint to the steering input shaft, aligning the marks.

17 Install the subframe bolts and tighten them to the torque listed in this Chapter's Specifications.

18 Install the steering shaft U-joint pinch bolt and tighten it to the torque listed in this Chapter's Specifications.

19 Connect the tie-rod ends to the steering knuckle arms and tighten them to the torque listed in this Chapter's Specification (see Section 17). Install new cotter pins.

20 The remainder of installation is the reverse of the removal procedure.

21 Fill the power steering fluid reservoir with the recommended fluid (see Chapter 1). Bleed the power steering system (see Section 21).

22 Have the alignment checked and, if necessary, adjusted.

20 Power steering pump - removal and installation

REMOVAL

➧ Refer to illustration 20.4

1 Disconnect the cable from the negative battery terminal (see Chapter 5, Section 1).

2 Using a large syringe or suction gun, suck as much fluid out of the power steering fluid reservoir as possible. Place a drain pan under the vehicle to catch any fluid that spills out when the hoses are disconnected.

3 Remove the drivebelt (see Chapter 1).

4 Detach the fluid suction hose from the pump (see illustration). Disconnect the electrical connector from the power steering pressure switch.

5 Disconnect the pressure line from the pump. Discard the sealing washers (new ones should be used when installing the line).

6 Disconnect the pressure switch.

7 Remove the mounting bolts and lift off the power steering pump.

INSTALLATION

8 Installation is the reverse of removal. Be sure to tighten the mounting bolts to the torque listed in this Chapter's Specifications, and use new sealing washers on the pressure line fitting.

9 Top up the fluid level in the reservoir (see Chapter 1) and bleed the system (see Section 21).

20.4 Power steering pump pressure line (A) and suction hose (B) connections (2001 through 2006 V6 models; other pumps similar)

21 Power steering system - bleeding

1 Following any operation in which the power steering fluid lines have been disconnected, the power steering system must be bled to remove all air and obtain proper steering performance.

2 With the front wheels in the straight-ahead position, check the power steering fluid level and, if low, add fluid.

3 Start the engine and allow it to idle. Recheck the fluid level and add more if necessary.

4 Bleed the system by turning the wheels fully from side to side, without hitting the stops. It may take several dozen turns to bleed the system. This will work the air out of the system. Keep the reservoir full of fluid as this is done.

➡ Note: This procedure can be done with the front of the vehicle raised with a jack and supported on jackstands. This makes it easier to turn the wheels back and forth during the bleeding process.

5 When the air is worked out of the system, return the wheels to the straight-ahead position and leave the vehicle running for several more minutes before shutting it off.

6 Road test the vehicle to be sure the steering system is functioning normally and noise free.

7 Recheck the fluid level to be sure it is up to the Hot mark on the dipstick while the engine is at normal operating temperature. Add fluid if necessary (see Chapter 1).

22 Subframe - removal and installation

Refer to illustration 22.10

1 Disconnect the cable from the negative battery terminal (see Chapter 5, Section 1).

2 Loosen the front wheel lug nuts, raise the front of the vehicle and support it securely on jackstands. Remove both front wheels.

Note: The jackstands must be behind the front suspension subframe, not supporting the vehicle by the subframe.

3 Remove any interfering front bumper trim components.

4 Disconnect the stabilizer bar links from the stabilizer bar (see Section 2).

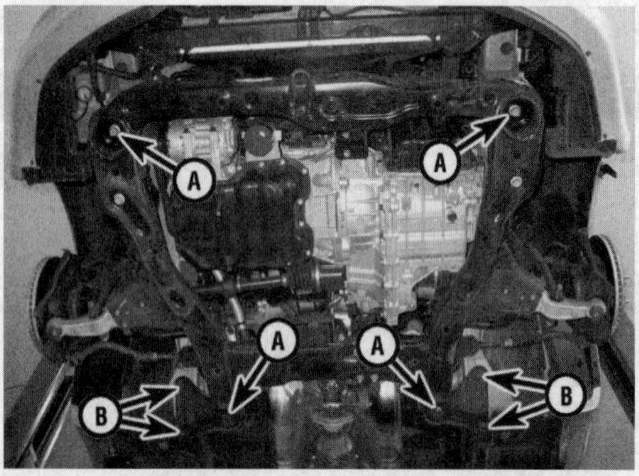

22.10 Subframe mounting bolts (A) and reinforcement bracket bolts (B)

5 Unbolt the lower balljoints from the steering knuckles (see illustration 6.3). Also unbolt the shock absorber forks from the control arms (see illustration 3.4).

6 Support the engine from above using an engine hoist or support fixture (see Chapter 2C).

WARNING:

DO NOT place any part of your body under the engine when it's supported only by a hoist or other lifting device.

7 Inspect the subframe for any hose, line or harness brackets that may be attached, and detach them.

8 Detach all engine and transaxle mounts from the subframe (see Chapter 2).

9 Using two floor jacks, support the subframe. Position one jack on each side of the subframe, midway between the front and rear mounting points.

10 With the jacks sufficiently supporting the subframe, remove the subframe mounting bolts and reinforcement bracket bolts (see illustration).

11 With the use of an assistant to steady the subframe, carefully lower the jacks far enough to access the steering gear mounting bolts. Remove the steering gear mounting bolts.

Note: Support the steering gear from above with a rope.

12 Lower the subframe to the ground.

13 Installation is the reverse of removal. Tighten all suspension and subframe fasteners to the torque listed in this Chapter's Specifications. Tighten the engine mount fasteners to the torque listed in the Chapter 2 Specifications.

23 Wheels and tires - general information

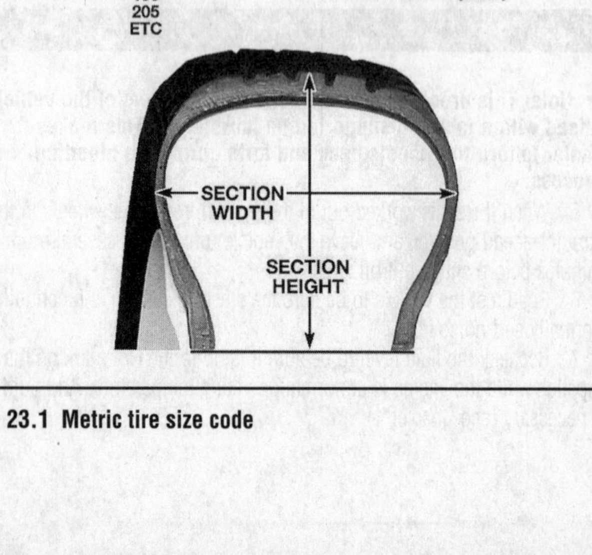

23.1 Metric tire size code

Refer to illustration 23.1

1 All vehicles covered by this manual are equipped with metric-sized fiberglass or steel belted radial tires (see illustration). Use of other size or type of tires may affect the ride and handling of the vehicle. Don't mix different types of tires, such as radials and bias belted, on the same vehicle as handling may be seriously affected. It's recommended that tires be replaced in pairs on the same axle, but if only one tire is being replaced, be sure it's the same size, structure and tread design as the other.

2 Because tire pressure has a substantial effect on handling and wear, the pressure on all tires should be checked at least once a month or before any extended trips (see Chapter 1).

3 Wheels must be replaced if they are bent, dented, leak air, have elongated bolt holes, are heavily rusted, out of vertical symmetry or if the lug nuts won't stay tight. Wheel repairs that use welding or peening are not recommended.

4 Tire and wheel balance is important in the overall handling, braking and performance of the vehicle. Unbalanced wheels can adversely affect handling and ride characteristics as well as tire life. Whenever a tire is installed on a wheel, the tire and wheel should be balanced by a shop with the proper equipment.

24 Wheel alignment - general information

Refer to illustration 24.1

A wheel alignment refers to the adjustments made to the wheels so they are in proper angular relationship to the suspension and the ground. Wheels that are out of proper alignment not only affect vehicle control, but also increase tire wear. The alignment angles normally measured are camber, caster and toe-in (see illustration).

Getting the proper wheel alignment is a very exacting process, one in which complicated and expensive machines are necessary to perform the job properly. Because of this, you should have a technician with the proper equipment perform these tasks. We will, however, use this space to give you a basic idea of what is involved with a wheel alignment so you can better understand the process and deal intelligently with the shop that does the work.

Toe-in is the turning in of the wheels. The purpose of a toe specification is to ensure parallel rolling of the wheels. In a vehicle with zero toe-in, the distance between the front edges of the wheels will be the same as the distance between the rear edges of the wheels. The actual amount of toe-in is normally only a fraction of an inch. On the front end, toe-in is controlled by the tie-rod end position on the tie-rod. On the rear end, it's controlled by cam bolts at the inner ends of the lower arms. Incorrect toe-in will cause the tires to wear improperly by making them scrub against the road surface.

Camber is the tilting of the wheels from vertical when viewed from one end of the vehicle. When the wheels tilt out at the top, the camber is said to be positive (+). When the wheels tilt in at the top the camber is negative (-). The amount of tilt is measured in degrees from vertical and this measurement is called the camber angle. This angle affects the amount of tire tread, which contacts the road and compensates for changes in the suspension geometry when the vehicle is cornering or traveling over an undulating surface.

Caster is the tilting of the front steering axis from the vertical. A tilt toward the rear is positive caster and a tilt toward the front is negative caster. Too little caster will make the front end wander, while too much caster can make the steering effort higher.

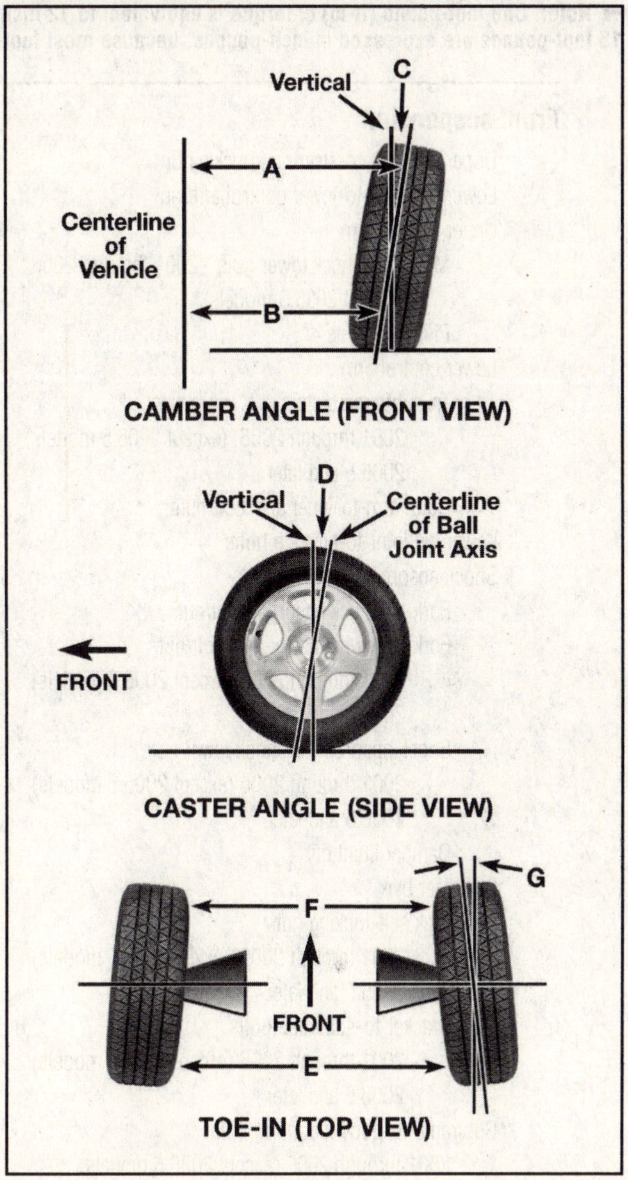

24.1 Camber, caster and toe-in angles

A minus B = C (degrees camber)
D = caster (expressed in degrees)
E minus F = toe-in (measured in inches)
G = toe-in (expressed in degrees)

Torque specifications	Ft-lbs (unless otherwise indicated)	Nm

➡ Note: One foot-pound (ft-lb) of torque is equivalent to 12 inch-pounds (in-lbs) of torque. Torque values below approximately 15 foot-pounds are expressed in inch-pounds, because most foot-pound torque wrenches are not accurate at these smaller values.

Front suspension

	Ft-lbs	Nm
Upper balljoint-to-steering knuckle nut	26 to 33	35 to 45
Lower balljoint-to-lower control arm nut	55 to 66	75 to 90
Upper control arm		
Mount-to-shock tower nuts - 2001 through 2006 (except 2006.5 models)	59 to 74	80 to 100
Pivot bolt nuts	40 to 48	55 to 65
Lower control arm		
To-subframe bolts		
2001 through 2006 (except 2006.5 models)	88	120
2006.5 and later	103 to 118	140 to 160
Outer arm-to-inner arm bolt/nuts	74 to 88	100 to 120
Lower balljoint-to-knuckle bolts	74 to 88	100 to 120
Shock absorber		
Fork-to-shock absorber bolt/nut	44 to 59	60 to 80
Fork-to-lower control arm bolt/nut		
2001 through 2006 (except 2006.5 models)	74 to 88	100 to 120
2006.5 and later	103 to 118	140 to 160
Shock absorber-to-shock tower nuts		
2001 through 2006 (except 2006.5 models)	30 to 37	40 to 50
2006.5 and later	33 to 44	45 to 60
Damper shaft nut	15 to 18	20 to 25
Stabilizer bar		
Link self-locking nut		
2001 through 2006 (except 2006.5 models)	26 to 33	35 to 45
2006.5 and later	74 to 88	100 to 120
Bracket-to-subframe bolts		
2001 through 2006 (except 2006.5 models)	22 to 33	30 to 45
2006.5 and later	33 to 40	45 to 55
Subframe-to-body mounting bolts		
2001 through 2006 (except 2006.5 models)	74 to 88	100 to 120
2006.5 and later		
Large bolts	101 to 115	137 to 156
Small bolts	33 to 43	44 to 58

Torque specifications (continued) — Ft-lbs (unless otherwise indicated) — Nm

➡ **Note: One foot-pound (ft-lb) of torque is equivalent to 12 inch-pounds (in-lbs) of torque. Torque values below approximately 15 foot-pounds are expressed in inch-pounds, because most foot-pound torque wrenches are not accurate at these smaller values.**

Rear suspension

Item	Ft-lbs	Nm
Rear hub spindle nut	148 to 206	200 to 260
Rear hub and bearing assembly-to-axle carrier bolts	52 to 66	70 to 90
Subframe mounting bolts	103 to 118	140 to 160
Shock absorber		
Upper mounting bolts		
2001 through 2006 (except 2006.5 models)	74 to 88	100 to 120
2006.5 and later	37 to 44	50 to 60
Lower mounting nuts		
2001 through 2006 (except 2006.5 models)	59 to 66	80 to 90
2006.5 and later	103 to 118	140 to 160
Damper shaft nut	15 to 18	20 to 25
Stabilizer bar		
Stabilizer bar link self-locking nuts		
2001 through 2006 (except 2006.5 models)	26 to 33	35 to 45
2006.5 and later	33 to 40	45 to 55
Stabilizer bushing/retainer bolts		
2001 through 2006 (except 2006.5 models)	26 to 33	35 to 45
2006.5 and later	33 to 40	45 to 55
Upper arm-to-shock bracket bolts - 2001 through 2006 (except 2006.5 models)	44 to 58	60 to 78
Upper arm-to-hub carrier bolt/nut - 2001 through 2006 (except 2006.5 models)	74 to 88	100 to 120
Upper arm-to-crossmember bolts (2006.5 and later)	74 to 88	100 to 120
Upper arm balljoint nuts (2006.5 and later)	59 to 66	80 to 90
Assist arm-to-hub carrier bolt/nut		
2001 through 2006 (except 2006.5 models)	74 to 88	100 to 120
2006.5 and later	103 to 118	140 to 160
Assist arm-to-crossmember bolt/nut		
2001 through 2006 (except 2006.5 models)	59 to 74	80 to 100
2006.5 and later	81 to 88	110 to 120
Center arm-to-hub carrier bolt/nut		
2001 through 2006 (except 2006.5 models)	44 to 53	60 to 72
2006.5 and later	103 to 118	140 to 160
Center arm-to-crossmember bolt/nut		
2001 through 2006 (except 2006.5 models)	74 to 88	100 to 120
2006.5 and later	81 to 88	110 to 120
Trailing arm-to-body bolt/nut		
2001 through 2006 (except 2006.5 models)	74 to 88	100 to 120
2006.5 and later	103 to 118	140 to 160
Trailing arm-to-carrier bolt/nut		
2001 through 2006 (except 2006.5 models)	74 to 88	100 to 120
2006.5 and later	103 to 118	140 to 160

Torque specifications (continued)	Ft-lbs (unless otherwise indicated)	Nm

➡ **Note: One foot-pound (ft-lb) of torque is equivalent to 12 inch-pounds (in-lbs) of torque. Torque values below approximately 15 foot-pounds are expressed in inch-pounds, because most foot-pound torque wrenches are not accurate at these smaller values.**

Steering system

Airbag module screws	72 to 96 in-lbs	8 to 11
Steering wheel nut	29 to 36	40 to 50
Steering gear mounting bolts/nuts	44 to 51	60 to 70
Steering shaft universal joint pinch bolt	132 in-lbs	16
Steering column mounting fasteners	156 in-lbs	18
Tie-rod end-to-steering knuckle nut	17 to 25	24 to 34
Tie-rod end lock nut	37 to 40	50 to 55
Power steering pump mounting bolts		
2001 through 2006 (except 2006.5 models)	44 to 59	60 to 80
2006.5 and later		
Four-cylinder engines	13 to 18	17 to 25
V6 engines	26 to 36	35 to 50
Wheel lug nuts	See Chapter 1	

11

BODY

Section

1 General information
2 Body - maintenance
3 Vinyl trim - maintenance
4 Upholstery and carpets - maintenance
5 Body repair - minor damage
6 Body repair - major damage
7 Hinges and locks - maintenance
8 Windshield and fixed glass - replacement
9 Hood - removal, installation and adjustment
10 Hood latch and release cable - removal and installation
11 Bumper covers - removal and installation
12 Front fender - removal and installation
13 Radiator grille - removal and installation
14 Cowl cover - removal and installation
15 Door trim panels - removal and installation
16 Door - removal, installation and adjustment
17 Door latch, lock cylinder and handle - removal and installation
18 Door window glass - removal and installation
19 Door window glass regulator and motor - removal and installation
20 Mirrors - removal and installation
21 Trunk lid - removal, installation and adjustment
22 Trunk lid latch, lock cylinder and handle - removal and installation
23 Center console - removal and installation
24 Dashboard trim panels - removal and installation
25 Steering column covers - removal and installation
26 Instrument panel - removal and installation
27 Seats - removal and installation
28 Rear parcel shelf - removal and installation

1 General information

These models feature a unibody layout, using a floor pan with integral side frame rails that support the body components, front and rear suspension systems and other mechanical components.

Certain components are particularly vulnerable to accident damage and can be unbolted and repaired or replaced. Among these parts are the body moldings, bumpers, front fenders, the hood and trunk lid, doors and all glass.

Only general body maintenance practices and body panel repair procedures within the scope of the do-it-yourselfer are included in this Chapter.

***** WARNING:**

The front seat belts on some models are equipped with pre-tensioners, which are pyrotechnic (explosive) devices designed to retract the seat belts in the event of a collision. On models equipped with pre-tensioners, do not remove the front seat belt retractor assemblies, and do not disconnect the electrical connectors leading to the assemblies. Problems with the pre-tensioners will turn on the SRS (airbag) warning light on the dash. If any pre-tensioner problems are suspected, take the vehicle to a dealer service department.

2 Body - maintenance

1 The condition of your vehicle's body is very important, because the resale value depends a great deal on it. It's much more difficult to repair a neglected or damaged body than it is to repair mechanical components. The hidden areas of the body, such as the wheel wells, the frame and the engine compartment, are equally important, although they don't require as frequent attention as the rest of the body.

2 Once a year, or every 12,000 miles, it's a good idea to have the underside of the body steam-cleaned. All traces of dirt and oil will be removed and the area can then be inspected carefully for rust, damaged brake lines, frayed electrical wires, damaged cables and other problems.

3 At the same time, clean the engine and the engine compartment with a steam cleaner or water-soluble degreaser.

4 The wheel wells should be given close attention, since undercoating can peel away and stones and dirt thrown up by the tires can cause the paint to chip and flake, allowing rust to set in. If rust is found, clean down to the bare metal and apply an anti-rust paint.

5 The body should be washed about once a week. Wet the vehicle thoroughly to soften the dirt, and then wash it down with a soft sponge and plenty of clean soapy water. If the surplus dirt is not washed off very carefully, it can wear down the paint.

6 Spots of tar or asphalt thrown up from the road should be removed with a cloth soaked in kerosene. Scented lamp oil is available in most hardware stores and the smell is easier to work with than straight kerosene.

7 Once every six months, wax the body and chrome trim. If chrome cleaner is used to remove rust from any of the vehicle's plated parts, remember that the cleaner also removes part of the chrome, so use it sparingly. On any plated parts where chrome cleaner is used, use a good paste wax over the plating for extra protection.

3 Vinyl trim - maintenance

Don't clean vinyl trim with detergents, caustic soap or petroleum-based cleaners. Plain soap and water works just fine, with a soft brush to clean dirt that may be ingrained. Wash the vinyl as frequently as the rest of the vehicle.

After cleaning, application of a high quality rubber and vinyl protectant will help prevent oxidation and cracks. The protectant can also be applied to weather stripping, vacuum lines and rubber hoses, which often fail as a result of chemical degradation, and to the tires.

4 Upholstery and carpets - maintenance

1 Every three months, remove the floormats and clean the interior of the vehicle (more frequently if necessary). Use a stiff whisk broom to brush the carpeting and loosen dirt and dust, and then vacuum the upholstery and carpets thoroughly, especially along seams and crevices.

2 Dirt and stains can be removed from carpeting with basic household or automotive carpet shampoos available in spray cans. Follow the directions and vacuum again, then use a stiff brush to bring back the nap of the carpet.

3 Most interiors have cloth or vinyl upholstery, either of which can be cleaned and maintained with a number of material-specific cleaners or shampoos available in auto supply stores. Follow the directions on the product for usage, and always spot-test any upholstery cleaner on an inconspicuous area (bottom edge of a backseat cushion) to ensure that it doesn't cause a color shift in the material.

4 After cleaning, vinyl upholstery should be treated with a protectant.

➡ **Note: Make sure the protectant container indicates the product can be used on seats - some products may make a seat too slippery.**

CAUTION:

Do not use protectant on steering wheels.

5 Leather upholstery requires special care. It should be cleaned regularly with saddlesoap or leather cleaner. Never use alcohol, gasoline, nail polish remover or thinner to clean leather upholstery.

6 After cleaning, regularly treat leather upholstery with a leather conditioner, rubbed in with a soft cotton cloth. Never use car wax on leather upholstery.

7 In areas where the interior of the vehicle is subject to bright sunlight, cover leather seating areas of the seats with a sheet if the vehicle is to be left out for any length of time.

5 Body repair - minor damage

FLEXIBLE PLASTIC BODY PANELS (FRONT AND REAR BUMPER FASCIA)

The following repair procedures are for minor scratches and gouges. Repair of more serious damage should be left to a dealer service department or qualified auto body shop. Below is a list of the equipment and materials necessary to perform the following repair procedures on plastic body panels. Although a specific brand of material may be mentioned, it should be noted that equivalent products from other manufacturers may be used instead.

Wax, grease and silicone removing solvent
Cloth-backed body tape
Sanding discs
Drill motor with three-inch disc holder
Hand sanding block
Rubber squeegees
Sandpaper
Non-porous mixing palette
Wood paddle or putty knife
Curved-tooth body file
Flexible parts repair material

1 Remove the damaged panel, if necessary or desirable. In most cases, repairs can be carried out with the panel installed.

2 Clean the area(s) to be repaired with a wax, grease and silicone removing solvent applied with a water-dampened cloth.

3 If the damage is structural, that is, if it extends through the panel, clean the backside of the panel area to be repaired as well. Wipe dry.

4 Sand the rear surface about 1-1/2 inches beyond the break.

5 Cut two pieces of fiberglass cloth large enough to overlap the break by about 1-1/2 inches. Cut only to the required length.

6 Mix the adhesive from the repair kit according to the instructions included with the kit, and apply a layer of the mixture approximately 1/8-inch thick on the backside of the panel. Overlap the break by at least 1-1/2 inches.

7 Apply one piece of fiberglass cloth to the adhesive and cover the cloth with additional adhesive. Apply a second piece of fiberglass cloth to the adhesive and immediately cover the cloth with additional adhesive in sufficient quantity to fill the weave.

8 Allow the repair to cure for 20 to 30 minutes at 60-degrees to 80-degrees F.

9 If necessary, trim the excess repair material at the edge.

10 Remove all of the paint film over and around the area(s) to be repaired. The repair material should not overlap the painted surface.

11 With a drill motor and a sanding disc (or a rotary file), cut a V along the break line approximately 1/2-inch wide. Remove all dust and loose particles from the repair area.

12 Mix and apply the repair material. Apply a light coat first over the damaged area; then continue applying material until it reaches a level slightly higher than the surrounding finish.

13 Cure the mixture for 20 to 30 minutes at 60-degrees to 80-degrees F.

14 Roughly establish the contour of the area being repaired with a body file. If low areas or pits remain, mix and apply additional adhesive.

15 Block sand the damaged area with sandpaper to establish the actual contour of the surrounding surface.

16 If desired, the repaired area can be temporarily protected with several light coats of primer. Because of the special paints and techniques required for flexible body panels, it is recommended that the vehicle be taken to a paint shop for completion of the body repair.

STEEL BODY PANELS

See photo sequence

Repair of minor scratches

17 If the scratch is superficial and does not penetrate to the metal of the body, repair is very simple. Lightly rub the scratched area with a fine rubbing compound to remove loose paint and built up wax. Rinse the area with clean water.

18 Apply touch-up paint to the scratch, using a small brush. Continue to apply thin layers of paint until the surface of the paint in the scratch is level with the surrounding paint. Allow the new paint at least two weeks to harden, and then blend it into the surrounding paint by rubbing with a very fine rubbing compound. Finally, apply a coat of wax to the scratch area.

19 If the scratch has penetrated the paint and exposed the metal of the body, causing the metal to rust, a different repair technique is required. Remove all loose rust from the bottom of the scratch with a pocket knife, and then apply rust inhibiting paint to prevent the formation of rust in the future. Using a rubber or nylon applicator, coat the scratched area with glaze-type filler. If required, the filler can be mixed with thinner to provide a very thin paste, which is ideal for filling narrow scratches. Before the glaze filler in the scratch hardens, wrap a piece of smooth cotton cloth around the tip of a finger. Dip the cloth in thinner and then quickly wipe it along the surface of the scratch. This will

ensure that the surface of the filler is slightly hollow. The scratch can now be painted over as described earlier in this Section.

Repair of dents

20 When repairing dents, the first job is to pull the dent out until the affected area is as close as possible to its original shape. There is no point in trying to restore the original shape completely as the metal in the damaged area will have stretched on impact and cannot be restored to its original contours. It is better to bring the level of the dent up to a point that is about 1/8-inch below the level of the surrounding metal. In cases where the dent is very shallow, it is not worth trying to pull it out at all.

21 If the back side of the dent is accessible, it can be hammered out gently from behind using a soft-face hammer. While doing this, hold a block of wood firmly against the opposite side of the metal to absorb the hammer blows and prevent the metal from being stretched.

22 If the dent is in a section of the body that has double layers, or some other factor makes it inaccessible from behind, a different technique is required. Drill several small holes through the metal inside the damaged area, particularly in the deeper sections. Screw long, self-tapping screws into the holes just enough for them to get a good grip in the metal. Now the dent can be pulled out by pulling on the protruding heads of the screws with locking pliers.

23 The next stage of repair is the removal of paint from the damaged area and from an inch or so of the surrounding metal. This is easily done with a wire brush or sanding disk in a drill motor, although it can be done just as effectively by hand with sandpaper. To complete the preparation for filling, score the surface of the bare metal with a screwdriver or the tang of a file or drill small holes in the affected area. This will provide a good grip for the filler material. To complete the repair, see the Section on filling and painting.

Repair of rust holes or gashes

24 Remove all paint from the affected area and from an inch or so of the surrounding metal using a sanding disk or wire brush mounted in a drill motor. If these are not available, a few sheets of sandpaper will do the job just as effectively.

25 With the paint removed, you will be able to determine the severity

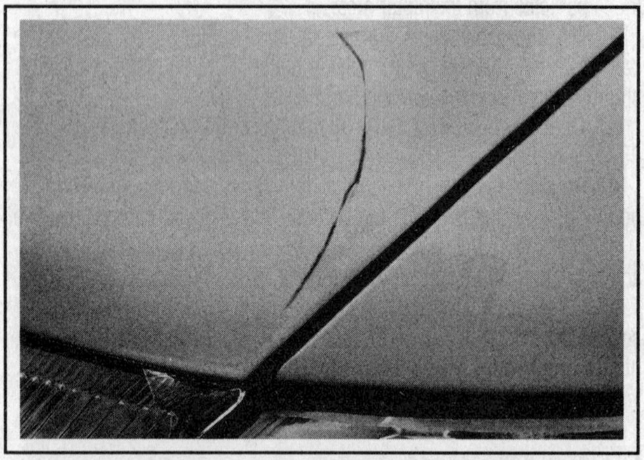

Make sure the damaged area is perfectly clean and rust free. If the touch-up kit has a wire brush, use it to clean the scratch or chip. Or use fine steel wool wrapped around the end of a pencil. Clean the scratched or chipped surface only, not the good paint surrounding it. Rinse the area with water and allow it to dry thoroughly

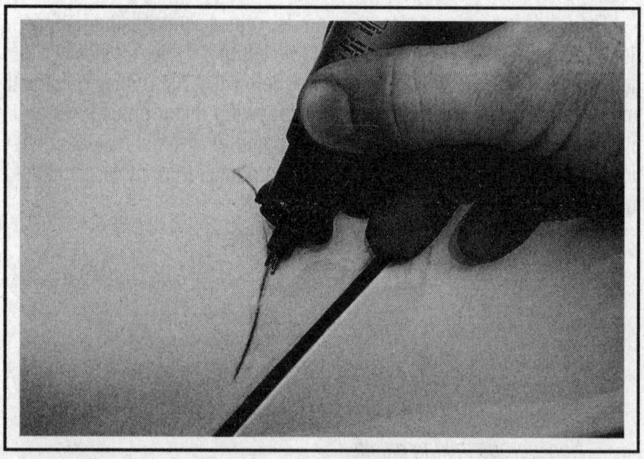

Thoroughly mix the paint, then apply a small amount with the touch-up kit brush or a very fine artist's brush. Brush in one direction as you fill the scratch area. Do not build up the paint higher than the surrounding paint

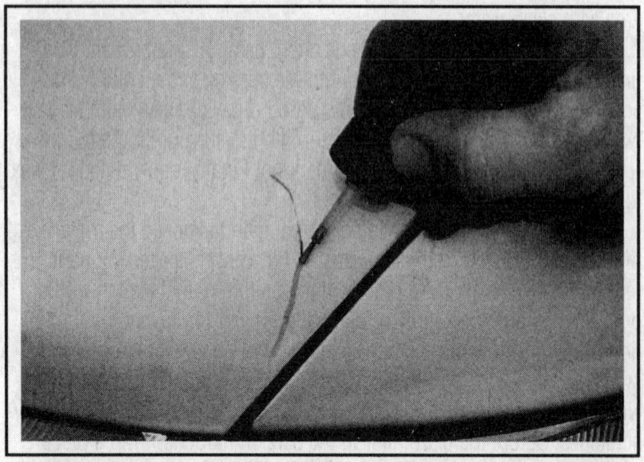

If the vehicle has a two-coat finish, apply the clear coat after the color coat has dried

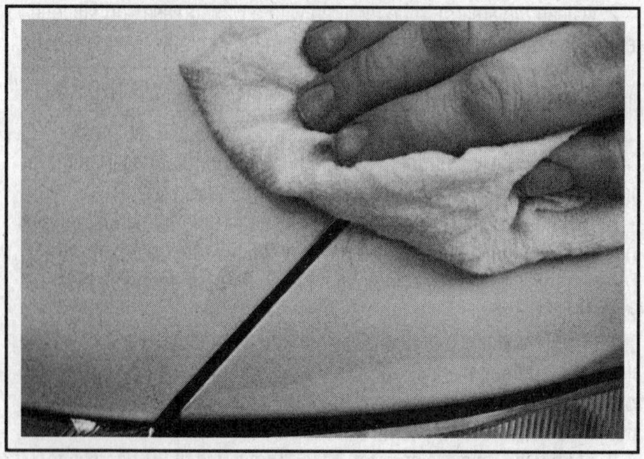

Wait a few days for the paint to dry thoroughly, then rub out the repainted area with a polishing compound to blend the new paint with the surrounding area. When you're happy with your work, wash and polish the area

These photos illustrate a method of repairing simple dents. They are intended to supplement Body repair - minor damage in this Chapter and should not be used as the sole instructions for body repair on these vehicles.

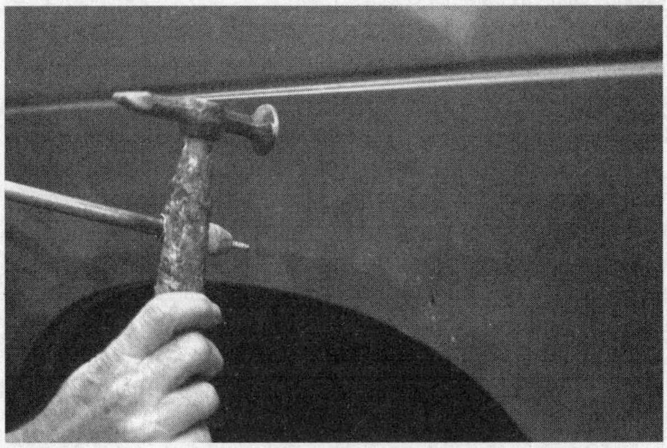

1 If you can't access the backside of the body panel to hammer out the dent, pull it out with a slide-hammer-type dent puller. Tap with a hammer near the edge of the dent to help 'pop' the metal back to its original shape, about 1/8-inch below the surface of the surrounding metal

2 Using coarse-grit sandpaper, remove the paint down to the bare metal. Clean the repair area with wax/silicone remover.

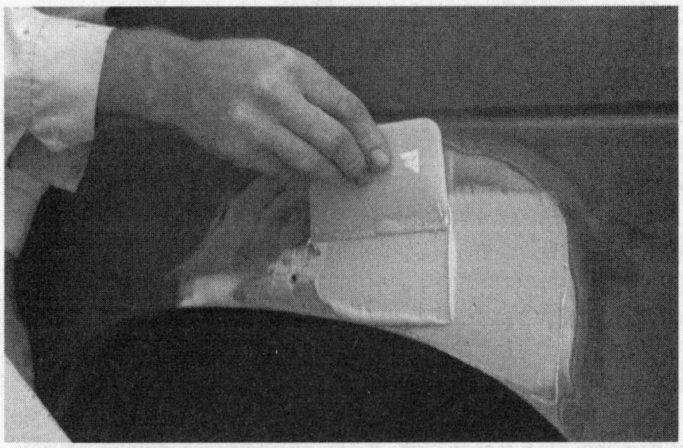

3 Following label instructions, mix up a batch of plastic filler and hardener, then quickly press it into the metal with a plastic applicator. Work the filler until it matches the original contour and is slightly above the surrounding metal

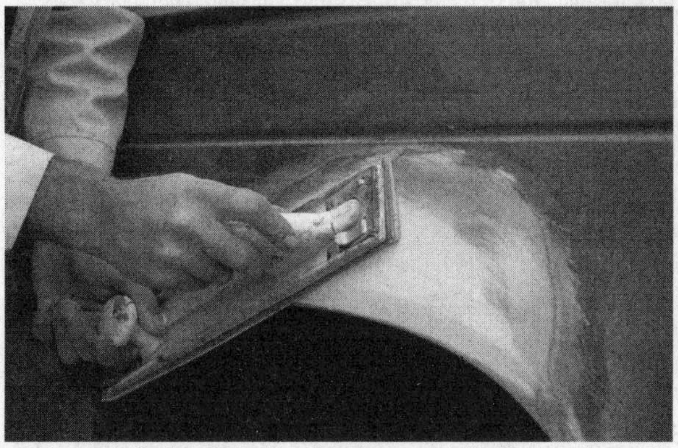

4 Let the filler harden until you can just dent it with your fingernail. File, then sand the filler down until it's smooth and even. Work down to finer grits of sandpaper - always using a board or block - ending up with 360 or 400 grit

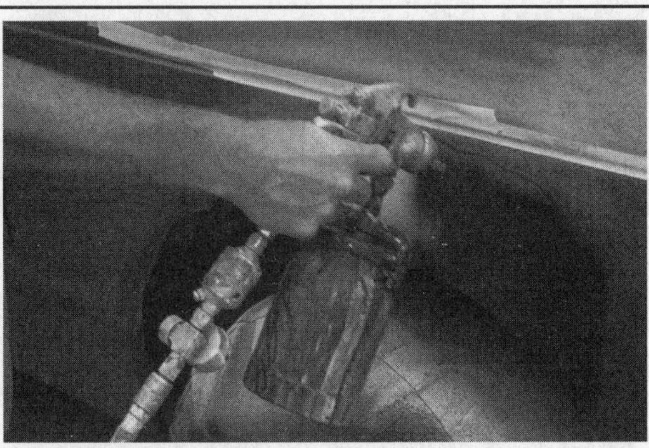

5 When the area is smooth to the touch, clean the area and mask around it. Apply several layers of primer to the area. A professional-type spray gun is being used here, but aerosol spray primer works fine

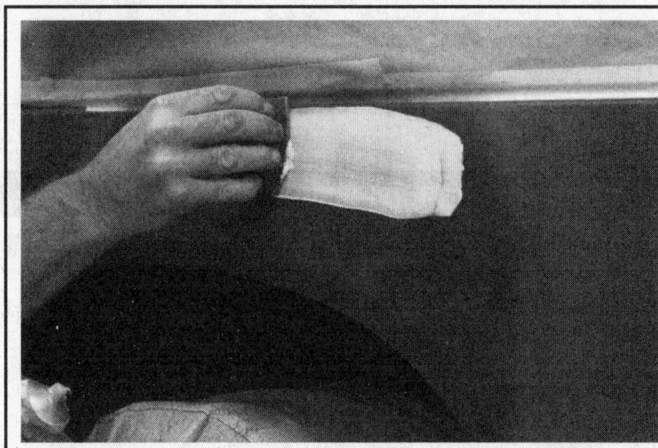

6 Fill imperfections or scratches with glazing compound. Sand with 360 or 400-grit and re-spray. Finish sand the primer with 600 grit, clean thoroughly, then apply the finish coat. Don't attempt to rub out or wax the repair area until the paint has dried completely (at least two weeks)

of the corrosion and decide whether to replace the whole panel, if possible, or repair the affected area. New body panels are not as expensive as most people think and it is often quicker to install a new panel than to repair large areas of rust.

26 Remove all trim pieces from the affected area except those which will act as a guide to the original shape of the damaged body, such as headlight shells, etc. Using metal snips or a hacksaw blade, remove all loose metal and any other metal that is badly affected by rust. Hammer the edges of the hole in to create a slight depression for the filler material.

27 Wire brush the affected area to remove the powdery rust from the surface of the metal. If the back of the rusted area is accessible, treat it with rust inhibiting paint.

28 Before filling is done, block the hole in some way. This can be done with sheet metal riveted or screwed into place, or by stuffing the hole with wire mesh.

29 Once the hole is blocked off, the affected area can be filled and painted. See the following subsection on filling and painting.

Filling and painting

30 Many types of body fillers are available, but generally speaking, body repair kits which contain filler paste and a tube of resin hardener are best for this type of repair work. A wide, flexible plastic or nylon applicator will be necessary for imparting a smooth and contoured finish to the surface of the filler material. Mix up a small amount of filler on a clean piece of wood or cardboard (use the hardener sparingly). Follow the manufacturer's instructions on the package; otherwise the filler will set incorrectly.

31 Using the applicator apply the filler paste to the prepared area. Draw the applicator across the surface of the filler to achieve the desired contour and to level the filler surface. As soon as a contour that approximates the original one is achieved, stop working the paste. If you continue, the paste will begin to stick to the applicator. Continue to add thin layers of paste at 20-minute intervals until the level of the filler is just above the surrounding metal.

32 Once the filler has hardened, the excess can be removed with a body file. From then on, progressively finer grades of sandpaper should be used, starting with a 180-grit paper and finishing with 600-grit wet-or-dry paper. Always wrap the sandpaper around a flat rubber or wooden block; otherwise the surface of the filler will not be completely flat. During the sanding of the filler surface, the wet-or-dry paper should be periodically rinsed in water. This will ensure that a very smooth finish is produced in the final stage.

33 At this point, the repair area should be surrounded by a ring of bare metal, which in turn should be encircled by the finely feathered edge of good paint. Rinse the repair area with clean water until all of the dust produced by the sanding operation is gone.

34 Spray the entire area with a light coat of primer. This will reveal any imperfections in the surface of the filler. Repair the imperfections with fresh filler paste or glaze filler and once more smooth the surface with sandpaper. Repeat this spray-and-repair procedure until you are satisfied that the surface of the filler and the feathered edge of the paint are perfect. Rinse the area with clean water and allow it to dry completely.

35 The repair area is now ready for painting. Spray painting must be carried out in a warm, dry, windless and dust free atmosphere. These conditions can be created if you have access to a large indoor work area, but if you are forced to work in the open, you will have to pick the day very carefully. If you are working indoors, dousing the floor in the work area with water will help settle the dust that would otherwise be in the air. If the repair area is confined to one body panel, mask off the surrounding panels. This will help minimize the effects of a slight mismatch in paint color. Trim pieces such as chrome strips, door handles, etc., will also need to be masked off or removed. Use masking tape and several thickness of newspaper for the masking operations.

36 Before spraying, shake the paint can thoroughly, and then spray a test area until the spray-painting technique is mastered. Cover the repair area with a thick coat of primer. The thickness should be built up using several thin layers of primer rather than one thick one. Using 600-grit wet-or-dry sandpaper, rub down the surface of the primer until it is very smooth. While doing this, the work area should be thoroughly rinsed with water and the wet-or-dry sandpaper periodically rinsed as well. Allow the primer to dry before spraying additional coats.

37 Spray on the top coat, again building up the thickness by using several thin layers of paint. Begin spraying in the center of the repair area and then, using a circular motion, work out until the whole repair area and about two inches of the surrounding original paint is covered. Remove all masking material 10 to 15 minutes after spraying on the final coat of paint. Allow the new paint at least two weeks to harden, then use a very fine rubbing compound to blend the edges of the new paint into the existing paint. Finally, apply a coat of wax.

6 Body repair - major damage

1 Major damage must be repaired by an auto body shop specifically equipped to perform unibody repairs. These shops have the specialized equipment required to do the job properly.

2 If the damage is extensive, the body must be checked for proper alignment or the vehicle's handling characteristics may be adversely affected and other components may wear at an accelerated rate.

3 Due to the fact that some of the major body components (hood, fenders, doors, etc.) are separate and replaceable units, any seriously damaged components should be replaced rather than repaired. Sometimes the components can be found in a wrecking yard that specializes in used vehicle components, often at considerable savings over the cost of new parts.

7 Hinges and locks - maintenance

Once every 3000 miles, or every three months, the hinges and latch assemblies on the doors, hood and trunk should be given a few drops of light oil or lock lubricant. The door latch strikers should also be lubricated with a thin coat of grease to reduce wear and ensure free movement. Lubricate the door and trunk locks with spray-on graphite lubricant.

8 Windshield and fixed glass - replacement

Replacement of the windshield and fixed glass requires the use of special fast-setting adhesive/caulk materials and some specialized tools and techniques. These operations should be left to a dealer service department or a shop specializing in glass work.

9 Hood - removal, installation and adjustment

➡ **Note: The hood is awkward to remove and install; at least two people should perform this procedure.**

REMOVAL AND INSTALLATION

➧ **Refer to illustrations 9.1, 9.2, 9.3 and 9.4**

⁂ CAUTION:

After opening the hood, be sure to put blankets or pads over the fenders and cowl area of the body to protect the body and paint as the hood is lifted off.

1 Disconnect the windshield washer lines, or detach the line clips from the underside of the hood (see illustration) and set the lines aside.

2 The upper ends of the hood support struts are secured to their hood brackets by small spherical bearings. On some models, a small metal clip secures the connection. Use a small screwdriver to pry off the clip (see illustration), then use a larger screwdriver to pop loose the spherical bearing from its hood bracket.

3 Make marks around the hood hinges to ensure proper alignment during installation (see illustration).

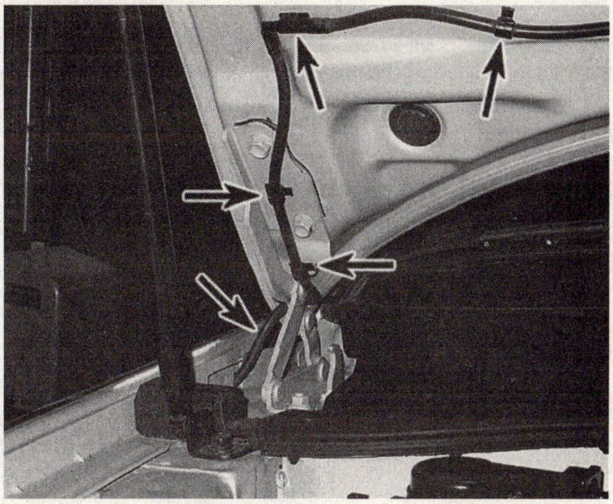

9.1 If the windshield washer lines are attached to the hood, disconnect them between the cowl area and the hood. If you're replacing the hood, detach all the washer line clips and set the lines aside

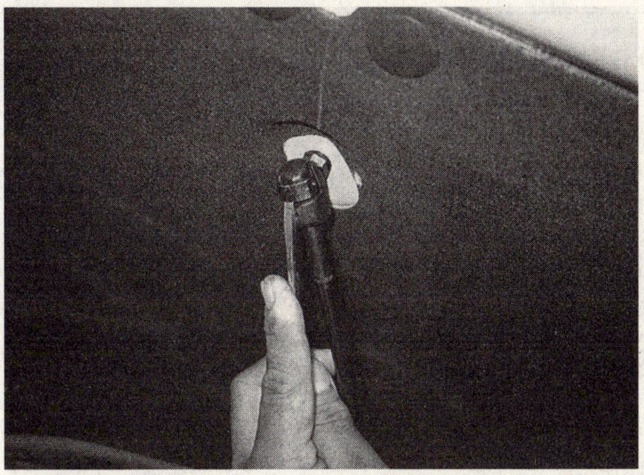

9.2 On some models, you have to pry off this clip before you can disconnect the hood support strut

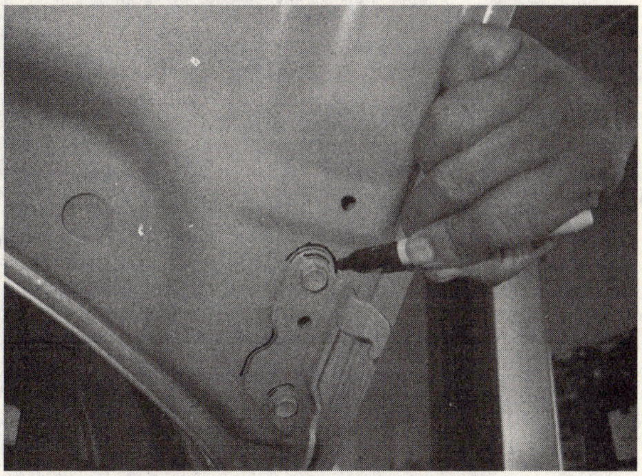

9.3 Draw alignment marks around the hood hinges to ensure proper alignment of the hood when it's reinstalled

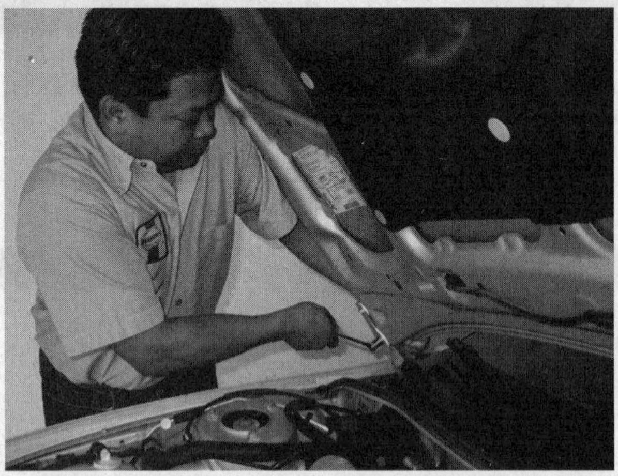

9.4 Support the hood with your shoulder while removing the hood bolts

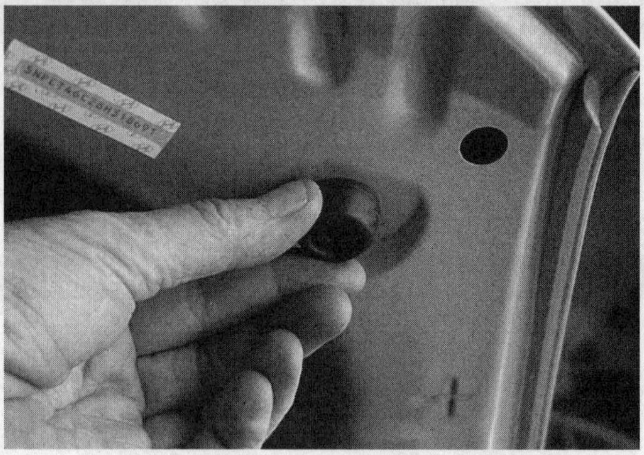

9.10 To adjust the vertical height of the leading edge of the hood so that it's flush with the fenders, rotate each edge cushion

4 Have an assistant support one side of the hood. Take turns removing the hinge-to-hood bolts and lift off the hood (see illustration).

5 Installation is the reverse of removal. Align the hinge bolts with the marks made in Step 3.

ADJUSTMENT

➧ Refer to illustration 9.10

6 Fore-and-aft and side-to-side adjustment of the hood is done by moving the hood in the hinge plate slots after loosening the bolts.

7 If you haven't done so already, mark around the entire hinge plate so you can determine the amount of movement.

8 Loosen the bolts and move the hood into correct alignment. Move it only a little at a time. Tighten the hinge bolts and carefully lower the hood to check the position.

9 If necessary after installation, the entire hood latch assembly can be adjusted up-and-down as well as from side-to-side on the radiator support, so the hood closes securely and flush with the fenders. Scribe a line or mark around the hood latch mounting bolts to provide a reference point, then loosen them and reposition the latch assembly, as necessary (see illustration 10.2). Following adjustment, retighten the mounting bolts.

10 Finally, adjust the hood bumpers at the front of the hood so when closed, it's flush with the fenders (see illustration). The bumpers are on the radiator support on 2001 through 2006 models and on the bottom front edge of the hood on 2006.5 and later vehicles.

11 The hood latch assembly, as well as the hinges, should be periodically lubricated with white lithium-base grease to prevent binding and wear.

10 Hood latch and release cable - removal and installation

10.2 Hood latch bolts

LATCH

➧ Refer to illustration 10.2

1 Remove the radiator guard or trim panel, if applicable.

2 Scribe a line around the latch to aid alignment when installing, then remove the retaining bolts securing the hood latch to the radiator support (see illustration). Remove the latch.

3 Disconnect the hood release cable by disengaging the cable from the latch.

4 Installation is the reverse of removal.

➡ Note: Adjust the latch so the hood engages securely when closed and the hood bumpers are slightly compressed.

CABLE

5 Working in the passenger compartment, lift the hood release handle lever upward, then pull down on the cable housing end and disengage the cable from the hood release lever handle.

6 Attach a piece of thin wire or string to the end of the cable.

7 Disconnect the hood release cable from the latch as described in Steps 1 and 2.

8 Remove the left inner plastic fenderwell.

9 Unclip all the cable retaining clips on the radiator support and the outer fenderwell.

10 Pull the cable forward into the wheel well until you can see the wire or string, then remove the wire or string from the old cable and fasten it to the new cable.

11 With the new cable attached to the wire or string, pull the wire or string back through the body until the new cable reaches the inside handle.

12 Working in the passenger compartment, install the new cable into the hood release lever, making sure the cable housing fits snugly into the notch in the handle bracket.

➡ Note: Pull on the cable with your fingers from the passenger compartment until the cable stop seats in the grommet on the body.

13 The remainder of the installation is the reverse of removal.

11 Bumper covers - removal and installation

FRONT BUMPER COVER

2001 through 2006 models

➧ Refer to illustrations 11.2, 11.4, 11.5a and 11.5b

1 Apply the parking brake, raise the vehicle and support it securely on jackstands.

2 Remove the upper bumper cover fasteners from the center part of the bumper (see illustration).

3 Remove the headlight housings (see Chapter 12).

4 Remove the bumper cover fasteners in and around each headlight opening (see illustration).

5 Remove the screws at the upper rear corners of the bumper cover that secure it to the fenders; one is accessible through the headlight housing (see illustration), the other through the front part of the wheel well (see illustration).

11.2 Typical front bumper cover fastener locations (2001 through 2006 models; exact location and number of fasteners varies with model year)

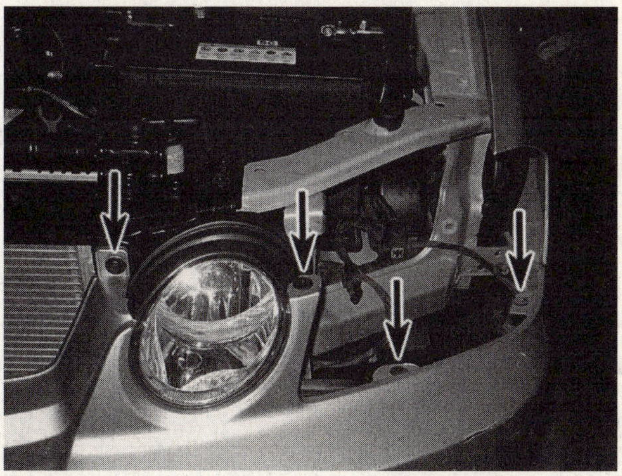

11.4 Typical front bumper cover fastener locations (2001 through 2006 models)

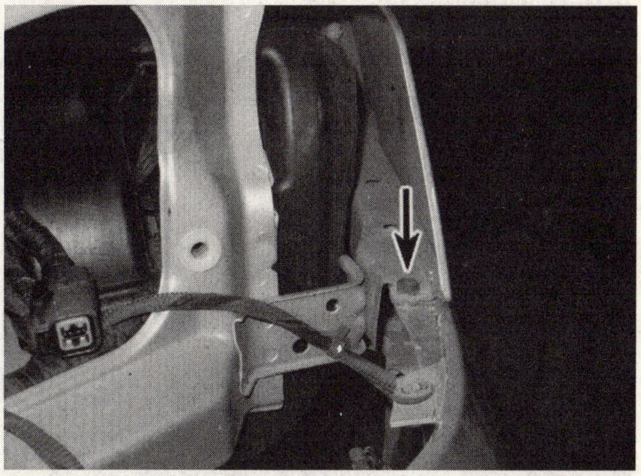

11.5a One front bumper cover-to-fender fastener is located in the headlight housing area . . .

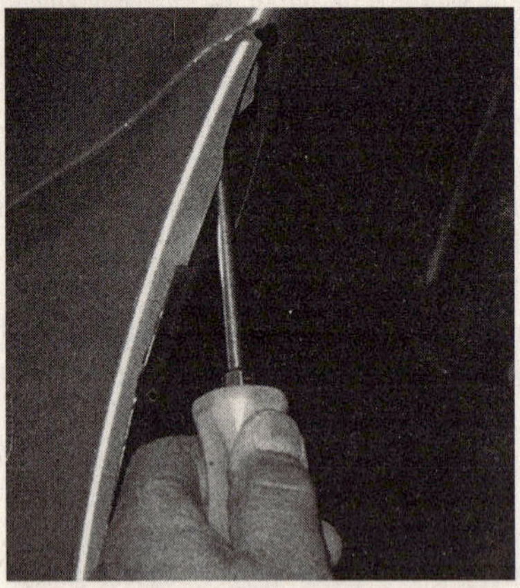

11.5b . . . the other is accessed through the wheel well (fastener not visible in this photo) (2001 through 2006 models)

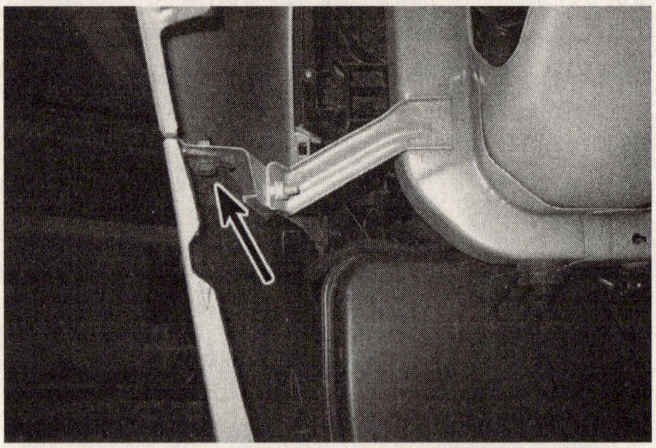

11.10 The front inner wheel well must be removed for access to the mounting bolts at the ends of the front bumper cover (2006.5 and later models)

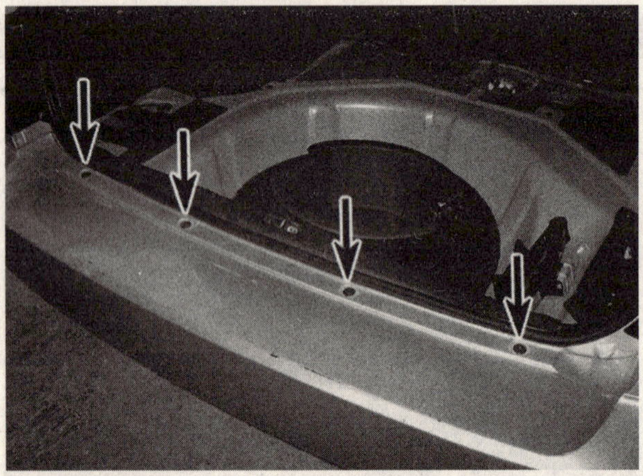

11.15 Rear bumper cover upper fasteners (2001 through 2006 models)

11.16a Remove the taillight housing mounting fasteners . . .

6 Remove the bumper cover. If it doesn't come off easily, check for any remaining fasteners, then try again.

7 Installation is the reverse of removal.

2006.5 and later models

➧ Refer to illustration 11.9

8 Apply the parking brake, raise the vehicle and support it securely on jackstands.

9 Working inside the wheel wells, remove the fasteners from the front parts of the inner fender splash shields and pull them back far enough to access the bumper cover fasteners.

10 Remove the fasteners that secure each end of the bumper cover to the front fenders (see illustration).

11 Remove the trim cover above the radiator.

12 Remove the fasteners from the top and underside of the bumper cover.

13 Remove the bumper cover. If it doesn't come off easily, check for any remaining fasteners, then try again.

14 Installation is the reverse of removal.

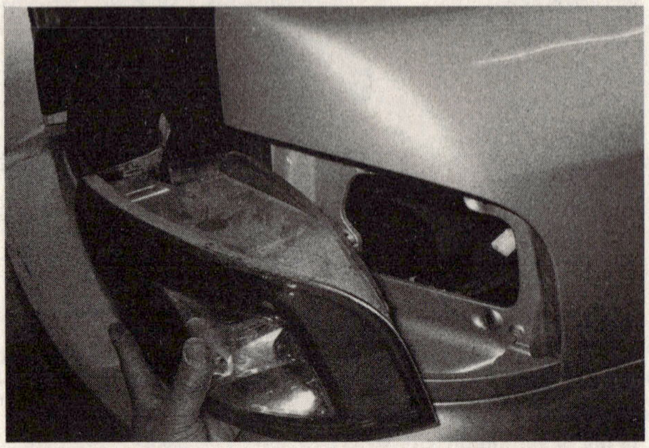

11.16b . . . and pull out each taillight housing (2001 through 2006 models; other models similar)

REAR BUMPER COVER

2001 through 2006 models

➧ Refer to illustrations 11.15, 11.16a, 11.16b, 11.17, 11.19 and 11.20

15 Open the trunk lid and remove the fasteners along the top edge of the bumper (see illustration).

16 Open the trunk lid and remove both taillight housing assemblies (see illustrations).

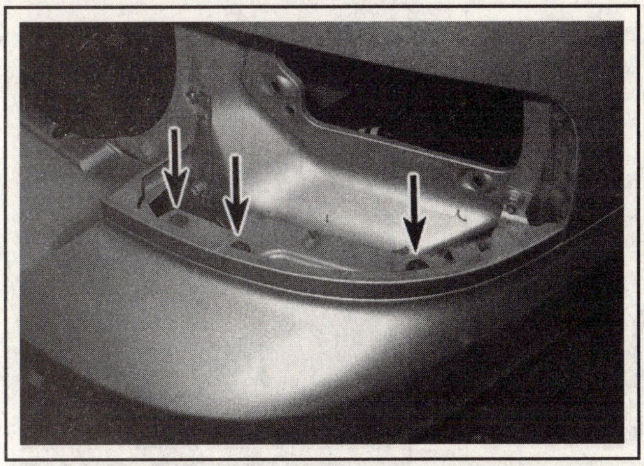

11.17 Rear bumper cover fastener locations - right side taillight housing shown (2001 through 2006 models)

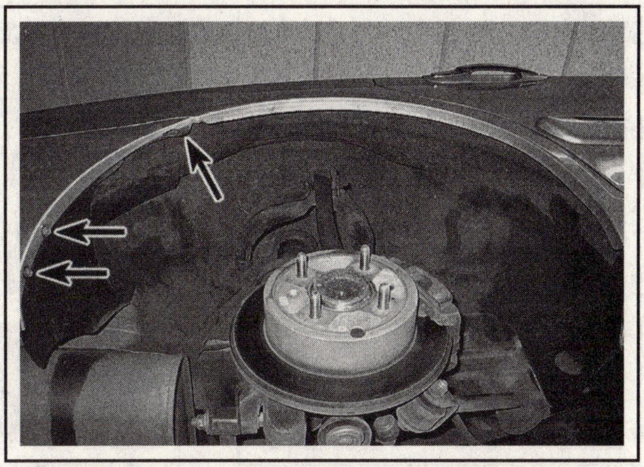

11.19 Rear bumper cover fastener locations - right side wheel well shown (2001 through 2006 models)

17 Remove the fasteners from the taillight areas (see illustration).
18 Raise the vehicle and place it securely on jackstands.
19 Remove the fasteners that secure the forward corners of the bumper cover to the rear wheel wells (see illustration).
20 Remove the fasteners from the lower leading edge of the bumper cover (see illustration) and remove the bumper cover.
21 Installation is the reverse of removal.

2006.5 and later models

22 Although the location, number and type of fasteners will vary somewhat, the procedure for removing the rear bumper cover on these models is similar to the procedure for earlier models (see Steps 15 through 21).

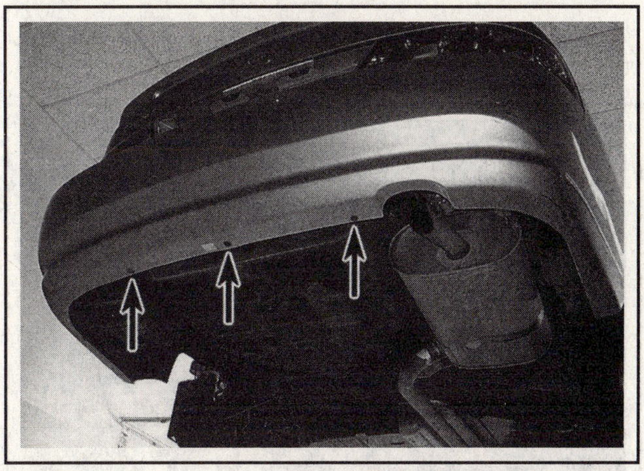

11.20 Rear bumper cover fastener locations (2001 through 2006 models)

12 Front fender - removal and installation

2001 THROUGH 2006 MODELS

Refer to illustrations 12.4, 12.5, 12.6, 12.7 and 12.8

1 Loosen the front wheel lug nuts. Raise the vehicle, support it securely on jackstands and remove the front wheel.
2 Remove the headlight housing (see Chapter 12).
3 Detach the front bumper cover from the fender (see illustrations 11.5a and 11.5b).
4 Remove the wheel well splash shield fasteners (see illustration) and remove the splash shield.

12.4 Inner fender splash shield fasteners (number and location of fasteners varies with year and model)

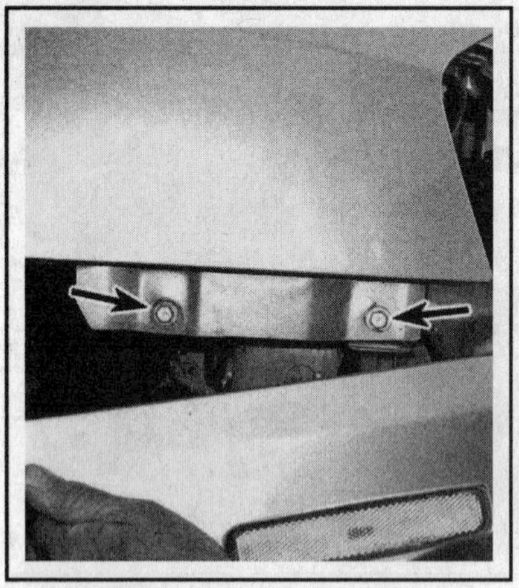

12.5 Remove these two front fender bolts

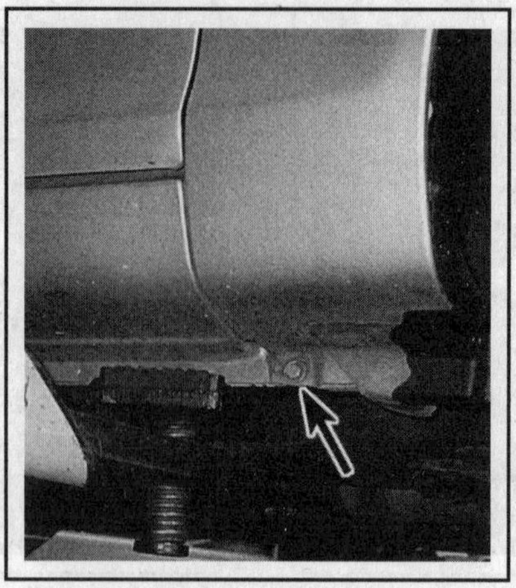

12.6 Lower fender bolt

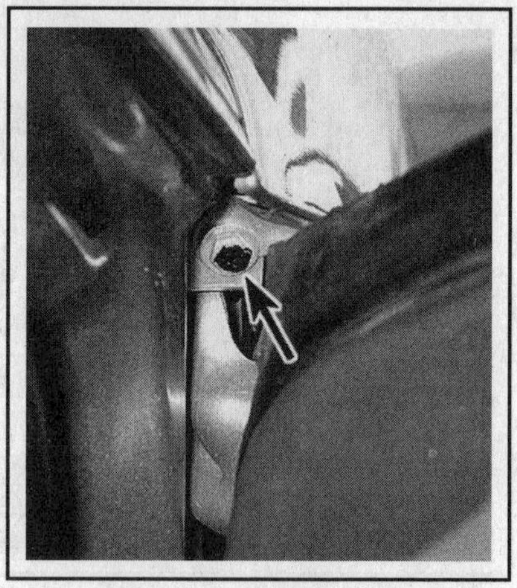

12.7 Upper rear fender bolt (open the door to access this bolt)

5 Pull the front bumper cover loose and remove the two front fender bolts (see illustration).

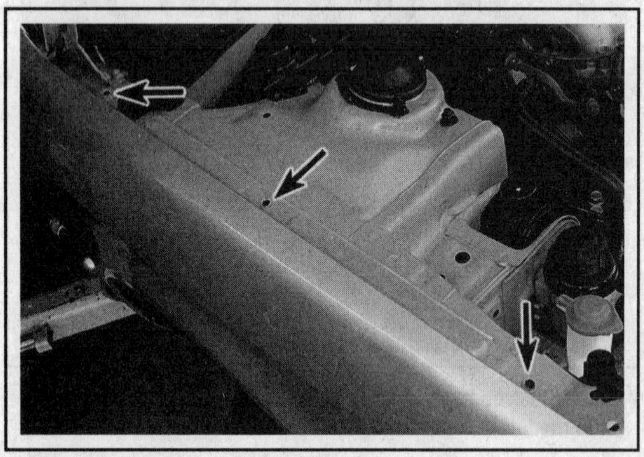

12.8 Fender upper mounting bolts

6 Remove the fender-to-body bolt from the lower rear corner of the fender, behind the wheel well (see illustration).

7 Open the door and remove the upper rear fender bolt (see illustration).

8 Open the hood and remove the upper fender bolts (see illustration).

9 Lift off the fender. It's a good idea to have an assistant support the fender while it's being moved away from the vehicle to prevent damage to the surrounding body panels.

10 Installation is the reverse of removal. Check the alignment of the fender to the hood and front edge of the door before final tightening the fender fasteners.

2006.5 AND LATER MODELS

11 Although the location, number and type of fasteners will vary somewhat, the procedure for removing a front fender on these models is similar to the procedure for earlier models (see Steps 1 through 10).

13 Radiator grille - removal and installation

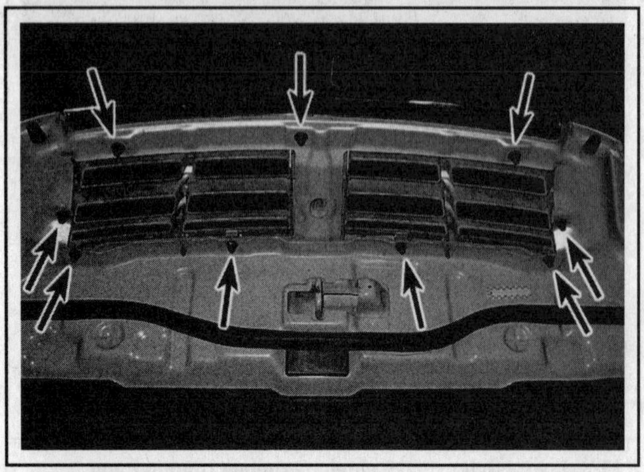

13.2 Grille fasteners (number and location of fasteners may vary with year and model)

2001 THROUGH 2006 MODELS

Refer to illustration 13.2

1 Open the hood.

2 Remove the grille fasteners (see illustration) and remove the grille.

3 Installation is the reverse of removal.

2006.5 AND LATER MODELS

4 Remove the front bumper cover (see Section 11).

5 Remove the grille fasteners and remove the grille from the bumper cover.

6 Installation is the reverse of removal.

14 Cowl cover - removal and installation

Refer to illustrations 14.2, 14.3a and 14.3b

1 Remove the wiper arms (see Chapter 12, Section 13).

2 Remove the plastic retainers at each end of the hood seal, if equipped (see illustration).

3 Pry up the cowl to release the clips that secure it, working from one end toward the other (see illustrations).

4 Installation is the reverse of removal.

14.2 Most models have clips securing the ends of the cowl weatherstrip

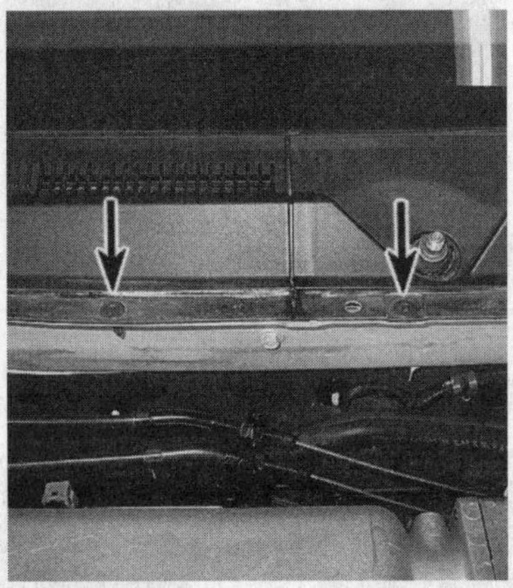

14.3a The cowl trim panel is secured by pop fasteners like these

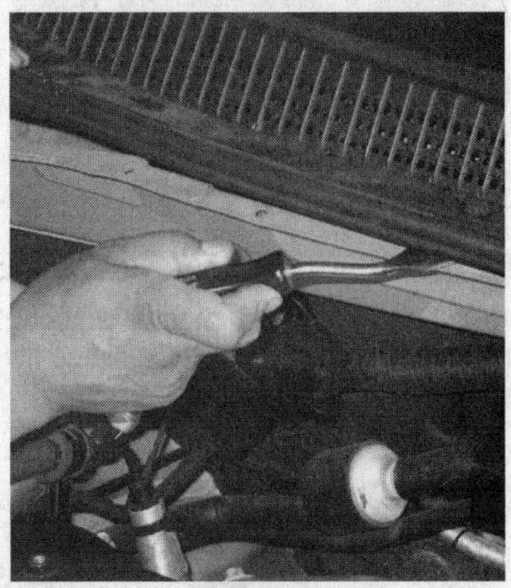

14.3b To disengage the cowl fasteners, carefully pry up the cowl trim with a trim panel removal tool

15 Door trim panel, watershield and door module - removal and installation

WARNING:

The models covered by this manual are equipped with Supplemental Restraint systems (SRS), more commonly known as airbags. Always disarm the airbag system before working in the vicinity of any airbag system component to avoid the possibility of accidental deployment of the airbag, which could cause personal injury (see Chapter 12).

CAUTION:

Wear gloves when working inside the door openings to protect against cuts from sharp metal edges.

1 Disconnect the cable from the negative battery terminal (see Chapter 5, Section 1).

2001 THROUGH 2006 MODELS

Refer to illustrations 15.2a, 15.2b, 15.3, 15.4a, 15.4b, 15.4c, 15.5, 15.6a, 15.6b, 15.7, 15.8 and 15.9

2 Pry the cover from the side mirror and disconnect the electrical connector for the mirror wiring (see illustrations).

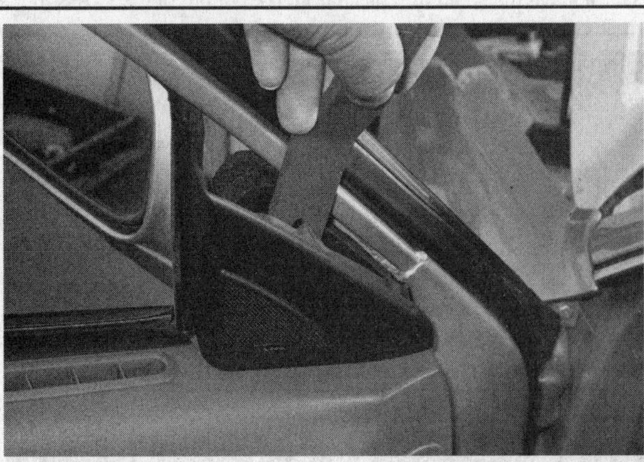

15.2a Use a trim removal tool to carefully pry off the trim cover for the outside mirror . . .

15.2b . . . then disconnect the electrical connector for the tweeter

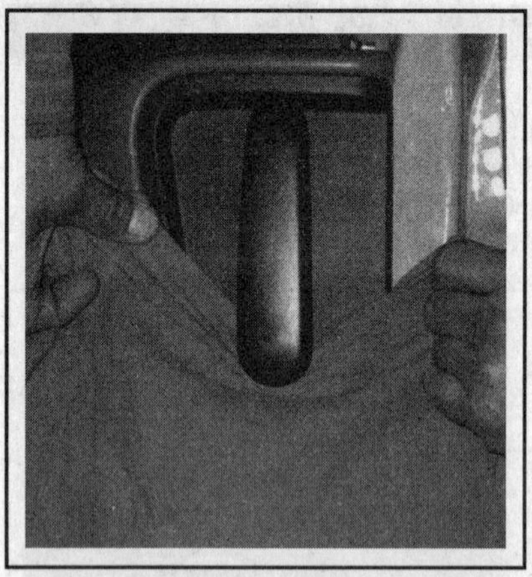

15.3 On vehicles with manual window regulators, use a cloth to disengage the spring clip from the handle

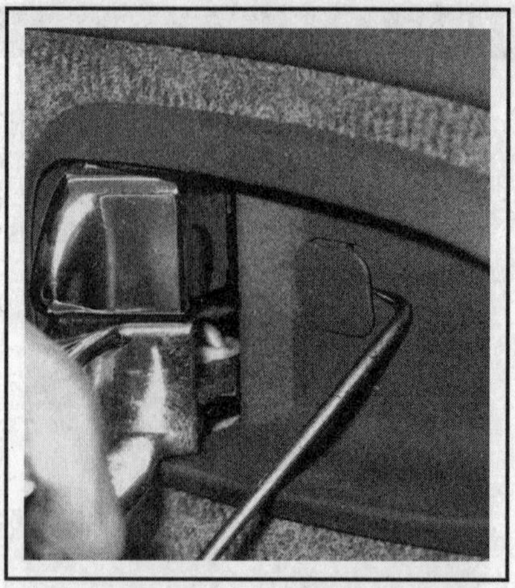

15.4a Carefully pry off this small trim cap in the inside door handle recess . . .

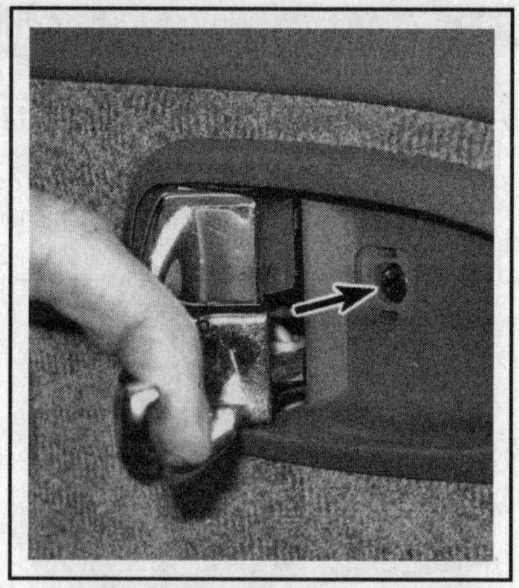

15.4b . . . remove the inside handle retaining screw . . .

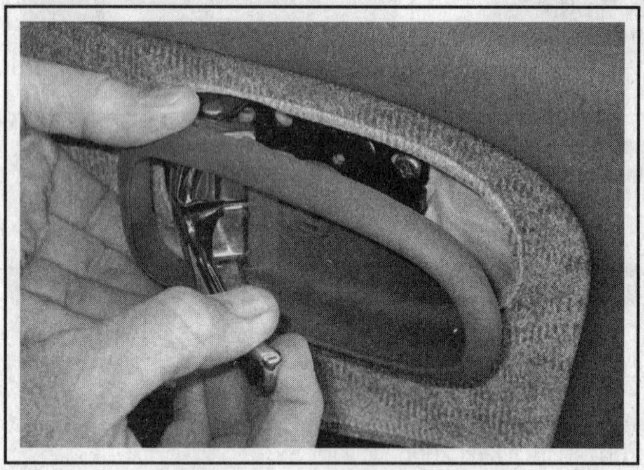

15.4c . . . and remove the inside handle trim panel

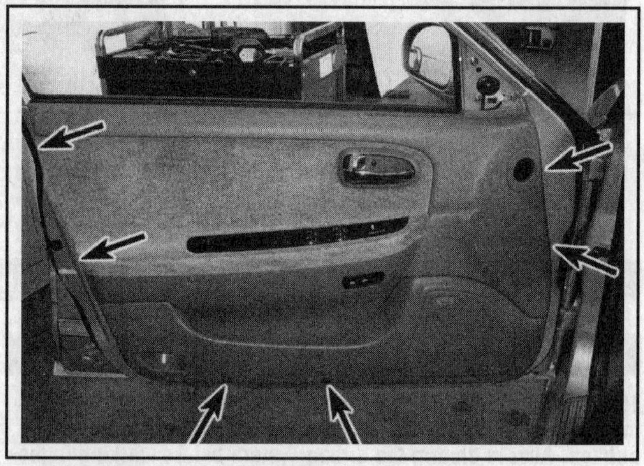

15.5 Door trim panel fastener locations

3 If you're working on a model with manual window regulators, fully shut the window, and note the position of the regulator handle. Release the spring clip by inserting a clean cloth between the handle and the door trim (see illustration). Using a sawing action, pull the cloth against the open ends of the clip to release it, simultaneously pulling the handle from the regulator shaft splines. Withdraw the handle and recover the clip.

4 Carefully pry off the small trim panel from the inside door handle, then remove the handle retaining screw and the inside handle trim panel (see illustrations).

5 Remove the door panel retaining screws (see illustration). Pry out the two small trim caps to access the rear screws, which are screwed into small threaded brackets (see illustration 15.8).

6 Remove the small trim piece from the bottom of the recess in the

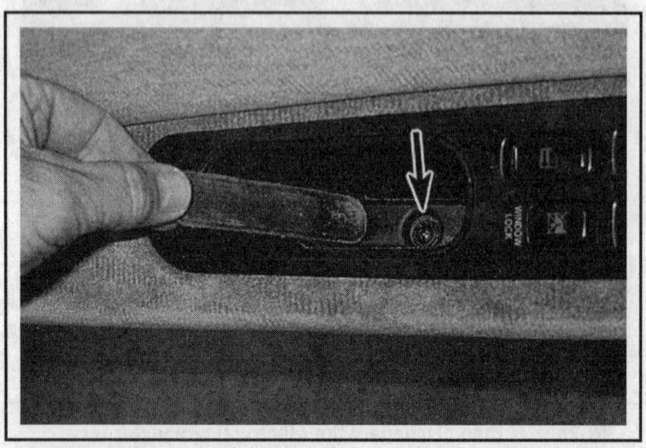

15.6a Remove this small trim piece from the recess in the armrest switch panel and remove the screw

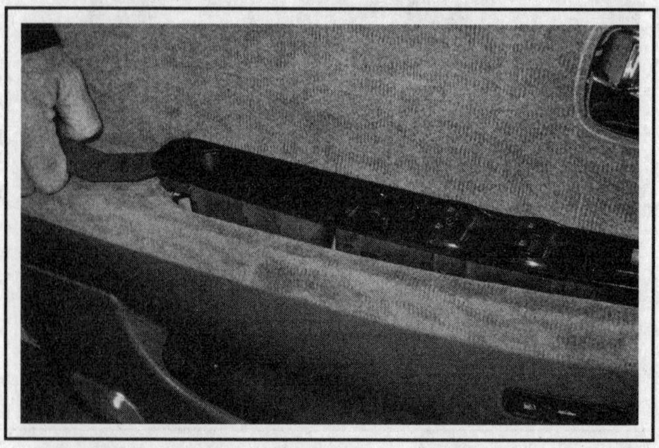

15.6b Pry out the switch panel

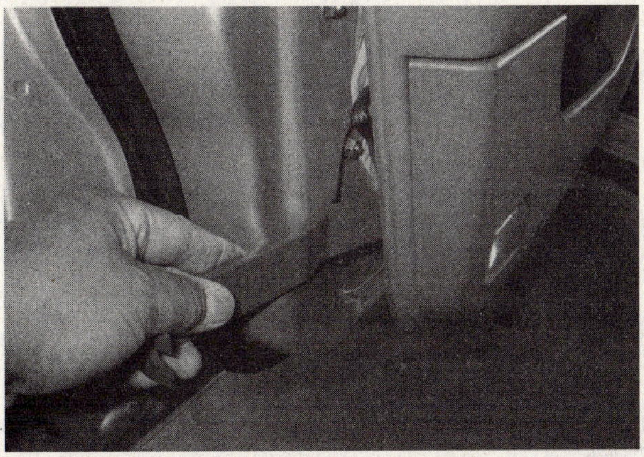

15.7 Use a trim removal tool to pry the door trim panel loose from the pop fasteners located around the circumference of the door

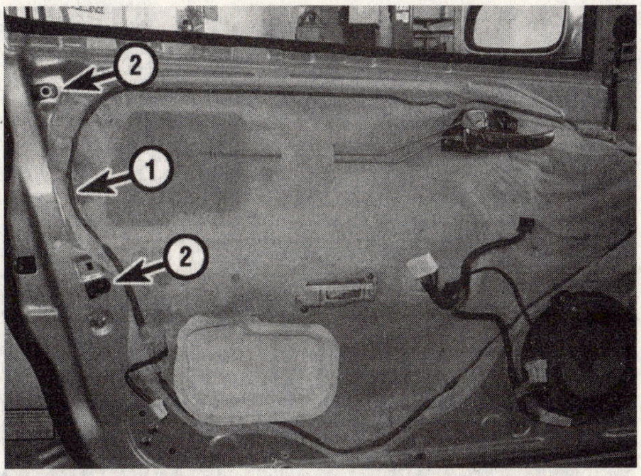

15.8 Door watershield adhesive bead (1) and threaded brackets for the rear trim panel screws (2)

15.9 Position of the clip, before installing the handle

armrest switch panel and remove the screw below the trim piece (see illustration), then pry out the switch panel (see illustration) and disconnect the electrical connectors.

7 Once all the door panel retaining screws are removed, use a trim panel removal tool or a putty knife to carefully pry the door panel loose at the lower edge and sides (see illustration). Lift up the upper edge of the door trim panel to disengage it from the lip that runs along the top of the door. Pull the upper edge toward you and disconnect the electrical connectors for all wiring harnesses between the door and the trim panel.

8 For access to the door latch, lock cylinder, door outside handle or the door window regulator, carefully peel back the plastic watershield. Use a sharp utility knife to separate the bead of adhesive that secures the watershield to the door (see illustration).

✲✲ CAUTION:

Be careful not to cut the watershield itself because it cannot be re-used.

9 Installation is the reverse of removal. On manual window models, install the retaining clip to the regulator handle before installing the handle to the regulator shaft (see illustration).

2006.5 AND LATER MODELS

10 The procedure for removing the door trim panel on later models is essentially the same as earlier models (see Steps 2 through 9), except that the locations of the fasteners around the edge of the trim panel will vary slightly.

11 These models do not use a watershield; they use a door module or inner panel - a large flat metal mounting plate on which the window regulator and motor, the inside door handle and other components are mounted. To remove the module, disconnect all electrical connectors, then remove all fasteners: four bolts (located around the lower and front edges of the module), one nut (located at the lower rear end of the module), and three screws (see illustration 17.9).

➡ Note: The latch assembly must be removed with the module; they can only be separated after removing the entire assembly from the door.

16 Door - removal, installation and adjustment

➡ Note: The door is heavy and awkward to handle - at least two people should perform this procedure.

REMOVAL AND INSTALLATION

➧ Refer to illustration 16.3

1 Raise the window completely in the door and disconnect the cable from the negative battery terminal (see Chapter 5, Section 1).

2 Open the door all the way and support it from the ground on jacks or blocks covered with rags to prevent damaging the paint.

3 From the door side, detach the rubber conduit between the body and the door (see illustration). If you can disconnect all wires between the body and the door at this location, proceed to Step 4. If not, remove the door trim panel (see Section 15), then disconnect the connectors for all wiring leading through the conduit. If any of the connectors inside

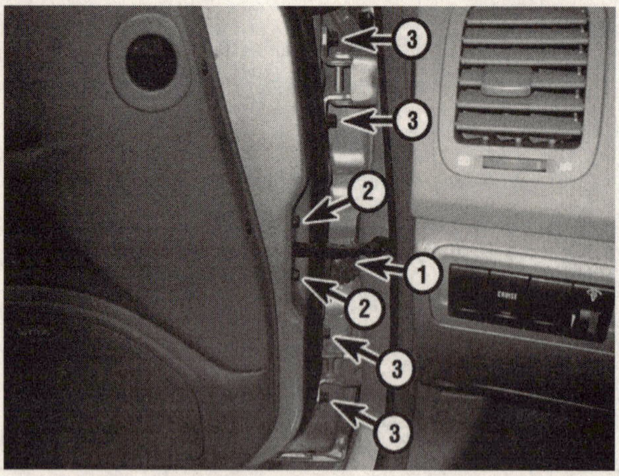

16.3 Door removal details:

1 *Rubber conduit for electrical wiring harnesses*
2 *Door stop strut bolts*
3 *Door hinge bolts*

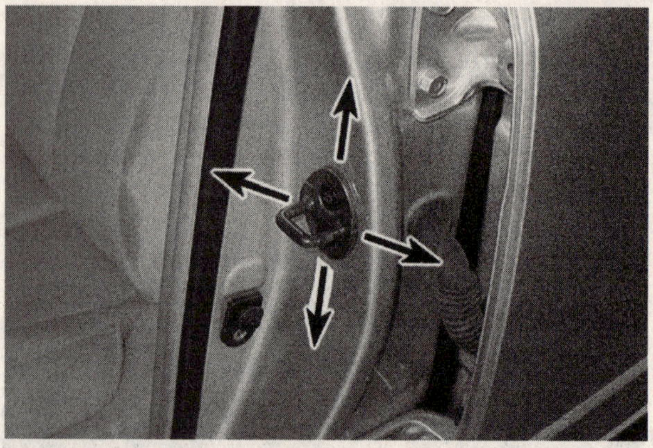

16.11 Adjust the door lock striker by loosening the mounting fasteners and gently tapping the striker in the desired direction

the door are inaccessible, remove either the watershield (2001 through 2006 models) or the door module (2006.5 and later models) (see Section 15). On all models, trace the wiring from its point of entry into the door to its electrical connector in the door and disconnect it. Pull the wiring harness through the conduit hole and remove it from the door.

4 Remove the door stop strut bolts.

5 Mark around the door hinges with a pen or a scribe to facilitate realignment during reassembly.

6 With an assistant holding the door, remove the hinge-to-door bolts and lift off the door.

7 Installation is the reverse of removal.

ADJUSTMENT

➧ **Refer to illustration 16.11**

8 Having proper door-to-body alignment is a critical part of a well-functioning door assembly. First check the door hinge pins for excessive play. Fully open the door and lift up and down on the door without lifting the body. If a door has 1/16-inch or more excessive play, the hinges should be replaced.

9 Door-to-body alignment adjustments are made by loosening the hinge-to-body bolts or hinge-to-door bolts and moving the door. Proper body alignment is achieved when the top of the doors are parallel with the roof section, the front door is flush with the fender, the rear door is flush with the rear quarter panel and the bottom of the doors are aligned with the lower rocker panel. If these goals can't be reached by adjusting the hinge-to-body or hinge-to-door bolts, body alignment shims may have to be purchased and inserted behind the hinges to achieve correct alignment.

10 To adjust the door-closed position, scribe a line or mark around the striker plate to provide a reference point, and then check that the door latch is contacting the center of the latch striker. If not, adjust the up and down position first.

11 Finally adjust the latch striker sideways position, so that the door panel is flush with the center pillar or rear quarter panel and provides positive engagement with the latch mechanism (see illustration).

17 Door latch, lock cylinder and handles - removal and installation

CAUTION:

Wear gloves when working inside the door openings to protect against cuts from sharp metal edges.

INSIDE DOOR HANDLE

➧ **Refer to illustration 17.2**

1 Remove the door trim panel (see Section 15).

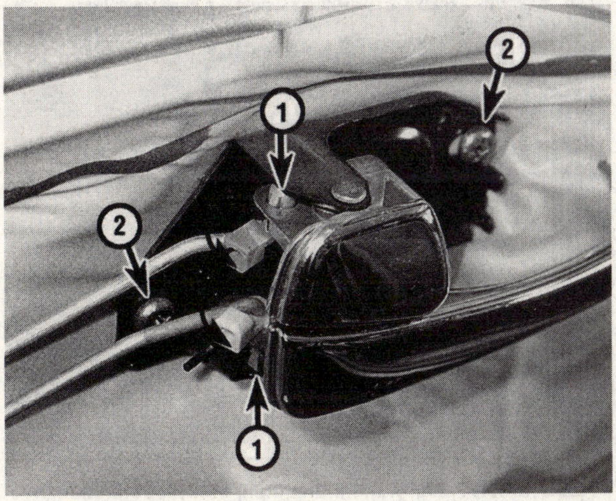

17.2 Inside door handle details:

1 *Lock rods (open the plastic locks, then push the ends of the rods out of their levers)*
2 *Inside door handle mounting screws*

2 Disconnect the lock rods from the inside handle (see illustration)
3 Remove the inside handle mounting screws and remove the handle.
4 Installation is the reverse of removal.

DOOR LATCH

2001 through 2006 models

Refer to illustrations 17.6 and 17.8

5 Remove the door trim panel and the watershield (see Section 15).
6 Working through the large access hole, disengage the rods from the inside handle (see illustration 17.2) and the lock cylinder (see illustration). The door lock rods are secured by plastic clips. Unsnap each plastic clip, then pull the rod out of its locating hole.
7 Disconnect the electrical connectors from the latch.
8 Remove the screws securing the latch to the door (see illustration) and remove the latch assembly through the access opening in the door.
9 Installation is the reverse of removal.

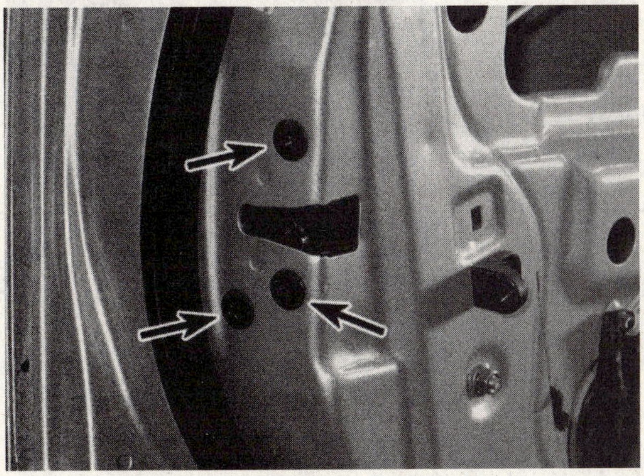

17.8 Door latch mounting screws

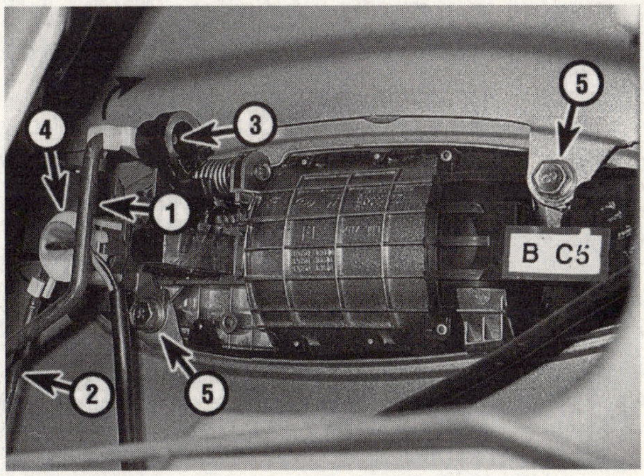

17.6 Outside handle and lock cylinder details (2001 through 2006 models):

1 *Lock cylinder-to-latch rod*
2 *Outside handle-to-latch rod*
3 *After flipping up each plastic lock, push each rod out of its lever*
4 *Lock cylinder electrical connector*
5 *Outside handle/lock cylinder assembly mounting bolts*

2006.5 and later models

10 Remove the door trim panel (see Section 15).
11 Remove the window glass (see Section 18).
12 Remove the inside door handle.
13 Remove the rear window glass channel.
14 Remove the door module assembly (see Step 11 in Section 15).
15 Unbolt and detach the latch from the door module.
16 Installation is the reverse of removal.

OUTSIDE HANDLE AND DOOR LOCK CYLINDER

CAUTION:

Take care not to scratch the paint on the outside of the door. Wide masking tape applied around the handle opening before beginning the procedure can help avoid scratches.

2001 through 2006 models

17 Remove the door trim panel and the watershield (see Section 15).
18 Working through the access hole, disengage the plastic clips that secure the door handle-to-latch rod and the lock cylinder-to-latch rod (see illustration 17.6).
19 Disconnect the electrical connector from the lock cylinder.
20 Remove the outside handle/lock cylinder mounting bolts and remove the outside handle/cylinder assembly from the door.
21 Installation is the reverse of removal.

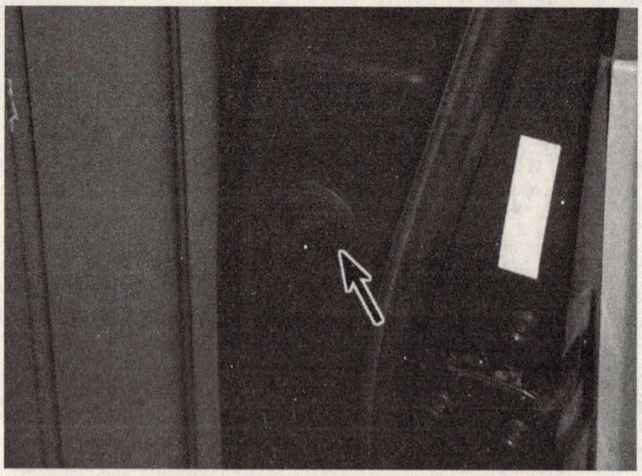

17.22a Remove this trim cap to access the outside door handle mounting bolt (2006.5 and later models)

17.22b Outside door handle mounting bolt (2006.5 and later models)

2006.5 and later models

Refer to illustrations 17.22a and 17.22b

22 Remove the access hole trim cap, then remove the fastener at the rear of the handle (see illustrations).

23 Slide the handle assembly to the rear and pull it out of its mounting hole in the door.

24 Installation is the reverse of removal.

18 Door window glass - removal and installation

Refer to illustration 18.4

CAUTION:

Wear gloves when working inside the door openings to protect against cuts from sharp metal edges.

1 Remove the door trim panel and, on 2001 through 2006 models, the plastic watershield (see Section 15).

2 Lower the window glass all the way into the door.

3 Remove the door window glass weatherstrip. Remove the glass run channel retaining screws and remove the run channel.

4 Raise the glass to access the window glass mounting bolts (see illustration). Loosen the two glass mounting bolts, then remove the glass by pulling it up and out.

Note: Access to the window glass mounting bolts on later models is farther down, below the door module.

5 Installation is the reverse of removal. Align the glass using the marks left by the glass retainers. If the glass doesn't operate easily it can be adjusted fore and aft. Check it before installing the door panel.

18.4 Window glass bolts (2001 through 2006 model shown; 2006.5 and later models similar)

19 Door window glass regulator and motor - removal and installation

CAUTION:

Wear gloves when working inside the door openings to protect against cuts from sharp metal edges.

2001 THROUGH 2006 MODELS

Refer to illustration 19.4

1 Remove the door trim panel and the watershield (see Section 15).
2 Remove the door window glass (see Section 18).
3 Disconnect the electrical connector from the regulator motor.
4 Remove the regulator assembly mounting fasteners (see illustration) and work the regulator out of the door through the large access hole.
5 Installation is the reverse of removal. Lubricate the rollers and wear points on the regulator with white grease before installation.

2006.5 AND LATER MODELS

Window motor

6 Remove the door trim panel (see Section 15).
7 Disconnect the electrical connector for the power window motor, then remove the fasteners securing the power window motor and remove the motor.
8 Installation is the reverse of removal.

Window regulator

9 Remove the door trim panel (see Section 15).
10 Remove the regulator motor (see Steps 6 and 7).
11 Remove the door window glass (see Section 18).
12 Remove the window regulator mounting nuts and remove the regulator through the larger access hole between the door module and the door.
13 Installation is the reverse of removal.

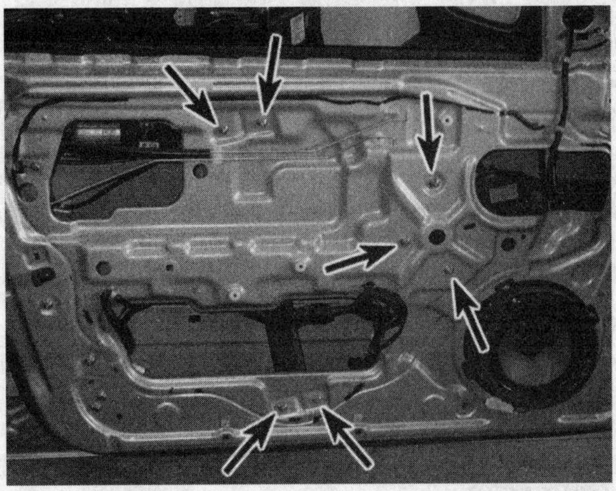

19.4 Regulator assembly mounting fasteners (2001 through 2006 models)

20 Mirrors - removal and installation

Refer to illustration 20.2

1 Remove the mirror trim panel (see illustration 15.2a).
2 Disconnect the electrical connector, remove the mounting fasteners, then remove the mirror (see illustration).
3 Installation is the reverse of removal.

20.2 To remove a mirror, disconnect the electrical connector (A), then remove the mounting fasteners (B)

21 Trunk lid - removal, installation and adjustment

➡ Note: The trunk lid is heavy and awkward to handle - at least two people should perform this procedure.

REMOVAL AND INSTALLATION

Refer to illustrations 21.2, 21.5 and 21.6

1 Open the trunk lid.
2 Remove the trunk lid trim panel by prying off the plastic retainers (see illustration).
3 Disconnect all electrical connections, ground wires and harness retaining clips from the trunk lid.

➡ Note: It is a good idea to label all connections to aid the reassembly process.

4 Pull the wiring harness through the opening and out of the trunk lid.
5 Detach the support struts using a small screwdriver to release the clip and separate the ball socket connection (see illustration). Have an assistant hold the weight of the trunk lid.
6 Mark around the trunk lid hinges with a pen or a scribe to facilitate realignment during reassembly (see illustration).
7 With the assistant still holding the trunk lid, remove the hinge-to-trunk lid bolts and lift the trunk lid off.
8 Installation is the reverse of removal.

ADJUSTMENT

9 Having proper trunk lid-to-body alignment is a critical part of a well-functioning trunk lid assembly. First check the hinge pins for excessive play. Fully open it and lift up and down on the trunk lid without lifting the body. If it has 1/16-inch or more excessive play, the hinges should be replaced.

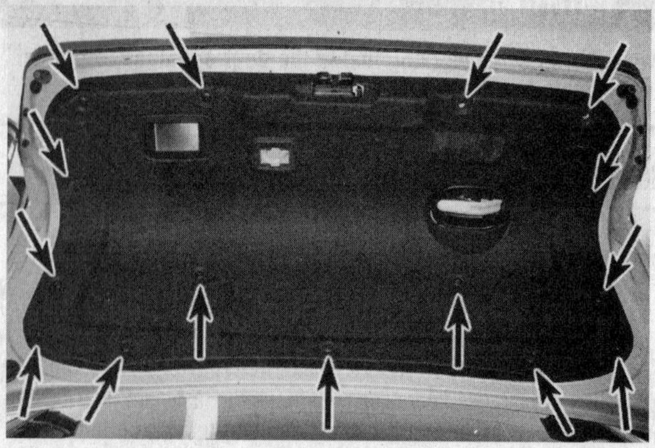

21.2 Remove the plastic retainers and screws securing the trunk lid trim panel

10 Trunk lid-to-body alignment adjustments are made by loosening the hinge-to-body bolts or hinge-to-lid bolts and moving the trunk lid. Proper body alignment is achieved when the top of the trunk lid is parallel with the roof section and the sides of it are flush with the quarter panels and the bottom of the lid is aligned with the lower sill. If these goals can't be reached by adjusting the hinge-to-body or hinge-to-trunk lid bolts, body alignment shims may have to be purchased and inserted behind the hinges to achieve correct alignment.
11 To adjust the trunk lid closed position, scribe a line or mark around the striker plate to provide a reference point, then check that the latch is contacting the center of the latch striker. If not, adjust the up and down position first.
12 Finally adjust the latch striker sideways position, so that the trunk lid panel is flush with the quarter panel and provides positive engagement with the latch mechanism.

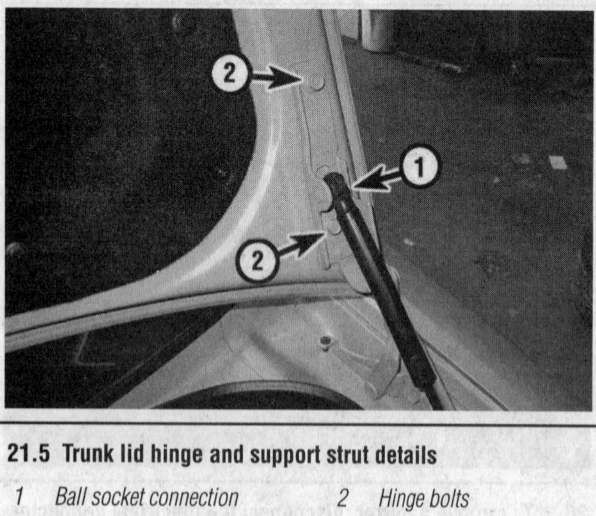

21.5 Trunk lid hinge and support strut details

1 Ball socket connection 2 Hinge bolts

21.6 Mark around the trunk lid hinges so it can be installed in exactly the same position

22 Trunk lid latch, lock cylinder and handle - removal and installation

Note: If the trunk latch fails to operate with the remote release, first check that the lock mechanism at the latch is set to the Unlock position.

TRUNK LID LATCH

Refer to illustrations 22.2a and 22.2b

1 Open the trunk and remove the trunk lid trim panel (see illustration 21.2).

2 Disconnect the electrical connector for the power lock, remove the plastic cover and disconnect the outside trunk release handle-to-latch cable (see illustrations), then disconnect the trunk lock cylinder-to-latch rod (see illustration 22.7a or 22.7b).

3 All trunk lid lock rods are attached by plastic clips. The plastic clips can be removed by unsnapping the portion engaging the connecting rod, then pulling the rod out of its locating hole.

4 Remove the fasteners securing the latch to the trunk lid. Remove the latch assembly.

5 Installation is the reverse of removal.

TRUNK LID LOCK CYLINDER

Refer to illustration 22.7a and 22.7b

6 Open the trunk and remove the trunk lid trim panel (see illustration 21.2).

7 Working through the large access hole, disengage the outside trunk lid lock cylinder-to-latch rod (see illustrations).

8 All trunk lid lock rods are attached by plastic clips. The plastic clips can be removed by unsnapping the portion engaging the connecting rod, then pulling the rod out of its locating hole.

9 Disconnect the wiring harness.

10 Remove the lock cylinder mounting fasteners. Remove the lock cylinder.

11 Installation is the reverse of removal.

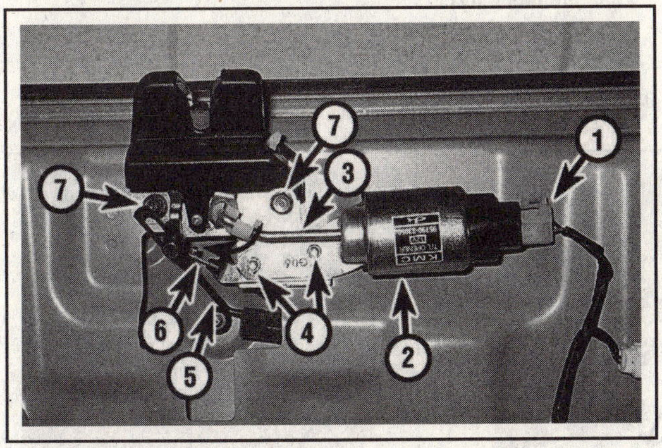

22.2a Trunk lid latch and solenoid assembly details (2001 through 2006 models):

1. *Solenoid electrical connector*
2. *Solenoid*
3. *Solenoid-to-latch rod*
4. *Solenoid mounting fasteners*
5. *Trunk lid lock cylinder-to-latch rod*
6. *Trunk release handle-to-latch cable*
7. *Latch mounting bolts*

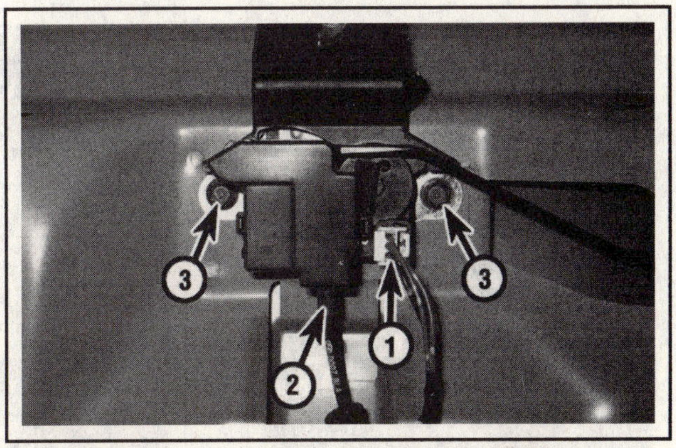

22.2b Trunk lid latch assembly details (2006.5 and later models)

1. *Power lock electrical connector*
2. *Trunk release handle-to-latch cable*
3. *Latch mounting fasteners*

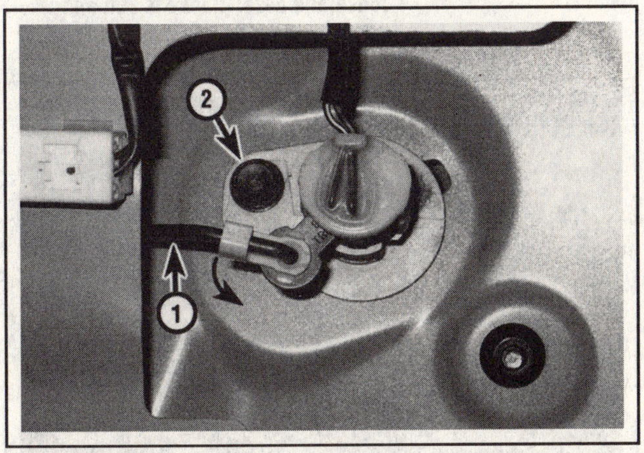

22.7a Trunk lock cylinder assembly details (2001 through 2006 models):

1. *Trunk lock cylinder-to-latch rod*
2. *Lock cylinder mounting bolt*

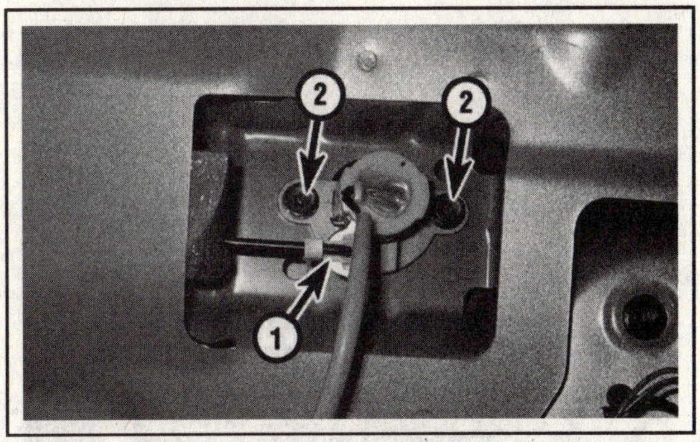

22.7b Trunk lock cylinder assembly details (2006.5 and later models)

1. *Lock cylinder-to-latch rod*
2. *Lock cylinder mounting fasteners*

23 Center console - removal and installation

➧ **Refer to illustrations 23.1a, 23.1b, 23.1c, 23.2a, 23.2b, 23.3, 23.4a, 23.4b and 23.5**

⁂ WARNING:

The models covered by this manual are equipped with Supplemental Restraint systems (SRS), more commonly known as airbags. Always disable the airbag system before working in the vicinity of any airbag system component to avoid the possibility of accidental deployment of the airbag, which could cause personal injury (see Chapter 12).

1 On 2001 through 2006 models, open the storage bin lid and remove the plastic liner (see illustration). On 2006.5 and later models, remove the mat from the floor of the storage bin, then remove the two bolts underneath it (see illustrations).

2 Using a trim removal tool, carefully pry off the bezel around the base of the shift lever and the upper trim piece around the bezel (see illustrations). Disconnect the electrical connectors from the switches on the upper trim piece and set it aside.

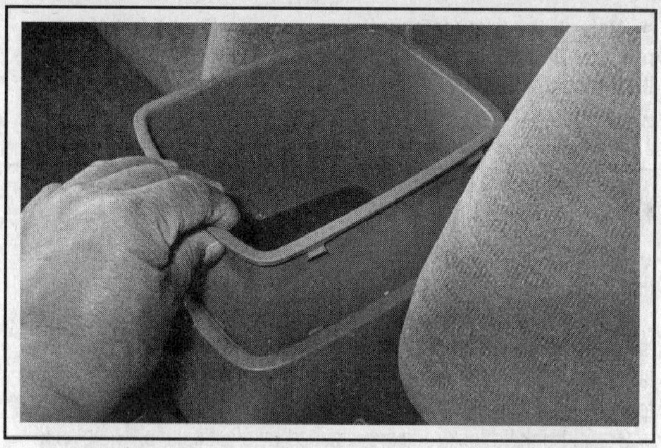

23.1a Remove the liner from the storage bin (2001 through 2006 models only)

3 On 2001 through 2006 models, remove the two screws ahead of the shift lever and the two screws behind it (see illustration).

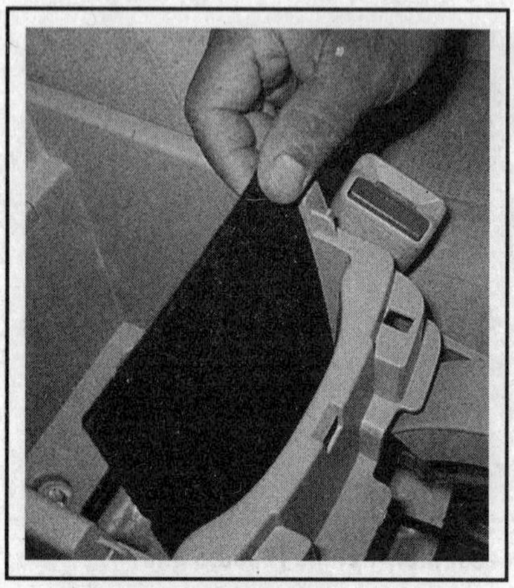

23.1b Remove the mat from the bottom of the storage bin . . .

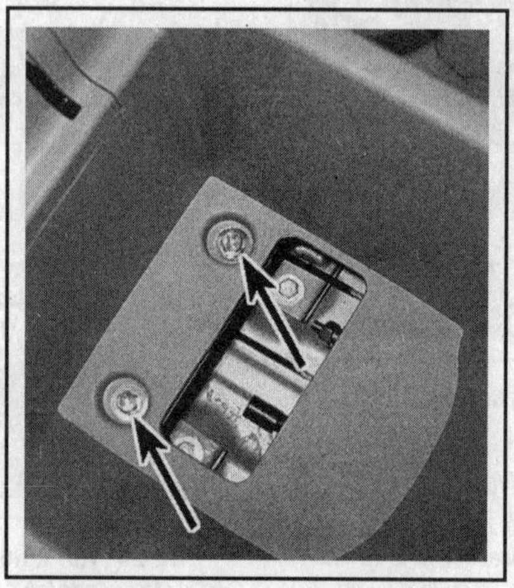

23.1c . . . and remove these two screws (2006.5 and later models only)

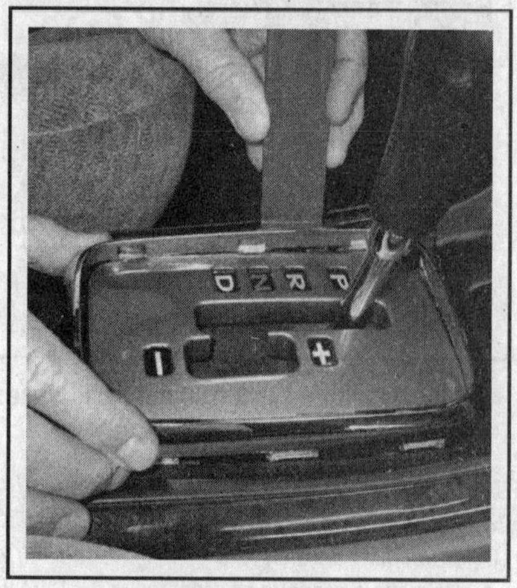

23.2a Use a plastic trim removal tool to carefully pry the shift lever bezel loose; the bezel plastic is soft and easily damaged

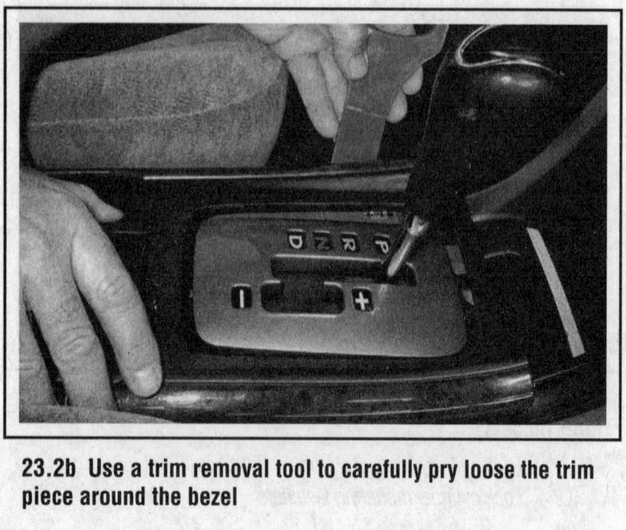

23.2b Use a trim removal tool to carefully pry loose the trim piece around the bezel

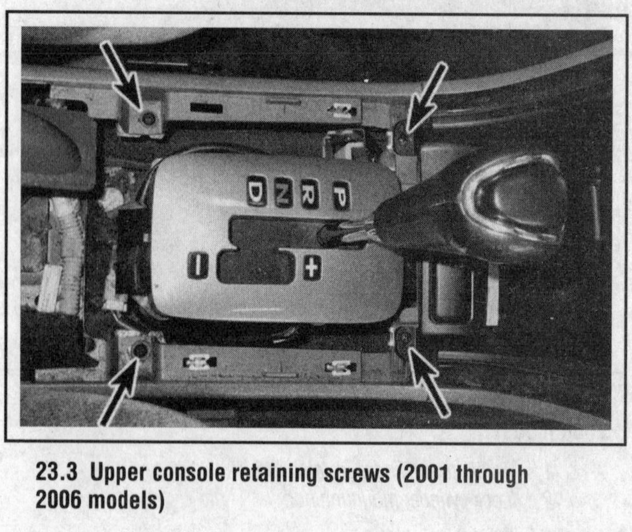

23.3 Upper console retaining screws (2001 through 2006 models)

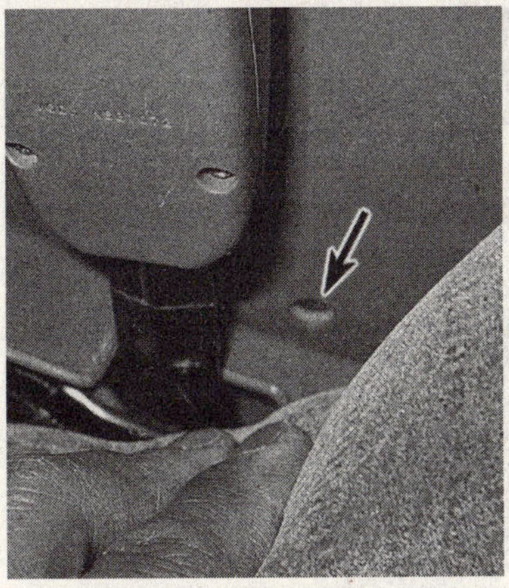

23.4a Near the back of the console on 2001 through 2006 models, there is one mounting screw on each side

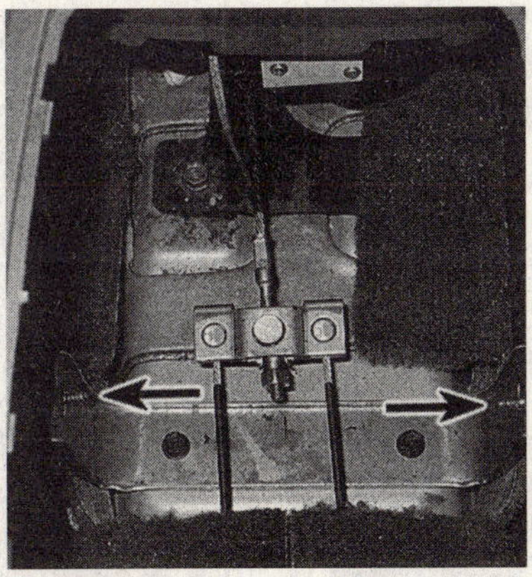

23.4b If you can't find the two rear console screws on 2001 through 2006 models, look inside the storage receptacle to see where they're located

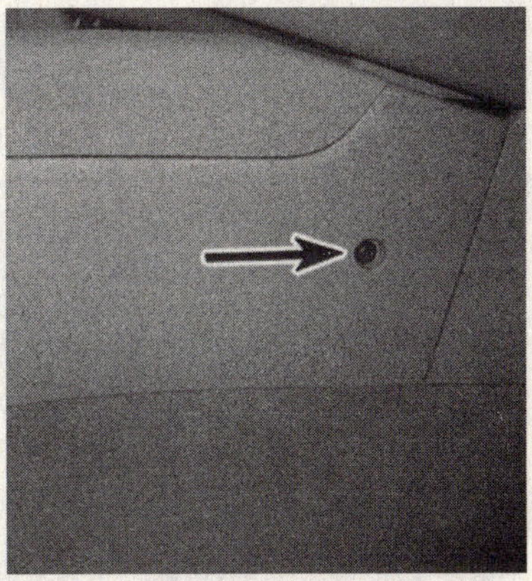

23.5 There is one screw on each side at the front end of the console used on 2001 through 2006 models (shown); there are two screws on each side on 2006.5 and later models

4 On 2001 through 2005 and some 2006 models, slide the front seats forward as necessary, then remove the two screws (see illustration) near the rear end (one on each side) of the console. You may need to look inside the storage bin for the threaded ends of the two screws protruding into the console at the bottom of the bin (see illustration).

5 Remove the two screws near the forward end of the console (see illustration). On 2001 through 2006 models, there is one screw on each side; on 2006.5 and later models there are two screws on each side.

6 Remove the console.

7 Installation is the reverse of removal.

24 Dashboard trim panels - removal and installation

⁂ WARNING:

Models covered by this manual are equipped with a Supplemental Restraint System (SRS), more commonly known as airbags. Always disable the airbag system before working in the vicinity of any airbag system component to avoid the possibility of accidental deployment of the airbag, which could cause personal injury (see Chapter 12).

➡ Note: Plastic trim parts are easy to scratch and they use a variety of clips and tabs that are easy to break. To protect them from scratches, use a plastic trim removal tool. If you don't have access to any trim removal tools, wrap the end of a flat-blade screwdriver with electrical tape.

1 Disconnect the cable from the negative battery terminal (see Chapter 5).

INSTRUMENT CLUSTER BEZEL

➧ Refer to illustrations 24.2 and 24.3

2 Remove the fasteners securing the cluster bezel (see illustration).

➡ Note: 2001 through 2006 models have three fasteners, 2006.5 and later models have two fasteners.

3 Carefully work the cluster bezel out (see illustration); be careful not to scratch any of the surrounding trim.

4 Installation is the reverse of removal.

24.2 Instrument cluster bezel fasteners (2001 through 2006 models; later models have two fasteners)

24.3 Carefully work the instrument cluster trim bezel out from its installed position

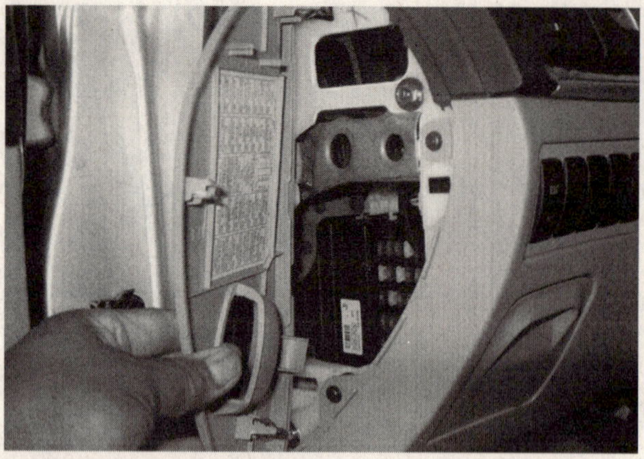

24.5 Carefully pry off the trim cover from the left end of the instrument panel (2006.5 and later models) (right cover removed the same way)

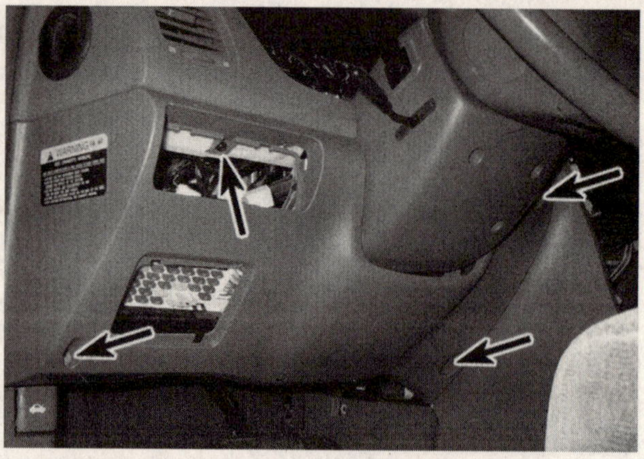

24.7a Knee bolster trim fasteners (2001 through 2006 models)

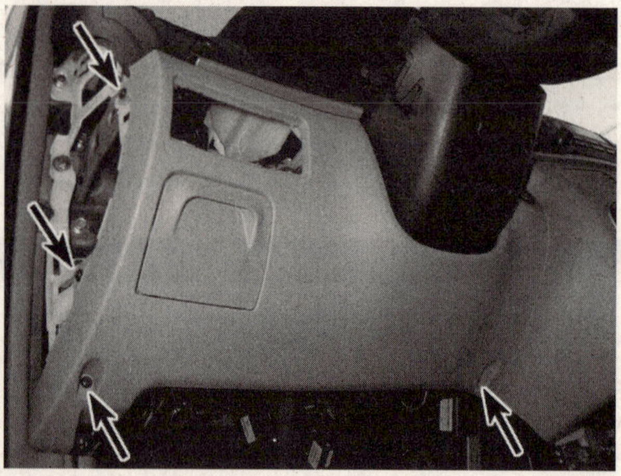

24.7b Knee bolster trim fasteners (2006.5 and later models)

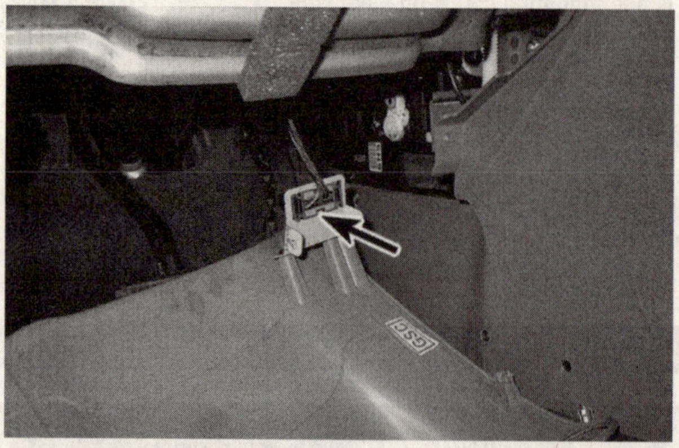

24.9 Before pulling off the knee bolster trim panel, make sure that there are no electrical connectors (like this Assembly Line Data Link connector) still attached

KNEE BOLSTER TRIM PANEL

Refer to illustrations 24.5, 24.7a, 24.7b and 24.9

5 On 2006.5 and later models, remove the left (driver's side) end cover (see illustration).

6 Remove the switch housing from the upper left corner of the knee bolster trim panel (see *Dashboard switches - removal and installation* in Chapter 12).

7 Remove the knee bolster fasteners (see illustrations).

8 Some knee bolster panels may be secured by clips as well as fasteners. If the panel doesn't come off easily, verify that you've removed all fasteners, then pull firmly on the panel to disengage it from its clips. Try not to damage or lose any plastic retainers; you'll need them to install the bolster trim panel.

9 Don't pull the knee bolster trim panel down until you've determined whether there are any wiring harnesses between the panel and the dashboard. Carefully lower the trim panel and disconnect any electrical connectors (see illustration), then remove the panel.

10 Installation is the reverse of removal. Be sure to replace any damaged plastic retainers so that each clip is securely engaged.

CENTER TRIM PANEL

Refer to illustration 24.11

11 Carefully pry off the panel with a trim removal tool (see illustration) or with a screwdriver wrapped with tape.

24.11 Detach the center trim panel by carefully prying if off with a trim removal tool. 2001 through 2006 models shown, 2006.5 and later models similar

24.15a Pull out the right stopper . . .

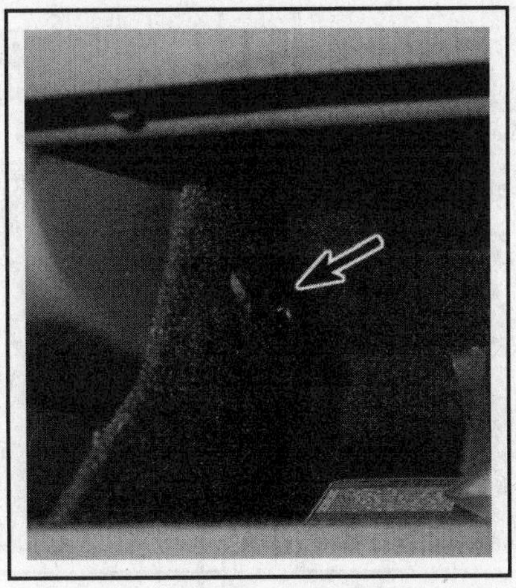

24.15b . . . and the left stopper

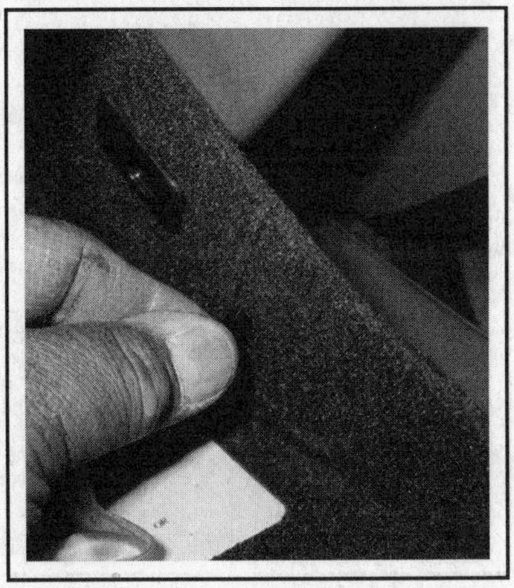

24.16a Push out the pin . . .

12 Disconnect all electrical connectors from the backside of the panel assembly and remove the panel.

13 If you need to remove any electrical components from the center trim panel, refer to Chapter 12.

14 Installation is the reverse of removal. Make sure that all panel mounting tabs snap into place.

GLOVE BOX

Refer to illustrations 24.15a, 24.15b, 24.16a, 24.16b, 24.18 and 24.19

15 Open the glove box and pull out the stopper from each side of the box (see illustrations).

16 Push out the pin for the stopper cable (see illustrations).

17 Allow the glove box to drop down.

18 On 2001 through 2006 models, remove the two bolts and two screws that secure the hinge (see illustration), then remove the glove box.

19 On 2006.5 and later models, push the hinge pins (see illustration) sideways and remove the glove box.

20 Installation is the reverse of removal.

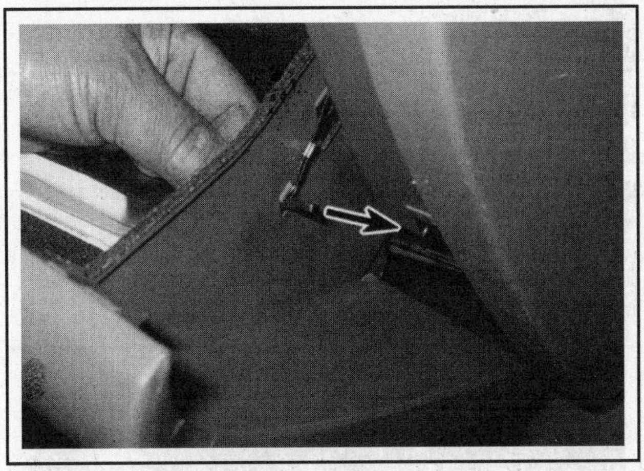

24.16b . . . for the stopper cable

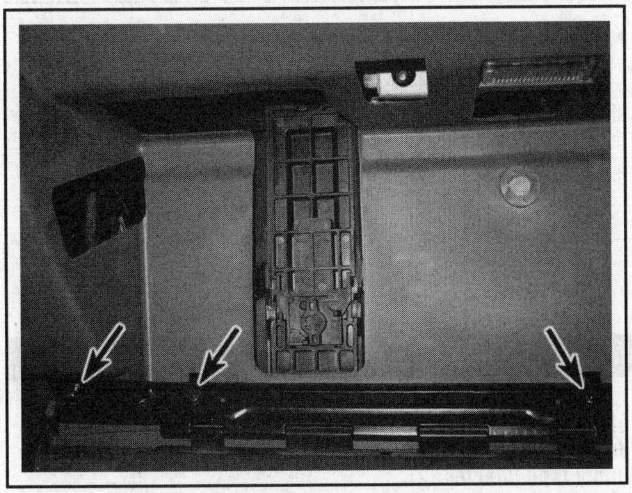

24.18 Glove box bolts and screws (right bolt not shown) on 2001 through 2006 models

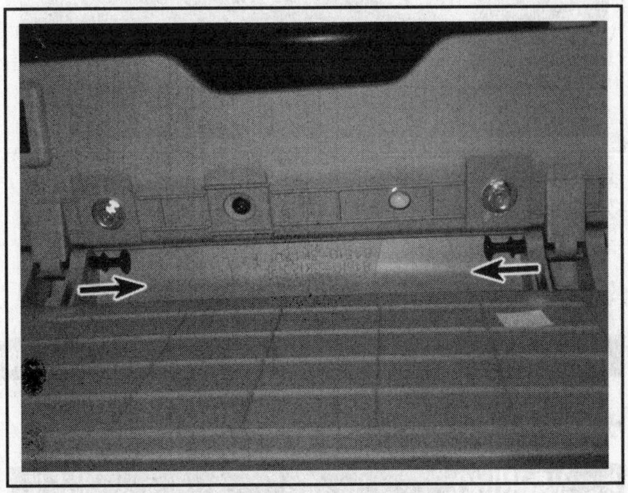

24.19 On 2006.5 and later models, slide the hinge pins toward one another to detach the glove box

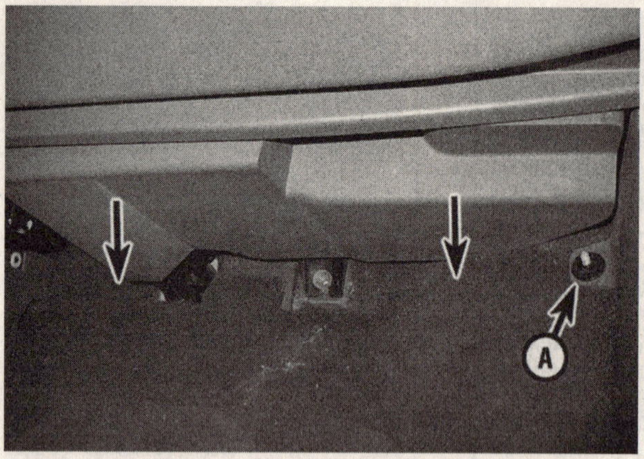

24.21 The instrument panel under cover is secured by three clips; to remove it, grasp it firmly and pull it straight down. The fastener (A) at the right secures the kick panel

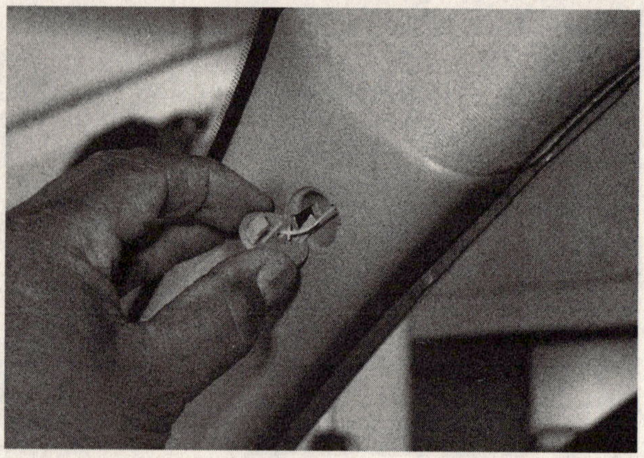

24.29 The A-pillars on 2006.5 and on later models have retaining screws under these small trim covers

RIGHT INSTRUMENT PANEL UNDER COVER

➧ Refer to illustration 24.21

21 The right (passenger's side) instrument panel under cover is secured to the underside of the instrument panel by metal clips (see illustration).

22 To remove the right under cover, grasp it firmly and pull it straight down (see illustration 24.21). Use a trim removal tool to give you more leverage if necessary.

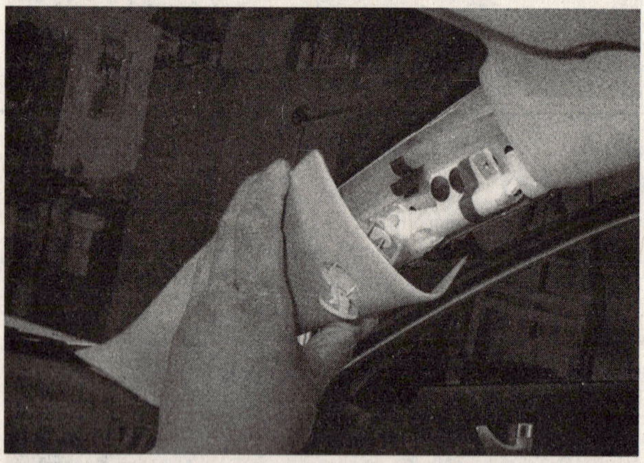

24.30 To remove an A-pillar cover, grasp it firmly and pull to disengage it from its retaining clips

23 Make sure that the clips are in good condition. Align the clips with their corresponding slots and firmly push the undercover up against the underside of the instrument panel.

KICK PANELS

24 Remove the door sill panels.

25 Remove the kick panel retaining fastener (see illustration 24.21), grasp the kick panel firmly and carefully pull the kick panel off to release the clips.

26 Installation is the reverse of removal.

INSTRUMENT PANEL SIDE TRIM PANELS

27 Pry the end panels off with a trim removal tool or a screwdriver wrapped with tape (see illustration 24.5).

28 Installation is the reverse of removal.

A-PILLAR TRIM COVERS

➧ Refer to illustrations 24.29 and 24.30

29 On 2006.5 and later models, remove the screw trim cover (see illustration), then remove the pillar retaining screw.

30 Grasp the pillar cover firmly and pull to disengage it from its retaining clips (see illustration).

31 Installation is the reverse of removal.

25 Steering column covers - removal and installation

➧ Refer to illustrations 25.3a and 25.3b

⁂ WARNING:

Models covered by this manual are equipped with a Supplemental Restraint System (SRS), more commonly known as airbags. Always disable the airbag system before working in the vicinity of any airbag system component to avoid the possibility of accidental deployment of the airbag, which could cause personal injury (see Chapter 12).

1 Disconnect the cable from the negative terminal of the battery (see Chapter 5, Section 1).

25.3a Remove the fasteners securing the two halves of the steering column covers (viewed from below) . . .

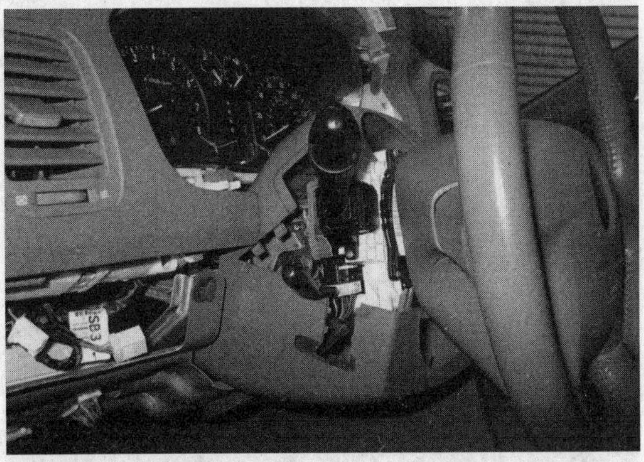

25.3b . . . then split the two halves of the cover and remove each half separately

2 Move the steering column to its lowest position.

3 Remove the screws from the lower half of the steering column cover assembly, then separate the two halves and remove the upper and lower steering column covers (see illustrations).

4 Installation is the reverse of the removal procedure.

26 Instrument panel - removal and installation

Refer to illustrations 26.9, 26.14a, 26.14b and 26.16

WARNING:

Models covered by this manual are equipped with a Supplemental Restraint System (SRS), more commonly known as airbags. Always disable the airbag system before working in the vicinity of any airbag system component to avoid the possibility of accidental deployment of the airbag, which could cause personal injury (see Chapter 12).

Note 1: This is a difficult procedure for the home mechanic. There are many hidden fasteners, difficult angles to work in and many electrical connectors to tag and disconnect/connect. We recommend that this procedure be done only by an experienced do-it-yourselfer.

Note 2: During removal of the instrument panel, make careful notes of how each piece comes off, where it fits in relation to other pieces and what holds it in place. If you note how each part is installed before removing it, getting the instrument panel back together again will be much easier.

Note 3: It is not necessary, but we suggest that you remove both front seats to give yourself more space, and to eliminate the possibility of seat damage during this procedure.

1 Disconnect the cable from the negative battery terminal (see Chapter 5, Section 1).

2 Remove the front seats to give yourself more room to work (see Section 27).

3 Remove the steering wheel (see Chapter 10).

4 Remove the multi-function switch assembly (see Chapter 12).

5 Remove the dashboard trim panels (see Section 24) and the center floor console (see Section 23).

6 Remove the heater and air conditioning control panel (see Chapter 3) and the audio unit (see Chapter 12).

7 Remove the instrument cluster (see Chapter 12), then remove the glove box (see Section 24).

8 Disconnect the passenger side airbag electrical connector.

Note: All airbag harness connectors are bright yellow.

9 Remove the driver's knee bolster (see illustration).

10 Unscrew the bolts securing the steering column to the instrument panel and lower it (see Chapter 10).

11 Remove both A-pillar trim panels (see illustrations 24.29 and 24.30).

12 Remove the kick panels (see illustration 24.21).

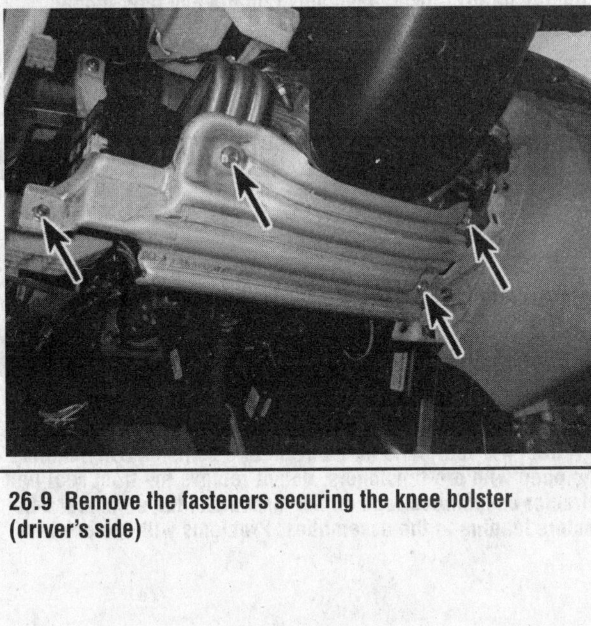

26.9 Remove the fasteners securing the knee bolster (driver's side)

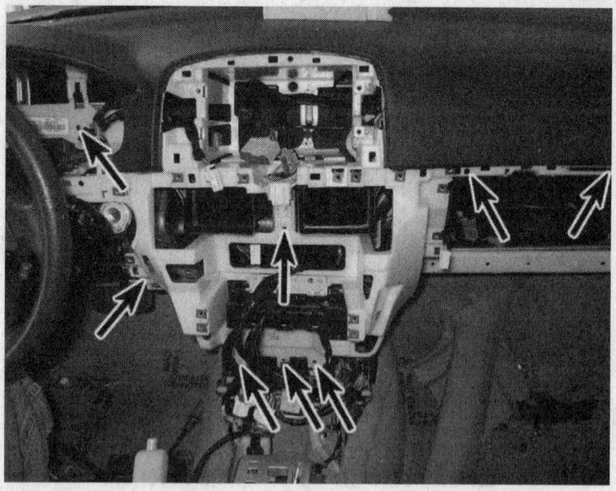

26.14a Remove the fasteners along the front side of the instrument panel (not all fasteners shown in this photo, and exact number and location of fasteners will vary with model year) . . .

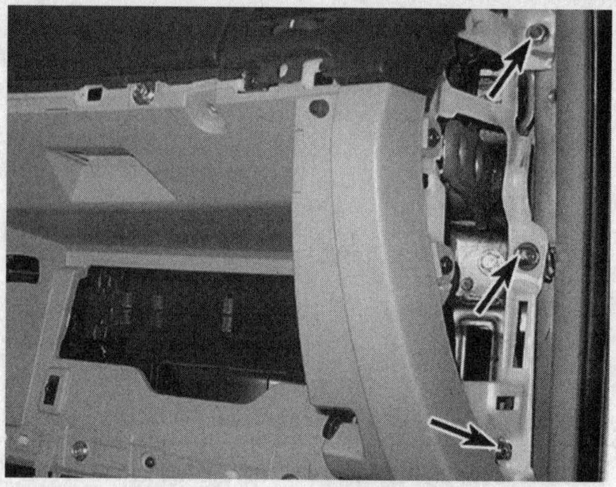

26.14b . . . and remove the fasteners from the ends of the instrument panel (2006.5 and later models shown, earlier models similar)

26.16 Removal of the support beam is an intensive task, requiring tagging and disconnecting many connectors, and finding hard-to-locate fasteners (2006.5 and later model shown, earlier models similar)

13 A number of electrical connectors must be disconnected in order to remove the instrument panel. Most connector halves are designed to fit only one other connector half, but if you have any doubts about certain connectors, mark them with masking tape and a marking pen before disconnecting them.

14 Remove all of the fasteners holding the instrument panel to the body (see illustrations).

15 Once all of the fasteners are removed, lift the panel, then pull it away from the windshield and take it out through the door opening.

➡ **Note: This is a two-person job.**

16 Removal of the support beam is a second difficult procedure. Many electrical connectors remain to disconnect, and most harnesses are clipped or clamped to this beam (see illustration). Unless you have to access the heating/air conditioning unit, don't remove the beam.

17 Installation is the reverse of removal.

27 Seats - removal and installation

FRONT SEAT

➧ **Refer to illustrations 27.2a and 27.2b**

✲✲ WARNING:

The front seat belts on some models are equipped with pre-tensioners, which are pyrotechnic (explosive) devices designed to retract the seat belts in the event of a collision. On models equipped with pre-tensioners, do not remove the front seat belt retractor assemblies, and do not disconnect the electrical connectors leading to the assemblies. Problems with the pre-tensioners will turn on the SRS (airbag) warning light on the dash. If any pre-tensioner problems are suspected, take the vehicle to a dealer service department. Also on these models, be sure to disable the airbag system (see Chapter 12).

✲✲ WARNING:

On models with side-impact airbags, be sure to disarm the airbag system before beginning this procedure (see Chapter 12).

1 Pry off any plastic covers to access the seat tracks and their

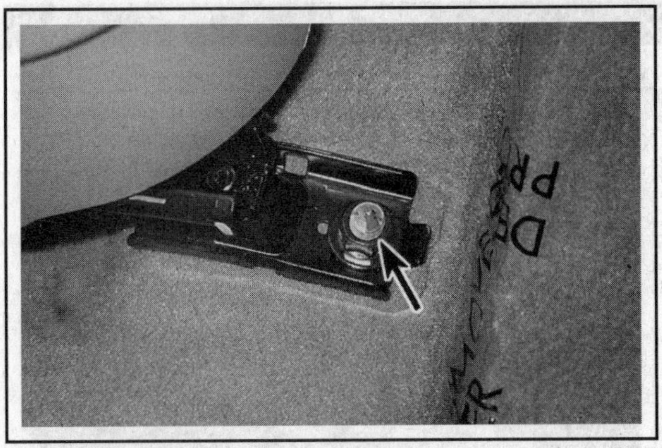

27.2a Front seat front mounting bolts

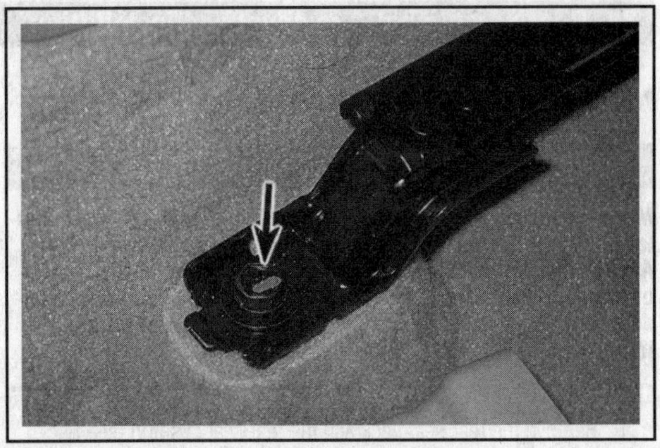

27.2b Front seat rear mounting detail

mounting bolts. Keep them in order, as they are not identical.

2 Remove the retaining bolts (see illustrations).

➡ Note: Be sure to disconnect the wiring from under each seat before trying to lift it out.

3 Tilt the seat upward to access the underside, then disconnect any electrical connectors and lift the seat from the vehicle.

4 Installation is the reverse of removal.

REAR SEAT

Seat cushion

➧ Refer to illustrations 27.5 and 27.6

5 Using a socket and an extension, remove the bolts at the back of the seat cushion, at the bottom of the seatback (see illustration). There are two bolts, one in the middle of each seat cushion.

6 Release the retainers at the bottom edge near each end of the seat cushion (see illustration).

7 Lift out the rear seat cushion.

8 Installation is the reverse of removal.

Seat back

➧ Refer to illustration 27.10

9 Remove the seat cushion (see Steps 5 through 7).

27.5 Use a socket and an extension to remove the bolts at the back of the seat cushion

10 Remove the two bolts at the bottom of the seat back (see illustration).

11 Release the lock buttons at the top of the seat back and lift the seat back up and out. The location and number of the lock buttons for the seat back varies with the model and year. Refer to your owner's manual.

12 Installation is the reverse of removal.

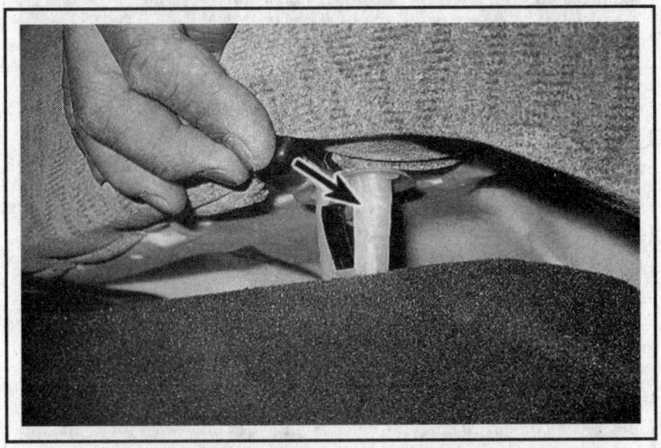

27.6 When the rear seat cushion is removed you can remove the lower rear seat back mounting bolts - the seat back is also secured with clips at the top

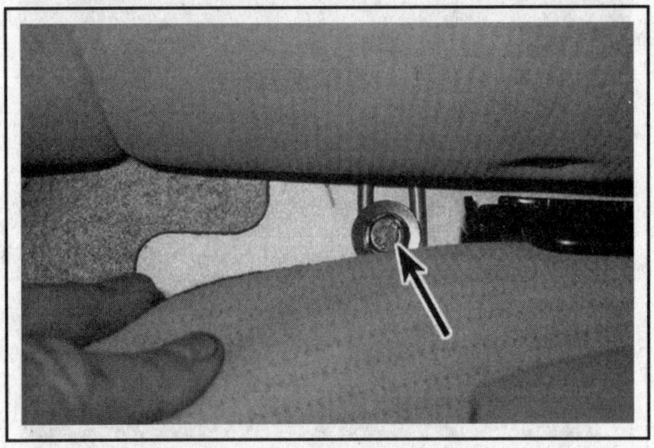

27.10 Once the rear seat cushion is removed you can remove the mounting bolts at the bottom of the seat back

28 Rear parcel shelf - removal and installation

➧ **Refer to illustrations 28.2a, 28.2b, 28.3, 28.4 and 28.5**

✲✲ WARNING:

Models covered by this manual are equipped with a Supplemental Restraint System (SRS), more commonly known as airbags. Always disable the airbag system before working in the vicinity of any airbag system component to avoid the possibility of accidental deployment of the airbag, which could cause personal injury (see Chapter 12).

1 Remove the rear seat back and the rear seat cushion (see Section 27).

2 Remove the side cushions (see illustrations).

3 Remove the left and right C-pillar trim panels (see illustration).

4 Remove the luggage compartment trim panel fasteners (see illustration) and remove the luggage compartment trim panel.

5 Remove the parcel shelf fasteners (see illustration).

6 Unbolt the rear seatbelts.

7 Carefully remove the parcel shelf.

8 Installation is the reverse of removal.

28.2a Remove the fastener at the bottom of the side cushion (right cushion shown) . . .

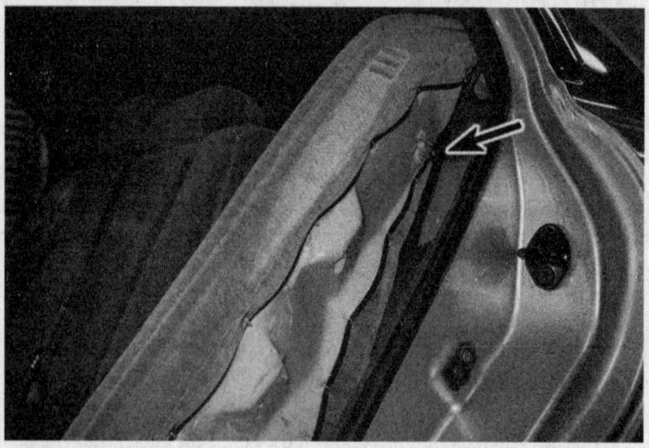

28.2b . . . then lift the cushion upward to release the top clip (left cushion shown)

28.3 Use a trim removal tool to pry off the C-pillar trim panels

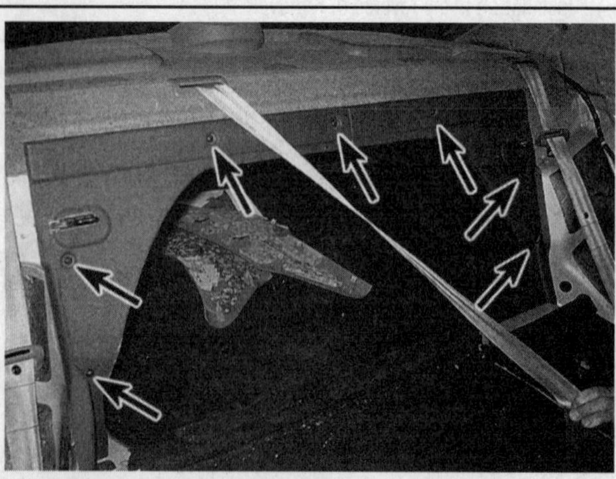

28.4 Luggage compartment trim panel fasteners (2001 through 2006 models shown, later models similar)

28.5 Rear parcel shelf fastener, right side (2001 through 2006 models shown, later models similar)

12 CHASSIS ELECTRICAL SYSTEM

Section

1 General information

The electrical system is a 12-volt, negative ground type. Power for the lights and all electrical accessories is supplied by a lead/acid-type battery, which is charged by the alternator.

This Chapter covers repair and service procedures for the various electrical components not associated with the engine. Information on the battery, alternator and starter motor can be found in Chapter 5.

It should be noted that when portions of the electrical system are serviced, the cable should be disconnected from the negative battery terminal to prevent electrical shorts and/or fires.

2 Electrical troubleshooting - general information

➧ Refer to illustrations 2.5a and 2.5b

A typical electrical circuit consists of an electrical component, any switches, relays, motors, fuses, fusible links or circuit breakers related to that component and the wiring and connectors that link the component to both the battery and the chassis. To help you pinpoint an electrical circuit problem, wiring diagrams are included at the end of this Chapter.

Before tackling any troublesome electrical circuit, first study the appropriate wiring diagrams to get a complete understanding of what makes up that individual circuit. For instance, noting whether other components related to the circuit are operating correctly can often narrow down potential causes of trouble. If several components or circuits fail at one time, chances are the problem is in a fuse or ground connection, because several circuits are often routed through the same fuse and ground connections.

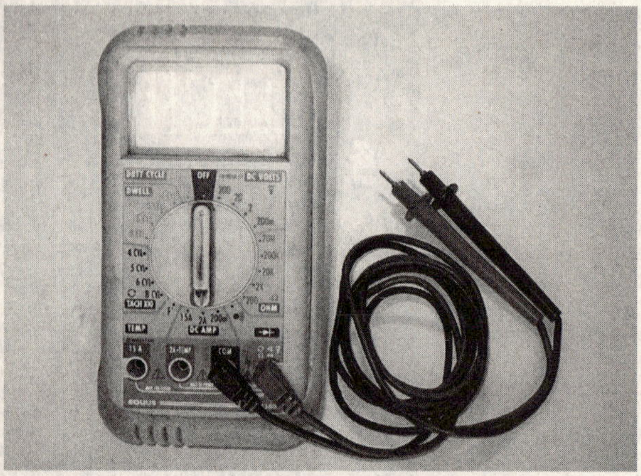

2.5a The most useful tool for electrical troubleshooting is a digital multimeter that can check volts, amps, and test continuity

2.5b A simple test light is a very handy tool for testing voltage

Electrical problems usually stem from simple causes, such as loose or corroded connections, a blown fuse, a melted fusible link or a failed relay. Visually inspect the condition of all fuses, wires and connections in a problem circuit before troubleshooting the circuit.

If test equipment and instruments are going to be utilized, use the diagrams to plan ahead of time where you will make the necessary connections in order to accurately pinpoint the trouble spot.

The basic tools needed for electrical troubleshooting include a circuit tester or voltmeter (a 12-volt bulb with a set of test leads can also be used), a continuity tester, which includes a bulb, battery and set of test leads, and a jumper wire, preferably with a circuit breaker incorporated, which can be used to bypass electrical components (see illustrations). Before attempting to locate a problem with test instruments, use the wiring diagram(s) to decide where to make the connections.

VOLTAGE CHECKS

➧ Refer to illustration 2.6

Voltage checks should be performed if a circuit is not functioning properly. Connect one lead of a circuit tester to either the negative battery terminal or a known good ground. Connect the other lead to a connector in the circuit being tested, preferably nearest to the battery or

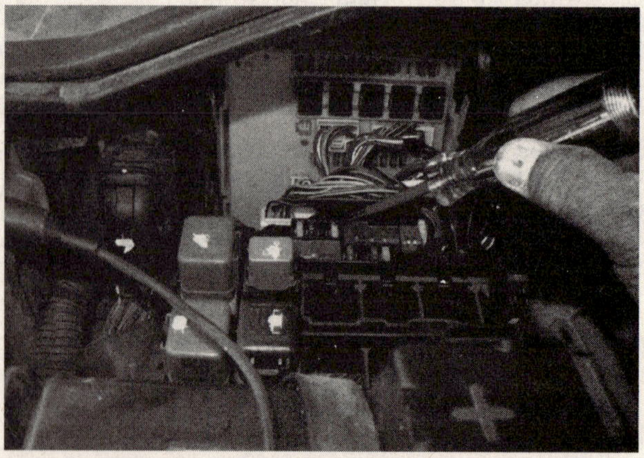

2.6 In use, a basic test light's lead is clipped to a known good ground, then the pointed probe can test connectors, wires or electrical sockets - if the bulb lights, the circuit being tested has battery voltage

fuse (see illustration). If the bulb of the tester lights, voltage is present, which means that the part of the circuit between the connector and the battery is problem free. Continue checking the rest of the circuit in the same fashion. When you reach a point at which no voltage is present, the problem lies between that point and the last test point with voltage. Most of the time the problem can be traced to a loose connection.

➡ **Note: Keep in mind that some circuits receive voltage only when the ignition key is in the Accessory or Run position.**

FINDING A SHORT

One method of finding shorts in a live circuit is to remove the fuse and connect a test light in place of the fuse terminals (fabricate two jumper wires with small spade terminals, plug the jumper wires into the fuse box and connect the test light). There should be voltage present in the circuit. Move the suspected wiring harness from side-to-side while watching the test light. If the bulb goes off, there is a short to ground somewhere in that area, probably where the insulation has rubbed through.

GROUND CHECK

Perform a ground test to check whether a component is properly grounded. Disconnect the battery and connect one lead of a continuity tester or multimeter (set to the ohm scale), to a known good ground. Connect the other lead to the wire or ground connection being tested. If the resistance is low (less than 5 ohms), the ground is good. If the bulb on a self-powered test light does not go on, the ground is not good.

CONTINUITY CHECK

➧ **Refer to illustration 2.9**

A continuity check is done to determine if there are any breaks in a circuit - if it is passing electricity properly. With the circuit off (no power in the circuit), a self-powered continuity tester or multimeter can be used to check the circuit. Connect the test leads to both ends of the circuit (or to the power end and a good ground), and if the test light comes on the circuit is passing current properly (see illustration). If the resistance is low (less than 5 ohms), there is continuity; if the reading is 10,000 ohms or higher, there is a break somewhere in the circuit. The same procedure can be used to test a switch, by connecting the continuity tester to the switch terminals. With the switch turned on, the test light should come on (or low resistance should be indicated on a meter).

FINDING AN OPEN CIRCUIT

When diagnosing for possible open circuits, it is often difficult to locate them by sight because the connectors hide oxidation or terminal misalignment. Merely wiggling a connector on a sensor or in the wiring harness may correct the open circuit condition. Remember this when an open circuit is indicated when troubleshooting a circuit. Intermittent problems may also be caused by oxidized or loose connections.

Electrical troubleshooting is simple if you keep in mind that all electrical circuits are basically electricity running from the battery, through the wires, switches, relays, fuses and fusible links to each electrical component (light bulb, motor, etc.) and to ground, from which it is passed back to the battery. Any electrical problem is an interruption in the flow of electricity to and from the battery.

CONNECTORS

Most electrical connections on these vehicles are made with multi-wire plastic connectors. The mating halves of many connectors are secured with locking clips molded into the plastic connector shells. The mating halves of large connectors, such as some of those under the instrument panel, are held together by a bolt through the center of the connector.

To separate a connector with locking clips, use a small screwdriver to pry the clips apart carefully, then separate the connector halves. Pull only on the shell; never pull on the wiring harness as you may damage the individual wires and terminals inside the connectors. Look at the connector closely before trying to separate the halves. Often the locking clips are engaged in a way that is not immediately clear. Additionally, many connectors have more than one set of clips.

Each pair of connector terminals has a male half and a female half. When you look at the end view of a connector in a diagram, be sure to understand whether the view shows the harness side or the component side of the connector. Connector halves are mirror images of each other, and a terminal shown on the right side end-view of one half will be on the left side end view of the other half.

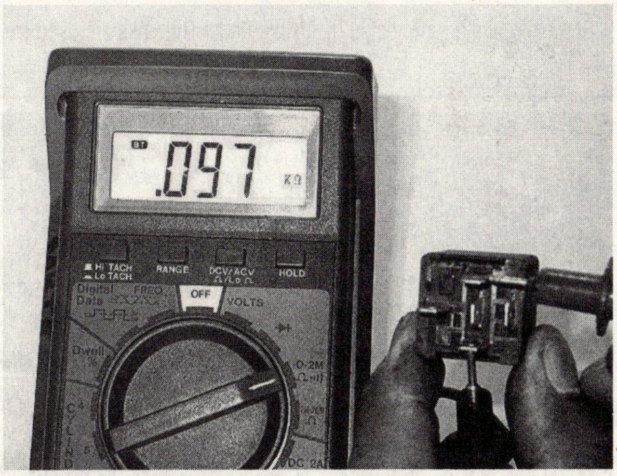

2.9 With a multimeter set to the ohm scale, resistance can be checked across two terminals - when checking for continuity, a low reading indicates continuity, a high reading or infinity indicates lack of continuity

3 Fuses and fusible links - general information

FUSES

Refer to illustrations 3.1a, 3.1b and 3.3

The electrical circuits of the vehicle are protected by a combination of fuses, circuit breakers and fusible links. The fuse boxes (see illustrations) are located in the engine compartment and either in the lower left part of the instrument panel (2001 through 2006 models) or in the left end of the instrument panel (2006.5 and later models).

Each of the fuses is designed to protect a specific circuit, and the various circuits are identified on the fuse panel cover.

Miniaturized fuses are employed in the fuse blocks. If an electrical component fails, always check the fuse first. The best way to check a fuse is with a test light. Check for power at the exposed terminal tips of each fuse. If power is present on one side of the fuse but not the other, the fuse is blown. A blown fuse can also be confirmed by visually inspecting it (see illustration).

Be sure to replace blown fuses with the correct type. Fuses of different ratings are physically interchangeable, but only fuses of the proper rating should be used. Replacing a fuse with one of a higher or lower value than specified is not recommended. Each electrical circuit needs a specific amount of protection. The amperage value of each fuse is molded into the fuse body.

If the replacement fuse immediately fails, don't replace it again until the cause of the problem is isolated and corrected. In most cases, this will be a short circuit in the wiring caused by a broken or deteriorated wire.

FUSIBLE LINKS

Some circuits are protected by fusible links. The links are used in circuits that are not ordinarily fused, such as the high-current side of the charging or starting circuits. Conventional inline fusible links, such as those used in the starter cable, were characterized by a bulge in the cable. Newer cartridge-type fusible links, which are similar in appearance to a large cartridge-type fuse, are located in their own fusible link block in the engine compartment fuse and relay box (see illustration 3.1a). After disconnecting the cable from the negative battery terminal, simply remove the fusible link and replace it with a unit of the same amperage.

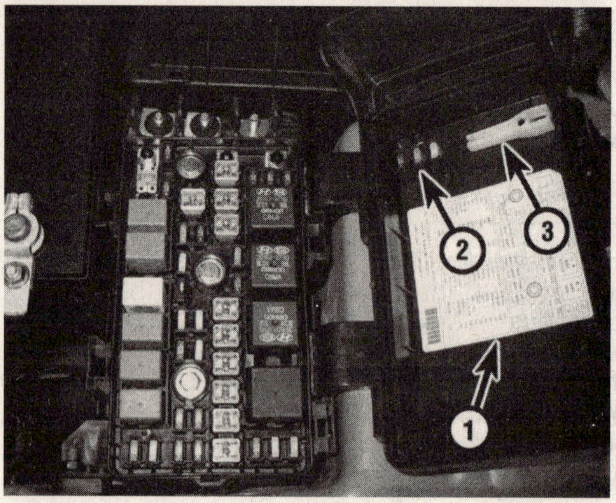

3.1a The engine compartment fuse and relay box is located at the left side of the engine compartment

1 Fuse locations label
2 Spare fuses
3 Fuse puller

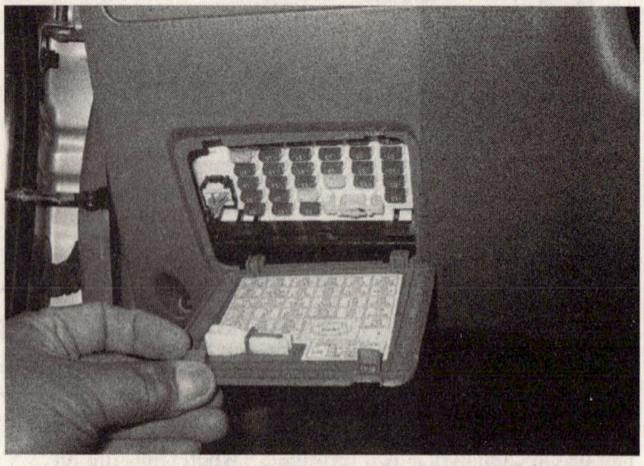

3.1b Interior fuse box location (2001 through 2006 models)

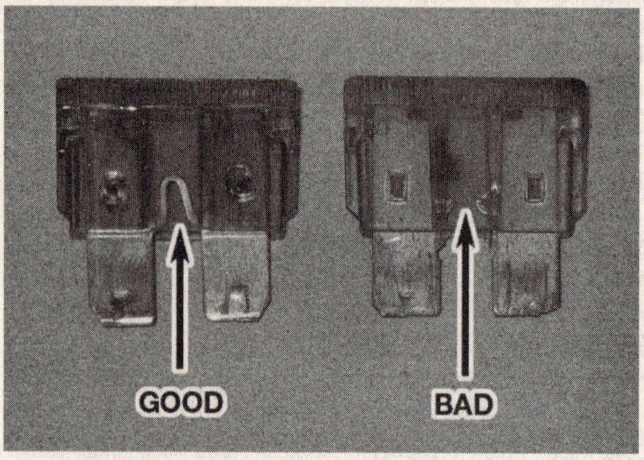

3.3 When a fuse blows, the element between the terminals melts

4 Circuit breakers - general information

Circuit breakers protect certain circuits, such as the power windows or heated seats. Depending on the vehicle's accessories, there might be circuit breakers in or near either of the fuse and relay boxes.

Because the circuit breakers reset automatically, an electrical overload in a circuit-breaker-protected system will cause the circuit to fail momentarily, and then come back on. If the circuit does not come back on, check it immediately.

For a basic check, pull the circuit breaker up out of its socket on the fuse panel, but just far enough to probe with a voltmeter. The breaker should still contact the sockets.

With the voltmeter negative lead on a good chassis ground, touch each end prong of the circuit breaker with the positive meter probe. There should be battery voltage at each end. If there is battery voltage only at one end, the circuit breaker must be replaced.

Some circuit breakers must be reset manually.

5 Relays - general information and testing

GENERAL INFORMATION

1 Several electrical accessories in the vehicle, such as the fuel injection system, horns, starter, and fog lamps use relays to transmit the electrical signal to the component. Relays use a low-current circuit (the control circuit) to open and close a high-current circuit (the power circuit). If the relay is defective, that component will not operate properly. Most relays are mounted in the engine compartment fuse/relay box, with some specialized relays located in the underhood box at the fender. If a faulty relay is suspected, it can be removed and tested using the procedure below or by a dealer service department or a repair shop. Defective relays must be replaced as a unit. Identification of the circuit the relay controls is often marked on the top of the relay, but the decal or imprint inside the cover of the relay box should also indicate which circuits they control.

TESTING

Refer to illustrations 5.3a, 5.3b and 5.6

2 Refer to the wiring diagrams for the circuit to determine the proper connections for the relay you're testing. If you can't determine the correct connection from the wiring diagrams, however, you may be able to determine the test connections from the information that follows.

3 There are four basic types of relays used on these models (see illustrations). Some are normally open type and some normally closed, while others include a circuit of each type.

4 On most relays, two of the terminals are the relay control circuit (they connect to the relay coil which, when energized, closes the large contacts to complete the circuit). The other terminals are the power circuit (they are connected together within the relay when the control-circuit coil is energized).

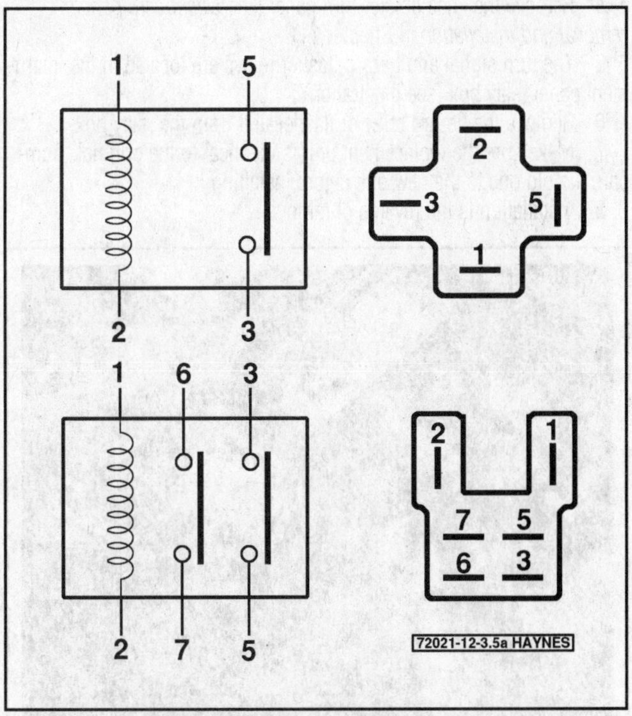

5.3a These two relays are typical normally open types; the one above completes a single circuit (terminal 5 to terminal 3) when energized - the lower relay type completes two circuits (6 and 7, and 3 and 5) when energized

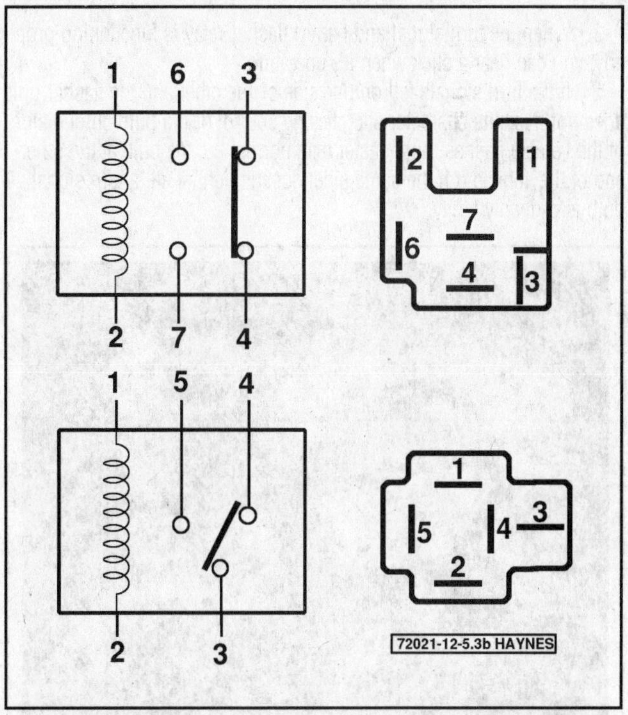

5.3b These relays are normally closed types, where current flows though one circuit until the relay is energized, which interrupts that circuit and completes the second circuit

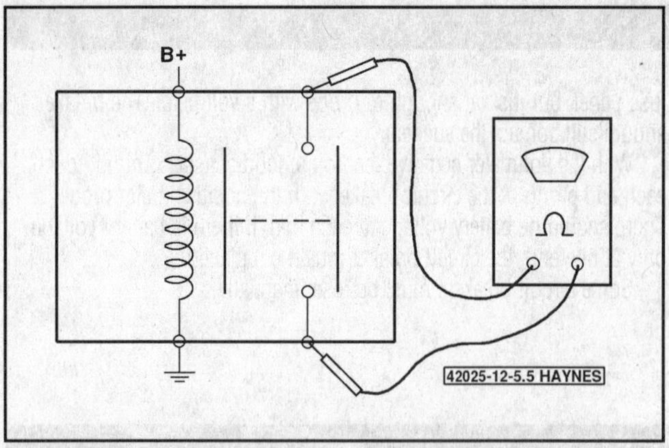

5.6 To test a typical four-terminal normally open relay, connect an ohmmeter to the two terminals of the power circuit - the meter should indicate continuity with the relay energized and no continuity with the relay not energized

5 Some relays may be marked as an aid to help you determine which terminals make up the control circuit and which make up the power circuit. If the relay is not marked, refer to the wiring diagrams at the end of this Chapter to determine the proper hook-ups for the relay you're testing.

6 To test a relay, connect an ohmmeter across the two terminals of the power circuit - continuity should not be indicated (see illustration). Now connect a fused jumper wire between one of the two control circuit terminals and the positive battery terminal. Connect another jumper wire between the other control circuit terminal and ground. When the connections are made, the relay should click and continuity should be indicated on the meter. On some relays, polarity may be critical, so, if the relay doesn't click, try swapping the jumper wires on the control circuit terminals.

7 If the relay fails the above test, replace it.

6 Turn signal and hazard flasher relay - check and replacement

⁂ WARNING:

The models covered by this manual are equipped with Supplemental Restraint Systems (SRS), more commonly known as airbags. Always disable the airbag system before working in the vicinity of any airbag system component to avoid the possibility of accidental deployment of the airbags, which could cause personal injury (see Section 24).

CHECK

1 When the turn signal and hazard flasher relay is functioning properly, you can hear a click when it's operating.

2 If the turn signals fail on one side or the other and the flasher unit does not make its characteristic clicking sound, or if a bulb on one side of the vehicle flashes much faster than normal but the bulb at the other end of the vehicle (on the same side) doesn't light at all, a turn signal bulb is probably faulty.

3 If both turn signals fail to blink, the problem might be a blown fuse, a faulty flasher unit, a defective switch or a loose or open connection. If a quick check of the fuse box indicates that the turn signal fuse has blown, check the wiring for a short before installing a new fuse.

REPLACEMENT

2001 through 2006 models

➧ Refer to illustration 6.5

4 Remove the knee bolster trim panel (see *Dashboard panels - removal and installation* in Chapter 11).

5 The turn signal and hazard flasher relays are located in the instrument panel relay box (see illustration).

6 Remove the hazard relay or flasher unit from the relay box.

7 Make sure the replacement unit is identical to the original. Compare the old one to the new one before installing it.

8 Installation is the reverse of removal.

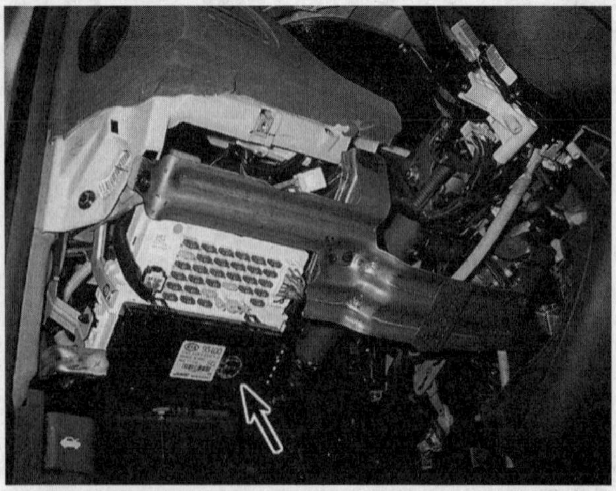

6.5 On 2001 through 2006 models, the turn signal and hazard flasher relays are located in the instrument panel relay box

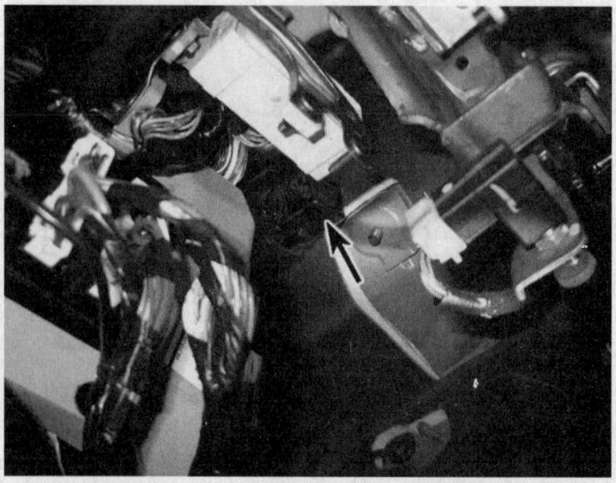

6.9 On 2006.5 and later models, the turn signal and hazard flasher relay is located under the left side of the instrument panel

2006.5 and later models

➧ Refer to illustration 6.9

9 The turn signal and hazard flasher relay is located under the left side of the instrument panel, above the junction box (see illustration).

10 Simply pull the relay straight out of the holder; it might be retained by a plastic tang.

11 Make sure the replacement unit is identical to the original. Compare the old one to the new one before installing it.

12 Installation is the reverse of removal.

7 Ignition switch and key lock cylinder - replacement

➧ Refer to illustrations 7.5, 7.6 and 7.8

⁂ WARNING:

The models covered by this manual are equipped with Supplemental Restraint Systems (SRS), more commonly known as airbags. Always disable the airbag system before working in the vicinity of any airbag system component to avoid the possibility of accidental deployment of the airbag(s), which could cause personal injury (see Section 24).

1 Disconnect the cable from the negative terminal of the battery (see Chapter 5, Section 1).

2 Remove the upper and lower steering column covers (see Chapter 11).

3 Refer to Chapter 11 and remove the driver's knee bolster panel and the reinforcement plate behind it.

4 The manufacturer recommends that you remove the steering column (see Chapter 10), but it is possible to gain access to the ignition switch screws by lowering the column without removing it.

5 Disconnect the wiring, remove the screws and remove the ignition switch from the back of the assembly (see illustration).

6 Disconnect the wiring, remove the screw and remove the key illumination ring from the lock cylinder (see illustration).

7 To remove the key lock cylinder, insert the key and turn it to the on position.

8 Use a small pointed tool to depress the lock (see illustration). Withdraw the cylinder.

9 Installation is the reverse of removal.

7.5 Top view of the ignition switch retaining screw (location) with the instrument panel removed

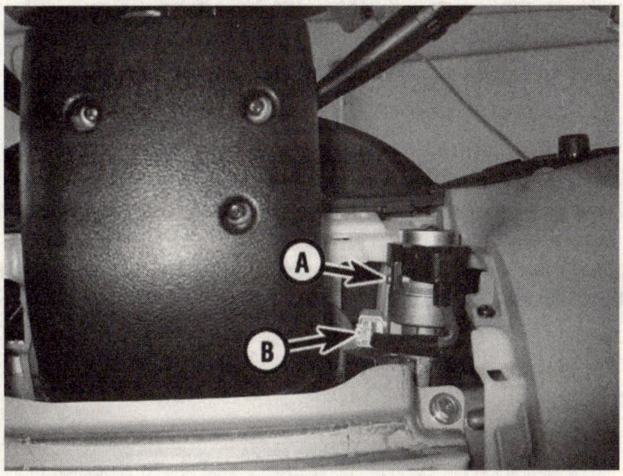

7.6 Key illumination ring retaining screw (A) and electrical connector (B)

7.8 Turn the key On, push in on this button with a pointed tool, then pull the lock cylinder out

8 Multi-function switches - replacement

WARNING:

The models covered by this manual are equipped with Supplemental Restraint Systems (SRS), more commonly known as airbags. Always disable the airbag system before working in the vicinity of any airbag system components to avoid the possibility of accidental deployment of the airbag(s), which could cause personal injury (see Section 24).

2001 THROUGH 2006 MODELS

Refer to illustrations 8.3a and 8.3b

Note: The multi-function switches (also referred to as combination switches or steering column switches) are two separate switch units connected to a central plastic housing known as the switch body, which encircles the steering column. The left multi-function switch controls the headlights and the turn signals; the right switch controls the windshield washer/wiper system. The switches can be replaced separately.

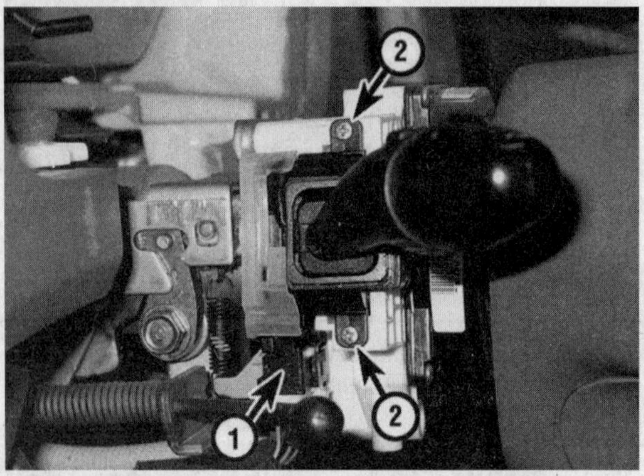

8.3a Headlight/turn signal switch details (2001 through 2006 models):

1 Electrical connector *2 Switch mounting screws*

1 Disconnect the cable from the negative terminal of the battery (see Chapter 5, Section 1).

2 Remove the steering column covers (see Chapter 11).

3 Disconnect the electrical connector from the switch (see illustrations).

4 Remove the switch mounting screws and remove the switch.

5 Installation is the reverse of removal.

2006.5 AND LATER MODELS

6 Disconnect the cable from the negative battery terminal.

7 Remove the steering column covers (see Chapter 11).

8 Each side of the multi-function switch can be removed independently of the other side by first disconnecting the wiring harness.

9 Push in the lock pin and pull the switch out.

10 Installation is the reverse of removal.

8.3b Windshield wiper/washer switch details (2001 through 2006 models):

1 Electrical connector *2 Switch mounting screws*

9 Instrument panel switches - replacement

WARNING:

The models covered by this manual are equipped with Supplemental Restraint Systems (SRS), more commonly known as airbags. Always disable the airbag system before working in the vicinity of any airbag system component to avoid the possibility of accidental deployment of the airbag(s), which could cause personal injury (see Section 24).

1 Disconnect the cable from the negative battery terminal (see Chapter 5, Section 1).

INSTRUMENT BRIGHTNESS CONTROL/CRUISE CONTROL SWITCH

Refer to illustrations 9.3a and 9.3b

2 On 2006.5 and later models, remove the fuse panel cover from the end of the instrument panel.

3 On 2006.5 and later models, reach through the opening and push the switch assembly out (see illustration). On 2001 through 2006

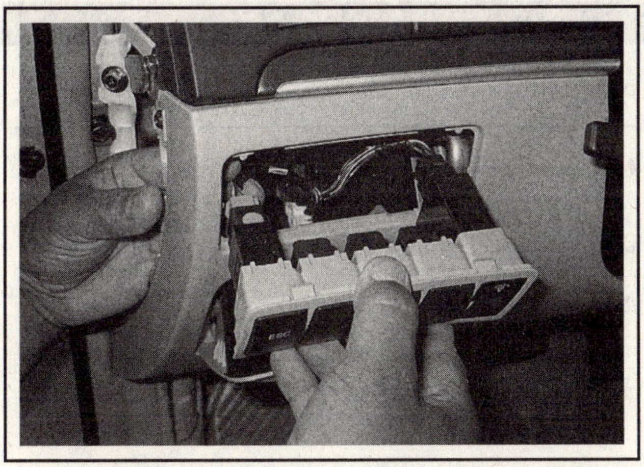

9.3a On 2006.5 and later models, reach through the opening for the fuse box in the end of the instrument panel and push out this instrument panel switch housing

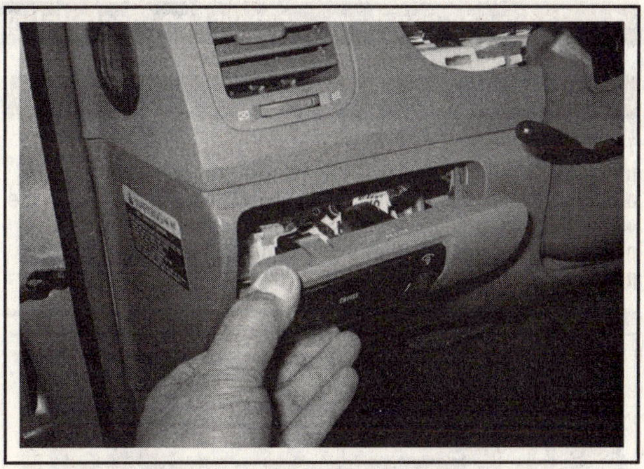

9.3b On 2001 through 2006 models, the switches can be pried out with a trim removal tool

models, pry out the switch housing with plastic trim removal tool (see illustration).

4 Disconnect the wiring harness.

5 Installation is the reverse of the removal procedure.

HAZARD WARNING SWITCH AND DIGITAL CLOCK

➧ Refer to illustration 9.8

6 Remove the center trim panel (see *Dashboard trim panels - removal and installation* in Chapter 11).

7 On 2006.5 and later models, remove the screws that secure the upper center trim panel above the center trim panel. Using a trim removal tool, carefully pry the upper center trim panel from the instrument panel and disconnect the electrical connectors.

8 Remove the switch or clock mounting screws (see illustration) and remove the switch or clock from the center trim panel.

9 Installation is the reverse of removal.

9.8 Digital clock and hazard warning switch mounting screws (2001 through 2006 models shown; other models similar)

10 Instrument cluster - removal and installation

➧ Refer to illustration 10.3

⁂ WARNING:

The models covered by this manual are equipped with Supplemental Restraint Systems (SRS), more commonly known as airbags. Always disable the airbag system before working in the vicinity of any airbag system component to avoid the possibility of accidental deployment of the airbag(s), which could cause personal injury (see Section 24).

1 Disconnect the cable from the negative battery terminal (see Chapter 5, Section 1).

2 Remove the instrument cluster bezel (see *Dashboard trim panels - removal and installation* in Chapter 11).

3 Remove the cluster mounting screws (see illustration) and pull the instrument cluster towards the steering wheel.

4 Disconnect the electrical connectors from the rear of the cluster.

5 Installation is the reverse of removal.

10.3 To detach the instrument cluster, remove the two lower mounting screws. Remove the two outer screws (A) on 2001 through 2006 models, or the upper screws (B) on 2006.5 and later models

11 Radio and speakers - removal and installation

⁂ WARNING:

The models covered by this manual are equipped with Supplemental Restraint Systems (SRS), more commonly known as airbags. Always disable the airbag system before working in the vicinity of any airbag system component to avoid the possibility of accidental deployment of the airbag(s), which could cause personal injury (see Section 24).

11.3 Radio mounting screws (2001 through 2006 models shown, other models similar)

11.7 Door speaker electrical connector and mounting screws

11.12 Tweeter mounting screws

RADIO

➧ Refer to illustration 11.3

1 Disconnect the cable from the negative battery terminal (see Chapter 5, Section 1).

2 Remove the center trim panel (see *Dashboard trim panels - removal and installation* in Chapter 11).

3 Remove the radio mounting screws (see illustration).

4 Pull out the radio and disconnect the antenna cable and electrical connectors from the radio assembly.

5 Installation is the reverse of removal.

SPEAKERS

Door speakers

➧ Refer to illustration 11.7

6 Remove the door trim panel (see Chapter 11).

7 Disconnect the electrical connector (see illustration).

8 Remove the speaker mounting screws and remove the speaker from the door.

9 Installation is the reverse of removal.

Front tweeters

➧ Refer to illustration 11.12

10 Remove the outside mirror trim panel (see Chapter 11).

11 Disconnect the tweeter electrical connector.

12 Remove the tweeter mounting screws (see illustration) and remove the tweeter from the outside mirror trim panel.

13 Installation is the reverse of removal.

Rear speakers

➧ Refer to illustration 11.16

14 Remove the rear package tray (see Chapter 11).

15 Working inside the trunk, locate the speaker electrical connector underneath the package tray area and disconnect it.

16 Remove the speaker mounting screws (see illustration) and remove the speaker from the top.

17 Installation is the reverse of removal.

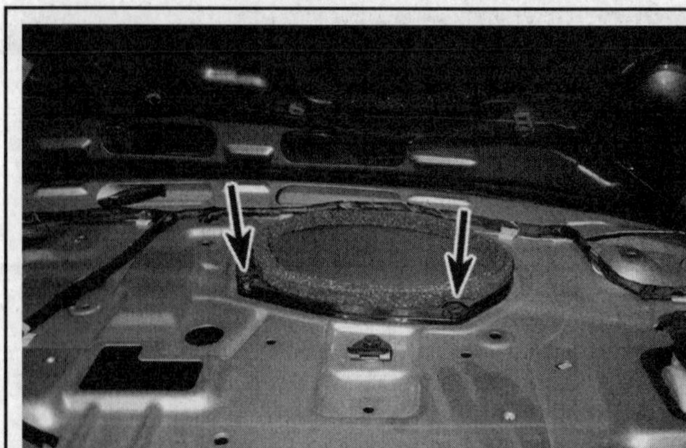

11.16 Rear speaker mounting screws (not all screws visible)

12 Antenna - replacement

2001 THROUGH 2006 MODELS

➧ **Refer to illustration 12.1**

1 To remove the antenna from its base, turn the hex at the bottom of the mast counterclockwise (see illustration).

2 Installation is the reverse of removal.

12.1 Use a small wrench to unscrew the hex at the lower end of the antenna mast (2001 through 2006 models)

2006.5 AND LATER MODELS

3 These models are equipped with a wire grid-type antenna attached to the rear window glass. If there's a problem with it, repair the antenna grid the same way that you'd repair the rear window defogger grid (see Section 14). Be sure to check the antenna connection at the rear of the audio unit before trying to diagnose a problem with the antenna itself.

13 Wiper motor - check and replacement

WIPER MOTOR CIRCUIT CHECK

➡ **Note: Refer to the wiring diagrams for the following checks. When checking for voltage, probe a grounded 12-volt test light to each terminal at a connector until it lights; this verifies voltage (power) at the terminal. If the following checks fail to locate the problem, have the system diagnosed by a dealer service department or other properly equipped repair facility.**

1 If the wipers work slowly, make sure that the battery is in good condition and has a strong charge (see Chapter 5). If the battery is in good condition, remove the wiper motor (see below) and operate the wiper arms by hand. Check for binding linkage and pivots. Lubricate or repair the linkage or pivots as necessary. Reinstall the wiper motor. If the wipers still operate slowly, check for loose or corroded connections, especially the ground connection. If all connections look OK, replace the motor.

2 If the wipers fail to operate when activated, check the fuse in the driver's side interior fuse panel. If the fuse is OK, connect a jumper wire between the wiper motor's ground terminal and ground, then retest. If the motor works now, repair the ground connection. If the motor still doesn't work, turn the wiper switch to the HI position and check for voltage at the motor.

➡ **Note: The cowl cover will have to be removed (see Chapter 11) to access the wiper motor electrical connector.**

3 If there's voltage at the connector, remove the motor and check it off the vehicle with fused jumper wires from the battery. If the motor now works, check for binding linkage (see Step 1). If the motor still doesn't work, replace it. If there's no voltage to the motor, check for voltage at the wiper control relays. If there's voltage at the wiper control relays and no voltage at the wiper motor, have the switch tested. If the switch is OK, the wiper control relay is probably bad. See Section 5 for relay testing.

4 If the interval (delay) function is inoperative, check the continuity of all the wiring between the switch and wiper control module.

5 If the wipers stop at the position they're in when the switch is turned off (fail to park), check for voltage at the park feed wire of the wiper motor connector when the wiper switch is OFF but the ignition is ON. If no voltage is present, check for an open circuit between the wiper motor and the fuse panel.

REPLACEMENT

➧ **Refer to illustrations 13.6, 13.7, 13.9, 13.11 and 13.12**

6 On 2006.5 and later models, remove the trim caps that cover the wiper arm mounting nuts.

➡ **Note: The windshield wiper arms on earlier models don't use trim caps.**

Remove the wiper arm mounting nuts (see illustration).

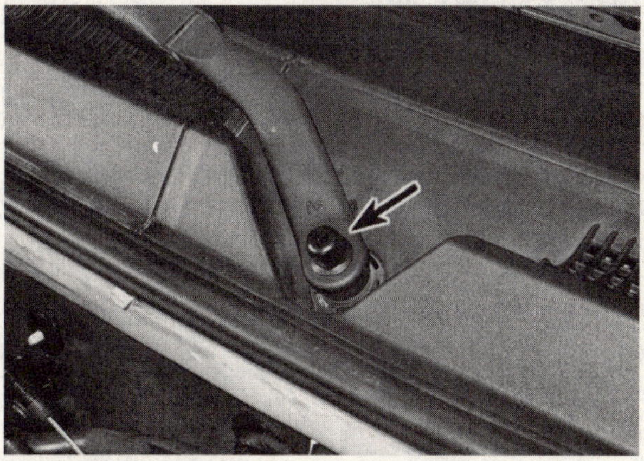

13.6 Remove the trim caps (2006.5 and later models) and unscrew the wiper arm retaining nuts . . .

13.7 . . . then mark the positions of the arms to the shafts so they can be correctly installed

7 Mark the position of each wiper arm to its shaft, then remove the arms (see illustration).

➡ **Note: If the arm is severely stuck to the shaft, use a battery terminal remover to pull it free.**

8 Remove the plastic cowl cover (see Chapter 11).

9 Disconnect the electrical connector from the wiper motor (see illustration).

10 Remove the wiper motor and link assembly mounting bolts (see illustration 13.9) and remove the wiper motor and link assembly from the cowl area.

11 Use a screwdriver to pry the linkage rod from the crank arm pivot of the wiper motor (see illustration).

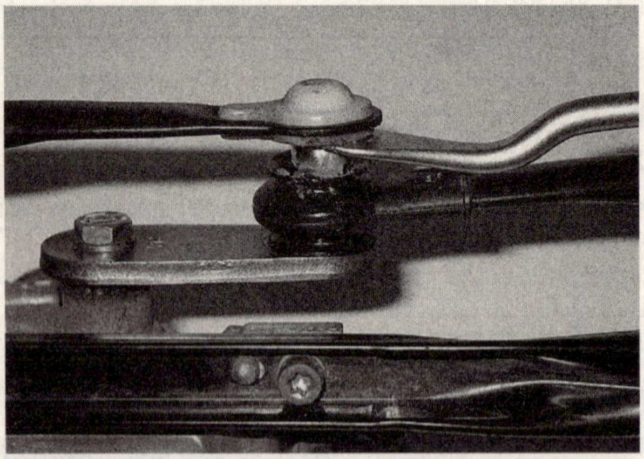

13.11 Pry the link from the crank arm; the crank arm can then be removed from the motor shaft if required

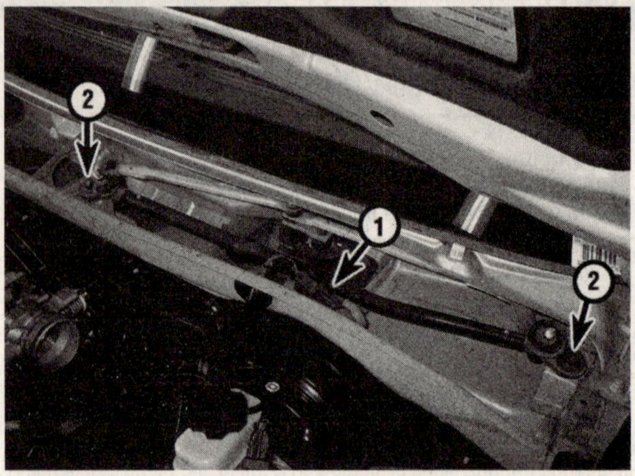

13.9 Typical windshield wiper assembly details (2001 through 2006 models shown; other models similar)

1 Electrical connector
2 Mounting bolts

12 Remove the crank arm nut (see illustration), mark the relationship of the crank arm to the motor shaft and remove the crank arm from the shaft.

13 Remove the wiper motor mounting bolts and detach the motor.

14 Installation is the reverse of removal.

13.12 Windshield wiper motor details (2001 through 2006 models shown; other models similar):

1 Wiper motor crank arm nut
2 Motor mounting nuts

14 Rear window defogger - check and repair

1 The rear window defogger consists of a number of horizontal elements baked onto the glass surface.

2 Small breaks in the element can be repaired without removing the rear window.

CHECK

➧ Refer to illustrations 14.4, 14.5 and 14.7

3 Turn the ignition switch and defogger system switches to the ON position. Using a voltmeter, place the positive probe against the defogger grid positive terminal and the negative probe against the ground terminal. If battery voltage is not indicated, check the fuse, defogger switch and related wiring. If voltage is indicated, but all or part of the defogger doesn't heat, proceed with the following tests.

4 When measuring voltage during the next two tests, wrap a piece of aluminum foil around the tip of the voltmeter positive probe and press the foil against the heating element with your finger (see illustration). Place the negative probe on the defogger grid ground terminal.

5 Check the voltage at the center of each heating element (see illustration). If the voltage is 5 or 6-volts, the element is okay (there is no break). If the voltage is zero, the element is broken between the center of the element and the positive end. If the voltage is 10 to 12-volts, the element is broken between the center of the element and ground. Check each heating element.

6 Connect the negative lead to a good body ground. The reading should stay the same. If it doesn't, the ground connection is bad.

7 To find the break, place the voltmeter negative probe against the defogger ground terminal. Place the voltmeter positive probe with the foil strip against the heating element at the positive terminal end and slide it toward the negative terminal end. The point at which the voltmeter deflects from several volts to zero is the point at which the heating element is broken (see illustration).

REPAIR

➧ Refer to illustration 14.13

8 Repair the break in the element using a repair kit specifically recommended for this purpose, available at most auto parts stores. Included in this kit is plastic conductive epoxy.

9 Prior to repairing a break, turn off the system and allow it to cool off for a few minutes.

10 Lightly buff the element area with fine steel wool, then clean it thoroughly with rubbing alcohol.

11 Use masking tape to mask off the area being repaired.

12 Thoroughly mix the epoxy, following the instructions provided with the repair kit.

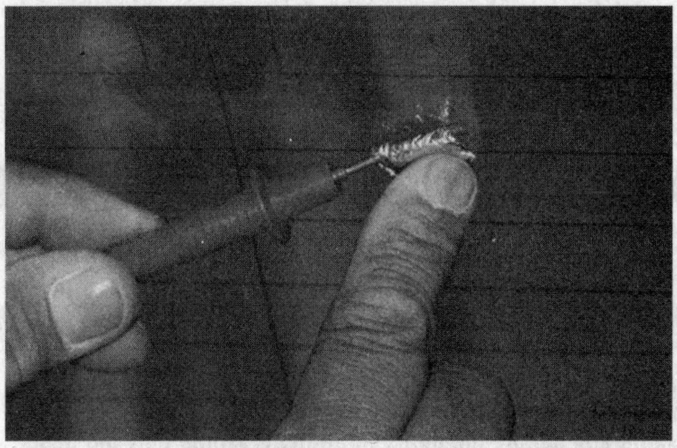

14.4 When measuring the voltage at the rear window defogger grid, wrap a piece of aluminum foil around the positive probe of the voltmeter and press the foil against the wire with your finger

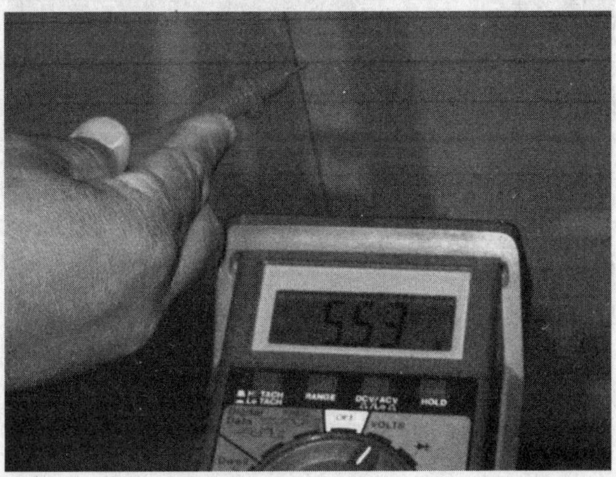

14.5 To determine if a heating element has broken, check the voltage at the center of each element - if the voltage is 5 or 6-volts, the element is unbroken - if the voltage is 10 or 12-volts, the element is broken between the center and the ground side - if there is no voltage, the element is broken between the center and the positive side

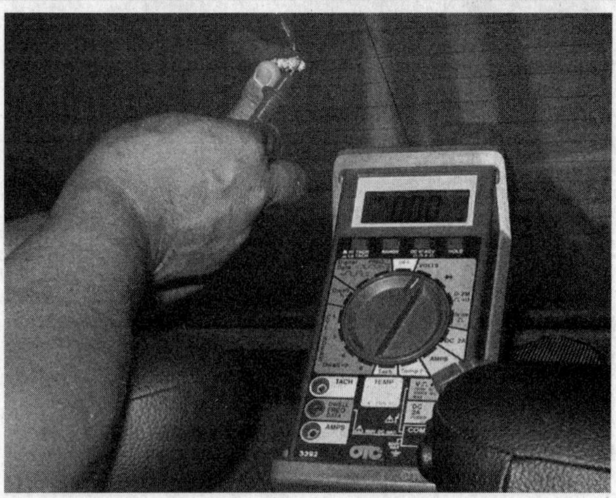

14.7 To find the break, place the voltmeter negative lead against the defogger ground terminal, place the voltmeter positive lead with the foil strip against the heating element at the positive terminal end and slide it toward the negative terminal end - the point at which the voltmeter reading changes abruptly is the point at which the element is broken

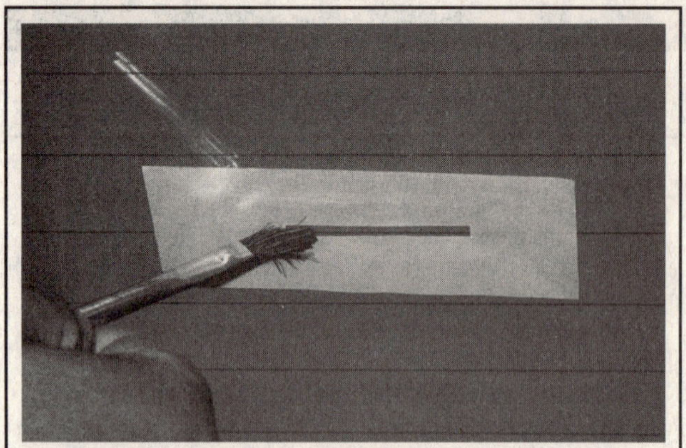

14.13 **To use a defogger repair kit, apply masking tape to the inside of the window at the damaged area, then brush on the special conductive coating**

13 Apply the epoxy material to the slit in the masking tape, overlapping the undamaged area about 3/4-inch on either end (see illustration).

14 Allow the repair to cure for 24 hours before removing the tape and using the system.

15 Headlight bulb - replacement

Refer to illustrations 15.2, 15.3, 15.4a and 15.4b

WARNING:

Halogen gas-filled bulbs are under pressure and may shatter if the surface is scratched or the bulb is dropped. Wear eye protection and handle the bulbs carefully, grasping only the base whenever possible. Do not touch the surface of the bulb with your fingers because the oil from your skin could cause it to overheat and fail prematurely. If you do touch the bulb surface, clean it with rubbing alcohol.

Note: On 2001 through 2006 models, the headlight housing contains the low-beam headlight bulb and the combination light housing contains the high-beam bulb. The bulbs are identical and are removed exactly the same way once you've removed the housing.

1 Remove the headlight housing (see Section 16).

2 Remove the cover from the rear of the housing (see illustration).

3 Disconnect the wiring (see illustration).

4 Release the retaining spring and pull out the old bulb (see illustrations).

15.2 Unscrew the cover from the rear of the headlight housing (turn it counterclockwise) . . .

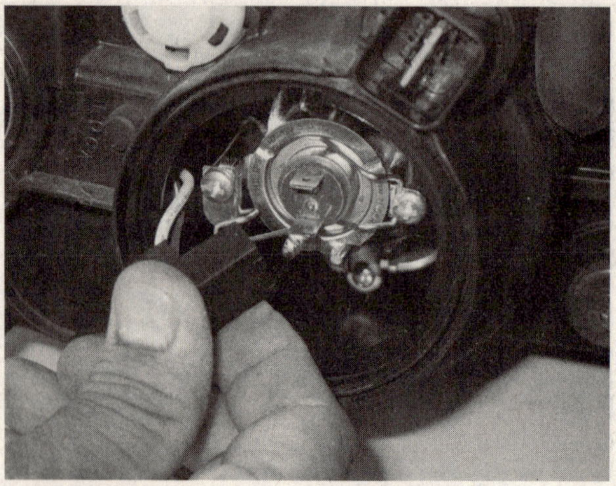

15.3 . . . then pull off the electrical connector

15.4a Unhook the spring-loaded wire that retains the bulb . . .

15.4b . . . then remove the bulb from the housing

5 Without touching the bulb glass with your bare fingers, insert the new bulb assembly into the headlight housing.

➡ **Note: If you touch the glass or if it becomes oily, clean it with rubbing alcohol before installing it.**

6 Attach the bulb retaining spring and connect the wiring.
7 Install the cover, connect the wiring harness and replace the headlight assembly.

16 Headlight housing - removal and installation

➧ Refer to illustrations 16.1a and 16.1b

⁂ WARNING:

These vehicles are equipped with gas-filled headlight bulbs that are under pressure and may shatter if the surface is damaged or the bulb is dropped. Wear eye protection and handle the bulbs carefully, grasping only the base whenever possible. Do not touch the surface of the bulb with your fingers because the oil from your skin could cause it to overheat and fail prematurely. If you do touch the bulb surface, clean it with rubbing alcohol.

16.1a The low beam headlight housing on 2001 through 2006 models has two upper bolts and another bolt at the inside edge, near the radiator, which cannot be accessed until the combination light housing is removed; 2006.5 and later models have one upper bolt and two bolts along the inner rear edge of the housing, near the radiator

1 Open the hood for access to the mounting bolts (see illustrations).
2 Remove the two (2001 through 2006 models) or three (2006.5 and later models) headlight mounting bolts and carefully work the headlight housing out from the fender and the bumper cover.
3 Once you've pulled out the headlight housing far enough, disconnect the electrical connectors from the backside of the housing.
4 Installation is the reverse of removal.
5 Check headlight adjustment (see Section 17).

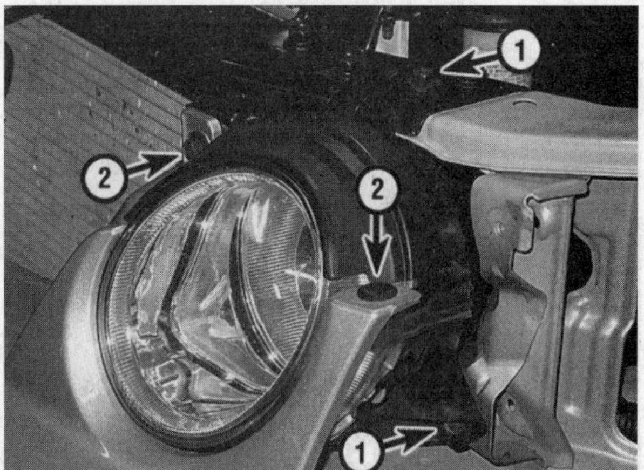

16.1b Combination light housing (high beam) details (2001 through 2006 models):

1 *Combination light housing bolts (one bolt, not visible here, on the inner edge of the housing, is not accessible until the bumper cover is detached)*
2 *Bumper cover fasteners*

17 Headlights - adjustment

Refer to illustrations 17.2, 17.5a and 17.5b

Note: The headlights must be aimed correctly. If adjusted incorrectly they could blind the driver of an oncoming vehicle and cause a serious accident or seriously reduce your ability to see the road. The headlights should be checked for proper aim every 12 months and any time a new headlight is installed or front-end bodywork is performed. It should be emphasized that the following procedure is only an interim step, which will provide temporary adjustment until a properly equipped shop can adjust the headlights.

1 There are several methods of adjusting the headlights. The simplest method requires masking tape, a blank wall and a level floor.

2 Position masking tape vertically on the wall in reference to the vehicle centerline and the centerlines of both headlights (see illustration).

3 Position a horizontal tape line in reference to the centerline of all the headlights.

Note: It may be easier to position the tape on the wall with the vehicle parked only a few inches away.

4 Adjustment should be made with the vehicle parked 25 feet from the wall, sitting level, the gas tank half-full and no unusually heavy load in the vehicle.

5 With the low beams on, position the high intensity zone so it is two inches below the horizontal line. Make the adjustment by turning the adjusting screw to raise or lower the beam (see illustrations).

6 With the high beams on, the high intensity zone should be vertically centered with the exact center just below the horizontal line.

Note: It may not be possible to position the headlight aim exactly for both high and low beams. If a compromise must be made, keep in mind that the low beams are the most used and have the greatest effect on driver safety.

7 Each headlight assembly is adjustable in the horizontal and vertical directions. On later models the screws are labeled.

8 Insert a long Phillips screwdriver through an adjustment hole so it engages with the adjustment wheel. Slowly turn the screwdriver until the desired setting is reached. Proceed to the next adjuster.

9 Have the headlights adjusted by a dealer service department or service station at the earliest opportunity.

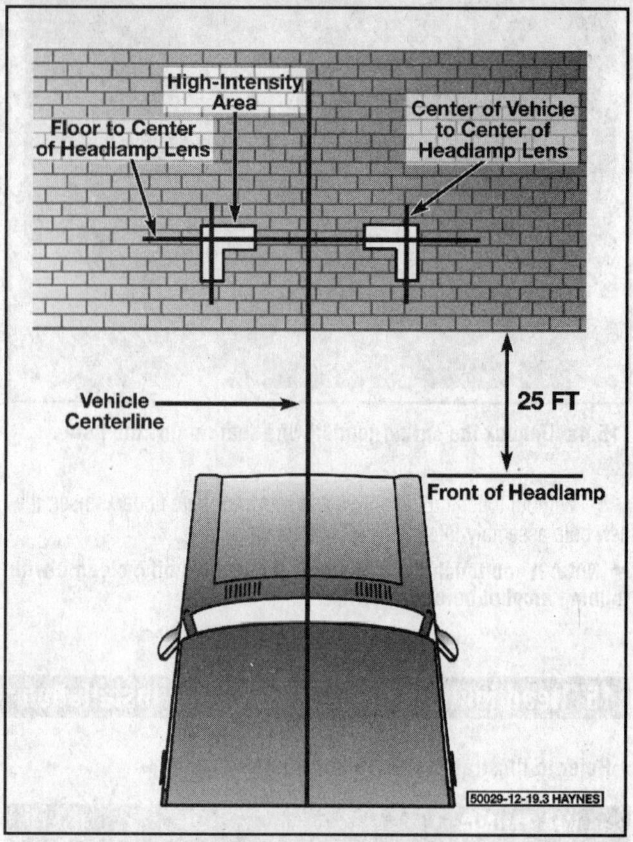

17.2 Headlight adjustment details

17.5a Headlight adjustment hole on 2001 through 2006 models

17.5b Combination light adjustment hole on 2006.5 and later models (no combination light housing on later models)

18 Horn(s) - check and replacement

⁂ WARNING:

The models covered by this manual are equipped with Supplemental Restraint Systems (SRS), more commonly known as airbags. Always disable the airbag system before working in the vicinity of any airbag system components to avoid the possibility of accidental deployment of the airbag(s), which could cause personal injury (see Section 24).

CHECK

➡ **Note: Check the fuses before beginning electrical diagnosis.**

1 Disconnect the electrical connector from the horn (see illustration 18.10).

2 To test the horn, connect battery voltage to the horn terminal with a jumper wire. If the horn doesn't sound, replace it.

3 If the horn does sound, check for voltage at the terminal when the horn button is depressed. If there's voltage at the terminal, check for a bad ground at the horn.

4 If there's no voltage at the horn, check the relay (see Section 5).

5 If the relay is OK, check for voltage to the relay power and control circuits. If either of the circuits is not receiving voltage, inspect the wiring between the relay and the fuse panel.

6 If both relay circuits are receiving voltage, depress the horn button and check the circuit from the relay to the horn button for continuity to ground. If there's no continuity, check the circuit for an open. If there's no open circuit, replace the horn button.

7 If there's continuity to ground through the horn button, check for an open or short in the circuit from the relay to the horn.

REPLACEMENT

➧ **Refer to illustration 18.10**

8 On 2001 through 2006 models, the horns are located in front of the condenser and are mounted on the hood latch assembly. Open the hood to access the horns.

9 On 2006.5 and later models, the horn is located behind the bumper cover. Remove the bumper cover (see Chapter 11).

10 Disconnect the electrical connector (see illustration).

11 Remove the bracket bolt.

12 Installation is the reverse of removal.

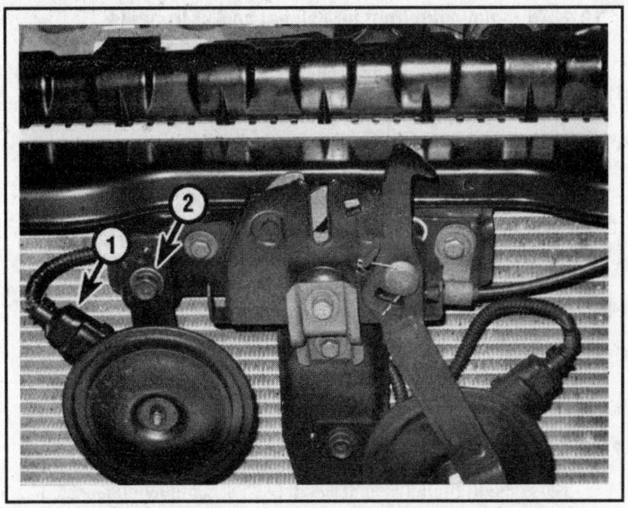

18.10 Typical horn assembly details (2001 through 2006 models shown; other models similar, except they have one horn):

1 Electrical connector *2 Mounting bolt*

19 Bulb replacement

EXTERIOR LIGHT BULBS

Front turn signal bulbs

➧ **Refer to illustrations 19.1, 19.2 and 19.3**

➡ **Note: The front turn signal bulbs are located in the headlight housing.**

1 Remove the headlight housing (see Section 16), then locate the front turn signal bulb (see illustration).

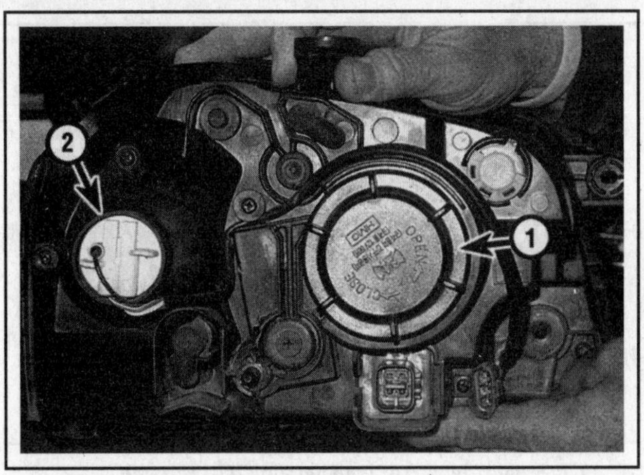

19.1 Headlight housing bulb locations (2001 through 2006 models shown; other models similar):

1 Headlight bulb (low beam) *2 Front turn signal bulb*

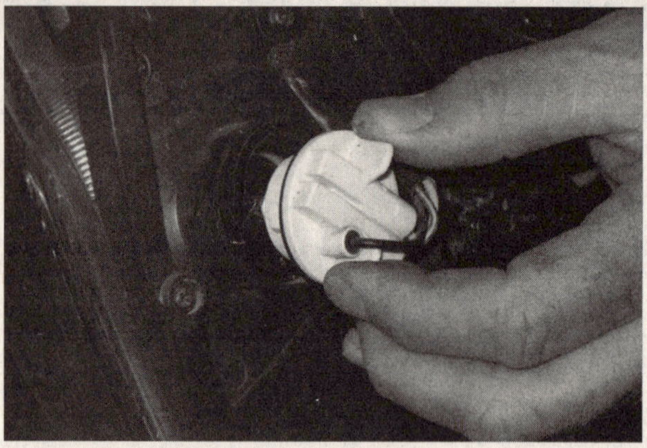

19.2 To remove the front turn signal socket from the headlight housing, turn it counterclockwise and pull it out (2001 through 2006 models shown; later models similar)

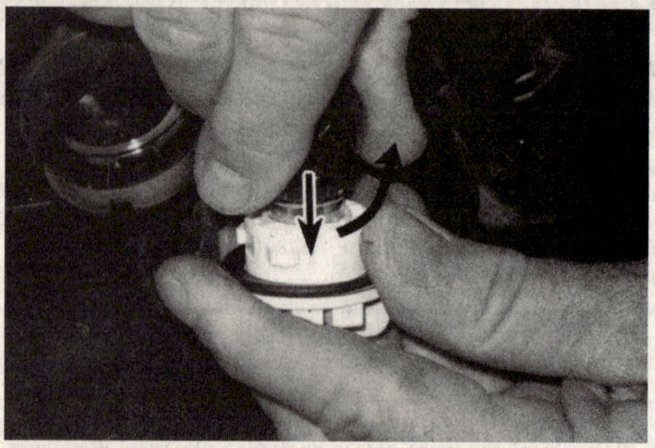

19.3 To remove the front turn signal bulb from its socket, push it down into the socket and turn it counterclockwise to release it, then pull it out

2 Remove the bulb holder from the headlight housing by twisting it counterclockwise (see illustration).

3 Remove the bulb from the holder by pushing it into the holder then turning it counterclockwise (see illustration). Install the new bulb by pushing it into the holder, then turning clockwise.

4 Insert the bulb holder into the headlight housing and turn it clockwise until it locks into place.

5 Installation is otherwise the reverse of removal.

Front side marker bulbs

➧ Refer to illustration 19.7

6 Raise the front of the vehicle and place it securely on jackstands, then detach the lower front part of the inner fender splash shield (see *Fender - removal and installation* in Chapter 11).

7 Disconnect the electrical connector from the side marker light (see illustration). Depress the large lock tab at the rear end of the side marker housing and push the housing out of the bumper cover.

8 Turn the bulb socket counterclockwise and pull it out of the side marker housing. Remove the side marker bulb from the socket.

9 Install a new bulb in the socket, then insert the socket into the side marker housing and turn it clockwise until it stops.

10 Make sure that the mounting tab at the front end of the side marker housing is on the inside of the bumper cover, then push the housing into the bumper cover until the large lock tab snaps into place. Installation is otherwise the reverse of removal.

Fog lamp bulbs

➧ Refer to illustration 19.12

⁂ WARNING:

Halogen gas-filled bulbs are under pressure and may shatter if the surface is scratched or the bulb is dropped. Wear eye protection and handle the bulbs carefully, grasping only the base whenever possible. Do not touch the surface of the bulb with your fingers because the oil from your skin could cause it to overheat and fail prematurely. If you do touch the bulb surface, clean it with rubbing alcohol.

11 Raise the front of the vehicle and place it securely on jackstands, then detach the lower front part of the inner fender splash shield (see *Fender - removal and installation* in Chapter 11).

12 Disconnect the electrical connector from the fog lamp bulb socket (see illustration), then turn the socket counterclockwise and pull it out

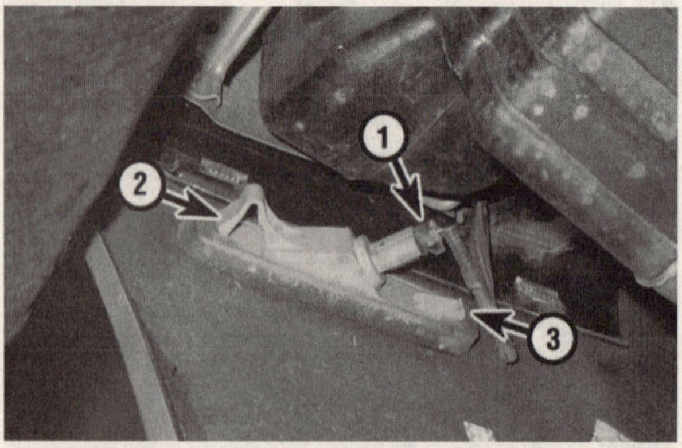

19.7 Front sidemarker light details (2001 through 2006 models):

1 *Electrical connector*
2 *Lock tab*
3 *Mounting tab*

19.12 Fog lamp details (2001 through 2006 models shown; other models similar):

1 *Wiring harness clip*
2 *Electrical connector*

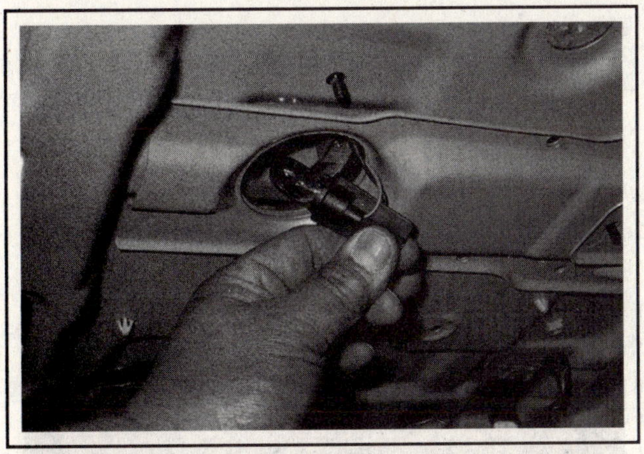

19.16 The center high-mounted brake light is located inside a housing above the parcel tray. It can be accessed through this hole in the underside of the tray (2001 through 2006 models shown; other models similar)

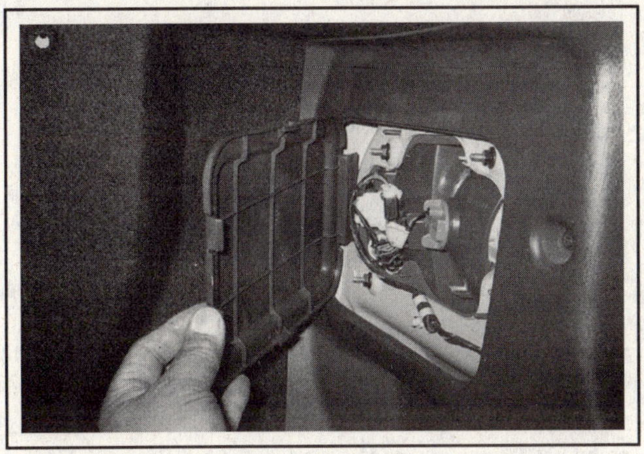

19.21 Open the trunk and pull open the cover for access to the taillight bulbs

of the fog lamp housing.

13 Remove the fog lamp bulb the same way you would remove a headlight bulb (see Section 15).

14 Insert the fog lamp bulb socket into the fog lamp housing, then turn it clockwise until it locks into place. Reconnect the electrical connector and secure the wiring harness clip.

15 Remove the jackstands and lower the front of the vehicle.

Center high-mounted brake light

➧ Refer to illustration 19.16

➡ Note: The center high-mounted brake light bulb is accessed through a hole in the underside of the parcel shelf.

16 Open the luggage compartment and remove the center high-mounted brake light socket from its housing by turning it counterclockwise and pull it out (see illustration).

17 To remove the old bulb, push it into the socket and turn it counterclockwise to release it, then pull it out of the socket.

18 To install the new bulb, insert it into the socket, then turn it clockwise until it stops. Pull on the bulb to verify that it's locked into place.

19 Insert the bulb socket into the center high-mounted brake light housing, then turn it clockwise until it stops. Pull on the socket to verify that it's locked into position.

20 Start the car, then apply the brake pedal and verify that the center high-mounted brake light comes on.

Rear brake/tail, turn signal, brake and back-up light bulbs

➧ Refer to illustrations 19.21, 19.22a, 19.22b and 19.23

21 Open the trunk. If you're replacing a bulb in the taillight housing located in the rear fender, remove the cover from the taillight assembly (see illustration).

22 Identify the bulb that you need to replace (see illustrations).

23 Remove the bulb socket from the taillight housing by turning it counterclockwise (see illustration).

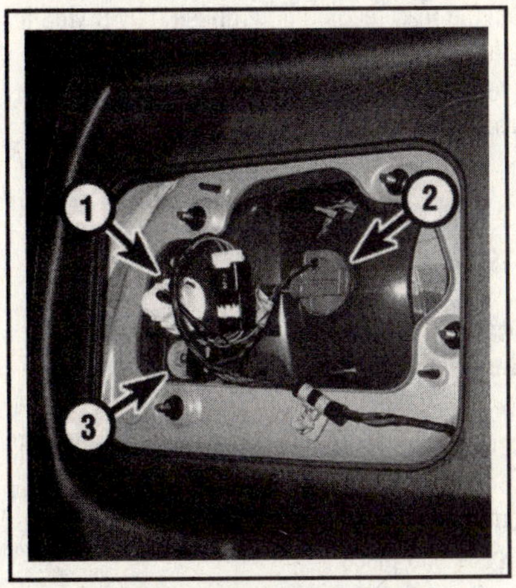

19.22a Taillight housing bulb details (2001 through 2006 models shown; other models similar):

1 *Back-up light bulb*
2 *Brake light/taillight bulb*
3 *Turn signal/side marker light bulb*

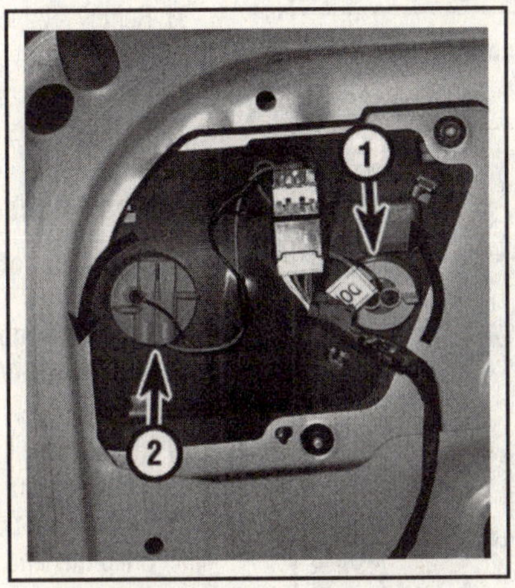

19.22b Taillight housing bulb details (2001 through 2006 models shown; other models similar):

1 *Back-up light bulb*
2 *Brake light/taillight bulb*

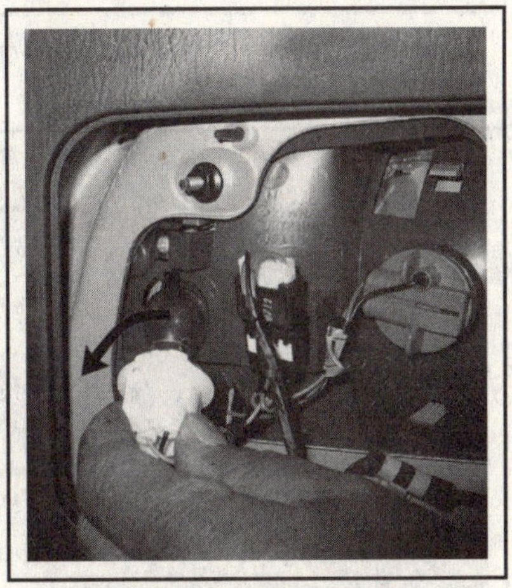

19.23 To remove a bulb socket from either taillight housing, turn it counterclockwise and pull it out

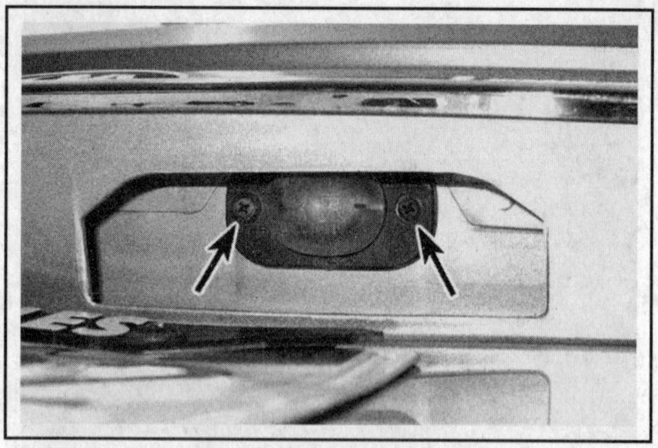

19.26 License plate light housing lens retaining screws (2001 through 2006 models shown; other models similar)

24 To remove a bulb from its socket, push it in and turn it counterclockwise, then pull it out of the socket. To install a new bulb, push it into the socket, then turn it clockwise until it stops. Pull on the bulb to verify that it's locked into place.

25 Installation is the reverse of removal.

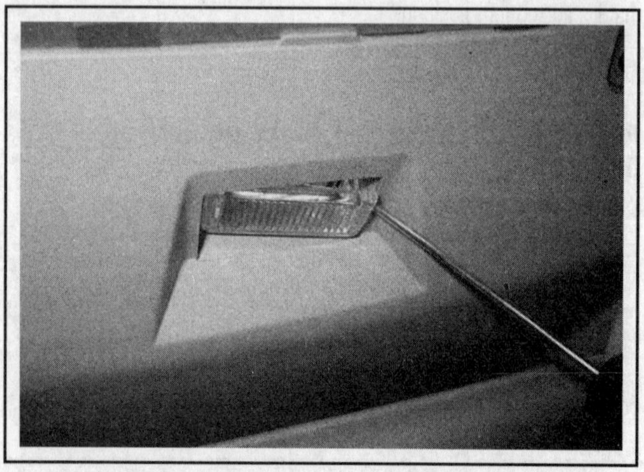

19.34 Carefully pry off the lens with a small screwdriver

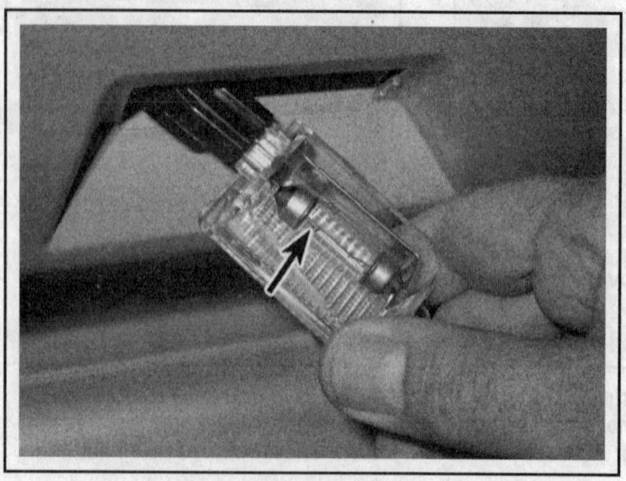

19.35 Pull the bulb from the holder

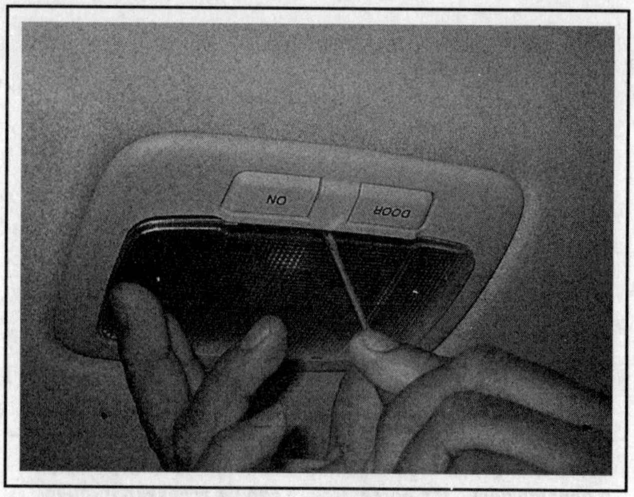

19.31 Carefully pry out the dome light lens

License plate light bulbs

➧ Refer to illustration 19.26

26 Remove the lens retaining screws (see illustration) and remove the lens.

27 Rotate the bulb socket counterclockwise and pull it out of the license plate light housing.

28 Pull the bulb straight out of the socket. To install the new bulb, insert it into the socket and push it in until it stops.

29 Insert the bulb socket into the license plate light housing and turn it clockwise to lock it into place.

30 Install the lens and tighten the lens retaining screws.

INTERIOR LIGHT BULBS

Dome light

➧ Refer to illustration 19.31

31 Remove the lens from the map reading light housing by prying it off with a screwdriver inserted into the small slot (see illustration).

32 Lift the lens off and remove the bulb from the terminals.

33 Installation is the reverse of removal.

Glove box light

➧ Refer to illustrations 19.34 and 19.35

➡ Note: Some models have glove box light bulbs that are replaceable by prying the lens down from inside the glove compartment.

34 Insert a small screwdriver into the small slot in the lens and pry it off (see illustration).

35 Remove the bulb from the holder and replace it (see illustration).

36 Snap the lens cover back into place.

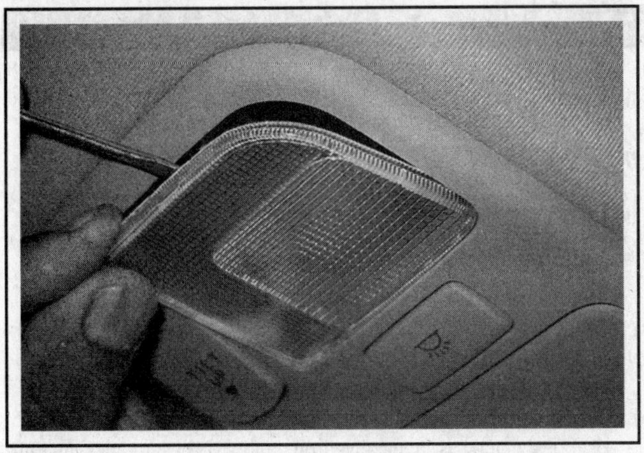

19.37 Pry at the rear of the map light to remove the lens

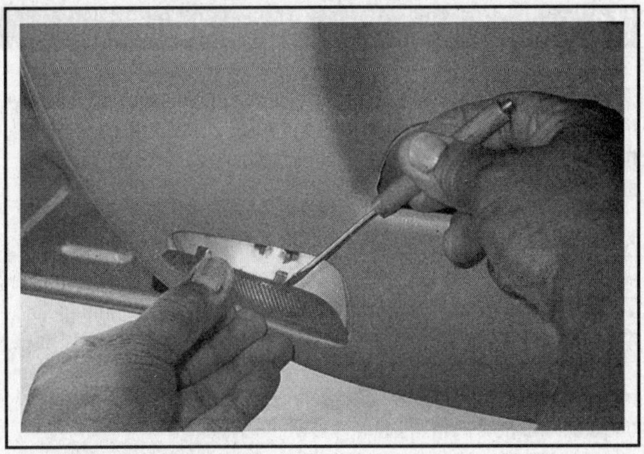

19.40 The door light lens is secured by plastic tabs - simply pry it off

Map light

Refer to illustration 19.37

37 Pry the lens off at the rear using a small screwdriver (see illustration).
38 Remove the bulb.
39 Snap the lens securely into place.

Door warning light

Refer to illustration 19.40

40 Pry the upper edge of the lens out with a small screwdriver (see illustration).
41 Replace the bulb.
42 Snap the lens back into place.

20 Electric side view mirrors - description

1 Most electric side view mirrors use two motors to move the glass; one for up and down adjustments and one for left-right adjustments.
2 The control switch has a selector portion that sends voltage to the left or right side mirror. With the ignition ON but the engine OFF, roll down the windows and operate the mirror control switch through all functions (left-right and up-down) for both the left and right side mirrors.
3 Listen carefully for the sound of the electric motors running in the mirrors.
4 If the motors can be heard but the mirror glass doesn't move, there's a problem with the drive mechanism inside the mirror. Remove and disassemble the mirror to locate the problem.
5 If the mirrors do not operate and no sound comes from the mirrors, check the fuse (see Section 3).
6 If the fuse is OK, remove the mirror control switch from the dashboard. Have the switch continuity checked by a dealership service department or other qualified automobile repair facility.
7 Test the ground connections. Refer to the wiring diagrams at the end of this Chapter.
8 If the mirror still doesn't work, remove the mirror and check the wires at the mirror for voltage.
9 If there's not voltage in each switch position, check the circuit between the mirror and control switch for opens and shorts.
10 If there's voltage, remove the mirror and test it off the vehicle with jumper wires. Replace the mirror if it fails this test.

21 Cruise control system - description

1 The cruise control system maintains vehicle speed with a vacuum actuated servo located in the engine compartment, which is connected to the throttle body by a cable. The system consists of the cruise control unit, brake switch, control switches, vacuum hose and vehicle speed sensor. Some features of the system require special testers and diagnostic procedures that are beyond the scope of this manual. Listed below are some general procedures that may be used to locate common problems.
2 Locate and check the fuse (see Section 3).
3 Check the brake light switch (see Chapter 9).
4 Visually inspect the control cable between the actuator assembly and the accelerator pedal for free movement - replace if necessary.
5 Test drive the vehicle to determine if the cruise control is now working. If it isn't, take it to a dealer for further diagnosis.

22 Power window system - description

1 The power window system operates electric motors, mounted in the doors, which lower and raise the windows. The system consists of the control switches, relays, the motors, regulators, glass mechanisms and associated wiring.

2 The power windows can be lowered and raised from the master control switch by the driver or by remote switches located at the individual windows. Each window has a separate motor that is reversible. The position of the control switch determines the polarity and therefore the direction of operation.

3 The circuit is protected by a fuse and a circuit breaker. Each motor is also equipped with an internal circuit breaker; this prevents one stuck window from disabling the whole system.

4 The power window system will only operate when the ignition switch is ON. In addition, many models have a window lockout switch at the master control switch that, when activated, disables the switches at the rear windows and, sometimes, the switch at the passenger's window also. Always check these items before troubleshooting a window problem.

5 These procedures are general in nature, so if you can't find the problem using them, take the vehicle to a dealer service department or other properly equipped repair facility.

6 If the power windows won't operate, always check the fuse and circuit breaker first.

7 If only the rear windows are inoperative, or if the windows only operate from the master control switch, check the rear window lockout switch for continuity in the unlocked position. Replace it if it doesn't have continuity.

8 Check the wiring between the switches and fuse panel for continuity. Repair the wiring, if necessary.

9 If only one window is inoperative from the master control switch, try the other control switch at the window.

➡ **Note: This doesn't apply to the driver's door window.**

10 If the same window works from one switch, but not the other, check the switch for continuity. Have the switch checked at a dealer service department or other qualified automobile repair facility.

11 If the switch tests OK, check for a short or open in the circuit between the affected switch and the window motor.

12 If one window is inoperative from both switches, remove the trim panel from the affected door and check for voltage at the switch and at the motor while the switch is operated.

13 If voltage is reaching the motor, disconnect the glass from the regulator (see Chapter 11). Move the window up and down by hand while checking for binding and damage. Also check for binding and damage to the regulator. If the regulator is not damaged and the window moves up and down smoothly, replace the motor. If there's binding or damage, lubricate, repair or replace parts, as necessary.

14 If voltage isn't reaching the motor, check the wiring in the circuit for continuity between the switches and motors. You'll need to consult the wiring diagram for the vehicle. If the circuit is equipped with a relay, check that the relay is grounded properly and receiving voltage.

15 Test the windows after you are done to confirm proper repairs.

23 Power door lock system - description

1 A power door lock system operates the door lock actuators mounted in each door. The system consists of the switches, actuators, a control unit and associated wiring. Diagnosis can usually be limited to simple checks of the wiring connections and actuators for minor faults that can be easily repaired.

2 Power door lock systems are operated by bi-directional solenoids located in the doors. The lock switches have two operating positions: Lock and Unlock. When activated, the switch sends a ground signal to the door lock control unit to lock or unlock the doors. Depending on which way the switch is activated; the control unit reverses polarity to the solenoids, allowing the two sides of the circuit to be used alternately as the feed (positive) and ground side.

3 Some vehicles may have an anti-theft system incorporated into the power locks. If you are unable to locate the trouble using the following general Steps, consult a dealer service department or other qualified repair shop.

4 Always check the circuit protection first. Some vehicles use a combination of circuit breakers and fuses.

5 Operate the door lock switches in both directions (Lock and Unlock) with the engine off. Listen for the click of the solenoids operating.

6 Test the switches for continuity. Remove the switches and have them checked by a dealer service department or other qualified automobile repair facility.

7 Check the wiring between the switches, control unit and solenoids for continuity. Repair the wiring if there's no continuity.

8 Check for a bad ground at the switches or the control unit.

9 If all but one lock solenoid operate, remove the trim panel from the affected door (see Chapter 11) and check for voltage at the solenoid while the lock switch is operated. One of the wires should have voltage in the Lock position; the other should have voltage in the Unlock position.

10 If the inoperative solenoid is receiving voltage, replace the solenoid.

11 If the inoperative solenoid isn't receiving voltage, check the relay for an open or short in the wire between the lock solenoid and the control unit.

➡ **Note: It's common for wires to break in the section of harness that goes between the body and door because opening and closing the door fatigues and eventually breaks the wires.**

24 Airbag system - general information

All models are equipped with a Supplemental Restraint System (SRS), more commonly known as the airbag system. The airbag system is designed to protect the driver and the front seat passenger from serious injury in the event of a head-on or frontal collision. It consists of the impact sensors, a driver's airbag module in the center of the steering wheel, a passenger's airbag module in the glove box area of the instrument panel and a sensing/diagnostic module mounted in the center of the floorpan, in the center console. Some models are also equipped with side-impact airbags.

AIRBAG MODULES

Driver's airbag

The airbag inflator module contains a housing incorporating the cushion (airbag) and inflator unit, mounted in the center of the steering wheel. The inflator assembly is mounted on the back of the housing over a hole through which gas is expelled, inflating the bag almost instantaneously when an electrical signal is sent from the system. A clockspring assembly on the steering column under the steering wheel carries this signal to the module. This clockspring assembly can transmit an electrical signal regardless of steering wheel position. The igniter in the airbag converts the electrical signal to heat and ignites the powder, which inflates the bag.

Passenger's airbag

The airbag is mounted inside the right end of the instrument panel, in the vicinity of the glove box compartment. It's similar in design to the driver's airbag, except that it's larger than the steering wheel unit. The passenger airbag is mounted between the instrument panel reinforcement bar and the underside of the instrument panel. The trim cover (on the side of the instrument panel that faces toward the passenger) is textured and colored to match the instrument panel and has a molded seam that splits open when the bag inflates.

Side impact airbags

Extra protection is provided by side-impact airbags on some models. These are smaller devices, which are located on the outer sides of the seat backs, and deploy in the event of a severe side-impact collision.

Curtain airbags

Curtain airbags are found on later models only. They are mounted behind the plastic trim that runs over each door opening. Like side impact bags, they deploy whenever the vehicle is struck from the side.

SENSING AND DIAGNOSTIC MODULE

The sensing and diagnostic module supplies the current to the airbag system in the event of the collision, even if battery power is cut off. It checks this system every time the vehicle is started, causing the AIR BAG light to go on then off, if the system is operating properly. If there is a fault in the system, the light will go on and stay on, flash, or the dash will make a beeping sound. If this happens, the vehicle should be taken to your dealer immediately for service.

DISARMING THE SYSTEM AND OTHER PRECAUTIONS

⁂ WARNING:

Failure to follow these precautions could result in accidental deployment of the airbag and personal injury.

Whenever working in the vicinity of the steering wheel, steering column or any of the other SRS system components, the system must be disarmed.

To disarm the airbag system:

- a) *Point the wheels straight ahead and turn the key to the Lock position.*
- b) *Disconnect the cable from the negative battery terminal.*
- c) *Wait at least two minutes for the back-up power supply to be depleted.*

Whenever handling an airbag module:

Always keep the airbag opening (the trim side) pointed away from your body. Never place the airbag module on a bench or other surface with the airbag opening facing the surface. Always place the airbag module in a safe location with the airbag opening facing up.

Never measure the resistance of any SRS component. An ohmmeter has a built-in battery supply that could accidentally deploy the airbag.

Never use electrical welding equipment on a vehicle equipped with an airbag without first disconnecting the electrical connector for each airbag.

Never dispose of a live airbag module. Return it to a dealer service department or other qualified repair shop for safe deployment and disposal.

COMPONENT REMOVAL AND INSTALLATION

Driver's side airbag module and clockspring

Refer to Chapter 10, *Steering wheel - removal and installation*, for the driver's side airbag module and clockspring removal and installation procedures.

Other airbag modules

We don't recommend removing any of the other airbag modules. These jobs are best left to a professional.

25 Remote keyless entry system - battery replacement

1 Here's how the transmitter inside the remote keyless entry fob should work:

a) *When you press the UNLOCK button, the driver's door unlocks. If you press the UNLOCK button a second time within four seconds, all the doors unlock.*
b) *Pressing the lock button sets the alarm and locks all of the doors.*

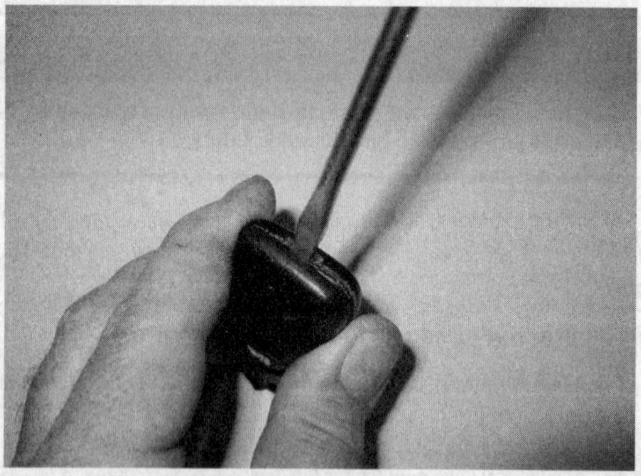

25.3 Carefully pry the halves of the transmitter apart

BATTERY REPLACEMENT

Refer to illustrations 25.3 and 25.4

2 When the transmitter becomes weak, operation will become intermittent and require you to be closer to the vehicle for it to work. Eventually it won't work at all.

3 To replace the transmitter battery, carefully pry open the keyless entry fob by inserting a coin or screwdriver into the notch in the body of the transmitter and separate the halves of the fob (see illustration).

4 Carefully push the old battery out with a small screwdriver (see illustration).

5 Installation is the reverse of removal. Make sure the two halves of the cover snap together tightly to keep out dirt, dust, humidity and rain.

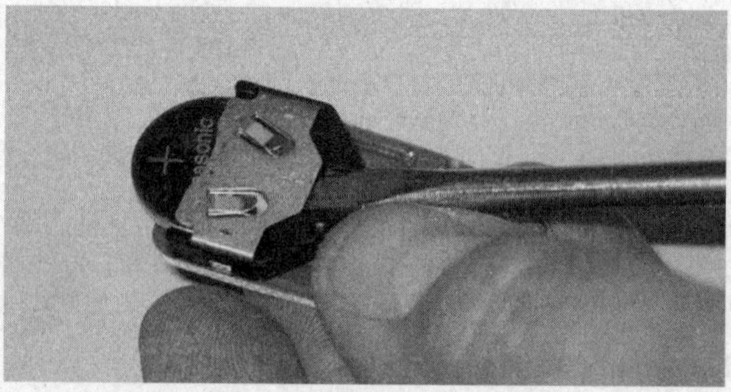

25.4 Using a small screwdriver, push the old battery out of the holder

26 Ignition key - programming

➡ **Note: This procedure is used for adding an additional master key if a master key (or both of them) has been lost. It will be necessary to have the ID key in order to perform this procedure. If the ID key has been lost, this procedure must be performed at a dealer service department or other repair shop equipped with a Hi-Scan diagnostic tool.**

1 Place the ID key into the ignition lock cylinder and turn it to the on position, then the off position.

2 With ten seconds, insert the key to be added into the ignition lock cylinder and turn it to the on position, then the off position. The new key is now registered to work with the immobilizer system.

3 If another key is to be added, repeat Step 2.

➡ **Note: Only two master keys can be registered.**

27 Wiring diagrams - general information

Since it isn't possible to include all wiring diagrams for every year covered by this manual, the following diagrams are those that are typical and most commonly needed.

Prior to troubleshooting any circuits, check the fuse and circuit breakers (if equipped) to make sure they're in good condition. Make sure the battery is properly charged and check the cable connections (see Chapter 1).

When checking a circuit, make sure that all connectors are clean, with no broken or loose terminals. When unplugging a connector, do not pull on the wires - pull only on the connector housings.

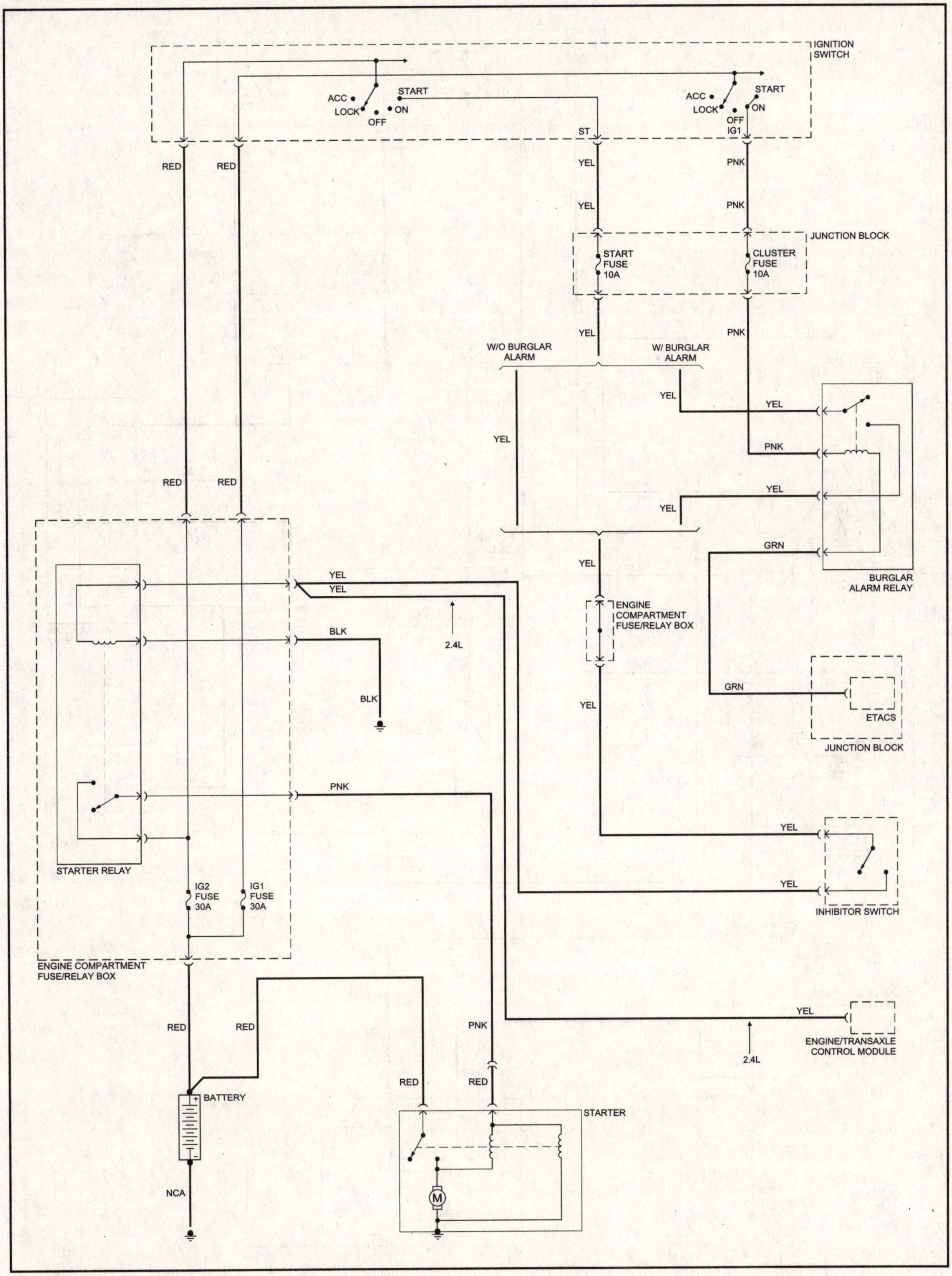

Starting system - 2006 and earlier models (automatic transaxle)

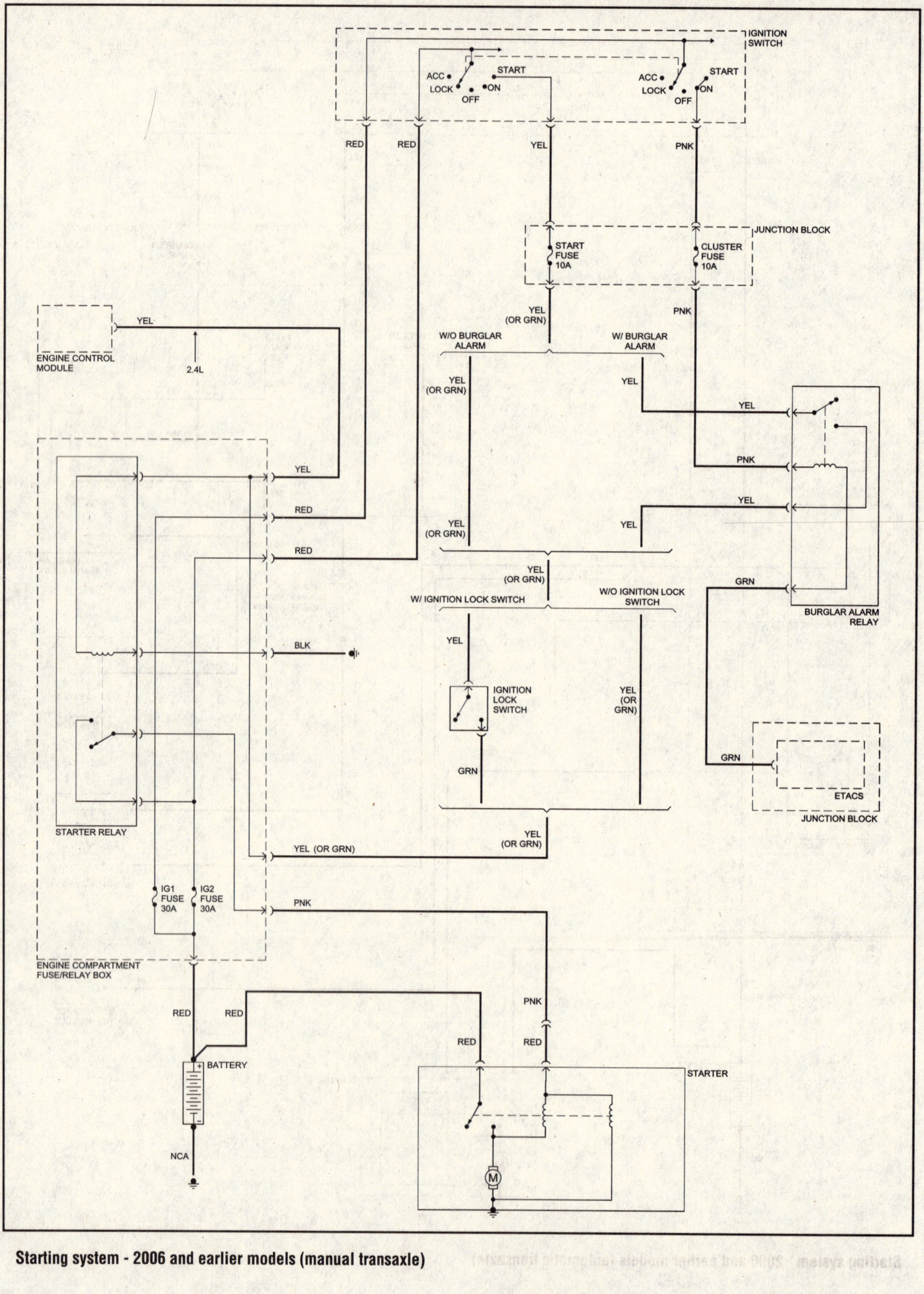

Starting system - 2006 and earlier models (manual transaxle)

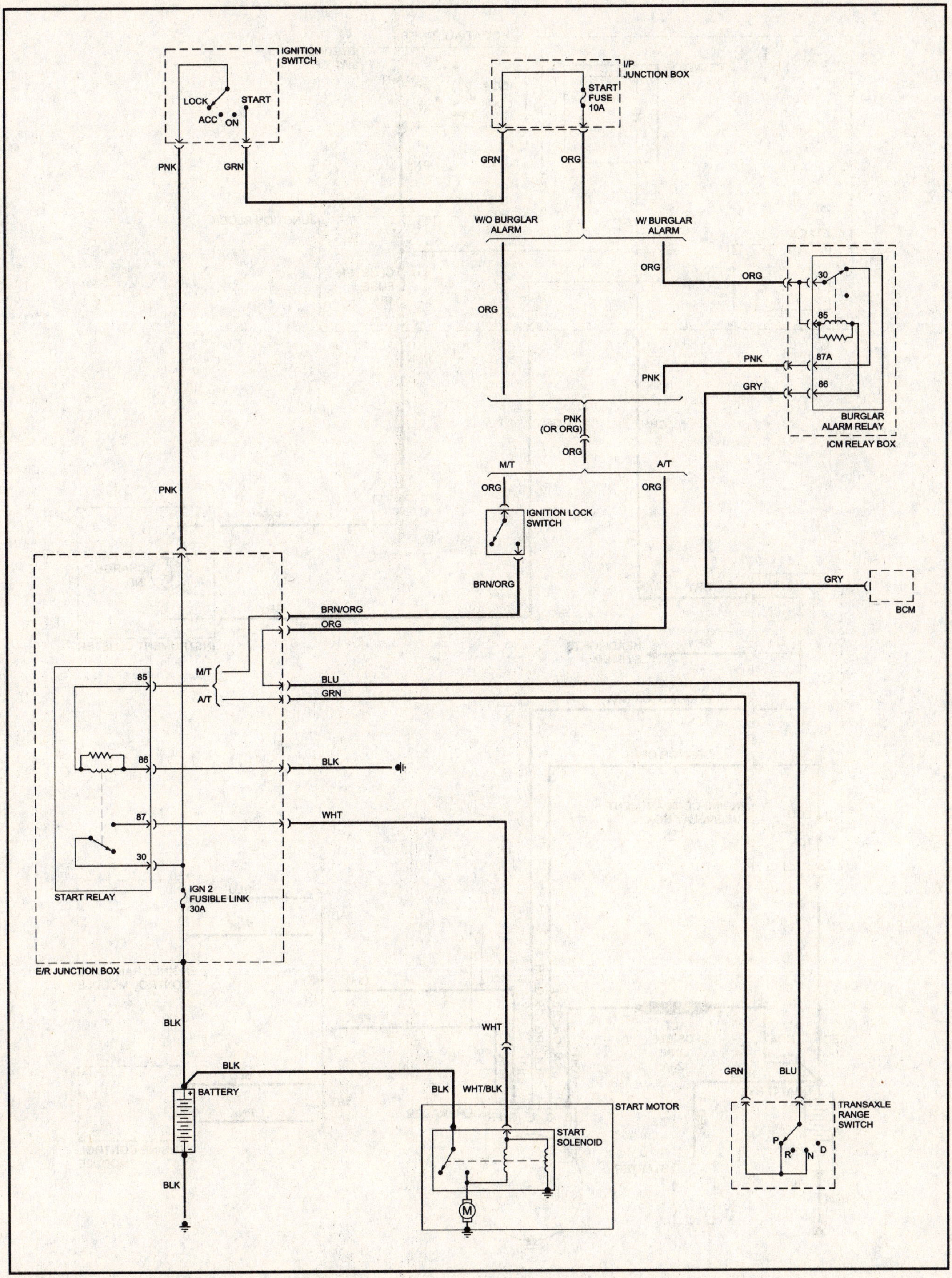

Starting system - 2006.5 and later models

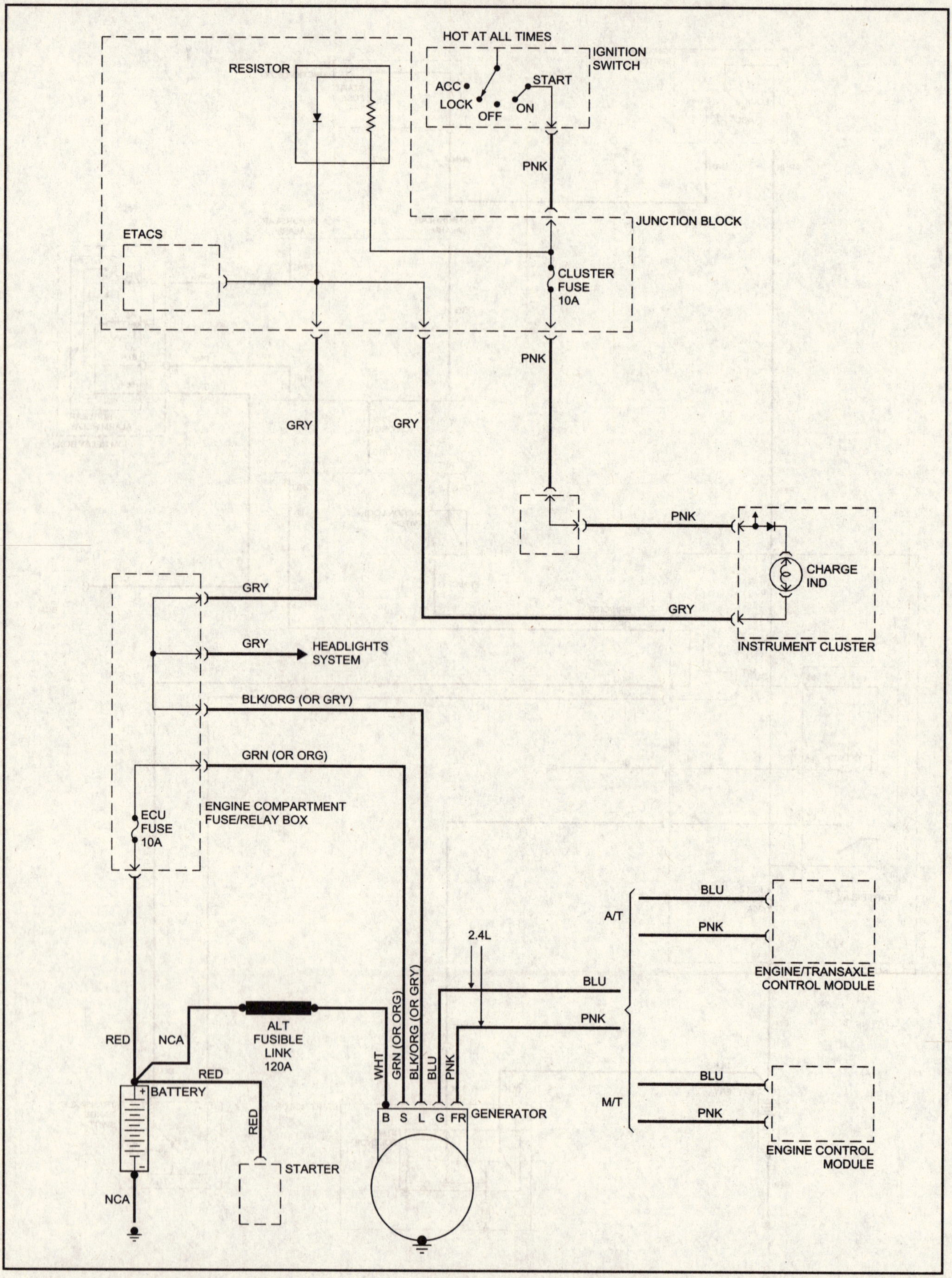

Charging system - 2006 and earlier models

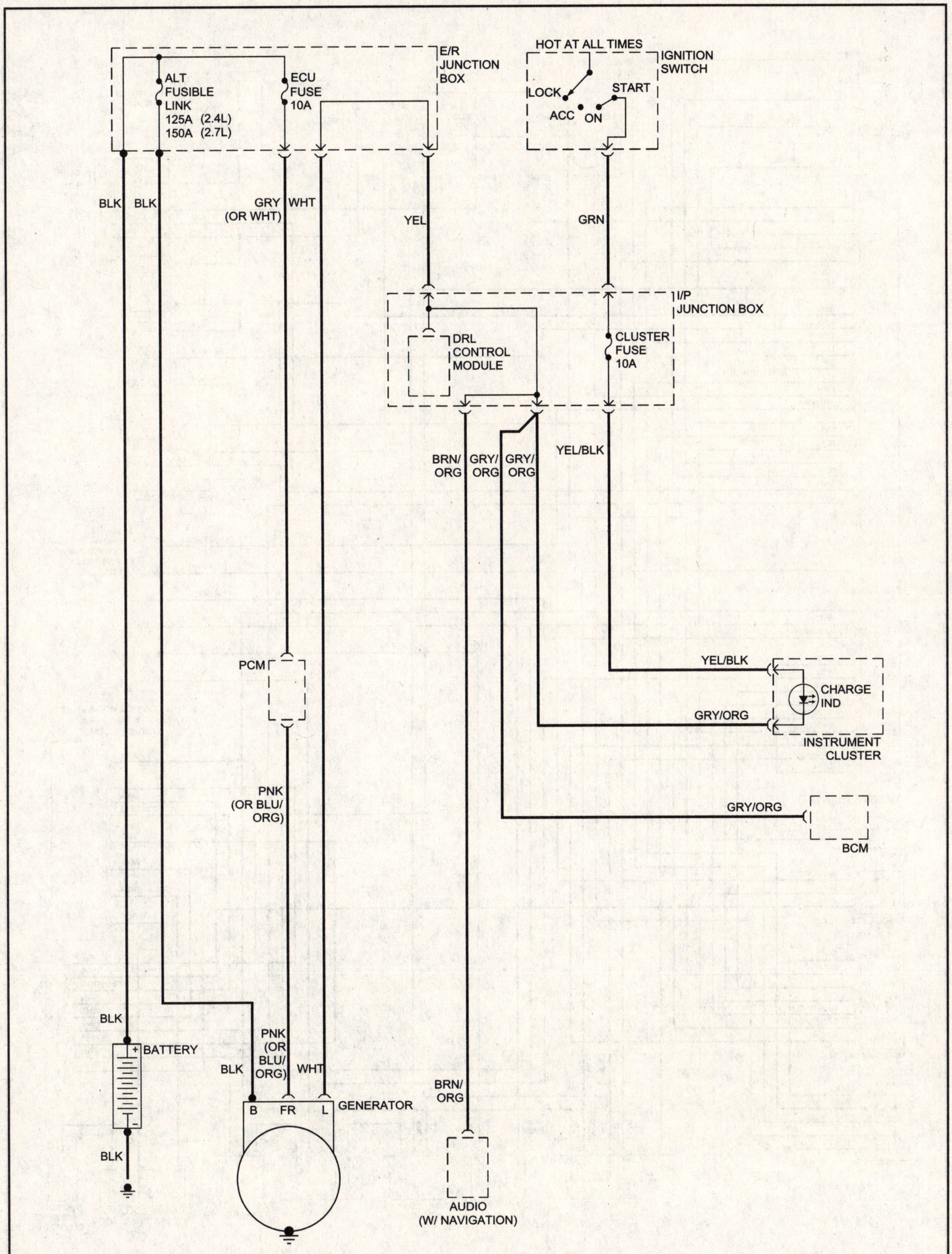

Charging system - 2006.5 and later models

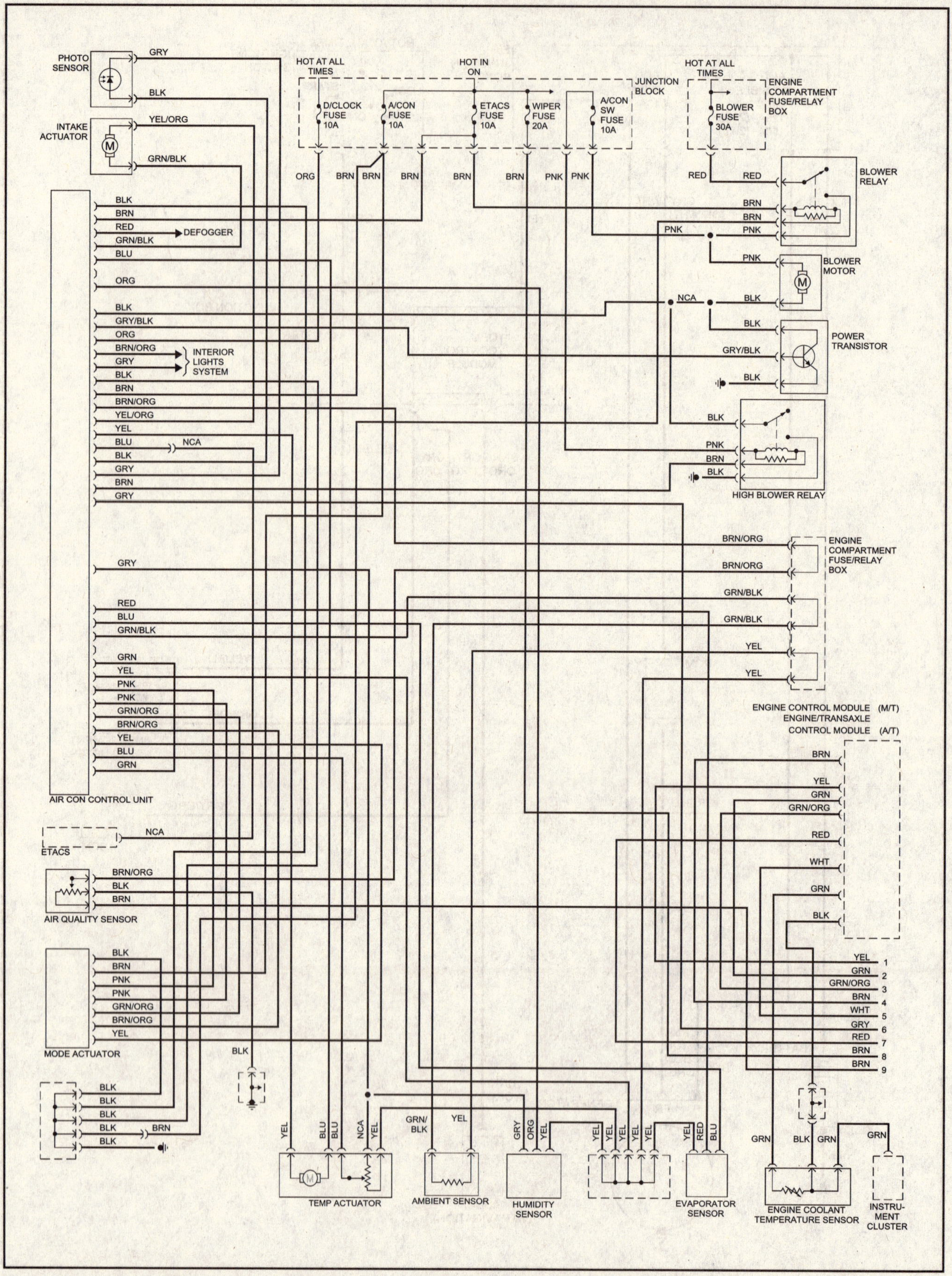

Air conditioning, heating and engine cooling fan system (automatic) - 2006 and earlier models (1 of 2)

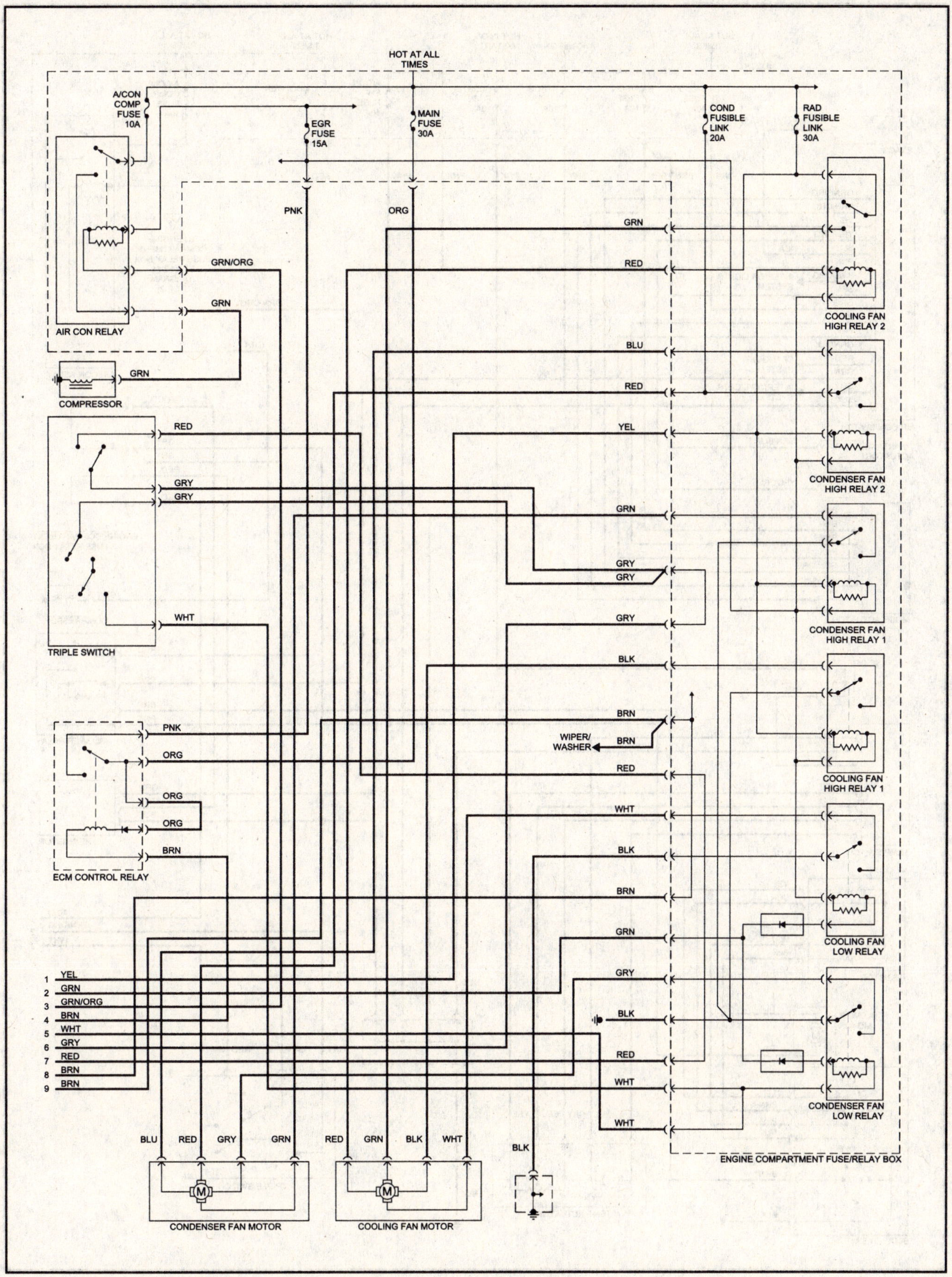

Air conditioning, heating and engine cooling fan system (automatic) - 2006 and earlier models (2 of 2)

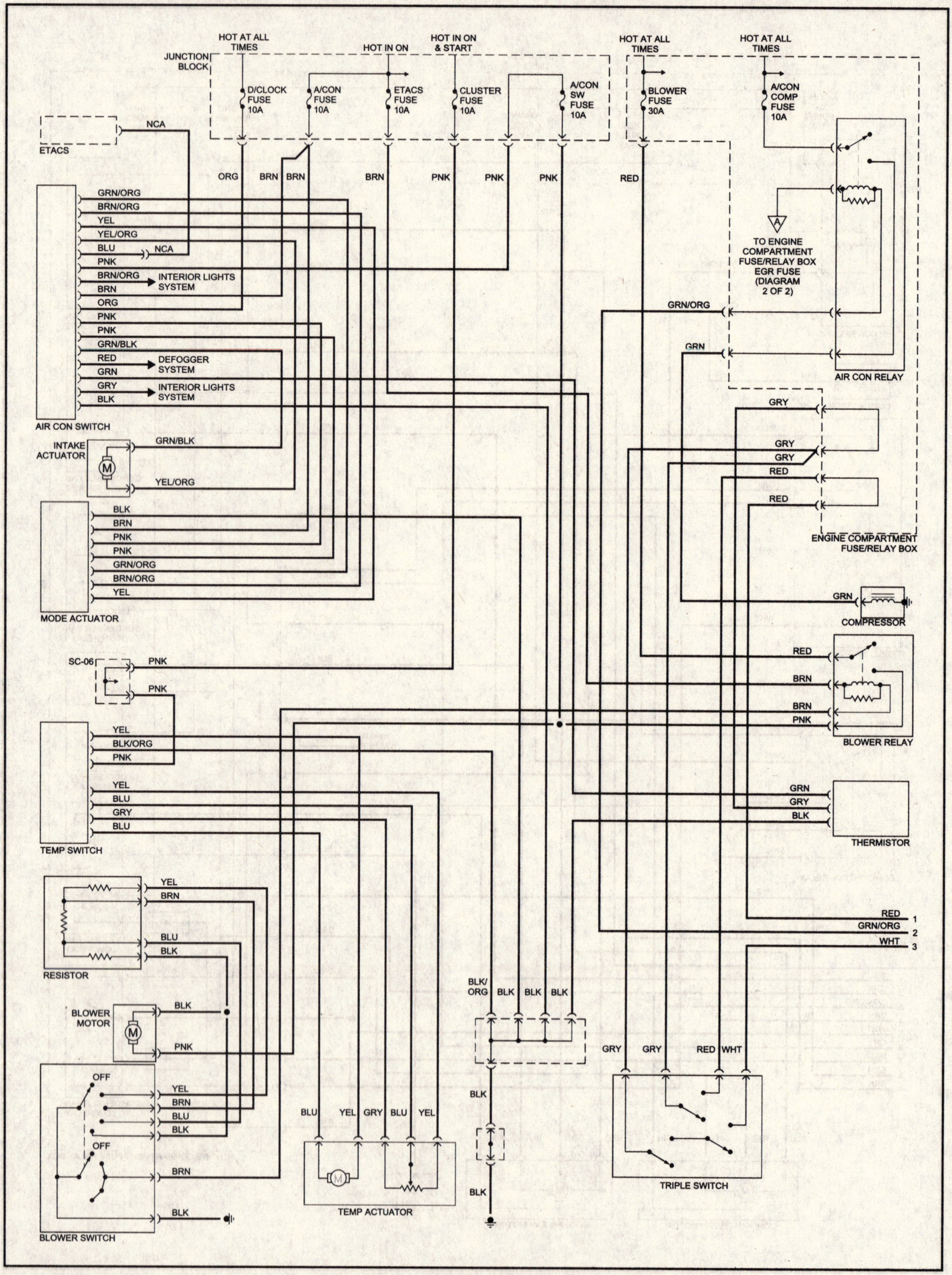

Air conditioning, heating and engine cooling fan system (manual) - 2006 and earlier models (1 of 2)

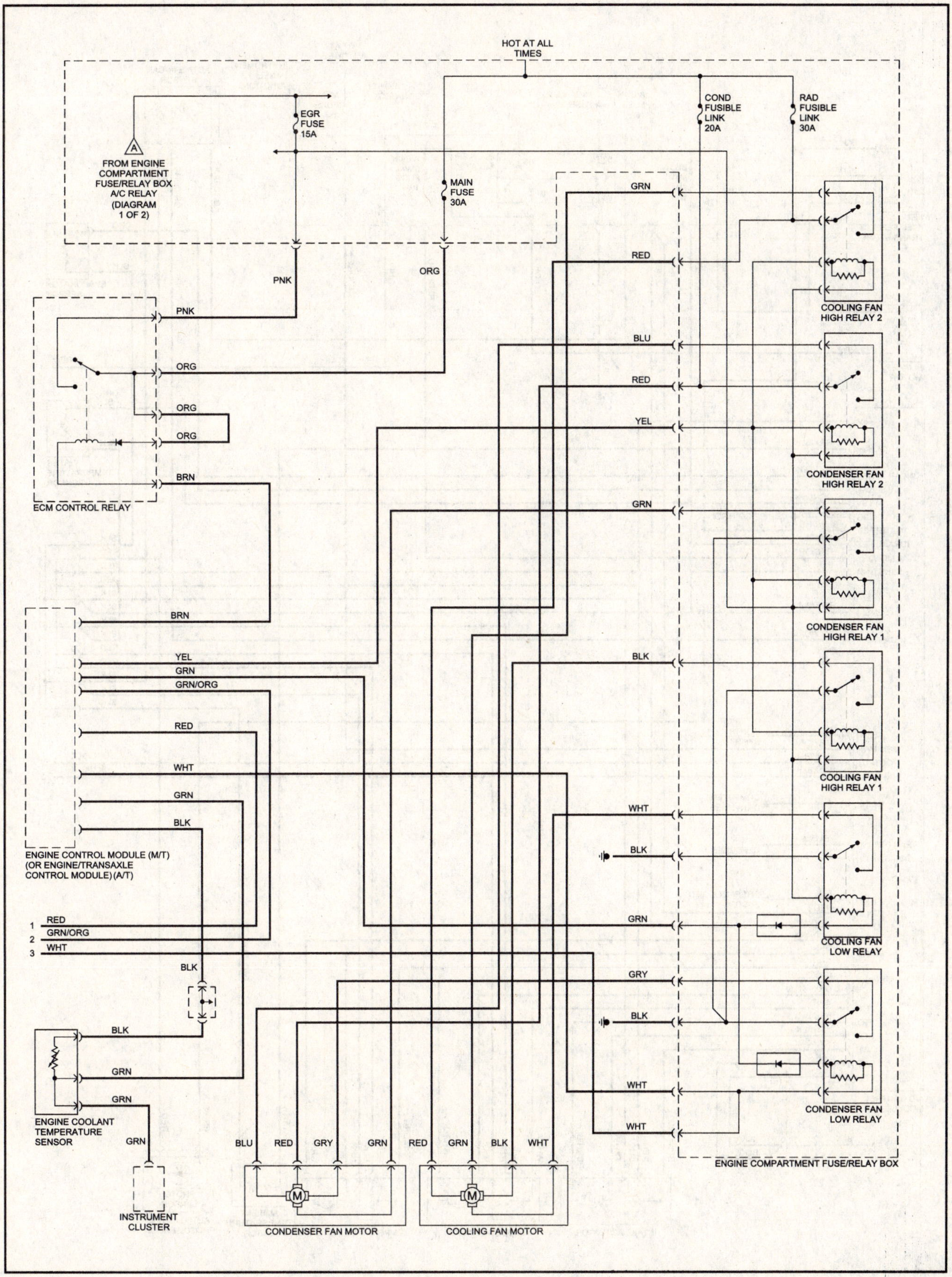

Air conditioning, heating and engine cooling fan system (manual) - 2006 and earlier models (2 of 2)

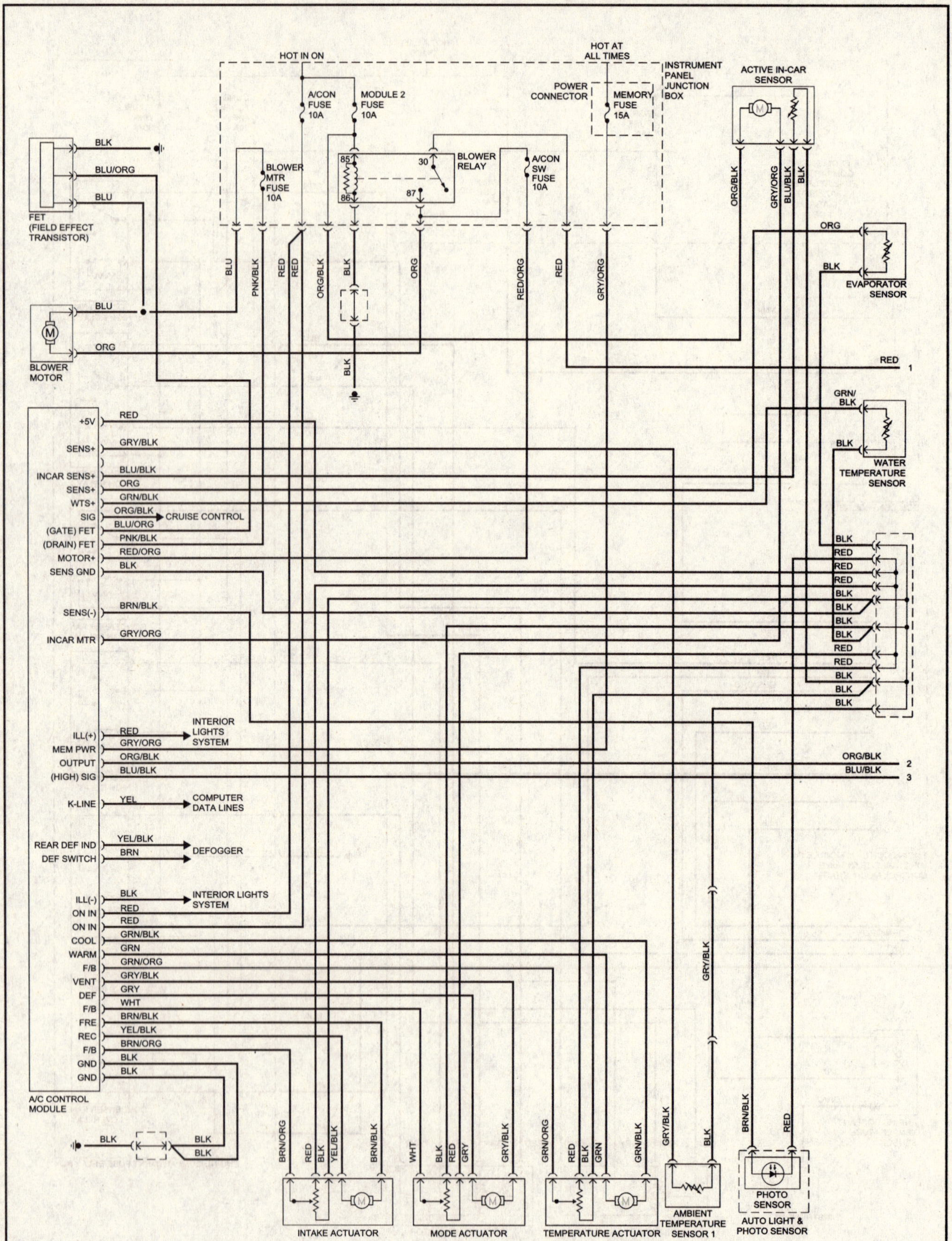

Air conditioning, heating and engine cooling fan system (automatic) - 2006.5 and later models (1 of 2)

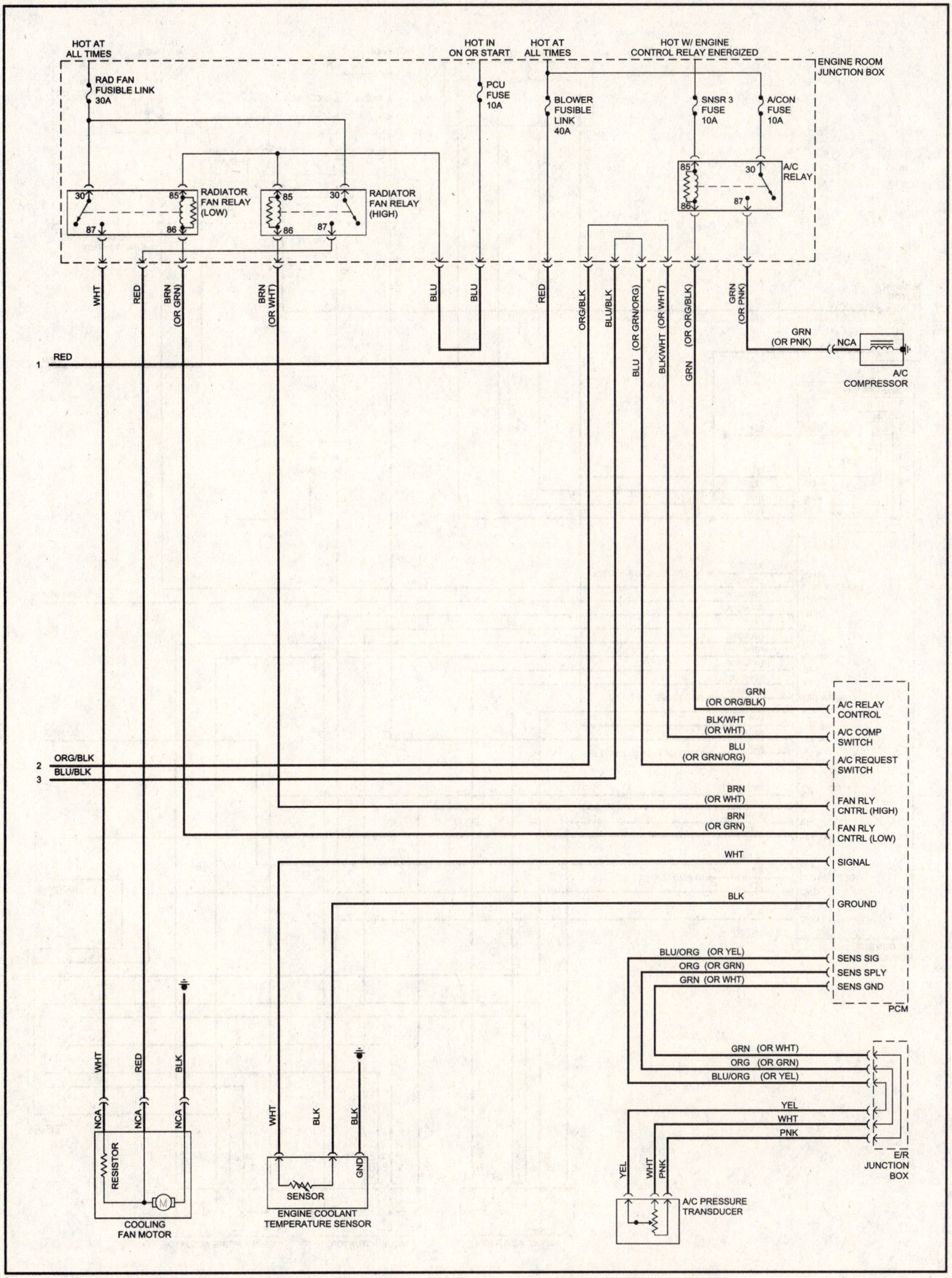

Air conditioning, heating and engine cooling fan system (automatic) - 2006.5 and later models (2 of 2)

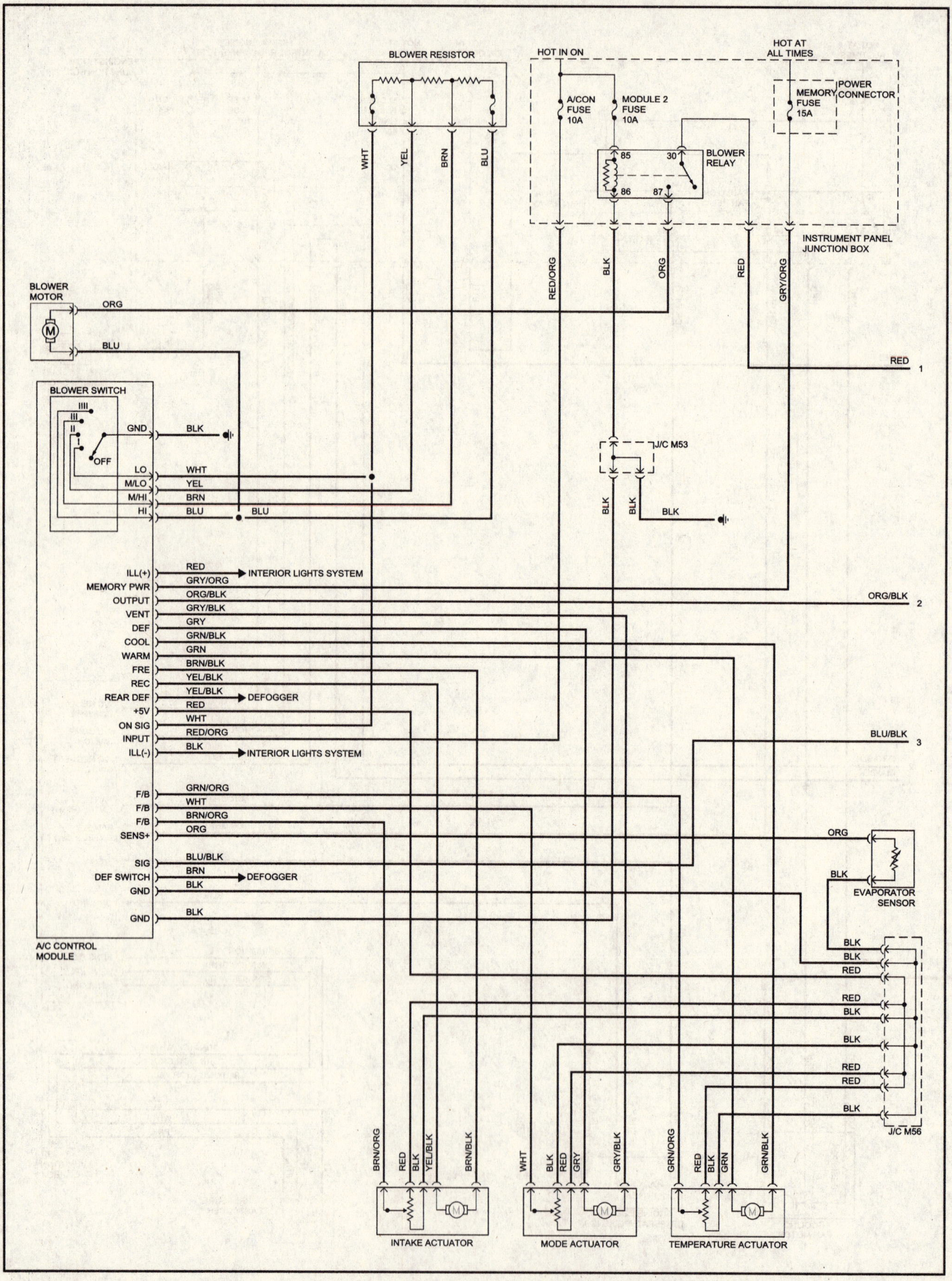

Air conditioning, heating and engine cooling fan system (automatic) - 2006.5 and later models (1 of 2)

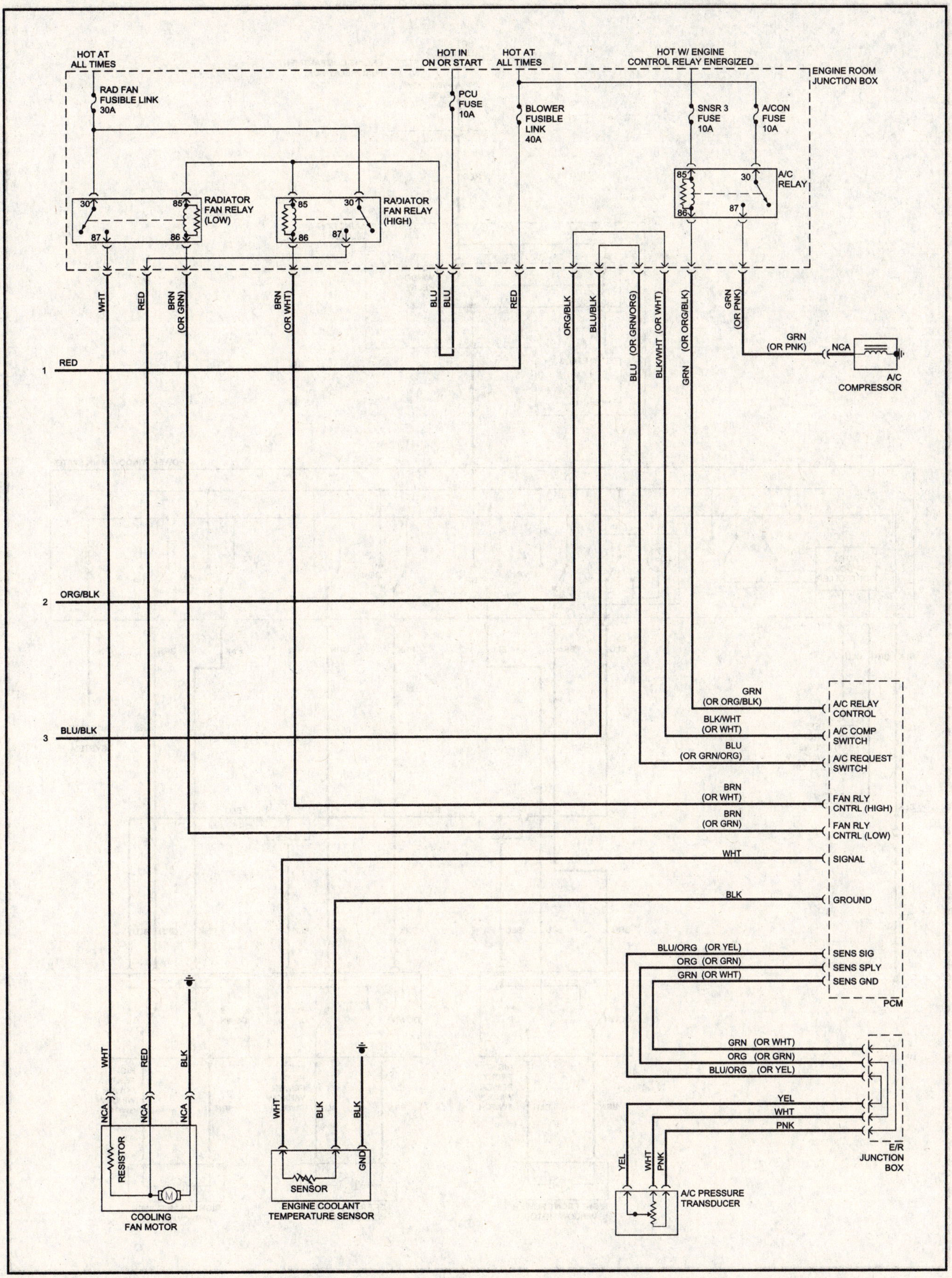

Air conditioning, heating and engine cooling fan system (automatic) - 2006.5 and later models (2 of 2)

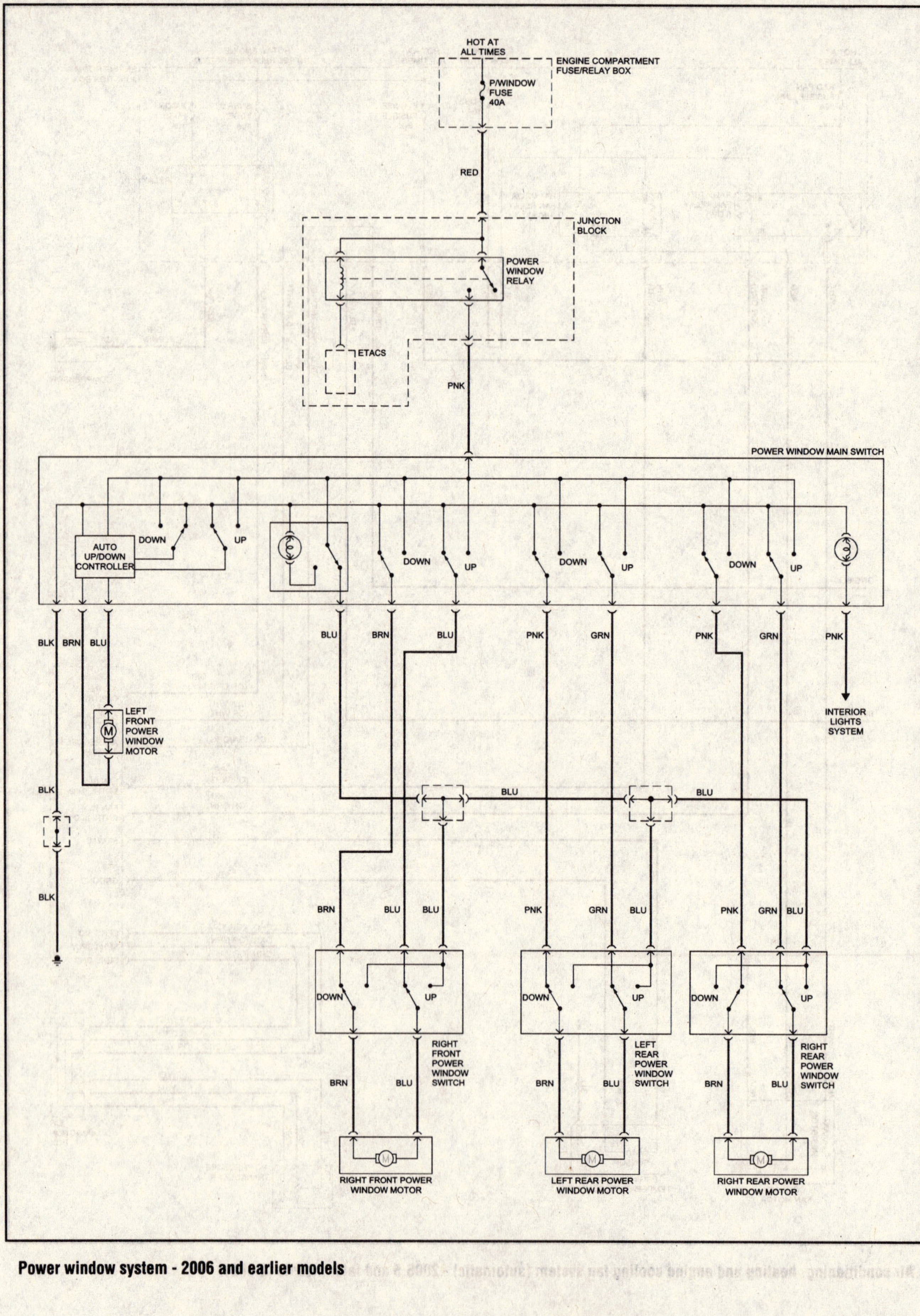

Power window system - 2006 and earlier models

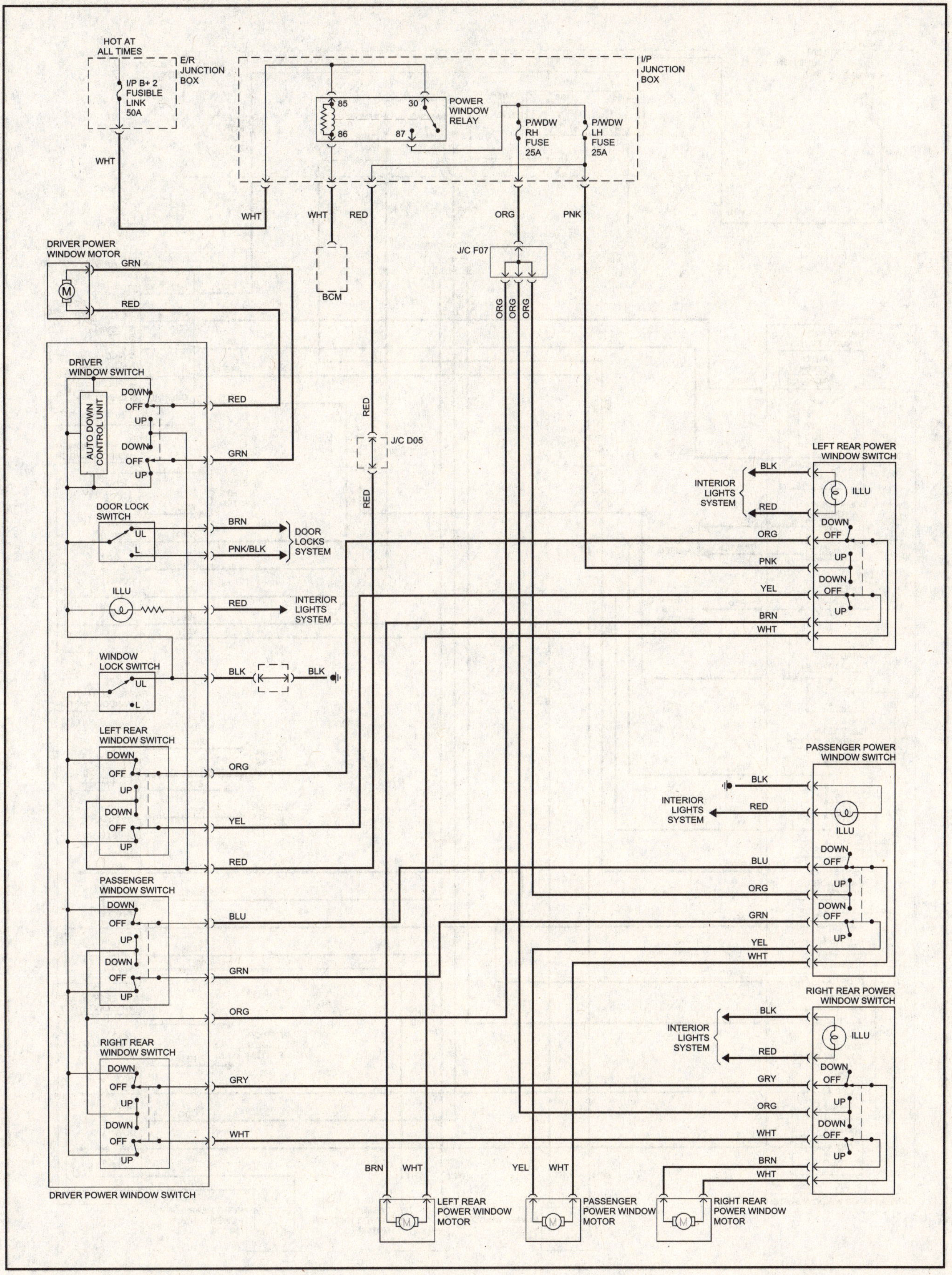

Power window system (without pinch protection) - 2006.5 and later models

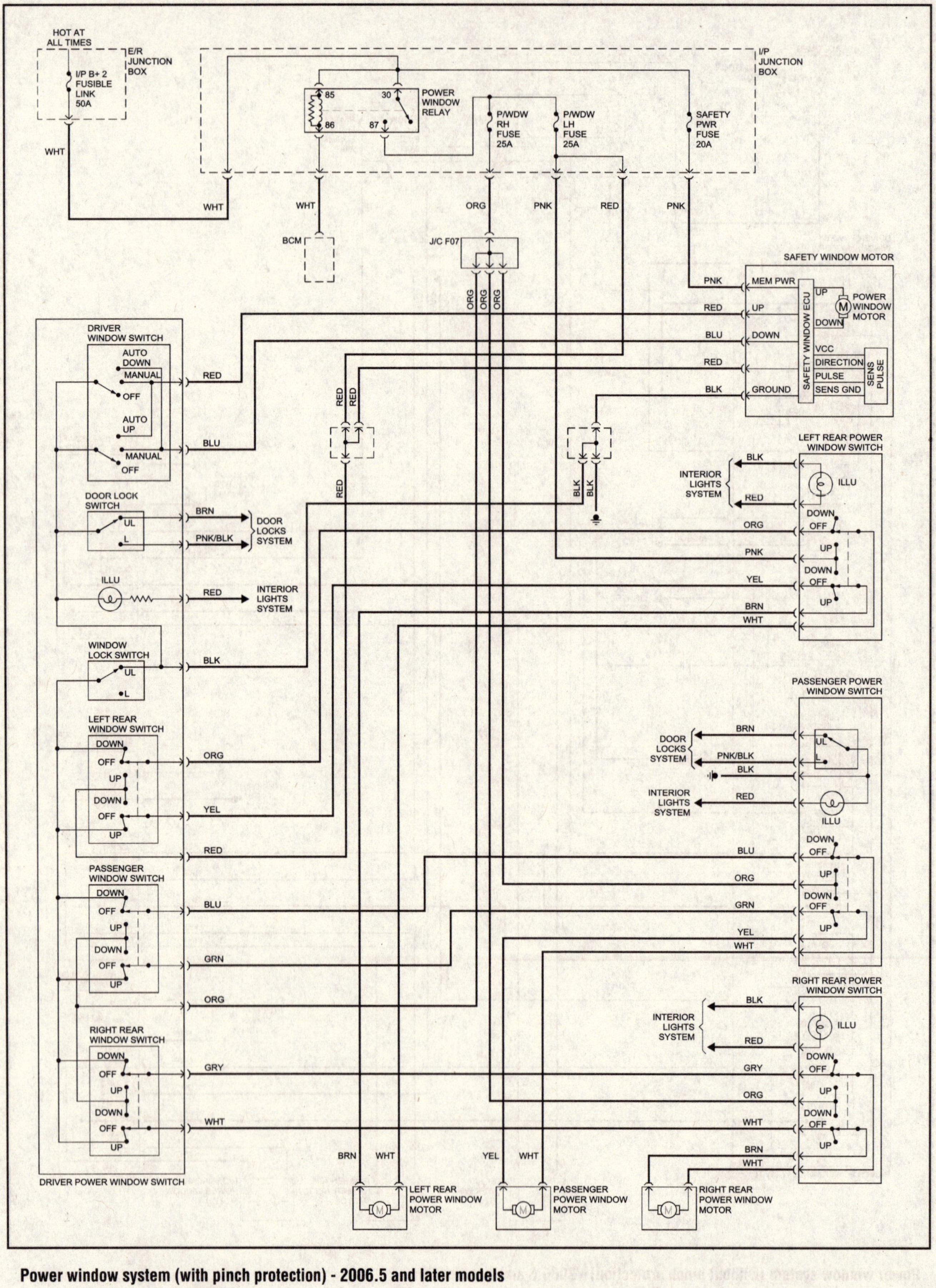

Power window system (with pinch protection) - 2006.5 and later models

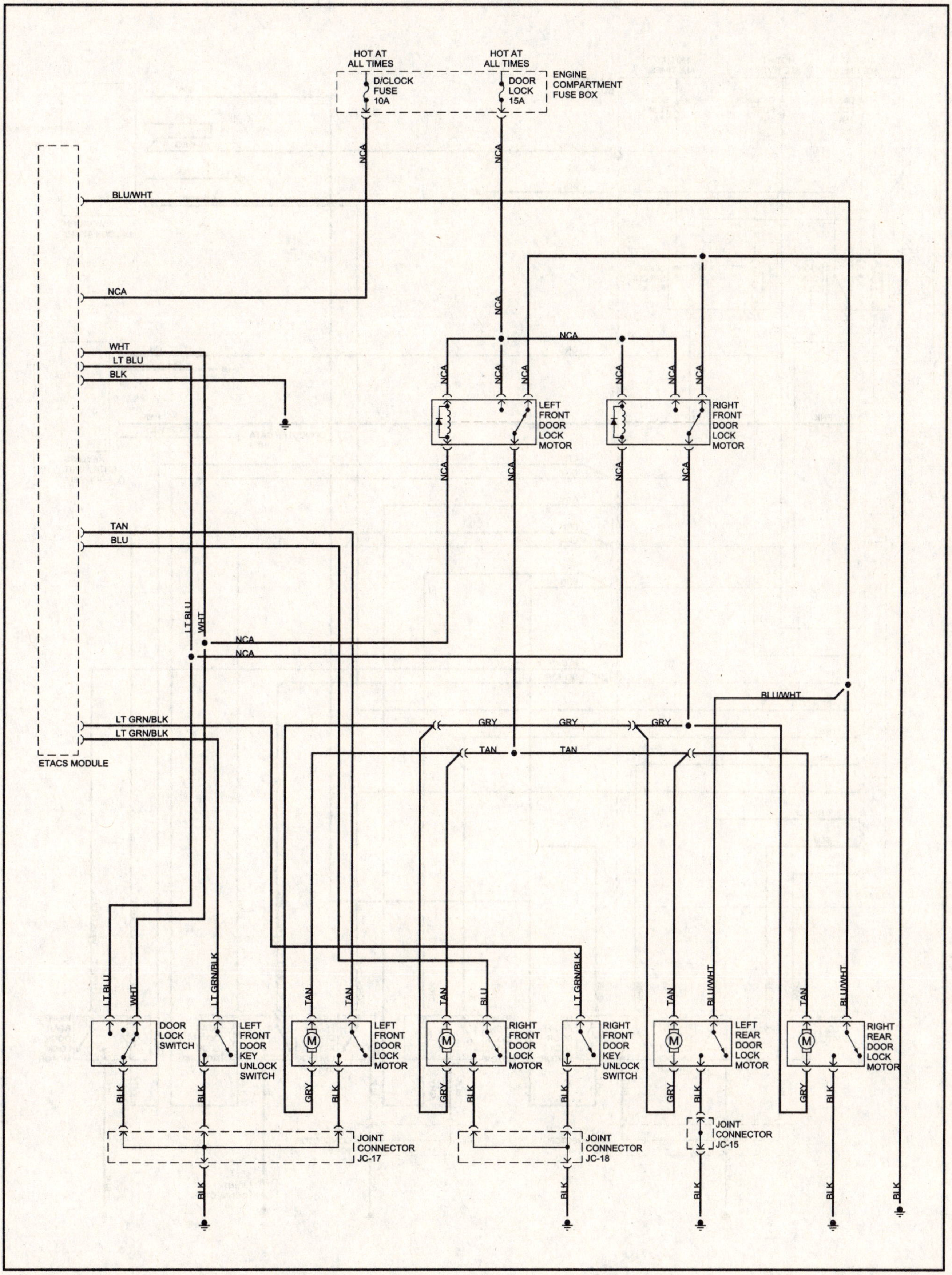

Power door lock system - 2001 and 2002 models

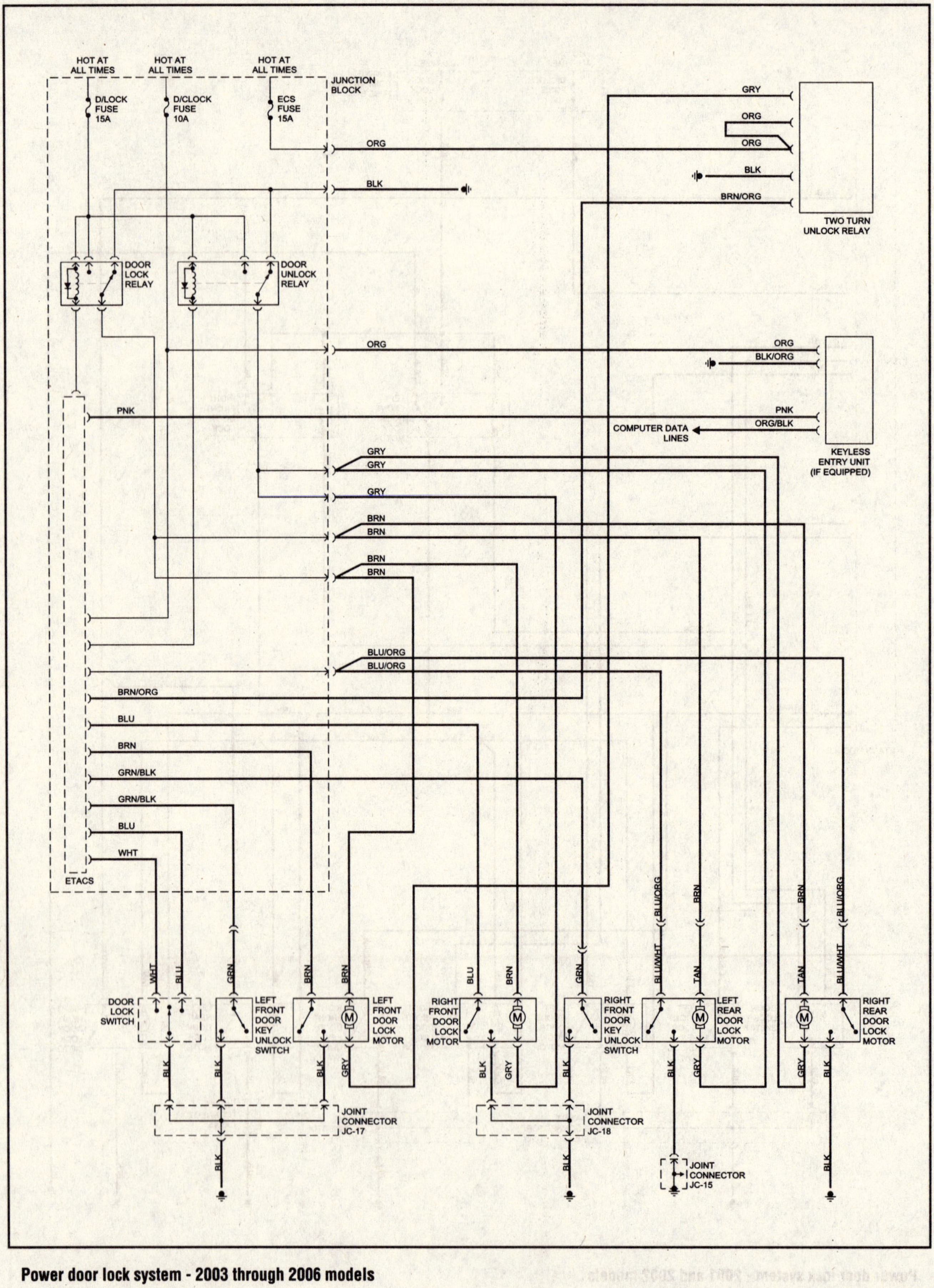

Power door lock system - 2003 through 2006 models

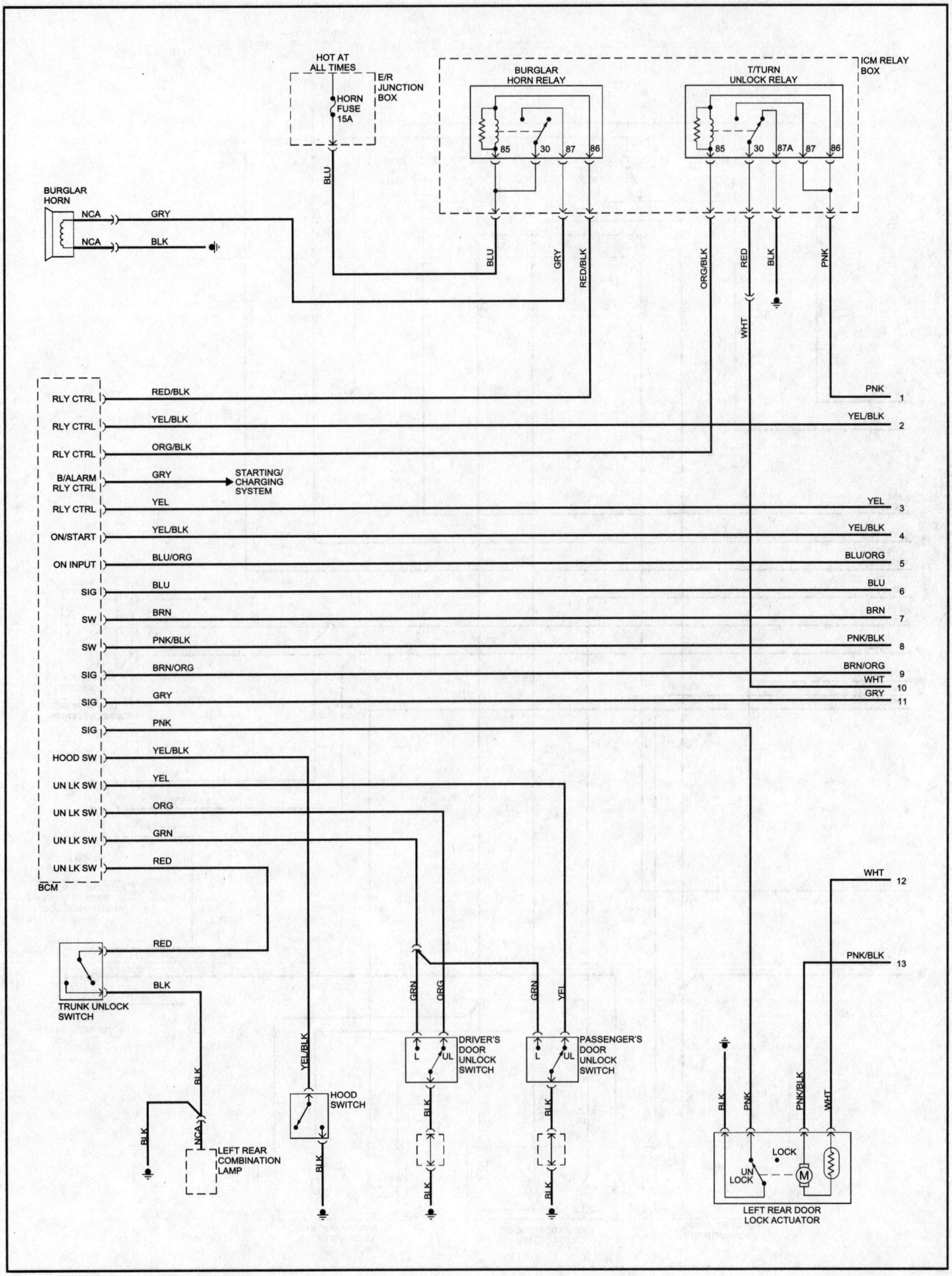

Power door lock system - 2006.5 and later models (1 of 2)

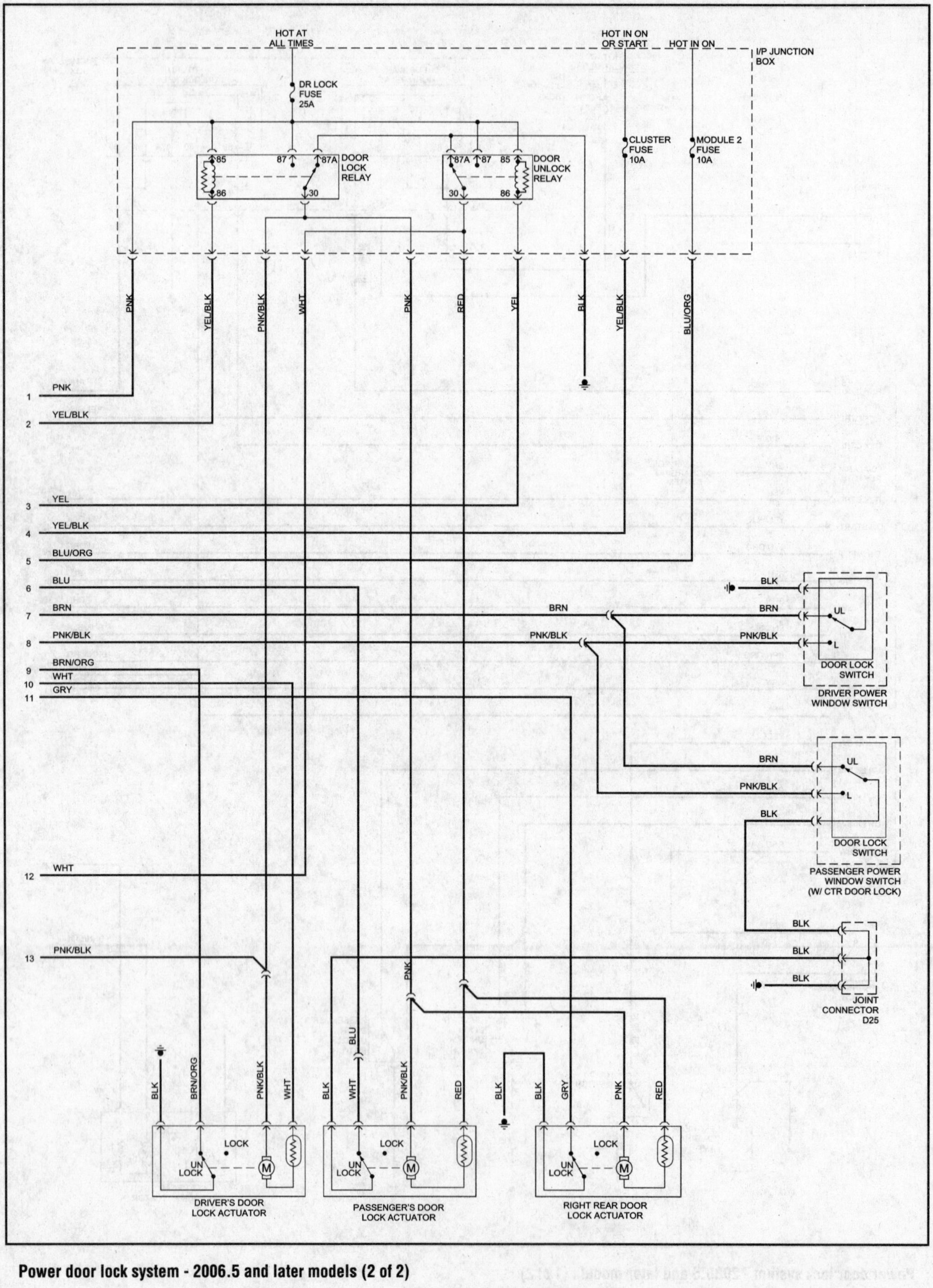

Power door lock system - 2006.5 and later models (2 of 2)

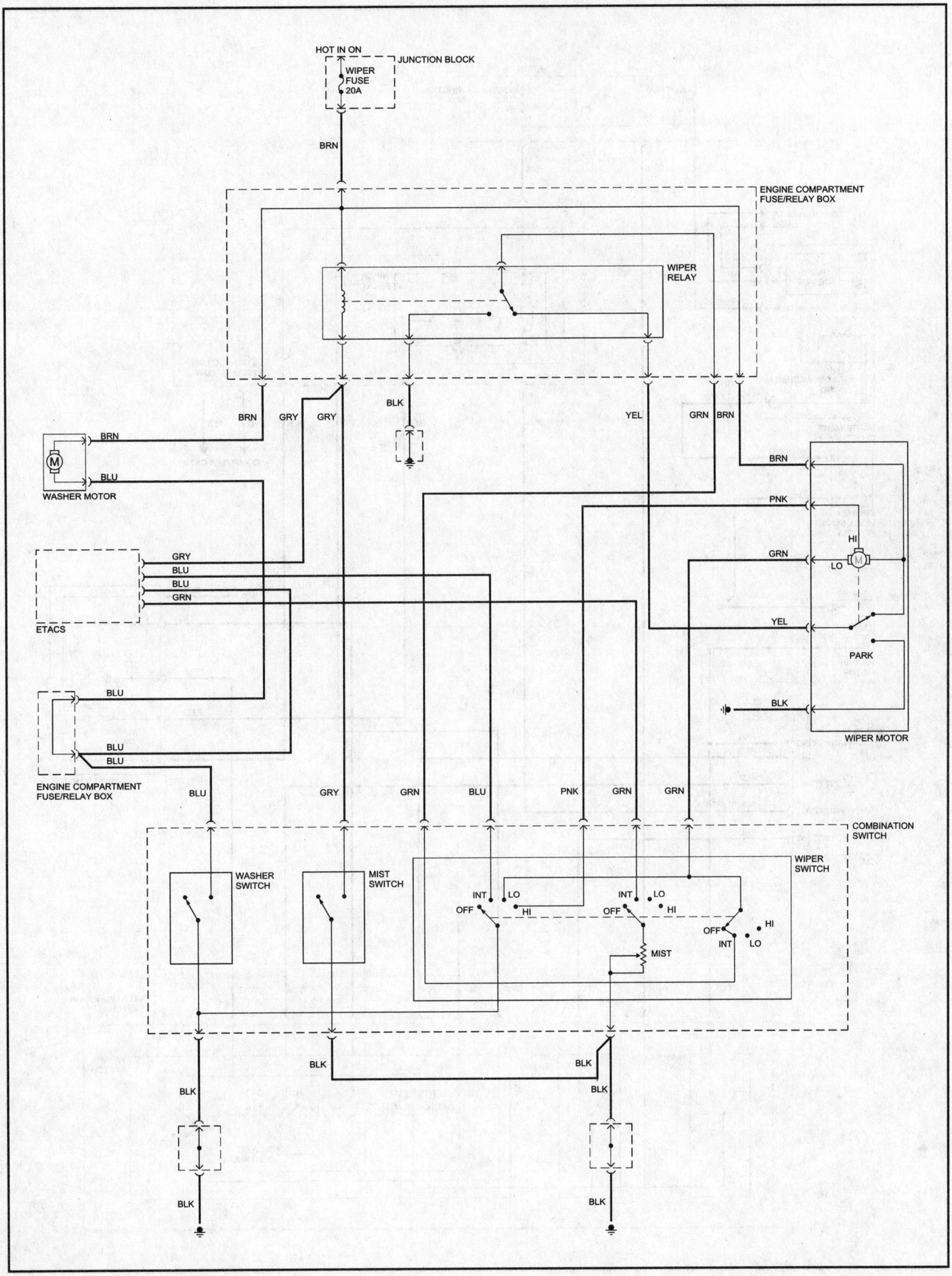

Windshield wiper/washer system - 2006 and earlier models

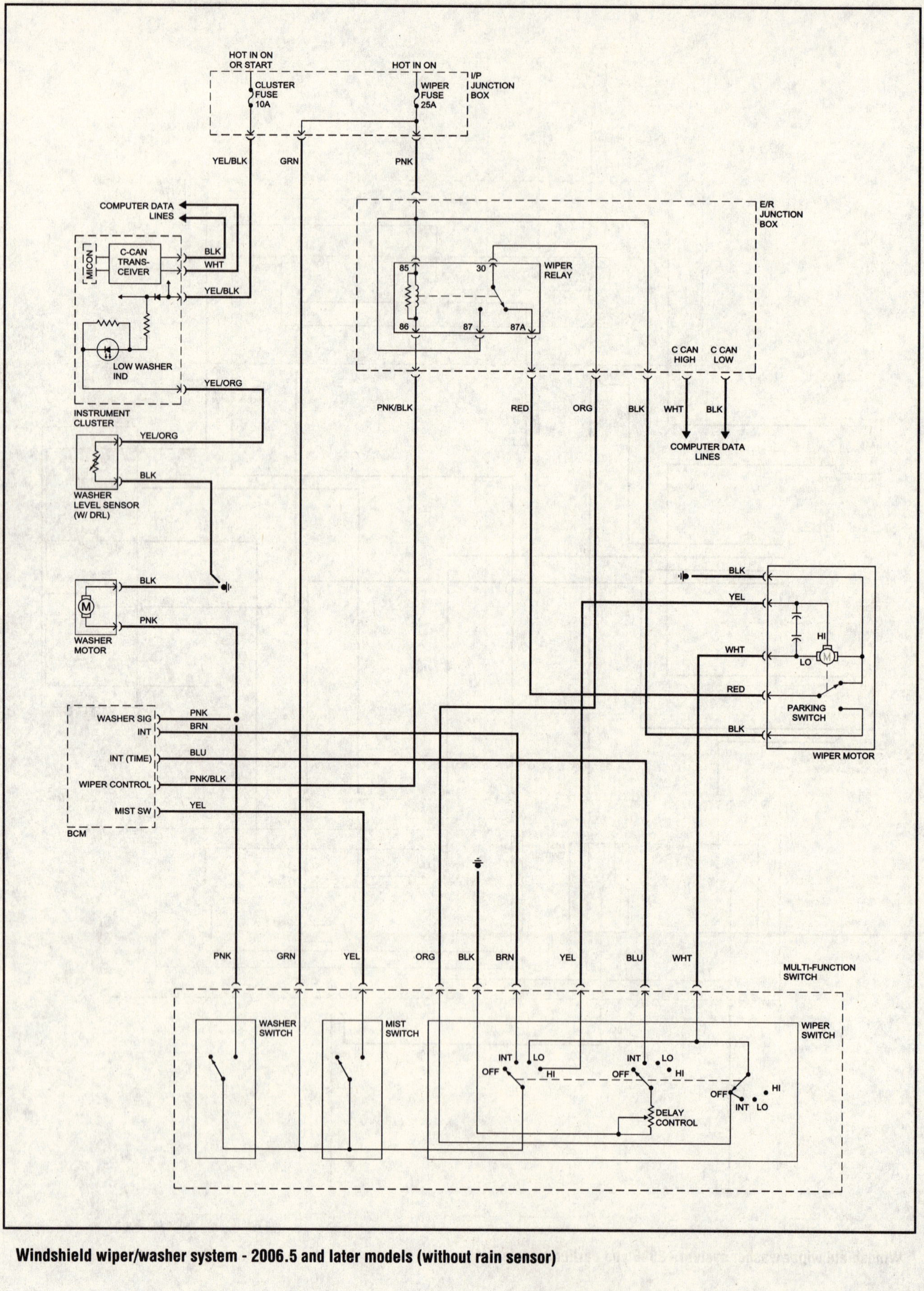

Windshield wiper/washer system - 2006.5 and later models (without rain sensor)

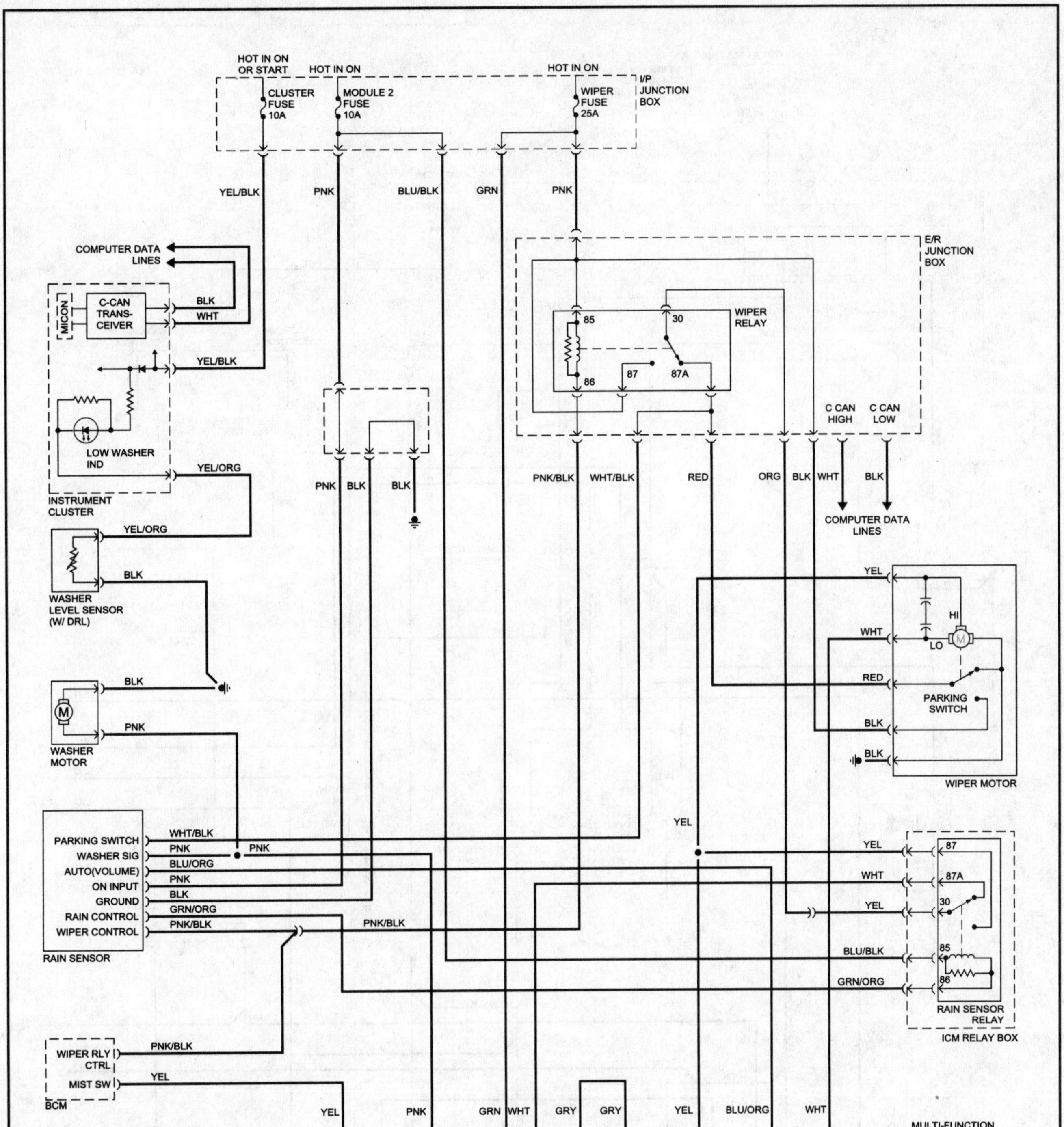

Windshield wiper/washer system - 2006.5 and later models (with rain sensor)

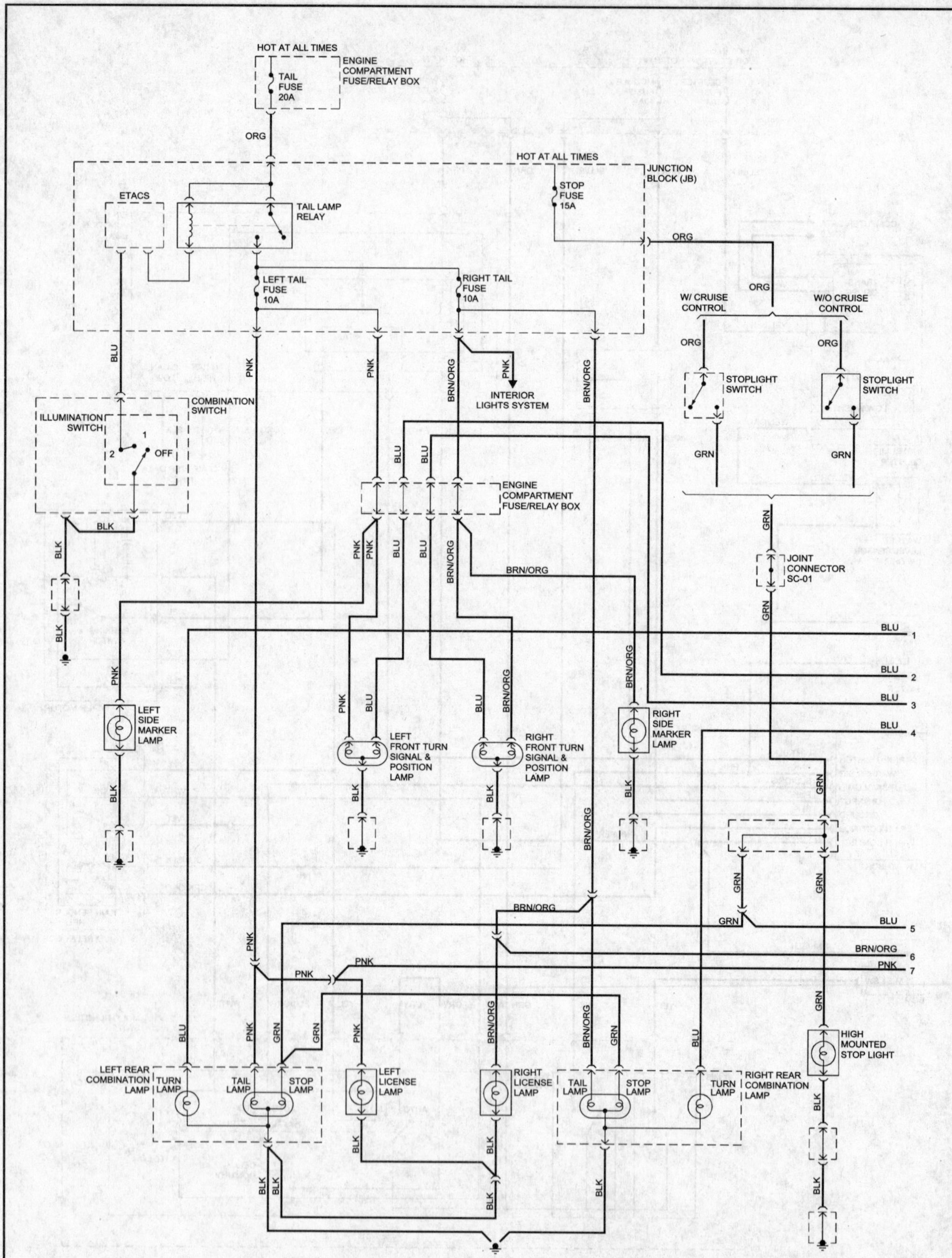

Exterior lighting system (except headlights and back-up lights) - 2006 and earlier models

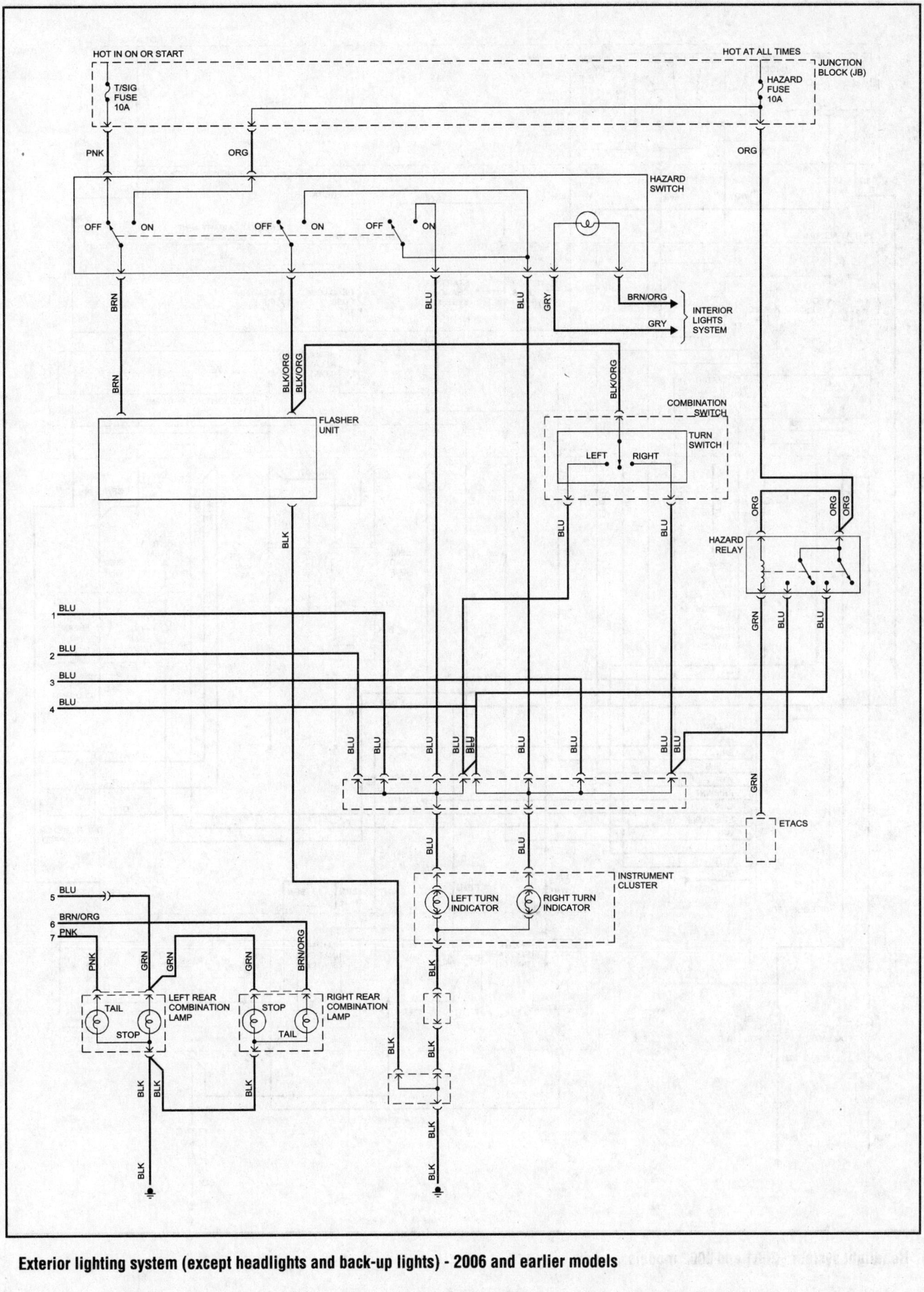

Exterior lighting system (except headlights and back-up lights) - 2006 and earlier models

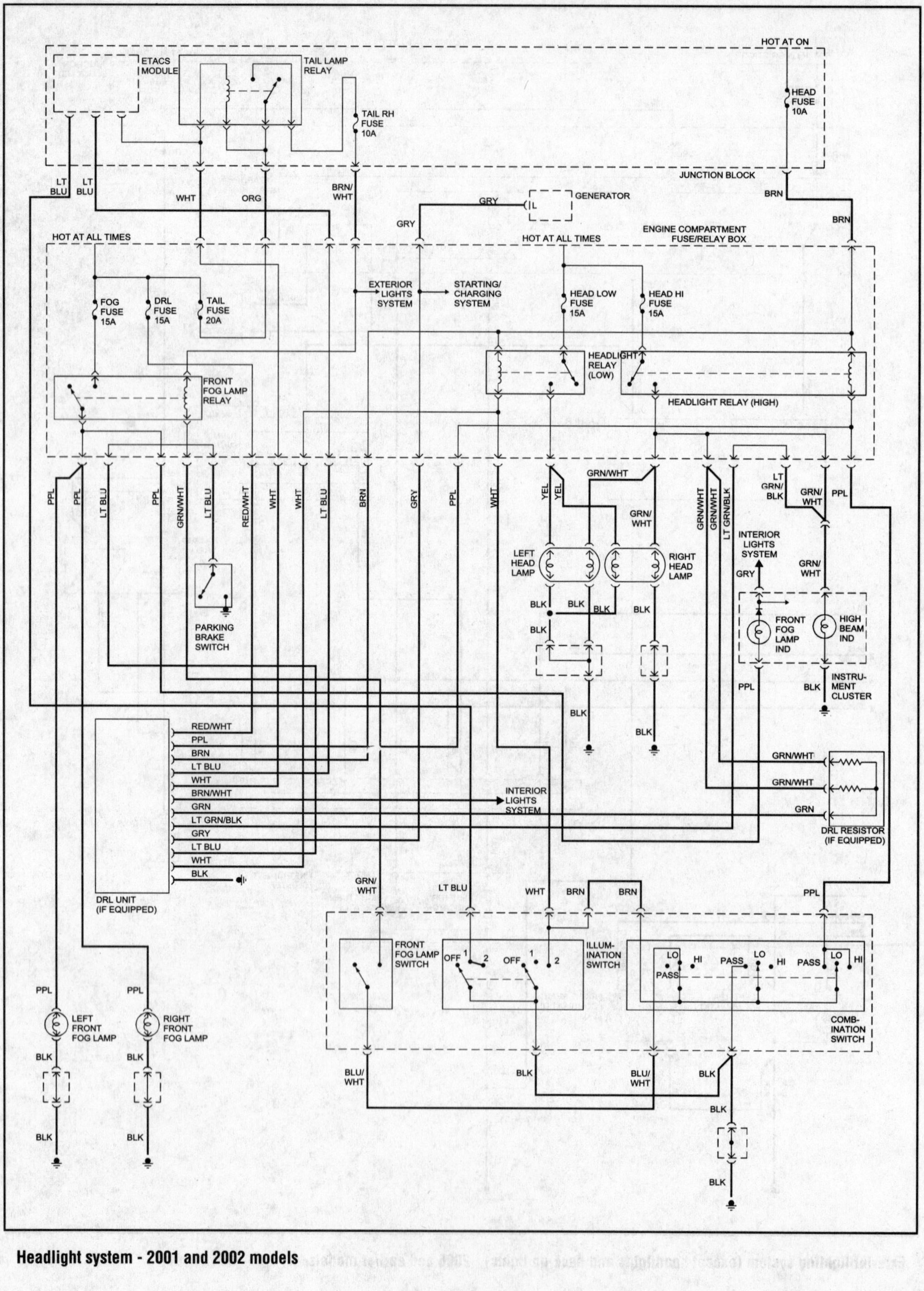

Headlight system - 2001 and 2002 models

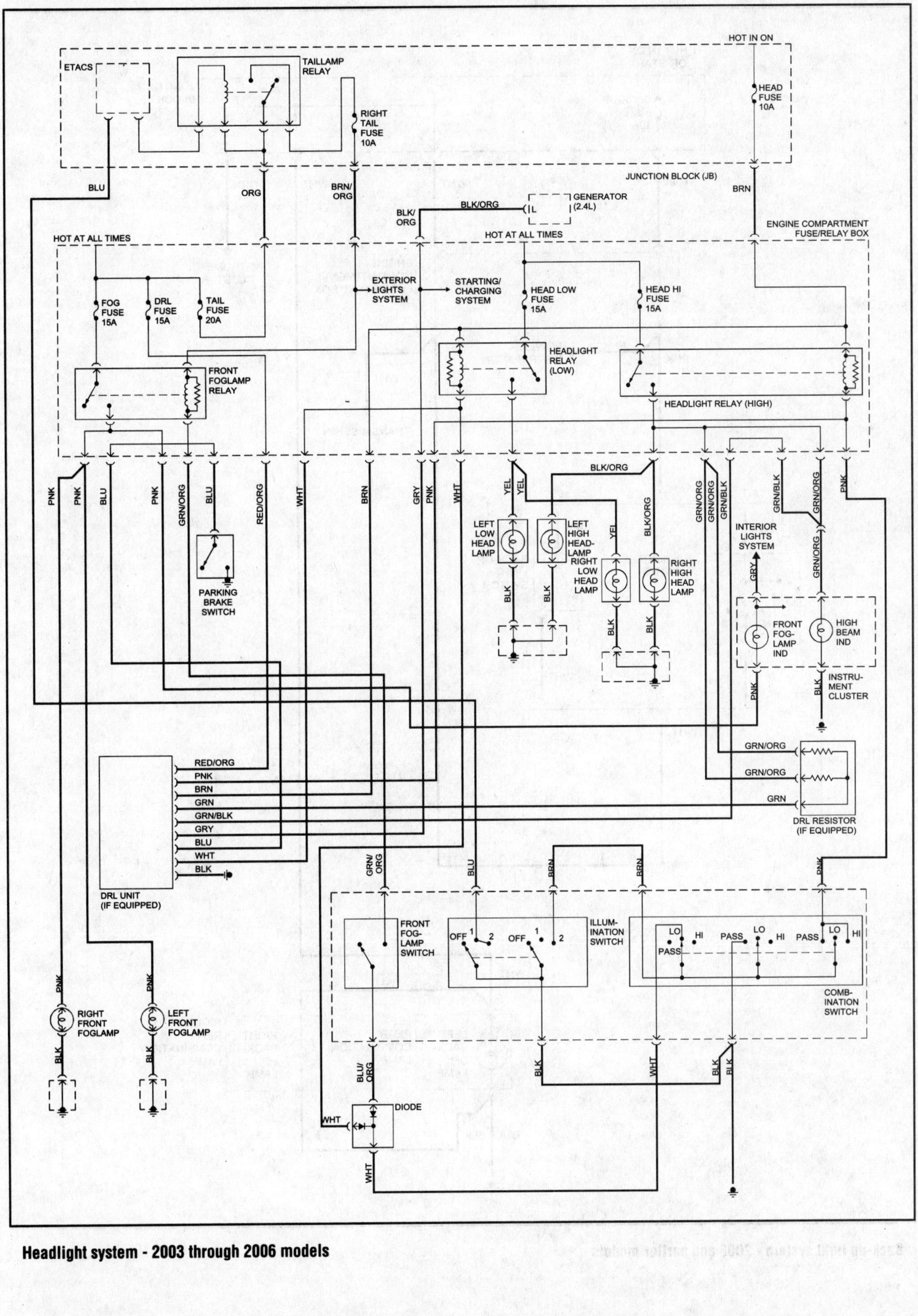

Headlight system - 2003 through 2006 models

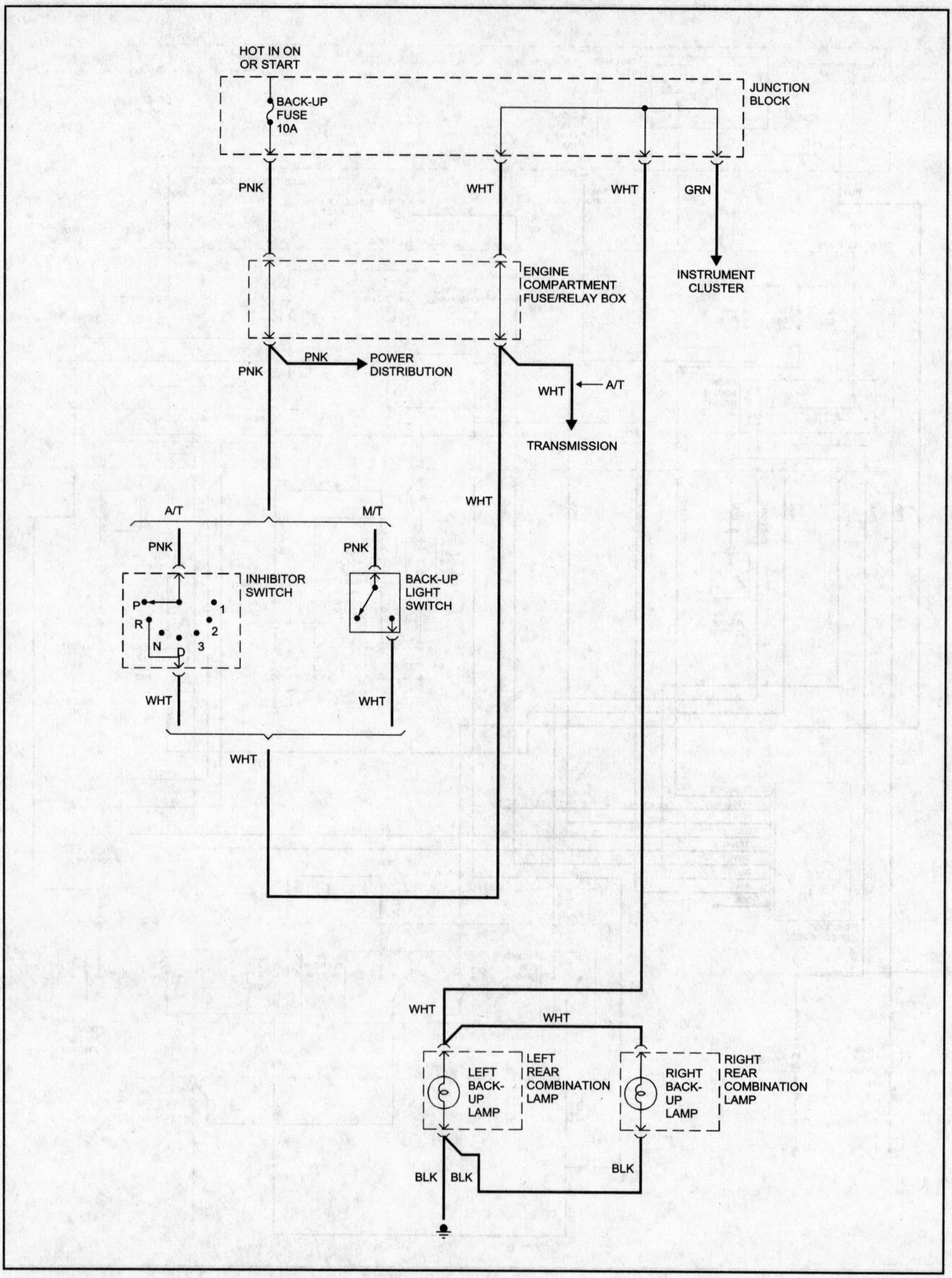

Back-up light system - 2006 and earlier models

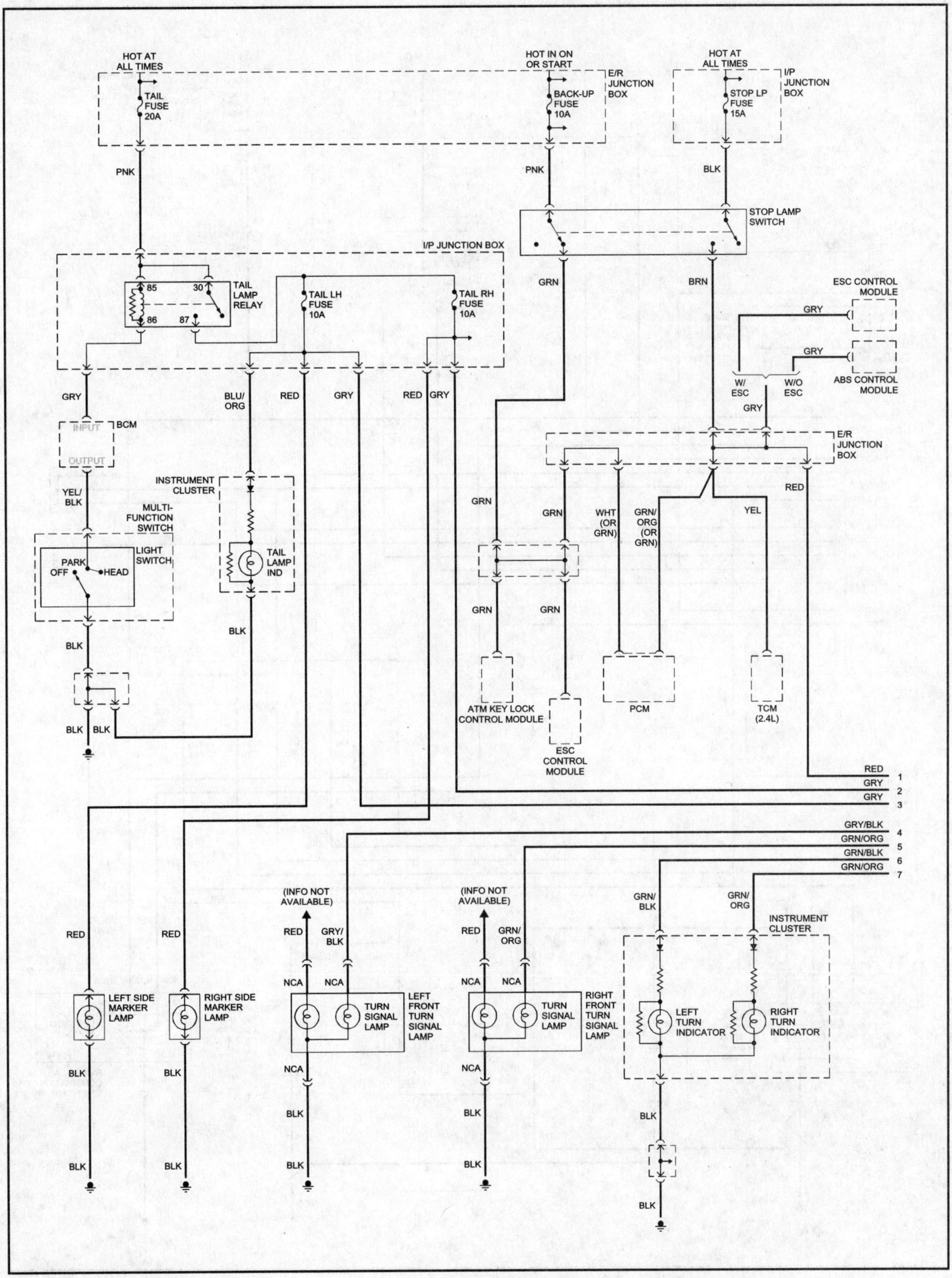

Exterior lighting system (except headlights and back-up lights) - 2006.5 through 2008 models (1 of 2)

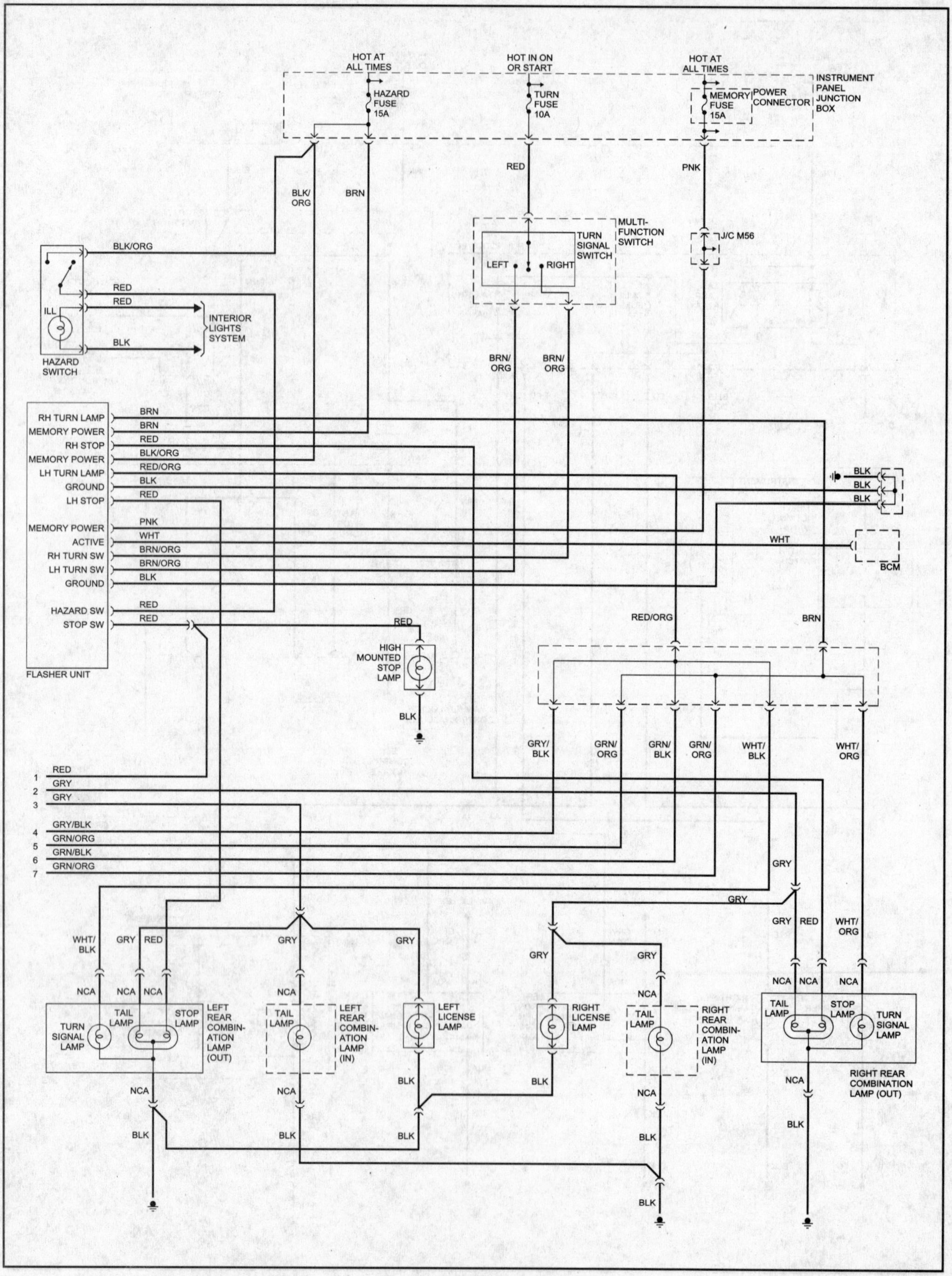

Exterior lighting system (except headlights and back-up lights) - 2006.5 through 2008 models (2 of 2)

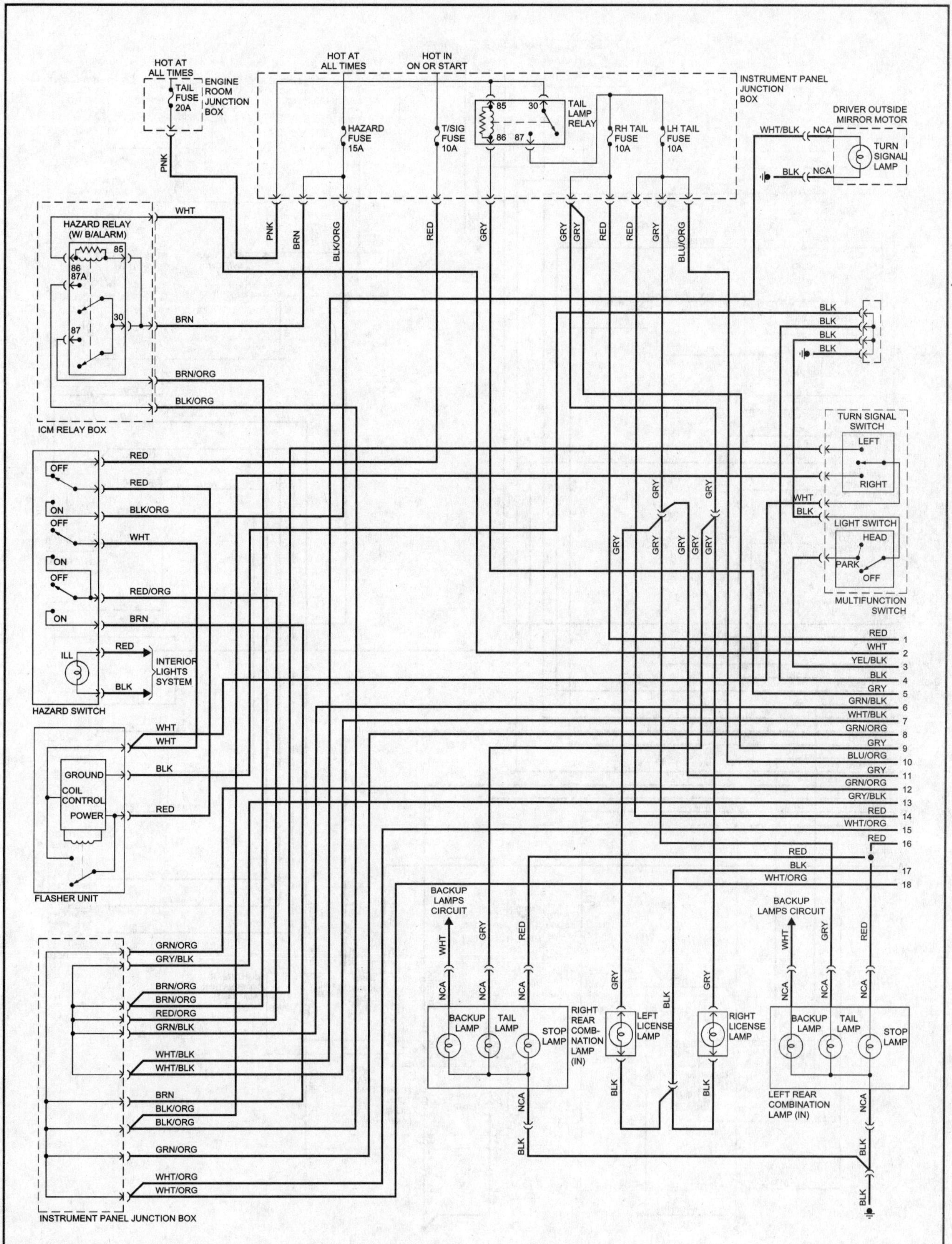

Exterior lighting system (except headlights and back-up lights) - 2009 and later models (1 of 2)

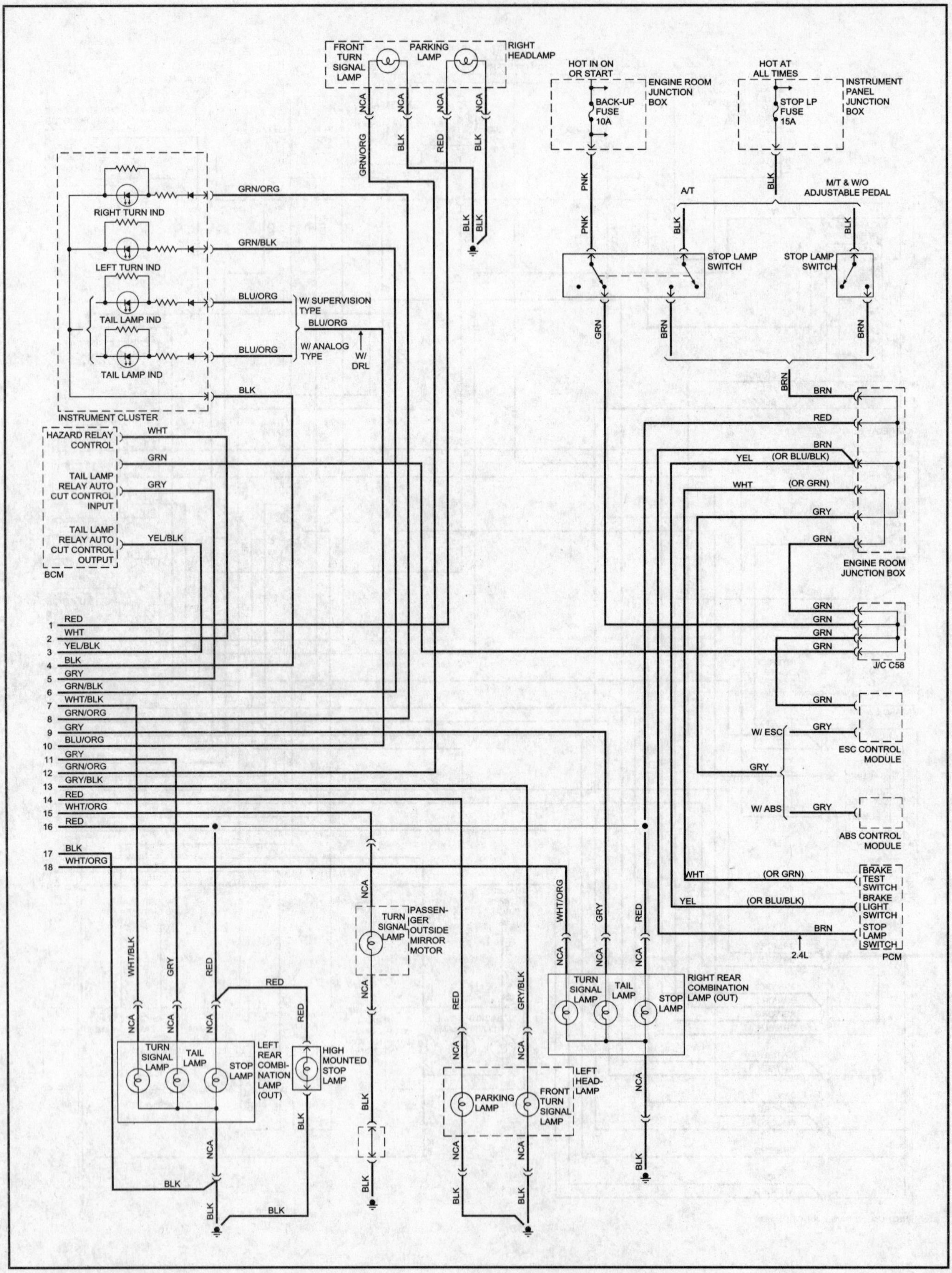

Exterior lighting system (except headlights and back-up lights) - 2009 and later models (2 of 2)

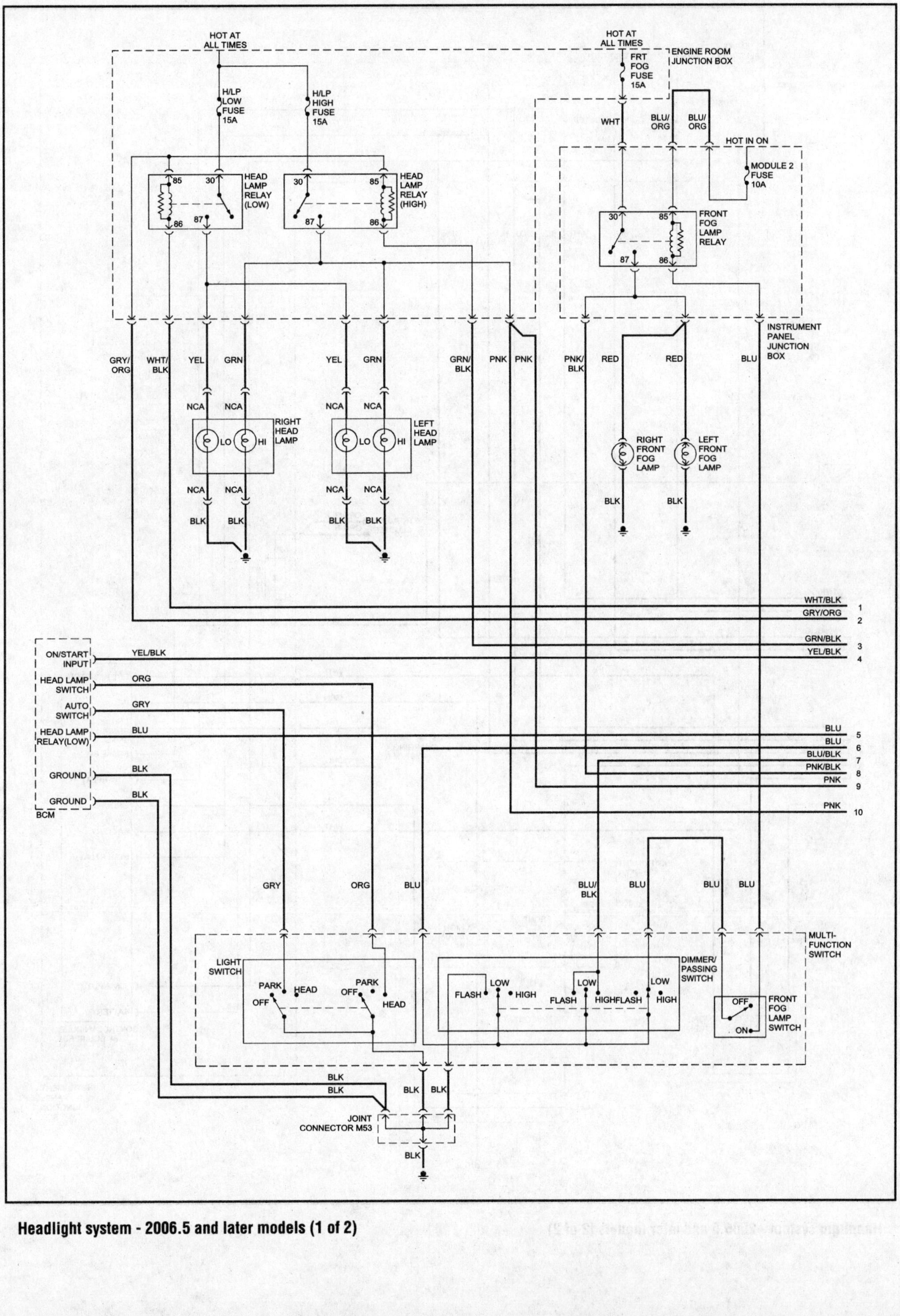

Headlight system - 2006.5 and later models (1 of 2)

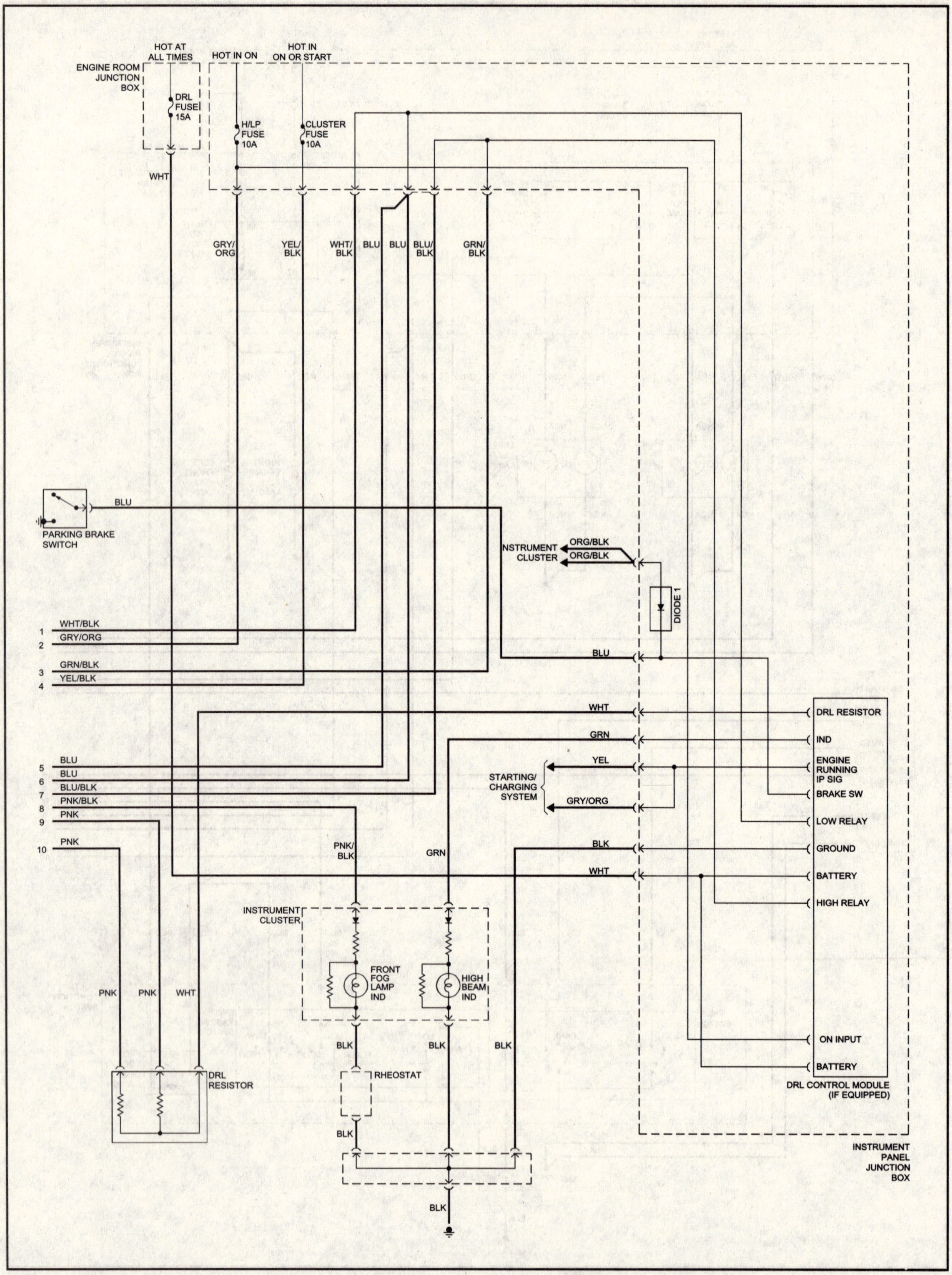

Headlight system - 2006.5 and later models (2 of 2)

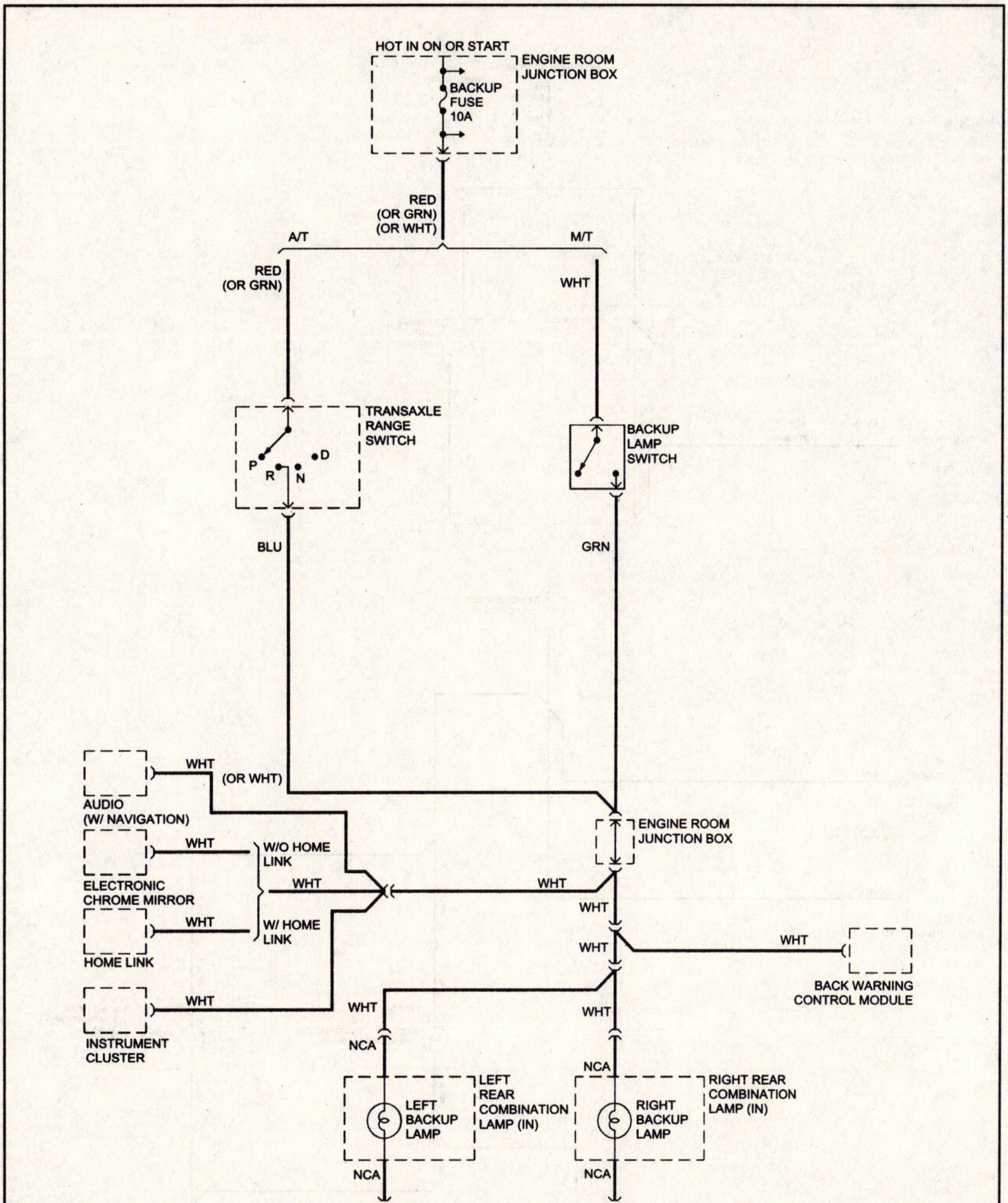

Back-up light system - 2006.5 through 2008 models

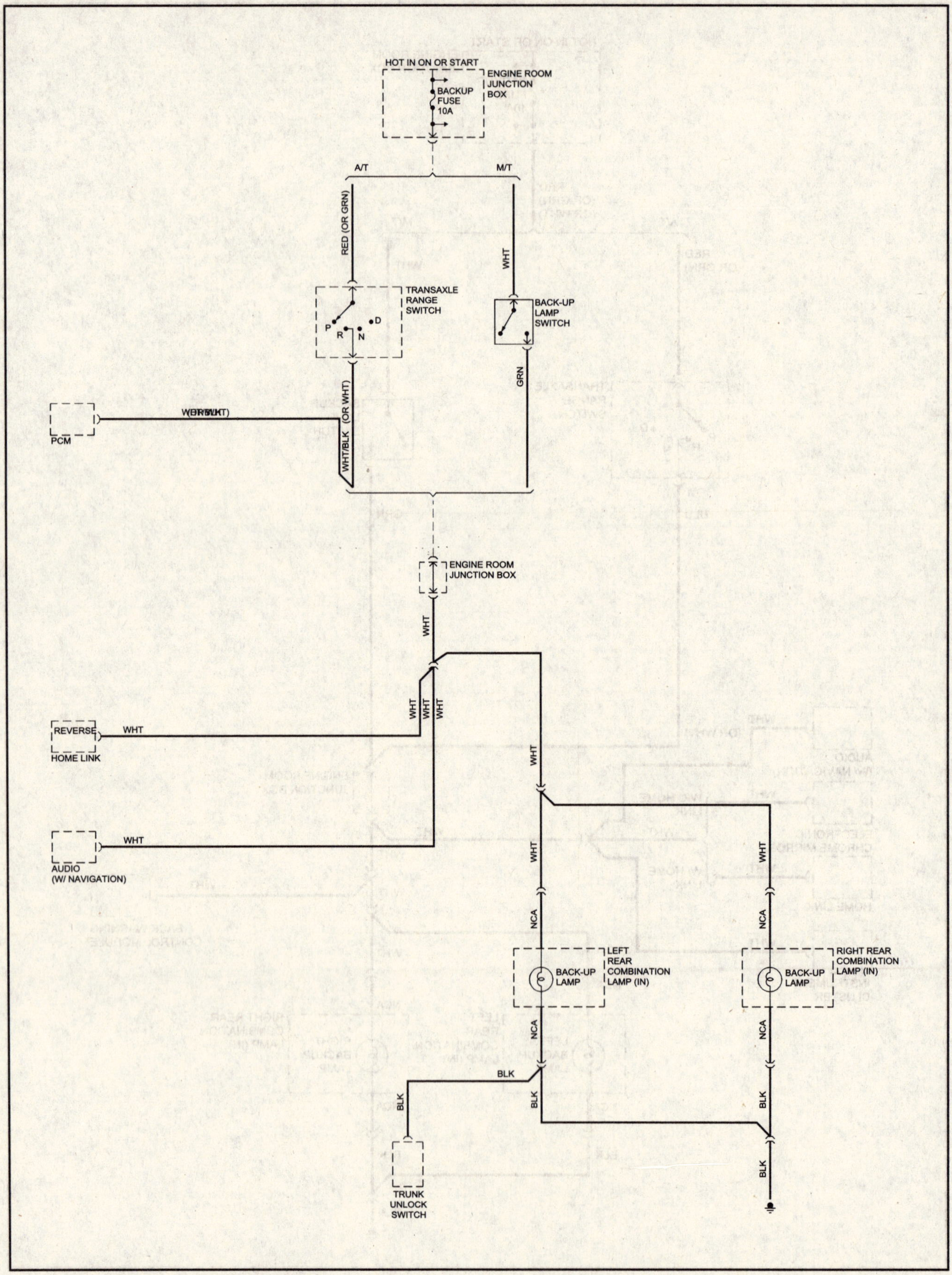

Back-up light system - 2009 and later models

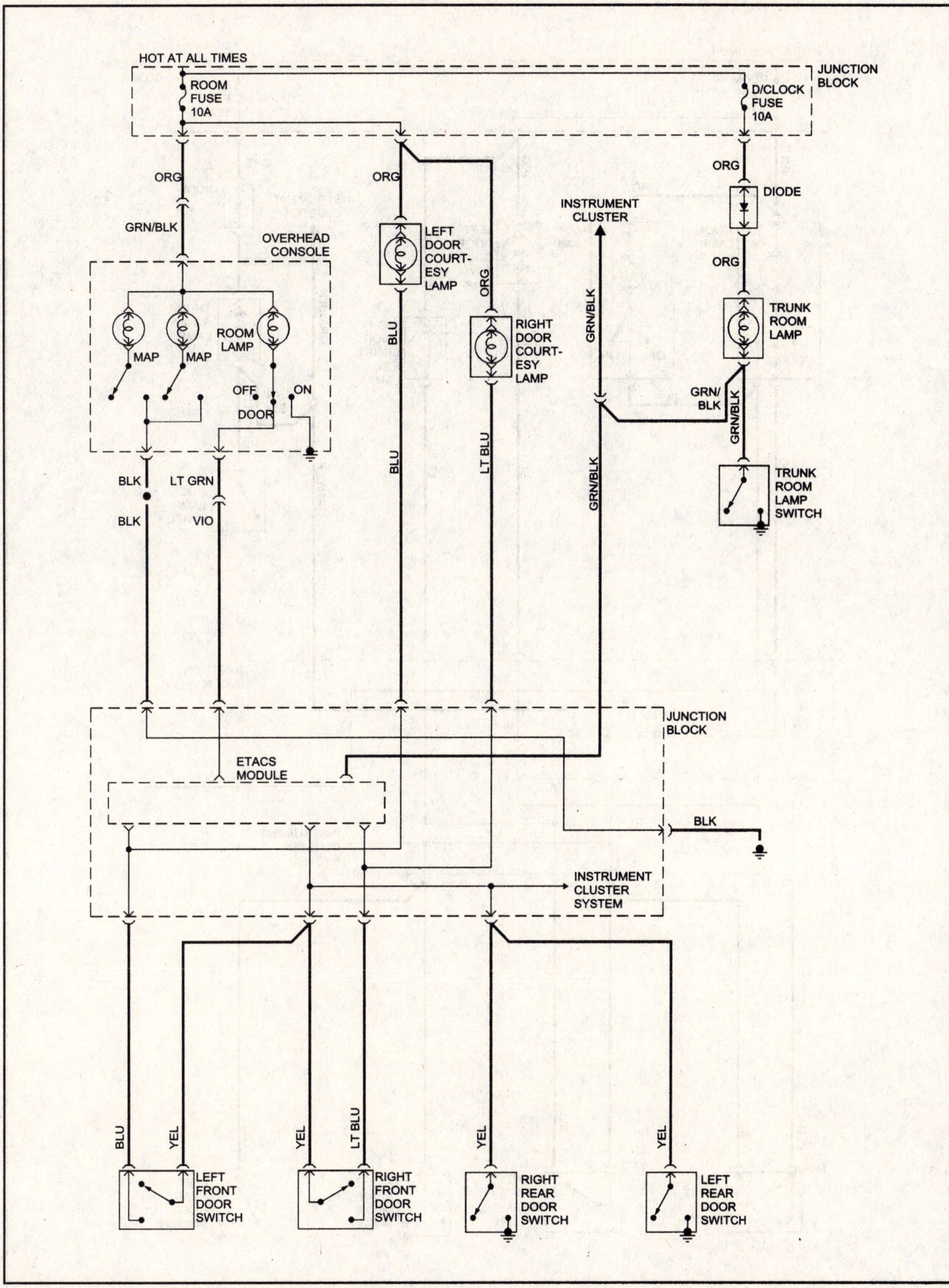

Interior lighting system - 2001 and 2002 models (with sunroof)

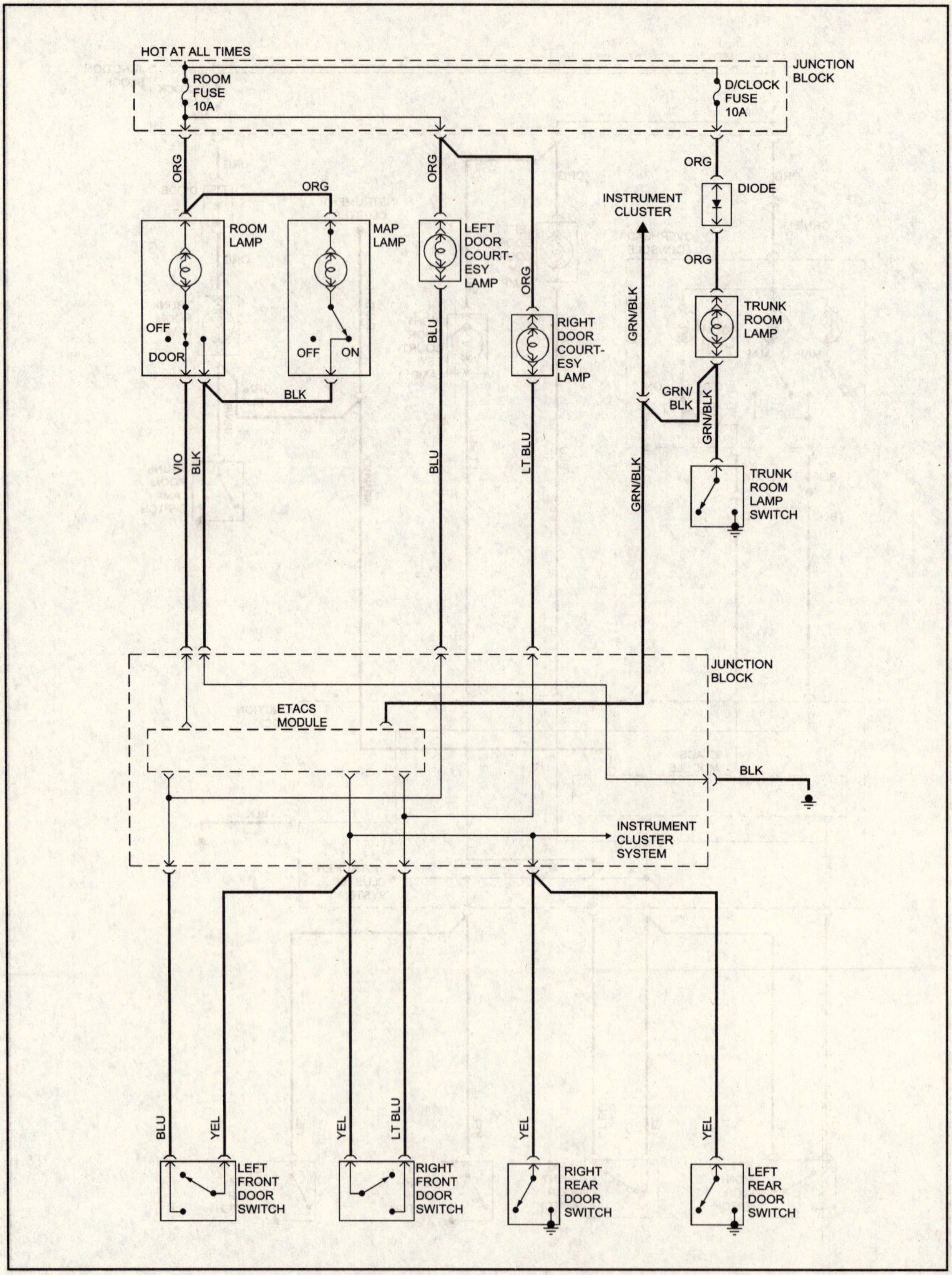

Interior lighting system - 2001 and 2002 models (without sunroof)

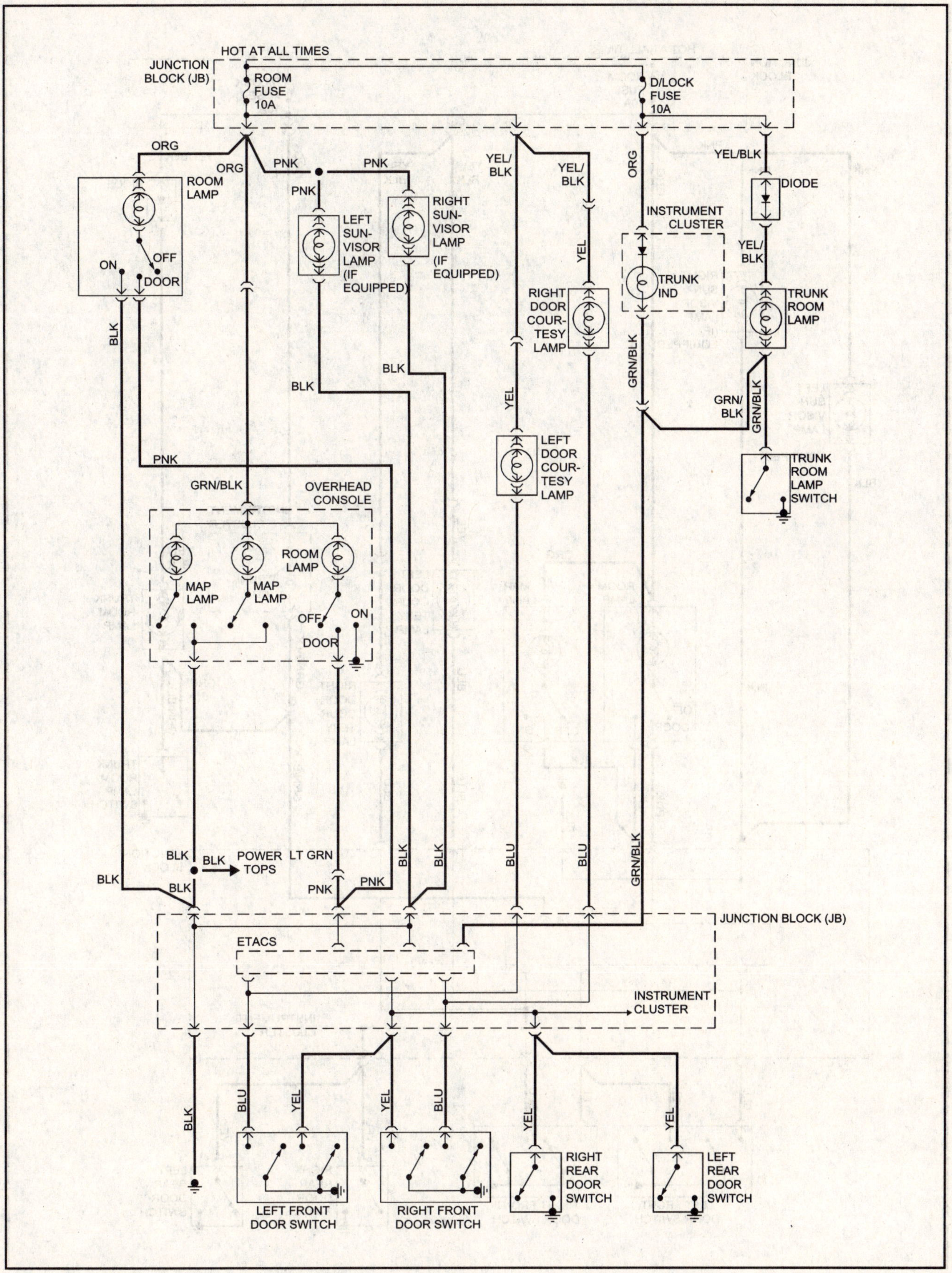

Interior lighting system - 2003 through 2006 models (with sunroof)

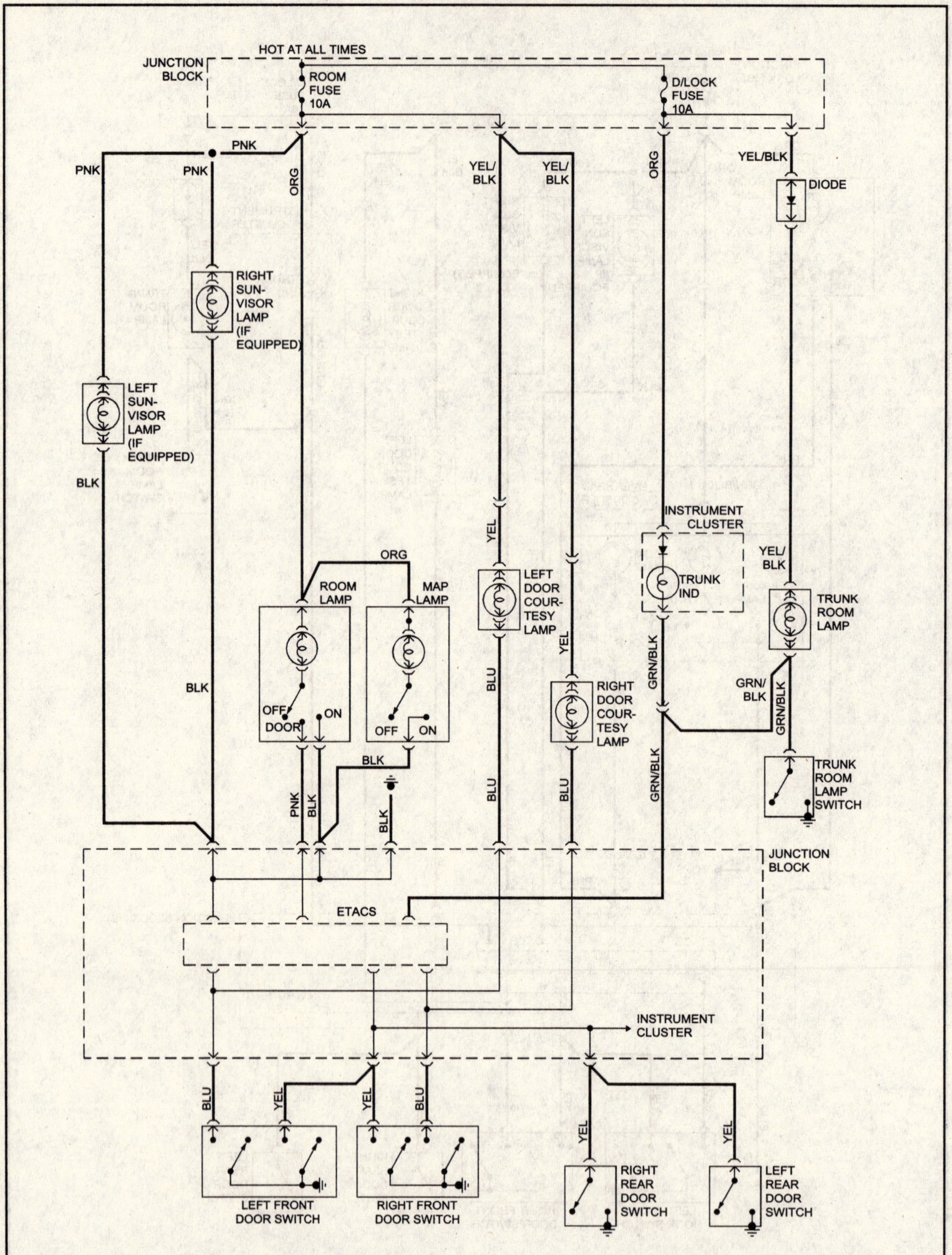

Interior lighting system - 2003 through 2006 models (without sunroof)

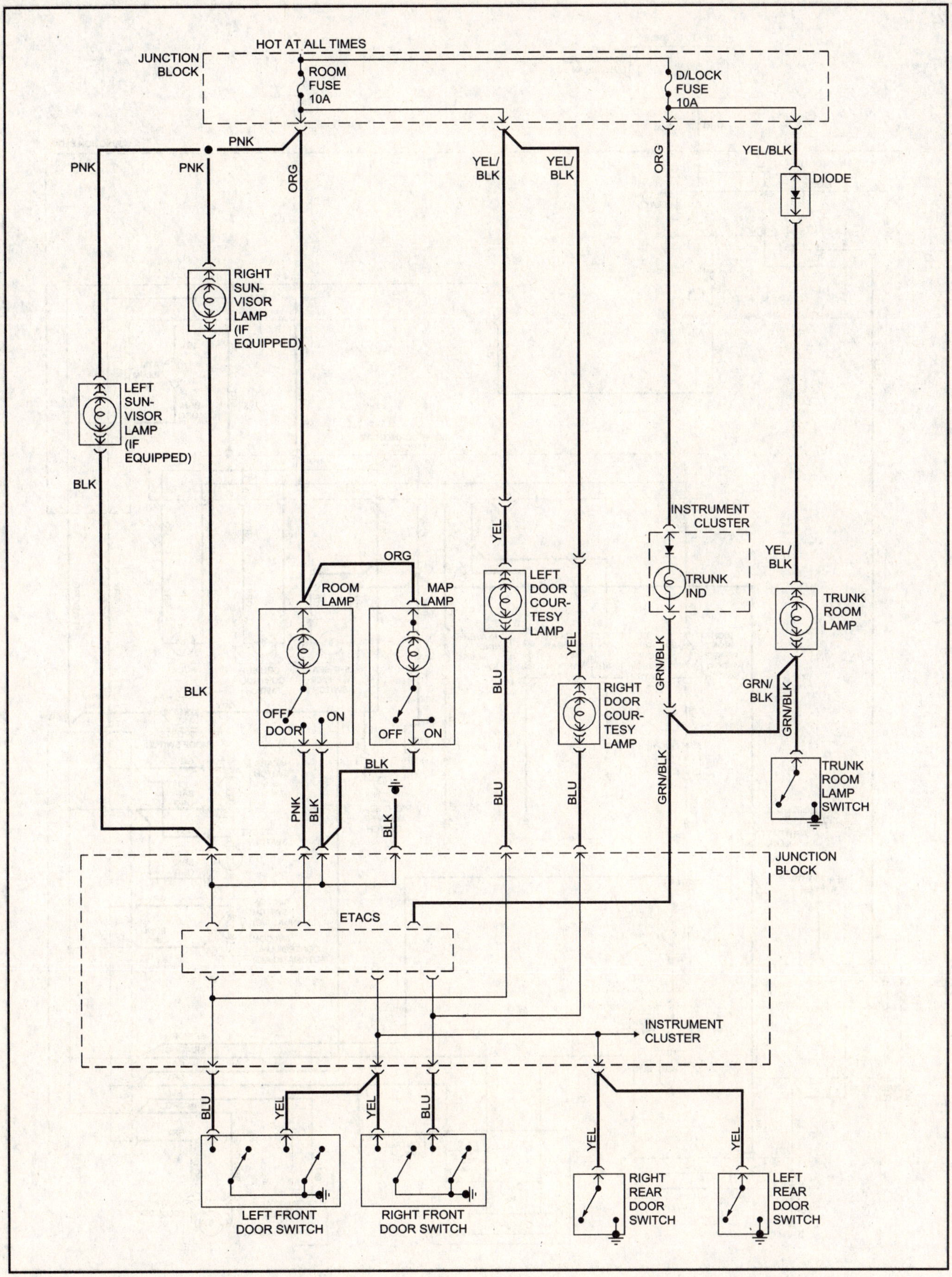

Interior lighting system - 2006.5 and later models

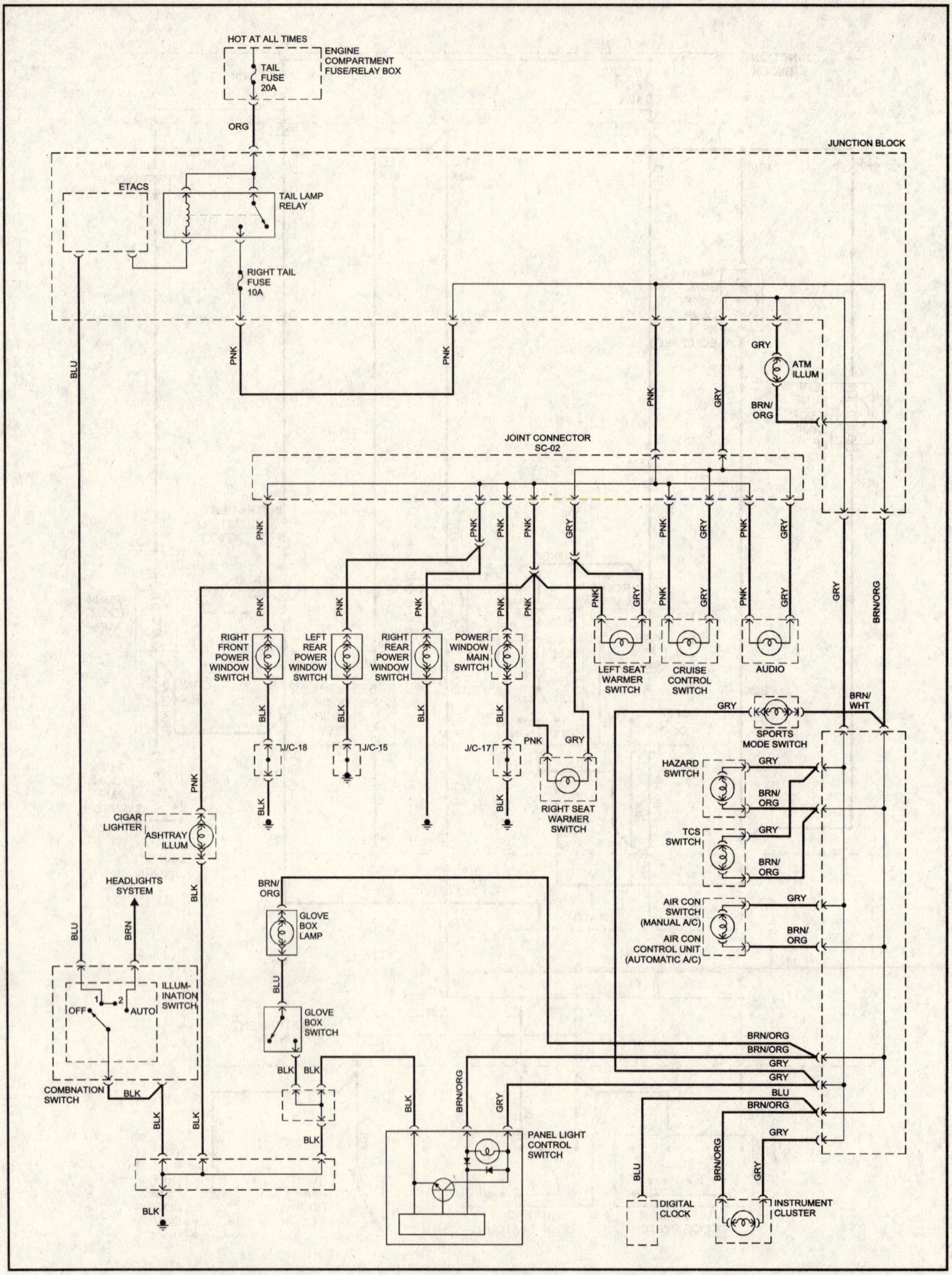

Instrument panel and switch illumination - 2006 and earlier models

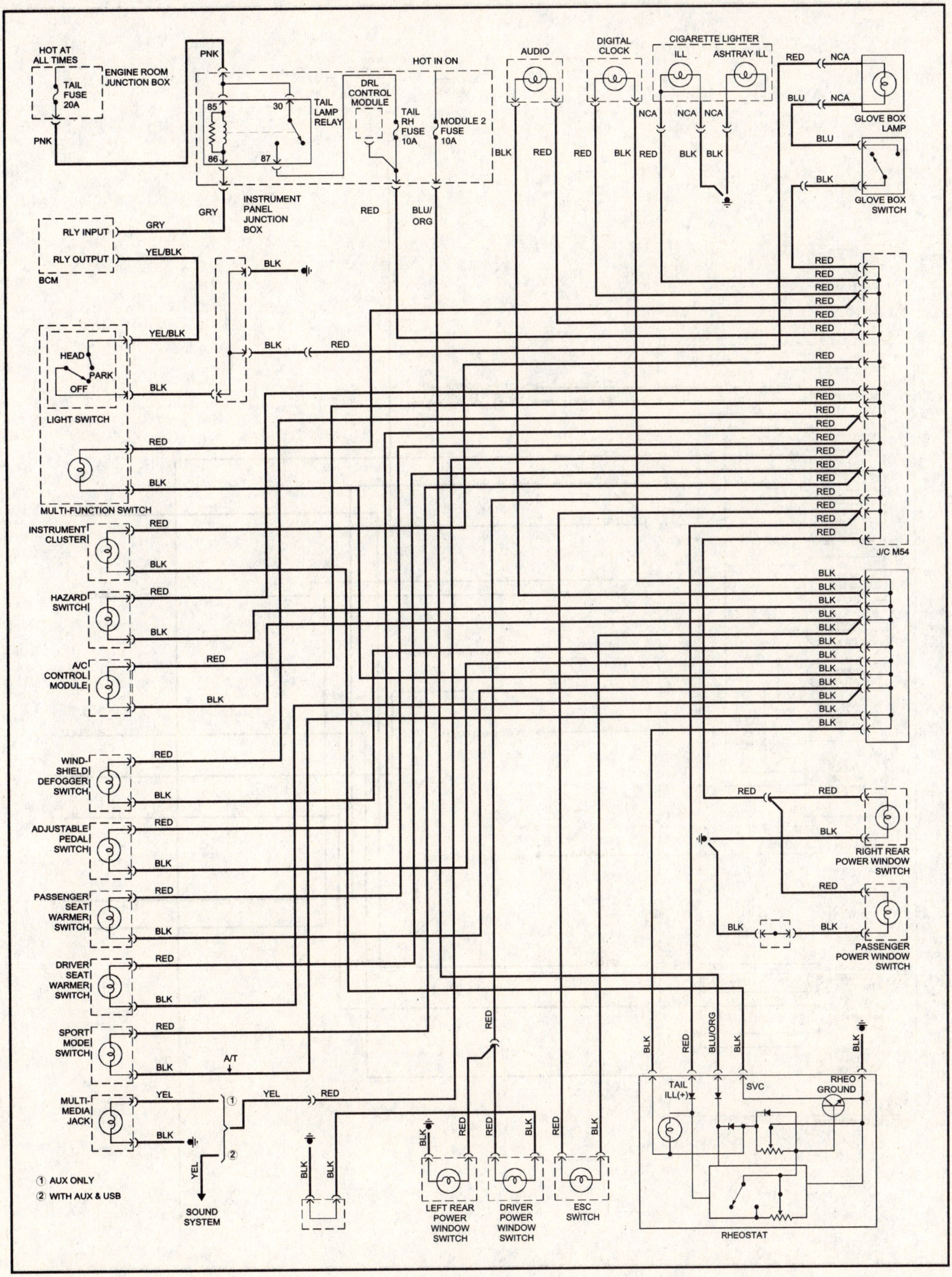

Instrument panel and switch illumination - 2006.5 and later models

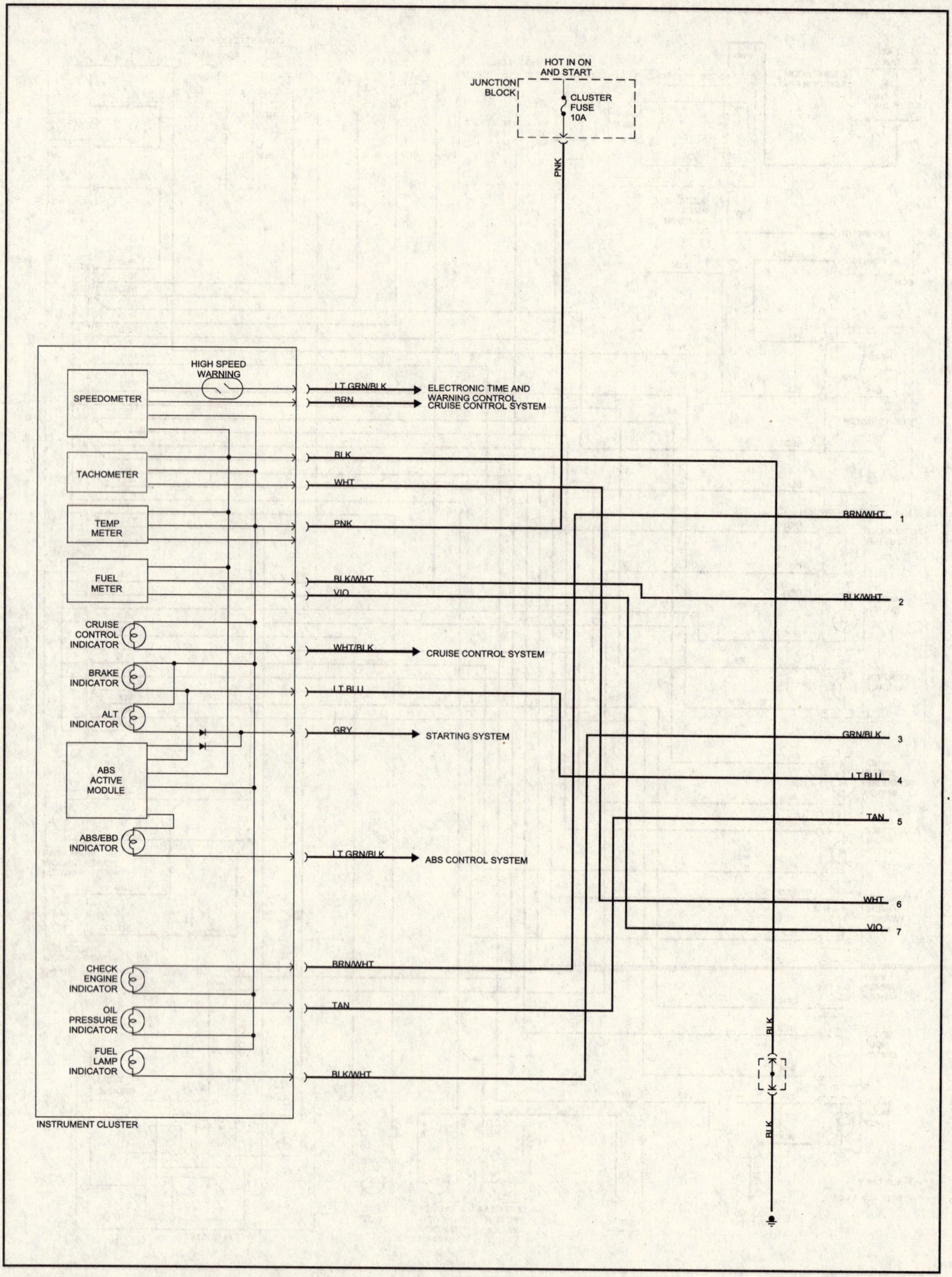

Warning lights and gauges - 2001 and 2002 models (1 of 2)

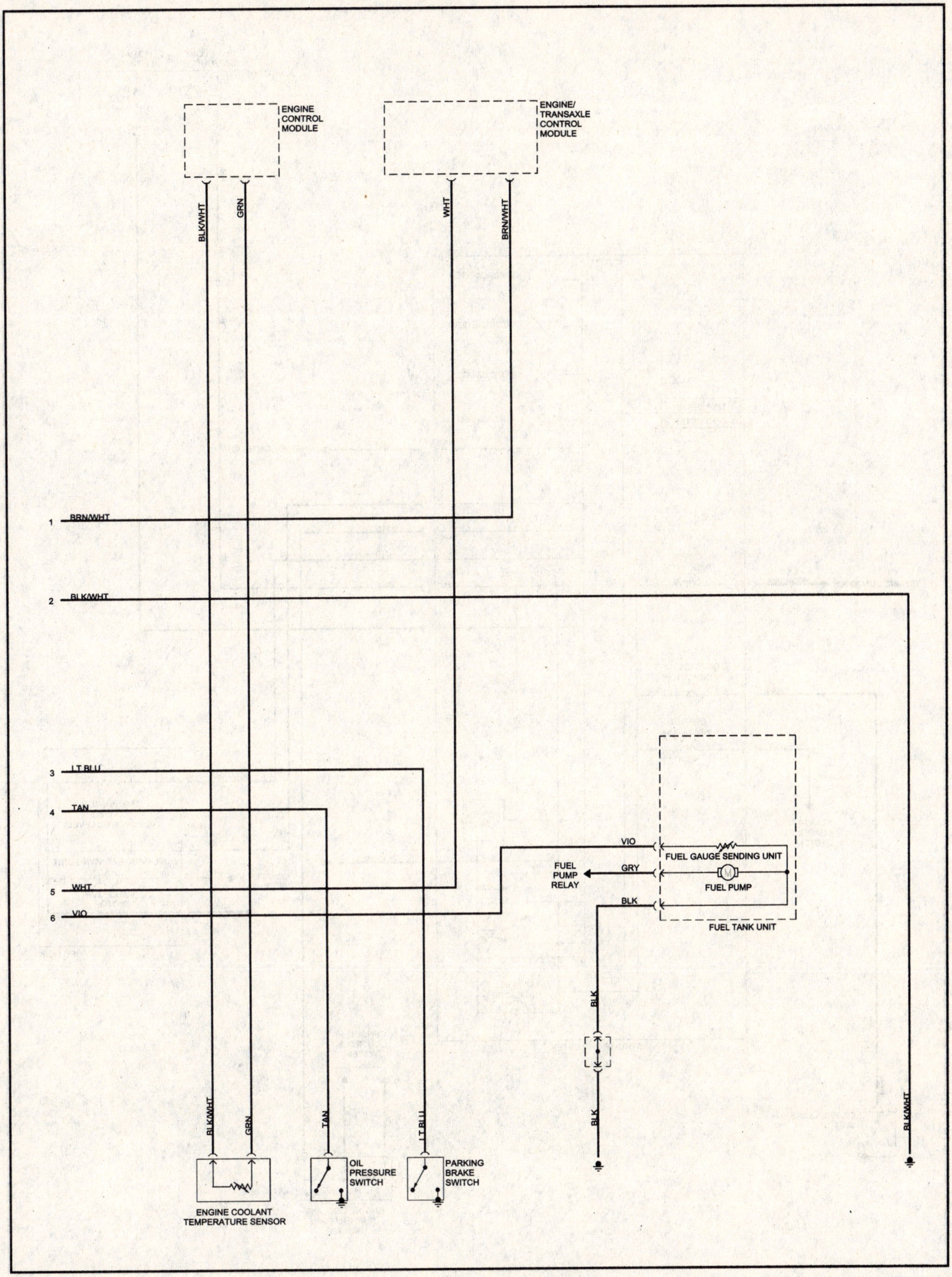

Warning lights and gauges - 2001 and 2002 models (2 of 2)

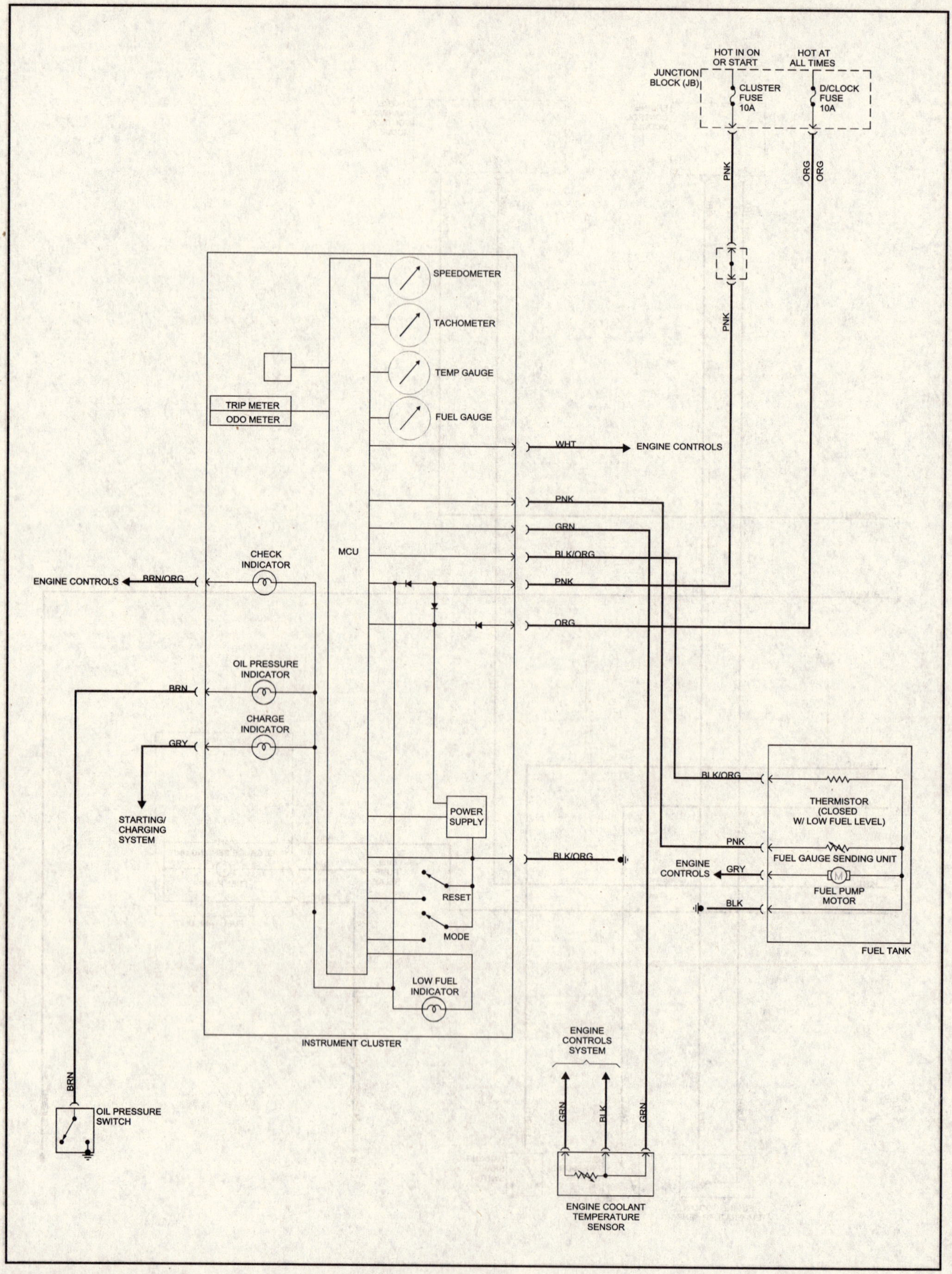

Warning lights and gauges - 2003 through 2006 models

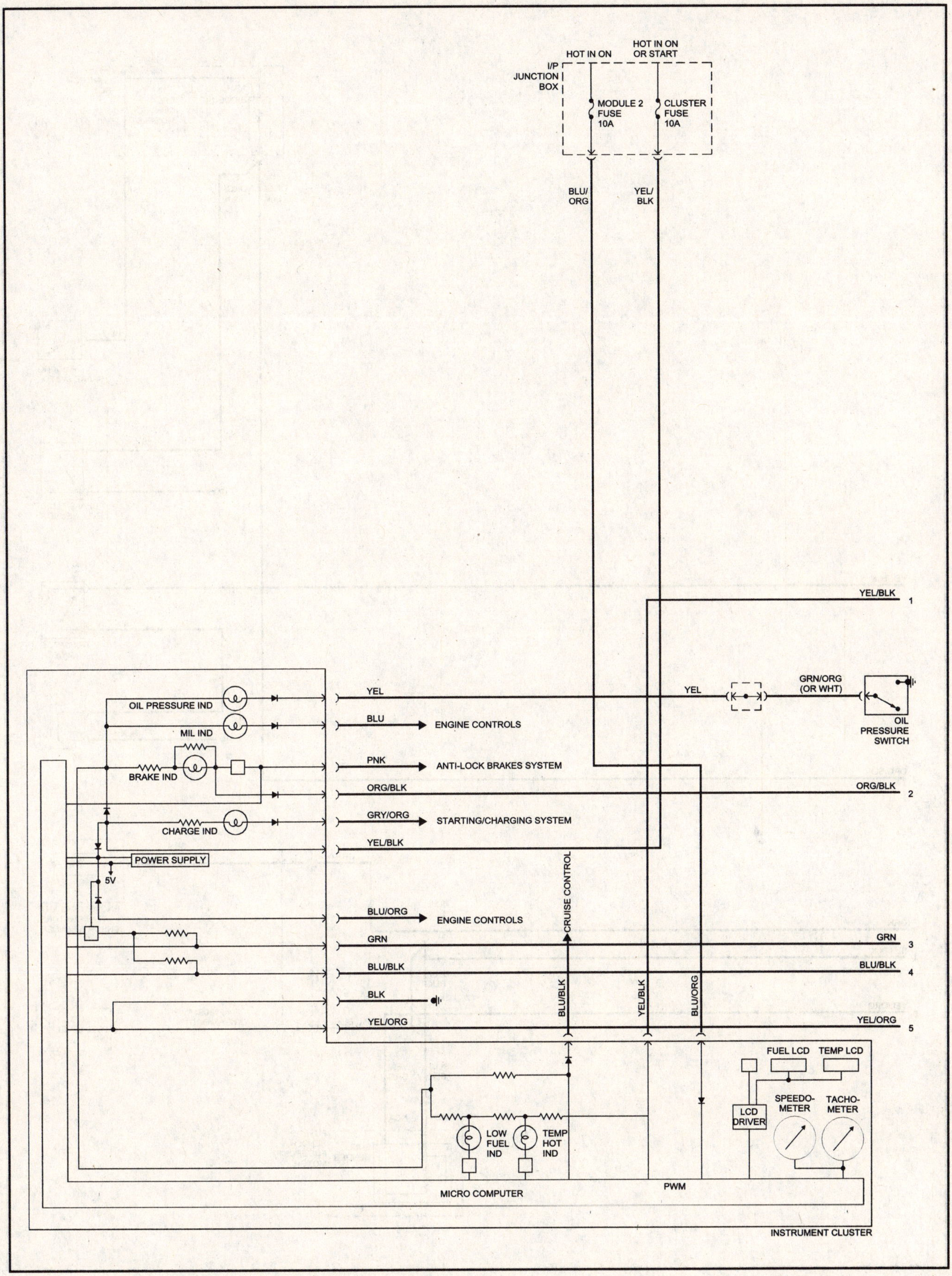

Warning lights and gauges - 2006.5 through 2008 models (1 of 2)

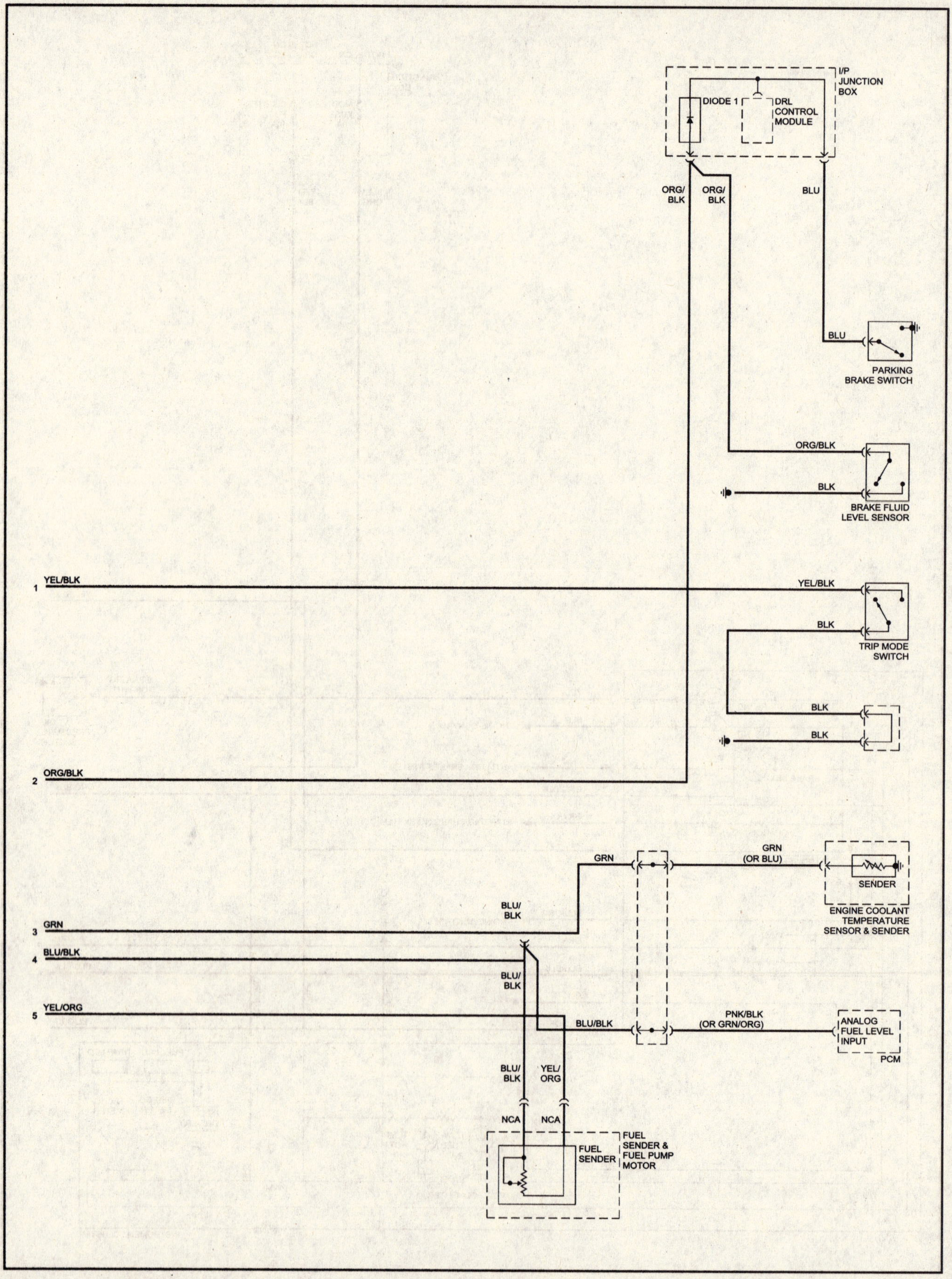

Warning lights and gauges - 2006.5 through 2008 models (2 of 2)

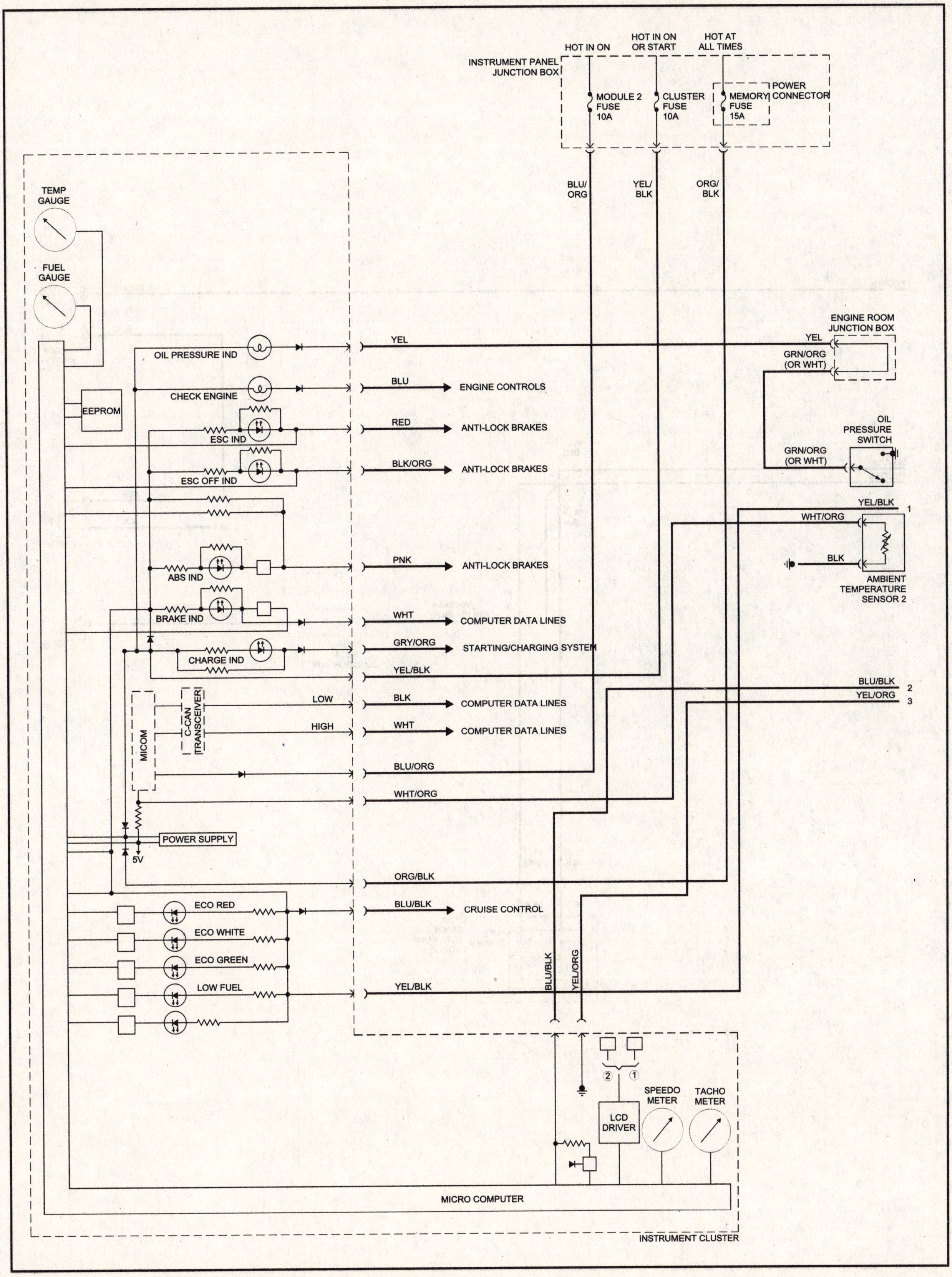

Warning lights and gauges - 2009 and later models (1 of 2)

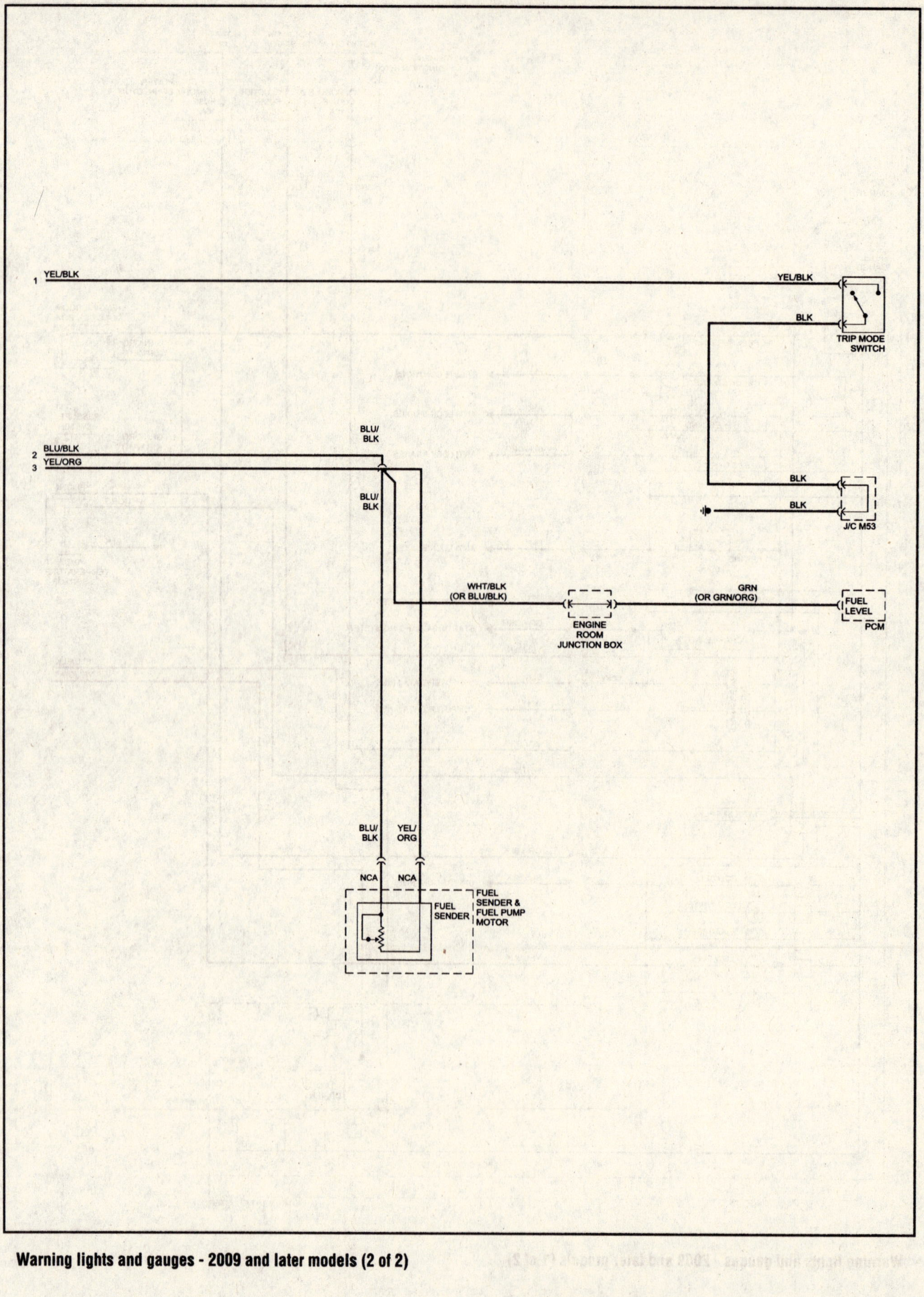

Warning lights and gauges - 2009 and later models (2 of 2)

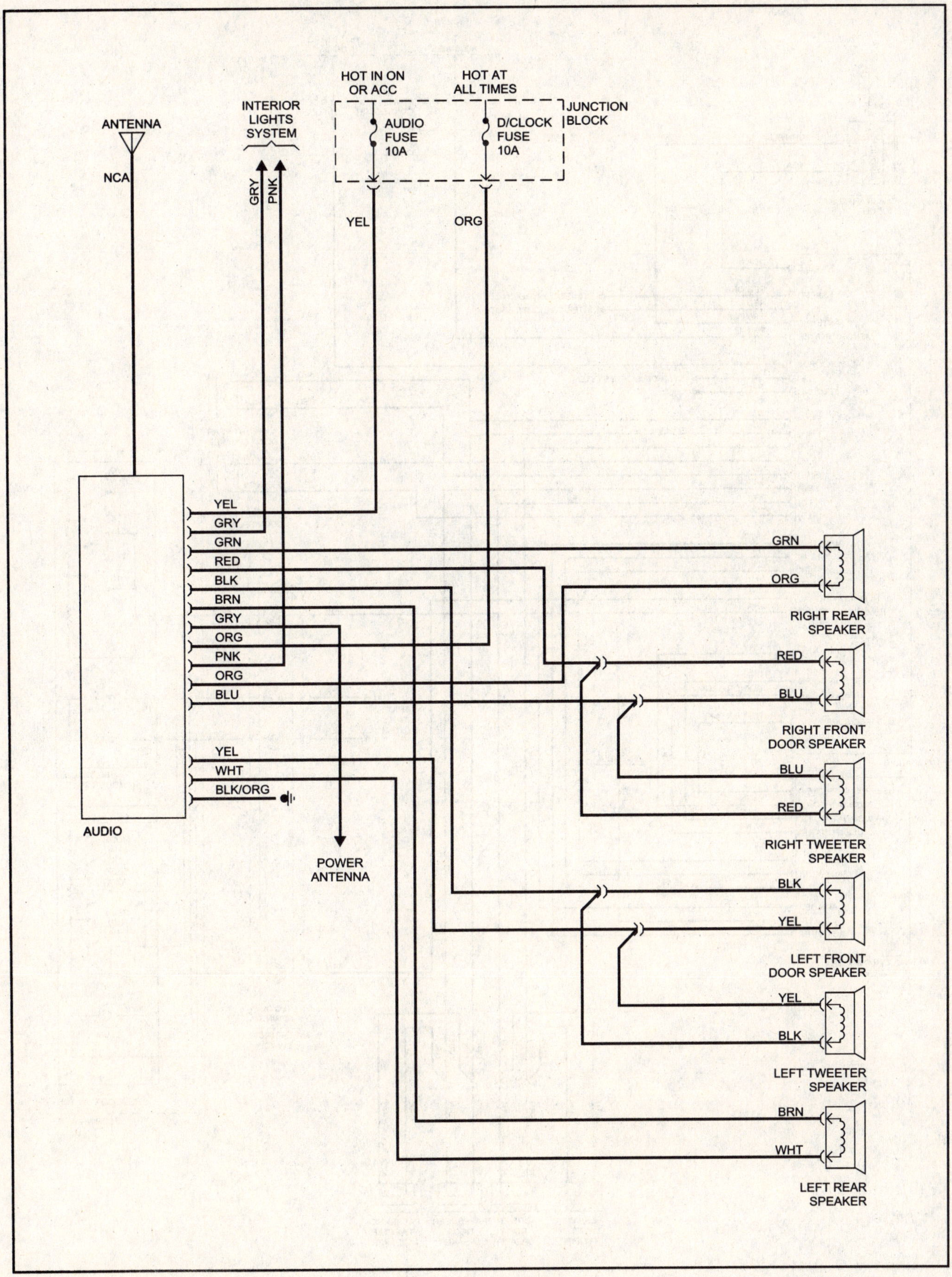

Audio system - 2006 and earlier models

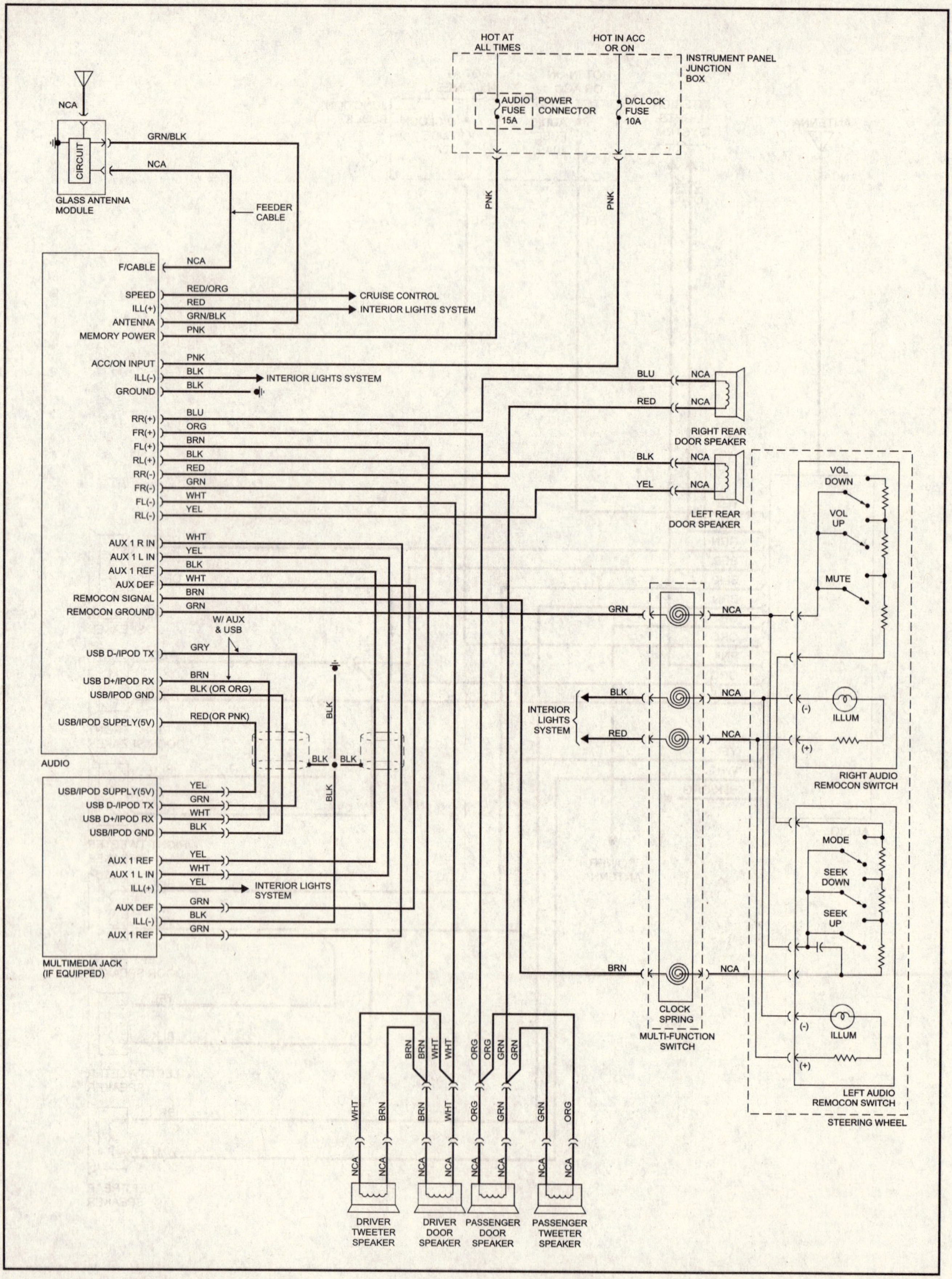

Audio system - 2006.5 and later models

GLOSSARY

AIR/FUEL RATIO: The ratio of air-to-gasoline by weight in the fuel mixture drawn into the engine.

AIR INJECTION: One method of reducing harmful exhaust emissions by injecting air into each of the exhaust ports of an engine. The fresh air entering the hot exhaust manifold causes any remaining fuel to be burned before it can exit the tailpipe.

ALTERNATOR: A device used for converting mechanical energy into electrical energy.

AMMETER: An instrument, calibrated in amperes, used to measure the flow of an electrical current in a circuit. Ammeters are always connected in series with the circuit being tested.

AMPERE: The rate of flow of electrical current present when one volt of electrical pressure is applied against one ohm of electrical resistance.

ANALOG COMPUTER: Any microprocessor that uses similar (analogous) electrical signals to make its calculations.

ARMATURE: A laminated, soft iron core wrapped by a wire that converts electrical energy to mechanical energy as in a motor or relay. When rotated in a magnetic field, it changes mechanical energy into electrical energy as in a generator.

ATMOSPHERIC PRESSURE: The pressure on the Earth's surface caused by the weight of the air in the atmosphere. At sea level, this pressure is 14.7 psi at 32°F (101 kPa at 0°C).

ATOMIZATION: The breaking down of a liquid into a fine mist that can be suspended in air.

AXIAL PLAY: Movement parallel to a shaft or bearing bore.

BACKFIRE: The sudden combustion of gases in the intake or exhaust system that results in a loud explosion.

BACKLASH: The clearance or play between two parts, such as meshed gears.

BACKPRESSURE: Restrictions in the exhaust system that slow the exit of exhaust gases from the combustion chamber.

BAKELITE: A heat resistant, plastic insulator material commonly used in printed circuit boards and transistorized components.

BALL BEARING: A bearing made up of hardened inner and outer races between which hardened steel balls roll.

BALLAST RESISTOR: A resistor in the primary ignition circuit that lowers voltage after the engine is started to reduce wear on ignition components.

BEARING: A friction reducing, supportive device usually located between a stationary part and a moving part.

BIMETAL TEMPERATURE SENSOR: Any sensor or switch made of two dissimilar types of metal that bend when heated or cooled due to the different expansion rates of the alloys. These types of sensors usually function as an on/off switch.

BLOWBY: Combustion gases, composed of water vapor and unburned fuel, that leak past the piston rings into the crankcase during normal engine operation. These gases are removed by the PCV system to prevent the buildup of harmful acids in the crankcase.

BRAKE PAD: A brake shoe and lining assembly used with disc brakes.

BRAKE SHOE: The backing for the brake lining. The term is, however, usually applied to the assembly of the brake backing and lining.

BUSHING: A liner, usually removable, for a bearing; an anti-friction liner used in place of a bearing.

CALIPER: A hydraulically activated device in a disc brake system, which is mounted straddling the brake rotor (disc). The caliper contains at least one piston and two brake pads. Hydraulic pressure on the piston(s) forces the pads against the rotor.

CAMSHAFT: A shaft in the engine on which are the lobes (cams) which operate the valves. The camshaft is driven by the crankshaft, via a belt, chain or gears, at one half the crankshaft speed.

CAPACITOR: A device which stores an electrical charge.

CARBON MONOXIDE (CO): A colorless, odorless gas given off as a normal byproduct of combustion. It is poisonous and extremely dangerous in confined areas, building up slowly to toxic levels without warning if adequate ventilation is not available.

CARBURETOR: A device, usually mounted on the intake manifold of an engine, which mixes the air and fuel in the proper proportion to allow even combustion.

CATALYTIC CONVERTER: A device installed in the exhaust system, like a muffler, that converts harmful byproducts of combustion into carbon dioxide and water vapor by means of a heat-producing chemical reaction.

CENTRIFUGAL ADVANCE: A mechanical method of advancing the spark timing by using flyweights in the distributor that react to centrifugal force generated by the distributor shaft rotation.

CHECK VALVE: Any one-way valve installed to permit the flow of air, fuel or vacuum in one direction only.

CHOKE: A device, usually a moveable valve, placed in the intake path of a carburetor to restrict the flow of air.

CIRCUIT: Any unbroken path through which an electrical current can flow. Also used to describe fuel flow in some instances.

CIRCUIT BREAKER: A switch which protects an electrical circuit from overload by opening the circuit when the current flow exceeds a predetermined level. Some circuit breakers must be reset manually, while most reset automatically.

COIL (IGNITION): A transformer in the ignition circuit which steps up the voltage provided to the spark plugs.

COMBINATION MANIFOLD: An assembly which includes both the intake and exhaust manifolds in one casting.

COMBINATION VALVE: A device used in some fuel systems that routes fuel vapors to a charcoal storage canister instead of venting them into the atmosphere. The valve relieves fuel tank pressure and allows fresh air into the tank as the fuel level drops to prevent a vapor lock situation.

COMPRESSION RATIO: The comparison of the total volume of the cylinder and combustion chamber with the piston at BDC and the piston at TDC.

CONDENSER: 1. An electrical device which acts to store an electrical charge, preventing voltage surges. 2. A radiator-like device in the air conditioning system in which refrigerant gas condenses into a liquid, giving off heat.

CONDUCTOR: Any material through which an electrical current can be transmitted easily.

CONTINUITY: Continuous or complete circuit. Can be checked with an ohmmeter.

COUNTERSHAFT: An intermediate shaft which is rotated by a mainshaft and transmits, in turn, that rotation to a working part.

CRANKCASE: The lower part of an engine in which the crankshaft and related parts operate.

CRANKSHAFT: The main driving shaft of an engine which receives reciprocating motion from the pistons and converts it to rotary motion.

CYLINDER: In an engine, the round hole in the engine block in which the piston(s) ride.

CYLINDER BLOCK: The main structural member of an engine in which is found the cylinders, crankshaft and other principal parts.

CYLINDER HEAD: The detachable portion of the engine, usually fastened to the top of the cylinder block and containing all or most of the combustion chambers. On overhead valve engines, it contains the valves and their operating parts. On overhead cam engines, it contains the camshaft as well.

DEAD CENTER: The extreme top or bottom of the piston stroke.

DETONATION: An unwanted explosion of the air/fuel mixture in the combustion chamber caused by excess heat and compression, advanced timing, or an overly lean mixture. Also referred to as "ping".

DIAPHRAGM: A thin, flexible wall separating two cavities, such as in a vacuum advance unit.

DIESELING: A condition in which hot spots in the combustion chamber cause the engine to run on after the key is turned off.

DIFFERENTIAL: A geared assembly which allows the transmission of motion between drive axles, giving one axle the ability to turn faster than the other.

DIODE: An electrical device that will allow current to flow in one direction only.

DISC BRAKE: A hydraulic braking assembly consisting of a brake disc, or rotor, mounted on an axle, and a caliper assembly containing, usually two brake pads which are activated by hydraulic pressure. The pads are forced against the sides of the disc, creating friction which slows the vehicle.

DISTRIBUTOR: A mechanically driven device on an engine which is responsible for electrically firing the spark plug at a predetermined point of the piston stroke.

DOWEL PIN: A pin, inserted in mating holes in two different parts allowing those parts to maintain a fixed relationship.

DRUM BRAKE: A braking system which consists of two brake shoes and one or two wheel cylinders, mounted on a fixed backing plate, and a brake drum, mounted on an axle, which revolves around the assembly.

DWELL: The rate, measured in degrees of shaft rotation, at which an electrical circuit cycles on and off.

ELECTRONIC CONTROL UNIT (ECU): Ignition module, module, amplifier or igniter. See Module for definition.

ELECTRONIC IGNITION: A system in which the timing and firing of the spark plugs is controlled by an electronic control unit, usually called a module. These systems have no points or condenser.

END-PLAY: The measured amount of axial movement in a shaft.

ENGINE: A device that converts heat into mechanical energy.

EXHAUST MANIFOLD: A set of cast passages or pipes which conduct exhaust gases from the engine.

FEELER GAUGE: A blade, usually metal, or precisely predetermined thickness, used to measure the clearance between two parts.

FIRING ORDER: The order in which combustion occurs in the cylinders of an engine. Also the order in which spark is distributed to the plugs by the distributor.

FLOODING: The presence of too much fuel in the intake manifold and combustion chamber which prevents the air/fuel mixture from firing, thereby causing a no-start situation.

FLYWHEEL: A disc shaped part bolted to the rear end of the crankshaft. Around the outer perimeter is affixed the ring gear. The starter drive engages the ring gear, turning the flywheel, which rotates the crankshaft, imparting the initial starting motion to the engine.

FOOT POUND (ft. lbs. or sometimes, ft.lb.): The amount of energy or work needed to raise an item weighing one pound, a distance of one foot.

FUSE: A protective device in a circuit which prevents circuit overload by breaking the circuit when a specific amperage is present. The device is constructed around a strip or wire of a lower amperage rating than the circuit it is designed to protect. When an amperage higher than that stamped on the fuse is present in the circuit, the strip or wire melts, opening the circuit.

GEAR RATIO: The ratio between the number of teeth on meshing gears.

GENERATOR: A device which converts mechanical energy into electrical energy.

HEAT RANGE: The measure of a spark plug's ability to dissipate heat from its firing end. The higher the heat range, the hotter the plug fires.

HUB: The center part of a wheel or gear.

HYDROCARBON (HC): Any chemical compound made up of hydrogen and carbon. A major pollutant formed by the engine as a byproduct of combustion.

HYDROMETER: An instrument used to measure the specific gravity of a solution.

INCH POUND (inch lbs.; sometimes in.lb. or in. lbs.): One twelfth of a foot pound.

INDUCTION: A means of transferring electrical energy in the form of a magnetic field. Principle used in the ignition coil to increase voltage.

INJECTOR: A device which receives metered fuel under relatively low pressure and is activated to inject the fuel into the engine under relatively high pressure at a predetermined time.

INPUT SHAFT: The shaft to which torque is applied, usually carrying the driving gear or gears.

INTAKE MANIFOLD: A casting of passages or pipes used to conduct air or a fuel/air mixture to the cylinders.

JOURNAL: The bearing surface within which a shaft operates.

KEY: A small block usually fitted in a notch between a shaft and a hub to prevent slippage of the two parts.

MANIFOLD: A casting of passages or set of pipes which connect the cylinders to an inlet or outlet source.

MANIFOLD VACUUM: Low pressure in an engine intake manifold formed just below the throttle plates. Manifold vacuum is highest at idle and drops under acceleration.

MASTER CYLINDER: The primary fluid pressurizing device in a hydraulic system. In automotive use, it is found in brake and hydraulic clutch systems and is pedal activated, either directly or, in a power brake system, through the power booster.

MODULE: Electronic control unit, amplifier or igniter of solid state or integrated design which controls the current flow in the ignition primary circuit based on input from the pick-up coil. When the module opens the primary circuit, high secondary voltage is induced in the coil.

NEEDLE BEARING: A bearing which consists of a number (usually a large number) of long, thin rollers.

OHM: (Ω) The unit used to measure the resistance of conductor-to-electrical flow. One ohm is the amount of resistance that limits current flow to one ampere in a circuit with one volt of pressure.

OHMMETER: An instrument used for measuring the resistance, in ohms, in an electrical circuit.

OUTPUT SHAFT: The shaft which transmits torque from a device, such as a transmission.

OVERDRIVE: A gear assembly which produces more shaft revolutions than that transmitted to it.

OVERHEAD CAMSHAFT (OHC): An engine configuration in which the camshaft is mounted on top of the cylinder head and operates the valve either directly or by means of rocker arms.

OVERHEAD VALVE (OHV): An engine configuration in which all of the valves are located in the cylinder head and the camshaft is located in the cylinder block. The camshaft operates the valves via lifters and pushrods.

OXIDES OF NITROGEN (NOx): Chemical compounds of nitrogen produced as a byproduct of combustion. They combine with hydrocarbons to produce smog.

OXYGEN SENSOR: Use with the feedback system to sense the presence of oxygen in the exhaust gas and signal the computer which can reference the voltage signal to an air/fuel ratio.

PINION: The smaller of two meshing gears.

PISTON RING: An open-ended ring with fits into a groove on the outer diameter of the piston. Its chief function is to form a seal between the piston and cylinder wall. Most automotive pistons have three rings: two for compression sealing; one for oil sealing.

PRELOAD: A predetermined load placed on a bearing during assembly or by adjustment.

PRIMARY CIRCUIT: the low voltage side of the ignition system which consists of the ignition switch, ballast resistor or resistance wire, bypass, coil, electronic control unit and pick-up coil as well as the connecting wires and harnesses.

PRESS FIT: The mating of two parts under pressure, due to the inner diameter of one being smaller than the outer diameter of the other, or vice versa; an interference fit.

RACE: The surface on the inner or outer ring of a bearing on which the balls, needles or rollers move.

REGULATOR: A device which maintains the amperage and/or voltage levels of a circuit at predetermined values.

RELAY: A switch which automatically opens and/or closes a circuit.

RESISTANCE: The opposition to the flow of current through a circuit or electrical device, and is measured in ohms. Resistance is equal to the voltage divided by the amperage.

RESISTOR: A device, usually made of wire, which offers a preset amount of resistance in an electrical circuit.

RING GEAR: The name given to a ring-shaped gear attached to a differential case, or affixed to a flywheel or as part of a planetary gear set.

ROLLER BEARING: A bearing made up of hardened inner and outer races between which hardened steel rollers move.

ROTOR: 1. The disc-shaped part of a disc brake assembly, upon which the brake pads bear; also called, brake disc. 2. The device mounted atop the distributor shaft, which passes current to the distributor cap tower contacts.

SECONDARY CIRCUIT: The high voltage side of the ignition system, usually above 20,000 volts. The secondary includes the ignition coil, coil wire, distributor cap and rotor, spark plug wires and spark plugs.

SENDING UNIT: A mechanical, electrical, hydraulic or electromagnetic device which transmits information to a gauge.

SENSOR: Any device designed to measure engine operating conditions or ambient pressures and temperatures. Usually electronic in nature and designed to send a voltage signal to an on-board computer, some sensors may operate as a simple on/off switch or they may provide a variable voltage signal (like a potentiometer) as conditions or measured parameters change.

SHIM: Spacers of precise, predetermined thickness used between parts to establish a proper working relationship.

SLAVE CYLINDER: In automotive use, a device in the hydraulic clutch system which is activated by hydraulic force, disengaging the clutch.

SOLENOID: A coil used to produce a magnetic field, the effect of which is to produce work.

SPARK PLUG: A device screwed into the combustion chamber of a spark ignition engine. The basic construction is a conductive core inside of a ceramic insulator, mounted in an outer conductive base. An electrical charge from the spark plug wire travels along the conductive core and jumps a preset air gap to a grounding point or points at the end of the conductive base. The resultant spark ignites the fuel/air mixture in the combustion chamber.

SPLINES: Ridges machined or cast onto the outer diameter of a shaft or inner diameter of a bore to enable parts to mate without rotation.

TACHOMETER: A device used to measure the rotary speed of an engine, shaft, gear, etc., usually in rotations per minute.

THERMOSTAT: A valve, located in the cooling system of an engine, which is closed when cold and opens gradually in response to engine heating, controlling the temperature of the coolant and rate of coolant flow.

TOP DEAD CENTER (TDC): The point at which the piston reaches the top of its travel on the compression stroke.

TORQUE: The twisting force applied to an object.

TORQUE CONVERTER: A turbine used to transmit power from a driving member to a driven member via hydraulic action, providing changes in drive ratio and torque. In automotive use, it links the driveplate at the rear of the engine to the automatic transmission.

TRANSDUCER: A device used to change a force into an electrical signal.

TRANSISTOR: A semi-conductor component which can be actuated by a small voltage to perform an electrical switching function.

TUNE-UP: A regular maintenance function, usually associated with the replacement and adjustment of parts and components in the electrical and fuel systems of a vehicle for the purpose of attaining optimum performance.

TURBOCHARGER: An exhaust driven pump which compresses intake air and forces it into the combustion chambers at higher than atmospheric pressures. The increased air pressure allows more fuel to be burned and results in increased horsepower being produced.

VACUUM ADVANCE: A device which advances the ignition timing in response to increased engine vacuum.

VACUUM GAUGE: An instrument used to measure the presence of vacuum in a chamber.

VALVE: A device which control the pressure, direction of flow or rate of flow of a liquid or gas.

VALVE CLEARANCE: The measured gap between the end of the valve stem and the rocker arm, cam lobe or follower that activates the valve.

VISCOSITY: The rating of a liquid's internal resistance to flow.

VOLTMETER: An instrument used for measuring electrical force in units called volts. Voltmeters are always connected parallel with the circuit being tested.

WHEEL CYLINDER: Found in the automotive drum brake assembly, it is a device, actuated by hydraulic pressure, which, through internal pistons, pushes the brake shoes outward against the drums.

Notes

MASTER INDEX

A

B

C

S

T

U

V

W